Causality and Development

Gerald Young

Causality and Development

Neo-Eriksonian Perspectives

Springer

Gerald Young
Department of Psychology
Glendon College
York University
Toronto, ON, Canada

ISBN 978-3-030-02492-5 ISBN 978-3-030-02493-2 (eBook)
https://doi.org/10.1007/978-3-030-02493-2

Library of Congress Control Number: 2018959760

This Springer imprint is published by the registered company Springer Nature Switzerland AG
The registered company address is: Gewerbestrasse 11, 6330 Cham, Switzerland

Acknowledgment

The constant encouragement and support of the editorial and production team at the publishers has been instrumental toward completing this book, in particular. I owe so much thanks to Sharon Panulla and Sylvana Ruggirello in the editorial office and Sharmila Saikumar in production. My staff has been responsible for the onerous task of typing and keeping track of the manuscript as it has been written. Joyce Chan and Jenny X. Wang have worked at it and kept it organized, and I am so thankful for that. My colleagues at Glendon College at York University have always supported my work as well as my teachers over the years. Finally, this book has been inspired by the need to have students see the big picture in psychology, and I thank mine for all their probing questions over the years.

Evidence-supported practice in psychology is important to the field, as it is in medicine, and I hope that this book contributes to that trend and the respect that science deserves. This book reflects the nature of science, its proponents, and its hardworking and insightful researchers who produce replicable results and refined theory. In this regard, this is my third book in the last few years having an integrative scientific theme on development and causality (also see Young, 2011, 2016). Finally, the book is dedicated to our grandchildren and to our daughters.

References

Young, G. (2011). *Development and causality: Neo-Piagetian perspectives*. New York: Springer Science + Business Media.

Young, G. (2016). *Unifying causality and psychology: Being, brain and behavior*. Cham, Switzerland: Springer International Publishing.

Contents

Part I Causality

Brief Biography

Gerald Young Ph.D., C. Psych., is a Full Professor in the Department of Psychology at Glendon College, York University, Toronto, Canada. He is a Fellow both of the American Psychological Association and the Association for Psychological Science. He has received an award for outstanding lifetime contributions for his trauma research from the Canadian Psychological Association and an award from the American Psychological Association about the journal he founded and edits – *Psychological Injury and Law* [PIL, springer.com]. He is the sole author or senior editor/co-author of multiple books. He has written integrative articles in multiple journals. In addition, he is a practicing psychologist. He has successfully testified in a case involving the Supreme Court of Canada on the rights of injured workers.

Chapter 1
Introduction

Abstract The first chapter in the book outlines the relevance of this third book in a series of three books on the topic of causality and development (see Young, Development and causality: Neo-Piagetian perspectives. Springer Science + Business Media, New York, 2011; Unifying causality and psychology: being, brain and behavior. Springer International Publishing, Cham, 2016). The first part of the book deals with the causality of handedness/hemispheric specialization development, and it includes the role in this regard of the author's developmental model and causal thinking. It emphasizes the centrality of activation – inhibition coordination in helping to describe both behavior and brain function. The second part of the book elaborates the Neo-Eriksonian portion of the author's Neo-Piagetian/Neo-Eriksonian 25-step developmental model. It shows how the model can inform not only development but also therapeutic practice. The chapter emphasizes the needed integration of causality as a unifying theme in psychology and that causality and development are not dissociable. The first part of the book on handedness/hemispheric specialization provides an extensive literature review and, in this sense, is empirically driven. Also, the Neo-Piagetian model is based on Piaget's rich observations of his children in the first year of life and also on other data that were used to support the competing models of Case and Fischer, in particular, and that apply as well to the present model. The Neo-Eriksonian portion of the book begins with the presentation of the concept of neo-stage, which permits empirical investigation of networking on sub-stage components and their advancement into more advanced sub-stages. However, the Neo-Eriksonian portion of the present model will require clinical application and insight before more rigorous empirical investigation can be undertaken. Nevertheless, the extent to which it greatly elaborates the Eriksonian lifespan developmental model of eight stages (not to mention Freud's precursor model of five stages) into a 25-step model warrants its investigation and also supports its potential utility and validity.

G. Young, *Causality and Development*,
https://doi.org/10.1007/978-3-030-02493-2_1

Book Introduction

This book, entitled *Causality and Development: Neo-Eriksonian Perspectives*, is the third in a series of books on the topic of development and causality. The first book in 2011 especially emphasized the Neo-Piagetian portion of the present Neo-Piagetian/Neo-Eriksonian stage/sub-stage model (*Development and Causality: Neo-Piagetian Perspectives*; Young, 2011). The second book in 2016 presented a broad view of causality in psychology and advocated both for an integration of causality perspectives and for considering causality as a central unifying theme in psychology (*Unifying Causality and Psychology: Being, Brain, and Behavior*; Young, 2016). This present third book in the series examines both causality in more depth and the Neo-Piagetian/Neo-Eriksonian model in more depth, but this time in elaborating the Neo-Eriksonian portion of the model (see Table 1.1 for the presentation of the present 25-step stage/sub-stage model). The 2016 book had presented novel aspects to the model, but not the Neo-Eriksonian aspect, nor did a 2012 article on the model (Young, 2012). There have been only a handful of books in psychology with the terms causality, causation, mechanism, and the like in the title, and there have been even less books in psychology with the terms unifying, unification, and the like (see Young, 2016), so that the present three-book series stand spout for its novel contributions to the field of psychology. The broad vision that I bring to my work on causality, development, unification, psychology, and stage modeling is consistent with my ethics book that described the basis for an integrated ethics code for mental health practice that extends from psychology to all other mental health disciplines, in general (Young, 2017), and my 2014 book on malingering that took an integrated biopsychosocial and forensic approach while addressing causality in the legal arena (Young, 2014).

Laterality Development and Its Causes

The first part of this book on causality and development focuses on the development of handedness and hemispheric specialization. These topics are ones of longstanding interest (Young, Segalowitz, Corter, & Trehub, 1983), but there has not been one integrated source on the topic since my early work on it. Aside from giving one integrated perspective on this area of study, the first part of the book relates the topic to the broader view of causality in psychology as described in my 2016 book. The approach in that book was to examine the multiplicity of ways that causality is studied in psychology toward integrating them, for example, under related themes of systems theory, network concepts, the biopsychosocial model, embodiment approaches, statistical and graph modeling, and so on. The concept of free will belief was underscored as part of a biopsychosocial perspective in that book. Also, the 2016 book emphasized one integrating causal concept that applies across behavior and brain in explaining their mechanisms of action – that of activation-inhibition

Table 1.1 Neo-Piagetian/Neo-Eriksonian model of development: lifespan stages and sub-stages

Neo-Piagetian		Neo-Eriksonian		Age ranges for stage X sub-stage combinations
Stage	Sub-stage	Stage	Sub-stage	
Reflex	Coordination	Nonparticipatory reflexive socio-emotions	Coordination	Reflex stage Earlier fetal life Quite premature Somewhat premature Full-term newborn 0–1 month
Sensori-motor	Hierarchization	Preparticipatory socio-affects	Hierarchization (includes Erikson's trust, initiative, identity, and generativity stages in the last four neo-Eriksonian stages)	Sensori-motor motor stage 1–4 month 4–8 8–12 12–18 18–24
Peri-operational (Piaget's preoperational and concrete operational stages)	Systematization	Peri-participatory social cognitions	Systematization	Peri-operational stage 2–3.5 year 3.5–5 5–7 7–9 9–11
Abstract (formal)	Multiplication	Hyper-participatory social mutuality	Multiplication (includes Erikson's autonomy, industry, intimacy, and ego integrity stages in the last four neo-Eriksonian stages)	Abstract stage 11–13 year 13–16 16–19 19–22 22–25
Collective Intelligence (post-formal)	Integration	Super-ordinate participatory collective sociality	Hierarchization	Collective intelligence stage 25–28 year 28–39 39–50 50–61 61 onward

Adapted from Young (1990a, 1990b, 2011, 2012, 2016)

Sub-stages 1 to 25 provide the basic cognitive, socio-emotional, and related (e.g., self) acquisitions at each sub-stage of Young's (2011, 2016) Neo-Piagetian/Neo-Eriksonian model. The initial steps in the model are reflexive and sensori-motor in nature before developing into more mature cognitive forms (operational). The 25-step sequence (five stages × five sub-stages) in the tables represents the only developmental model that is fully lifespan, illustrating how Neo-Piagetian sub-stage acquisitions prepare for Neo-Eriksonian acquisitions. The Neo-Eriksonian acquisitions might lag behind their paired cognitive acquisitions due to nonoptimal environmental support, abuse, etc.

coordination. The latter concept is given much prominence in the first part of the present book on handedness and brain lateralization development.

The first part of this book on handedness/hemispheric specialization development gives a multifaceted view of the causality of the development of these phenomena, aside from arguing for the centrality of the concept of activation-inhibition coordination in explaining the development. In this sense, it is a natural follow-up to my 2016 book on causality in psychology. Also, it includes as part of its multifactorial approach to causality in psychology how my own stage/sub-stage model and other related models might contribute to understanding the topics of development under review.

In short, the first part of the present book provides a comprehensive review of integration of the literature on one aspect of development (handedness/hemispheric specialization) and places the review in the context of a wider understanding of causality in psychology, thereby opening it to new avenues of conceptualization and empirical research. This section of the book is reference-heavy because it examines all major psychology databases/engine searches for articles and books (chapters) on the topic over the last few years into the second half of 2018 (PsycINFO, PubMed/MEDLINE, Scopus, Web of Science, Google Scholar) by using the combined term of "Handedness or Hemispheric Specialization or Laterality or Cerebral Dominance." In this sense, the first part of the book can stand on its own as a monograph. However, by showing the relation of the topic to the present (sub)stage model of development, it serves as a segue for the second part of the book, which is more directly on the (sub)stage model. For these reasons, the two parts of the book are seamless.

There is another reason for including the two parts of the book under one umbrella. The first part is heavily empirical in the sense that it reviews hundreds of empirical studies, presents their methods and findings with the sufficient depth needed, and then gives commentaries, insights, and interim conclusions as the work proceeds, leading to the modeling section in the last part. This first part of the book thus illustrates the meticulous evidentiary base that I use in my approach to the study of development, as was also demonstrated in the first two books in the series (Young, 2011, 2016).

Neo-Eriksonian Development

The second part of the book, on the Neo-Eriksonian portion of my combined Neo-Piagetian/Neo-Eriksonian (sub)stage model, begins with a comprehensive literature review of recent stage-related literature, which is consistent with my general approach in scientific, scholarly works presenting my views. However, although a lengthy literature review introduces the second part of the present book, on the stage/sub-stage model, the chapters that actually present the Neo-Eriksonian sub-stages over the lifespan barely have any references. Rather, they delve into explaining the sub-stages and showing their utility for helping patients, but essentially without recourse to research references (there are just a few). That is, the second part of the book, which gives for the first time the details of my Neo-Eriksonian model, is a theoretical exercise more than an empirical one, although it leads to much description of development that can be tested empirically. Had time and space permitted, I would have examined in depth the relevant literature toward culling studies that illustrate or elaborate the descriptions given. Under the circumstances, this phase of the elaboration of the present model is delayed.

Nevertheless, the current approach to the relationship between cognitive and socio-affective development is consistent with contemporary positions. Bjorklund (2018) maintained that the development of non-social cognitive ability should not be viewed as what conditions or is the foundation of social behavior, an assumption that was the implicit and often explicit assumption held by Piaget. Rather, according to Bjorklund (2018) social behavior constitutes the driver of cognitive development through social cognition, the social brain, and related concepts. Therefore, even though the present modeling describes the steps in cognitive development as laying the groundwork for the development of parallel socio-affective steps, the model is not insisting that cognitive development is about schemes and operations developing through information processing, solving cognitive problems on objects, and so on. Instead, the material for cognitive development derives from any contextual problem that confronts the developing individual, whether physical, social, or both.

Table 1.2 presents the original eight-step (stage) Eriksonian model. The theoretical leap evident in the present Neo-Eriksonian model is exponentially relative to prior models of this type, in that they all have few stages compared to the present one of 25 steps. The refined splicing of development in the socio-affective arena afforded by the present model of 25 lifespan steps will allow for greater precision and thus better operationalization and testing of the concepts involved. Moreover, the model gives the therapeutic implications of having problems stemming from any one step of the model, which thus includes 25 possible scenarios, while discussing how problems at the different steps can multiply or be yoked together in individual ways.

Note that Chaps. 13 to 17 describe in depth the 25 steps of the current Neo-Eriksonian model of socio-affective develop. Each of the five chapters present the five x sub-stages in these regards associated with the stage being described. Each sub-stage description starts with a very brief statement on what the step is about. The collection of these 25 brief statements are presented together toward the end of the book in Chap. 18 as a summary of the Neo-Eriksonian model in the book. As well, the 25 steps so presented are described simple enough to be used clinically or towards developing an inventory.

Table 1.2 The issues-crises in Erikson's psychosocial developmental stages

Stage (and normative age)		Issue-crisis
1	*Trust vs. mistrust* (0–1)	First year devoted to acquiring sentiment of trust in self and environment. Mothers, in particular, satisfy infants' basic needs, creating this feeling of positive self-worth. Inconsistent, discontinuous, or rejecting care may result in a sense of loss, perception of world as dangerous, and view of the world as unreliable
2	*Autonomy vs. shame/doubt* (1–3)	In the following years, toddlers and young children learn the tasks of self-sufficiency such as feeding, dressing, cleaning self. They separate from the parents and learn the rules of their culture. Problems in attaining a sense of independence may produce self-doubt in capacities, expectation of defeat in a struggle involving will, and feelings of shame
3	*Initiative vs. guilt* (3–6)	Preschoolers' energy and imagination lead not only to communication, curiosity, pretend play, acceptance of responsibility, and trying to act grown-up but also intrusive activities and consuming fantasies. The latter happenings can lead to conflicts with family members and also guilt. Excessive guilt can dampen initiative, so a balance of initiative and respect of others' requirements is needed. Children's conscience emerges here
4	*Industry vs. inferiority* (6–12)	The school-age period before puberty sees children master complex social and academic skills. Comparisons with peers are made. The reward for accepting instruction is praise for success, producing a sense of efficacy and self-assurance. The potential crisis is that a sense of personal inadequacy can develop if these skills escape children in their life at school or at home, causing them to avoid new activities
5	*Identity vs. identity diffusion* (12–18)	Adolescents integrate childhood identification to create a self-identity concerning their pubertal drives, skills, social roles, and potential work roles. They choose whom to become from among the multiple possible selves available. They may want to tryout many selves but must be moderate. Confusion at these levels is temporarily unavoidable, and the risk is of role ambiguity, diffusion, or negativity (oppositional behavior against peers' or parents' wishes)
6	*Intimacy vs. isolation* (20s)	Young adults secure in their identity can establish a feeling of intimacy with the (20s) inner self and the outer world (friends, love partner). They can share all aspects of oneself with others without fearing the loss of identity. A deep sentiment of loneliness may be incurred if individuals cannot fully enter into an intimate relationship due to a fear of losing their identity
7	*Generativity vs. self-absorption* (20s +)	In middle adulthood, mature individuals strive to establish and guide the following *absorption* (20s +) generation. Responsibilities concern family, work, the role of mentor, and whatever standards the culture defines. Problems here yield self-centered, self-absorbed behavior and a feeling of interpersonal emptiness
8	*Ego integrity vs. despair* (50s +)	With intimacy and acceptance of one's efforts at generativity, elder persons can look *despair* (50s +) back at their lives as meaningful, productive, satisfying, and happy. They actively reminisce about the past, enthusiastically anticipate the future, and seemingly possess wisdom. At issue is whether the dominant mood will be one of contentment or disappointment with unfulfilled goals, leading to sadness, displeasure, disgust

(continued)

Table 1.2 (continued)

Erikson wrote his major works in the 1950s and 1960s (Erikson, 1980). He ameliorated the classical Freudian view of psychosexual stages in several important ways. First, he referred to the stages as psychosocial instead of psychosexual, acknowledging their contextual and mutuality influences. The developing person is not just the seat of libidinal impulses and the battles to control them as well as the psychodynamic conflicts that they engender. The ego has a role to play in the person's psychic apparatus and mediates with the surround. Therefore, each stage is marked by a polarity of a new developmental challenge, crisis, issue, or danger, and the developing person negotiates each one in context. The stages stretch into adulthood; Erikson realized that development is lifelong and the psychosexual stage of the adolescent and adult period is not the last one to develop; the genital investment that it involves modifies with new psychosocial polarities at major life junctures

Elaborations of Book Content

The first part of the book on causality (handedness/hemispheric specialization development) consists of three major parts, each with two chapters. After a brief introductory chapter, the reader will find two chapters each on the development of handedness/hemispheric specialization, the causes of handedness/hemispheric specialization, and the review and elaboration of relevant models on the topic, including new approaches offered by the author. The most important in these regards concerns his concept of activation-inhibition coordination, which was developed to help explain the exquisite coordination required of the young infant reaching toward and then opening the hand to grasp an object. I had shown early in my career that the right hand already expresses this type of specialization, which is consistent with a model of the left hemisphere being specialized for activation-inhibition coordination generally (e.g., speech/verbal skills require the same type of coordination).

The first of the developmental chapters on handedness/hemispheric specialization considers the early years, and the second one examines the later years as well as aspects such as applications in research, including on hemisphericity. The first chapter in the second part of this first component of the book on causality considers the causality of handedness/hemispheric specialization from the point of view of human research. Inevitably, genetic models are considered primary, but environmental contributions through epigenesis, culture, stress, and so on also are considered. The chapter on animal research opens the topic to the evolutionary origins of handedness/hemispheric specialization. The research reviewed is mostly with great apes/non-human primates (chimpanzees, in particular). The different models reviewed might emphasize a manual-first or gestural (communication)-first evolutionary origin to lateralized behavior and brain, but I argue that the concept of activation-inhibition coordination might undergird both views (and others). The third part of this causality component of the present book considers the various models that could explain the development and evolution of handedness/manual specialization. One of the chapters especially reviews various concepts and studies that support the present contention that, typically, the right hand and left hemisphere are specialized for activation-inhibition coordination. The next chapter considers newer models that might help understand handedness/hemispheric specialization development, especially network ones. Nevertheless, the latter type of modeling is not inconsistent with ones involving activation-inhibition coordination.

The second part of the book (Development) on the 25-step Neo-Eriksonian model begins with chapters that review the literature in Erikson's model, which is quite restricted to the identity stage, in particular. As for research on the associated Neo-Piagetian model, the review indicates that it is quite restricted to Piaget's original model of stages and the causes that might apply to them.

One can ask why there is little direct research on these two theories. On one hand, they were not formulated with the rigor required in today's empirical environment in psychology. They have relatively few stages contained within them (e.g., four in Piaget) and so might not have precise boundaries and common transformative mechanisms associated with the stages. Granted, the two primary Neo-Piagetian stages (Fischer, Case) include sub-stages, but they are still limited to a total of 15 or so sub-stages in their models, and they do not cover the complete lifespan in a differentiated way, unlike with my own model that had been built on theirs (Young, 2011). Further, the Case and Fischer Neo-Piagetian stage/sub-stage models of cognitive development are quite different despite superficial similarities (e.g., each has a three sub-stage cyclical recursion of sub-stages at each stage, but they are not placed at the same age ranges), as documented in Young (2011), which might confuse empirical researchers.

Adding to the difficulty of using these models as a starting point in research on cognitive development is the impression that Piaget and Erikson developed their theories in an earlier time, and so any revisions reflect an outdated approach to psychology. Also, these theories are grand ones, which have less currency in contemporary times in which empirical/reductionist approaches hold sway.

The danger of the latter view is that isolated silos of study in psychology propagate without any or much cross-talk. There are hot topics of study in psychology, to be sure, that garner much conceptual and empirical support, but they remain silos, nonetheless, albeit of a more advanced nature.

Dismissal of the silos that mark the study of psychology is not sufficient to return to grand theories because they do have their own problems. Rather, my approach has been to update and modernize the major stage theories in psychology while making them amenable to empirical testability. In effect, the grand theory proposed in the present case (Neo-Piagetian/Neo-Eriksonian) does not suffer from imprecision and from a lack of falsifiability, which are valid worries for any theory, due to the types of revisions undertaken.

Further, I did not hearken back to "imperialist" traditions in psychology that attempted to inefficiently subsume understanding of behavior in grand narratives. Rather, the manner in which I undertook the updating/modernizing of my model has allowed for it to reveal linkages with other grand approaches that are emerging (e.g., networks, system, biopsychosocial) in psychology. Moreover, the inclusion of much contemporary work in my approach, over the three books in the series, permits finding common cause across the various sub-disciplines in psychology through an appreciation that causality can cohere them toward unification.

It is a truism that psychology seeks both to describe and to understand the causes of behavior. But there has been little attempt to unify causal study, which would help to unify psychology. These are grand projects, and perhaps that is all we can expect, to grasp the critical projects that we need to undertake in order to create more cohesion in the field. This third book on the series on Development and Causality aspires to further support the importance of these unifying, yet forever ongoing, projects needed in the field.

The sticking points in any stage model are, first, how can the contents of a stage cohere into an organized structure and, second, how can the qualitatively distinct stages appear so abruptly and especially without any accepted mechanism in place to explain the qualitative shifts that are required for the transitions. This type of questioning leads to the second chapter of the introductory material prior to the presentation of the 25 steps of the current Neo-Eriksonian model. As mentioned, the first chapter of the two provides a literature review of both recent Piagetian/Neo-Piagetian and Eriksonian/Neo-Eriksonian scholarly works. Except for the identity question in the latter, there has not been much work in these regards. As for the second chapter, it introduces the concept of "Neo-stage." This concept includes networking concepts and presents a contemporary view of stages that addresses both how any one (sub)stage might cohere and how they might transition from one to the next. This concept illustrates how the present stage modeling that has been undertaken to update/modernize Piaget's and Erikson's (and indeed Freud's) original stage theories meets contemporary criteria for having qualitative distinct steps in development (sub-stage/stage model) and for having effective transition mechanisms that could account for their qualitative shifts and transformations.

The crux of the second portion of the book on development includes multiple chapters on the 25 steps of the Neo-Eriksonian model presented. First, a brief chapter outlines the present approach in describing the 25 steps. Then, five chapters ensue based on each of the five stages of the present model, with five sub-stages described for each stage. The organizational structure for the presentation of each of the 25 steps in the present Neo-Eriksonian model is held constant, so there is consistency in how they are described.

Crucially, the five stages (and five sub-stages in each of them) in the Neo-Piagetian portion of the present model serve as the basis for the 25 steps that comprise the Neo-Eriksonian model that has been elucidated, giving it a firm foundation. The corresponding Neo-Piagetian stages in the present model consist of (a) reflexive activity; (b) sensori-motor activity; (c) peri-operations (pre-operational, concrete operational); (d) abstract, formal operations; and (e) post-formal operations/collective intelligence. This series of five stages in cognitive development is consistent with Piaget's sequence of stages, with some modification.

Each of the five chapters that present the details of the Neo-Eriksonian model has particular labels meant to give their primary characteristics. The five stages, then, in this regard refer to (a) nonparticipatory reflexive socio-emotions, (b) pre-participatory socio-affects, (c) peri-participatory social cognition, (d) hyperparticipatory social mutuality, and (e) super-ordinate participatory collective sociality. These labels indicate that the relational co-regulation in the dynamics between self and other increases as development moves through these stages.

The Neo-Piagetian cognitive reflexive stage in development underwrites the first Neo-Eriksonian socio-affective stage of nonparticipatory reflexive socio-emotions. The stage concerns prenatal development, prematurity, birth, and the first month of life. Therefore, relative to other succeeding stages, it is nonparticipatory as well as reflexive. That being said, it does concern some basic emotions vital to life, including those not only related to satisfaction of physical needs but also ones with a more behavioral (psychological) component.

The second stage in development involves Piagetian sensori-motor cognitive development, which is associated with preparticipatory socio-affects. The types of interactions with care-givers in the first year of life involves much scaffolding and guided participation in the interactivity created, but not the same mutuality in participation evoked later in development. That said, the infant is highly social at this age, and emotions are linked to sociality.

The young child entering the age period of 2 years is capable of representational thought, which I refer to as peri-operations (pre-operations develop and then concrete operations). These cognitive acquisitions allow for Neo-Eriksonian peri-participatory social cognition. The child soon develops a theory of mind, engages well with the other, etc.

In the next abstract stage in cognitive development, the teenager develops a hyper-participatory social mutuality. The teen is deeply engaged with the other; initiates identity searching, which is often related to the other; and so on.

In the last stage of development, the super-ordinate abstract adult mind allows for super-ordinate participatory collective sociality. Erikson's stage of generativity fits nicely here.

The sub-stages in the Neo-Eriksonian sequence have the same characteristics as the Neo-Piagetian ones: (a) coordination, (b) hierarchization, (c) systematization, (d) multiplication, and (e) integration. However, the labels given to the sub-stages within each stage follow the Eriksonian tradition of using oppositions between positive and negative poles. My innovation in these regards was to refer to them as acts, e.g., Trust vs. Mistrust Acts.

The five stages in the proposed Neo-Eriksonian sequence give the titles for the chapters that present the stages. The contents of the chapters do not describe much the stages generally, in that they focus mostly on the five sub-stages of the chapter involved. The headings and subheadings of the chapters, both for this portion of the book and the first one, are numerous and should help the reader digest a long, complex monograph.

Conclusions

Overall, the present book on *Development and Causality: Neo-Eriksonian Perspectives* is innovative and makes contributions toward understanding both causality in psychology and Neo-Eriksonian development. The first part on causality illustrates how the topic of handedness/hemispheric specialization development can be studied from a broadened view of causality in psychology, including in terms of the present stage/sub-stage model, and on the underlying activation-inhibition coordination process that is championed in that approach. The second part of the book on development renders a 25-step model of socio-affective development based on the present five stage × five sub-stage Neo-Piagetian model as applied to (Neo-Eriksonian) socio-affective development. This model is much more elaborate than any prior socio-affective Eriksonian-related model, or its Freudian precursors, which typically are limited to eight (or five, as the case may be) stages in development (and without sub-stages).

To conclude this part of the book introduction, I emphasize that this third book in the series on Development and Causality completes a cycle of books that give a broad, unifying view of causality and psychology while indicating how its 25-step lifespan model can be applied therapeutically to the socio-affective context. Its particular set of concepts and empirical suggestions require further work, but its theoretical value and clinical utility might already be demonstrated.

Although the book has two portions, one on causality and one on development, these two topics are indissociable. The causality portion is about a developmental topic, and the development section is about change processes in development and therapy. Change processes by definition are causal. The environmental impacts on development discussed in this portion, by definition, are causal. Causality and development really constitute one overarching theme in psychology. Every aspect of psychology is developmental. One cannot fully address learning, perception, thinking, motivation, personality, psychopathology, the brain, neurosciences, and so on without including the developmental aspect. This might suggest that development is the unifying cement in psychology, and I have toyed with that theme. However, development is about the "what" and the "why" of developing behavior, which brings us back to causality as the unifying project to psychology. Moreover, to proclaim one psychology discipline as most central might be considered insular, although I would not have phrased the argument that way. Returning to the idea of change as primary in psychology, whether developmental, in therapy, or otherwise, this is a fruitful theme to consider as part of the unifying causality aspect of my work. I have shown the similarities, for example, across the five longer term developmental sub-stages in the present model (coordination, hierarchization, systematization, multiplication, and integration) and the five shorter term stages of change model (Prochaska, Norcross, & DiClemente, 1994) that has been applied to topics, such as changing disordered behavior.

To summarize, development and causality are part of the very nature of psychology, and the book addresses the two central aspects of this unity project. First, it examines the development of brain-behavior relationships through the lens of developmental models, including my own. Then, it shifts into an elaboration of the socio-affective component of the model. In a certain sense, the reaching hand of the young infant, which I studied at the start of my academic career, extends not only toward the target object but also toward the very essence of what makes us human and growing throughout our lifespan.

The remainder of this book introduction chapter provides a brief chapter-by-chapter description of the contents of the book. They emphasize the book's contributions.

Chapter Summaries

Chapter 1

This chapter introduces the book, explaining how causality and development are interrelated in the book. It underscores the concept of activation-inhibition coordination for causality, among others, and the author's 25-step lifespan model of Neo-Eriksonian development, which has therapeutic applications.

Chapter 2

The second chapter of the book briefly introduces its first portion on the development of laterality. It gives basic terminology, methodological issues, and the historical course in the study of the topic.

Chapter 3

Chapter 3 examines the research on the development of early laterality, both for manual behavior and for hemispheric specialization. Right from the prenatal period on, the developing fetus demonstrates the equivalent of the adult pattern in these regards. The concept of activation-inhibition coordination can help explain early right-hand preference in infancy and corresponding early left hemisphere specialization.

Chapter 4

Chapter 4 continues to present the developmental laterality research, focusing on children in particular. Results vary with method, among other factors, but the pattern continues to be adult-like. The chapter examines associations of handedness with cognition, language, and atypicality. It concludes by presenting connectivity and network research on laterality.

Chapter 5

This chapter presents more conceptualization and research on the concept of activation-inhibition coordination in lateralization. Then, it considers how a concept that has fallen out of favor in laterality research – that of hemisphericity – can be revised and be useful in understanding laterality.

Chapter 6

Chapter 6 examines the multi-factorial influences on the development of laterality. The genetic influences involved are polygenic, and any one gene explains very little of the variance in laterality. The environmental influences include culture, parent modeling, stress, early adversity, and so on. Cultural neuroscience indicates interactive influences in these regards as well.

Chapter 7

This chapter examines the animal research on laterality, along with evolutionary models of lateralization. Studies on invertebrates and fossils of the earliest species indicate that asymmetry has a long evolutionary history. The research on our hominin ancestors and great apes/non-human primates indicates the evolutionary origins of laterality in our species. The chapter reviews evidence for the tool-use-first and gestural communication-first hypotheses in the evolution of lateralization, a debate which continues.

Chapter 8

The eighth chapter of the book examines in more depth the activation-inhibition coordination model as applied to lateralization, mostly in terms of adult research this time. Also, it examines models related to it. It examines research on disorders in which inhibition is problematic. It considers activation-inhibition coordination as a general dynamic underlying both behavior and brain function. It concludes by examining network and biopsychosocial concepts.

Chapter 9

The last chapter of the book on laterality reviews the major models on lateralization that have been highlighted in the prior chapters. For example, it presents a combined progressive development and invariant development model, once more emphasizes the activation-inhibition coordination model, and presents new ones that might contribute to understanding laterality, such as the embodiment, nonlinear dynamical systems theory, and attractor models. The author's more speculative models also are considered in these regards.

Chapter 10

This first chapter of the second portion of the book argues for the value of stage models in psychology. It presents current research on Piaget's and Erikson's stage models. It examines their perspectives on the nature of stages. It suggests that grand theories such as these in psychology can help with its empirical (replication) crisis.

Chapter 11

This chapter describes in more depth, by tabular format, the current Neo-Piagetian/ Neo-Eriksonian model, focusing on the Neo-Piagetian portion. It examines some other Neo-Piagetian models, finding some inconsistencies and oversights. The chapter especially presents the concept of Neo-stage, which renders the stage concept more contemporary and testable, including for the Neo-Eriksonian portion of the model.

Chapter 12

This chapter introduces the 25-step Neo-Eriksonian model and how it reflects the parallel 25-step Neo-Piagetian model. The attributes of each of the steps in the Neo-Eriksonian model were constructed based on the corresponding cognitive acquisitions in the Neo-Piagetian model. The 17 steps in the Neo-Eriksonian model that were added to the original eight Eriksonian steps were constructed by examining the corresponding Neo-Piagetian acquisitions and the Eriksonian stages near them in the sequence.

Chapter 13

This chapter constitutes the first one of those on the 25 steps in the present Neo-Eriksonian model. It examines the age period from the prenatal period into the first month of life. The stage involved has five sub-stages, and none correspond to any in Erikson's original eight-stage sequence.

Chapter 14

This chapter describes in depth the Neo-Eriksonian model proposed by the author for the infancy period. It consists of five sub-stages, and two of them reflect Erikson's original model, including the Eriksonian stage of Trust vs. Mistrust. The active attachment period follows the trust one in this model.

Chapter 15

The chapter on the childhood period spans the ages of 2 years to the preteen years and so witnesses vast changes in development. The child passes through the Eriksonian stages of Initiative and of Industry, but they are sandwiched between three others, including on identification and role/personality tryouts.

Chapter 16

This chapter on the teen years and the early adult ones covers a wide age range that witnesses the development of abstract thought, consciousness, and so on and ends with thinking of the wider world and acting for it. The Neo-Eriksonian challenges include Identity and Intimacy, and the present model has added sub-stages related to consciousness and nurturing, for example.

Chapter 17

The last stage of life covers the later 20s to the end of life. It spans setting up work/family, engaging in generativity, and ending life with a sense of catharsis. Problems at this level include despair, for example.

Chapter 18

The book ends with a brief chapter on its promise. It addresses its role in the scientific pursuit in psychology.

Chapter 19

This chapter provides appendices on Chaps. 13, 14, 15, 16, and 17 that illustrate the prior work published on matters related to the Neo-Eriksonian model of development. It consists of 25 appendices, or one for each step of the model.

Chapter Conclusions

The first portion of the book is on the causality of behavior, using the development of handedness/hemispheric specialization as the primary example. This portion of the book illustrates the value of the concept of activation-inhibition coordination in behavior and shows how the present stage model can also apply to illuminating this topic.

The second portion of the book consists of presenting a 25-step lifespan Neo-Eriksonian model, showing what develops in socio-affectivity and how it can be treated when it goes awry. It begins with the concept of neo-stage, which allows for a reliable and valid, testable model.

References

Bjorklund, D. F. (2018). A metatheory for cognitive development (or "Piaget is dead" revisited). *Child Development, 89*, 2288–2302.

Erikson, E. H. (1980). *Identity and the life cycle*. New York: Norton.

Prochaska, J. O., Norcross, J. C., & DiClemente, C. C. (1994). *Changing for good: The revolutionary program that explains the six stages of change and teaches you how to free yourself from bad habits*. New York: Morrow.

Young, G. (1990a). The development of hemispheric and manual specialization. In G. Hammond (Ed.), *The cerebral control of speech and limb movements* (pp. 79–139). Amsterdam, The Netherlands: North Holland.

Young, G. (1990b). Early neuropsychological development: Lateralization of functions – Hemispheric specialization. In C. A. Hauert (Ed.), *Developmental psychology: Cognitive, perceptuo-motor and neuropsychological perspectives* (pp. 113–181). Amsterdam, The Netherlands: North Holland.

Young, G. (2011). *Development and causality: Neo-Piagetian perspectives*. New York: Springer Science + Business Media.

Young, G. (2012). A unitary Neo-Piagetian/ Neo-Eriksonian model of development: Fundamental assumptions and meta-issues. *New Ideas in Psychology, 30*, 241–249. https://doi.org/10.1016/j.newideapsych.2011.11.002

Young, G. (2014). *Malingering, feigning, and response bias in psychiatric/psychological injury – Implications for practice and court*. New York: Springer Science + Business Media.

Young, G. (2016). *Unifying causality and psychology: Being, brain and behavior*. Cham, Switzerland: Springer International Publishing.

Young, G. (2017). *Revising the APA ethics code*. Cham, Switzerland: Springer International Publishing.

Young, G., Segalowitz, S. J., Corter, C. M., & Trehub, S. E. (Eds.). (1983). *Manual specialization and the developing brain*. New York: Academic Press.

Part I
Causality

Development of Evolution of Handedness, Manual Specialization, and Hemispheric Specialization: Activation-Inhibition Coordination Model

Chapter 2
Introducing Laterality

Abstract This brief chapter provides an introduction to the first portion of the present book, which is especially on the development of handedness/hemispheric specialization. The literature review focuses on the early years, in particular. In addition, this portion of the book deals with the causes of behavioral and brain laterality, including their evolution, leading to a review of non-human primate research, in particular. Modeling emphasizes activation-inhibition coordination. The various terms in the field include manual specialization, cerebral dominance, asymmetry in brain function, etc., and they are defined and differentiated in this chapter. The concept of activation-inhibition specialization is examined carefully in these regards, as well. Other areas in the chapter include methodological issues and the historical course in the study of laterality.

Outline of the First Portion of the Book on Causality

The first portion of this book on *Development and Causality: Neo-Eriksonian Perspectives* focuses on causality. It reviews pertinent developmental and animal research on sidedness biases in manual and related behavior and function, toward elucidating better developmental and evolutionary models of handedness, manual specialization, and hemispheric specialization. The development of handedness concerns preference on daily tasks. Manual specialization refers to skill on complex tasks. Hemispheric specialization (the differential skills/functions of the hemispheres) conditions the direction of sidedness in manual specialization, and both specializations are evident in the human neonate. This suggests an invariant model of hemispheric specialization rather than an equi-potential or progressive one. The literature review on early manual behavior and hemispheric specialization supports an early lateralization manually and hemispherically along adult lines, but with development still taking place; therefore, a combined invariant-equi-potential/progressive lateralization model is supported. The present work considers other aspects of human lateralization, including hemisphericity and causality. For the former, it

G. Young, *Causality and Development*,
https://doi.org/10.1007/978-3-030-02493-2_2

proposes renewal of its study. For the latter, it examines research on genetics, epigenetics, experience, culture, and so on, supporting a biopsychosocial and multi-factorial model. Ultimately, manual and cerebral lateralizations should be explained through common underlying functions, such as activation-inhibition coordination. The present work considers the left hemisphere the seat of these advanced skills. As for the evolution and study of non-human primate manual behavior and hemispheric specialization, the research supports a right-sided bias, especially for chimpanzees and gorillas in tool use and communicative gesturing. Other lines of study support behavioral lateralizations in invertebrates, consistent with an evolutionary model of sweeps in phylogenesis that have selected for behavioral and neural lateralizations. Discussion focuses on different models in this regard, including on networked connectivities. Other models reviewed concern the author's including his stage/sub-stage model of development, which prepares the way for the second portion of the book on 25 lifespan developmental steps from a Neo-Eriksonian perspective. To summarize, this comprehensive review of the early development of handedness, manual specialization, and hemispheric specialization describes clearly the conceptual and empirical issues in the field. It indicates the central importance of laterality development to understanding human behavior, its development, and its evolution.

Introduction and Human Research

Introduction

Topics and Topical Issues

The first portion of the book reviews conceptualization and research on the early development of handedness, manual specialization, and hemispheric specialization while exploring a multi-factorial approach to understanding lateralization in brain and behavior, including in terms of non-human primate lateralizations and evolutionary pathways. It considers novel models that can help integrate the field, especially in terms of activation-inhibition coordination and network connectivities. The first part outlines its contributions to the field, preparing the way for a background section and then the literature review section.

There have been only a handful of books on handedness, and most concern the fascinating topic of left handedness (e.g., Kushner, 2017; McManus, 2004; Porac, 2016; Smits, 2012; Wright, 2007). One new book has appeared related to the topic (Asenova, 2018), but it deals especially with developmental disorders. Three recent related books treat laterality mostly with respect to animals and humans, respectively, and handedness and manual or upper limb preference is a central topic, but not exclusively, in that brain function, manual dexterity, and related topics also are considered. Also, developmental aspects of both human handedness and brain function/asymmetry are not given much space in these three books (see, for mostly animals, Rogers & Vallortigara, 2017; Rogers, Vallortigara, & Andrew, 2013; general: Ocklenburg & Güntürkün, 2018). The present work fills the void of there being no recent academic monographs that examine generally the development of handedness and related phenomena.

Conceptually, we need to distinguish handedness and various lateralized functions related to brain and behavior. The development of handedness concerns trajectories in hand preferences on simpler or daily tasks, including in drawing and writing. For example, handedness is studied using grasping and reaching tasks even in the prenatal period and just after birth, which are complex tasks for that age period. The development of manual specialization involves tasks that are more complex than this, depending on the age, including coordinated bimanual activity. Hemispheric specialization concerns the differential skills and functioning of the left and right hemispheres, typically related to verbal and visuo-spatial functions, respectively, aside from the hemispheres' different manual skills. In this regard, the left hemisphere is considered especially more fine motor and sequential, and the right hemisphere is considered especially more spatial and holistic (Porac, 2016; Young, 2011, 2016; Young et al., 1983). However, careful examination of the developmental research is required from one age period to the next to determine exactly how the development of handedness and lateralization proceeds, for example, if it is invariant in some ways or developing progressively.

The study of the development of handedness, manual specialization, and hemispheric specialization is interlinked and involves three complex phenomena, the knowledge of which is rapidly evolving and differentiating in new directions. The present review consists of three parts. After providing background information on definitions of terms, measures, and concepts, the first part of this portion of the book examines the developmental literature from the prenatal period to early childhood, both in terms of manual behavior and brain structure and function. The second part of this portion of the book delves into the multi-factorial causes that influence the development of handedness, manual lateralization, and hemispheric specialization. It includes a review of biological (e.g., genetic) and evolutionary bases to lateralized behavior and brain behavior function while presenting, as well, notions related to the environment and culture in the causes of the lateralization. The third part of this first portion of the present work engages in discussion and implications, including presentation of coherent models that cut across the empirical findings related to developing handedness, manual specialization, and hemispheric specialization, such as on activation-inhibition coordination both in behavior and the brain and network connectivities in this regard. It considers broader issues related to evolution, culture, causality, and the biopsychosocial model.

Contributions and Innovations

The present work of handedness, manual specialization, and hemispheric specialization early in life stands as an original contribution to the field, beyond the comprehensiveness of its review, in terms of its conceptualizations and modeling. This contribution to the field includes the following.

First, the present work examines the differences among handedness and specializations behaviorally and in the developing brain from the point of view of the invariant and "equi-potential" progressive lateralization models. The work finds them complementary and consistent with an *invariant progressive lateralization model*.

Second, consistent with the exquisite synchrony in the reaching and grasping right hand of the very young infant (e.g., Young et al., 1983; Young, Segalowitz, Misek, Alp, & Boulet, 1983), the book proposes a common metric for both behavior and brain asymmetries in terms of *activation-inhibition coordination* (Young, 1990a, 1990b, 2011, 2016; Young et al., 1983; Young & Gagnon, 1990; Young, Segalowitz, Misek, et al., 1983). Behavior is expressed by activation in balance with inhibition, and the same function takes place in the brain, both in a macro sense (e.g., the behavioral activation and inhibition systems; Gray, 1982) and at the level of the neuron, in that its processes have been described in terms of activation (or excitation) and inhibition.

Specifically, activation-inhibition coordination concerns the integration of activation and inhibition processes in the brain, behavior, or both, such that the functional activity involved is dynamically refined, skillful, organized, fine-tuned, efficient, economical, well-sequenced, exquisitely responsive, contextually adaptive, ongoing and online, goal-directed and optimal for goal success, as well as without any interfering processes, or with a control of such interfering processes, that hinder, disrupt, or otherwise compromise the quality of the activation-inhibition process and resultant output/activity. The action/behavior that results could be movement-related/motoric, emotional/social, or perceptual/cognitive and could involve coordination with other(s). The aim of the activation-inhibition coordination is to keep engaged to the degree possible on a continual interactive basis with the internal system at issue (e.g., monitoring thoughts) or the external environment at issue (e.g., monitoring effects of actions and interactions). The coordination involved is conducive to the left hemisphere because of the structural and functional properties that are consistent with it. The right hemisphere, in contrast, appears specialized for less complex inhibitory skills, such as outright suppression of activity or activation-inhibition coordination of a brief nature.

The present work examines other generic models that have been proposed related to the differences between the left and right brain, and it indicates that they can be subsumed under the present generic model concerning activation, inhibition, and their coordination. Through this compare/contrast process relating other models to the present one, the parsimony and the broad-ranging value of the present one becomes highlighted.

Third, the book extends the concept of activation and inhibition coordination to network and related models on neural and behavioral connections over nodes, for example, in terms of small-world hubs and measures of centrality (e.g., Borsboom, 2008; Sporns, 2011, 2012), so that the reworking of the differential functioning of the left and right hemispheres hypothesized in terms of activation-inhibition coordination places the hemispheres at the heart of new approaches to brain and behavior. In short, the reaching and grasping hand of the neonate holds indices that can help decipher the grand scheme of evolution and the development of behavior and the brain through reworking according to these cogent contemporary models of brain and behavior.

Fourth, the first portion of the present work proposes that behavior and brain specializations need to consider individual differences in hemisphere use, for example, according to what has been called hemisphericity or hemisphere preference. This concept has fallen out of favor because of problems in its measurement, conceptualization, and associations in studies of its convergent validity. However, it could be revitalized conceptually, leading to renewed empirical investigation, including developmentally. In this regard, it is proposed that hemisphericity is reconceptualized as *cerebral hemisphere activation/preference*, whether intrinsically or extrinsically.

Fifth, the present work speaks to the causality of behavior generally because handedness has been related to genetics, certain genes, experience, culture, gene-culture coevolution, and so on. This would place the study of the development of handedness and related phenomena in the framework of the broad biopsychosocial model of causality and close the circle of the present argument that manual and hemispheric specialization are both about invariance from birth and progressive development. Only by adopting a "systems" view of handedness, manual specialization, hemispheric specialization, and related phenomena can the complexity of their evolution and development be ascertained, and only if the various models proposed in these regards are examined for their systemic coherence and complementarity can the conceptual ambiguities and empirical contradictions in the field be explained and lead to better research and theory in the area. For example, the social theory of the evolution of lateralization (e.g., Vallortigara & Rogers, 2005) may be too specific and focus too much on only one domain in lateralization in function.

Comment

Although the present review intends to emphasize these five major theoretical contributions to the study of the development and evolution of handedness, manual specialization, and hemispheric specialization (as well as the in-depth literature review in the early developmental period related to the topic), it is not organized to explicitly make these points by using them as five organizers to the paper. Rather, the work is organized in terms of traditional topics and addresses the major contributions made as exposition or commentary at the appropriate intervals in the review. Moreover, in presenting the empirical literature, often it is accomplished by first describing the research at face value, but, nevertheless, the present work would then offer evaluative comments on them either immediately after the research description or before it. This is especially true of the portion of the present work that describes lateralization in behavior and brain at each phase early in life, which is found after the next background section. The latter section defines the various terms used in the field, as well as reviewing critical tasks and measures used in its study.

Background

History

From a scientific perspective, historically, the study of left-right differences in brain and behavior began with Paul Broca's (1861) work on the effects of left hemisphere stroke on language production, which led to an understanding of localization of language function asymmetrically in the cerebral hemispheres. Shortly thereafter, Wernicke (1874) further specified that more temporal regions of the brain, and not only frontal ones, were involved in language control (reception) on the left side of the brain. The French father-son Dax duo (Marc, Gustave) also has been credited with initiating the scientific study of lateralized effects in the brain in the nineteenth century (Manning & Thomas-Antérion, 2011). That said, interest in the phenomenon of handedness began at least in biblical times, with the right hand being considered more cunning and the left hand being considered more sinister, for example (Treves, Goldschmidt, & Korczyn, 1983).

Terms

Handedness has status as a descriptive term of manual behavior both for any one individual and any one population. Handedness refers to the hand preferred, used, or favored on simpler daily tasks by an individual (Marchant, 2017), which, for an adult, includes writing but, for a young child, might include other activities, such as drawing (Hepping, Ploegmakers, Geertzen, Bulstra, & Stevens, 2015). Also, handedness can refer to population-level asymmetries, as in humans being considered mostly right-handed. While handedness is an enduring pattern for an individual or for species-wide manual behavior (Marchant & McGrew, 2013) on simpler tasks, it does not refer to manual dexterity on more complex tasks, which involves manual specialization. Manual specialization is a term reserved for performance on more complex tasks, demanding skill and dexterity, as elaborated below.

Manual preference is a generic term that relates to manual choices in hand use on any type of task, whether simpler or more complex. Manual preference could be applied to behavior on simpler tasks, as in handedness ones, or more complex tasks, as in those related to manual specialization. Manual preference concerns laterality on a specific task for a specific subject (human, non-human), and the limb preferred might not be the same as for handedness in the person. Manual preference applies to the individual, although workers in the field might apply it to a particular population, but that might be confusing (Vallortigara, 2015).

Manual specialization is related to hemispheric specialization rather than handedness. Hemispheric specialization refers to the differential function, skill, or processing qualities of the left and right hemispheres (Young, Segalowitz, Corter, & Trehub, 1983; also see Tzourio-Mazoyer & Seghier, 2016). The hand preferred on complex tasks demanding specialized skills, as in manual specialization, varies over individuals, their ages, their species, and so on. For more efficient and successful performance, tasks of this nature require the hemispheric specializations of the individual, at the ages involved, and for the species involved (or the contralateral side of the brain or nervous system, depending on the phylogenetic and evolutionary status of the species at issue). Many factors affect whether a complex task at hand evokes left or right manual use (and the corresponding hemisphere associated with the hand used), but the specialized qualities that differentiate the hemispheres rank primary among them.

The classic difference between the hemispheres is that, typically, the left hemisphere is specialized for language and the right hemisphere is specialized for spatial functions, as reviewed below. Lateralization and asymmetry concern differential-side specialization, for example, in hemispheric function but also in downstream effects, whether manual or behavioral. They are concepts about relative advantages and not absolute differences, as is the case with handedness. Moreover, they are all exquisitely developmental, conditioned by evolution, and have implications beyond hand use and language, for example, to cognition.

Lateralized activity could take place manually, in other appendages or limbs, have functions associated with them, and might be underpinned by morphological differences, as well as other associations, such as between the brain and behavior. Specifically, for the brain, the differential specializations of the hemispheres might refer to functional lateralizations, for example, to qualities of information processing (e.g., global vs. local). Also, hemispheric specialization (or cerebral lateralization, hemispheric dominance, asymmetry of the brain) might refer to structural differences in the brain between the left and right hemispheres.

Manual lateralization refers to the hand preferred for more complex tasks, and the bias typically reflects the differential skills and specializations associated with the hemispheres (Young, Segalowitz, Corter, et al., 1983). The term has been used in other ways, such as to reflect lateralization within subjects across tasks (e.g., Marchant & McGrew, 2013). But, as used presently, it allows for differential specializations in the right and left hands depending on the underlying hemispheric specialization consistent with each of the differential behaviors at issue (e.g., holding for support with one hand and manipulating with the other).

In this regard, handedness needs to be differentiated from other lateralized functions, such as hemispheric specialization and manual specialization, both of which also begin to develop early in life. Manual specialization differs from handedness by the greater demands involved in task complexity and the different behaviors that might be needed on the task at hand. For example, handedness generally involves simpler unimanual behaviors, while manual lateralization might concern bimanual ones, such as in bimanual coordination to stabilize a tube or to open a jar in order to retrieve a target object. Handedness is differentiated from the term of hemispheric specialization by being quite orthogonal to it. Whereas manual specialization is related to underlying hemispheric specialization, handedness involves preferences on simpler task not typically examined in manual specialization. Therefore, the hemisphere seemingly associated with the preferred hand on handedness tasks might be the same only because of serendipitous factors or third variable factors more than because of any direct association, per se.

That said, manual specializations might influence the development of handedness. That is, on more complex tasks, the differential skills of the hands should reflect the differential skills of the hemispheres, which retain a contralateral and not an ipsilateral organization, as in left hemisphere motoric control while the right fingers move. Manual specializations to one side or the other might be evoked consistently, depending on a variety of variables for an individual, especially in terms of hemispheric specialization. The typical hand uses governed by underlying hemispheric specializations could influence general hand preference in handedness, such that the side of handedness and manual specialization are quite related, but there are so many variables involved, for example, experientially, context, the tasks used, the measures, and so on, that this type of influence should be weak at best (Young, Corter, Segalowitz, & Trehub, 1983).

As with the term lateralization, generally, laterality or sidedness can refer to differential hemispheric function or to differential preference in manual function; in handedness, these terms are broader ones that encapsulate any type of manual or hemispheric difference. In this sense, at the manual level, these terms cover both specialized manual skills and simpler preferred manual activity, such as in handedness. Also, the terms apply to brain and not only behavior, both structurally and functionally, as in lateralized brain function. Note that dominance also applies to both manual and brain function. The dominant hand is considered the right one. The left hemisphere specialization for language function has led it to be referred to as the dominant cerebral hemisphere (Tzourio-Mazoyer & Seghier, 2016). One last term to consider is task specialization (Marchant & McGrew, 2013), which refers to whether an individual using a hand on one type of task uses it similarly on related tasks, or consistently over tasks.

Measures and Tasks

Often, handedness is measured with questionnaires, such as the Edinburgh Handedness Inventory (EHI; Oldfield, 1971). Another common handedness questionnaire concerns the Waterloo Handedness Questionnaire (WHQ; Steenhuis & Bryden, 1989). Flindall and Gonzalez (2018) found that a combined EHI and WHQ (E-WHQ) scored on a 5-point scale for each of its 22 items lacked reliability and validity. Nelson, Gonzalez, El-Asmar, Fouad Ziade, and Abu-Rustum (2018) developed a parent administered handedness questionnaire with unimanual and bimanual behaviors. Veale (2014) developed a short form of the EHI involving four items – writing, throwing, using a toothbrush, and using a spoon. However, for young children, drawing would be a better item than writing. Other measures of handedness include performance on tasks, such as pegboard speed for older children and reaching and bimanual coordination for younger children (Scharoun & Bryden, 2014). To examine differences in the left and right hemispheres, aside from querying the effects of hemispheric injuries and stroke, one can give participants dichotic listening and information processing tasks (Ocklenburg, 2017). Also, researchers can determine task-specific or resting-state hemispheric activations, for example, with functional magnetic resonance imaging (fMRI; Li et al., 2014) and functional transcranial Doppler (fTCD) ultrasound (Groen, Whitehouse, Badcock, & Bishop, 2013). Conducting observational research is important in laterality research in infancy, especially pertaining to reaching and grasping (e.g., Fagard, Margules, Lopez, Granjon, & Huet, 2017). Sacco, Moutard, and Fagard (2006) developed a baby handedness test. It consists of five items on simple grasping behavior and two on precision grasping behavior. Badcock et al. (2018) developed a language lateralization test for infants as young as 1 year of age, involving both Doppler ultrasonography and an animation of a face engaged in object search to capture attention and then asking the infant "What is this?" following replacement of the face by an object.

Aside from considering variations in laboratory task or task observed, one needs to consider whether the measure is categorical (left, mixed, right) or places handedness on a continuum. Also, research has shown that the strength in lateralization might be more determinant of relevant associations functionally than the direction of lateralization, per se. Any task or measure used might be run in a laboratory but should end up being ecologically valid or generalizable. Finally, modality is critical, for example, findings in the visual modality might not be isomorphic with those auditorially (Rogers, 2017). Despite all these potential variations in manual behavior and the qualities of hemispheric function, often researchers consider handedness as unitary and the specializations of the hemispheres as categorical (Corballis & Häberling, 2017), and they work especially with the primary direction involved (e.g., the right side for handedness and the left side for hemispheric specialization for language).

Conclusion

The field of development of laterality has historical roots stretching back thousands of years, and, at the same time, its present methodologies are specifying and differentiating concepts and measures so that the research is state of the art. The research stretches from fine-grained analysis of infant manual behavior to advanced functional brain scanning techniques that can determine brain-behavior relations. Missteps in this area include having too global measures of behavior and imputing localized brain functions in certain regions without considering networked connectivities.

References

Asenova, I. V. (2018). *Brain lateralization and developmental disorders: A new approach to unified research.* Milton Park, UK: Taylor & Francis.

Badcock, N. A., Spooner, R., Hofmann, J., Flitton, A., Elliott, S., Kurylowicz, L., et al. (2018). What box: A task for assessing language lateralization in young children. *Laterality: Asymmetries of Body, Brain, and Cognition, 23*, 391–408.

Borsboom, D. (2008). Psychometric perspectives on diagnostic systems. *Journal of Clinical Psychology, 64*, 1089–1108. https://doi.org/10.1002/jclp.20503
Broca, M. P. (1861). New observation of aphasia produced by a lesion in the posterior half of the second and third left frontal circumvolutions. *Bulletin de la Société Anatomique, 36*, 398–407.
Corballis, M. C., & Häberling, I. S. (2017). The many sides of hemispheric asymmetry: A selective review and outlook. *Journal of International Neuropsychological Society, 23*, 710–718. https://doi.org/10.1017/S1355617717000376
Fagard, J., Margules, S., Lopez, C., Granjon, L., & Huet, V. (2017). How should we test infant handedness? *Laterality: Asymmetries of Body, Brain and Cognition, 22*, 294–312. https://doi.org/10.1080/1357650X.2016.1192186
Flindall, J. W., & Gonzalez, C. L. R. (2018). Wait wait, don't tell me: Handedness questionnaires do not predict hand preference for grasping. *Laterality: Asymmetries of Body, Brain, and Cognition*. https://doi.org/10.1080/1357650X.2018.1494184
Gray, J. A. (1982). *The neuropsychology of anxiety: An enquiry into the functions of the septohippocampal system*. Oxford, UK: Oxford University Press.
Groen, M. A., Whitehouse, A. J. O., Badcock, N. A., & Bishop, D. V. M. (2013). Associations between handedness and cerebral lateralisation for language: A comparison of three measures in children. *PLoS One, 8*, e64876. https://doi.org/10.1371/journal.pone.0064876
Hepping, A. M., Ploegmakers, J. J. W., Geertzen, J. H. B., Bulstra, S., & Stevens, M. (2015). The influence of hand preference on grip strength in children and adolescents: A cross-sectional study of 2284 children and adolescents. *PLoS One, 10*, e0143476. https://doi.org/10.1371/journal.pone.0143476
Kushner, H. I. (2017). *On the other hand: Left hand, right brain, mental disorder, and history* (1st ed.). Baltimore, MD: Johns Hopkins University Press.
Li, G., Nie, J., Wang, L., Shi, F., Lyall, A. E., Lin, W., et al. (2014). Mapping longitudinal hemispheric structural asymmetries of the human cerebral cortex from birth to 2 years of age. *Cerebral Cortex, 24*, 1289–1300. https://doi.org/10.1093/cercor/bhs413
Manning, L., & Thomas-Antérion, C. (2011). Marc Dax and the discovery of the lateralisation of language in the left cerebral hemisphere. *Revue Neurologique, 167*, 868–872. https://doi.org/10.1016/j.neurol.2010.10.017
Marchant, L. F. (2017). Handedness. In A. Fuentes (Ed.), *The international encyclopedia of primatology* (pp. 1–2). New York: Wiley.
Marchant, L. F., & McGrew, W. C. (2013). Handedness is more than laterality: Lessons from chimpanzees. *Annals of the New York Academy of Sciences, 1288*, 1–8. https://doi.org/10.1111/nyas.12062
McManus, C. (2004). *Right hand, left hand: The origins of asymmetry in brains, bodies, atoms, and cultures*. London: Harvard University Press.
Nelson, E. L., Gonzalez, S. L., El-Asmar, J. M., Fouad Ziade, M., & Abu-Rustum, R. S. (2018). The home handedness questionnaire: Pilot data from preschoolers. *Laterality: Asymmetries of Body, Brain and Cognition*. https://doi.org/10.1080/1357650X.2018.1543313.
Ocklenburg, S. (2017). Tachistoscope viewing and dichotic listening. In L. J. Rogers & G. Vallortigara (Eds.), *Lateralized brain functions: Methods in human and non-human species* (pp. 3–26). New York: Springer SBM.
Ocklenburg, S., & Güntürkün, O. (2018). *The lateraized brain: The neuroscience and evolution of hemispheric asymmetries*. Cambridge, MA: Elsevier.
Oldfield, R. C. (1971). The assessment and analysis of handedness: The Edinburgh inventory. *Neuropsychologia, 9*, 97–113.
Porac, C. (2016). *Laterality: Exploring the enigma of left-handedness*. London: Elsevier.
Rogers, L. J. (2017). Eye and ear preferences. In L. J. Rogers & G. Vallortigara (Eds.), *Lateralized brain functions* (pp. 79–102). New York: Springer SBM.
Rogers, L. J., & Vallortigara, G. (2017). *Lateralized brain functions: Methods in human and non-human species*. New York: Springer SBM.
Rogers, L. J., Vallortigara, G., & Andrew, R. J. (2013). *Divided brains: The biology and behaviour of brain asymmetries*. Cambridge, MA: Cambridge University Press.

Sacco, S., Moutard, M. L., & Fagard, J. (2006). Agenesis of the corpus callosum and the establishment of handedness. *Developmental Psychobiology, 48*, 472–481. https://doi.org/10.1002/dev.20162

Scharoun, S. M., & Bryden, P. J. (2014). Hand preference, performance abilities, and hand selection in children. *Frontiers in Psychology, 5*, 82. https://doi.org/10.3389/fpsyg.2014.00082

Smits, R. (2012). *The puzzle of left-handedness*. London: Reaktion Books.

Sporns, O. (2011). *Networks of the brain*. Cambridge, MA: MIT Press.

Sporns, O. (2012). *Discovering the human connectome*. Cambridge, MA: MIT Press.

Steenhuis, R. E., & Bryden, M. (1989). Different dimensions of hand preference that relate to skilled and unskilled activities. *Cortex, 25*, 289–304.

Treves, T., Goldschmidt, I., & Korczyn, A. D. (1983). Development of manual laterality and language function. In G. Young, S. J. Segalowitz, C. M. Corter, & S. E. Trehub (Eds.), *Manual specialization and the developing brain* (pp. 395–400). New York: Academic.

Tzourio-Mazoyer, N., & Seghier, M. L. (2016). The neural bases of hemispheric specialization. *Neuropsychologia, 93*, 319–324. https://doi.org/10.1016/j.neuropsychologia.2016.10.010

Vallortigara, G. (2015). Handedness: What kangaroos tell us about our lopsided brains. *Current Biology, 25*, R654–R676. https://doi.org/10.1016/j.cub.2015.06.036

Vallortigara, G., & Rogers, L. J. (2005). Survival with an asymmetrical brain: Advantages and disadvantages of cerebral lateralization. *Behavioral and Brain Sciences, 28*, 575–589. https://doi.org/10.1017/S0140525X05000105

Veale, J. F. (2014). Edinburgh handedness inventory – Short form: A revised version based on confirmatory factor analysis. *Laterality: Asymmetries of Body, Brain and Cognition, 19*, 164–177. https://doi.org/10.1080/1357650X.2013.783045

Wernicke, C. (1874). The symptom complex of aphasia. A psychological study on an anatomical basis (Translated from German; G. H. Eggert, Trans.). In *Wernicke's work on aphasia: A sourcebook and review*. The Hague: Mouton, 1977.

Wright, E. (2007). *A left-handed history of the word*. Eastbourne, UK: Gardners Books.

Young, G. (1990a). The development of hemispheric and manual specialization. In G. Hammond (Ed.), *The cerebral control of speech and limb movements* (pp. 79–139). Amsterdam, The Netherlands: North Holland.

Young, G. (1990b). Early neuropsychological development: Lateralization of functions – Hemispheric specialization. In C.-A. Hauert (Ed.), *Developmental psychology: Cognitive, perceptuo-motor and neuropsychological perspectives* (pp. 113–181). Amsterdam, The Netherlands: North Holland.

Young, G. (2011). *Development and causality: Neo-Piagetian perspectives*. New York: Springer Science + Business Media.

Young, G. (2016). *Unifying causality and psychology: Being, brain and behavior*. Cham, Switzerland: Springer International Publishing.

Young, G., Bowman, J. G., Methot, C., Finlayson, M., Quintal, J., & Boissonneault, P. (1983). Hemispheric specialization development: What (inhibition) and how (parents). In G. Young, S. J. Segalowitz, C. M. Corter, & S. E. Trehub (Eds.), *Manual specialization and the developing brain* (pp. 119–140). New York: Academic.

Young, G., Corter, C. M., Segalowitz, S. J., & Trehub, S. E. (1983). Manual specialization and the developing brain: An overview. In G. Young, S. J. Segalowitz, C. M. Corter, & S. E. Trehub (Eds.), *Manual specialization and the developing brain* (pp. 3–12). New York: Academic.

Young, G., & Gagnon, M. (1990). Neonatal laterality, birth stress, familial sinistrality, and left brain inhibition. *Developmental Neuropsychology, 6*, 127–150.

Young, G., Segalowitz, S. J., Corter, C. M., & Trehub, S. E. (Eds.). (1983). *Manual specialization and the developing brain*. New York: Academic.

Young, G., Segalowitz, S. J., Misek, P., Alp, I. E., & Boulet, R. (1983). Is early reaching left-handed? Review of manual specialization research. In G. Young, S. J. Segalowitz, C. M. Corter, & S. E. Trehub (Eds.), *Manual specialization and the developing brain* (pp. 13–32). New York: Academic.

Chapter 3
Developmental Laterality Research: Infancy

Abstract The first comprehensive chapter of the book examines in depth the developmental literature on early laterality. It reviews recent publications both on manual behavior and on findings related to the brain. The research reviewed is organized by age and cuts fine. It keeps the age range limited in each section of the chapter in order to present a clear developmental picture. The chapter begins with research in the prenatal period and continues with the newborn and early months of life, before moving on to the second half of the first year and then the second year. The major empirical issue is when laterality first manifests in the infant, because one of the major views is that the brain is equi-potential early in life and that manual behavior does not demonstrate its normal right-hand preference. In contrast, the major opposing view in this regard is that the early brain is specialized already along adult lines, which is the approach of invariant lateralization. The research demonstrates that when tasks and measures are used that are age specific, whether examining manual specialization or hemispheric specialization, the empirical results reflect the later adult pattern, supportive of the invariant lateralization model. In this regard, there is sufficient data even in the prenatal period that the developing fetus demonstrates a right-hand preference for behaviors indicative of manual preference. Moreover, associated brain development findings support that early hemispheric specialization at this age period is organized in a way that parallels later left hemisphere verbal skills and later right hemisphere visuo-spatial ones. Moreover, the models that can best explain the findings include the one of activation-inhibition coordination. The model of cascades in development helps explain longitudinal findings.

G. Young, *Causality and Development*,
https://doi.org/10.1007/978-3-030-02493-2_3

Research Review

Human Populations

Introduction

There are two major sections to the present work in terms of the research reviewed, with the first part on human research and the second part on animal research. The latter section begins with discussion on causality. The first part of the human research section presents a literature review of recent work on the development of handedness and related lateralizations. This area is burgeoning, and new concepts and findings arise continuously. The second part on human research in relation to lateralizations examines hemisphericity, which is a concept that has almost disappeared from the research scene but does have some validity and should be resurrected. The section after the review of the human research turns to animal research and causality. It begins with a discussion of the causes and mechanisms underlying handedness and related development. It is oriented biopsychosocially, covering the role of genes, epigenesis, experience, culture, and so on, as well as psychological factors. Then, the present work shifts to the animal and evolutionary research, before concluding the last section that presents other concepts and models that contribute to the field.

Developmental Research on Handedness, Manual Specialization, and Hemispheric Specialization

Introduction

The present section of the book describes developmental findings in lateralized manual behavior, handedness, and hemispheric specialization. The structure of the review involves presentation of the research according to the chronological age of the children, beginning prenatally and up to the preschool years. Also, two categories of research are reviewed, one on manual behavior, including handedness, and the other on the developing brain and its lateralization.

Note that the review is selective because there is so much empirical research on the two topics, and it is impossible to describe it all. Moreover, the review does not present much of the details of the research, or else it would be prohibitively long. Also, it intersperses comments as the review proceeds, which elaborate, amplify, criticize, and so on, by using the italicized phrase of *as a comment*, and without using the subheading "Comment," which is used in later sections of this first portion of the present book, where the structure lends itself more readily to using this subheading. Conceptually, this part of the book emphasizes the activation-inhibition coordination and connectivity network approaches to the brain and to behavior and how they can help understand lateralized behavior and lateralized brain function.

Prenatal

Manual Behavior Hepper (2013) reviewed the research on fetal laterality from his laboratory. First, he noted that Hepper, Shahidullah, and White (1991) had taken scans showing that thumb sucking is right-handed in the fetus. Also, fetuses turn the head rightward (Hepper, McCartney, & Shannon, 1998). As for other fetal behaviors, McCartney and Hepper (1999) showed that the fetus moves the right arm more than the left. Finally, Hepper, Wells, and Lynch (2005) found that fetal right thumb sucking predicted right-handedness in 10- to 12-year-old children.

Note that the developmental relationship in longitudinal research does not involve an earlier behavior exclusively determining a later one. In this particular case of early fetal behavior predicting later lateralization, the predictions found are not direct, in that there are intervening variables and other changes with age that do not reflect the initial lateralizations. The more appropriate interpretation of the findings is that the earlier lateralizations might lead to further lateralization changes that reflect developmental cascades of influence (Marcinowski, Campbell, Faldowski, & Michel, 2016). It is not that early thumb sucking directly causes later side of hand preference, but it sets in motion dynamical experiences that condition its emergence on the same side of the sucking.

Michel (2018) reviewed his research that early prenatal head turning takes place more to the right and predicts later head turning and manual asymmetries. Specifically, neonates prefer to turn the head to the right, and this appears to relate to later infant preference in object contact and retrieval (Michel, 1981; Michel & Harkins, 1986).

In research by other groups, Parma, Brasselet, Zoia, Bulgheroni, and Castiello (2017) found that, at 18-week gestational age, kinematically evaluated fetal arm movements as measured during four-dimensional fetal ultrasonography were faster toward the eye and mouth regions compared to the uterine wall, which requires less precision. Movement time (MT) in fetal reaching was the best measure in predicting handedness side at 9 years of age, as measured by maternal report. The right hand was used more than the left in fetuses who ended up right-handed, and future left-handed fetuses showed a different pattern. The authors concluded that the future dominant hand (evident as mostly right one even at this age) was the one that planned precise movements with better skill.

Other Lateralized Factors Prenatally

Reissland, Francis, Aydin, Mason, and Exley (2014) found that mouth opening movements were more left lateralized at 24- to 36-week gestation. Typically, left lateralization and mouth opening movements during speech are taken as a sign of left hemisphere activation for language (Graves, Goodglass, & Landis, 1982).

Chan and Loh (2016) remarked the differences in oxygenation in the right and left subclavian arteries by the 9th week of fetal life might be a factor in the development of various lateralizations. For example, they refer to handedness in this regard. Another fetal factor in the development of handedness relates to testosterone.

Papadatou-Pastou and Martin (2017) related later language lateralization to the influence of fetal testosterone. Beking et al. (2018) related prenatal testosterone assays at 15- to 18-week measures prenatally to 15-year-old lateralization during cognitive activity, but only for boys and only in interaction with pubertal testosterone level. The cognitive tasks were mental rotation, chimeric faces, and word generation. The lateralization was measured with functional transcranial Doppler (fTCD) ultrasonography. For example, low prenatal testosterone led to pubertal testosterone effects on the right hemisphere (see the study for the specifics of the complex results).

Brain de Kovel et al. (2017) studied embryonic spinal cord development in the 4- to 8-week fetal period and its mirror development in the hindbrain. They found that the right side matured faster for the former, and the left for the latter. They noted that this finding has been the developmentally earliest research finding on left-right differences in the development of the brain. In this regard, Ocklenburg et al. (2017) found evidence that gene activity in the spinal cord is asymmetric fetally and might help explain handedness development.

Im et al. (2010) found the first cortical signs in favor of the left hemisphere, being in the superior temporal sulci. Specifically, the left side showed more sulcal pits (also see Habas et al., 2012). Habas et al. (2012) also found many areas of the fetal brain that expressed a right-sided advantage, as did Kasprian et al. (2011) and Li et al. (2014), for example, with respect to the posterior temporal operculum (PTO) and middle temporal gyrus (MTG) in these regards). In an fNIRS (functional near-infrared spectroscopy) study with prematures born between 26 to 39 weeks gestational age, Arimitsu, Minagawa, Yagihashi, Uchida, Matsuzaki, Ikeda, and Takahashi (2018) demonstrated that the pattern of hemsiphere specialization exhibited in the hemodynamic response to phonetic changes of speech gradually developed to resemble the pattern in term infants. In an fMRI study with premature infants at 29 weeks gestation, Mahmoudzadeh et al. (2013) determined that the left hemisphere activated more for processing syllable changes.

Other findings about the prenatal lateralized brain have shown a larger temporal lobe on the left side between 18 and 37 weeks of gestation (Kasprian et al., 2011). Kooistra and Heilman (1988) had previously found the globus pallidus has a greater left-side volume. Note that the temporal lobe is involved in language reception and the globus pallidus in movement, the early development of which in the left hemisphere might help serve its specializations for language and for fine motor control, respectively.

Note that although developmental findings implicate hemisphere cortical and subcortical differences in the fetal brain, the trajectories differ over region, and early patterns do not continue into the end of term. Part of the reason relates to the way the developing brain grows fetally, with torque twisting, ventral and dorsal differences as much as left and right ones, and so on.

In this regard, Andescavage et al. (2017) conducted a volumetric analysis of the growth trajectories of the developing fetal brain using three-dimensional fMRI in healthy fetuses from 18 to 27 and 28 to 39 weeks gestation. The brain areas studied included cortical grey matter, white matter, deep sub-cortical structures, and the cerebellum. All but the white matter had larger left-side volumes in the earlier gestational period. However, in the second one, there were no left-right volumetric brain differences that were evident, except for the continuation of the greater left hemisphere volume for cortical grey matter. These results are consistent with results with newborns showing a greater left hemisphere volume for gray matter in particular (Gilmore et al., 2007).

Additionally, a study with premature infants using well-adapted technology to obtain fMRI readings has shown that functional lateralization along adult lines appears present prenatally in the human brain (Scheef et al., 2017). The researchers examined fMRI responses in the sensori-motor cortex in 8 premature infants aged 26 weeks when they were passively stimulated in the right arm. For the most part, they found only contralateral responses. At 2 years of age, testing revealed normal neuro-developmental outcome. The authors concluded that, even in the age period studied in the prematures, a considerable amount of functional lateralization appears to have developed, at least for sensori-motor circuits.

Using cortical auditory evoked responses (CAERs) to click stimuli in 30 healthy newborns (30–38 post-menstrual weeks), Kaminska, Delattre, Laschet, Dubois, Labidurie, Duval, Manresa, Magny, Hovhannisyan, Mokhtari, Ouss, Boissel, Hertz-Pannier, Sintsov, Minlevbaev, Khazipov, and Chiron (2018) demonstrated predominant right-side EEG power in delta and gamma frequency bands over the middle and posterior temporal brain regions. The authors related the results to a prenatal right hemisphere specialization in the indicated age period for tone dictation/ discrimination (also citing Mento, Suppiej, Altoè, & Bisiacchi, 2010). As for the left hemisphere in this age period, Kaminska et al. (2018) cited the research of Mahmoudzade, Dehaene-Lambertz, Fournier, Kongolo, Goudjil, Dubois, Grebe, and Wallois (2013) who found that at birth this hemisphere appears specialized for specific speech properties.

As a comment, the evidence is clear that the equi-potential model of the left and right hemispheres in the human case does not meet the critical test empirically for both brain and behavior. The nature of the findings prenatally fit the age period and refers to lateralized patterns in brain development that do not necessarily map onto the equivalent patterns in the child or adult due to the relatively primitive status of the behavioral and brain development involved. Nevertheless, these lateralizations have far-reaching consequences, by setting in process the lateralization development that is a fundamental attribute of human behavior and brain.

However, findings are not always fully compatible with the invariant lateralization model implicated by many of the findings in the field. For example, the volumetric analysis of the cortical, subcortical, and cerebellum for left-right differences and their changes from the middle to the third trimester in fetuses revealed less lateralization to the left as development proceeded. That said, the lateralized brain volume differences in the middle trimester could have had functional implications developmentally even as the right hemisphere eventually caught up in volume in these regards. Moreover, other research supports structural and functional differences in the hemispheres neonatally and thereafter.

Neonates

Manual Behavior Research has shown that the grasping reflex is more evident in the right hand (Tan, Ors, Kürkçüoglu, & Kutlu, 1992), as is object holding as measured in time in the hold (Caplan & Kinsbourne, 1976). Fagard, Margules, Lopez, Granjon, and Huet (2017) reviewed the early research on stronger hand and arm right-side reflexes in neonates but referred to contradictory results, too. As cited in Ittyerah (2017), Streri and Gentaz (2003) found that newborns can recognize visually the shape of an object that had been previously manipulated out of sight by the right hand.

As a comment, note that there is no contradiction in the right hand being preferred not only for a reflex but also for a functional activity such as object holding, because grasping facilitates object holding. Therefore, we can conclude that the neonatal pattern in grasping motorically reflects the adult pattern in hemispheric specialization, that is, a left-sided advantage for more complex fine motor behavior.

Nagy, Pal, and Orvos (2014) found a better left-hand skill for imitation of finger movements in 2-day-olds, which is consistent with the right hemisphere advantage for spatial skills generally. The results speak to early development of the right hemisphere's superior spatial skills, which complement other findings of the early development of the left hemisphere's superior verbal skills.

At the behavioral level, these results are consistent with the similar functional findings of Young, Bowman, et al. (1983) and of Young and Gagnon (1990). Respectively, they had found that 1-month-olds exhibit a right-handed reaching and that 2-day-olds exhibit a right-sided head turning to verbal stimuli compared to matched musical ones.

Specifically, Young, Bowman, et al. (1983) found that 1-month-olds sitting upright reached more with the right hand to objects presented at the midline, opened the right hand more just before contact, and contacted the object more with the right hand, all compared to the left hand, while the left hand moved more generally in a non-directed way, as if helping in determining the spatial relationship of the target object to the body.

Young and Gagnon (1990) showed that 2-day-olds turned more to the right than left to hear low-intensity speech from behind at the midline compared to matched low-intensity musical tone sounds, which is consistent with an early left hemisphere specialization for language. Together, these results support the invariant lateralization model of the developing brain compared to the equi-potential, progressive one, which is a conclusion amplified below in terms of a combined model.

Activation-Inhibition Coordination Young, Corter, Segalowitz, and Trehub (1983) distinguished early manual specialization from handedness. Also, they argued that early hemispheric specialization followed the adult model, with manual skills, as they develop, mapping onto their related differential skills of the hemispheres.

That is, the critical manual behavior emerging at the age of 1 month in development concerns visually directed reaching (Piaget; e.g., Young, 2011), and this complex manual behavior requires much activation-inhibition coordination. Thus, it should begin by being right-handed, as found in Young, Bowman, et al. (1983), through mapping onto the specialization of the left hemisphere, which is posited to involve activation-inhibition coordination. That is, it was found to be a right-handed activity at the indicated age presumably because of the activation-inhibition coordination involved.

In the other study by Young and colleagues (Young & Gagnon, 1990; on 2-day-old head turning to low-intensity sounds presented from behind), it could be argued that speech sounds are more complex than musical ones in terms of the activation-inhibition coordinations required to process them, or at least verbal production requires these skills, to the point that any verbal task ends up shunted to the left hemisphere even if pre-speech in development, as was found. Once more, it appears that an early critical behavior emerges and seems to require activation-inhibition coordination; this leads to its mapping onto the left hemisphere even if it is early in life, because the left hemisphere already at this age period can accommodate to the demand due to its activation-inhibition coordination skills.

Brain Research on the development of lateralization of the brain involves investigating both functional concomitants to differential left and right hemisphere activity and structural bases that might underlie the functional differences in these regards. At the functional level, in neonates, Bertoncini et al. (1989) found a right-ear advantage for processing speech stimuli in newborns, which reflects left hemisphere processing for language.

As elaborated in Tzourio-Mazoyer, Perrone-Bertolotti, Jobard, Mazoyer, and Baciu (2017), in a neuroimaging study of 2-day-olds, Perani et al. (2011) showed that on the left side of the brain, the inferior frontal gyrus (IFG) and the superior temporal gyrus (STG) are synchronized homotopically during sentence listening, and without intra-hemispheric connectivity, although the right auditory cortex was implicated more generally in the neural network for language in these newborns. For auditory stimuli in 2-month-olds, Dehaene-Lambertz (2000) found that ERP (event-related potential) amplitude was larger over the left hemisphere relative to the right hemisphere.

Lori et al. (2017) conducted a somatosensory evoked potential (SEP) study with 2-day-olds who were either 37- to 39-week gestational age or 40- to 41-week gestational age. The EEG (electroencephalogram)-related N1-P1 complex was higher in mean amplitude in the younger group for left hemisphere readings.

Peña et al. (2003) and Dehaene-Lambertz, Dehaene, and Hertz-Pannier (2002) both related left hemisphere speech processing to the temporal lobe. In contrast,

Homae, Watanabe, Nakano, Asakawa, and Taga (2006) found that prosody and intonation, nonverbal in nature, elicited right temporo-parietal blood flow at this age.

Structurally, Li et al. (2014) used surface-based morphometry of magnetic resonance imaging (MRI) not only for participants at birth but also at 1–2 years of age. Consistent with the invariant lateralization model, they found that the left planum temporale was both larger and deeper than the right one at all three ages. Dehaene-Lambertz (2017) concluded after her review of the research on lateralized neonatal brain structure for language-related skills that the left hemisphere is primed from birth for its later linguistic skills.

Levman, MacDonald, Lim, Forgeron, and Takahashi (2017) showed similar findings with their structural MRI study, with ages of participants varying from 0 to 32 years. I calculated their left-right hemisphere differences for the number of findings revealing greater left or right hemisphere asymmetries (see their Table 5.1). For surface area, five of the seven findings concerned a left hemisphere advantage; for number of vertices, the findings favored the left side in a ratio of 7 to 2, with the same results for gray matter volume. The only result for white matter volume favored the left side. The authors concluded that a left dominance in language-related and other areas was observed in the MRI findings, although the neonatal period was not singled out, per se, in these regards.

Ratnarajah et al. (2014) used diffusion tensor imaging scans (DTI) in neonates. They tracked white matter axonal pathways involving interregional connections both in the cortex and subcortex. They used network concepts and showed tight connections and short paths in both hemispheres but more efficient structural connections in the left hemisphere. Specifically, the neonatal left hemisphere showed better intraregional integration and interconnection segregation both locally and globally. Other results found more left hemisphere connectivity according to "betweenness centrality." They concluded that there are more efficient circuit paths in the left hemisphere and that they facilitate quicker information transfer and flow compared to the right hemisphere.

As a comment, Tzourio-Mazoyer et al. (2017) echoed Perani et al. (2011) that, in infancy, there is more inter-hemispheric functional connectivity and that as development proceeds, it becomes more intra-hemispheric. In terms of the model being espoused in the present work of the generalized mechanism that undergirds hemispheric specialization, this increased inter-hemispheric communication in the development process might allow better activation-inhibition coordination not only within the left hemisphere but also by the left hemisphere with the right one as development proceeds.

Further, the finding that the left hemisphere exhibits better efficiency and shorter circuit paths (Ratnarajah et al., 2014) speaks to the differential connectivity of the hemispheres from the neonatal period and onward. The research is finding not only a lack of equi-potentiality in the organization of the cerebral hemispheres early in life but also a structural basis for the invariant lateralization model of hemispheric specialization and its functional implications for the neonate and older child. At the same time, the left hemisphere language lateralization that develops early in life continues to develop, for example, in terms of better intra-hemispheric connectivity (Tzourio-Mazoyer et al., 2017).

First Year

Manual Behavior As previously described, Young, Bowman, et al. (1983) had found that 1-month-olds reach more efficiently with the right hand, both in terms of direction in the reach and hand opening before contact, let alone contact itself, and the left hand engages in more non-directed and spatially related behavior. Young, Bowman, et al. (1983) noted that if one adds together the total of left- and right-hand movements, because there are so much more non-directed compared to directed behaviors, the overall impression is that the 1-month-old is left-handed, just like how Gesell and Ames (1947) had proposed. However, by differentiating manual function in hemisphere skill in consistent ways (that is, skilled reaching vs. non-directed and spatial), the results actually revealed the opposite finding – that the baby begins life right-handed.

Note that Morange-Majoux, Lemoine, and Dellatolas (2013) found similar reaching results for infants aged 20–30 weeks, especially in terms of approach time to object being shorter for the left hand and grasping latency time shorter with the right hand. Also, Morange-Majoux (2010) found that 4- to 6-month-old infants pressed and tapped the hard part of an object with the right hand and the softer parts by passive touch with the left hand. Morange-Majoux, Peze, and Bloch (2000) observed reaching movements in 5- to 8-month-old infants. They found that when an object was presented at a reachable distance, movement time was consistently shorter for the right hand compared to the left. Also, the right hand was oriented more directly toward the object, and it made less corrective changes than the left hand. Morange-Majoux and Devouche (2014) also demonstrated that the right hand reaches better in 6-month-olds. Further, Morange-Majoux, Devouche, Lemoine-Lardennois, and Orriols (2017) noted that 6-month-olds watching the right hand manipulate objects ipsilaterally behaved differently compared to the left hand on the same task. Specifically, the infants looked more at objects when the objects were placed to the right and more around the objects when they were to the left.

As a comment, note that, collectively, these findings are quite consistent with Young, Bowman, et al.'s (1983) approach that the right hand already at 1 month of age engages in more directed hand movements toward objects. In contrast, early in life, already the left hand engages in more non-directed or spatial movements.

The results of research with older infants confirm the general tendency for the right and left hands to behave in ways indicative of an early manual laterality that is consistent with the adult model. Michel's research team studied 6-month-olds and used multiple objects in their testing. They found a right-hand preference in object acquisition and manipulation at 6 months of age (Campbell, Marcinowski, Babik, & Michel, 2015; Campbell, Marcinowski, Latta, & Michel, 2015; Michel, Babik, Shue, & Campbell, 2013, respectively).

Fagard, Spelke, and von Hofsten (2009) determined that 8-month-olds exhibited a right-hand preference as they reached for moving objects. Note, however, that the 6-month-olds and the 10-month-olds who were also studied did not show this right-hand preference.

Vauclair and Imbault (2009) studied 10- to 40-month-olds in pointing. They found that even children who were left-handed or ambidextrous used the right hand for pointing.

As a comment, note developmental research on handedness and on manual specialization profits from longitudinal research designs. These types of studies need to choose differing age-appropriate tasks at different ages with the goal to establish in the best way cross-age relations. Also, they tackle diverse questions, such as the relationship of different types of manual behavior and other developmental aspects, for example, related to symbols and language.

In the 6- to 14-month age period, Marcinowski et al. (2016) studied the development of hand preference on manual tasks involving manipulation of objects of various shapes and sizes, and they observed stacking when the infants were 10–14 months of age. They found that the right hand was preferred either stably or as a trend in 57.6% of the sample, with left handers at 12.2% and non-handers at 30.2%. Also, stable right or left handers developed faster and better stacking skills at 14 months. Another study by the Michel group, by Campbell, Marcinowski, Latta, et al. (2015), examined monthly classifications of hand preference from 8- to 14-month-olds on the same tasks as Marcinowski et al. (2016) and other tasks from the Fagard group (refer to Esseily, Jacquet, & Fagard, 2011). The former Michel tasks showed that 45% of the infants expressed a right-preferring developmental trajectory, while only 5% showed a left-preferring one, with 50% showing no clear preference. The latter Fagard tasks indicated two trajectories, one 70% right-handed and the other 30% with no preference. In a similar study by Campbell, Marcinowski, and Michel (2017) using the Michel tasks, and with the participants being 6–14 months of age, 32% were early right-handed in the age period, and 25% were later right-handed, for a total of 57%. Also, early-handed infants were more advanced neuro-motorically according to Touwen's test (Touwen, 1976). Morange-Majoux and Adrien (2016) reported an unpublished study in which 6-month-olds used their left hand to hold an object as they heard music, implying a right hemisphere activation.

Jacobsohn, Rodrigues, Vasconcelos, Corbetta, and Barreiros (2014) studied children from birth to 2 years of age in eight time periods for lateral manual asymmetry. They used age-appropriate tasks. Object-related manual activity to a cube presented at midline was observed in the 6- to 9-month period, and midline reaching to a plastic ball was observed from 12 to 18 months. The authors found an emergence of right-hand lateralization in manual behavior at 9 months and an increase in this preference over the developmental time frame. The authors did not find lateralized manual behavior at birth and in the first and third month, perhaps because the infants were placed in a supine position, unlike other studies that use seating position (e.g., Young, Bowman, et al., 1983).

Another methodological consideration in laterality research relates to the laterality formula used. For example, Fagard et al. (2017) showed that there are three different laterality formulae one can use in their study of 9- and 11-month-olds. Also, results varied for uni-manual tasks compared to bimanual tasks, as well as the number of trials. As for left-right differences in behaviors, their results agree that there was a higher percentage of right- than left-handers for the tasks used in the age period studied.

As a comment, these sets of results indicate that, on the one hand, handedness for tasks that are simpler for a specific age period, such as reaching at 6–10 months of age, do not necessarily exhibit a consistent right-hand preference. This is because more complex tasks are needed for the age period being studied so as to elicit a manual specialization and one that is consistent with an underlying hemispheric specialization. These results also indicate that more complex manual behaviors for a specific age period, such as happens with pointing in 10-month-olds, are capable of activating the underlying hemispheric specialization involved and do so independently of the general hand preference of the infant or its lack.

Similarly, for 12- to 20-month-olds, Potier, Meguerditchian, and Fagard (2013) studied right-hand grasping and manipulations in bimanual coordinated actions when precision compared to whole-hand gripping was involved in the tasks. Generally, the children were right-handed, and right-hand preference increased with age. More to the point, from 12 months of age, the right hand excelled in grasping, removing pieces, and transferring, which are complex tasks for the age period. Further in this regard, the right hand showed its preference more clearly in the precision grip mode.

Even the relationships of manual behavior to complex outcomes, such as in language, confirm that laterality differences are evident and important at the age under review. Mumford and Kita (2016) examined the relationship between pointing and receptive vocabulary scores in 10- to 12-month-olds. They found that the more the right hand was used for pointing, the larger was receptive vocabulary. Pointing was observed when a desired toy was placed in front of the infant, and receptive vocabulary was measured using the Oxford Communicative Development Inventory (CDI; Hamilton, Plunkett, & Schafer, 2000).

As a comment, the developmental research on early manual laterality has proliferated in the first year of life because it is a crucial age to study and is easier to study than in neonates. The findings indicate changing developmental trajectories consistent with the predominant adult model on manual specialization, but with developmental links forming, for instance, to the language function.

The next study reviewed relates to early right hemisphere specialization for a spatial function but took place with a functional task and so is included in the behavioral section. It illustrates, as with Young and Gagnon's (1990) study with 2-day-olds, that discovering underlying hemispheric differences is quite possible by studying functional differences in dealing with information, for example, speech versus nonspeech.

Specifically, Bulf, de Hevia, Gariboldi, and Macchi Cassia (2017) studied 7-month-olds, who are preverbal, while they learned higher-order, rule-like patterns in sequences of visually presented geometric shapes when the sequences were presented either in the direction left to right or that of right to left. The method used involved a habituation paradigm, with mean looking times calculated. The results showed superior rule learning of visually presented novel geometric shapes (as evidenced by longer looking at novel stimuli on test trials) for the left to right and not the right to left sequences. The presentation of left to right sequence is similar to the direction of reading in English and Western languages, so one could argue that a left to right advantage would be found because of cultural factors, such as watching how adults read. However, the results in this direction also would be consistent with an early right hemisphere advantage for functionally dealing with visuo-spatial tasks (de Hevia, Girelli, & Macchi Cassia, 2012), as argued by the authors, without ruling out cultural influences. In another relevant study, with 5- to 7-month-olds and older infants, Morange-Majoux and Devouche (2019) replicated Young and Gagnon's (1990) neonatal finding that even very young infants are predisposed to processing music in the right hemisphere relative to speech sounds–the youngest infants in Morange-Majoux and Devouche (2019), but not the older ones, used the left hand to reach while listening to classical music, unlike the case for reaching when listening to adult speech.

Finally, in a study bridging the next section on the brain research in the first year of life, the cognitive implications of a well-developing left hemisphere in the motor area was accentuated by de Oliveira et al. (2017). For full-term and premature 6-month-olds, the degree of hemodynamic activity during a motor task, as measured by functional near-infrared spectroscopy (fNIRS), was positively associated with motor scale results on the Bayley Scales of Infant Development III (Bayley, 2009; a composite measure was calculated for the fine and gross motor scale results).

Brain Kobayashi, Macchi Cassia, Kanazawa, Yamaguchi, and Kakigi (2018) studied face processing in the visual modality in 9-month-olds and found a right hemisphere function. Specifically, using near-infrared spectroscopy (NIRS), they found that, for adult face stimuli, the right temporal lobe was more active hemodynamically. In a fast-periodic visual stimulation (FPVS) paradigm study with 4- to 6-month-olds, de Heering and Rossion (2015) found a strong right lateralized electroencephalogram (EEG) response in the occipito-temporal region selectively to faces. Face images were inserted in the stream in 20% of the stimuli. Research with children has not found similar findings, although it has with adults, suggesting to Behrmann and Plaut (2013) that right hemisphere face perception begins only after the left hemisphere language lateralization firmly develops once reading is mastered. Lochy, de Heering, and Rossion (2017) used the same methodology as in their infant research, finding an absence of lateralization in children who were 5 years. They argued that when the developmental trajectory is examined for right hemisphere lateralized face perception, a nonlinear model fits the data.

As a comment, essentially, this collection of research studies supports a combined model of early lateralization in the brain for the area of face perception along adult lines (right lateralized), but with variability in the developmental course before stability obtains later in development. This pattern is the one that seems to fit much of the developmental research on lateralization in infants and children, for example, in the stability of handedness preference.

Hane, Fox, Henderson, and Marshall (2008) studied infants from 4 to 9 months of age in a longitudinal research. The results showed that infants who were "positively reactive" showed more approach behavior as well as left frontal region electroencephalographic (EEG) asymmetry. As for "negatively reactive" infants, they showed more avoidance and, also, more right frontal EEG asymmetry. The authors concluded that behavioral activity in infants is related to approach/withdrawal and specialized in the left and right frontal areas of the hemispheres accordingly.

This research follows up on the original work by Fox and Davidson (1984) on the left vs. right frontal hemisphere differences in emotional control and expression. The model that they have developed has been referred to as the approach-withdrawal model of hemispheric specialization for emotions (Davidson, 1983), as reviewed in Palmiero and Piccardi (2017). A similar model referred to as the valence model was developed by Heller (1990). In this model, the left hemisphere is considered specialized for positive emotions and the right hemisphere for negative emotions. The problem with this model concerns how anger fits into it. Another model about left vs. right hemisphere differences concerning emotions is the "capability model" (Coan, Allen, & McKnight, 2006), which adds a contextual aspect in either responding or inhibiting emotionally. Recent reviews of frontal EEG asymmetries do not particularly mention the role of inhibition differentially in the hemispheres and emphasize, instead, a left hemisphere positive emotion/approach/motivation configuration relative to a right hemisphere negative emotion/withdrawal activity (Allen, Keune, Schönenberg, & Nusslock, 2018; Harmon-Jones & Gable, 2018; Helwig, 2018; Reznik & Allen, 2018).

Palmiero and Piccardi (2017) described that a recent model on the differentiation of emotions in the hemispheres has been proposed by Grimshaw and Carmel (2014). Grimshaw and Carmel also included inhibition in their model. They described different types of inhibitions in the two hemispheres, for example, as mediated by mechanisms in the dorsolateral prefrontal cotex (dlPFC) and as related to executive function. Specifically, in the Grimshaw-Carmel inhibitory model of the hemispheres, the left frontal cortex acts to inhibit negative distractors and the right frontal cortex similiarly inhibits positive distractors. For example, if the left frontal activity is low, the person has difficulty disengaging attention from negative stimuli, as in depression (Cisler & Koster, 2010). In contrast, if right frontal activity is low, the person has difficulty in inhibiting positive distractions, such as those related to addiction (Goldstein & Volkow, 2011). The Grimshaw-Carmel model is reviewed in more depth later in the present article.

Palmiero and Piccardi (2017) concluded that, as applied to the review of hemispheric asymmetries and mood, the evidence especially supports the approach-withdrawal and valence models. They argued, for example, that the findings of Engels et al. (2010) do not support the differential left-right hemisphere distractor inhibition model of Grimshaw and Carmel (2014).

Yet there is research that supports differential inhibitory aspects of the hemispheres in development. For example, in a longitudinal study spanning 18 years, Schwartz et al. (2010) found that children who were more socially outgoing compared to inhibited (or low reactive compared to high reactive) at 4 months of age later developed at 18 years a thicker left orbito-frontal cortex, especially in the transverse orbital sulcus, as revealed by an MRI investigation. In contrast, the high-reactive infants developed a thicker right orbito-frontal cortex.

Also, the newer models on differential inhibitory skills in the hemispheres, such as that of Grimshaw and Carmel (2014), are interesting by attempting to translate the emotional models into inhibitory ones. In this sense, they are consistent with the present approach of activation-inhibition coordination differences in the hemispheres. This concept is elaborated in much depth later in this article.

Returning to the Hane et al. (2008) results described above for infant emotions, they are consistent with adult models of hemispheric specialization for emotions and related behavior. In this regard, Shobe (2014) posited that the left hemisphere specializes for coding emotional information verbally and propositionally. It is the conscious interpreter of emotions, regulating them, and so on. But it has a "positivity" bias. In contrast, the right hemisphere deals with unconscious processing of emotional stimuli, and it is the seat of subjective feelings. It has a "negativity" bias, and so both hemispheres are needed in dealing with emotions.

Missana and Grossmann (2014) found evidence that the right hemisphere is specialized already early in life for positive emotions, as is the case for the adult. They tested infants at 4–8 months of age. In the study, Missana and Grossmann measured frontal EEG alpha asymmetry as evoked by dynamically presented body expressions in the stimuli that were either "happy" or "fearful" and which were either upright or inverted As for the results, 8-month-olds (but not 4-month-olds) showed left frontal activation to the upright "happy" stimuli and also right frontal activation to the upright "fearful" stimuli.

Aslin, Shukla, and Emberson (2015) found right hemisphere asymmetry for face processing, not only in the 8-month-old but also in the 4-month-old, with the findings accumulated over five studies (e.g., Nakato, Otsuka, Kanazawa, Yamaguchi, & Kakigi, 2011). Beyond this finding, their review also found some left hemisphere specialization for aspects of face processing (e.g., in the left fronto-polar cortex, the left prefrontal channel, and the left posterior temporal area; Grossmann, Parise, & Friederici, 2010; Lloyd-Fox et al., 2009).

As a comment, these complementary laterality findings in the first year of life in terms of the brain for a basic function (emotions) are consistent with those related to manual specialization, for example, with respect to bimanual coordination in which the right and left hands have their specific specializations. Generally, the patterns in behavioral and brain lateralization by the end of the first year are quite in the direction and strength found for older children, teens, and adults, but with more instabilities and variance.

Year One

Manual Behavior The research with older infants has produced more differentiated results in right-hand specializations. For example, Corbetta, Friedman, and Bell (2014) found that 1-year-olds reached with the right hand to grasp a small toy, but only if they were experienced walkers and not novice or non-walking infants. Sacrey, Arnold, Whishaw, and Gonzalez (2013) studied reaching-to-eat compared to reaching-to-grasp movements in 1-year-olds. The reach-to-eat behavior was more right lateralized compared to the reach-to-grasp one at this age period. Vauclair and Cochet (2013) studied the pointing gesture at 12 months, and it was shown to be more right-handed than left-handed. Furthermore, the more the infants were right-handed in pointing, the higher was their developmental quotient on a language measure (for scores above 100, measured by the Brunet-Lézine test, a subtest of the Brunet-Lézine subscale (Josse, 1997)).

Brain The complexity of emotional specialization in the brain is illustrated in attachment research with infants. Gander and Buchheim (2015) reported research by Dawson and colleagues (e.g., Dawson, 1994) that infants who are attached securely to their mothers exhibited greater right frontal lateralization in EEG when their mothers walked to the door, but only if their mothers were nondepressed. In contrast, for depressed mothers, the infants' frontal activity was greater for the left hemisphere (Dawson et al., 2001). Gander and Buchheim (2015) concluded that the children of depressed mothers who are securely attached engage in left hemisphere frontal activity as an index of their negative emotion suppression. Conversely, I would add that, for nondepressed mothers, their securely attached children can express their negative emotions and exhibit less left frontal activation.

Year Two

Manual Behavior The manual behaviors that are specialized in year two for the left or right side continue to include behaviors such as grasping and pointing, but they also include tool use and drawing. Furthermore, the relationships to other measures, such as word production and reading achievements, are noteworthy.

In these regards, Gonzalez, Flindall, and Stone (2015) replicated the finding of Sacrey et al. (2013) that 1-year-olds are more right-handed for eating-type behavior than other behavior. Specifically, they found that even at 2 years of age, for the right hand, children would grasp to eat more than grasp to construct.

Esseily et al. (2011) studied 14-month-olds and found that preference for right-sided pointing related to word production. Cox and Smitman (2018) examined action perseveration in 14-, 24-, and 36-month olds according to dynamical modeling that took into account prior action history, handedness, and age, while accounting for individual variability. They noted that handedness on midline spoon presentation varied over age, from essentially 50 to 80%. Rat-Fischer, O'Regan, and Fagard (2013) studied using a rake to get a toy out of reach in 16-month-olds. They found a right-hand preference in grasping in raking the toy. Wilbourn, Gottfried, and Kee (2011) found a consistency for hand preference in manual drawing for hand preference in 18- to 24-month-old girls and a relationship with verbal intelligence and reading achievement when they were 10–17 years of age. The same results were not found for boys. This indicates that the well-known hemispheric differences in language specialization according to gender might begin to develop in some senses in toddlerhood.

Nelson et al., (2017) conducted a longitudinal study of the development of laterality biases in bimanual coordination from 18 to 24 months of age ($N = 90$, monthly evaluations), with a follow-up on language development at 3 years of age ($N = 60$). The authors referred to bimanual coordination as role-differentiated bimanual manipulation (RDBM), and they elicited it by presenting for 20 seconds at midline 29 objects requiring one hand in support and the other in manipulation (e.g., removal, unlatching, unzipping, peeling). Language development was assessed using the Preschool Language Scales, Fifth Edition (PLS-5; Zimmerman, Steiner, & Pond, 2011), which includes two scales, one for receptive auditory comprehension and one for expressive communication (production). The children were given handedness index scores based on which hand was the active manipulator on tasks (HI = $(R - L)/(R + L)$).

As for the data analysis conducted in the study by Nelson et al. (2017), latent class growth analysis (LCGA) statistical procedures were used to establish three patterns or trajectories over the 7 months studied in lateralized manipulation. The right-hand group of toddlers (40%) was the largest and had only "mild" left-hand use. Another trajectory involved "moderate" left-hand use in a right-hand group (36%). Finally, the left-hand group (24%) was found to use the right hand moderately. These results indicate that almost 80% of the toddlers were consistently right-handed in bimanual coordination. The stability of the preferences in the group was evident in the results, as indicated by slopes that did not differ from zero, being flat and not quadratic, for example. Finally, the stronger right-hand lateralized group was found to have the highest language scores one year after the lateralized manual determination, especially expressively, although for all groups the language scores were in the "typical" range. The results indicate that hand preference even for complex tasks in the toddler period reaches a relative stability from 18 to 24 months of age and in favor of the right hand while predicting language development one year later at 3 years of age.

As a comment, these results do not suggest that there is a cognitively representational element in the bimanual coordination strategies of young infants, given that they predict later language development. Rather, they indicate that as particular age-related complex, or apex, left hemisphere related skills emerge early in development, and earlier for some compared to others, the underpinning bases for the skills similarly allow for earlier language development at a later point for those developmentally advanced young children, at a point in time when language becomes the apex behavior in development. That is, sensori-motor advances or sensori-motor learning related to the left hemisphere earlier in life predispose that hemisphere to apply its underlying skills to newly emerging behaviors consistent with it at a later point in development, such as in language, even if they are representational and not sensori-motor ones. In discussing object banging and percussive tool use, Lockman and Kahrs (2017) reached a similar conclusion in how early sensori-motor object use in animals and in human infants transforms to higher-order or representational tool-use patterns later in the human case, a finding that should not be used to ascribe higher-order cognitive skills to young infants or to animals. At the same time, research does not always support a relationship between manual preference in the 18- and 24-month-old period and language lateralization (Fagard, Sirri, & Rämä, 2014). However, do note that in Fagard et al. (2014), the proportion in 18-month-olds with high vocabulary was greater for right handers than for non-handed children. Also, these 18-month-olds had a more pronounced N400 effect in semantic priming relative to the non-handers.

Note that Nelson et al. (2017) referred to the cascade model of development in explaining their longitudinal findings (e.g., Michel, 2002, 2013). However, this model should not be considered a uniform one in the sense that, conceptually, one developmental track could refer to cascades or transformations within a domain and another track could refer to longitudinal effects across domains, as in a transfer over domains due to a common mechanism. In this regard, the within-domain track in the cascade model relates to right-sided motor biases from prenatal and neonatal head turning to early postnatal visual regard of the reaching hand to later bimanual coordination and ultimately with influence on stabilized handedness. A second track in the developmental cascade process concerns the common mechanisms being accentuated in the left and right hemisphere and how they apply to not only motor behavior but adjunct behavior such as language.

In this regard, this latter across-domain cascade in development could be addressed by the currently proposed activation-inhibition dynamic in brain organization and behavior. This skill relates to both better manual behavior and language, and the more the left hemisphere can excel in this foundational function, the more its manifestations in behavioral and language function that depend on it will be secured (and correlate or relate over developmental periods).

Brain The left hemisphere advantage for more positive emotions and social behavior in infants is evidenced by the study by Paulus, Kühn-Popp, Licata, Sodian, and Meinhardt (2013). They found that, in the second year of life, empathic responding/comforting was associated with the activation of the left frontal hemisphere. In contrast, the behavior of instrumental helping was associated with the activation of the right temporal lobe.

As a comment, note that manual behavior and hemispheric specializations to the left or to the right side are not absolute but only relative. Therefore, in the present case, for example, it is not being argued that empathy is exclusively left lateralized and instrumental helping is exclusively right lateralized.

Conclusion

The period of prenatal development and infancy-toddlerhood witnesses rapid advances in brain development including in terms of laterality. The earliest prenatal weeks witness a lateralization in development, presaging and predicting later development. Even side of foetal manual activity and of head turning relate to later handedness. By observing and measuring age-specific behaviors and brain activity in this period, the concept of the equi-potential, progressively developing brain and its lateralization has been found untenable. Rather, the data in this age period already support the invariant, adult-like model of laterality in behavior and brain.

References

Allen, J. J. B., Keune, P. M., Schönenberg, M., & Nusslock, R. (2018). Frontal EEG alpha asymmetry and emotion: From neural underpinnings and methodological considerations to psychopathology and social cognition. *Psychophysiology, 55*, e13028. https://doi.org/10.1111/psyp.13028

Andescavage, N. N., du Plessis, A., McCarter, R., Serag, A., Evangelou, I., Vezina, G., et al. (2017). Complex trajectories of brain development in the healthy human fetus. *Cerebral Cortex, 27*, 5274–5283. https://doi.org/10.1093/cercor/bhw306

Arimitsu, T., Minagawa, Y., Yagihashi, T., Uchida, M. O., Matsuzaki, A., Ikeda, K., & Takahashi, T. (2018). The cerebral hemodynamic response to phonetic changes of speech in preterm and term infants: The impact of postmenstrual age. *NeuroImage: Clinical, 19*, 599–606.

Aslin, R. N., Shukla, M., & Emberson, L. L. (2015). Hemodynamic correlates of cognition in human infants. *Annual Review of Psychology, 66*, 349–379. https://doi.org/10.1146/annurev-psych-010213-115108

Bayley, N. (Ed.). (2009). *Bayley scales of infant development: Administration manual* (3rd ed.). San Antonio, TX: Harcourt Assessment.

Behrmann, M., & Plaut, D. C. (2013). Distributed circuits, not circumscribed centers, mediate visual recognition. *Trends in Cognitive Sciences, 17*, 210–219. https://doi.org/10.1016/j.tics.2013.03.007

Beking, T., Geuze, R. H., van Faassen, M., Kema, I. P., Kreukels, B. P. C., & Groothuis, T. G. G. (2018). Prenatal and pubertal testosterone affect brain lateralization. *Psychoneuroendocrinology, 88*, 78–91. https://doi.org/10.1016/j.psyneuen.2017.10.027

Bertoncini, J., Morais, J., Bijeljac-Babic, R., McAdams, S., Peretz, I., & Mehler, J. (1989). Dichotic perception and laterality in neonates. *Brain and Language, 37*, 591–605. https://doi.org/10.1016/0093-934X(89)90113-2

Bulf, H., de Hevia, M. D., Gariboldi, V., & Macchi Cassia, V. (2017). Infants learn better from left to right: A directional bias in infants' sequence learning. *Scientific Reports, 7*, 2437. https://doi.org/10.1038/s41598-017-02466-w

Campbell, J. M., Marcinowski, E. C., Babik, I., & Michel, G. F. (2015). The influence of a hand preference for acquiring objects on the development of a hand preference for unimanual manipulation from 6 to 14 months. *Infant Behavior and Development, 39*, 107–117. https://doi.org/10.1016/j.infbeh.2015.02.013

Campbell, J. M., Marcinowski, E. C., Latta, J., & Michel, G. F. (2015). Different assessment tasks produce different estimates of handedness stability during the eight to 14 month age period. *Infant Behavior and Development, 39*, 67–80. https://doi.org/10.1016/j.infbeh.2015.02.003

Campbell, J. M., Marcinowski, E. C., & Michel, G. F. (2017). The development of neuromotor skills and hand preference during infancy. *Developmental Psychobiology*. https://doi.org/10.1002/dev.21591

Caplan, P. J., & Kinsbourne, M. (1976). Baby drops the rattle: Asymmetry of duration of grasp by infants. *Child Development, 2*, 532–534. https://doi.org/10.2307/1128815

Chan, Y. K., & Loh, P. S. (2016). Handedness in man: The energy availability hypothesis. *Medical Hypotheses, 94*, 108–111. https://doi.org/10.1016/j.mehy.2016.06.018

Cisler, J. M., & Koster, E. H. W. (2010). Mechanisms of attentional biases towards threat in anxiety disorders: An integrative review. *Clinical Psychology Review, 30*, 203–216. https://doi.org/10.1016/j.cpr.2009.11.003

Coan, J. A., Allen, J. J. B., & McKnight, P. E. (2006). A capability model of individual differences in frontal EEG asymmetry. *Biological Psychology, 72*, 198–207. https://doi.org/10.1016/j.biopsycho.2005.10.003

Corbetta, D., Friedman, D. R., & Bell, M. A. (2014). Brain reorganization as a function of walking experience in 12-month-old infants: Implications for the development of manual laterality. *Frontiers in Psychology, 5*, 245. https://doi.org/10.3389/fpsyg.2014.00245

Cox, R. F. A., & Smitsman, A. W. (2018). Action-selection perseveration in young children: Advances of a dynamic model. *Developmental Psychobiology*. https://doi.org/10.1002/dev.21776

Davidson, R. J. (1983). Hemispheric specialization for cognition and affect. In A. Gale & J. Edwards (Eds.), *Physiological correlates of human behavior* (pp. 203–216). London: Academic.

Dawson, G. (1994). Development of emotional expression and emotion regulation in infancy: Contributions of the frontal lobe. In G. Dawson & K. W. Fischer (Eds.), *Human behavior and the developing brain* (pp. 346–379). New York: Guilford Press.

Dawson, G., Ashman, S. B., Hessl, D., Spieker, S., Frey, K., Panagiotides, H., et al. (2001). Autonomic and brain electrical activity in securely- and insecurely-attached infants of depressed mothers. *Infant Behavior and Development, 24*, 135–149. https://doi.org/10.1016/S0163-6383(01)00075-3

de Heering, A., & Rossion, B. (2015). Rapid categorization of natural face images in the infant right hemisphere. *eLife, 4*, 1–14. https://doi.org/10.7554/eLife.06564

de Hevia, M. D., Girelli, L., & Macchi Cassia, V. (2012). Minds without language represent number through space: Origins of the mental number line. *Frontiers in Psychology, 3*, 466. https://doi.org/10.3389/fpsyg.2012.00466

de Kovel, C. G. F., Lisgo, S., Karlebach, G., Ju, J., Cheng, G., Fisher, S. E., et al. (2017). Left-right asymmetry of matruation rations in human embryonic neural development. *Biological Psychiatry, 82*, 204–212. https://doi.org/10.1016/j.biopsych.2017.01.016

de Oliveira, S. R., de Paula Machado, A. C. C., de Paula, J. J., de Moraes, P. H. P., Nahin, M. J. S., Magalhães, L. C., et al. (2017). Association between hemodynamic activity and motor performance in six-month-old full-term and preterm infants: A functional near-infrared spectroscopy study. *Neurophonetics, 5*, 011016. https://doi.org/10.1117/1.NPh.5.1.011016

Dehaene-Lambertz, G. (2000). Cerebral specialization for speech and non-speech stimuli in infants. *Journal of Cognitive Neuroscience, 12*, 449–460.

Dehaene-Lambertz, G. (2017). The human infant brain: A neural architecture able to learn language. *Psychonomic Bulletin & Review, 24*, 48–55. https://doi.org/10.3758/s13423-016-1156-9

Dehaene-Lambertz, G., Dehaene, S., & Hertz-Pannier, L. (2002). Functional neuroimaging of speech perception in infants. *Science, 298*, 2013–2016. https://doi.org/10.1126/science.1077066

Engels, A. S., Heller, W., Spielberg, J. M., Warren, S. L., Sutton, B. P., Banich, M. T., et al. (2010). Co-occurring anxiety influences patterns of brain activity in depression. *Cognitive, Affective, & Behavioral Neuroscience, 10*, 141–156. https://doi.org/10.3758/CABN.10.1.141

Esseily, R., Jacquet, A.-Y., & Fagard, J. (2011). Handedness for grasping objects and pointing and the development of language in 14-month-old infants. *Laterality: Asymmetries of Body, Brain and Cognition, 16*, 565–585. https://doi.org/10.1080/1357650X.2010.499911

Fagard, J., Margules, S., Lopez, C., Granjon, L., & Huet, V. (2017). How should we test infant handedness? *Laterality: Asymmetries of Body, Brain and Cognition, 22*, 294–312. https://doi.org/10.1080/1357650X.2016.1192186

Fagard, J., Sirri, L., & Rämä, P. (2014). Effect of handedness on the occurrence of semantic N400 priming effect in 18- and 24-month-old children. *Frontiers of Psychology, 5*, 1–8. https://doi.org/10.3389/fpsyg.2014.00355

Fagard, J., Spelke, E., & von Hofsten, C. (2009). Reaching and grasping a moving object in 6-, 8-, and 10-month-old infants: Laterality and performance. *Infant Behavior & Development, 32*, 137–146. https://doi.org/10.1016/j.infbeh.2008.12.002

Fox, N. A., & Davidson, R. (1984). Hemispheric substrates of affect: A developmental model. In N. A. Fox & R. Davidson (Eds.), *The psychobiology of affective development* (pp. 353–381). Hillsdale, NJ: Erlbaum.

Gander, M., & Buchheim, A. (2015). Attachment classification, psychophysiology and frontal EEG asymmetry across the lifespan: A review. *Frontiers in Human Neuroscience, 9*, 79. https://doi.org/10.3389/fnhum.2015.00079
Gesell, A., & Ames, L. (1947). The development of handedness. *Journal of Genetic Psychology, 70*, 155–175.
Gilmore, J. H., Lin, W., Prastawa, M. W., Looney, C. B., Vetsa, Y. S. K., Knickmeyer, R. C., et al. (2007). Regional gray matter growth, sexual dimorphism, and cerebral asymmetry in the neonatal brain. *Journal of Neuroscience, 27*, 1255–1260. https://doi.org/10.1523/JNEUROSCI.3339-06.2007
Goldstein, R. Z., & Volkow, N. D. (2011). Dysfunction of the prefrontal cortex in addiction: Neuroimaging findings and clinical implications. *Nature Reviews: Neuroscience, 12*, 652–669. https://doi.org/10.1038/nrn3119
Gonzalez, C. L. R., Flindall, J. W., & Stone, K. D. (2015). Hand preference across the lifespan: Effects of end-goal, task nature, and object location. *Frontiers in Psychology, 5*, 1579. https://doi.org/10.3389/fpsyg.2014.01579
Graves, R., Goodglass, H., & Landis, T. (1982). Mouth asymmetry during spontaneous speech. *Neuropsychologia, 20*, 371–381.
Grimshaw, G. M., & Carmel, D. (2014). An asymmetric inhibition model of hemispheric differences in emotional processing. *Frontiers in Psychology, 5*, 489. https://doi.org/10.3389/fpsyg.2014.00489
Grossmann, T., Parise, E., & Friederici, A. D. (2010). The detection of communicative signals directed at the self in infant prefrontal cortex. *Frontiers in Human Neuroscience, 4*, 201. https://doi.org/10.3389/fnhum.2010.00201
Habas, P. A., Scott, J. A., Roosta, A., Rajagopalan, V., Kim, K., Rousseau, F., et al. (2012). Early folding patterns and asymmetries of the normal human brain detected from in utero MRI. *Cerebral Cortex, 22*, 13–25. https://doi.org/10.1093/cercor/bhr053
Hamilton, A., Plunkett, K., & Schafer, G. (2000). Infant vocabulary development assessment with a British Communicative Development Inventory: Lower scores in the UK than the USA. *Journal of Child Language, 27*, 689–705.
Hane, A. A., Fox, N. A., Henderson, H. A., & Marshall, P. J. (2008). Behavioral reactivity and approach-withdrawal bias in infancy. *Developmental Psychology, 44*, 1491–1496. https://doi.org/10.1037/a0012855
Harmon-Jones, E., & Gable, P. A. (2018). On the role of asymmetric frontal cortical activity in approach and withdrawal motivation: An updated review of the evidence. *Psychophysiology, 55*, e12879. https://doi.org/10.1111/psyp.12879
Heller, W. (1990). The neuropsychology of emotion: Developmental patterns and implications of psychopathology. In N. Stein, B. L. Leventhal, & T. Trabasso (Eds.), *Psychological and biological approaches to emotion* (pp. 167–211). Hillsdale, NJ: Erlbaum.
Helwig, J. (2018). Intentionality in frontal asymmetry research. *Psychophysiology, 55*, e12852. https://doi.org/10.1111/psyp.12852
Hepper, P. G. (2013). The developmental origins of laterality: Fetal handedness. *Developmental Psychobiology, 55*, 588–595. https://doi.org/10.1002/dev.21119
Hepper, P. G., McCartney, G. R., & Shannon, E. A. (1998). Lateralised behavior in first trimester human fetuses. *Neuropsychologia, 36*, 531–534.
Hepper, P. G., Shahidullah, S., & White, R. (1991). Handedness in human fetus. *Neuropsychologia, 29*, 1107–1111.
Hepper, P. G., Wells, D. K., & Lynch, C. (2005). Prenatal thumb sucking is related to postnatal handedness. *Neuropsychologia, 43*, 313–315. https://doi.org/10.1016/j.neuropsychologia.2004.08.009
Homae, F., Watanabe, H., Nakano, T., Asakawa, K., & Taga, G. (2006). The right hemisphere of sleeping infants perceives sentential prosody. *Neuroscience Research, 54*, 276–280. https://doi.org/10.1016/j.neures.2005.12.006

Im, K., Jo, H. J., Mangin, J. F., Evans, A. C., Kim, S. I., & Lee, J. M. (2010). Spatial distribution of deep sulcal landmarks and hemispherical asymmetry on the cortical surface. *NeuroImage, 58*, 716–723. https://doi.org/10.1093/cercor/bhp127

Ittyerah, M. (2017). Emerging trends in the multimodal natural of cognition: Touch and handedness. *Frontiers in Psychology, 8*, 844. https://doi.org/10.3389/fpsyg.2017.00844

Jacobsohn, L., Rodrigues, P., Vasconcelos, O., Corbetta, D., & Barreiros, J. (2014). Lateral manual asymmetries: A longitudinal study from birth to 24 months. *Developmental Psychobiology, 56*, 58–72. https://doi.org/10.1002/dev.21091

Josse, D. (1997). *Revised Brunet- Lézine: Scale of psychomotor development in infancy* [Brunet-Lézine revisé: Echelle de développement psychomoteur de la première enfance]. Issy-les-Moulineaux, France: EAP.

Kaminska, A., Delattre, V., Laschet, J., Dubois, J., Labidurie, M., Duval, A., Manresa, A., Magny, J-F., Hovhannisyan, S., Mokhtari, M., Ouss, L., Boissel, A., Hertz-Pannier, L., Sintsov, M., Minlevbaev, M., Khazipov, R., & Chiron, C. (2018). Cortical auditory-evoked responses in preterm neonates: Revisited by spectral and temporal analyses. *Cerebral Cortex, 28*, 3429–3444. https://doi.org/10.1093/cercor/bhx206

Kasprian, G., Langs, G., Brugger, P. C., Bittner, M., Weber, M., Arantes, M., et al. (2011). The prenatal origin of hemispheric asymmetry: An in utero neuroimaging study. *Cerebral Cortex, 21*, 1076–1083. https://doi.org/10.1093/cercor/bhq179

Kobayashi, M., Macchi Cassia, V. M., Kanazawa, S., Yamaguchi, M. K., & Kakigi, R. (2018). Perceptual narrowing towards adult faces is a cross-cultural phenomenon in infancy: A behavioral and near-infrared spectroscopy study with Japanese infants. *Developmental Science, 21*, e12498. https://doi.org/10.1111/desc.12498

Kooistra, C. A., & Heilman, K. M. (1988). Motor dominance and lateral asymmetry of the globus pallidus. *Neurology, 28*, 388–390.

Levman, J., MacDonald, P., Lim, A. R., Forgeron, C., & Takahashi, E. (2017). A pediatric structural MRI analysis of healthy brain development from newborns to young adults. *Human Brain Mapping, 38*, 5931–5942. https://doi.org/10.1002/hbm.23799

Li, G., Nie, J., Wang, L., Shi, F., Lyall, A. E., Lin, W., et al. (2014). Mapping longitudinal hemispheric structural asymmetries of the human cerebral cortex from birth to 2 years of age. *Cerebral Cortex, 24*, 1289–1300. https://doi.org/10.1093/cercor/bhs413

Lloyd-Fox, S., Blasi, A., Volein, A., Everdell, N., Elwell, C. E., & Johnson, M. H. (2009). Social perception in infancy: A near infrared spectroscopy study. *Child Development, 80*, 986–999. https://doi.org/10.1111/j.1467-8624.2009.01312.x

Lochy, A., de Heering, A., & Rossion, B. (2017). The non-linear development of the right hemispheric specialization for human face perception. *Neuropsychologia*. https://doi.org/10.1016/j.neuropsychologia.2017.06.029

Lockman, J. J., & Kahrs, B. A. (2017). New insights into the development of human tool use. *Current Directions in Psychological Science, 26*, 330–334. https://doi.org/10.1177/0963721417692035

Lori, S., Gabbanini, S., Bastianelli, M., Bertini, G., Corsini, I., & Dani, C. (2017). Multimodal neurophysiological monitoring in healthy infants born at term: Normative continuous somatosensory evoked potentials data. *Developmental Medicine & Child Neurology, 59*, 959–964. https://doi.org/10.1111/dmcn.13430

Mahmoudzadeh, M., Dehaene-Lambertz, G., Fournier, M., Kongolo, G., Goudjil, S., Dubois, J., et al. (2013). Syllabic discrimination in premature human infants prior to complete formation of cortical layers. *Proceedings of the National Academy of Sciences of the United States of America, 110*, 4846–4851. https://doi.org/10.1073/pnas.1212220110

Marcinowski, E. C., Campbell, J. M., Faldowski, R. A., & Michel, G. F. (2016). Do hand preferences predict stacking skill during infancy? *Developmental Psychobiology, 58*, 958–967. https://doi.org/10.1002/dev.21426

McCartney, G., & Hepper, P. G. (1999). Developmental of lateralised behavior in the human fetus from 12 to 27 weeks' gestation. *Developmental Medicine and Child Neurology, 41*, 83–86.

Mento, G., Suppiej, A., Altoè, G., & Bisiacchi, P. S. (2010). Functional hemispheric asymmetries in humans: Electrophysiological evidence from preterm infants. *European Journal of Neuroscience, 31*, 565–574.
Michel, G. F. (1981). Right-handedness: A consequence of infant supine head-orientation preference? *Science, 212*, 685–687.
Michel, G. F. (2002). Developmental of infant handedness. In D. J. Lewkowicz & R. Lickliter (Eds.), *Conceptions of development: Lessons from the laboratory* (pp. 165–186). New York: Psychology Press.
Michel, G. F. (2013). The concept of homology in the development of handedness. *Developmental Psychobiology, 55*, 84–91. https://doi.org/10.1002/dev.21038
Michel, G. F. (2018). How might the relation of the development of hand preferences to the development of cognitive functions be examined during infancy: A sketch? *Frontiers in Neuroscience, 11*, 739. https://doi.org/10.3389/fnins.2017.00739
Michel, G. F., Babik, I., Shue, C.-F., & Campbell, J. M. (2013). Latent classes in the developmental trajectories of infant handedness. *Developmental Psychology, 50*, 349–359. https://doi.org/10.1037/a0033312
Michel, G. F., & Harkins, D. A. (1986). Postural and lateral asymmetries in the ontogeny of handedness during infancy. *Developmental Psychobiology, 19*, 247–258. https://doi.org/10.1002/dev.420190310
Missana, M., & Grossmann, T. (2014). Infants' emerging sensitivity to emotional body expressions: Insights from asymmetrical frontal brain activity. *Developmental Psychology, 51*, 151–160. https://doi.org/10.1037/a0038469
Morange-Majoux, F. (2010). Manual exploration consistency (soft vs hard) and handedness in infants from 4 to 6 months old. *Laterality: Asymmetries of Body, Brain and Cognition, 16*, 292–312. https://doi.org/10.1080/13576500903553689
Morange-Majoux, F., & Adrien, J.-L. (2016). Motor function and handedness in infants with Autism spectrum disorder: A new approach for exploration of disorders, based on a literature review [Translated]. *Devenir, 28*, 213–227. https://doi.org/10.3917/dev.164.0213
Morange-Majoux, F., & Devouche, E. (2014). Social encouragement can influence manual preference in 6-month-old-infants. *Frontiers in Psychology, 5*, 1225. https://doi.org/10.3389/fpsychg.2014.01225
Morange-Majoux, F., & Devouche, E. (2019). Language or music? Environmental influences on infants' handedness from 5 to 12 months. *Brain and Cognition, 129*, 1–8.
Morange-Majoux, F., Devouche, E., Lemoine-Lardennois, C., & Orriols, E. (2017). *Visual exploration of reaching space during left and right arm movements in 6-month-old infants.* Psychologie Française. https://doi.org/10.1016/j.psfr.2017.06.003
Morange-Majoux, F., Lemoine, C., & Dellatolas, G. (2013). Early manifestations of manual specialization in infants: A longitudinal study from 20 to 30 weeks. *Laterality: Asymmetries of Body, Brain and Cognition, 18*, 231–250. https://doi.org/10.1080/1357650X.2012.660163
Morange-Majoux, F., Peze, A., & Bloch, H. (2000). Organisation of left and right hand movement in a prehension task: A longitudinal study from 20 to 30 weeks. *Laterality: Asymmetries of Body, Brain and Cognition, 5*, 351–362. https://doi.org/10.1080/713754386
Mumford, K. H., & Kita, S. (2016). At 10-12 months, pointing gesture handedness predicts the size of receptive vocabularies. *Infancy, 21*, 751–765. https://doi.org/10.1111/infa.12138
Nagy, E., Pal, A., & Orvos, H. (2014). Learning to imitate individual finger movements by the human neonate. *Developmental Science, 17*, 841–857. https://doi.org/10.1111/desc.12163
Nakato, E., Otsuka, Y., Kanazawa, S., Yamaguchi, M. K., & Kakigi, R. (2011). Distinct differences in the pattern of hemodynamic response to happy and angry facial expressions in infants – A near-infrared spectroscopic study. *NeuroImage, 54*, 1600–1606. https://doi.org/10.1016/j.neuroimage.2010.09.021
Nelson, E. L., Gonzalez, S. L., Coxe, S., Campbell, J. M., Marcinowski, E. C., & Michel, G. F. (2017). Toddler hand preference trajectories predict 3-year language outcome. *Developmental Psychobiology, 59*, 876–887. https://doi.org/10.1002/dev.21560

Ocklenburg, S., Schmitz, J., Moinfar, Z., Moser, D., Klose, R., Lor, S., et al. (2017). Epigenetic regulation of lateralized fetal spinal gene expression underlies hemispheric asymmetries. *eLife, 6*. https://doi.org/10.7554/eLife.22784

Palmiero, M., & Piccardi, L. (2017). Frontal EEG asymmetry of mood: A mini-review. *Frontiers in Behavioral Neuroscience, 11*, 224. https://doi.org/10.3389/fnbeh.2017.00224

Papadatou-Pastou, M., & Martin, M. (2017). Cerebral laterality for language is related to adult salivary testosterone levels but not digit ratio (2D:4D) in men: A functional transcranial Doppler ultrasound study. *Brain and Language, 166*, 52–62. https://doi.org/10.1016/j.bandl.2016.12.002

Parma, V., Brasselet, R., Zoia, S., Bulgheroni, M., & Castiello, U. (2017). The origin of human handedness and its role in pre-birth motor control. *Scientific Reports, 7*, 16804. https://doi.org/10.1038/s41598-017-16827-y

Paulus, M., Kühn-Popp, M., Licata, M., Sodian, B., & Meinhardt, J. (2013). Neural correlates of prosocial behavior in infancy: Different neurophysiological mechanisms support the emergence of helping and comforting. *NeuroImage, 66*, 522–530. https://doi.org/10.1016/j.neuroimage.2012.10.041

Peña, M., Maki, A., Kovačić, D., Dahaene-Lambertz, G., Koizumi, H., Bouquet, F., et al. (2003). Sounds and silence: An optical topography study of language recognition at birth. *Proceedings of the National Academy of Science of the United States of America, 100*, 11702–11705. https://doi.org/10.1073/pnas.1934290100

Perani, D., Saccuman, M. C., Scifo, P., Anwander, A., Spada, D., Baldoli, C., et al. (2011). Neural language networks at birth. *Proceedings of the National Academy of Science of the United States of America, 108*, 38. https://doi.org/10.1073/pnas.1102991108

Potier, C., Meguerditchian, A., & Fagard, J. (2013). Handedness for bimanual coordinated actions in infants as a function of grip morphology. *Laterality: Asymmetries of Body, Brain and Cognition, 18*, 576–593. https://doi.org/10.1080/1357650X.2012.732077

Rat-Fischer, L., O'Regan, J. K., & Fagard, J. (2013). Handedness in infants' tool use. *Developmental Psychobiology, 55*, 860–868. https://doi.org/10.1002/dev.21078

Ratnarajah, N., Rifkin-Graboi, A., Fortier, M. V., Chong, Y. S., Kwek, K., Saw, S. M., et al. (2014). Structural connectivity asymmetry in the neonatal brain. *NeuroImage, 75*, 187–194. https://doi.org/10.1016/j.neuroimage.2013.02.052

Reissland, N., Francis, B., Aydin, E., Mason, J., & Exley, K. (2014). Development of prenatal lateralization: Evidence from fetal mouth movements. *Physiology & Behavior, 131*, 160–163. https://doi.org/10.1016/j.physbeh.2014.04.035

Reznik, S. J., & Allen, J. J. B. (2018). Frontal asymmetry as a mediator and moderator of emotion: An updated review. *Psychophysiology, 55*, e12965. https://doi.org/10.1111/psyp.12965

Sacrey, L.-A., Arnold, B., Whishaw, I. Q., & Gonzalez, C. L. (2013). Precocious hand use preference in reach-to-eat behavior versus manual construction in 1- to 5-year-old children. *Developmental Psychobiology, 55*, 902–911. https://doi.org/10.1002/dev.21083

Scheef, L., Nordmeyer-Massner, J. A., Smith-Collins, A. P., Müller, N., Stegmann-Woessner, G., Jankowski, J., et al. (2017). Functional laterality of task-evoked activation in sensorimotor cortex of preterm infants: An optimized 3 T fMRI study employing a customized neonatal head coil. *PLoS One, 12*, 1–17. https://doi.org/10.1371/journal.pone.0169392

Schwartz, C. E., Kunwar, P. S., Greve, D. N., Moran, L. R., Viner, J. C., Covino, J. M., et al. (2010). Structural differences in adult orbital and ventromedial prefrontal cortex predicted by infant temperament at 4 months of age. *Archives of General Psychiatry, 67*, 78–84. https://doi.org/10.1001/archgenpsychiatry.2009.171

Shobe, E. R. (2014). Independent and collaborative contributions of the cerebral hemispheres to emotional processing. *Frontiers in Human Neuroscience, 8*, 230. https://doi.org/10.3389/fnhum.2014.00230

Streri, A., & Gentaz, E. (2003). Cross-modal recognition of shape from hand to eyes in human newborns. *Neuropsychologia, 42*, 1365–1369. https://doi.org/10.1016/j.neuropsychologia.2004.02.012

Tan, U., Ors, R., Kürkçüoglu, M., & Kutlu, N. (1992). The lateralization of the grasp reflex in human newborns. *International Journal of Neuroscience, 62*, 1–8.

Touwen, B. (1976). *Neurological development in infancy*. Lavenham, Suffolk: The Lavenham Press, Ltd.

Tzourio-Mazoyer, N., Perrone-Bertolotti, M., Jobard, G., Mazoyer, B., & Baciu, M. (2017). Multi-factorial modulation of hemispheric specialization and plasticity for language in healthy and pathological conditions: A review. *Cortex, 86*, 314–339. https://doi.org/10.1016/j.cortex.2016.05.013

Vauclair, J., & Cochet, H. (2013). Hand preference for pointing and language development in toddlers. *Developmental Psychobiology, 55*, 757–765. https://doi.org/10.1002/dev.21073

Vauclair, J., & Imbault, J. (2009). Relationship between manual preferences for object manipulation and pointing gestures in infants and toddlers. *Developmental Science, 12*, 1060–1069. https://doi.org/10.1111/j.1467-7687.2009.00850.x

Wilbourn, M. P., Gottfried, A. W., & Kee, D. W. (2011). Consistency of hand-preference across the early years: Long-term relationship to verbal intelligence and reading achievement in girls. *Developmental Psychology, 47*, 931–942. https://doi.org/10.1037/a0023834

Young, G. (2011). *Development and causality: Neo-Piagetian perspectives*. New York: Springer Science + Business Media.

Young, G., Bowman, J. G., Methot, C., Finlayson, M., Quintal, J., & Boissonneault, P. (1983). Hemispheric specialization development: What (inhibition) and how (parents). In G. Young, S. J. Segalowitz, C. M. Corter, & S. E. Trehub (Eds.), *Manual specialization and the developing brain* (pp. 119–140). New York: Academic.

Young, G., Corter, C. M., Segalowitz, S. J., & Trehub, S. E. (1983). Manual specialization and the developing brain: An overview. In G. Young, S. J. Segalowitz, C. M. Corter, & S. E. Trehub (Eds.), *Manual specialization and the developing brain* (pp. 3–12). New York: Academic.

Young, G., & Gagnon, M. (1990). Neonatal laterality, birth stress, familial sinistrality, and left brain inhibition. *Developmental Neuropsychology, 6*, 127–150.

Zimmerman, I. L., Steiner, V. G., & Pond, R. E. (2011). *Preschool language scales, fifth edition* (PLS-5). Bloomington, MA: Pearson.

Chapter 4
Developmental Laterality Research: Childhood

Abstract The second chapter on early laterality continues with research on children; and the same patterns are found as for infancy – the right hand exhibits a manual preference/handedness – but there are task and measure variations. The left hemisphere appears specialized not only for manual skills but also for verbal ones. The common underlying variable to these skills appear to be activation-inhibition coordination. The right hemisphere has its visuospatial and related skills. The chapter gives some research with adolescents and adults, too, on the topic at hand. Also, it considers questions such as the relationship of handedness/laterality and cognition and atypical development. The chapter presents research on how circuitry and connectivity networks distinguish the left and right hemispheres. The data indicate that the differential organization of the hemispheres might relate to efficiency, linkaging, "small worlds," and other novel concepts in the field.

Children

Manual Behavior Some of the research for children in terms of preferences is straightforward, such as Faria, Diniz, and Barreiros (2017) finding a right-hand or dominant-hand facility in tapping in 6- to 7-year-olds. Some of this research with children's laterality is not on manual behavior but is still relevant. For example, Streuli, Obrist, and Brugger (2017) found spontaneous left-turning preference in children who average 8 years of age. Cochet (2016) conducted a literature review on manual lateralization and hemispheric specialization in children, citing Flindall and Gonzalez (2014), who showed that more precision requirements during the pre-shaping phase of reaching and then grasping to eat could be the factor that leads to greater right-hand preference for this behavior relative to other manual behaviors.

Cochet, Centelles, Jover, Plachta, and Vauclair (2015) investigated manual asymmetry in 3- to 5-year-olds on tasks involving reaching, pointing, and symbolic gestures (e.g., to represent "hi"). For all tasks at all ages, the participants were strongly lateralized to the right. These results suggest stability in basic hand function laterality in the preschool period. In contrast, Hodgson, Hirst, and Hudson (2016) found

G. Young, *Causality and Development*,
https://doi.org/10.1007/978-3-030-02493-2_4

that children were more lateralized on an electronic pegboard task the younger they were in the 3- to 10-year period involved in the study, although both handedness and speech lateralization were quite set by age 3. Moreover, both Hodgson et al. (2016) and Doyen, Lambert, Dumas, and Carlier (2017) found that the non-dominant hand was more indicative of performance level than the dominant hand. Their results related to (a) a study of children in the preschool/kindergarten period and later and (b) atypical speech lateralization and literacy acquisition, respectively. Consequently, the research on manual lateralization stabilization in the preschool period leaves open many questions.

In this regard, Scharoun and Bryden (2014) pointed out that different lateralized results are obtained depending on the measure involved, that is, there are three types – hand preference on basic tasks, performance ability on more complex ones, and observation of hand preference. For them, young children in the 3- to 5-year-old period generally show "weak" and "inconsistent" hand preference tendencies. Similarly, Sivagnanasunderam et al. (2015) found variations in manual asymmetries in 4- to 5-year-olds on various tasks, such as pegboard and tapping.

Thevenot, Fayol, and Barrouillet (2018) investigated the putative right-hemisphere mediated bias to represent increasing magnitudes in a display from left to right. The authors studied 84 3- to 5-year-old children as they added or removed objects from displays. Only the right-handers in the sample manipulated the displays more at that right end, consistent with the right hemisphere spatial skill (attentional bias to the left side) hypothesis. The absence of the same findings in left-handers indicated a "weaker" brain lateralization in the preschoolers. A different study, however, on functional connectivities with 6- to 10-year-olds implicated the left hemisphere in visual attention (Gracia-Tabuenca, Moreno, Barrios, & Alcauter, 2018). The different tasks involved seem to be the factor in the different results, as per the next study reviewed.

Girelli, Marinelli, Grossi, and Arduino (2017) investigated spatial laterality biases in different age groups, beginning with preschoolers (3- to 5-year-olds) and 8-year-olds, as well as adults. Generally, the 8-year-olds exhibited the expected adult pattern but not the preschoolers. Specifically, because the tasks involved word bisection as well as the more familiar line bisection and figure string bisection, the predisposition for right hemisphere activation for line bisection at any age was complemented by a left hemisphere preference for word bisection, but only at 8 years of age once reading is well-established. The authors concluded that spatial biases reflect the interaction of biological and environmental (cultural exposure to written material) factors. As for right hemispheric specialization for monaural tonal stimuli, Yamazaki et al. (2017) determined that it is evident already in 5-year-olds.

As a comment, these results raise the question whether the lateralization process for both manual behavior and brain relationships to the behavior are fixed early in life without further development, as might be one implication of the invariant lateralization model, or whether manual and brain specialization continues to develop throughout childhood. In fact, there is no inconsistency indicated in that the developing cerebral hemispheres reflect an invariant lateralization process as well that lateralization in behavior and brain continues throughout development. With proper tasks and behaviors observed or measured, invariant lateralization could appear evident developmentally. However, the lateralization still could be fragile and susceptible to environment and contextual variation and become more ingrained as the hemispheric specialization associated with it solidifies and entrenches. Therefore, when research shows that there are developmental shifts in hemispheric function, for example, to the left for the language function, that take place progressively over time (e.g., Friederici, Brauer, & Lohmann, 2011), this cannot be taken to deny the invariant lateralization model or uniquely support a model of progressive lateralization of the brain. The same would apply to results showing that developmental changes in manual behavior, including in handedness, its direction, its consistency, its stability, and so on. Therefore, any conclusions that either lateralized manual behavior or handedness are fixed from early in life (or progressively change throughout life) are unequivocally supported would be inappropriate.

Gonzalez et al. (2014) studied 4- to 5-year-olds for both grasping small food items and discriminating the articulation of "sh" and "s" sounds. They found that more the children were right lateralized in grasping, the better they could discriminate the two sounds. The authors proceeded to study younger and older children (5- to 6- vs. 9- to 10-year-olds) for right-hand grasping and its relationship to executive function (EF), as measured by the Behavioral Rating Inventory of Executive Function (BRIEF; Gioia, Isquith, Guy, & Kenworthy, 2000). They found that more right-hand grasping was related to higher EF scores. They related the results to a better structural efficiency in the left hemisphere, which allows for better EF.

Most of the research described at this point in the article on the topic of manual behavior has focused on reaching, grasping, and dexterity. Beyond these topics, Nelson, Gonzalez, El-Asmar, Fouad Ziade, and Abu-Rustum (2018) developed home handedness questionnaires that parents administered to their 3-year-olds. It included unimanual and bimanual tasks. The N of the study was 64, and 52 participants or 81.25% were right-handed for the unimanual tasks. The equivalent percentage for the bimanual tasks was 76.56 %. Right-hand preference for both types of tasks was 70%. The authors concluded that there is a lot of variability in 3-year-old hand preferences on this instrument. In another vein, Hepping, Ploegmakers, Geertzen, Bulstra, and Stevens (2015) determined that, even at 4 years of age, the right hand is 10% stronger in grip strength than the left. The results applied to right-handers. However, left-preferring girls were generally stronger with their preferred hand.

As for research with teenagers, in an electroencephalogram (EEG) study examining cortico-cortico coherence, Blais, Amarantini, Albaret, Chaix, and Tallet (2018) found that, in 13-year-old bimanual coordination learning, the right hemisphere was involved in the increase because the task involved the selection of spatial responses. The left hemisphere is skilled for bimanual coordination, generally, so the findings serve to illustrate that the hemisphere specialization recruited for the task at hand depends on the underlying function called for.

Brain Kikuchi et al. (2011) studied preschoolers on language-related tasks and theta band activity in a magnetoencephalographic (MEG) study. They found that theta band (6–8 Hz) activity coherence in the parietotemporal region was associated with better language performance. The language measure was derived from the KABC (Kaufman Assessment Battery for Children; Kaufman & Kaufman, 1983). The authors concluded that the left hemisphere contains better long-distance phase-locked connectivity in the temporal and parietal regions.

Centanni et al. (2018) studied 5- to 6-year-old letter sensitivity and letter specificity in relation to fusiform gyri (FG) fMRI activity (i.e., greater activation to lower-case letters compared to face presentations and false font presentations, respectively). They found that greater left FG activation to letters compared to false fonts correlated positively with word reading scores on the Woodcock (1998). Also, the results indicated that as the left hemisphere becomes more involved linguistically, it appears to crowd out face perception to the right hemisphere.

In an fMRI study, Alcauter, García-Mondragón, Gracia-Tabuenca, Moreno, Ortiz, and Barrios (2017) related reading speed in 6- to 9-year-olds to mostly left-lateralized resting-state functional connectivity of the prefrontal cortex and the superior temporal cortices, in particular. The regions extended beyond Broca's and Wernicke's and other regions associated with language in the left hemisphere, as they included the subcortical left caudate, putamen, and thalamus, in what can be referred to as a reading network in the brain.

Comparing 6-year-old preterms and controls, in a study of white matter tract fractional anisotropy (FA), the preterms only demonstrated differential white matter pathways for receptive and expressive language. Both groups demonstrated that the arcuate fasciculus (AF) of the left hemisphere mediated phonological awareness skill (as indexed by three subtests of the Comprehensive Test of Phonological Processing, CTOPP; Wagner, Torgesen, & Rashotte, 1999; elision, sound matching, and blending words).

In a 2-year longitudinal auditory event-related potential (AERP) electroencephalogram (EEG) study of 7-year-olds (Clunies-Ross et al., 2018), the left hemisphere was found specialized for processing rapidly presented tone stimuli (50 ms inter-stimulus interval, ISI), while the right hemisphere evidenced specialization for slower stimuli (ISI = 100 and 200 ms). Notably, at the younger age, greater leftward lateralization to the rapidly presented tones positively predicted 9-year-old phonemic coding skill. In a rule induction task with 7- to 10-year-olds, Du, Cao, He, and Li (2018) measured ERPs and found that the P3b (300 plus ms) portion of the P3 wave, as measured by parietal electrodes, indicated that the children processed the key information in the task in the left side of the brain.

In an fMRI study, Demir-Lira et al. (2018) determined that 8- to 10-year-olds express gesture-speech integration in association with activity in the frontal gyri, the right middle temporal gyrus, and the left superior temporal gyrus. Although the methods relative to research with adults are not fully comparable (Dick, Mok, Raja Beharelle, Goldin-Meadow, & Small, 2014), the results show a narrowing of gesture-speech integration to the left hemisphere developmentally.

As for results that involve better right hemisphere activity in children, Yaakoby-Rotem and Geva (2014) found that the learning efficiency in 5- to 6-year-olds evidenced a right-hemisphere advantage for stimuli displayed as targets in the left compared to right visual fields. In a near-infrared spectroscopy study (NIRS), Suzuki et al. (2018) found that 7- to 12-year-olds evidenced right prefrontal cortex (PFC) specialization for visuospatial working memory, especially for sequential presentation of the stimuli involved.

For adolescent research, Lahat et al. (2018) found an association among right hemisphere (frontal) EEG activity and shyness, in particular, in girls who had been maltreated and then followed longitudinally at 14–17 years. Specifically, unlike the controls (N = 25), the girls were recruited through child protection services (N = 38–55, depending on the analysis). Shyness was measured using the Shyness and Sociability Scale (SSS; Cheek & Buss, 1981). Somewhat comparable results were found for related measures, e.g., on neuroticism and anxiety symptoms. The results speak to the approach-withdrawal model of left and right frontal lobe specialization. Another study on the relationship of neuroticism to hemispheric differences in adolescence (Madsen, Jernigan, Vestergaard, Mortensen, & Baaré, 2018) found sex differences, especially in the left and right cingulum related to neuroticism.

In terms of relationships to left hemisphere specialization for language and effects on developmental variables, MacDonald, Ganjavi, Collins, Evans, and Karama (2014) found that 6- to 18-year-olds exhibited a positive correlation between intelligence quotient (IQ), as measured by the Wechsler Abbreviated Scale of Intelligence (WASI; Wechsler, 1999), and left striatal (caudate nucleus and putamen) volume.

The present work does not deal much with sex differences in lateralization, but Gur and Gur (2017) have reviewed the literature showing that sex differences in lateralization are robust and accelerate in adolescence with the onset of puberty. Generally, females perform better in tasks involving memory and social cognition. Males excel in tasks involving spatial processing and motor speed. In terms of brain dynamics, females express greater inter-hemispheric connectivity, within-module connectivity, or inter-modularity, while males express greater intra-hemispheric connectivity, between-module connectivity, or modularity.

As a comment, the latter study points to the wider implications of the early development of handedness, manual specialization, and hemispheric specialization. The next section expands on these implications for cognition, language, and atypicality.

Applications

Cognition For normal development, behavioral and brain lateralization has been investigated for their associations. Michel, Campbell, Marcinowski, Nelson, and Babik (2016) reviewed research on infant hand preference in relation to cognitive abilities. They found that, in the longitudinal research examined, the development of early hand preferences in object acquisition and manipulation significantly predicted expressive language, object construction, object management skills, and tool use. They posited that developmental trajectories could be affected in a cascading manner such that more general cognitive functioning and brain organization that emerges later in development also is associated with early lateralized manual behavior. In systematic review/meta-analyses, research has found a marginal relationship between right-handedness and IQ (Ntolka & Papdatou-Pastou, 2017). Sala, Signorelli, Barsuola, Bolognese, and Gobet (2017) found that variance in mathematical task scores for 6- to 17-year-old Italian students was related to handedness, but the results were obtained by using a continuous measure of handedness strength rather than a categorical measure of right or left handedness.

Language Research has shown that more pronounced language lateralization relates to higher verbal IQs and better reading capacity (Chiarello, Welcome, Halderman, & Leonard, 2009; Everts et al., 2009; as per Güntürkün & Ocklenburg, 2017). Note that the same relationship is not found with handedness and verbal ability (Somers, Shields, Boks, Kahn, & Sommer, 2015). Moreover, Bartha-Doering, Kollndorfer, Kasprian, Novak, Schuler, Fischmeister, Alexopoulos, Gaillard, Prayer, Seidl, and Berl (2018) also found results in contradiction to the view that stronger language lateralization confers advantages in language performance. Specifically, they examined 35 7- to 16-year-old right handers in an fMRI (functional magnetic resonance imaging) scan study. They determined the relationship of both in-scanner performance and out-of-scanner performance to a comprehensive language-memory battery, taking measures in the frontal, temporal, and parietal lobes. For the former, less lateralization was associated with better semantic decision task accuracy and verbal fluency (in-scan and out-scan, respectively). For the latter, advantages of less lateralization were found for out-of-scanner verbal learning memory tasks. The results for the temporal lobe were not significant. Overall, the authors concluded that less brain lateralization is associated with better language vocabulary and verbal fluency in the childhood period. Bartha-Doering et al. (2018) maintained that their results differ from those of Everts et al. (2009) and others due to different sample sizes, imaging methods, and tasks used. I would add that different ages, health statuses, culture, and other demographic factors might be involved, as well. Clearly, more conceptualization and research is needed, for example, on the role of inter-hemispheric coupling activation-inhibition, and their coordination before a complete picture obtains on degree of hemispheric lateralization in relation to language performance as determined by fMRI and language and related measures in children and adolescents.

Atypicality About laterality in non-normal development, Finch, Seery, Talbott, Nelson, and Tager-Flusberg (2017) found that 12-month-olds with autism spectrum disorder (ASD) expressed reversed lateralization of the brain for language function. Also, Markou, Ahtam, and Papadatou-Pastou (2017) conducted three meta-analyses and found that atypical handedness (left, mixed, and undetermined) characterized children with ASD. Rysstad and Pedersen (2018) obtained similar results. There are many developmental disorders that have been related to atypical lateralization beyond the ones mentioned. For example, see Blais et al. (2018) in this regard with respect to developmental coordination disorder.

As for early brain damage and central plasticity related to lateralized brain function, Krägeloh-Mann, Lidzba, Pavlova, Wilke, and Staudt (2017) reviewed the literature and found that early plasticity coexisted with limits in compensation due to the impacts of early brain damage on the left hemisphere (e.g., in right hemisphere "crowding"). Specifically, they found that the young brain that is damaged on the left side compensates by right hemisphere recruitment for language function, but there are limits in this regard. Similarly, Dinomais et al. (2017) found that neonatal stroke led to more left handedness than expected 7 years later, specifically by the loss of the ability of the left hemisphere to inhibit the right hemisphere and keep its normal dominance.

Comment Different aspects of the development of brain lateralization take place in different trajectories, so that simple developmental models of asymmetric brain and behavior relationships should be avoided (Tzourio-Mazoyer, 2016). There is an absence of sufficient well-designed developmental research on the development of early handedness and related behaviors, such as bimanual preferences (Gonzalez & Nelson, 2015), although the research of Michel and colleagues especially has been filling the void. Also, the research on types of tasks that best elicit manual preferences in infancy is constantly subject to revision and testing (e.g., Domellöf, Barbu-Roth, Fagard, Rönnqvist, Jacquet, & Fagard, 2015). It has even been queried whether the hands relative to the feet are the best limbs for the study of developing laterality (Kamson, Juhász, Chugani, & Jeong, 2015). Finally, the developmental research varies on which laterality index is used, a confounder that might create inconsistencies in the data (Fagard, Margules, Lopez, Granjon, & Huet 2017). For example, should the formula involve simply right (R) minus left (L) aspects of a behavior being studied divided by the total of R plus L? Or should bimanual behaviors be included in the denominator? Other variations in laterality indices include finding the square root of the denominator.

This concludes the review of the developmental research on lateralized manual and hemispheric functions. It includes research related to handedness as well as manual lateralization, but the dividing line between them sometimes is fuzzy early in life. For example, reaching might be right-sided very early in life, but does this reflect a nascent early handedness on simpler tasks or a specialization manually on more complex tasks? The field needs careful operationalization of its measures and tasks in conducting its research as well as continued quality longitudinal research that can determine predictive outcomes of early manual and hemisphere functional lateralizations.

The present work turns to the adult period for relevant research that depicts the status of manual and hemispheric specializations and handedness, but only for a select set of recent studies and papers on modeling because of the mammoth literature in the area. The review highlights the dynamic, changing nature of the research and theory in the field, as has been shown for the early developmental research, as well.

Adults

Manual

Right Generally, handedness is not perfectly correlated with the side of hemispheric dominance for language. The model is not that the adult uses one hand or the other in his or her handedness and also that the hand used serves as a biomarker of the hemisphere that is specialized for language function. That said, the correspondence between adult handedness and language control in the left hemisphere is notable. Corballis (2014) noted that 95–99% of adults who are right-handed in handedness are specialized for language in the left brain. This illustrates that typically lateralized brain and behavior function control proceeds from the brain to the limbs, peripheral sensory modalities, and so on, in a manner exhibiting contralateral (opposite side) control. For example, when we move our right fingers, an exclusive control takes place in the left hemisphere. However, when we move our right arm, the control is not exclusively contralateral and there are ipsilateral pathways involved, too. Nevertheless, generally, right arm movements are controlled by the left hemisphere, especially in the case of right handers. The same relative dominance by the left hemisphere in the control of language function obtains, with the left hemisphere especially involved relative to the right hemisphere, but not uniquely. This is illustrated in the case of left-sided brain damage, particularly earlier in life, in that the brain evidences plasticity of function and the right hemisphere can take over language function to a degree (Lidzba, de Haan, Wilke, Krägeloh-Mann, & Staudt, 2017). It is important to note that even 70–80% of adult left-handers exhibit left hemisphere control for language (Corballis, 2014; Tzourio-Mazoyer & Seghier, 2016). Left-handers are not mirror right-handers in either manual or brain lateralizations (Nelson, Berthier, & Konidaris, 2017).

Left This latter fact illustrates that the study of left-handers and their development is as interesting as the study of right-handers and their development, because the patterns and consequences both in the brain and behavior might be different and revealing (Porac, 2016). Similarly, the study of ambidextrous individuals presents challenges, and the study of developmentally compromised individuals, such as in the case of early developing autism, presents unique opportunities and windows for the investigation of laterality and its developmental and evolutionary origins. About non-right-handers, for example, Johnston, Nicholls, Shah, and Shields (2009) found that children performed significantly worse if they are left-handed and mixed handed rather than right-handed for nearly all developmental measures investigated. Their own empirical investigation examined Australian children in this regard, with left handedness associated with lower levels of cognitive ability, for example, on the Peabody Picture Vocabulary Test, Third Edition (PPVT-III; Dunn & Dunn, 1997), and with mixed handers performing even worse.

Despite these intriguing findings related to left-handers, the present review is limited in dealing with them and investigates more so the modal right-hander and left hemisphere dominance. At the same time, it is concerned with individual differences in lateralization, as shall be more evident as the article proceeds.

Much of the present work examines the empirical literature on developmental lateralization early in life. However, the lateralization continues throughout childhood into adolescence and even into the elderly years (see Nenert et al., 2017; also see Kang et al., 2017). Once more, although the results are intriguing, the scope of the present work does not allow for much description of lateralization beyond childhood.

Brain

Torque Li, Crow, Hopkins, Gong, and Roberts (2018) examined MRI scans of humans and chimpanzees in order to differentiate the dynamic structure of the human brain. Only the humans demonstrated torque twisting in conjunction with hemispheric differences. Specifically, the human pattern consisted of a right frontal combined with a left occipital "petalia." Also, a bending that was downward and rightward was found for the occipital pole. Next, the authors found a leftward displacement, especially anteriorly of the temporal lobe and the superior temporal sulcus (STS), consistent with results of a greater depth of the STS in the right relative to the left hemisphere (Leroy et al., 2015) and in keeping with similar results antenatally and neonatally (Glasel et al., 2011; Kasprian et al., 2011, respectively) Also, there were asymmetries posteriorly relating to the left occipitotemporal surface along with a clockwise rotation of the left sylvan fissure around the left-right axis. The sex differences were few and not certain for the authors. The authors concluded that the human cerebral torque process proceeds from the right frontal to left occipital regions, with prominence in the posterior or sensory portion of the cerebrum.

Circuits Right hemisphere language regions relate to nonverbal aspects. Again, the present work is limited into discussing this aspect, dealing more with language functions. For a brief review of right hemisphere functions, consider that they relate to facial and spatial processing (Chen & Spence, 2017). In addition, the brain circuits involved as having a cerebral organization reflective of cerebral asymmetry in structure and lateralization of function are multiple, including the right hemisphere ones for spatial attention and not just the left hemisphere ones for language (Badzakova-Trajkov, Corballis, & Häberling, 2016).

So far, the topic of lateralized brain function has been considered in the present work from the point of view that it is uniform in one half brain or the other. However, research with adults point to independent lateralized areas and functions in each hemisphere. For example, Tzourio-Mazoyer, Perrone-Bertolotti, Jobard, Mazoyer, and Baciu (2017) found that left hemisphere dominance for language in adults is based in intra-hemispheric associative bundles (e.g., arcuate fasciculus) and inter-hemispheric transcallosal (corpus callosum) connections. In this regard, Liu,

Stufflebeam, Sepulcrea, Heddena, and Buckner (2009) conducted a brain imaging study in participants with the brain at rest. They found four different and uncorrelated dimensions of asymmetric regional activation by factor analysis. One region corresponded to the language area of the brain, and the three others were related to the functions of vision, attention, and internal thought, with vision and attention lateralized to the right hemisphere and internal thought to the left, as with language. In another study that speaks of the issue, Groen, Whitehouse, Badcock, and Bishop (2013) found little relationship between handedness measures and variance in cerebral lateralization. They used a variety of handedness measures and still found this result, while the cerebral lateralization was examined using functional transcranial Doppler ultrasound during a language production task (also see Häberling, Corballis, & Corballis, 2016; Hodgson et al., 2016). Note that the relationship of lateralized brain structure and language function varies to a degree based on handedness, but the relationship is not strong (see Nenert et al., 2017; also see the research by Kang et al., 2017, on handedness and brain morphology).

Connectivity Networks The recent research in the field is evolving rapidly and is pointing to new directions in understanding differential organization of the left and right hemispheres that underlie their respective advantages. Specifically, connectivity-based research in scan studies is finding that even early in life the hemispheres differ in their connectivities in ways that are consistent with their respective skills. For example, Hervé, Zago, Petit, Mazoyer, and Tzourio-Mazoyer (2013) conducted a literature review of neuro-imaging research, which showed that the left hemisphere contains more "crucial" networked "hub" regions, as per Iturria-Medina et al. (2011), while the right hemisphere shows greater interregional connectivity (that is, being more efficiently organized). The authors surmised that the tasks associated with the left hemisphere are more "highly demanding," such as in language, and so require a hub organization, while the skills of the right hemisphere are broader, such as in visuospatial integration, and so require more interregional connectivity (also see Serrien & Sovijärvi-Spapé, 2016, for work on better motor efficiency in the left hemisphere).

However, more research is needed on the question because other researchers have found opposite patterns in connectivity in the hemispheres. For example, Caeyenberghs and Leemans (2014) used fiber tractography in 45 nodes and found that the topology of the left hemisphere was more efficient than the right hemisphere. The differences in the two sets of research could relate to the different definitions, methods used, and so on. For example, the better efficiency for one hemisphere or the other in the two publications could be complementary, with the left hemisphere evidencing the efficiency locally (Hervé et al., 2013) and the right hemisphere globally (Caeyenberghs & Leemans, 2014). At any rate, Caeyenberghs and Leemans (2014) related their results to a better left than right hemisphere information processing. They found that efficiency in the left hemisphere was both local and global in network interconnections over regions.

As a comment, note that the different results in Caeyenberghs and Leemans (2014) and in Hervé et al. (2013) refer to tractography, white matter, and structural connectivities. Connectivity is also studied functionally, and the results for each of "small world" (high clustering with short characteristic path length, Young, 2016); "rich club" (with high-degree nodes); core nodes; integration, efficiency, short/long nodes; interregional/intraregional hubs; and so on in connectivities need further elucidation for left and right hemispheric differences and their relationship to structural connectivity differences in the hemispheres. That said, the results of Ratnarajah et al. (2014) implicate a tighter and more efficient organization right from the neonatal period onward for the left hemisphere. This would support the comprehensive literature review of Hervé et al. (2013) about how the left hemisphere possesses "small world" properties.

Comment Proper review of the literature on adult manual and brain lateralization helps determine the end point of the developmental trajectory of the lateralizations involved. It is a truism that, at the level of content, the left hemisphere is specialized for language skills and the right for visuospatial skills, and this impacts behavioral lateralization, including in-hand preference/handedness manually. However, the literature also is invested in finding the underlying common elements to the diverse specializations in behavior and brain lateralities, such as small world properties in the left hemisphere.

However, one could ask what ultimate function is served by this networked connectivity organization in one hemisphere or the other. In this regard, the next section of the article examines the diverse explanations offered for understanding early lateralizations, including genetically. It considers a model of activation-inhibition coordination, as proposed by the author, beginning with his developmental research on reaching at 1 month of age. The infant's lateralized manual behavior has much to reveal about all forms of behavior and its evolution.

The next part of the present works turns to how to explain the lateralized developmental findings related to manual behavior and the brain. It begins with a review of the early manual behavior and brain research for lateralization findings and then considers a revised invariant lateralization model to explain them. This next section then considers the causation of early lateralizations more broadly, such as in the activation-inhibition coordination model and in hemisphericity, which might be beneficial to examine anew.

References

Alcauter, S., García-Mondragón, L., Garcia-Tabuenca, Z., Moreno, M. B., Ortiz, J. J., & Barrios, F. A. (2017). Resting state functional connectivity of the anterior striatum and prefrontal cortex predicts reading performance in school-age children. *Brain and Language, 174*, 94–102. https://doi.org/10.1016/j.bandl.2017.07.007

Badzakova-Trajkov, G., Corballis, M. C., & Häberling, I. S. (2016). Complementarity or independence of hemispheric specializations? A brief review. *Neuropsychologia, 93*, 386–393. https://doi.org/10.1016/j.neuropsychologia.2015.12.018

Bartha-Doering, L., Kollndorfer, K., Kasprian, G., Novak, A., Schuler, A-L., Fischmeister, F. P. S., Alexopoulos, J., Gaillard, W. D., Prayer, D., Seidl, R., & Berl, M. M. (2018). Weaker semantic language lateralization associated with better semantic language performance in healthy right-handed children. *Brain and Behavior*. https://doi.org/10.1002/brb3.1072

Blais, M., Amarantini, D., Albaret, J.-M., Chaix, Y., & Tallet, J. (2018). Atypical inter-hemispheric communication correlates with altered motor inhibition during learning of a new bimanual coordination pattern in developmental coordination disorder. *Developmental Science, 21*, e12563. https://doi.org/10.1111/desc.12563

Caeyenberghs, K., & Leemans, A. (2014). Hemispheric lateralization of topological organization in structural brain networks. *Human Brain Mapping, 35*, 4944–4957. https://doi.org/10.1002/hbm.22524

Centanni, T. M., Norton, E. S., Park, A., Beach, S. D., Halverson, K., Ozernov-Palchik, O., et al. (2018). Early development of letter specialization in left fusiform is associated with better word reading and smaller fusiform face area. *Developmental Science*, e12658. https://doi.org/10.1111/desc.12658

Cheek, J. M., & Buss, A. H. (1981). Shyness and sociability. *Journal of Personality and Social Psychology, 41*, 330–339. https://doi.org/10.1037/0022-3514.41.2.330

Chen, Y.-C., & Spence, C. (2017). Hemispheric asymmetry: Looking for a novel signature of the modulation of spatial attention in multisensory processing. *Psychonomic Bulletin & Review, 24*, 690–707. https://doi.org/10.3758/s13423-016-1154-y

Chiarello, C., Welcome, S. E., Halderman, L. K., & Leonard, C. M. (2009). Does degree of asymmetry relate to performance? An investigation of word recognition and reading in consistent and mixed handers. *Brain and Cognition, 69*, 521–530. https://doi.org/10.1016/j.bandc.2008.11.002

Clunies-Ross, K. L., Campbell, C., Ohan, J. L., Anderson, M., Reid, C., & Fox, A. M. (2018). Hemispheric asymmetries in rapid temporal processing at age 7 predict subsequent phonemic decoding 2 years later: A longitudinal event-related potential (ERP) study. *Neuropsychologia, 111*, 252–260. https://doi.org/10.1016/j.neuropsychologia.2018.01.035

Cochet, H. (2016). Manual asymmetries and hemispheric specialization: Insight from developmental studies. *Neuropsychologia, 93*, 335–341. https://doi.org/10.1016/j.neuropsychologia.2015.12.019

Cochet, H., Centelles, L., Jover, M., Plachta, S., & Vauclair, J. (2015). Hand preference in preschool children: Reaching, pointing and symbolic gestures. *Laterality: Asymmetries of Body, Brain and Cognition, 20*, 501–516. https://doi.org/10.1080/1357650X.2015.1007057

Corballis, M. C. (2014). Left brain, right brain: Facts and fantasies. *PLoS Biology, 12*, e1001767. https://doi.org/10.1371/journal.pbio.1001767

Demir-Lira, Ö., Asaridou, S. S., Raja Beharelle, A., Holt, A. E., Goldin-Meadow, S., & Small, S. L. (2018). Functional neuroanatomy of gesture-speech integration in children varies with individual differences in gesture processing. *Developmental Science*, e12648. https://doi.org/10.1111/desc.12648

Dick, A. S., Mok, E. H., Raja Beharelle, A., Goldin-Meadow, S., & Small, S. L. (2014). Frontal and temporal contributions to understanding the iconic co-speech gestures that accompany speech. *Human Brain Mapping, 35*, 900–917. https://doi.org/10.1002/hbm.22222

Dinomais, M., Thébault, G., Hertz-Pannier, L., Gautheron, V., Nguyen The Tich, S., Fluss, J., et al. (2017). Is there an excess of left-handedness after neonatal stroke? *Cortex, 96*, 161–164. https://doi.org/10.1016/j.cortex.2017.08.007

Domellöf, E., Barbu-Roth, M., Rönnqvist, L., Jacquet, A.-Y., & Fagard, J. (2015). Infant manual performance during reaching and grasping for objects moving in depth. *Frontiers in Psychology, 6*, 1142. https://doi.org/10.3389/fpsyg.2015.01142

Doyen, A.-L., Lambert, E., Dumas, F., & Carlier, M. (2017). Manual performance as predictor of literacy acquisition: A study from kindergarten to grade 1. *Cognitive Development, 43*, 80–90. https://doi.org/10.1016/j.cogdev.2017.02.011

Du, B., Cao, B., He, W., & Li, F. (2018). Different electrophysiological responses to informative value of feedback between children and adults. *Frontiers in Psychology, 9*, 346. https://doi.org/10.3389/fpsyg.2018.00346

Dunn, L. M., & Dunn, L. M. (1997). *Peabody picture vocabulary test – Third edition (PPVT-III)*. Circle Pines, MN: American Guidance Service.

Everts, R., Lidzba, K., Wilke, M., Kiefer, C., Mordasini, M., Schroth, G., et al. (2009). Strengthening of laterality of verbal and visuospatial functions during childhood and adolescence. *Human Brain Mapping, 30*, 473–483. https://doi.org/10.1002/hbm.20523

Fagard, J., Margules, S., Lopez, C., Granjon, L., & Huet, V. (2017). How should we test infant handedness? *Laterality: Asymmetries of Body, Brain and Cognition, 22*, 294–312. https://doi.org/10.1080/1357650X.2016.1192186

Faria, I., Diniz, A., & Barreiros, J. (2017). Manual asymmetries in bimanual isochronous tapping tasks in children. *Acta Psychologica, 172*, 41–48. https://doi.org/10.1016/j.actpsy.2016.11.005

Finch, K. H., Seery, A. M., Talbott, M. R., Nelson, C. A., & Tager-Flusberg, H. (2017). Lateralization of ERPs to speech and handedness in the early development of autism spectrum disorder. *Journal of Neurodevelopmental Disorders, 9*, 1–14. https://doi.org/10.1186/s11689-017-9185-x

Flindall, J. W., & Gonzalez, C. L. R. (2014). Eating interrupted: The effect of intent on hand-to-month actions. *Journal of Neurophysiology, 112*, 2019–2025. https://doi.org/10.1152/jn.00295.2014

Friederici, A. D., Brauer, J., & Lohmann, G. (2011). Maturation of the language network: From inter- to intrahemispheric connectivities. *PLoS One, 6*, e20726. https://doi.org/10.1371/journal.pone.0020726

Gioia, G. A., Isquith, P. K., Guy, S. C., & Kenworthy, L. (2000). *Behavior rating inventory of executive function (BRIEF)*. Odessa, FL: Psychological Assessment Resources.

Girelli, L., Marinelli, C. V., Grossi, G., & Arduino, L. S. (2017). Cultural and biological factors modulate spatial biases over development. *Laterality: Asymmetries of Body, Brain, and Cognition, 22*, 725–739. https://doi.org/10.1080/1357650X.2017.1279623

Glasel, H., Leroy, F., Dubois, J., Hertz-Pannier, L., Mangin, J. F., & Dehaene-Lambertz, G. (2011). A robust cerebral asymmetry in the infant brain: The rightward superior temporal sulcus. *NeuroImage, 58*, 716–723. https://doi.org/10.1016/j.neuroimage.2011.06.016

Gonzalez, C. L. R., Mills, K. J., Genee, I., Li, F., Piquette, N., Rosen, N., et al. (2014). Getting the right grasp on executive function. *Frontiers in Psychology, 5*, 285. https://doi.org/10.3389/fpsyg.2014.00285

Gonzalez, S. L., & Nelson, E. L. (2015). Addressing the gap: A blueprint for studying bimanual hand preference in infants. *Frontiers in Psychology, 5*, 560. https://doi.org/10.3389/fpsyg.2015.00560

Gracia-Tabuenca, Z., Moreno, M. B., Barrios, F. A., & Alcauter, S. (2018). Hemispheric asymmetry and homotopy of resting state functional connectivity correlate with visuospatial abilities in school-age children. *NeuroImage, 174*, 441–448. https://doi.org/10.1016/j.neuroimage.2018.03.051

Groen, M. A., Whitehouse, A. J. O., Badcock, N. A., & Bishop, D. V. M. (2013). Associations between handedness and cerebral lateralisation for language: A comparison of three measures in children. *PLoS One, 8*, e64876. https://doi.org/10.1371/journal.pone.0064876

Güntürkün, O., & Ocklenburg, S. (2017). Ontogenesis of lateralization. *Neuron, 94*, 249–263. https://doi.org/10.1016/j.neuron.2017.02.045

Gur, R. C., & Gur, R. E. (2017). Complementarity of sex differences in brain and behavior: From laterality to multimodal imaging. *Journal of Neuroscience Research, 95*, 189–199. https://doi.org/10.1002/jnr.23830

Häberling, I. S., Corballis, P. M., & Corballis, M. C. (2016). Language, gesture, and handedness: Evidence for independent lateralized networks. *Cortex, 82*, 72–85. https://doi.org/10.1016/j.cortex.2016.06.003

Hepping, A. M., Ploegmakers, J. J. W., Geertzen, J. H. B., Bulstra, S., & Stevens, M. (2015). The influence of hand preference on grip strength in children and adolescents: A cross-sectional study of 2284 children and adolescents. *PLoS One, 10*, e0143476. https://doi.org/10.1371/journal.pone.0143476.

Hervé, P. Y., Zago, L., Petit, L., Mazoyer, B., & Tzourio-Mazoyer, N. (2013). Revisiting human hemispheric specialization with neuroimaging. *Trends in Cognitive Sciences, 17*, 69–80. https://doi.org/10.1016/j.tics.2012.12.004

Hodgson, J. C., Hirst, R. J., & Hudson, J. M. (2016). Hemispheric speech lateralisation in the developing brain is related to motor praxis ability. *Developmental Cognitive Neuroscience, 22*, 9–17. https://doi.org/10.1016/j.dcn.2016.09.005

Iturria-Medina, Y., Pérez Fernández, A., Morris, D. M., Canales-Rodríguez, E. J., Haroon, H. A., García Pentón, L., et al. (2011). Brain hemispheric structural efficiency and interconnectivity rightward asymmetry in human and non-human primates. *Cerebral Cortex, 21*, 56–67. https://doi.org/10.1093/cercor/bhq058

Johnston, D. W., Nicholls, M. E. R., Shah, M., & Shields, M. A. (2009). Nature's experiment? Handedness and early childhood development. *Demography, 46*, 281–301. https://doi.org/10.1353/dem.0.0053

Kamson, D. O., Juhász, C., Chugani, H. T., & Jeong, J.-W. (2015). Novel diffusion tensor imaging technique reveals developmental streamline volume changes in the corticospinal tract associated with leg motor control. *Brain & Development, 37*, 370–375. https://doi.org/10.1016/j.braindev.2014.07.001

Kang, S. J., Kang, K. A., Jang, H., Lee, J. Y., Kee, K. I., Kwoen, M. S., et al. (2017). Brain morphology according to age, sex, and handedness. *Annals of Clinical Neurophysiology, 19*, 93–100. https://doi.org/10.14253/acn.2017.19.2.93

Kasprian, G., Langs, G., Brugger, P. C., Bittner, M., Weber, M., Arantes, M., et al. (2011). The prenatal origin of hemispheric asymmetry: An in utero neuroimaging study. *Cerebral Cortex, 21*, 1076–1083. https://doi.org/10.1093/cercor/bhq179

Kaufman, A., & Kaufman, N. (1983). *Kaufman assessment battery for children: Administration and scoring manual*. Circle Pines, MN: American Guidance Service.

Kikuchi, M., Shitamichi, K., Yoshimura, Y., Ueno, S., Remijn, G. B., Hirosawa, T., et al. (2011). Lateralized theta wave connectivity and language performance in 2- to 5-year-old children. *Journal of Neuroscience, 31*, 14984–14988. https://doi.org/10.1523/JNEUROSCI.2785-11.2011

Krägeloh-Mann, I., Lidzba, K., Pavlova, M. A., Wilke, M., & Staudt, M. (2017). Plasticity during early brain development is determined by ontogenetic potential. *Neuropediatrics*. https://doi.org/10.1055/s-0037-1599234

Lahat, A., Tang, A., Tanaka, M., Van Lieshout, R. J., MacMillan, H. L., & Schmidt, L. A. (2018). Longitudinal associations among child maltreatment, resting frontal electroencephalogram asymmetry, and adolescent shyness. *Child Development*. https://doi.org/10.1111/cdev.13060

Leroy, F., Cai, Q., Bogart, S. L., Dubois, J., Coulon, O., Monzalvo, K., et al. (2015). New human-specific brain landmark: The depth asymmetry of superior temporal sulcus. *Proceedings of the National Academy of Sciences of the United States of America, 112*, 1208–1213. https://doi.org/10.1073/pnas.1412389112

Li, X., Crow, T. J., Hopkins, W. D., Gong, Q., & Roberts, N. (2018). Human torque is not present in chimpanzee brain. *NeuroImage, 165*, 285–293. https://doi.org/10.1016/j.neuroimage.2017.10.017

Lidzba, K., de Hann, B., Wilke, M., Krägeloh-Mann, I., & Staudt, M. (2017). Lesion characteristics driving right-hemispheric language reorganization in congenital left-hemispheric brain damage. *Brain & Language, 173*, 1–9. https://doi.org/10.1016/j.bandl.2017.04.006

Liu, H., Stufflebeam, S. M., Sepulcrea, J., Heddena, T., & Buckner, R. L. (2009). Evidence from intrinsic activity that asymmetry of the human brain is controlled by multiple factors. In *Proceedings of the National Academy of Sciences of the United States of America* (Vol. 26, pp. 198–208). https://doi.org/10.1073/pnas.0908073106

MacDonald, P. A., Ganjavi, H., Collins, D. L., Evans, A. C., & Karama, S. (2014). Investigating the relation between striatal volume and IQ. *Brain Imaging and Behavior, 8*, 52–59. https://doi.org/10.1007/s11682-013-9242-3

Madsen, K. S., Jernigan, T. L., Vestergaard, M., Mortensen, E. L., & Baaré, W. F. C. (2018). Neuroticism is linked to microstructural left-right asymmetry of frontolimbic fibre tracts in adolescents with opposite effects in boys and girls. *Neuropsychologia, 114*, 1–10. https://doi.org/10.1016/j.neuropsychologia.2018.04.010

Markou, P., Ahtam, B., & Papadatou-Pastou, M. (2017). Elevated levels of atypical handedness in autism: Meta-analysis. *Neuropsychology Review*. https://doi.org/10.1007/s11065-017-9354-4

Michel, G. F., Campbell, J. M., Marcinowski, E. C., Nelson, E. L., & Babik, I. (2016). Infant hand preference and the development of cognitive abilities. *Frontiers in Psychology, 7*, 410. https://doi.org/10.3389/fpsyg.2016.00410

Nelson, E. L., Berthier, N. E., & Konidaris, G. D. (2017). Handedness and reach-to-place kinematics in adults: Left-handers are not reversed right-handers. *Journal of Motor Behavior*, 1–11. https://doi.org/10.1080/00222895.2017.1363698

Nelson, E. L., Gonzalez, S. L., El-Asmar, J. M., Fouad Ziade, M., & Abu-Rustum, R. S. (2018). The home handedness questionnaire: Pilot data from preschoolers. *Laterality: Asymmetries of Body, Brain and Cognition*. https://doi.org/10.1080/1357650X.2018.1543313

Nenert, R., Allendorfer, J. B., Martin, A. M., Banks, C., Vannest, J., Holland, S. K., et al. (2017). Age-related language lateralization assessed by fMRI: The effects of sex and handedness. *Brain Research, 1674*, 20–35. https://doi.org/10.1016/j.brainres.2017.08.021

Ntolka, E., & Papadatou-Pastou, M. (2017). Right-handers have marginally higher IQ scores than left-handers: Systematic review and meta-analyses. *Neuroscience & Biobehavioral Reviews*. https://doi.org/10.1016/j.neubiorev.2017.08.007

Porac, C. (2016). *Laterality: Exploring the enigma of left-handedness*. London: Elsevier.

Ratnarajah, N., Rifkin-Graboi, A., Fortier, M. V., Chong, Y. S., Kwek, K., Saw, S. M., et al. (2014). Structural connectivity asymmetry in the neonatal brain. *NeuroImage, 75*, 187–194. https://doi.org/10.1016/j.neuroimage.2013.02.052

Rysstad, A. L., & Pedersen, A. V. (2018). There are indeed more left-handers within the autism spectrum disorder compared with in the general population, but the many mixed-handers is the more interesting finding. *Journal of Autism and Developmental Disorders*. https://doi.org/10.1007/s10803-018-3553-6

Sala, G., Signorelli, M., Barsuola, G., Bolognese, M., & Gobet, F. (2017). The relationship between handedness and mathematics is non-linear and is moderated by gender, age, and type of task. *Frontiers in Psychology, 8*, 948. https://doi.org/10.3389/fpsyg.2017.00948

Scharoun, S. M., & Bryden, P. J. (2014). Hand preference, performance abilities, and hand selection in children. *Frontiers in Psychology, 5*, 82. https://doi.org/10.3389/fpsyg.2014.00082

Serrien, D. J., & Sovijärvi-Spapé, M. M. (2016). Manual dexterity: Functional lateralization patterns and motor efficiency. *Brain and Cognition, 108*, 42–46. https://doi.org/10.1016/j.bandc.2016.07.005

Sivagnanasunderam, M., Gonzalez, D. A., Bryden, P. J., Young, G., Forsyth, A., & Roy, E. A. (2015). Handedness throughout the lifespan: Cross-sectional view on sex differences as asymmetries change. *Frontiers in Psychology, 5*, 1556. https://doi.org/10.3389/fpsyg.2014.01556

Somers, M., Shields, L. S., Boks, M. P., Kahn, R. S., & Sommer, I. E. (2015). Cognitive benefits of right-handedness: A meta-analysis. *Neuroscience and Biobehavioral Reviews, 51*, 48–63. https://doi.org/10.1016/j.neubiorev.2015.01.003

Streuli, J. C., Obrist, G., & Brugger, P. (2017). Childrens' left-turning preference is not modulated by magical ideation. *Laterality: Asymmetries of Body, Brain, and Cognition, 22*, 90–104. https://doi.org/10.1080/1357650X.2015.1134565

Suzuki, K., Kita, Y., Oi, Y., Okumura, Y., Okuzumi, H., & Inagaki, M. (2018). Right prefrontal cortex specialization for visuospatial working memory and developmental alterations in prefrontal cortex recruitment in school-age children. *Clinical Neurophysiology, 129*, 759–765. https://doi.org/10.1016/j.clinph.2018.01.010

Thevenot, C., Fayol, M., & Barrouillet, P. (2018). Spatial numerical associations in preschoolers. *Thinking & Reasoning, 24*, 221–233. https://doi.org/10.1080/13546783.2017.1375013

Tzourio-Mazoyer, N. (2016). Intra- and inter-hemispheric connectivity supporting hemispheric specialization. In H. Kennedy, D. C. Van Essen, & Y. Christen (Eds.), *Micro-, meso- and macro-connectomics of the brain* (pp. 129–146). Cham, Switzerland: Springer International Publishing.

Tzourio-Mazoyer, N., Perrone-Bertolotti, M., Jobard, G., Mazoyer, B., & Baciu, M. (2017). Multi-factorial modulation of hemispheric specialization and plasticity for language in healthy and pathological conditions: A review. *Cortex, 86*, 314–339. https://doi.org/10.1016/j.cortex.2016.05.013

Tzourio-Mazoyer, N., & Seghier, M. L. (2016). The neural bases of hemispheric specialization. *Neuropsychologia, 93*, 319–324. https://doi.org/10.1016/j.neuropsychologia.2016.10.010

Wagner, R. K., Torgesen, J. K., & Rashotte, C. A. (1999). *Comprehensive test of phonological processing (CTOPP)*. Austin, TX: Pro-Ed.

Wechsler, D. (1999). *Wechsler abbreviated scale of intelligence (WASI)*. San Antonio, TX: The Psychological Corporation.

Woodcock, R. W. (1998). *Woodcock reading mastery tests, revised*. Circle Pines, MN: American Guidance Service.

Yaakoby-Rotem, S., & Geva, R. (2014). Asymmetric attention networks: The case of children. *Journal of the International Neuropsychological Society, 20*, 434–443. https://doi.org/10.1017/S1355617714000150

Yamazaki, H., Easwar, V., Polonenko, M. J., Jiwani, S., Wong, D. D. E., Papsin, B. C., et al. (2017). Cortical hemispheric asymmetries are present at young ages and further develop into adolescence. *Human Brain Mapping*. https://doi.org/10.1002/hbm.23893

Young, G. (2016). *Unifying causality and psychology: Being, brain and behavior*. Cham, Switzerland: Springer International Publishing.

Chapter 5
Other Human Laterality Research

Abstract This chapter briefly reviews the equi-potential and invariant lateralization models before shifting into an in-depth exposition of the activation-inhibition coordination model. This includes examining in more depth the research that the author has cited in support of the latter model. Next, the chapter focuses especially on hemisphericity. The concept used to be heavily researched but fell out of favor due to the absence of positive findings in the research. However, I propose that a revised version of the concept might be useful. The chapter reviews the sparse recent research being conducted on the topic. It concludes by examining how different models, such as the biopsychosocial one, can help to update the concept of hemisphericity. In this regard, the concept of activation-inhibition coordination might also be useful.

Explaining the Development of Handedness, Manual Specialization, and Hemispheric Specialization

Review of Findings and Models

Alternative models of the development of handedness had considered it beginning with a left-hand preference in early infancy, with alterations across the hands over the first year. Handedness development was considered a maturational phenomenon (Gesell & Ames, 1947). However, Young, Segalowitz, Misek, Alp, and Boulet (1983b) showed that this type of result in the early literature on developing handedness was an artifact, for example, of not observing separately non-directed and directed behavior to objects, such that the non-directed ones contributing to the total are left-handed and relatively frequent, thereby masking the critical directed behaviors that are right-handed generally, even if relatively infrequent.

Research has shown that even in fetal development, the right hand is preferred for the activity of thumb sucking (Hepper, 2013). Further, in the neonatal period, the right hand is preferred for directed reaching-type activities, as mentioned, while the

G. Young, *Causality and Development*,
https://doi.org/10.1007/978-3-030-02493-2_5

left hand is preferred for more spatial activities (e.g., Young, Bowman, et al., 1983a; Young, Segalowitz, et al., 1983b). These preferential tendencies in hand use reflect that the early manual specializations at these ages are consistent with the patterns for adults and reflect underlying hemispheric specializations (Young, 2011, 2016; Young, Bowman, et al., 1983a; Young & Gagnon, 1990; Young, Segalowitz, et al., 1983b). That said, lateralization of behavior and the brain continue throughout development, especially in the early years, for example, in developing consistency and stability in the general right-side preferences in handedness and on complex manual tasks and in solidifying the left hemisphere specialization for language.

As for early concepts of the development of hemispheric specialization, the two hemispheres were considered equi-potential at first and they were considered to develop their adult-like specializations gradually (progressively) over the first years. Lenneberg (1967) enunciated this point of view, and it contrasts with the invariant lateralization model (e.g., Bryden, Hécaen, & deAgostini, 1982), as summarized in Hämäläinen and Takio (2010, also see Kinsbourne and Hiscock, 1976). The research especially supports the invariant lateralization model because there are early signs of left and right hemisphere specialization. However, the developing brain still shows progressive changes in its lateralization, so that the article supports a combined invariant/equi-potential/progressive model of lateralized brain development as well as manual specialization development.

One could ask which drives the other, the manual or the language development, in their association. The developmental research on handedness, manual specialization, and hemispheric specialization indicates patterns early in life that are consistent with the invariant model of lateralization, such that the left and right hemispheres express their respective advantages right from the beginning of their development. However, this does not imply that handedness, which is a general manual preference, maps onto the hemisphere that is better specialized for more advanced manual skills, that is, the left hemisphere. Rather, the results show that if both handedness and complex manual activities are right lateralized, the lateralizations are coincident more than causal. For example, there is a lot of variation in early handedness and there is room for environmental influence on its development.

As new behaviors mature or otherwise develop, they could map onto the existing skills of one hemisphere or the other, while others that had been already lateralized hemispherically become less important behaviorally and less of an index of ongoing hemispheric specialization development. That is, at each age, new and different behaviors can serve as expressions of the constant and unchanging underlying skills and functions of the hemispheres, depending on the developmental acquisitions that take place. This type of longitudinal development is also reflected in the ongoing dynamic of newly developing manual skills and their relationship to critical language acquisitions in the age period in which they emerge and at a later point, as well.

Activation-Inhibition Coordination

Model As noted, Young (1990a, 1990b, 2011, 2016) and colleagues (Young, Bowman, et al., 1983a; Young & Gagnon, 1990; Young, Segalowitz, et al., 1983b) have developed a model of differential left and right hemisphere specialization in terms of activation-inhibition coordination. He proposed that the left hemisphere is better at refined and continual activation-inhibition coordination, as in the early right-handed reaching of infants with the goal to grasp, while the right hemisphere is specialized for less complex or different inhibition skills, such as inhibition alone or non-continual activation-inhibition coordination.

This section of the paper further elucidates the left hemisphere advantage for inhibitory skills in concert with activating ones while describing those of the right hemisphere as well (see Table 5.1). Specifically, the left hemisphere is specialized for any behavior or function, including in information processing, which demands immediate, ongoing, and millisecond-by-millisecond integration of the activation and inhibitory processes that govern behavior and its workings. It does not engage in simpler activation and inhibition coordinations, nor does it engage in outright

Table 5.1 Different types of activation-inhibition functions in the left and right cerebral hemisphere

Hemisphere	Type	Description
Left	Longer-term synchrony	Complex, sophisticated, interweaving (see next)
	Sophisticated synchrony	Sophisticated, subtle interweaving of activation and inhibitory skills, with appropriate activations taking place because of the suppression of interference due to inappropriate alternative behavior, both when selecting adaptive goal-directed activity and during its (movement) transitions. Both subtle competing movements and gross interfering ones are countered and controlled
	Altering synchrony	Majorly modifying/disrupting sequential activation-inhibition coordinations
Right	Adjusting synchrony	Minorly adapting/refining sequential activation-inhibition coordinations
	Long damping	Full suppression/damping activity over time
	Short synchrony	Activation-inhibition synchrony instantaneously or for a short time period. In spatial processes, some information as figure highlighted and some as ground moderated

The left hemisphere specializes in a sophisticated interweaving of activation and inhibitory skills. Activation-inhibition coordination especially involves the suppression of interference due to inappropriate alternative behavior, both when selecting adaptive goal-directed activity and during its (movement) transitions (e.g., in both language and fine motor activities). Moreover, activation-inhibition inter-coordination takes place not only within the left hemisphere but also by the left hemisphere with the right one. The hemispheres collaborate to produce functionally adaptive behavior. The specialization of each hemisphere is relative, and some redundancy is built into the system

Adapted from Young (1990a, 1990b, 2011, 2016)

inhibition without activation for the most part. These alternate activation and inhibition functions are left to the right hemisphere, and the hemispheres work together in an ultimate synchronization but with the left hemisphere governing that control through its cross-hemisphere inhibitory skills. Moreover, the developmental evidence considered in the piece to this point support an early development of left and right hemisphere differential activation and inhibition coordination skills.

To remind, the two hemispheres work in concert in any functional activity, behavioral, information processing, or otherwise. Neither hemisphere has superior skills; language is not more important than spatial skills, also activation-inhibition coordination is not more important than outright inhibition. Indeed, much of behavior involves inhibition more than activation, as in self-control. Furthermore, the network studies imply that each hemisphere has its advantages in efficiency, with the left organized better locally and the right globally in this regard (for example, Brederoo, Nieuwenstein, Lorist, & Cornelissen, 2017). We can project that whatever model eventually best describes the hemispheres and the new findings that they will predict and find, both hemispheres will be considered specialized and there will be no "left over" or secondary functioning attributed to one or the other hemisphere, as has been attributed to the right hemisphere in the past (e.g., Corballis, 2017).

Initial and Later Evidence When first presented (Young, Bowman, et al., 1983a), the activation-inhibition coordination model emphasized this skill in the left hemisphere and even for the human neonate. The following presents a sampling of the research cited in Young's publication on differential inhibition skills in the two cerebral hemispheres. Young Bowman, et al. (1983a) referred to a pegboard study with adults by Annett, Annett, Hudson, and Turner (1979). The data seemed to imply that the left hemisphere was better in inhibiting both the preferred and non-preferred hands, which is consistent with the general view that the left hemisphere compared to the right hemisphere has better cross-hemisphere inhibitory skills, as discussed elsewhere in the paper. Also, Kimura (1980) reported research on left hemisphere damaged patients that revealed both "perseverative" errors within manual sequences and irrelevant movements that impinged on them, thereby supporting a left hemisphere inhibition deficit in these patients. In 1990, Young et al. published three works concerning the activation-inhibition coordination model of left hemisphere specialization (Young, 1990a, 1990b; Young & Gagnon, 1990). Young's 1990 works cited evidence that the left hemisphere is specialized in this way in terms of (a) early left hemisphere inhibition skills (e.g., Liederman, 1983), stutterers being disturbed in intra- and inter-hemispheric activation-inhibition balancing (Greiner, Fitzgerald, & Cooke, 1986), and (c) the left hemisphere acquiring inhibitory control of the right for emotional expression control in infancy (Fox & Davidson, 1984). Young (2011) cited Vauclair and Imbault (2009), who studied pointing gestures in 10–40-month-olds. The authors referred to a better "facilitatory/inhibitory" system in the left hemisphere. Also, he cited Aron (2008), who referred to the frontal cortex ability to "inhibit and activate" representations in other brain regions. Young (2016) cited Reid and Serrien (2012), who studied adults on a bimanual task and found results indicating that right handers appear to manifest intra- and inter-hemispheric inhibitory asymmetries in processing. Also, Ocklenburg, Ness, Güntürkün, Suchan, and Beste (2013) found that, in adults, initial verbal information processing takes place in the left hemisphere, thereby leading to better left hemisphere response inhibition. Similar results were found for the right hemisphere for a facial stimulus task.

Elaboration As originally described (Young, Bowman, et al., 1983a), "the activation-inhibition coordination model referred not only to the better coordination involved in the left compared to the right hemisphere but also to a hierarchical model in this regard. Specifically, the authors described that the left hemisphere is better in its hierarchical organization, such as in selecting appropriate macro and micro-paths in behavior to follow, even socially." That is, "one hierarchic motor, verbal, processing, or social plan is chosen and skillfully descended via a specific node pathway, with nodes often being sub-hierarchies, looping subsystems, and so on, while other hierarchies and nodes within the chosen hierarchy are inhibited in order to minimize interference" (p. 127). Patients, then, might be unable to select hierarchies, navigate them, deploy the correct inhibition in using them, and so on.

Comment Cochet (2016) noted that the association between the development of predominant right-hand use and left hemispheric specialization for language needs to consider broader concepts, and, in this regard, she referred to cerebral networks common to gesture in language and to complex multimodal integration. In effect, Young and colleagues' activation-inhibition coordination model speaks to this type of broader conceptualization of the common bases in manual specialization and hemispheric specialization. The present work concludes below with further suggestions about Young's model in terms of manual and cerebral connectivities and networks as governed by the activation-inhibition coordination dynamic.

The next part of the research review with humans considers the concept of hemisphericity and how it could be revised. Then, the review moves to animal research and discussion of evolution, before considering discussion, modeling, and so on.

Hemisphericity

Introduction

Morton (2013) documented the decline of the concept of hemisphericity, emphasizing difficulties with its conceptualization and measurement, which have served to produce conflicting results. The concept originated with Bogen (1969) and refers to a gradient rather than a categorical orientation to differences in left and right thinking between the two hemi-brains and their associated behavioral properties. Hemisphericity, then, is referred to as differential hemisphere-related behavioral orientations or behavioral laterality style. Morton (2013) noted, of course, that the hemispheres have different areas of the brain that are structurally different on one side compared to the other and properties related to behavior that are associated with them. The types of instruments used to detect hemisphere differences in behavioral orientation style include questionnaires, motor behavior, line bisection, and dichotic listening.

The behavioral qualities found to differentiate left and right hemisphere preferring individuals include logical orientation, types of consciousness, fear level and sensitivity, social and professional orientation, and pair bonding and spousal dominance style. That hemisphere preference and use can have such drastic effects on behavior needs to be verified with different procedures. Moreover, Morton's approach to hemisphere style differences is one involving a binary, left-right hemisphere preference difference, but psychological constructs often are expressed along continua. Therefore, his approach to reject the dimensional approach in favor of a categorical one for the area of hemisphericity (which he refers to as "hemisity") might be premature.

Questionnaire Research

Genovese (2005) compared three hemisphericity questionnaires for their psychometric properties and found that the original preference test (PT; Zenhausern, 1978) had better psychometric properties than Morton's later polarity questionnaire (PQ; Morton, 2002). Merckelbach, Muris, Pool, de Jong, and Schouten (1996) also found that the PQ had acceptable psychometric properties, for example, the required two-factor structure, as did Russo, Persegani, Papeschi, Nicolini, and Trimarchi (2000). Genovese (2005) studied a third instrument, the Wagner Preference Inventory II (WAPI II; Wagner & Wells, 1985), finding it acceptable psychometrically. Research has related PQ scores to mid-frontal EEG asymmetries (Merckelbach, Muris, Horselenberg, & de Jong, 1997; Russo et al., 2001).

Also, some research has found relations between the PQ and behavioral measures. For example, Vlachos, Andreou, and Delliou (2013) found a relationship between dyslexia and right brain preference using the PQ. Díaz-Morales and Barreno (2014) found a relationship between left brain orientation in PQ scores and adolescent school marks. Also see Genovese, Sparks, and Little (2017) for study of left-right differences in tympanic membrane temperature and hemispheric cognitive style as measured by an unpublished questionnaire.

Other Research

The most recent study found on the topic of hemisphere preference (Herzog, Farchi, & Gidron, 2017) reported intriguing results with a short version of the PQ and referred to the valence model of emotions in the hemispheres as a model of hemispheric preference (Davidson, 1992, 2004; and see the research described above by Fox and colleagues (Fox & Davidson, 1984; Hane, Fox, Henderson, & Marshall,

2008) for an equivalent approach-withdrawal model. In the valence model relating hemispheric activation to emotions or affective style, which functions like a trait, the left hemisphere (especially the prefrontal cortex) is considered the seat of positive emotions and of other approach emotions such as anger. In contrast, the right hemisphere is considered specialized for negative emotions, withdrawal, and stress/arousal (also see Martin & Altarriba, 2017).

As for the investigation, itself, in Herzog et al. (2017), they studied an N of 186 southern Israelis who had been exposed to missile attacks in 2014. They used a short version of the PQ, involving two questions aimed at left hemisphere (on reading, synonyms) and two at the right (on creativity, using symbols), with all questions scored on a 10-point Likert scale. The total right from left scores were subtracted and the extreme 40% of the sample at the high end and low end of the distribution were considered as RP or LP (right or left hemisphere preferring). Herzog et al. (2017) used another measure that is used frequently in hemisphericity research, that of line bisection of pre-bisected lines of about 23 cm (The two measures – one related to perceived cognitive style and one on neuro-visual bias – were not correlated but gave similar results). In this second task, 15 lines are presented as equally bisected, and those considered LPs will generally indicate the right side is bigger, with an RP individual indicating the opposite. Posttraumatic stress disorder (PTSD) was evaluated using a 4-item scale.

The results showed that being LP, and unlike the case for RP, protected against the development of PTSD after having been exposed to missiles. Herzog et al. (2017) concluded that the LF could protect against the negative effects of severe life stress. The left hemisphere is specialized better for resilience compared to the right hemisphere. They also related their findings to research showing that stress can shift the typical left hemisphere functioning to the right side (Lewis, Weekes, & Wang, 2007). This shows that the LP or RP style might be conditioned by cumulative stress experiences that shift natural hemisphere activation patterns. A study by Herzog, Killianova, Pauwels, Germeys, and Gidron (2014) supported the authors' conclusions by finding that an experimentally induced stress elicited more perceived stress in RPs compared to LPs.

Note that Mutlauer et al. (2017) adopted a different neuro-protective model of the left hemisphere, arguing that in extreme child abuse, for those who dissociate, for example, in cases of PTSD with the dissociative subtype, the left prefrontal cortex thickens. One can presume that the mechanism helps avoid the deleterious chronic stress response associated with the right hemisphere, which might otherwise activate more often in these circumstances.

Comment

But this begs the question why few reliable, consistent correlations involving relevant questionnaires and behavioral properties have been found that validate the concept of hemisphericity. On the one hand, the items on the PQ are written, so might not effectively tap into a gradient of left-right hemisphere differences in behavioral style. Sample PQ items beyond those mentioned include right preferring, RP, Are you logical, and left preferring, LP, How often does your thinking consist of mental images or pictures. On the other hand, the items reflect older conceptions of how the hemispheres differ and newer research findings might lead to the addition of items to this and related questionnaires that would increase their validity. In this regard, after presentation of his results, Genovese (2005) suggested that different models of hemisphericity should be considered, such as dual dimensional and dual processing models (Epstein, Pacini, Denes-Raj, & Heier, 1996; Riding & Rayner, 1998).

Interim Conclusion

Hemisphericity appears to reflect hemisphere use preferences that might develop because of the specialized skills of the hemispheres and variables that make their use more likely than would be otherwise. For example, perhaps the left hemisphere language skills for one individual are so pervasively evident and effective that they push the individual to use the left hemisphere more than would be the case otherwise, creating an LP. The same argument might apply to RPs, who might use spatial skills and the right hemisphere more than expected because of learning to rely on the right hemisphere for reasons of efficacy and positive feedback after strategic implementation of this hemisphere and its skills. These types of explanations are more intrinsic to the nature of the hemisphere as drivers of RP or LP individuals. However, extrinsic factors might also be involved, although there is no clear separation between such factors. For example, the study by Iuşcă (2014) provided evidence that experience can affect hemisphericity. She used the Hemispheric Mode Indicator instrument (McCarthy, 1993) to categorize left and right brain orientation and found that music students were mostly right-brained, while the more-experienced philharmonic performers were accentuated in left hemisphericity. Finally, perhaps the most important driver in the development of hemispheric preference relates to the core hemisphere that is activated emotionally – the left more positively and the right more negatively, for example. Perhaps experiences related to emotions over the life course affect the predisposition to use one hemisphere or the other beyond situations that are emotional, as in cognitive style.

Given these new developments in understanding left and right hemisphere styles, it might be possible to create a novel hemisphericity questionnaire with the following elements. First, the items should not be only written, in that pictures and lines might be useful, as well. Second, the questions might be chosen to reflect several dimensions in left and right hemisphere differences beyond the classic verbal-spatial, analysis-synthesis dichotomies, including with respect to concepts related to information processing, approach-avoidance, positive and negative emotions, and so on. Third, the items should be chosen to afford convergent validity correlations with contemporary concepts related to the hemispheres, such as inhibition, activation, and their coordination.

Morton (2013) referred to thousands of studies with inconsistent findings on hemisphericity and that, because of this factor, it is much less researched today than in its heyday. However, the concept can be revived with appropriate conceptualization and measurement, and the research can improve on the few positive results still emerging in its support. The terms to denote it should avoid facile and incorrect ones, such as "brainedness" (Corballis, 2017).

Development

Conceptually, the hemispheres develop, and hemisphericity is rarely discussed in terms of its development. All matters related to lateralization develop, and if there are tendencies to use more one hemisphere compared to the other, even when balance is called for, then how the preference emerges needs to be established. Moreover, in that development, as with any developmental phenomenon, there are bound to be multiple and interacting causes, including experiential ones. More than likely, the cascade model that has been applied to handedness and manual lateralization development applies to hemisphericity development. Perhaps there is an initial hemisphere bias use or preference, and it gets magnified in a positive feedback loop each time the hemisphere at issue is used preferentially. As with the development of temperament or other developmental attributes, the hemisphere-based patterns, styles, and so on become more ingrained, more stable, less variable, and more consistent and exhibit appropriate correlations, both concurrently and longitudinally. The cascades, therefore, take place both for intrinsic and extrinsic reasons, with extrinsic ones related to reinforcements by the environment and the feedback provided by positive outcomes to the application of the hemisphere at issue, for example.

One study speaks indirectly to the development of hemisphericity (Garcia & Teixeira, 2017). They biased 4–5-year-old children who were right-handed according to a drawing task to use their left hands spontaneously to reach and grasp after an intervention, and the left-hand preference continued at 14 days post-intervention. Experiences can alter naturally occurring lateralization tendencies in the hand, and presumably in the brain, as well, including in the developmental period.

Hemispheric Activation/Use Proclivity

As for the correct model to use in referring to hemisphericity, it might be more appropriate to replace the term with a more descriptive one that does not have its baggage. Hemisphericity refers to orientation, style, or preference in hemisphere use, everything else being equal. It does not refer to the typical activation, use, or application of a hemisphere and its attributes best suited to a task or problem at hand or a thinking style consistent with it that the context requires (i.e., appropriate use of hemispheric skills and the deployment of the hemispheres in context). Hemisphericity might be described categorically, but it reflects the degree to which a hemisphere is used when a balanced use is more appropriate or when a hemisphere is required to an extent but is used even more than that extent. That is, relative to normative use, either at the population level for a specific context, or even for the typical use by an individual, one hemisphere or the other is used statistically more often than expected as a state, and it becomes a state to which the system involved gravitates generally, creating trait.

Moreover, hemispheres can be biased in their use by priming effects, as in the third study by Agroskin, Jonas, Klackl, and Prentice (2016) in which inhibitory primes activated differentially outcomes. That is, experiential biasing of the hemispheres might start early in life through parental, schooling, cultural, and related factors, as well as through individual proclivities, but proximally, there might be experiences that induce the use of one or the other hemisphere preferentially, too. Moreover, these primes might be powerful enough to override the typical hemispheric preference.

A last conceptual point worth underscoring about hemisphericity is that any label for it should refer to cerebral hemisphericity. This suggestion acknowledges, however, that cortical regions are not the only ones involved, through pathways and circuits to lower-order levels, such as the amygdala and hippocampi, as well as any lateralized usage predilections inherent in these areas/hemi-areas.

Given these considerations, an appropriate term to use instead of hemisphericity would be *cerebral hemisphere activation/use preference* or *predisposition/proclivity*. Simply, perhaps a term for the proposed concept to replace the hemisphericity one could be hemispheric activation/use proclivity. Moreover, as they develop, hemispheric proclivities need to be considered from the perspective of a cascade or augmenting positive feedback loop process, whether the sources are intrinsic or extrinsic. Finally, until considered a valid developmental topic, hemispheric preference or related concepts will miss aspects that would improve them as constructs and as valid causes of behavior.

Biopsychosocial

One goal in addressing hemisphericity was to emerge with a more comprehensive biopsychosocial model of handedness and lateralized function, whether hemispheric or manual. Hemisphere preferences or use activations beyond the expected for any one individual appear to take place and has consequences for behavior. Moreover, handedness and lateralized behavior, including manual ones, would appear to be reciprocally related to hemisphericity or related concepts by co-activation processes that more deeply ingrain them, like attractor basins that get deeper in their wells with repeated usage (Young, 2016). In this sense, one more influence on handedness development might be the hemisphericity processes in development that reciprocally influence hand use preference or handedness-related tasks. Moreover, the same type of mutually interacting and side use or laterality strengthening that could be taking place in hemisphere use and handedness might occur even more forcefully for hemispheric preference and manual lateralizations, given their reflections of underlying hemispheric specializations.

Activation-Inhibition Coordination

Finally, the discussion of hemisphericity could be reworked into the language of inhibitory processes and the concept of activation-inhibition coordination. The latter concept can help translate disparate behavioral and central phenomena into a common metric.

Consider that the left compared to right hemisphere has been qualified as more involved in self-control, while the right hemisphere is more involved in external orientation (Zhang, Hu, Chao, & Li, 2017). In this regard, Agroskin et al. (2016) related right hemisphere frontal activation to an inhibitory style (BIS, behavioral inhibition system) and mortality salience. This model is consistent with the model of the left and right hemispheres, respectively, being related to routines-sequences and external orientation, for example, predator escape (Vallortigara & Versace, 2017). Also, it is consistent with the activation-inhibition model of hemispheric differences as proposed by Young et al. (Young, 1990a, 1990b, 2011, 2016; Young, Bowman, et al., 1983a; Young & Gagnon, 1990; Young, Segalowitz, et al., 1983b). That is, for these authors, the left hemisphere is better at activation-inhibition coordination, such as refined integration of activation and inhibition processes toward creating effective and efficient online adaptive behavior for a task at hand, as in coordinated reaching and then grasping. In contrast, the right hemisphere is specialized for other types of inhibition that are less complex, such as full-scale suppression without activation or short term, less complex activation-inhibition coordination.

In this regard, and especially for the question of hemisphericity, one could translate a left hemisphere advantage for efficient motor routines as a subtle, rapid ongoing activation-inhibition coordination over time that economizes motor and underlying cognitive activity, such as in planning. Further, one could add that the success that an individual has in deploying this skill feeds back to reinforcing it such that it is preferred, everything else being equal, and so encouraging a left hemisphere preference. Or, there might be an adaptive advantage in using other types of activation and inhibition skills, including those that are right-hemisphere based, leading to a right hemisphere preference. Referring back to the terminology of left hemisphere being more verbal and analytic and the right hemisphere being more spatial and holistic, for example, and keeping in mind the connections between various left and right hemisphere skills because of underlying commonalities, this could mean that, for any one person who is developing a left hemisphere preference, the other aspects of network of skills in the left hemisphere that are related to activation-inhibition coordination and language would become preferred through the connections that they have, for example, through the common activation-inhibition coordination processes that are reinforced as preferences for the person. The same type of logic applies to generalized right hemisphere preference use that individuals might develop in relation to that hemisphere's superior spatial-related skills and its own activation-inhibition coordination specializations.

This conclusion leads into a more general discussion of the causes and mechanisms in handedness development and related lateralization developments. First, the literature review continues with respect to the influence on lateralization of genes, environment, and related factors, such as epigenesis and culture. Then the review shifts to animal research and evolution with respect to lateralization.

Comment

The first component of this portion of the book has dealt with human developmental research, in particular. The next section on multi-factorial causality also deals with research with humans, for example, related to the genetic influences on handedness. Moreover, the research review component of this portion of the book continues in the multi-factorial causality section by the review of the animal research on lateralization.

In terms of contributions to the literature, the first goal of the present portion of the book, as outlined at the outset, had been to present a combined invariant lateralization/progressive developmental model, and this has been accomplished in the human developmental literature review above. Another goal had been to present Young's activation-inhibition coordination model of lateralization in brain and behavior, which has been introduced above and which continues in depth below. A third goal had been to point to the value of examining the need to revitalize the concept of hemisphericity, which had essentially been abandoned in the scientific studies of lateralization, and this has been accomplished. A fourth goal of the present work was related to presenting novel concepts that had been applied or that could be applied to the study of lateralization, such as networks in brain function. The human developmental review above has shown that, already in the neonatal period, the left hemisphere appears to be networked differently than the right hemisphere, for example, being more "small world," efficient, and so on. The concern of the present work for presenting new models in the areas in the study of lateralization continues in depth in the following chapters.

References

Agroskin, D., Jonas, E., Klackl, J., & Prentice, M. (2016). Inhibition underlies the effect of high need for closure on cultural closed-mindedness under mortality salience. *Frontiers in Psychology, 7*, 1583. https://doi.org/10.3389/fpsyg.2016.01583

Annett, J., Annett, M., Hudson, P. T. W., & Turner, A. (1979). The control of movement in the preferred and nonpreferred hands. *Quarterly Journal of Experimental Psychology, 31*, 641–652. https://doi.org/10.1080/14640747908400755

Aron, A. R. (2008). Progress in executive-function research: From task to functions to regions networks. *Current Directions in Psychological Science, 17*, 124–129. https://doi.org/10.1111/j.1467-8721.2008.00561.x

Bogen, J. E. (1969). The other side of the brain. II. An appositional mind. *Bulletin of the Los Angeles Neurological Societies, 34*, 135–162.

Brederoo, S. G., Nieuwenstein, M. R., Lorist, M. M., & Cornelissen, F. W. (2017). Hemispheric specialization for global and local processing: A direct comparison of linguistic and non-linguistic stimuli. *Brain and Cognition, 119*, 10–16.

Bryden, M. P., Hécaen, H., & deAgostini, M. (1982). *Patterns of cerebral organization*. Waterloo, ON: University of Waterloo.

Cochet, H. (2016). Manual asymmetries and hemispheric specialization: Insight from developmental studies. *Neuropsychologia, 93*, 335–341. https://doi.org/10.1016/j.neuropsychologia.2015.12.019

Corballis, M. C. (2017). The evolution of lateralized brain circuits. *Frontiers in Psychology, 8*, 1021. https://doi.org/10.3389/fpsyg.2017.01021

Davidson, R. J. (1992). Anterior cerebral asymmetry and the nature of emotion. *Brain and Cognition, 20*, 125–151. https://doi.org/10.1016/0278-2626(92)90065-T

Davidson, R. J. (2004). What does the prefrontal cortex "do" in affect: Perspectives on frontal EEG asymmetry research. *Biological Psychology, 67*, 219–234. https://doi.org/10.1016/j.biopsycho.2004.03.008

Díaz-Morales, J. F., & Barreno, C. E. (2014). Hemisphere preference test: Psychometric properties and relations with academic performance among adolescents. *Laterality: Asymmetries of Body, Brain and Cognition, 19*, 677–689. https://doi.org/10.1080/1357650X.2014.897350

Epstein, S., Pacini, R., Denes-Raj, V., & Heier, H. (1996). Individual differences in intuitive-experiential and analytical-rational thinking styles. *Journal of Personality and Social Psychology, 71*, 390–405.

Fox, N. A., & Davidson, R. (1984). Hemispheric substrates of affect: A developmental model. In N. A. Fox & R. Davidson (Eds.), *The psychobiology of affective development* (pp. 353–381). Hillsdale, NJ: Erlbaum.

Garcia, J. M., & Teixeira, L. A. (2017). Modulating children's manual preference through spontaneous nondominant hand use. *Perceptual and Motor Skills, 124*, 932–945. https://doi.org/10.1177/0031512517720565

Genovese, J. E. C. (2005). Hemispheric cognitive style: A comparison of three instruments. *The Journal of Genetic Psychology, 166*, 467–481. https://doi.org/10.3200/GNTP.166.4.467-482

Genovese, J. E. C., Sparks, K. E., & Little, K. D. (2017). Tympanic membrane temperature and hemispheric cognitive style. *The Journal of Genetic Psychology, 178*, 298–302. https://doi.org/10.1080/00221325.2017.1351418

Gesell, A., & Ames, L. (1947). The development of handedness. *Journal of Genetic Psychology, 70*, 155–175.

Greiner, J., Fitzgerald, H., & Cooke, P. (1986). Speech fluency and hand performance on a sequential tapping task in left- and right-handed stutterers and non-stutterers. *Journal of Fluency Disorders, 11*, 55–69.

Hämäläinen, H., & Takio, F. (2010). Integrating auditory and visual asymmetry. In K. Hugdahl & R. Westerhausen (Eds.), *The two halves of the brain: Information processing in the cerebral hemispheres* (pp. 417–437). Cambridge, MA: MIT Press.

Hane, A. A., Fox, N. A., Henderson, H. A., & Marshall, P. J. (2008). Behavioral reactivity and approach-withdrawal bias in infancy. *Developmental Psychology, 44*, 1491–1496. https://doi.org/10.1037/a0012855

Hepper, P. G. (2013). The developmental origins of laterality: Fetal handedness. *Developmental Psychobiology, 55*, 588–595. https://doi.org/10.1002/dev.21119

Herzog, D., Farchi, M., & Gidron, Y. (2017). The relationship between exposure to missiles and PTSD symptoms as a function of hemispheric preference in Israelis. *Journal of Trauma & Dissociation*, 1–16. https://doi.org/10.1080/15299732.2017.1304487

Herzog, D., Killianova, T., Pauwels, S., Germeys, P., & Gidron, Y. (2014). Hemispheric lateralization moderates the life events-distress relationship. *Stress and Health, 32*, 47–54. https://doi.org/10.1002/smi.2577

Iuşcă, D. (2014). Brain hemisphericity and music performance level in undergraduate music student and phiharmonic musicians. *Procedia – Social and Behavioral Sciences, 142*, 59–63. https://doi.org/10.1016/j.sbspro.2014.07.588

Kimura, D. (1980). Neuromotor mechanisms in the evolution of human communication. In H. D. Steklis & M. J. Raleigh (Eds.), *Neurobiology of social communication in primates* (pp. 197–220). New York: Academic Press.

Kinsbourne, M., & Hiscock, M. (1976). Does cerebral dominance develop? In S. J. Segalowitz & F. A. Gruber (Eds.), *Language development and neurological theory* (pp. 171–191). New York: Academic Press.

Lenneberg, D. S. (1967). *Biological foundations of language*. New York: Wiley.

Lewis, R. S., Weekes, R. S., & Wang, T. H. (2007). The effect of a naturalistic stressor on frontal EEG asymmetry, stress, and health. *Biological Psychology, 75*, 239–247. https://doi.org/10.1016/j.biopsycho.2007.03.004

Liederman, J. (1983). Mechanisms underlying instability in the development of hand preference. In G. Young, S. J. Segalowitz, C. M. Corter, & S. E. Trehub (Eds.), *Manual specialization and the developing brain* (pp. 71–92). New York: Academic Press.

Martin, J. M., & Altarriba, J. (2017). Effects of valence on hemispheric specialization for emotion word processing. *Language and Speech*, 1–17. https://doi.org/10.1177/0023830916686128

McCarthy, B. (1993). *The hemispheric mode indicator*. Illinois, MI: Excel.

Merckelbach, H., Muris, P., Horselenberg, R., & de Jong, P. J. (1997). EEG correlates of a paper-and-pencil test measuring hemisphericity. *Journal of Clinical Psychology, 53*, 739–744.

Merckelbach, H., Muris, P., Pool, K., de Jong, P. J., & Schouten, E. (1996). Reliability and validity of a paper-pencil test measuring hemispheric preference. *European Journal of Personality, 10*, 221–231.

Morton, B. E. (2002). Outcomes of hemispheric questionnaires correlate with unilateral dichotic deafness. *Brain and Cognition, 49*, 63–72. https://doi.org/10.1006/brcg.2001.1485

Morton, B. E. (2013). Behavioral laterality of the brain: Support for the binary construct of hemisity. *Frontiers in Psychology, 4*, 683. https://doi.org/10.3389/fpsyg.2013.00683

Mutlauer, T., Şar, V., Kose-Demiray, C., Arslan, H., Tamer, S., Inal, S., et al. (2017). Lateralization of neurobiological response in adolescents with post-traumatic stress disorder related to severe childhood sexual abuse: The tri-modal reaction (T-MR) model of protection. *Journal of Trauma & Dissociation*, 1–10. https://doi.org/10.1080/15299732.2017.1304489

Ocklenburg, S., Ness, V., Güntürkün, O., Suchan, B., & Beste, C. (2013). Response inhibition is modulated by functional cerebral asymmetries for facial expression perception. *Frontiers in Psychology, 4*, 879. https://doi.org/10.3389/fpsyg.2013.00879

Reid, C. S., & Serrien, D. J. (2012). Handedness and the excitability of cortical inhibitory circuits. *Behavioral Brain Research, 230*, 144–148. https://doi.org/10.1016/j.bbr.2012.02.008

Riding, R., & Rayner, S. (1998). *Cognitive styles and learning strategies*. London: Fulton.

Russo, P., Persegani, C., Carucci, C., Vallini, I., Papeschi, L. L., & Trimarchi, M. (2001). Interaction between cognitive style and school environment: Consequences on self-evaluated anxiety and depression. *International Journal of Neuroscience, 110*, 79–90. https://doi.org/10.3109/00207450108994223

Russo, P., Persegani, C., Papeschi, L. L., Nicolini, M., & Trimarchi, M. (2000). Sex differences in hemisphere preference as assessed by a paper and pencil test. *International Journal of Neuroscience, 100*, 29–37. https://doi.org/10.3109/00207450008999676

Vallortigara, G., & Versace, E. (2017). Laterality at the neural, cognitive, and behavioral levels. In J. Call, G. M. Burghardt, I. M. Pepperberg, C. T. Snowdon, & T. Zentall (Eds.), *APA handbook of comparative psychology: Basic concepts, methods, neural substrate, and behavior* (Vol. 1, pp. 557–577). Washington, DC: American Psychological Association.

Vauclair, J., & Imbault, J. (2009). Relationship between manual preferences for object manipulation and pointing gestures in infants and toddlers. *Developmental Science, 12*, 1060–1069. https://doi.org/10.1111/j.1467-7687.2009.00850.x

Vlachos, F., Andreou, E., & Delliou, A. (2013). Brain hemisphericity and developmental dyslexia. *Research in Developmental Disabilities, 34*, 1536–1540. https://doi.org/10.1016/j.ridd.2013.01.027

Wagner, R. F., & Wells, K. A. (1985). A refined neurobehavioral inventory of hemispheric preference. *Journal of Clinical Psychology, 41*, 671–676.

Young, G. (1990a). The development of hemispheric and manual specialization. In G. Hammond (Ed.), The cerebral control of speech and limb movements (pp. 79–139). Amsterdam: North Holland.

Young, G. (1990b). Early neuropsychological development: Lateralization of functions – Hemispheric specialization. In C.-A. Hauert (Ed.), *Developmental psychology: Cognitive, perceptuo-motor and neuropsychological perspectives* (pp. 113–181). Amsterdam: North Holland.

Young, G. (2011). *Development and causality: Neo-Piagetian perspectives*. New York: Springer Science + Business Media.

Young, G. (2016). *Unifying causality and psychology: Being, brain and behavior*. Cham, Switzerland: Springer International Publishing.

Young, G., Bowman, J. G., Methot, C., Finlayson, M., Quintal, J., & Boissonneault, P. (1983). Hemispheric specialization development: What (inhibition) and how (parents). In G. Young, S. J. Segalowitz, C. M. Corter, & S. E. Trehub (Eds.), *Manual specialization and the developing brain* (pp. 119–140). New York: Academic Press.

Young, G., & Gagnon, M. (1990). Neonatal laterality, birth stress, familial sinistrality, and left brain inhibition. *Developmental Neuropsychology, 6*, 127–150.

Young, G., Segalowitz, S. J., Misek, P., Alp, I. E., & Boulet, R. (1983). Is early reaching left-handed? Review of manual specialization research. In G. Young, S. J. Segalowitz, C. M. Corter, & S. E. Trehub (Eds.), *Manual specialization and the developing brain* (pp. 13–32). New York: Academic Press.

Zenhausern, R. (1978). Imagery, cerebral dominance, and style of thinking: A unified field model. *Bulletin of the Psychonomic Society, 12*, 381–384.

Zhang, S., Hu, S., Chao, H. H., & Li, C. R. (2017). Hemispheric lateralization of resting-state functional connectivity of the ventral striatum: An exploratory study. *Brain Structure and Function, 222*, 2573–2583. https://doi.org/10.1007/s00429-016-1358-y

Chapter 6
Multi-factorial Causality in Laterality

Abstract This chapter considers the causes of developing laterality and adopts a multi-factorial perspective. It reviews genetic and environmental contributions, in particular. Genetically, simple Mendelian models do not work, and polygenetic models have more traction. But any one allele suggested as influencing handedness and related lateralities explains very little of the data. Environmental factors include the influence of culture; for example, some cultures might train out left-handedness. Also, parents might model more right-handedness. Further, stress can have indirect environmental effects, such as influencing laterality development prenatally or through early postnatal adversity. Epigenetics provides one influence on laterality development and is burgeoning in the research undertaken. Epigenesis concerns silencing the promoter region of alleles that contributes to a behavioral or nervous system characteristic, such as handedness, for example, through DNA methylation. Stress could be one factor in this gene silencing process. The result is that the alleles involved do not transcribe the proteins to which their function is dedicated, thereby altering development. The chapter concludes with research on cultural neuroscience, illustrating how laterality is influenced by culture, depending on differential neuroscientific/brain patterns over culture. These findings illustrate that laterality development is a biopsychosocial expression as much as other areas of development.

Multi-factorial Causality and Animal Research

Genes and Environment

Introduction

The genetic models that first emerged were consistent with the times and sought unique genes involved in handedness and sought, as well, models that could explain why most individuals ended up right handed. For example, according to the "right-shift" model, 80% of individuals are born with the genetic underpinnings for

G. Young, *Causality and Development*,
https://doi.org/10.1007/978-3-030-02493-2_6

right-handedness and the remaining 20% split between left- and right-handedness according to encountered environmental parameters (Annett, 1985), accounting for the typical 90–10% split for right- and left-handedness, respectively.

Studies of cultural differences in the prevalence of right- and left-handedness suggest a bio-cultural basis for handedness development (Rozin, Moscovitch, & Imada, 2016; who referred to biological and cultural co-evolution in this regard). The typical nature–nurture debate is sterile in psychology, generally, and the same should apply to the development of handedness and related phenomena. First, the article reviews the nurture side of influences on handedness and related development. Then it moves to genetic and epigenetic research, before turning to more general models.

Culture

The environment exists at multiple levels and at the macro level includes cultural factors on the expression of handedness. For example, Porac (2016) and Mandal and Dutta (2001) showed that right-handedness varies with cultural and geographic locations, being less common in oriental cultures, such as India and China.

Schmitz, Metz, Güntürkün, and Ocklenburg (2017) conducted a literature review of non-genetic factors that can influence handedness, confirming that, in Japan, parents strongly encourage right hand use (Konishi, Mikawa, & Suzuki, 1986) and harbor negative stereotypes of left-handers (Uwaezuoke, Eke, & Nwobi, 2015). Schmitz, Metz, et al. (2017) reported low rates of handedness in Japan, as well. Schmitz, Metz, et al. (2017) indicated that China and other countries actively engage in societal pressure against expressing left-handedness (e.g., Kushner, 2013), and also for two of every three people in the world, on average, negative stereotypical views predominate about left handers. Societies that have schools reduce left-handedness expression (Geuze et al., 2012), and those that develop away from traditional roles, also such as agriculture, and have less negative attitudes toward left-handers reduce the expression of left-handedness (e.g., Beukelaar & Kroonenberg, 1986). Attitudes about breast-feeding vary with cultures, and this factor has been associated with right-handedness (Denny, 2012; Johnston, Nicholls, Shah, & Shields, 2010).

Note that findings concerning family, culture, and related factors on handedness do not deny other factors in this regard, especially maternal stress in pregnancy, birth stress (even if minorly), and fetal hormones, for example, testosterone (as studied by research on DES intake in pregnancy; see, respectively, Reissland, Aydin, Francis, & Exley, 2015; Smith & Hines, 2000; Van der Elst et al., 2011).

Aside from possible reasons for differential handedness across cultures that relates to pressures to conformity, such as in agricultural societies, left-handedness has been related to clumsiness, dirtiness, mental disorder, and even evil in some societies (Corballis, 1991; Harris, 1980, as cited in Laland, 2008). Cultures change, however, over epochs, in their attitudes, and even in Western societies, the proportion of right handers is increasing (Corballis, 1991). Cultural neuroscience is confirming that the brains of Western- and Eastern-raised individuals might differ in hemispheric laterality. For example, Rozin et al. (2016) found a greater right hemispheric bias in "Asian" groups (raised at least for 15 years in Asia) on lateralized tasks relative to Western groups (born and raised in USA), with the tasks involving demands such as locating the nose in a scrambled face. The authors concluded that the right hemisphere is more specialized for holistic face processing in the Eastern compared to the Western groups. Generally, the right hemisphere appears specialized for emotions, but there are many qualifications in this regard (see below), including experiential/cultural influences, as well.

Environment

Of course, in all cultures studied, despite minor variations within cultures, the right hand is generally the preferred one in terms of handedness, so it appears to be a universal human trait (e.g., Marchant & McGrew, 2013). However, relative to hemispheric specialization and manual specialization, handedness appears more liable to the influence of experience and culture as it develops.

Because most adults are right-handed no matter what is the culture, evidence related to genetic influences on handedness has appeared. Therefore, one might think that handedness in children also reflects a right-side bias with a strong biological basis (Milliken, 2017). However, the development of handedness is a dynamic process, and right-handedness reflects the interaction of biological and experiential factors beginning with the prenatal period (Corballis, 2014). For example, Campbell, Marcinowski, Babik, and Michel (2015) pointed out that parenting influences, such as imitation of hand use and playful interaction, as well as social encouragement (Morange-Majoux & Devouche, 2014), might also affect a child's hand preference. Michel (2018) described the parental shaping of infant hand preference as unintentional, in that it involved own-dominant hand use in dyadic play. Laland (2008) described a "parental bias" that "shapes" their children's handedness in these regards. [Also see Young et al., 1983, in this regard.] Ocklenburg and Güntürkün (2018) added that early lateralized sensori-motor experiences, such as from right head turning biases, right-side eye-hand coordination, and right hand object manipulation, reinforce inherent right-side use tendencies. For adults, Sandve, Lorås, and Vorland Pedersen (2018) showed that two weeks of practice can alter right-hand writing in strong right handers to the left side.

Experience

The environment also includes macro factors, both post-natally and prenatally. For the latter, Reissland et al. (2015) found that, at 24–36 weeks gestation, scan results showed that maternal stress level was related positively to left-handed self-touching in the fetuses. Maternal stress level was evaluated using the Perceived Stress Scale (PSS; Cohen & Williamson, 1988). In the study, there was a slight advantage in right-hand fetal self-touching, generally, according to chi-square statistical testing. Schmitz, Kumsta, Moser, Güntürkün, and Ocklenburg (2017a) listed multiple prenatal experiential factors that have been related to left-handedness, especially in prenatal maternal stress (Searleman, Porac, & Coren, 1989). They related early stressors such as this to epigenetic influences on genes that help govern lateralization development (see below).

Aside from the experience of maternal stress fetally, as described above, the side to which the head is oriented when the fetus's body position is inverted (supine) serves to influence experiences to the left or right and is associated with later head turning preference and handedness (Fagard, 2013; Michel, 1981, 2018). For example, as the infant reaches for objects from 1 to 4 months of age, and considering that the typical head position is to the right (Fagard, 2013), the infant preferentially uses the right hand to do so. Thus, in this developmental period, the infant is getting more visuo-motor coordination on the right side, which brings with it related experiences. This happens through cascades of experience that differentially influence sidedness in behavior through the experiences afforded by the behavior on one side or the other. For example, the head turns one way, the hand reaches on that side, and that hand is seen more on the side, leading to better visuo-motor coordination on that side, and ultimately a more generalized handedness.

Further, post-natally, it appears that mothers hold their baby preferentially on the left side of their bodies (Todd & Banerjee, 2016; Ocklenburg, Packheiser, Schmitz, Rook, Güntürkün, Peterburs, & Grimshaw, 2018). Mothers appear to do this in order to better monitor their infant's state (with the information consequently being forwarded to the right hemisphere and better analyzed there because of its social-emotional processing advantage). Karenina, Giljov, Ingram, Rowntree, and Malashichev (2017) have shown the left side holding preference by mothers early in life cuts across many mammalian species and so indicates a precursor in the evolution in the right hemisphere in mammals for "social processing." This evolutionary application of these findings does not negate the experiential influences that left-side cradling affords the young infant in terms of lateralization (Jones, 2017). That being said, the biological basis for left-side cradling appears to reside in right hemisphere advantage for the processing of the female face in the temporo-parietal cortex (Prete, Malatesta, & Tommasi, 2017). [For a study with infant holding after separation in relation to the left hemisphere of fathers but not mothers, see Ito, Fujiwara, Monden, Yamagata, & Ohira, 2017.]

Stress

The role of maternal stress fetally as a factor that influences lateralization has been supported empirically, as mentioned (Searleman et al., 1989). Children who are exposed to stress post-natally also have their lateralization affected. Also, PTSD is associated with atypical lateralization (see below for the research). [For review of PTSD symptoms and causes, refer to Friedman, Keane, & Resick, 2014; Young, 2016, 2017.]

Ocklenburg, Korte, Peterburs, Wolf, and Güntürkün (2016) reviewed the literature on stress and laterality, showing that both chronic and acute stress are related to right hemisphere function or shifting to its function. The stress response has both a fast-acting adrenalin releasing system and a slower cortisol releasing system, related to the hypothalamus-pituitary-adrenal (HPA) axis. Aversive environmental events lead to stress responses and associated negative emotions, so priming the right hemisphere (Davidson, 2004; Rutherford & Lindell, 2011).

Ocklenburg, Korte, et al. (2016) noted that acute stress was associated with faster responses to angry faces in the left visual field and happy faces to the right visual field, unlike for controls, who did not exhibit asymmetries on this task (Brüne, Nadolny, Güntürkün, & Wolf, 2013). Also noted was that Madsen et al. (2012) found that higher cortisol awakening was associated positively with leftward fractional anisotropy (FA) asymmetries in the uncinate fasciculus, a limbic white matter tract, and negatively with rightward FA asymmetry in the cingulum. PTSD is associated with volume reductions in various left hemisphere areas (Kühn & Gallinat, 2013). Aside from differential hemisphere functions in response to stress, another avenue related to laterality in this regard is that stress could de-activate the normal left hemisphere inhibition of the right hemisphere, producing a less lateralized functional brain.

Similar findings in the present review substantiate the viewpoint of Ocklenburg, Korte, et al. (2016) on the relationship between stress and laterality. Behaviorally, non-right handedness is a risk factor for PTSD (Goetz, Pitman, Tanev, Pitman, & Chemtob, 2016). As for studies of the lateralized brain regions involved in PTSD, the frontal cortex appears primary, either for PTSD itself (Meyer et al., 2016) or for the effects of early childhood adversity (Miskovic, Schmidt, Georgiades, Boyle, & MacMillan, 2009; Moran et al., 2017; Schalinski, Moran, Elbert, Reindl, & Wienbruch, 2017). Other findings relate compromised left and accentuated right hippocampal functioning in PTSD (Luo et al., 2017; Rosso, Crowley, Silveri, Rauch, & Jensen, 2017), as well as the right supramarginal gyrus (Harricharan et al., 2017).

Note that other types of early stressors have been related to effects on the left hemisphere. For example, in a morphometry investigation, Besteher, Gaser, Spalthoff, and Nenadić (2017) related a higher rate of living in an urban environment throughout the first 15 years of life to reduced left frontal and other brain region thicknesses (in the left dorsolateral prefrontal cortex, left superior temporal cortex, and left para-hippocampal cortex, among others).

At the same time, stress is partly a product of appraisal. El Khawli et al. (2018) showed that habitual use of "re-appraisal" strategies (as measured by the Emotion Regulation Questionnaire (ERQ; Gross & John, 2003) of early occurring life stress (in terms of emotional abuse, EA, as measured by the Childhood Trauma Questionnaire; CTQ; Bernstein & Fink, 1998) could mitigate fMRI-determined amygdala-centered resting state functional connectivity (RSFC) and negative mood (as measured by the Positive and Negative Affect Schedule, Expanded version; PANAS-X, Watson & Clark, 1999). Specifically, in early-life EA, the use of re-appraisal strategies was associated with RSFC between left centro-medial amygdala

(CMA) and ventro-lateral prefrontal cortex (VPFC), while participants with low early-life EA had their re-appraisal indexed mostly in the RSFC between the right CMA and pre-motor/supplementary motor regions. That is, depending on early-life EA, for high re-appraisal, the CMA associated RSFC network was either left-centered or right-centered (for high vs. low early EA, respectively).

Genes

Corballis (2014) reviewed the genetics of handedness and cerebral asymmetry, as has Paracchini and Scerri (2017). Readers interested further in genetic research on brain and behavior asymmetries should consult the excellent resource by Paracchini and Scerri (2017).

Paracchini and Scerri (2017) reported a "weak" genetic component for "hand preference." Schmitz, Metz, et al. (2017) reported that heritability estimates for handedness from twin studies are only about 0.25 (Medland et al., 2009), so that there is large room for environmental influences on handedness, such as culture. The estimate is higher for family studies (0.66; Risch & Pringle, 1985), which leads to the question of missing heritability (Maher, 2008), or factors that could explain the difference, such as in epigenesis (Eichler et al., 2010), for example, by DNA methylation (adding a methyl $-CH_3$ group to CpG (cytosine guanine di-nucleotides) sites (Nikolova & Hariri, 2015; see below).

Further, the research does not support a single gene model in the development of these lateralizations. Rather, multi-locus or polygenetic models appear implicated (also see Armour, Davison, and McManus (2014) and Somers, Shields, Boks, Kahn, and Sommer (2015) for GWAS (genome-wide association studies) and linkage analysis studies, respectively).

In his review, Corballis (2014) emphasized that two genes implicated in some ways in laterality research include the pro-protein convertase subtilisin/kexin type 6 (*PCSK6*) variable number tandem repeat (VNTR) polymorphism and leucine rich repeat trans-membrane neuronal 1 (*LRRTM1*). However, no candidate genes have been established for certainty, and, even if many are found to contribute to a multi-gene model, each should be found to play small roles and contribute minimally when considered in isolation to explaining the degree of variance involved. In this regard, Tzourio-Mazoyer and Seghier (2016) indicated that genome-wide association scans have not detected any genetic polymorphisms having a substantial effect on human handedness. Partially because of the difficulties in finding specific handedness genes, genetic research is investigating genes associated with generalized laterality functions, such as left-right symmetry in the central nervous system. Ocklenburg, Arning, Gerding, Hengstler, Epplen, Güntürkün, Beste, and Akkad (2016; and as replicated by Crespi, Read, & Hurd, 2017a) showed that a particular haplotype of *SETDB2* (SET domain, bifurcated 2, located in intron 1 on the human chromosome 13q14), which is involved in symmetry in the central nervous system (CNS), probably through epigenetic modulation via histone H3 methylation, might be involved in handedness of adults. Specifically, they noted that individuals homozygous for the A allele (specifically haplotype 2, which includes the homozygous A allele of the single nucleotide polymorphism (SNP) *rs 4942830,* the option being the T allele) obtained a lower handedness laterality quotient.

To summarize, Schmitz, Metz, et al. (2017) list possible candidate genes related to handedness (although with each explaining only a small amount of the variability involved), as androgen receptor gene (*AR*) (Arning et al., 2015); polyprotein E gene (*APOE*) (Piper et al., 2013), catechol-*O*-methyltransferase (*COMT*) gene (Savitz, van der Merwe, Solms, & Ramesar, 2007); leucine-rich repeat trans-membrane neuronal 1 (*LRRTM1*) (Francks et al., 2007); proprotein convertase subtilisin/kexin type 6 (*PCSK6*) (Robinson, Hurd, Read, & Crespi, 2016); and SET domain bifurcated 2 (*SETDB2*) (Ocklenburg, Arning, et al., 2016; see next).

The research has related functional brain asymmetries involving language to a different set of genes. These include genetic variations in glutamate ionotropic receptor N-methyl-D-aspartate (NMDA) type subunit 2B (*GRIN2B*) and cholecystokinin A receptor (*CCKAR*), which were found to be associated with dichotic listening performance. Also, the gene forkhead box protein P2 (*FOXP2*) has been associated with language lateralization, especially the SNPs *rs2396753* and *rs12533005* (Ocklenburg et al., 2013). A more recent study found that the SNPs *rs7799109* and *rs1456013* are also relevant in this regard (Crespi, Read, & Hurd, 2017b).

In an intriguing research, Schmitz, Lor, Klose, Güntürkün and Ocklenburg (2017) determined that the gene complexes and their downstream effects differ in the case of handedness and language lateralization. The former case of handedness was associated with genes related to anatomical structure, asymmetry formation, and general morphogenetic regulation that appear to exert their effects in the early embryonic stage, including for relevant bodily asymmetries. The latter case of language lateralization was associated with genes related to different effects, such that the respective gene ontology sets barely overlapped in the two cases. The association of handedness genetic effects with the TGF-beta signaling pathway is consistent with this interpretation, in that it concerns left-right body asymmetries. This association was not found for language lateralization.

One common factor in the two cases of language lateralization and handedness involved downstream biological regulation mediation. Generally, the gene ontology sets were more complex for language lateralization, but the results are too complex to present here, though. Suffice it to say, there is much independence in the two gene sets (and their downstream ontologies) that are involved in handedness and language lateralization, such that a model of partial pleiotropy helps in explaining the few commonalities they have in their downstream effects.

As a comment, note that the relative independence of the two gene ontogeny sets does not deny the mutual interactions and experiential contributions of the two phenotypes developmentally. Also, the findings are consistent with the present approach to distinguish handedness and the other lateralizations manually and hemispherically. Also, note that the relationship of lateralization processes to downstream gene expressions is supported in the work of Muntané et al. (2017), who related receptor-enrichment in the posterior superior temporal cortex (STC) to left hemisphere language lateralization.

Schmitz, Metz, et al. (2017) further specified that genes are expressed asymmetrically in language regions of the brain, especially for functional gene groups. The areas studies included the superior temporal sulcus and Heschl's gyrus (Karlebach & Francks, 2015). Ocklenburg et al. (2017) found that there was more gene expression in the spinal cord segments that innervate the arms and hands at 8 weeks after conception, with right-side spinal cord expression asymmetries generally favored in the genes' effects (also see de Kovel et al., 2017).

Epigenetics

Evolutionary mechanisms relate to genetic bases that enable the inter-generational transmission of traits that confer fitness advantages, and not much evidence has been found relating candidate genes to handedness, so promoting evolutionary models. However, epigenetic processes serve to silence genes, presenting confounds to straightforward Mendelian genetics. Schmitz, Metz, et al. (2017) reported that Sparrow et al. (2016) related right corticospinal tract shape development in prematures to DNA methylation. Klengel et al. (2013) found that DNA methylation of a gene that is important in the stress response is associated with the volume of the right (and not left) hippocampus, the gene being FK506 binding protein 5 (*FKBP5*).

Leach, Prefontaine, Hurd, and Crespi (2014) related the gene *LRRTM1* to handedness through its epigenetic methylation in its promotor region even if variations in *LRRTM1* SNPs were not found to relate to handedness. For their epigenetic analysis, they analyzed methylation at 19 block representative CpG (cytosine guanine di-nucleotides) sites in relation to handedness in a non-clinical population, because CpG islands tend to be close to promotor regions and are generally unmethylated. For a sample N of 45, they found that the level of methylation especially in the contiguous CpG 78–85 block of sites within the *LRRTM1* CpG island that was analyzed was associated with mixed handedness, as measured by the Waterloo Handedness Questionnaire (WHQ; Steenhuis & Bryden, 1989). The authors concluded that environmental factors that could induce the DNA methylations involved might relate to fetal testosterone levels (and perhaps to postnatal insecure psychological attachment to care-givers, as mentioned later in the article). This conclusion leaves open the question of what variables might affect fetal testosterone levels in mixed handers. For example, prenatal (maternal) stress might be one influential factor in fetal testosterone levels acting in epigenetic influence on developing handedness.

Crow (2010) has offered a different model of epigenetic variation in the evolutionary origin of cerebral asymmetries. First, he described the Mendelian model of Annett (1985). She posited, as mentioned above, that there is a genetically determined right-shift factor for cerebral language dominance and right-handedness that is at work in 80% of the population. The remaining 20% divide evenly according to environmental factors, which accounts for the approximate 90–10% split in handedness. Crow (2010) preferred to describe a more general genetic influence on lateralization of behavior, though, while including epigenetic factors.

Crow's (2010) model of the environmental contribution to the evolution of handedness differs from the model of Laland (e.g., Laland, Kumm, Van Horn, & Feldman, 1995). It de-emphasizes culture in the trans-generational transmission of laterality and does emphasize epigenesis in these regards. However, in its proposed epigenetic mechanism for handedness, it describes a gene complex that is quite different than other candidate genes that have been related to handedness. Specifically, Crow (2010) postulated that the gene involved is in the X–Y homologous class, which evolved about six million years ago (mya) or about the time of the split in the common human-non-human primate ancestor into separate non-human primate and hominin lineages. The gene is *Protocadherin11XY* – the X and Y versions are homologues; males have the Y version and both sexes have the X. The Y version is present only in humans, while the X one is found in all mammals, including humans. The gene pair codes for the transcription of an adhesion molecule on cell surfaces and, for example, it is expressed in the cortical germinal cell layer. The interaction of the two proteins derived from the genes leads to the torque of cerebral asymmetry, and epigenesis plays a role by acting in male meiosis, through random pairings.

Crow (2010) concluded that the model helps explain sex differences in cerebral torque and its evolution. He considered that the origin of the homologous gene pair conferred the capacity to walk upright, with all the adaptive advantages that this trait offered. He related the torque in cerebral asymmetry to the period of about 160,000 years ago when modern humans evolved. However, modern humans were not the first to evidence cerebral torque in phylogenesis, and the evidence is consistent with its presence even in our common ancestor (Rogers & Vallortigara, 2017). Therefore, this inconsistency in the model might not be its failing, because perhaps it can be applied in part to the earliest origins in the appearance of the gene involved in evolution.

A comprehensive model of the epigenesis process in affecting handedness considered birth stress as a factor that could induce DNA methylation in the gene *NEUROD6* (Schmitz, Kumsta, et al., 2017a). Schmitz, Kumsta, et al. (2017a) described *NEUROD6* as a gene that helps in differentiating neural precursor cells as the CNS develops right in the fetal period. Specifically, among other things, lack of *NEUROD6* is associated with less glutamatergic network activity in neocortical projections of the corpus callosum and of other commissural fibers, as well as disruptions in these projections. *NEUROD6* is situated in chromosome 7, with the promoter lying between the start and end points 31380009 and 3138208, respectively. Schmitz, Kumsta, et al. (2017a) tested 11 target CpG sites in this region in 30 right handers and 30 left handers. They found a relationship between birth stress and cg10265323 methylation. They concluded that birth stress might be the environmental variable that is partly responsible for left–/right-handedness differences through its epigenetic effects on *NEUROD6*, considering that it is expressed asymmetrically in the brains of fetuses. Beyond this novel finding related to epigenetics and handedness, Schmitz, Kumsta, et al. (2017a) also found a relationship in the DNA methylation of CpG sites in three asymmetrically expressed genes (*LMO4*, *MT2A*, and *STK35*). Ocklenburg and Güntürkün (2018) added that *LMO4* (LIM domain only 4) is differentially expressed in the right relative to the right hemisphere while another gene is expressed relatively more in the left one (*HEY1*; hairy/enhancer-of-split related with YRPW motif 1). Moreover, Schmitz, Kumsta, et al. (2017a) reminded that various candidate genes, such as *LRRTM1* and *PCSK6,* explain only a small amount of the variation in handedness expression.

In further research by this team, Schmitz, Kumsta, Moser, Güntürkün, and Ocklenburg (2017b), demonstrated that epigenesis in relation to genes that might be involved in lateralization of brain function can be modified epigenetically and contribute to the development of dyslexia. The article indicates how one particular gene contributes to lateralization, can be affected epigenetically, and involves basic asymmetries even in ciliogenesis that have cascading effects from the embryonic period onward, thus affecting cerebral lateralization.

Specifically, Schmitz, Kumsta, et al. (2017b) studied DNA methylation of the gene *KIAA0319*, finding that it helps predict dichotic listening performance in healthy adults in conditions in which their attention is forced to one side or the other and either in concert with natural tendencies to report the presence of right- or left-sided stimuli (congruent), depending on the stimulus involved or in conflict with the expected side (incongruent). The N of the study was small at 59 healthy adults and the dichotic listening stimuli consisted of consonant-vowel sounds; the study reported sex differences in the results, but the small N precludes giving them much importance. Generally, the dichotic listening results were consistent with left hemisphere lateralization for the language processes involved. As for the epigenetic results, two CpG sites predicted lateralization in forced-left dichotic listening conditions (cg16906346 and cg26531923).

The authors explained that a region on the sixth chromosome that includes the first four exons of *KIAA0319* has been associated with reading ability, dyslexia, lateralized brain function for language dominance (the other regions involving *ACO T13* and *TDP2*). *KIAA0319* not only contains genetic variations to consider in asymmetry development but also can be affected by DNA methylation, as explained. Further, genes like this one involved in asymmetry of behavioral and brain function have their origin in their effects in early bodily asymmetries, in the Nodal cascade. Motile primary cilia rotate, inducing a leftward nodal fluid flow, which is sensed by primary cilia that are immotile. The result is a stronger left-sided Nodal cascade in gene expression leading to the formation of the left-right body axis. Brandler and Paracchini (2014; also see Paracchini, Diaz, & Stein, 2016) have related this early embryonic asymmetry development to later development of brain hemisphere lateralization.

Comment

We can conclude that continued research on the genetics and the epigenetics of handedness will narrow the search to specific genes and epigenetic effects. However, this will take place in the context of supporting polygenetic models that include major environmental effects on handedness.

Note that epigenetic models of development are broadening to include terms like co-action (Lerner & Overton, 2017). We need to avoid in terms such as "epigenetic determinism" and its reductionism as much as any reductionist model that ignores relational activity (Moore, 2017) in order to "transcend" the nature-nurture debate (Witherington & Lickliter, 2017) as well as to avoid to consider the concept of relational activity as just an "add-on" (Saunders, 2017). Epigenetics must be perceived as developmental, as in "developmental epigenetics." In addition, one should note that it should to be perceived as evolutionary, as in "evolutionary epigenetics" (Kronholm, 2017).

Together, the work of Gottlieb (e.g., Gottlieb, 2007) on probabilistic epigenesis and of Waddington (e.g., Waddington, 1957) on the developmental landscape presages the contemporary work in epigenetics (e.g., Meaney, 2010). Their efforts are broader in conceptualization and essentially refer to multi-factorial causality in development rather than gene silencing by methylation and like processes. These earlier models remind that the contemporary version of epigenetics inserts into a broader understanding of development. This notion prepares the way for presentation of the biopsychosocial model and like models (see below).

Clearly further research is needed on the genetics of handedness and related behavioral and cerebral asymmetries, while acknowledging the role of the environment, including epigenetically (e.g., gene silencing through DNA methylation). More likely than not, the type of genes found to influence handedness would not be directly related to brain areas and neither to the manual activities of the hand but to general brain development embryo-genetically. In this regard, Güntürkün and Ocklenburg (2017) referred to the nodal signaling cascade in the lateralization of the developing embryonic brain. The cascade relates to the developing left-right body axis in relation to the midline during neurulation in the left lateral plate mesoderm. This type of early embryo-genetic origin of lateralized body and brain structure speaks to the finding of lateralized behavior and neuronal structure in species such as fish, toads, nematodes, and bees (Güntürkün & Ocklenburg, 2017; and see the extensive discussion below), which supports its evolution in the earliest life forms.

Generally, the classic distinction between nature and nurture influences on development is unfounded. Development is multifactorial. Similarly, evolutionary models that exclude development are unfounded. Michel, Babik, Nelson, Campbell, and Marcinowski (2018) referred to "inheritance holism" in this regard, which refers to phenotypic traits being expressions of complex causal coactions in genes, epigenesis, the organism, and the environment during development.

Cultural Neuroscience and Teaching

Cultural neuroscience research is explicating nature-nurture interactions and showing how cultural variation can depend on different prevalence rates and function of different alleles of the same gene (Sasaki & Kim, 2017). For example, in gene-environment interactions, different cultures might have different and even opposite reactions if they have susceptibility genes (Belsky et al., 2009) compared to those who do not, although no matter the cultural variation, the reactions will be strong and pronounced. In this regard, Chen et al. (2014) and Khan, Schmidt, and Chen (2017) noted that the homozygous paired short (s/s) alleles in the serotonin transporter gene (*5-HTTLPR*) are associated with behavioral inhibition in North American children but the long (l/l) variant is associated with behavioral inhibition in Chinese children.

Inter-generational teaching and learning is referred to as a process of vertical transmission of cultural information (Mullon & Lehmann, 2017). Mesoudi (2016) noted that trans-generational cultural change is subject to Darwinian evolutionary processes. This does not happen through memes; culture confers adaptive fitness benefits and cultural selection processes work on selecting adaptive options in cultural variation. Genes by themselves do not constitute the ultimate cause of evolutionary change. Humans are the only species that index cumulative cultural evolution.

Legare (2017) amplified that humans are the only species that engages in cumulative cultural learning, with human care-givers uniquely motivated to transmit to children information by teaching in a natural pedagogy (Whiten, 2017; Whiten, Ayala, Feldman, & Laland, 2017). Young children do this well (Herrmann, Call, Hernàdez-Lloreda, Hare, & Tomasello, 2007). Teaching does take place in other animals but through different evolutionary mechanisms (Hoppitt et al., 2008).

In general, the notions of the uniqueness of human teaching and the receptivity to the teaching of the human child through imitation, copying, and over-learning speak to the mechanisms by which culture is transmitted, including about handedness, such as in the concept of devious left handers. Also, these notions help explain the powerful shaping forces in the expression of handedness in children, such as in conformity effects in traditional or agricultural societies.

Conclusion

If behavior is found to be present neonatally, it does not necessarily mean that it is inborn or innate. For example, the environment can have an effect pre-natally. Also, as development proceeds, the environment can influence the behavior. Also, if behavior is found to have a genetic influence, as in heritability, or even specific alleles of certain genes associated with it, this does not exclude possible influence of the environment on the behavior. Generally, behavior is considered as influenced both by nature and nurture or biology and environment. Young (2016) has shown that a biopsychosocial and systems developmental model can apply to understanding the causes of behavior and that neither nature nor nurture should be favored in this regard. Also, as development proceeds, the person him or herself has more of a say in development. The latter aspect has not been applied to the study of handedness and lateralized brain and behavior function, but it serves to illustrate, once more, that these behaviors are not determined solely by inheritance. Michel, Babik,

Shue, and Campbell (2013) proposed a similar construct in handedness development – that it is a product of a "multifaceted biosocial developmental process."

Young's (2016) extensive review of the causality of behavior emphasizes the biopsychosocial point of view and others (systems) that try to be integrative. The amount of research on these perspectives is increasing exponentially, and it is beyond the scope of the present work to integrate those views. Nevertheless, current reviews of the literature promote the integrative utility of these perspectives (e.g., Holt-Lunstad, 2018; Tremblay, Vitaro, & Côte, 2018; respectively). Also, see Pakulak, Stevens, and Neville (2018) and Jones, Moore, and Kobor (2018) on epigenetic and early adversity models, which relate to the biopsychosocial approach.

This concludes the section of the present book on research on human lateralization of behavior and function manually and hemispherically. The general message is that the patterns found later in life in these regards can be found earlier using appropriate methodologies and that the early developments along these lines influence the later developments. Moreover, the causation in the development of lateralities is multi-factorial.

However, a full understanding of the development of handedness, manual specialization, and hemispheric specialization cannot obtain without investigating their evolutionary origins. The next section examines the animal research, including in great ape non-human primates and earlier evolved species, as well as evolutionary models and relevant early hominin findings.

References

Annett, M. (1985). *Left, right, hand and brain: The right shift theory*. London: Erlbaum.

Armour, J. A., Davison, A., & McManus, J. C. (2014). Genome-wide association study of handedness excludes simple genetic models. *Heredity, 112*, 221–225. https://doi.org/10.1038/hdy.2013.93

Arning, L., Oklenburg, S., Schulz, S., Ness, V., Gerding, W. M., Hengstler, J. G., et al. (2015). Handedness and the X chromosome: The role of androgen receptor CAG-repeat length. *Scientific Reports, 5*, 8325. https://doi.org/10.1038/srep08325

Belsky, J., Jonassaint, C., Pluess, M., Stanton, M., Brummett, B., & Williams, R. (2009). Vulnerability genes or plasticity genes? *Molecular Psychiatry, 14*, 746–754. https://doi.org/10.1038/mp.2009.44

Bernstein, D. P., & Fink, L. (1998). *Childhood trauma questionnaire: A retrospective self-report manual*. San Antonio, TX: The Psychological Corporation.

Besteher, B., Gaser, C., Spalthoff, R., & Nenadić, I. (2017). Associations between urban upbringing and cortical thickness and gyrification. *Journal of Psychiatric Research, 95*, 114–120. https://doi.org/10.1016/j.jpsychires.2017.08.012

Beukelaar, L. J., & Kroonenberg, P. M. (1986). Changes over time in the relationship between hand preference and writing hand among left-handers. *Neuropsychologia, 24*, 301–303.

Brandler, W. M., & Paracchini, S. (2014). The genetic relationship between handedness and neurodevelopmental disorders. *Trends in Molecular Medicine, 20*, 83–90. https://doi.org/10.1016/j.molmed.2013.10.008

Brüne, M., Nadolny, N., Güntürkün, O., & Wolf, O. T. (2013). Stress induces a functional asymmetry in an emotional attention task. *Cognition & Emotion, 27*, 558–566. https://doi.org/10.1080/02699931.2012.726211

Campbell, J. M., Marcinowski, E. C., Babik, I., & Michel, G. F. (2015). The influence of a hand preference for acquiring objects on the development of a hand preference for unimanual manipulation from 6 to 14 months. *Infant Behavior and Development, 39*, 107–117. https://doi.org/10.1016/j.infbeh.2015.02.013

Chen, X., Zhang, G., Liang, Z., Zhang, M., Way, N., Yoshikawa, H., et al. (2014). The association between 5-HTTLPR gene polymorphism and behavioral inhibition in Chinese toddlers. *Developmental Psychobiology, 56*, 1601–1608. https://doi.org/10.1002/dev.21253

Cohen, S., & Williamson, G. (1988). Perceived stress in probability sample of the United States. In S. Spacapan & S. Oskamp (Eds.), *The social psychology of health: Claremont symposium on applied social psychology* (pp. 31–67). Newbury Park, CA: Sage.

Corballis, M. C. (1991). *The lopsided ape: Evolution of the generative mind*. New York: Oxford University Press.

Corballis, M. C. (2014). Left brain, right brain: Facts and fantasies. *PLoS Biology, 12*, e1001767. https://doi.org/10.1371/journal.pbio.1001767

Crespi, B., Read, S., & Hurd, P. (2017a). The SETDB2 locus: Evidence for a genetic link between handedness and atopic disease. *Heredity*. https://doi.org/10.1038/s41437-017-0004-7

Crespi, B., Read, S., & Hurd, P. (2017b). Segregating polymorphisms of FOXP2 are associated with measures of inner speech, speech fluency and strength of handedness in healthy population. *Brain & Language, 173*, 33–40. https://doi.org/10.1016/j.bandl.2017.06.002

Crow, T. J. (2010). A theory of the origin of cerebral asymmetry: Epigenetic variation superimposed on a fixed right-shift. *Laterality: Asymmetries of Body, Brain and Cognition, 15*, 289–303. https://doi.org/10.1080/13576500902734900

Davidson, R. J. (2004). What does the prefrontal cortex "do" in affect: Perspectives on frontal EEG asymmetry research. *Biological Psychology, 67*, 219–234. https://doi.org/10.1016/j.biopsycho.2004.03.008

de Kovel, C. G. F., Lisgo, S., Karlebach, G., Ju, J., Cheng, G., Fisher, S. E., et al. (2017). Left-right asymmetry of maturation rations in human embryonic neural development. *Biological Psychiatry, 82*, 204–212. https://doi.org/10.1016/j.biopsych.2017.01.016

Denny, K. (2012). Breastfeeding predicts handedness. *Laterality: Asymmetries of Body, Brain and Cognition, 17*, 361–368. https://doi.org/10.1080/1357650X.2011.579131

Eichler, E. E., Flint, J., Gibson, G., Kong, A., Leal, S. M., Moore, J. H., et al. (2010). Missing heritability and strategies for finding the underlying causes of complex disease. *Nature Reviews. Genetics, 11*, 446–450. https://doi.org/10.1038/nrg2809

El Khawli, E., Fan, Y., Aust, S., Wirth, K., Bönke, L., Stevense, A., et al. (2018). Early-life stress modulates neural networks associated with habitual use of reappraisal. *Behavioural Brain Research, 337*, 210–217. https://doi.org/10.1016/j.bbr.2017.09.018

Fagard, J. (2013). The nature and nurture of human infant hand preference. *Annals of the New York Academy of Sciences, 1288*, 114–123. https://doi.org/10.1111/nyas.12051

Francks, C., Maegawa, S., Lauren, J., Abrahams, B. S., Velayos-Baeza, A., Medland, S. E., et al. (2007). LRRTM1 on chromosome 2p12 is a maternally suppressed gene that is associated paternally with handedness and schizophrenia. *Molecular Psychiatry, 12*, 1129–1139. https://doi.org/10.1038/sj.mp.4002053

Friedman, M. J., Keane, T. M., & Resick, P. A. (2014). *Handbook of PTSD: Science and practice* (2nd ed.). New York: Guilford Press.

Geuze, R. H., Schaafsma, S. M., Lust, J. M., Bouma, A., Schiefenhövel, W., & Groothuis, T. G. G. (2012). Plasticity of lateralization: Schooling predicts hand preference but not hand skill asymmetry in a non-industrial society. *Neuropsychologia, 50*, 612–620. https://doi.org/10.1016/j.neuropsychologia.2011.12.017

Goetz, J. M., Pitman, S. R., Tanev, K. S., Pitman, R. K., & Chemtob, C. M. (2016). Mixed-handedness in identical twins discordant for combat exposure in Vietnam: Relationship to posttraumatic stress disorder. *Journal of Neuropsychiatry and Clinical Neurosciences, 28*, 45–48. https://doi.org/10.1176/appi.neuropsych.15040090

Gottlieb, G. (2007). Probabilistic epigenesis. *Developmental Science, 10*, 1–11. https://doi.org/10.1111/j.1467-7687.2007.00556.x

Gross, J. J., & John, O. P. (2003). Individual differences in two emotion regulation processes: Implications for affect, relationships, and well-being. *Journal of Personality and Social Psychology, 85*, 348–362. https://doi.org/10.1037/0022-3514.85.2.348

Güntürkün, O., & Ocklenburg, S. (2017). Ontogenesis of lateralization. *Neuron, 94*, 249–263. https://doi.org/10.1016/j.neuron.2017.02.045

Harricharan, S., Nicholson, A. A., Densmore, M., Théberge, J., McKinnon, M. C., Neufeld, R. W. J., et al. (2017). Sensory overload and imbalance: Resting-state vestibular connectivity in PTSD and its dissociative subtype. *Neuropsychologia, 106*, 169–178.

Harris, L. J. (1980). Left handedness: Early theories, facts and fancies. In J. Herron (Ed.), *Neuropsychology of left handedness* (pp. 3–78). London: Academic.

Herrmann, E., Call, J., Hernàdez-Lloreda, M. V., Hare, B., & Tomasello, M. (2007). Humans have evolved specialized skills of social cognition: The cultural intelligence hypothesis. *Science, 317*, 1360–1366. https://doi.org/10.1126/science.1146282

Holt-Lunstad, J. (2018). Why social relationships are important for physical health: A systems approach to understanding and modifying risk and protection. *Annual Review of Psychology, 69*, 437–458. https://doi.org/10.1146/annurev-psych-122216-011902

Hoppitt, W. J. E., Brown, G. R., Kendal, R., Rendell, L., Thornton, A., Webster, M. W., et al. (2008). Lessons from animal teaching. *Trends in Ecology & Evolution, 23*, 486–493. https://doi.org/10.1016/j.tree.2008.05.008

Ito, J., Fujiwara, T., Monden, Y., Yamagata, T., & Ohira, H. (2017). Association of Oxytocin and parental prefrontal activation during reunion with infant: A functional near-infrared spectroscopy study. *Frontiers in Pediatrics, 5*, 271. https://doi.org/10.3389/fped.2017.00271

Johnston, D. W., Nicholls, M., Shah, M., & Shields, M. A. (2010). *Handedness, health and cognitive development: Evidence from children in the NLSY* (IZA Discussion Paper 4774). Retrieved from http://ftp.iza.org/dp4774.pdf

Jones, M. J., Moore, S. R., & Kobor, M. S. (2018). Principles and challenges of applying epigenetic epidemiology to psychology. *Annual Review of Psychology, 69*, 459–485. https://doi.org/10.1146/annurev-psych-122414-033653

Jones, S. J. (2017). Cradling bias occurrence and purpose. *Medical & Clinical Research, 2*. Retrieved from http://medclinres.org/pdfs/cradling-bias-occurrence-and-purpose-mcr-17.pdf

Karenina, K., Giljov, A., Ingram, J., Rowntree, V. J., & Malashichev, Y. (2017). Lateralization of mother-infant interactions in a diverse range of mammal species. *Nature Ecology and Evolution, 1*. https://doi.org/10.1038/s41559-016-0030

Karlebach, G., & Francks, C. (2015). Lateralization of gene expression in human language cortex. *Cortex, 67*, 30–36. https://doi.org/10.1016/j.cortex.2015.03.003

Khan, A., Schmidt, L. A., & Chen, X. (2017). Cultural neuroscience of emotion: Toward a developmental framework. *Psychology & Neuroscience, 10*, 11–40. https://doi.org/10.1037/pne0000078

Klengel, T., Mehta, D., Anacker, C., Rex-Haffner, M., Pruessner, J. C., Pariante, C. M., et al. (2013). Allele-specific FKBP5 DNA demethylation mediates gene-childhood trauma interactions. *Nature Neuroscience, 16*, 33–41. https://doi.org/10.1038/nn.3275

Konishi, Y., Mikawa, H., & Suzuki, J. (1986). Asymmetrical head-turning of preterm infants: Some effects on later postural and functional lateralities. *Developmental Medicine and Child Neurology, 28*, 450–457.

Kronholm, I. (2017). Adaptive evolution and epigenetics. In T. O. Tollefsboll (Ed.), *Handbook of epigenetics: The new molecular and medical genetics* (2nd ed., pp. 427–439). London: Academic.

Kühn, S., & Gallinat, J. (2013). Gray matter correlates of posttraumatic stress disorder: A quantitative meta-analysis. *Biological Psychiatry, 73*, 70–74. https://doi.org/10.1016/j.biopsych.2012.06.029

Kushner, H. I. (2013). Why are there (almost) no left-handers in China? *Endeavour, 37*, 71–81. https://doi.org/10.1016/j.endeavour.2012.12.003

Laland, K. N. (2008). Exploring gene-culture interactions: Insights from handedness, sexual selection and niche-construction case studies. *Philosophical Transactions of the Royal Society B: Biological Sciences, 363*, 3577–3589. https://doi.org/10.1098/rstb.2008.0132

Laland, K. N., Kumm, J., Van Horn, J. D., & Feldman, M. W. (1995). A gene-culture model of human handedness. *Behavior Genetics, 25*, 433–445.

Leach, E. L., Prefontaine, G., Hurd, P. L., & Crespi, B. J. (2014). The imprinted gene LRRTM1 mediates schizotypy and handedness in a nonclinical population. *Journal of Human Genetics, 59*, 332–336. https://doi.org/10.1038/jhg.2014.30

Legare, C. H. (2017). Cumulative cultural learning: Development and diversity. In *Proceedings of National Academy of Sciences of the United States of America* (Vol. 114, pp. 7877–7883). https://doi.org/10.1073/pnas.1620743114

Lerner, R. M., & Overton, W. F. (2017). Reduction to absurdity: Why epigenetics invalidates all models involving genetic reduction. *Human Development, 60*, 107–123. https://doi.org/10.1159/000477995

Luo, Y., Liu, Y., Qin, Y., Zhang, X., Ma, T., Wu, W., et al. (2017). The atrophy and laterality of the hippocampal subfields in parents with or without posttraumatic stress disorder who lost their only child in China. *Neurological Sciences, 38*, 1241–4247. https://doi.org/10.1007/s10072-017-2952-3

Madsen, K. S., Jernigan, T. L., Iversen, P., Frokjaer, V. G., Mortensen, G. M., Knudsen, G. M., et al. (2012). Cotisol awakening response and negative emotionality linked to asymmetry in major limbic fibre bundle architecture. *Psychiatry Research, 201*, 63–72. https://doi.org/10.1016/j.pscychresns.2011.07.015

Maher, B. (2008). Personal genomes: The case of the missing heritability. *Nature, 456*, 18–21. https://doi.org/10.1038/456018a

Mandal, M. K., & Dutta, T. (2001). Left handedness: Facts and figures across cultures. *Psychology and Developing Societies, 13*, 173–191. https://doi.org/10.1177/097133360101300204

Marchant, L. F., & McGrew, W. C. (2013). Handedness is more than laterality: Lessons from chimpanzees. *Annals of the New York Academy of Sciences, 1288*, 1–8. https://doi.org/10.1111/nyas.12062

Meaney, M. J. (2010). Epigenetics and the biological definition of gene x environment interactions. *Child Development, 81*, 41–79. https://doi.org/10.1111/j.1467-8624.2009.01381.x

Medland, S. E., Duffy, D. L., Wright, M. J., Geffen, G. M., Hay, D. A., Levy, F., et al. (2009). Genetic influences on handedness: Data from 25,731 Australian and Dutch twin families. *Neuropsychologia, 47*, 330–337. https://doi.org/10.1016/j.neuropsychologia.2008.09.005

Mesoudi, A. (2016). Cultural evolution: A review of theory, findings, and controversies. *Evolutionary Biology, 43*, 481–497. https://doi.org/10.1007/s11692-015-9320-0

Meyer, T., Quaedflieg, C. W. E. M., Weijland, K., Schruers, K., Merckelbach, H., & Smeets, T. (2016). Frontal EEG asymmetry during symptom provocation predicts subjective responses to intrusions in survivors with and without PTSD. *Psychophysiology*, 1–21. https://doi.org/10.1111/psyp.12.779

Michel, G. F. (1981). Right-handedness: A consequence of infant supine head-orientation preference? *Science, 212*, 685–687.

Michel, G. F. (2018). How might the relation of the development of hand preferences to the development of cognitive functions be examined during infancy: A sketch? *Frontiers in Neuroscience, 11*, 739. https://doi.org/10.3389/fnins.2017.00739

Michel, G. F., Babik, I., Nelson, E. L., Campbell, J. M., & Marcinowski, E. C. (2018). Evolution and development of handedness: An evo-devo approach. *Progress in Brain Research.* https://doi.org/10.1016/bs.phr.2018.06.007

Michel, G. F., Babik, I., Shue, C.-F., & Campbell, J. M. (2013). Latent classes in the developmental trajectories of infant handedness. *Developmental Psychology, 50*, 349–359. https://doi.org/10.1037/a0033312

Milliken, G. W. (2017). Laterality (handedness). In J. Vonk & T. K. Shackelford (Eds.), *Encyclopedia of animal cognition and behavior* (pp. 1–4). Cham, Switzerland: Springer International Publishing.

Miskovic, V., Schmidt, L. A., Georgiades, K., Boyle, M., & MacMillan, H. L. (2009). Stability of resting frontal electroencephalogram (EEG) asymmetry and cardiac vagal tone in adolescent females exposed to child maltreatment. *Developmental Psychobiology, 51*, 474–487. https://doi.org/10.1002/dev.20387

Moore, D. S. (2017). The potential of epigenetics research to transform conceptions of phenotype development. *Human Development, 60*, 69–80. https://doi.org/10.1159/000477992

Moran, J. K., Crombach, A., Elbert, T., Nandi, C., Bambonyé, M., Wienbruch, C., et al. (2017). The individual contribution of DSM 5 symptom clusters of PTSD, life events, and childhood adversity to frontal oscillatory brain asymmetry in a large sample of active combatants. *Biological Psychology, 129*, 305–313. https://doi.org/10.1016/j.biopsycho.2017.09.014

Morange-Majoux, F., & Devouche, E. (2014). Social encouragement can influence manual preference in 6-month-old-infants. *Frontiers in Psychology, 5*, 1225. https://doi.org/10.3389/fpsychg.2014.01225

Mullon, C., & Lehmann, L. (2017). Invasion fitness for gene-culture co-evolution in family-structured populations and an application to cumulative culture under vertical transmission. *Theoretical Population Biology, 116*, 33–46. https://doi.org/10.1016/j.tpb.2017.06.003

Muntané, G., Santpere, G., Verendeev, A., Seeley, W. W., Jacobs, B., Hopkins, W. D., et al. (2017). Interhemispheric gene expression differences in the cerebral cortex of humans and macaque monkeys. *Brain Structure and Function, 222*, 3241–3254. https://doi.org/10.1007/s00429-017-1401-7

Nikolova, Y. S., & Hariri, A. R. (2015). Can we observe epigenetic effects on human brain function? *Trends in Cognitive Sciences, 19*, 366–373. https://doi.org/10.1016/j.tics.2015.05.003

Ocklenburg, S., Arning, L., Gerding, W. M., Epplen, J. T., Güntürkün, O., & Beste, C. (2013). Cholecystokinin A receptor (CCKAR) gene variation is associated with language lateralization. *PLoS One, 8*, e53643. https://doi.org/10.1371/journal.pone.0053643

Ocklenburg, S., Arning, L., Gerding, W. M., Hengstler, J. G., Epplen, J. T., Güntürkün, O., et al. (2016). Left-right axis differentiation and functional lateralization: A haplotype in the methyltransferases encoding gene SETDB2 might mediate handedness in healthy adults. *Molecular Neurobiology, 53*, 6355–6361. https://doi.org/10.1007/s12035-015-9534-2

Ocklenburg, S., & Güntürkün, O. (2018). *The lateraized brain: The neuroscience and evolution of hemispheric asymmetries*. Cambridge, MA: Elsevier.

Ocklenburg, S., Korte, S. M., Peterburs, J., Wolf, O. T., & Güntürkün, O. (2016). Stress and laterality – The comparative perspective. *Physiology & Behavior, 164*, 321–329. https://doi.org/10.1016/j.physbeh.2016.06.020

Ocklenburg, S., Packheiser, J., Schmitz, J., Rook, N., Güntürkün, O., Peterburs, J., & Grimshaw, G. M. (2018). Hugs and kisses - The role of motor preferences and emotional lateralization for hemispheric asymmetries in human social touch. *Neuroscience and Biobehavioral Reviews, 95*, 353–360.

Ocklenburg, S., Schmitz, J., Moinfar, Z., Moser, D., Klose, R., Lor, S., et al. (2017). Epigenetic regulation of lateralized fetal spinal gene expression underlies hemispheric asymmetries. *eLife*, 6. https://doi.org/10.7554/eLife.22784

Pakulak, E., Stevens, C., & Neville, H. (2018). Neuro-, cardio-, and immunoplasticity: Effects of early adversity. *Annual Review of Psychology, 69*, 131–156. https://doi.org/10.1146/annurev-psych-010416-044115

Paracchini, S., Diaz, R., & Stein, J. (2016). Advances in dyslexia genetics – New insights into the role of brain asymmetries. *Advances in Genetics, 96*, 53–97. https://doi.org/10.1016/bs.adgen.2016.08.003

Paracchini, S., & Scerri, T. (2017). Genetics of human handedness and laterality. In L. J. Rogers & G. Vallortigara (Eds.), *Lateralized brain functions: Methods in human and non-human species* (pp. 523–552). New York: Springer SBM.

Piper, B. J., Yasen, A. L., Taylor, A. E., Ruiz, J. R., Gaynor, J. W., Dayger, C. A., et al. (2013). Non-replication of an association of Apolipoprotein E2 with sinistrality. *Laterality: Asymmetries of Body, Brain and Cognition, 18*, 251–261. https://doi.org/10.1080/1357650X.2012.660164

Porac, C. (2016). *Laterality: Exploring the enigma of left-handedness*. London: Elsevier.

Prete, G., Malatesta, G., & Tommasi, L. (2017). Facial gender and hemispheric asymmetries: A hf-tRNS study. *Brain Stimulation, 10*, 1145–1147. https://doi.org/10.1016/j.brs.2017.08.002

Reissland, N., Aydin, E., Francis, B., & Exley, K. (2015). Laterality of fetal self-touch in relation to maternal stress. *Laterality: Asymmetries of Body, Brain and Cognition, 20*, 82–94. https://doi.org/10.1080/1357650X.2014.920339

Risch, N., & Pringle, G. (1985). Segregation analysis of human hand preference. *Behavioral Genetics, 15*, 385–400. https://doi.org/10.1007/BF01070896

Robinson, K. J., Hurd, P. L., Read, S., & Crespi, B. J. (2016). The PCSK6 gene is associated with handedness, the autism spectrum, and magical ideation in a non-clinical population. *Neuropsychologia, 84*, 205–212. https://doi.org/10.1016/j.neuropsychologia.2016.02.020

Rogers, L. J., & Vallortigara, G. (2017). *Lateralized brain functions: Methods in human and non-human species*. New York: Springer SBM.

Rosso, I. M., Crowley, D. J., Silveri, M. M., Rauch, S. L., & Jensen, J. E. (2017). Hippocampus glutamate and N-acetyl aspartate markers of excitotoxic neuronal compromise in posttraumatic stress disorder. *Neuropsychopharmacology, 42*, 1698–1705. https://doi.org/10.1038/npp.2017.32

Rozin, P., Moscovitch, M., & Imada, S. (2016). Right: Left: East: West. Evidence that individuals from East Asian and South Asian cultures emphasize right hemisphere functions in comparison to Euro-American cultures. *Neuropsychologia, 90*, 3–11. https://doi.org/10.1016/j.neuropsychologia.2016.06.027

Rutherford, H. J. V., & Lindell, A. K. (2011). Thriving and surviving: Approach and avoidance motivation and lateralization. *Emotion Review, 3*, 333–343. https://doi.org/10.1177/1754073911402392

Sandve, H., Lorås, H., & Vorland Pedersen, A. (2018). Is it possible to change handedness after only a short period of practice? Effects of 15 days of intensive practice on life-hand writing in strong right handers. *Laterality: Asymmetries of Body, Brain and Cognition*. https://doi.org/10.1080/1357650X.2018.1534856

Sasaki, J. Y., & Kim, H. S. (2017). Nature, nurture, and their interplay: A review of cultural neuroscience. *Journal of Cross-Cultural Psychology, 48*, 4–22. https://doi.org/10.1177/0022022116680481

Saunders, P. T. (2017). Epigenetic and evolution. *Human Development, 60*, 81–94. https://doi.org/10.1159/000477993

Savitz, J., van der Merwe, L., Solms, M., & Ramesar, R. (2007). Lateralization of hand skill in bipolar affective disorder. *Genes, Brain, and Behavior, 6*, 698–705. https://doi.org/10.1111/j.1601-183X.2006.00299.x

Schalinski, I., Moran, J. K., Elbert, T., Reindl, V., & Wienbruch, C. (2017). Oscillatory magnetic brain activity is related to dissociative symptoms and childhood adversities – A study in women with multiple trauma. *Journal of Affective Disorders, 218*, 428–436. https://doi.org/10.1016/j.jad.2017.05.009

Schmitz, J., Kumsta, R., Moser, D., Güntürkün, O., & Ocklenburg, S. (2017a). DNA methylation in candidate genes for handedness predicts handedness direction. *Laterality: Asymmetries of Body, Brain and Cognition*, 1–21. https://doi.org/10.1080/1357650X.2017.1377726

Schmitz, J., Kumsta, R., Moser, D., Güntürkün, O., & Ocklenburg, S. (2017b). *KIAA0319* promoter DNA methylation predicts dichotic listening performance in forced-attention conditions. *Behavioural Brain Research, 30*(337), 1–7. https://doi.org/10.1016/j.bbr.2017.09.035

Schmitz, J., Lor, S., Klose, R., Güntürkün, O., & Ocklenburg, S. (2017). The functional genetics of handedness and language lateralization: Insights from gene ontology, pathway, and disease association analyses. *Frontiers in Psychology, 8*, 1144. https://doi.org/10.3389/fpsychg.2017.01144

Schmitz, J., Metz, G. A. S., Güntürkün, O., & Ocklenburg, S. (2017). Beyond the genome – Towards an epigenetic understanding of handedness ontogenesis. *Progress in Neurobiology*. https://doi.org/10.1016/j.pneurobio.2017.10.005

Searleman, A., Porac, C., & Coren, S. (1989). Relationship between birth order, birth stress, and lateral preferences: A critical review. *Psychological Bulletin, 105*, 397–408.

Smith, L. L., & Hines, M. (2000). Language lateralization and handedness in women prenatally exposed to diethylstilbestrol (DES). *Psychoneuroendocrinology, 25*, 497–512.

Somers, M., Shields, L. S., Boks, M. P., Kahn, R. S., & Sommer, I. E. (2015). Cognitive benefits of right-handedness: A meta-analysis. *Neuroscience and Biobehavioral Reviews, 51*, 48–63. https://doi.org/10.1016/j.neubiorev.2015.01.003

Sparrow, S., Manning, J. R., Cartier, J., Anblagan, D., Bastin, M. E., Piyasena, C., et al. (2016). Epigenomic profiling of preterm infants reveal DNA methylation differences at sites associated with neural function. *Translational Psychiatry, 6*, e716. https://doi.org/10.1038/tp.2015.210

Steenhuis, R. E., & Bryden, M. P. (1989). Different dimensions of hand preference that relate to skilled and unskilled activities. *Cortex, 25*, 289–304.

Todd, B. K., & Banerjee, R. (2016). Lateralization of infant holding by mothers: A longitudinal evaluation of variations over the first 12 weeks. *Laterality: Asymmetries of Body, Brain and Cognition, 21*, 12–33. https://doi.org/10.1080/1357650X.2015.1059434

Tremblay, R. E., Vitaro, F., & Côte, S. M. (2018). Developmental origins of chronic physical aggression: A bio-psycho-social model for the next generation of preventive interventions. *Annual Review of Psychology, 69*, 383–407. https://doi.org/10.1146/annurev-psych-010416-044030

Tzourio-Mazoyer, N., & Seghier, M. L. (2016). The neural bases of hemispheric specialization. *Neuropsychologia, 93*, 319–324. https://doi.org/10.1016/j.neuropsychologia.2016.10.010

Uwaezuoke, S. N., Eke, C. B., & Nwobi, E. A. (2015). Left-hand dominance in children: Prevalence and maternal stereotypes in a South-East Nigerian city. *Laterality: Asymmetries of Body, Brain and Cognition, 20*, 530–542. https://doi.org/10.1080/1357650X.2015.1006642

Van der Elst, W., Hurks, P. P. M., Wassenberg, R., Meijs, C. J. C., Van Boxtel, M. P. J., & Jolles, J. (2011). On the association between lateral preferences and pregnancy/birth stress events in a nonclinical sample of school-aged children. *Journal of Clinical and Experimental Neuropsychology, 33*, 1–8. https://doi.org/10.1080/13803391003757825

Waddington, C. H. (1957). *The strategy of the genes*. London: Allen and Unwin.

Watson, D., & Clark, L. A. (1999). *The PANAS-X: Manual for the positive and negative affect schedule – Expanded form*. Iowa City, IA: Department of Psychological and Brain Sciences Publications. Retrieved from https://ir.uiowa.edu/cgi/viewcontent.cgi?article=1011&context=psychology_pubs

Whiten, A. (2017). Culture extends the scope of evolutionary biology in the great apes. In *Proceedings of National Academic Science in United States of America* (Vol. 114, pp. 7790–7797). https://doi.org/10.1073/pnas.1620733114

Whiten, A., Ayala, F. J., Feldman, M. W., & Laland, K. N. (2017). The extension of biology through culture. In *Proceedings of National Academic Science in United States of America* (Vol. 114, pp. 7775–7781). https://doi.org/10.1073/pnas.1707630114

Witherington, D. C., & Lickliter, R. (2017). Transcending the nature-nurture debate through epigenetics: Are we there yet? *Human Development, 60*, 65–68. https://doi.org/10.1159/000478796

Young, G. (2016). *Unifying causality and psychology: Being, brain and behavior*. Cham, Switzerland: Springer International Publishing.

Young, G. (2017). PTSD in court. Part II. Risk factors, endophenotypes, and biological underpinnings. *International Journal of Law and Psychiatry, 51*, 1–21. https://doi.org/10.1016/j.ijlp.2017.02.002

Young, G., Bowman, J. G., Methot, C., Finlayson, M., Quintal, J., & Boissonneault, P. (1983). Hemispheric specialization development: What (inhibition) and how (parents). In G. Young, S. J. Segalowitz, C. M. Corter, & S. E. Trehub (Eds.), *Manual specialization and the developing brain* (pp. 119–140). New York: Academic.

Chapter 7
Animal Laterality Research

Abstract This chapter shifts gears from research with humans to animal research. It gives some findings for invertebrates and, through fossil evidence, indicates that lateralization processes were evident in the earliest life forms, well over 1 billion years ago. The chapter also examines laterality in extant species; the ubiquity of lateralization in species, such as bees, points to the evolutionary basis to the characteristic. The chapter also considers laterality in early hominins; the evidence, for example, through tool use, also indicates an early presence of laterality in the lineage leading to modern humans. The best evidence in this regard concerns the study of lateralization in great apes/non-human primates, such as chimpanzees. Once methodological care is taken, these species also manifest a right-side lateralization for critical manual behaviors such as in the tube task and also in the wild. Even developing great apes/non-human primates exhibit this pattern. The evidence also indicates right hemispheric specialization in these species for its typical skills. At times, the evidence also reveals contradictory patterns of results related to great ape/non-human primate and human comparisons, including the brain areas involved (e.g., Broca). As for evolutionary models on lateralization, some are very broad and refer to asymmetries stretching into the earliest species, while others focus on our more recent ancestry in the hominid line. The evidence does not uniquely support the primary hypotheses in the area, for example, a tool-use first or gestural communication first origin. Also, issue arises about the evolutionary continuity in lateralization and whether dextralization has arisen multiply and independently over the course of evolution. The chapter concludes on the relevance of the concept of activation-inhibition coordination as a common function in these different evolutionary models.

G. Young, *Causality and Development*,
https://doi.org/10.1007/978-3-030-02493-2_7

Animals and Evolution

Animals

Introduction

Lateralization in behavior, brain, and neurons stretches back to the earliest life forms because differential left–right morphology provides adaptive advantages. However, complementary structures on the two sides of the body do so, as well. The basic opposition between the two patterns concerns whether redundancy over side proffers advantages relative to the costs, and conversely, whether the differentiation in lateralization of whatever structure, behavior, or function is involved affords adaptive advantages by increasing options (see Corballis, 2017a, who refers to an evolutionary trade-off in this regard). Evolutionary phylogenetic parallels could reflect analogy because of the common adaptive advantages for the structure or behavior to different phylogenetically unrelated species. Or, the parallel involved could reflect continuity in phylogenesis through intermediate forms, even with changing structure and behavior as the evolution proceeds. That said, if the latter holds, careful scrutiny might reveal common functional underpinnings that explain the putative surface differences over phylogenesis.

Of course, without a genetic basis to lateralized behavior and function, the search for its evolutionary origins is compromised. However, increasingly, the research is pointing to genetic origins in lateralized behavior (as per the review above, e.g., Paracchini & Scerri, 2017) Moreover, the research on the evolution of laterality in contemporary species across the phylogenetic spectrum is burgeoning, as well (Rogers & Vallortigara, 2017). Moreover, researchers are attempting to combine findings with humans and animals in order to address the nature of the divided brain, the behaviors and functions involved, and the evolutionary course leading to the lateralizations (Rogers & Vallortigara, 2017; Rogers, Vallortigara, & Andrew, 2013).

The review that follows on animal lateralization examines laterality research bearing on these issues, first, in animals not as advanced as great ape non-human primates and, then, in great ape non-human primates. However, there are methodological differences to consider in the studies involved, such as using ecologically valid tasks for the species investigated (e.g., Rogers & Vallortigara, 2017). As with the question of laterality in early human development, for which the invariant nature of the lateralization has been revealed by proper operationalization and methods, the same holds true for the laterality studies of invertebrate and earlier evolved vertebrate species – new techniques have discovered how extensive is lateralization in many living species, with implications for the phylogenesis and origin of the phenomena. Moreover, even the study of fossils related to early hominins has proved fruitful in this regard, a topic that is reviewed briefly before proceeding to the extensive animal research.

Invertebrate and Vertebrate Asymmetries

Earliest Evolutionary Signs

Findings Evidence suggests a right-side bias evolved toward 500 mya in the Cambrian period. The evidence for this conjecture relates to Babcock and Robison's (1989) finding that fossilized remains of trilobites demonstrate a 3 to 1 right vs. left distribution of bite marks dorsally. Trilobites lived in rivers and were attacked from the rear, so that either predators tended to bite on the right side of the trilobites or the trilobites were swerving to the right in order to try to escape.

Comment However, if the research on extinct animal species speaks to the evolutionary origins of the earliest signs of structural and functional lateralization, consider that even roundworms evidence neural asymmetry in function, as discussed later in the paper. Generally, lateralization might be as much a hallmark of adaptive animal functioning as much as symmetry.

Hominins and Humans

Findings The evolution of lateralized brain circuits has taken place in many species even prior to the ancestors of non-human primates, with evolutionary continuity going back to at least 30 if not 40 mya (Lindell, 2013; Marie et al., 2018). Research on hominin ancestors (including Neanderthals) and contemporary tribes that might index their behavior indicates that the creation of tools (e.g., flaking, knapping, knife use) might reflect lateralized activity, as does ancestral constructed rock art (Steele & Uomini, 2009). In both cases, the left hand appears to have undertaken the supporting role and the right hand the more complex manipulations. This pattern is consistent with the data found both for human infants and adults (see above) and great ape non-human primates and adults (see below).

Comment The most recent estimate of the time of the early evolution of right-handedness in early hominins dates back to 1.8 mya (Frayer, 2016; Lozano et al., 2017). Perhaps the time lines in the reconstruction of the evolutionary origins of lateralization in proto-hominins is being altered as new data is unearthed, but the implication is still clear – lateralization has been part and parcel of the traits that have defined our species in its origins. The differential yet complementary functions of the hemispheres and hands might have been critical to our adaptive success through the greater span of tasks that could be resolved through this structural and organizational phenotypic attribute. Granted, these types of attributes might have evolved through increased degrees of freedom afforded by other adaptations, such as upright posture and walking that had served to free the hands for more complex manual behavior and vocal tract developments that allowed for more rapid vocal communicative skills (see, for example, Corbetta, 2003; MacNeilage, 2007; Versace & Vallortigara, 2015).

Findings Consistent with the review of Steele and Uomini (2009), Cavanagh, Berbesque, Wood, and Marlowe (2016) examined handedness in contemporary hunter-gatherers as they hunted and foraged. The results showed that Hadza of Tanzania used the right hand for 96% of tool-based tasks. These data indicate that, everything else being equal, different human groups gravitate to nearly universal right-handedness for behavior on tasks that have been related to our evolutionary origin and should have appeared at about this rate in proto-hominins.

Comment To conclude, these results with respect to manual laterality in both ancestral hominins and modern hunter-gatherers reveal the probable time frame of manual lateralization expression in the human lineage, as well as its phylogenesis, and the types of behavior on critical tasks that appear to have been selected. The manual behaviors, such as tool use, are taken to reflect underlying hemispheric specializations, especially left hemisphere complex manual activity requiring coordination, as in left-hand support for right-hand flaking in tool construction and use. At the same time, lateralization appears to have evolved even earlier in the evolution of life, as discussed next.

Invertebrates and Vertebrates

Findings Vallortigara and Versace (2017) have reviewed the literature on asymmetries in sensory reception, behavior, and any associated peripheral and neuronal structure and function pertaining to invertebrates, in particular, and Rogers and Vallortigara (2017) have presented a compendium of methods and results that apply even to the earliest evolved species (their extant descendants).

In this regard, for invertebrates, consider that, according to the references to the studies in Vallortigara's works, roundworms demonstrate a left-side and not a right-side taste neuron that triggers forward movement (Suzuki et al., 2008). Fruit flies use their antennas to track olfactory signals, and the gradient is skewed to left-side sensory signals (Duistermars, Chow, & Frye, 2009). Honey bees have better olfactory memories on the right side of the brain, but longer-term memory retrieval is more effective in the left honey bee brain (Rogers & Vallortigara, 2008).

Other research supports the views and research presented by Vallortigara and Versace (2017) with respect to lateralization in invertebrate species. For example, Hori et al. (2017) found that fish, while Wiper's review of the literature (2017) found that toads, exhibit consistent lateralized behavior for behaviors pertinent to their survival, such as turning tendencies (Lippolis, Bisazza, Rogers, & Vallortigara, 2002; Vallortigara, Rogers, Bisazza, Lippolis, & Robins, 1998). Frasnelli (2017) indicated similar lateralizations in invertebrate species.

Comment These results can be interpreted in multiple ways for the nature of invertebrate lateralization, which is discussed further below. For example, are the central, peripheral, and behavioral patterns discerned in lateralization in invertebrate species indicative of locally adaptive outcomes for each species and no generalized adaptive function is found? Do they concern selected behaviors that help in survival and reproduction or more generalized functions? Are the behaviors domain-general or more specific and modular? For example, one could argue that the results of the study in invertebrate lateralization reflect generalized approach-withdrawal differences in the hemispheres that are quite consistent over species, both extant and extinct, or torque-related turning tendencies that are consistent with torque findings in embryonic development. Or, perhaps they relate to efficiencies in behavior and underlying neural activity that are better on the left side of the neural architecture. As might be evident at this point in the paper, the preferred interpretation of the author is that, specifically, any such generalized function in lateralization involves the activation-inhibition coordination dynamic.

Findings As for vertebrates, other examples confirm the extensive presence of lateralization. Domestic chicks express a left-hemisphere controlled bias for grain pecking (e.g., in discriminating grains from a distracting background, that is, a right-eye input bias) (Andrew, Tommasi, & Ford, 2000). Birds and more recent evolutionary descendant species, including great apes, express a left hemisphere advantage in executing well-practiced motoric sequences (e.g., manipulating objects, not just prey catching; Rutledge & Hunt, 2004; Hopkins, 2006, 2007, respectively). Findings such as these emphasize motor and related behavioral influences (e.g., manual) in selecting lateralization in brain and behavior, with left-brain side proficiencies in these regards underscored.

As for the right hemisphere, escaping predators consistently exhibits associations with the right hemisphere, for instance, in toads, birds, and mammals (Lippolis et al., 2002; Koboroff, Kaplan, & Rogers, 2008; Lippolis, Westman, McAllan, & Rogers, 2005; respectively). Once more, the behaviors at issue in putative right-brain side specializations in invertebrate and vertebrate species reflect the motoric saliency in the selection that must have taken place.

The comparative data includes manual and other behavior related to handedness and preference. For example, European toads use the right forepaw in swiping (Bisazza, Cantalupo, Robins, Rogers, & Vallortigara, 1997), which is consistent with left-brain side models involving manual behavioral lateralization. In contrast, the blue gourami fish uses its ventral fin while tactilely inspecting novel objects that are close by and prefers the left one in doing so (Bisazza, Lippolis, & Vallortigara, 2001). This behavior is consistent with functions attributed to the right side of brain, such as spatial exploration.

Comment One can query whether the data related to motoric selection pressures on lateralization are sufficient to explain it, independent of the nature of the behaviors involved and the generalized function they may represent. In development, behaviors cannot be expressed if the neurological substrate does not permit them, everything else being equal. In evolution, the same applies; perhaps certain behaviors would be adaptive, but they cannot be expressed if the underlying neural or central nervous system architecture and function do not permit them. Therefore, (a) do we emphasize as drivers in evolution the underlying substrate having been selected outright or to a degree that it is readily poised to do so with minor adjustments, in order to allow the behavior of interest to manifest in the ecological niche involved, or (b) do we emphasize as drivers in the evolutionary process the behaviors or functions themselves? The former strategy might implicate some generalized function in the brain, for example, while the latter might implicate a more specific process. Either way, the genetic substrate and consequent phenotype of the individual organism that develops partly through it must support the evolutionary selection involved.

Findings About findings on lateralization across species, both vertebrate and invertebrate, Vallortigara and Versace (2017) gave the example for vertebrates of the right hippocampus possessing properties that facilitate large-scale environmental information and navigation processing, from chicks to humans (e.g., Tommasi, Gagliardo, Andrew, & Vallortigara, 2003; Maguire, Woollett, & Spiers, 2006, respectively). Similarly, the right hippocampus even has pre-wired synaptic neuronal differences in mice, with the left compared to the right CA3-CA1 synapses generating stronger long-term potentiation (e.g., Shipton et al., 2014).

Thus, conceivably, the right side of the brain might have evolved its skills before the leftside of the brain because they concerned basic spatial functions in support of survival modes related to predator escape and any related neuronal activity supportive of this function. Nutrient acquisition cannot take place without survival itself and so specializations in lateralization might have been selected on that basis, with survival-related behaviors (although considered more primitive than feeding and related ones and which appear associated with the left side of the brain) advantaged in the right side of the brain, given the latter's specializations.

This argument is admittedly tentative, but it comports with the current hypothesis that the cerebral hemispheres are differentiated in their activation-inhibition coordination. It could be that simpler skills in these regards evolved first and that the locus was the right side of the brain, while more advanced skills along these lines evolved later, with its locus being the left side of the brain. The thrust of the literature review throughout this paper supports the argument that the left hemisphere expresses more advanced activation-inhibition coordination skills.

Comment Thus, more advanced activation-inhibition coordination skills might not have been quite necessary for survival in earlier, lower-order species, for which inhibitory function itself would have been more beneficial adaptively. In this evolutionary scenario, as the right side of the body and left side of neuronal system/brain evolved escape and underlying inhibitory capacities, the complementary function of activation-inhibition coordination only gradually evolved and anchored as the predominant function and correspondingly in the left side of the body and right side of neuronal system/brain in lateralization processes.

The argument, then, in this context is that the first side of the brain to be dominant in evolution was the right one. It could have been specialized for immediate survival-related behavior, such as spatial navigation to avoid predators. In this scenario, the right side of the brain might be analogous to an alarm system that stops all activity other than what is needed to resolve the immediate crisis at hand threatening survival. The left side of the brain might have evolved complementary skills later on, related to prey capture, foraging, and so on, which require more complex behavioral coordinations and lacking the immediacy of survival. This type of logic would confront the predominant paradigm of the left hemisphere being the dominant one with evidence and models based on them that reverse the prominence of the hemispheres in their evolutionary origins in terms of adaptive survival and consequent reproductive processes.

This type of argument is also consistent with the activation-inhibition coordination hypothesis of the different left and right hemisphere specialization skills in the human, beginning with the newborn and to the adult. That is, the prior literature review has shown that the left hemisphere appears specialized for activation-inhibition coordination right from the early prenatal and neonatal periods for motor sequences, reaching and grasping, and so on, and then developmentally onwards, because coordinated motor sequencing is a refined skill that calls upon the skills of the left hemisphere. Perhaps the left side of the brain had evolved its skills as an add-on to basic inhibitory skills that had already evolved in the right side of the brain, leading to the left appearing dominant because of the greater complexity involved in its skill. But this hypothesis might not do justice to an evolutionary scenario in which the right side of the brain was the first dominant one for the basic function that appears to differentiate the sides of the brain – the inhibition component of the activation-inhibition coordination function.

Findings Other recent research confirms that lateralized behavior and function evolved early in the animal kingdom. Güntürkün and Ocklenburg (2017) noted that lateralization has evolved repeatedly in evolution because of its local adaptive advantages (that is, in this sense, the evolution is convergent in nature and it does not reflect phylogenetic passing on the characteristic in conserved or homologous evolution). According to Güntürkün and Ocklenburg (2017), the generalized advantage in asymmetry in brain and behavior is that it increases neural capacity (In this regard, also see Levy, 1977).

Comment Generally, research on invertebrate and vertebrate cerebral hemispheric lateralization suggests a broad range of lateralized sensory and functional behavior related to prey capture and avoidance of predators. That is, there appears to be evolutionary continuity in basic behavioral processes in terms of capturing food items and avoiding predators.

But the question arises how much more specific can we be about the nature of laterality differences that evolve homologously over species and so constitute either conserved tendencies or precursors to differential structure and behavior that confer survival and reproductive advantages to extant humans. Do models that emphasize neural efficiency, information processing, and the like generally capture the lowest common salient denominator of differential sidedness in behavior, brain, and neural function? To answer this type of question, survey of the non-human primate literature for lateralization is as important to consider as that of the species that have evolved before them, which is the topic examined in the next section. The reader will gather that the evidence in our closest surviving animal relatives supports the present emphasis on the activation-inhibition coordination model of differential lateralizations in brain and behavior.

Laterality in Great Ape Non-human Primates

Introduction

The study of handedness and lateralized function in the behavior and brain of our closest living species, the great ape non-human primates, has proven especially fruitful. There are four major species of extant apes, including chimpanzees, gorillas, bonobos, and orangutans. The most studied species involves the chimpanzees, which are being increasingly shown to be quite right-handed on critical tasks, including in early development. Gorillas might even be more right-handed for some tasks, given their terrestrial niche and the greater personal space that they require. Bonobos had been thought to exhibit less lateralization in behavior than chimpanzees and gorillas, but that view is changing with recent targeted research. Orangutans appear less lateralized than the other three species, but they are older phylogenetically in terms of their evolutionary split from the others, at least in terms of their ancestral forebears.

Hopkins (2006) clarified that the common ancestor of chimpanzees and of humans appeared about 5.6 mya, with even earlier evolutionary divergence found for the lines of gorillas (about 7.8 mya) and orangutans (about 13–15 mya) relative to the human line. Despite these differences in lateralized manual behaviors in extant species of great ape non-human primates (and their phylogenetically different origins), the evidence can help recreate the evolutionary pathways in lateralized manual and related behaviors and so address the nature of that lateralization in humans.

Note that there is research on New World as well as Old World monkey lateralization, but the present review does not deal with these other species, which have fewer implications for the evolution of our lateralizations. However, I do note that comparative research with humans can be illuminating even for monkeys. In this regard, a monkey pointing to an experimenter about the location of a hidden object so that it could be fetched involves the right hand not only in human infants but also in baboons and rhesus monkeys (not in tufted capuchins, though; Meunier, Vauclair, & Fagard, 2012) [Also, see Nelson and Kendall (2018) for a study on task type/context and complexity in eliciting laterality results for goal-directed tail use in Columbian spider monkeys.]

Findings Returning to the question of lateralization in chimpanzees, Corballis (2014) noted that about two-thirds of chimpanzees are right-handed for behaviors such as gesturing and throwing. Note that the percentages involved do not approach the one for human handedness, which typically demonstrates a 90–10% split in favor of the right hand.

Comment The difference in degree of handedness lateralization in chimpanzees compared to humans might relate more to practice than brain or genetic underpinnings, though, given the extent of differential right-left manual practice in humans, including in young children in school. Also, the differences in handedness in chimpanzees and humans might be related to task differences. Humans have a classic index of handedness in writing (drawing in young children), and there are longer and brief handedness questionnaires that have evolved through factor analysis. As far as is known, there is no equivalent handedness inventory or observational system related to critical indices of handedness for chimpanzees.

Findings Also, for Corballis (2014), in terms of the cortical areas that are equivalent in chimpanzees to the primary areas of the human brain involved in language production and understanding, that is, Broca's and Wernicke's areas, respectively, the research shows that the left side is "enlarged" relative to the right in chimpanzees (Figure 1 in Corballis, 2014). The paper returns to this topic below in more depth.

Comment Briefly, these results indicate the phylogenetic continuity in the evolution of lateralization in later evolved species. Broca's and Wernicke's areas are equivalents that had evolved in our common ancestor with proto great ape non-human primates, but not to underwrite the language function. That is, the primary language areas have evolved their lateralization in common ancestors to surviving great ape non-human primates when language had not been adaptively present and so must reflect other aspects onto which language functions could have mapped. Once more, we need to ask if specific or generalized functions in the brain were the evolutionary drivers in lateralization evolution, and pose similar questions about the selection pressures on the specific behaviors involved, such as tool use. Or, it could be that a common function to brain and behavior, and this article is advocating for the activation-inhibition coordination in this regard, had underlain both the particular generalized and specific drivers in the evolution of the pre-adapted (exapted) Broca's and Wernicke's area equivalents millions of years ago in the hominid lineage, as well as their behavioral manifestations.

Development

Preface The research on the evolution of the development of handedness is sparse, so that examination of developmental patterns in extant great ape non-human primates might shed some light on the question. The evolutionary value of finding manual specialization in great ape non-human primates would be enhanced if similar lateralization in manual behavior were evidenced right from the earliest phases of life.

Findings In this regard, Boesch et al. (2017) found that the youngest of chimpanzees observed in the Bakoun forest in Guinea while they used tools to get nutrient-rich fresh water algae demonstrated lateralization in their manual behavior. Specifically, the youngest chimpanzees used the right hand in their tool-using activity and even more so than in adults.

Hopkins (2006) reviewed the little developmental evidence on handedness in the four great ape species. For example, neonatal chimpanzees express a right-sided grasping bias (Fagot & Bard, 1995), hand-to-mouth movements (Hopkins & Bard, 1993), and lead limb in locomoting (Hopkins, Bard, & Griner, 1997). As with humans, early lateral asymmetries in chimpanzees predict later asymmetries; for example, this applies to neonatal head orientation and 4- to 5-year-old coordinated bimanual action (Hopkins & Bard, 2000).

Comment This type of research illustrates the value of knowing what behaviors and tasks represent the functional specializations of the hemispheres or otherwise the left and right side of the neural architecture for different species that one wishes to study. The lateralization will emerge in concert with predicted models when the right methodological tools are used. Similarly, studying lateralization is difficult enough with animals, but its research base with developing members of a species at issue must be undertaken for a more complete picture of lateralization in extant species, including for the reasons of better formulating models about evolution based on the findings.

Adults

Findings According to Vallortigara and Versace (2017), semi-wild apes use the right hand in removing a reward inside a tube (McGrew & Marchant, 1997). The tube task is used often in manual laterality research with apes.

Hopkins et al. (2011) found a right preference on a tube task in 777 chimpanzees, gorillas, and bonobos, but not orangutans. Similarly, Wild Western gorillas in the Republic of Congo demonstrated right-hand shaking of termite mound pieces with the goal to collect termites (Salmi, Rahman, & Doran-Sheehy, 2016).

Forrester (2017) maintained that, across non-human primate groups, the evidence strongly supports population-level right-handedness over a range of rearing histories. Particularly, Forrester, Leavens, Quaresmini, and Vallortigara (2011) and Forrester, Quaresmini, Leavens, Speizio, and Vallortigara (2012) found a right-side preference for uni-manual inanimate object-directed behavior in chimpanzees and gorillas (but not to social targets). In addition, generally, great ape non-human primates use the right-hand in gesturing (Vallortigara & Versace, 2017).

Forrester, Rawlings, and Davila Ross (2016) observed bimanually coordinated behavior during natural feeding bouts on hard-shelled "strychnos" fruits in 33 semi-wild chimpanzees aged 5 to 31 years and found a group right-side bias. Of the 33 chimpanzees, as per their Table 5.1, 22 expressed a right-side bias, 10 a left one, with one ambidextrous. The proportion of right-handers relative to other handedness types is robust at two-thirds (67%).

Prieur, Pika, Barbu, and Blois-Heulin (2017) studied the social function of dyadic gestures intra-specifically in captive chimpanzees and gorillas living in socio-ecologically relevant conditions. For example, they observed clapping, embracing, touching, and punching, while coding for auditory, tactile, and visual gestures, and then compared the results across species. Gorillas typically demonstrate more social cohesion, with chimpanzees show more social flexibility. Gorillas keep a greater social spacing. This would facilitate auditory gestures for them relative to chimpanzees. In terms of lateralization of gestures, the study found that gorillas compared to chimpanzees demonstrated more right-hand auditory gesturing, showing the influence of social structure and dynamics in evolutionary selection pressures that shaped lateralization. The results support the social theory of the evolution of laterality (Vallortigara & Rogers, 2005; discussed more below).

Neufuss, Humle, Cremaschi, and Kivell (2016) are the first researchers to show that bonobos are among the great ape non-human primates that evidence right-hand bias in a tool use behavior. They studied nut-cracking behavior in rehabilitated, wild-born bonobos living in a natural environment in a sanctuary in the Democratic Republic of Congo. Two-thirds of the bonobos (66%) use the right-hand exclusively in nut-cracking while using a variety of precision and power grips. Prior research on bonobos had not studied larger samples or more complex tasks, such as nut-cracking, accounting for the lack of laterality findings previously for this species.

Meguerditchian et al. (2015) studied side preference in uni-manual reaching and grasping for small food items in four captive great ape species samples: chimpanzees, gorillas, bonobos, and orangutans. Aside from a generalized right-hand preference in all four species, precision grasping with the thumb and index finger was found to elicit more prevalent right-hand use. Moreover, on the tube task, which requires more complex coordinated bimanual behavior, right-hand preference was accentuated for chimpanzees and gorillas, with only orangutans being left-handed among the four species that had been studied. Although gorillas were not more right-handed than the case for the other three species in reaching, they were on the tube task. The authors noted that gorillas are more terrestrial than the other species studied, which could be the factor helping to explain the results, through ecological, postural, and biomechanical mechanisms.

Comment However, despite the proliferation of non-human primate research on lateralization, can we conclude that great ape non-human primates generally are right-sided in their manual skills like humans, especially if they are examined on complex tasks? The response to this question is that there is no universal pattern over all non-human primate species and that context is important to consider. Nevertheless, the research is telling when the correct tasks are used to determine non-human primate lateralization, including developmentally. There is little doubt that, generally, patterns in brain and behavior in non-human primate lateralization is right-sided and right-handed, respectively, as much as is the case for humans, but perhaps not as extensively. This does not deny that a common evolutionary function could be underwriting lateralizations in both humans, and their forebears, and surviving extant species of the forebears other than humans. Although the present work has championed the activation-inhibition coordination framework in these regards, there are multiple competing hypotheses, and they are explored below.

Hopkins is a leader in the field of research on non-human primate lateralization, and his work covers both manual behavior and the brain. The following reviews some of his research on the matter beyond what has been mentioned above and illustrates the changing landscape of models related to the evolutionary origins and functions of lateralization in great ape non-human primates.

Models

Model 1 Hopkins et al. (2005) studied captive chimpanzee laterality in manual gestures compared to reaching, tool use, and bimanual actions. Manual gestures were not only more right-handed than left-handed, independent of rearing history (at about a 3 to 1 ratio) but, as well, they were predicted by reaching 10 years prior when the chimpanzees were 3- to 4-year-olds. Also, the chimpanzee manual gestures were more right-handed when they were accompanied by concurrent vocalizations. Gestures were elicited in food item tasks, bimanual coordinations on a tube task, and tool use by skewers put into pipes for food retrieval. The authors concluded that the evolutionary origins of left-hemisphere language/speech skills in humans involve pre-existing lateralizations related to communicative manual gestures rather than to tool use (Corballis, 2002; Hopkins & Fernandez-Carriba, 2002).

Model 2 In a later publication, Hopkins and colleagues presented a different hypothesis for the evolutionary origins of lateralized behavior and its corresponding central correlates. Specifically, Hopkins, Russell, and Schaeffer (2012) reasoned that, after the evolutionary bifurcation from our common ancestor with great ape non-human primates, early hominins were subject to intense evolutionary pressures related to throwing. The authors studied throwing in chimpanzees that was not aimed at food gathering but to communicate socially, being used as "social tools." About half of the 78 chimpanzees studied were reliable throwers. Prior research had established that captive chimpanzees prefer to throw with the right hand (Hopkins, Russell, Cantalupo, Freeman, & Schapiro, 2005). The research under discussion determined whether right or left hand throwing in reliable throwers (N = 78, varying from 6 to 51 years of age) was associated with parameters in the part of the chimpanzee brain that is homologous with the human's language-related Broca's area and whether the association involved any lateralization. In this regard, using magnetic resonance imaging (MRI), the authors studied differences in the ratio of white matter (WM) to gray matter (GM) in the chimpanzees' brains in the inferior frontal gyrus (IFG), as well as in another motor area, the motor hand area of the pre-central gyrus (termed the KNOB).

According to calculated asymmetry quotients (AQ), the findings in Hopkins, Russell, and Schaeffer (2012) revealed that chimpanzees who were right- compared to left-hand throwers showed greater WM/ GM left-sided compared to right-sided brain asymmetries in both the IFG and KNOB areas. Further, based on cognitive task performance, throwers were more advanced in communication than non-throwers, but no laterality differences were evident in these results. Hopkins, Russell, and Schaeffer (2012) concluded that learning to throw socially alters the connectivity between the pre-motor and primary cortical regions of the chimpanzee brain. Moreover, throwing functioned as an evolutionary pre-adaptation for later evolutionary neural advances in motor programming necessary for complex motor actions, including for language/speech.

Model 3 Hopkins and colleagues conducted another recent chimpanzee study examining the relationship between manual behavior and central measures, and this time they supported an evolutionary view that placed primacy on tool use (Hopkins et al., 2017). The manual task involved a pipe with food in it and using sticks to get it out. The MRI scans (N = 189) were of the same regions as in the prior study, with the KNOB also referred to as the "pli-de-passage frontal-parietal moyen" (PPFM). As a group, the chimpanzees were not right lateralized on the manual task, but those who performed better with the right hand indexed greater leftward asymmetries in the two brain regions studied. The authors concluded that the evolution of tool usage was associated with an increased left hemisphere specialization for motor skills. The underlying skill involved related to motor planning, with the evolved left hemisphere specialization of this aspect being associated with the right-side manual preference in the associated behavior.

Comment Hopkins and colleagues have conducted research with great ape non-human primates that point to the evolutionary origins of lateralization alternately in communicative gestures, tool use, or other manual behavior. However, although language-related left hemisphere cerebral dominance is perhaps the most marked lateralized brain function in humans, there is little evidence of a direct, unvarying homologous evolution in the common ancestors with great ape non-human primates, although pre-adaptations are implicated in Broca's and Wernicke's areas and related regions. That said, continued research is needed to disambiguate which model is the most cogent in terms of the evolution of lateralization in hominins and great ape non-human primates, although the different models that have been proposed, such as tool use first and gestural communication first, could be complementary, revealing of a common function, or both.

Evolution

Introduction

The lines of research on lateralization in this book so far suggest that there are developmental, biological, environmental, and evolutionary bases to lateralized behavior and brain structure and function. Furthermore, they indicate that evolution might retain morphological or behavioral traits somewhat homologously, but that there are variations over evolution on which they build. Generally, the evolution of lateralizations involve pre-adaptations (exaptations), which concern traits that are adaptive for one reason at one evolutionary period and evolve to fit another function at a later one, building on what has been conferred in the earlier one(s). Understanding evolution at this level provides a proper foundation in examining both the evolutionary changes in phylogenesis that might be postulated and the developmental changes that speak to them. However, pre-adaptations and later adaptations might be more similar than the impression left at the surface, for example, through deep commonalities in structure and function even over diverse evolutionary epochs in phylogenesis.

The example of flying illustrates the various evolutionary patterns. House flies and birds both fly, but this parallel evolution has taken place through convergent analogous processes and not through evolutionary pathways over ancestors of the two species and all extinct intermediate species between them, that is, involving conservation of adaptive structures and functions or variations over evolution that evidence plausible linkages from one species to the next in the adaptive changes involved. At the same time, birds evolved from dinosaurs and dinosaurs had evolved flight over millions of years from featherlike pre-adaptations (exaptations) that had served different functions than flying (heat conservation related). This demonstrates the types of plausible changes that could have taken place in evolution leading from one type of structure and function to another that might appear extremely different but through speciation linkaging can be demonstrated not to be the case (e.g., Bard, 2017). Moreover, common functions might explain surface differences in changed adaptations over speciation, although for the function of dinosaur feathers (e.g., heat retention related) and bird feathers (flight), this is not the case.

Marchant and McGrew (2013) offered a similar argument in that, for them, the literature does not unequivocally support right-handedness in chimpanzees, as distinct from manual specializations on complex tasks. That is, assuming the conclusions is supported as research with extant great apes continue, we can read into this that humans evolved lateralizations in brain and behavior out of a general evolutionary conserved advantage for asymmetry but in a de novo evolutionary manner for the specific behavior of handedness, with much experiential influences involved, as well.

That is, the findings with great apes on hemispheric specialization, differential hemispheric structure, and so on support the evolution of brain lateralization of some kind in great ape ancestors (as per the Broca's area research reported by Corballis, 2014). That is, unlike the case for handedness on simpler, daily tasks, where a right-side preference might be less established in great ape non-human primates relative to humans, there is sufficient evidence for a right-sided bias in these extant species for specializations on complex functions in brain and behavior, that is, for manual specialization and hemispheric specialization. Thus, for the lateralized specializations of behavior and brain, the evidence consistently shows a right- or left-side advantage in great ape non-human primates for skills and processes that are similar in humans, and a common function in hand and brain sidedness might be the reason, such as activation-inhibition coordination, as has been argued above.

Evolutionary models of lateralization of function vary in whether they emphasize tool use as the driver in evolution, whether in this regard they emphasize other manual activity that is more symbolic, such as gestures, or whether they emphasize language-related activity, and so on. These diverse models might be nonexclusive and interrelated, for example, having common underlying functions over them, as per Young's activation-inhibition coordination model (e.g., Young, 2011, 2016); Young proposed a common metric for both evolutionary acquisitions in activation-inhibition coordination.

The next sections review in more depth models of lateralization applicable to evolution in terms of the brain, manually, and then for common functions. In effect, the following section elaborates models on the development and evolution of lateralization that might be beneficial in explicating both processes. The models are more complementary that in competition, much like the hands and hemispheres in their specializations. Throughout the presentation of the contemporary models on the topic, by way of commentary, the value of the present model of activation-inhibition coordination for both brain and behavior functions is underscored in depth, as well.

Brain Models

Model Vallortigara and Versace (2017) noted that certain aspects of language have not been passed on in evolution because they are uniquely human. Also, as shown above, some aspects of brain structure related to lateralization are not quite the same in humans relative to homologous areas in contemporary chimpanzees.

Vallortigara and Versace (2017) provided supplementary data to those of Hopkins on the matter. Specifically, Leroy et al. (2015) found that the superior temporal gyrus ventral to Heschel's gyrus in the right hemisphere in humans is deeper than for the left hemisphere yet the asymmetry is quite reduced in chimpanzees (Leroy et al., 2015). At the same time, according to Vallortigara and Versace (2017), for the critical left hemisphere language production area, Broca's region, the region is equivalently large in the left hemisphere compared to the right not only in humans but also in chimpanzees (as well as bonobos and gorillas) even though humans have more of a language function (Cantalupo & Hopkins, 2001).

Forrester (2017) also addressed the function of the left hemisphere's structure in great ape non-human primates, preferring a more generalized model. She reported that Broca's area underwrites different functions in great apes and humans but may have a common super-ordinate function of being a "supra-modal hierarchical processor" that allows for efficient sequential organization, whether in speech or motorically, so that it did not evolve as a specific human language production area, per se (also see the study by Higuchi, Chaminadeb, Imamizua, & Kawato, 2009).

Comment The models related to the brain for the evolution of lateralization in humans and our ancestors relate to specific areas of the brain and their specific functions or their generalized functions. For the latter, lateralized brain structures have been found in extant great ape non-human primate species that speak to areas equivalent to them that are associated with the human language function. As for more generalized processes that might be involved in lateralized brain organization, the model offered recently integrated concepts such as motor routines and sequences but goes beyond them by implicating a supra-modal hierarchical processor. This terminology is consistent with the proposed activation–inhibition coordination model in this regard, which has super-ordinate aspects for both brain and behavior and functions hierarchically in doing so.

Manual Models

Model In work prior to her 2017 publication, Forrester preferred to emphasize the manual driver to the evolution of lateralization. Forrester et al. (2016) opined that it is possible that the right-side bias in manual behavior in great apes will approach the proportion in humans, once thorough investigations are undertaken. The reason for this is that the left hemisphere in the common ancestor to humans and great ape non-human primates had already evolved to specialize in abilities that favored contralateral right-hand use, that is, for "routine sequences" in action.

Comment This manual model in the evolution of lateralization relative to the brain one illustrates that there is another debate whether the manual tool use or the gestural communication/throwing behaviors served as the evolutionary drivers in lateralization, as per the Hopkins research above. The workers in the field appear to vacillate in their views, with Forrester representing another researcher with varied opinions in this regard. Below, the paper explores further this debate and considers the common function argument as well.

However, we need to keep in mind that the proclivity for right-hand use in humans might be accentuated by our consistent upright posture, which frees the hands more so than in other non-human primates, thereby facilitating manual exploration and consequent manual specialization. This differential postural effect might lead to a more frequent right-side manual specialization in the human case relative to the great ape non-human primate case, even with ideal test task usage or ideal natural observations, despite some commonalities derived from having a common ancestor with some common left hemisphere skills. However, the degree of lateralization manually in humans compared to chimpanzees, for example, might be only in frequency and not in strength. That is, the typical right-side preferences for manual behavior on complex tasks might be found as much in chimpanzees as humans, at least in the right testing conditions and environment. Only with ideal research tasks that tap into the manual and hemispheric specializations of great ape non-human primates will their right-side lateralizations approach the proportions in humans; however, this might not mean that it translates into the typical human right-hand usage on most tasks confronted by great ape non-human primates in their daily activities, differential context and species differences aside.

Moreover, Forrester et al. (2016) speculated that the differences in proportions of right- hand preferences on manual tasks over species, with the proportion in humans more right-sided than for other species, might reflect several steps in phylogenesis, with initial, intermediate, and later lateralization patterns. For example, the left hemisphere specialization and associated right-side manual bias might have accentuated in evolution when early hominins began using sophisticated tools manually and began communicating skillfully at the verbal level (Marchant & McGrew, 2013). Here, Forrester (and colleagues) are arguing that steps in evolution might not relate to different structures, behaviors, and functions from one evolutionary epoch to the next in phylogenesis but to increasing demands for and ability in sophisticated, skillful behaviors and output, which is exactly the way the proposed common evolutionary function in lateralization of activation-inhibition coordination is described (see Table 5.1).

Common Models

Model What might be the generalized function that underscores commonalities in hemispheric specialization and related lateralities? Although the present work has argued that the common function involved relates to activation-inhibition coordination, another major hypothesis is that, generally, left-sided and right-sided hemispheric specialization allows for increased neural capacity, parallel processing, and simultaneous incompatible response elicitation (Rogers, 2002; Vallortigara, 2000).

Forrester et al. (2016) also addressed the generalized skill in the left hemisphere that would permit it a relative advantage in complex manual and in verbal behavior. In this regard, they referred to the left hemisphere being specialized for executive, top-down control of routine sequences in behavior (such as in approach and feeding) and the right hemisphere being specialized for processing novel/urgent stimuli (such as avoiding predators) [as per MacNeilage, Rogers, & Vallortigara, 2009; Rogers et al., 2013; Vallortigara & Rogers, 2005]. The evidence in favor of this hypothesis typically refers to right hemisphere dominance (left visual field advantage) in tasks such as monitoring conspecifics (e.g., Hews & Worthington, 2001;

Karenina et al., 2010; and Quaresmini, Forrester, Speizio, & Vallortigara, 2014; for lizards, beluga whales, and gorillas, respectively) and to left hemisphere dominance in tasks such as prey capture, foraging and manipulating food items, and object manipulation, for example, in apes (e.g., Forrester, Quaresmini, Leavens, Mareschal, & Thomas, 2013).

Comment The best common models of the evolution of lateralization should be able to incorporate under its aegis other proposed models. The models might exist at different levels of generality, be complementary, and so on, but the search for one generalized driver in the evolution of lateralization can bring with it an economy in modeling and supportive research. The models that have been proposed in this regard relate both to behavior (e.g., predator-prey relations) and neuronal architecture and function (capacity, processing), but neither of these types of modeling capture both behavior and neuronal architecture structure and function, unlike the case for the activation-inhibition coordination hypothesis, which was foundationally constructed based on the premise that a common function in brain and behavior exists.

Before addressing other drivers in the evolution of lateralization, the role of the environment in the process is given due consideration in the following. That is, in gene-culture interaction, which is a model that applies to handedness as much as other areas, the prominence of the environment in lateralization causation is highlighted (Laland, 2008).

Gene-Culture Model

Model Laland (2008) referred to the steps in lateralization phylogenesis that might have taken place in evolution as "selective sweeps" of handedness "distorters." The steps might each have lasted several hundred thousand years to millions of years. With each sweep, at the genetic level, another "dextralizing allele" was added to influence right-hand preference. Moreover, in the human case, because parents will be more right-handed, they will influence their offspring to be more right-handed independent of any added dextral alleles that they might have inherited. That is, according to Laland (2008), a gene-culture co-evolutionary model might best explain the steps in phylogenesis of increasing right-handedness. Furthermore, cultural factors that promoted right-handedness could also have included constructing environments that accommodated to the right-hand majority. Also, new behavior patterns could have been instituted culturally if they "benefited" from right-handedness.

Comment Laland's (2008) work on gene-culture interactions in the evolution of handedness is important because it supports an active participation by parents and culture in handedness development no matter what the hominid evolutionary epoch. For example, he indicated that not only do genes and culture co-evolve and reciprocally interact as they influence behavior, but also their interaction is more dominant than either aspect functioning alone – they are co-directors of behavior and evolutionary events and, moreover, humans are "active constructors" in this regard. The conformity in agricultural societies that leads to increased right handedness, then, should not be considered a passive phenomenon, just as the construction of "traditional" societies as ones that "modernize" should not be considered a passive process.

If culture has contributed to the evolutionary process in the way indicated, one should specify what aspect of trans-generational transmission in lateralization is liable to cultural learning as well as genetic underpinning, in a reciprocal constructive process. The following returns to the question raised by Hopkins, Forrester, and colleagues, among others, as reviewed above, whether language and related communications, such as gestures, or other manual aspects, such as tool use, as well as their brain-related underpinnings, have provided the initiating fertile selective grounds for the evolution of lateralization. Or could there be a more general driver in this regard, as has been posited?

Tools or Language First?

Model There have been several directions taken in modeling of the evolutionary course of hemispheric specialization and manual specialization in hominid evolution, with the tool use first and language or gestural communication first models being primary. In the former model, first, the left hemisphere became specialized for fine sequential type skills, which led to its generalized use in manual handedness tasks. In the latter model, first, the left hemisphere evolved specializations related to language precursors, and they led to evolved generalizations for other skills, including the manual.

The non-human primate tool using research, as reviewed above, suggests a tool-use evolutionary origin for lateralized manual behavior in hominins. However, other research supports other models – in particular, the alternative language-first scenario, as with the research on lateralized non-human primate communicative gestures.

Mangalam, Desai, and Singh (2016) underscored that manual symmetries reflect division of manual labor, which is economical evolutionarily. Specifically, they looked at research on bonnet macaques and capuchin monkeys in these regards, referring to maneuvering three-dimensional space and physical strength as the kinds of functions involved. They noted that Young, Corter, Segalowitz, and Trehub (1983) had differentiated the concepts of manual specialization and hand preference in the case of infants, which Fagot and Vauclair (1991) generalized the concept to work with great ape non-human primates.

Corballis (2014) also presented a division of labor model of hemisphere function and consequent differential hand skills. Specifically, he argued that the left hemisphere has a bias for "action dynamics," for example, with respect to gestures, speech, and tool use, such that there is a common precursor to these skills. He related the evolution of lateralized brain function in these regards to mirror neurons, which are involved in both understanding and producing manual actions. Further, he related this evolved left-hemisphere mirror neuron system to the evolution of skills in vocalization and "grammar-like complexity" (Corballis, 2003). Häberling, Corballis, and Corballis (2016) elaborated further that, in this evolutionary model of an initial left-hemisphere specialization that is action-based and embedded in the mirror system, the system involved first bifurcated evolutionarily into a language-related system and another related to observation and execution of manual actions, which itself further fissioned, including into a sub-system involving hand preference (also see Corballis, 2017b).

Thus, evolutionary scholars make a distinction between handedness and manual role specialization. For them, the latter refers to complementary coordination on skilled bimanual tasks (Steele & Uomini, 2009). To remind, these types of tasks are distinguished from the typical tasks used to establish handedness, which are unimanual (such as in writing). The term dominant hand, which is usually the right one, relates more to the concept of handedness than manual specialization.

Comment However, once more, one can ask to what extent an action dynamic or motor planning perspective makes sense as sufficient generalized primary evolutionary driver of lateralization? Is it the common function that can explain the priority in tool use or other manual behaviors drivers as selective pressures in lateralization evolution? The concept of motor planning or action dynamic can help explain the language function, which is dynamically planned motorically as much as is manual behavior, so in this sense the model works. However, earlier evolved species without motor planning capacities yet demonstrating lateralized structure and function exist. And so the dynamic action and motor planning model cannot work as a generalized common function across diverse species expressing lateralities. Further, adding in to these models a role for the motoric mirror system is intriguing but needs empirical verification. In this sense, as already explained, the activation-inhibition coordination model works and so is more elegant for the question asked relative to the planning model, the dynamic action one, the mirror neuron one, or any related ones.

Neither Tools nor Language First

Introduction The various models of drivers that have been proposed to explain the evolutionary origins of handedness and related manual and hemispheric specializations are not mutually exclusive, despite the search for a common function model that cuts across specializations and species. Cochet and Byrne (2013) summarized approaches to understanding especially how handedness had evolved, and examination of the models supports the need for a more generalized, integrating approach. Next, the present work reviews and comments on their approach to the question.

First, Cochet and Byrne (2013) indicated that human handedness is multidimensional and expresses much variability, for instance, in age, sex, and culture. For example, traditional societies vary in right-handedness (Faurie & Raymond, 2005), and, developmentally, the degree of right-hand asymmetries does not stabilize before middle childhood (McManus et al., 1988).

Gestures Communicative pointing gestures compared to object-related bimanual manipulative activities manifest less developmental change in humans in terms of the "strength" of right-handedness (Cochet & Vauclair, 2012; Vauclair & Cochet, 2013). For example, in infants, communicative pointing gestures for complex functions exhibit a strong right-hand preference (Cochet & Vauclair, 2010). Finally, for the hand preferred for tool use in infants and for communicative gestures, of the two types, the hand preference is less right-handed for tool use.

The same result applies to great ape non-human primates (Jacquet, Esseily, Rider, & Fagard, 2012). Further, intentional gestures in extant great ape non-human primates exhibit a right-side advantage (Hopkins, Pika, et al., 2012; Hopkins, Russell, & Schaeffer, 2012). Vauclair and Cochet (2013) conducted a cross-publication analysis of the strength of handedness for the two indicated behaviors with respect to human infants (Vauclair & Imbault, 2009), and human adults (Cochet & Vauclair, 2012) compared to chimpanzees (Meguerditchian, Vauclair, & Hopkins, 2010) and showed that the strength of handedness was strongest for both human ages. Versace and Vallortigara (2015) added that the review of Meguerditchian, Vauclair, and Hopkins (2013) found a pronounced preference for the right hand in great ape non-human primates for various gestures.

Comment The collection of results in these studies suggests that gestural communication might have been the primary manual driver of evolution of handedness, assuming developmental patterns can inform evolutionary phylogenesis. These results suggest that right-handedness and manual specialization might have evolutionary precursors but still strengthen through successive punctuated events in evolution, such as in the ancestral non-human primate-ancestral hominin split. However, note that there is insufficient developmental data in ancestral great ape non-human primates and hominins concerning handedness and manual specialization to determine whether developmental changes mark strengthening lateralization differences from one developmental period to the next in these ancestral species such that it is premature to map manual patterns developmentally across phylogeny and ontogeny in these regards. For example, did neoteny play a role in the evolution of handedness and related behaviors (Gould, 1977)?

My own approach to the question is that with careful selection of behaviors that fit the developing lateralized brain capacities in extant great ape non-human primates and contemporary humans, a better insight into the question can be obtained. Moreover, it should support an invariant model of lateralized functions over development, whether for modern humans or contemporary great ape non-human primates but with similar progressive stabilization over development of the behaviors involved. Finally, similar patterns in lateralized manual behavior and related specializations should be found in the evidence gathered about developing ancestral species in the phylogenesis that has led to human laterality.

Tool Use Again In explaining the developmental and evolutionary origins of lateralization, Cochet and Byrne (2013) indicated that genetic models are insufficient, as are environmental ones. In this regard, Cochet and Byrne (2013) referred to functional models with respect to handedness and hemispheric specialization as being important. The first hypothesis that they presented in these regards proposed that laterality evolved with the selection pressure of the differential demands on the hands in bimanual tool use. In support of this model, and has been described already above, Cochet and Byrne (2013) referred to the findings that contemporary chimpanzees and gorillas will use the right hand in actions toward inanimate compared to animate targets (Forrester et al., 2011, 2012) and that common neural processes in Broca's area, typically related to language production, are involved in tool use and language function (Higuchi et al., 2009). Among the evidence against the hypothesis for Cochet and Byrne (2013) is that, developmentally, gestural communication is more right-lateralized in infants compared to the case for tool use (e.g., Jacquet et al., 2012).

Gestures Again As for the gesture-first evolutionary hypothesis on the drivers of laterality in phylogenesis, especially as related to human and non-human primate ancestors, Cochet and Byrne (2013) cited imaging research that common neural networks are involved in language and gesturing (e.g., Xu, Gannon, Emmorey, Smith, & Braun, 2009). That is, gestural communication could have evolved in ancestors of human and non-human primates and then continued to evolve through intermediate steps into the current configuration that we have of left hemisphere cerebral dominance for language and related functions, as well as concordant manual lateralizations, including for gestures.

Counter evidence to the hypothesis was not offered, but Cochet and Byrne (2013) did refer the evolutionary precursors of language as perhaps involving vocalizations and gestures simultaneously (Hopkins & Cantero, 2003; Masataka, 2008). Cochet and Byrne (2013) continued to offer explanations of the relationship of gestures and manipulation, emphasizing that both reflect asymmetries related to actions generally. For example, as mentioned, both gestures and speech are associated with common networks in left lateralized inferior frontal and posterior temporal regions (e.g., Willems & Hagoort, 2007), and neurons have been found that are related to grasping movements both manually and with the mouth (Gentilucci & Dalla Volta, 2007).

Hierarchies For Cochet and Byrne (2013), one model that would encompass all lateralized activity is that the left hemisphere specializes for "processing hierarchical structures" of a certain degree of complexity in organization and execution, for example, in manipulation, gestures, and speech (Hauser, Chomsky, & Fitch, 2002).

The essential characteristic in these regards appears to be the organization of structured sequences in elements of action (e.g., Forrester & Quaresmini, 2013). Evidence that favors the hypothesis that laterality involves super-ordinate specialization for complex, hierarchical sequential organization includes the finding that right-side advantage has been found for chimpanzee tool use in nut-cracking (Lonsdorf & Hopkins, 2005). Cochet and Byrne (2013) did not present evidence against the hypothesis, although some of the evidence in support of it was shown to be inconsistent. The model resembles greatly the hierarchical model proposed in the Forrester research, as presented and analyzed above and also further below.

Goal State Left brain lateralization has been required to facilitate successful functional manipulation of objects by actions that are precisely timed sequences or skilled, serial motor movements deployed hierarchically to reach a goal state (Forrester et al., 2013). The movements represent an external physical "syntax" as objects are manipulated toward arriving at the goal state. Evidence for the hypothesis involve showing that all four surviving great ape species, and not just chimpanzees, as had been reviewed above in the Hopkins research, exhibit neuro-anatomical asymmetries in the left hemisphere that are homologous to the human Broca's area (e.g., Hopkins, Russell, & Cantalupo, 2007). Moreover, all four species are tool users.

Intentionality Another common function for manual manipulation, gesturing, and language that might underlie the evolution of laterality relates to intentionality (Cochet & Byrne, 2013). For example, gesture and speech processing related to communicative intentionality appears to engage a common neural network (Enrici, Adenzato, Cappa, Bara, & Tettamanti, 2011). Also, chimpanzees express a right-hand bias in throwing (Hopkins, Pika, et al., 2012; Hopkins, Russell, & Schaeffer, 2012), with associations found between throwing and communication ability. In evolution, throwing might have strengthened connections between the primary motor cortex and the homologue of Broca's area in applicable ancestral hominin ancestors.

Comment The search for general functions that could underlie tool use, gestures, and related activities have led Cochet and Byrne (2013) to visit models that concern higher-order functions that might underlie more advanced activities, such as dealing with a goal state and intentionality. However, for a general model of skills that apply differentially to the left and right hemispheres, one needs a concept that can apply differentially to the left and right hemispheres and, moreover, apply to species and behaviors that are less advanced yet still exhibit applicable left-right differences. In this sense, the lowest common denominator among language, tool use, communicative gestures, and so on seems to concern the presently promoted concept of activation-inhibition coordination. Further, this function can apply across the full range of behaviors, processes, and subsumed functions that are expressed differentially by sidedness. Finally, the concept lends itself to specifying both left- and right-side differences in all these regards, whether behaviorally or neuron/brain-wise, for example, by having more advanced skills lateralized to the right side (or left-brain part) and less advanced or different skills to the left side (or right-brain part).

Cochet and Byrne (2013) concluded that the various hypotheses about the evolution of laterality are not mutually exclusive, implying compatibility. Moreover, they might exist in parallel, implying independence in contribution (Liu, Stufflebeam, Sepulcrea, Heddena, & Buckner, 2009). For example, although the evolutionary time scales for different lateralizations might be contiguous, they might but have evolved for different adaptive reasons; the same independence might apply developmentally to hand preferences and hemispheric specializations (Cochet & Vauclair, 2010).

Note that Cochet and Byrne (2013) did not deal with theories of the evolution of lateralization that involved evidence related to pre-hominins and species that had evolved prior to great ape non-human primate ancestors, including invertebrates. There is rich evidence of lateralization in ancestor lineages extending well before the lateralized tool use in early hominins that has been dated to about 2.5 mya (Hopkins, 2006). Specifically, the work of Vallortigara and Rogers (e.g., Rogers & Vallortigara, 2017; Vallortigara & Versace, 2017) had addressed early evolutionary origins of lateralizations in social activities, for example. Only by examining the full gamut of lateralized species and by attempting to establish the phylogeny in the evolutionary process of its adaptive selection can adequate generalized models be constructed with sufficient validity. For lateralization, factors such as neural and information processing efficiency have been proposed in this regard, as have others not yet mentioned, as per the following.

Super-Structure The task of determining the evolutionary bases of lateralized behavior, brain function, and handedness is complicated by possible changes in evolutionary advantages over evolution. For example, it has been posited that, in prosimians who had engaged in clinging vertically to capture insects, the dominant (clinging) hand was the right one, although postural support in human infants, for example, to facilitate reaching, typically involves the left hand in the supportive role. That is, those early prosimians appeared to use the right hand for postural support while using the left hand for insect capture, unlike human infants, who reach and grasp for objects more with the right hand. MacNeilage (2014) elaborated that, based on the earlier right-hand postural support function in arboreal prosimians, later simians evolved different adaptations for the right hand (in manipulation, in right hand leading in bimanual coordination, in throwing, and in manual communication). This led to the evolution of right-hand tool use and to related left hemisphere language lateralization, together working in a "super-structure." The hypothesis is that, as evolution proceeded, an early type of manual specialization related to postural support allowed different types of manual skills to map on to it and the underlying differential hemisphere specializations associated with it. However, this took place with a behavior diametrically opposite in sidedness from one evolutionary epoch to the next.

Comment Although the sequence of evolutionary adaptations in this type of reasoning how postural support initially evolved as right-handed or dominant in arboreal non-human primate species and ended up in the human case as left-handed and not dominant makes logical sense, it appears convoluted even with the addition of the super-structure component integrating manual and language lateralizations. A more elegant and integrative solution involves the current concept of activation-inhibition coordination, which is a generalized behavior and brain function onto which can map any crucial behavior at any developmental or evolutionary epoch for dominant hand and cerebral preference. In this sense, an early postural support in evolution for arboreal species could have been very demanding according to this metric, even more so than in any fruit and related picking (e.g., insect prey capture) in the opposing free hand and so mapped onto the left hemisphere and its functional skills in this regard. Later in evolution, the postural support became less demanding relative to the manual manipulations, such as in tool use, and so was shunted to the left side (right hemisphere), with the tool use mapped onto the left hemisphere in its turn.

The description of this postural support by the right forelimb in early primates is quite consistent with this interpretation of the postural behavior involved. MacNeilage, Studdert-Kennedy, and Lindblom (1987) and MacNeilage (2007), as cited in Rogers et al. (2013), noted that in their postural origins theory of hemispheric specialization, the right hand was used for postural support because it required sustained, prolonged grasping with strength. This activity grasping appears consistent with the present theory of activation-inhibition coordination in behavior as underpinning the skills of the left hemisphere, despite the postural nature of the activity.

Prey/Predators Vallortigara and Versace (2017) explicated an evolutionary model of lateralized behavior and function that stretches over invertebrate and vertebrate evolution. The left side of the brain is involved in controlling well-established patterns of behavior required in ordinary and familiar circumstances. The right side of the brain, in contrast, is specialized for the detection of and response to stimuli that are unexpected, novel, dangerous, and requiring urgent, rapid response, as in dealing with predators (MacNeilage et al., 2009). Thus, the prey-seeking of predators is organized in the left part of the brain, unlike the case of predator escape in the prey, which is organized in the right part of the brain. According to Versace and Vallortigara (2015), this hypothesis has its origins in Andrew (2002), who postulated that lateralization emerged in the earliest vertebrates, in that their mouth was located on the left side of the head, thereby facilitating control perceptually and motorically in feeding.

Comment This model of hemispheric specialization and earlier left-right brain part specializations is *inconsistent* with the earliest fossil record of trilobites being either bitten on the tail to the right by predators or turning to the right to escape predators (see above). More likely, lateralization with respect to predator-prey behavior varied with the behavior required in the activity, as would be the case for any feeding and foraging behavior. The function of the activity should not be the determining factor of its lateralization but rather its behavioral and neural complexity, with the left hemisphere being more adaptive for more complex behavior in these regards.

Earlier evolved lateralities in escaping prey might have involved turning tendencies, generally, for example, to create a uniform pattern in groupings of prey so as not to isolate any and allow for easier predation. Also, turning tendencies relate to spatial navigation, which is generally a right-brain part function. Therefore, behavioral patterns in escape might require the specialized skills of the right side of the brain or neuronal architecture as much as the left.

Thus, the putative evolutionary selective pressure involving prey-predation might have contributed to the lateralization of left- and right-sided behavior and left and right neuronal architecture but for more general reasons than prey-predator relations themselves. Moreover, the side needed along these lines could vary by the nature of the escape behavior required. In this regard, if the activation-inhibition coordination model is correct, and the left side of the neural architecture even early in evolution works along these lines, turning to the right could reflect an activation-inhibition coordination skill programmed in the left part of the neuronal architecture and so might be right-side fostered behaviorally for this reason. Similarly, escape behaviors organized in the right hemisphere might be associated with that hemisphere because of a lesser complexity in terms of activation-inhibition coordination.

Social The predator-prey relationship is a powerful driver in evolution and is the mechanism behind well-known evolutionary arm races. In the end, it is a social phenomenon, especially for more complex species. As species evolved, and as the left and right parts of the brain took on structures akin to the left and right hemispheres, the social pressures on the evolution of differential functioning in the left and right brains continued. In this sense, a generalized pattern has been noted, with the right hemisphere evolved to have specific skills within a species socially, such as discrimination of social companions. In contrast, the left hemisphere became specialized to distinguish conspecifics vs. hetero-specifics (Vallortigara & Versace, 2017).

Comment Although plausible, the explanation of the social tendencies of the left and right hemispheres as involving essentially within and between species behavior belies the complexity in the two types of interaction. In the activation-inhibition coordination model, the left hemisphere is considered specialized for the complex synchronies of activation and inhibition, and the intra-species social dynamic must be the most complex manifestation of this function, even as much or more so than any language or manual production. In contrast, avoiding predation or otherwise dealing with other species might not evoke the social complexities evident in intra-species social interaction and so could be shunted to the right hemisphere (or will require more spatial and holistic processing and thus fit the activation-inhibition coordination skills of the right hemisphere, that is, global but more immediate and less ongoing integrations along these lines, as per the following).

Cognitive Consistent with the general thrust of the literature, for Vallortigara and Versace (2017), the right hemisphere is concerned with global and contextual representation of objects (think its spatial skills). The left hemisphere is concerned with rapidly assigning a stimulus to a category and in routine responses (Vallortigara, Rogers, & Bisazza, 1999). These skills presage later evolved skills related to them cognitively.

Comment Although, this conceptualization of the hemispheres captures some of the central ways they have been conceptualized as differential but complementary functional structures in the brain, there are some inconsistencies that should be pointed out. First, the left hemisphere also deals with objects through the manipulatory activities that it facilitates. Also, the actions so facilitated might be far from routine, as in the active exploration of novel objects. Indeed, one could argue that as activities become more automatic and chunked, they might be prone to right hemisphere control. Shifts in hemispheric control do take place, such as in good child readers who shift from right to left hemisphere strategies when they start to engage in phonemic decomposition of words, which is a demanding task (e.g., Gebauer et al., 2012; also see Nora et al., 2017, for a study of the particular issue; and see Xiao et al., 2016, for similar shifting in the language network in Chinese 3- to 5-year-olds). That is, hemispheric activity is not task-dependent but function-dependent and, as the task changes in demands in development, the hemisphere control could, too.

Ultimately, the presently proposed activation-inhibition coordination model could help explain these shifts in hemispheric task control developmentally. That is, it is the relative properties in this sense that determine when tasks are demanding enough to require a dynamic synchronization in these regards and so lead to left hemisphere control or when they are not demanding enough to require that anymore (or at all to begin with) and so lead to right-hemisphere control.

Attention Perhaps the most comprehensive model of left-right brain differences in function has been elaborated by Rogers et al. (2013). They have written a comprehensive survey of the literature over multiple extant animal species and also related to fossils and other evidence of evolution, to emerge with an integrated model of behavior and brain asymmetries. It includes the various specific models analyzed in the last few pages on the work of Vallortigara and colleagues, which include the coauthors of the book. Specifically, Rogers et al. (2013) proposed that the left hemisphere is specialized for the perceptual function of focal attending to stimuli features (local features, similarities, or invariances) in order to determine category or class to which stimuli belong. The left hemisphere engages in sustained response. Its perceptual properties prime more specific memory recall. The categories are products of rule-based strategies that are learned and followed. Noteworthy, Rogers et al. (2013) added that the organism engages in the left-hemisphere focal attention during routines so that it is not distracted easily by extraneous stimuli, while the left hemisphere keeps control, via the parasympathetic nervous system, of sympathetic nervous system activation and arousal. In addition, the left hemisphere can inhibit the right one and responds with its skills after the right hemisphere uses its own. The right hemisphere has the initial advantage, which is superseded by left hemisphere assessment and intervention and control or modulation of response, even to the point of determining which hand to use on a task. If required, the left hemisphere will assume full control and do so even if the situation is "disturbing."

In contrast, in Rogers et al.'s (2013) attentional model, the right hemisphere focuses on variable or novel stimuli, fixating on unique, minor differences between stimuli. However, in doing so, it can get easily distracted. Its attention is diffuse and global, allowing for the panoramic view of the spatial environment and its details in order to notice the miniscule stimuli differences mentioned. This aspect of its function translates into a corresponding global memory. In addition, the right hemisphere also "takes charge" in situations of emergency, with concomitant activation of the sympathetic system.

Comment Rogers et al.'s (2013) attentional model of hemispheric specialization covers more than attention. It includes basic perceptual processes, memory, and other cognitive aspects, with implications in relating to conspecifics and other species. It seems to cover a broad range of differential functions in the two hemispheres, but it might lack one overarching principle that differentiates them. It is more a compendium of what each hemisphere is specialized for rather than an attempt to explain the common principles underpinning the specializations in each hemisphere.

Careful examination of the properties attributed to the left hemisphere by Rogers et al. (2013) shows that they are consistent with the present overarching model of hemispheric specialization. For example, the sustaining and control aspect referred to as part of the left hemisphere's function correlate with the concept of activation-inhibition coordination. Similarly, for the right hemisphere, Rogers et al. (2013) refer to its more global properties, its role in emergency responses, etc., and these do not require such sophistication. That is, all this seems like a description of a lesser activation-inhibition coordination.

Predictivity Of the various models for lateralization that have been proposed, the one by Sainburg (2014) serves as a good bridge from others to my own. He has a good generic model of lateralized motor control and brain function, and it can be reworked into the concept of activation-inhibition coordination.

Sainburg (2014) presented a model of handedness and brain lateralization that is quite consistent with the one in the present work. In terms of motor control processes, he maintained that the left hemisphere specializes for predictive behavior of the effects of body/environment dynamics. This allows for energetic efficiency or precise trajectories and coordinated motor patterns. In contrast, the right hemisphere specializes for possible error control. This renders the left hemisphere biased for well-established behavior and the right hemisphere biased for unpredictable behavior. Overall, the left hemisphere leads in acuity, efficiency, precision, and coordination. In a transcranial direct current stimulation study (tDCS), Avenanti, Paracampo, Annella, Tidoni, and Aglioti (2017) also emphasized the predictive efficiency of the left hemisphere relative to the right hemisphere, specifically, in action prediction in relation to the inferior frontal cortex (IFC).

More recent research supports the information flow approach to left hemisphere specialization. In an fMRI study involving 4D spatio-temporal frequencies and granularity, Agcaoglu, Miller, Mayer, Hugdahl, and Calhoun (2016) found more fluctuations especially in the left hemisphere high-spatial frequency bands. They concluded that the left hemisphere processes information in smaller regions and more intensely than the right hemisphere, which is specialized for more diffuse, global, and smoother processing. Similarly, Avena-Koenigsberger et al. (2017) referred to a left hemisphere advantage in information segregation, in particular. Also, the left hemisphere could be activated for its functions, as in Avenanti et al. (2017) or can be disinhibited by individual characteristics, such as responding emotionally in a vicarious way to the pain of another (Giummarra et al., 2017).

Finally, in a peripheral electrodermal study, Bracco, Turriziani, Smirni, Giuseppa Mangano, and Oliveri (2017) not only showed that the left hemisphere is specialized for parasympathetic activity and the right hemisphere for sympathetic activity but also that the left hemisphere's motor cortical area has excitatory and inhibitory circuits that correlate positively, while the circuit activity in the right hemisphere motor cortical area is correlated negatively. These results support the differential activation-inhibition coordination model of the left and right hemispheres, as elaborated next.

Comment These concepts and research data that have been reviewed in the above fit Young's activation-inhibition coordination model (e.g., Young, 2011, 2016; Young, Bowman, et al., 1983). Specifically, Sainburg (2014) refers to the left hemisphere as being more coordinative and possessing properties that facilitate coordination, such as acuity and precision and intense and segregated information processing. Moreover, the left hemisphere is considered better in establishing predictions, which is a refined capacity consistent with activation-inhibition coordination. For example, predicting involves assembling ongoing patterns of body/environment dynamics and projecting the optimal pattern that should continue in context in these regards. Relative to the hypothesized right hemisphere skills, which especially concern brief activation-inhibition coordinations, not as complex ones, or inhibition by itself, prediction constitutes a poor fit with them.

Although Young's activation-inhibition coordination model has the advantage of being applicable across behavior and brain function, thus providing common metric to understand the fundamental processes underlying brain and behavior, as well as their lateralization, the model can be reworked to fit other concepts, and vice versa. This proviso applies especially to the new concepts related to networks and connectivities that have been applied both to brain and behavior, as well as lateralization.

Conclusion

Recent research keeps pushing back estimates of various aspects of the evolution of lateralization. For example, Marie et al. (2018) noted that the origin of cerebral specialization might relate to the common ancestor of humans, great apes, and non-human primates, which emerged about 30–40 mya. Their research focused on the planum temporale (PT), which is involved in the functional language network and is left lateralized in humans. They showed the same result in olive baboons. Durston, Peres, and Cohen (2018) related vertebrate handedness to embryonic counter-clockwise spiraling somatigenetic waves. Juan et al. (2018) related, in part, animal left-right asymmetry to an early-evolved regulator of acto-myosin chirality in the cytoskeleton (Myo1D; Myosin1D). Together, these results move the origins of left-right asymmetry to both the earliest phases embryonically and in our evolutionary history. Other research reminds of differential evolution of lateralization even with Hominidae. Regaiolli, Spiezo, and Hopkins (2018) did not find a one-sided cradling bias across Barbary macaque mothers in captivity. They suggested that there might be phylogenetic differences in maternal lateralization even within the primate order. Results in a study by Harris, Cárdenas, Stewart, and Almerigi (2018) support a left-hold selectivity bias in human mothers in this regard.

Multiple models have been proposed to explain both the relative advantages of the left and right hemispheres and how they evolved over species. As has been reviewed in the above, the models range from specific adaptations in specific domains, such as motor, social, planning, and the like, to more general factors, such as hierarchies and super-structures. However, despite the efforts to find broad models of hemispheric specialization by contemporary workers, the models that have been proposed are diverse, not consistent with all the evidence, limited in general applicability, and lacking in specificity. The present work supports an activation-inhibition dynamic in this regard, both in terms of how the hemispheres differ and how they evolved. The model is general enough to cover the simplest of behaviors and underpinning neural aspects that might be lateralized as well as more advanced ones. It allows for a unified approach to the development of lateralization in brain and behavior in humans and the evolution of lateralization from the earliest life forms onward exhibiting any kind of lateralization.

The activation-inhibition coordination model has implications for research and practice, because it asks that we consider the most parsimonious and broadest model proposed of lateralization differences in brain and behavior before advocating for other ones. This does not mean that other ones hold no relevance for the matter at hand, because they might constitute partial mini-theories that help elucidate lateralization processes and outcomes. That is, models might vary in complexity, generality, and specificity and so be complementary. That said, without considering the activation-inhibition coordination one as primary in understanding basis lateralization in brain and behavior, the more constrained ones might be too local and less generalizable. Furthermore, the activation-inhibition-coordination hypothesis of hemispheric specialization and related lateralizations lends itself to specific, testable predictions, such as the types of motor coordinations in early manual activity, as per Young's research. Also, it might help shed light on the nature of more complex functions and behaviors attributed to control by one hemisphere or the other, such as impulsivity in the right hemisphere, which can translate into difficulties with activation-inhibition coordination or outright inhibition in context.

The present portion of the book on causality, research with animals, and evolution concludes the literature undertaken on the development of lateralization and its evolution. The section on causality has emphasized the multi-factorial determinants of handedness, manual specialization, and hemispheric specialization, including genetically and environmentally. The section on genetics included material related to epigenetics and the section on the environment included material related to culture. The general approach in this section was consistent with the biopsychosocial model.

As for the section on animal research above, the first conclusion is that lateralization has been a ubiquitous and salient adapted trait in evolution stretching back multiple millions of years and into the earliest life forms. That said, the process of phylogenesis witnessed changes in the modality of lateralization and its underlying structure, for example, in the neuron and brain. Therefore, in terms of its expression in great ape non-human primates, the research is showing that the types of manual and communicative behaviors that are lateralized are consistent with the human model. Moreover, even the developmental research in these species now appears consistent with that model. Third, the nature of the specializations in these species speaks to models of the evolutionary origins of lateralization in brain and behavior in our hominin ancestors, for example, with respect to tool use and/or gestural communication in behavior and with respect to areas of the brain in these species that resemble Broca's and related areas in humans.

As with the first section of this portion of the book on handedness/lateralization development, which included human developmental research, this section of the book has considered that the concept of activation-inhibition coordination is an important one in understanding the causality of lateralization, as well as lateralization in extant great ape non-human primates and the evolution of lateralization. The section below continues by emphasizing this model for understanding better lateralization in brain and behavior; at the same time, it introduces other models that are pertinent in these regards, including with respect to networks.

References

Agcaoglu, O., Miller, R., Mayer, A. R., Hugdahl, K., & Calhoun, V. D. (2016). Increased spatial granularity of left brain activation and unique age/gender signatures: A 4D frequency domain approach to cerebral lateralization at rest. *Brain Imaging and Behavior, 10*, 1004–1014. https://doi.org/10.1007/s11682-015-9463-8

Andrew, R. J. (2002). The earliest origins and subsequent evolution of lateralization. In L. J. Rogers & R. J. Andrew (Eds.), *Comparative vertebrate lateralization* (pp. 70–93). Cambridge, UK: Cambridge University Press.

Andrew, R. J., Tommasi, L., & Ford, N. (2000). Motor control by vision and the evolution of cerebral lateralization. *Brain and Language, 73*, 220–235. https://doi.org/10.1006/brln.2000.2304

Avena-Koenigsberger, A., Mišić, B., Hawkins, R. X. D., Griffa, A., Hagmann, P., Goñi, J., et al. (2017). Path ensembles and a tradeoff between communication efficiency and resilience in the human connectome. *Brain Structure and Function, 222*, 603–618. https://doi.org/10.1007/s00429-016-1238-5

Avenanti, A., Paracampo, R., Annella, L., Tidoni, E., & Aglioti, S. M. (2017). Boosting and decreasing action prediction abilities through excitatory and inhibitory tDCs of inferior frontal cortex. *Cerebral Cortex*, 1–15. https://doi.org/10.1093/cercor/bhx041

Babcock, L. E., & Robison, R. A. (1989). Preferences of Palaeozoic predators. *Nature, 337*, 695–696. https://doi.org/10.1038/337695c0

Bard, J. (2017). *Principles of evolution: Systems, species, and the history of life*. New York: Garland Science.

Bisazza, A., Cantalupo, C., Robins, A., Rogers, L. J., & Vallortigara, G. (1997). Pawedness and motor asymmetries in toads. *Laterality: Asymmetries of Body, Brain and Cognition, 2*, 49–64. https://doi.org/10.1080/713754252

Bisazza, A., Lippolis, G., & Vallortigara, G. (2001). Lateralization of ventral fins use during object exploration in the blue gourami (Trichogaster trichopterus). *Physiology and Behavior, 72*, 575–578. https://doi.org/10.1016/S0031-9384(01)00417-6

Boesch, C., Kalan, A. A., Agbor, A., Arandjelovic, M., Dieguez, V., & Kühl, H. S. (2017). Chimpanzees routinely fish for algae with tools during the dry season in Bakoun, Guinea. *American Journal of Primatology, 79*. https://doi.org/10.1002/ajp.22613

Bracco, M., Turriziani, P., Smirni, D., Giuseppa Mangano, R., & Oliveri, M. (2017). Relationship between physiological excitatory and inhibitory measures of excitability in the left vs. right human motor cortex and peripheral electrodermal activity. *Neuroscience Letters, 641*, 45–50.

Cantalupo, C., & Hopkins, W. D. (2001). Asymmetric Broca's area in great apes. *Nature, 414*, 505. https://doi.org/10.1038/35107134

Cavanagh, T., Berbesque, J. C., Wood, B., & Marlowe, F. (2016). Hadza handedness: Lateralized behavior in a contemporary hunter-gatherer population. *Evolution and Human Behavior, 37*, 202–209. https://doi.org/10.1016/j.evolhumbehav.2015.11.002

Cochet, H., & Byrne, R. W. (2013). Evolutionary origins of human handedness: Evaluating contrasting hypotheses. *Animal Cognition, 16*, 531–542. https://doi.org/10.1007/s10071-013-0626-y

Cochet, H., & Vauclair, J. (2010). Pointing gestures produced by toddlers from 15 to 30 months: Different functions, hand shapes and laterality patterns. *Infant Behavior and Development, 33*, 432–442. https://doi.org/10.1016/j.infbeh.2010.04.009

Cochet, H., & Vauclair, J. (2012). Hand preferences in human adults: Noncommunicative actions versus communicative gestures. *Cortex, 48*, 1017–1026. https://doi.org/10.1016/j.cortex.2011.03.016

Corballis, M. C. (2002). *From hand to mouth: The origins of language*. Princeton, NJ: Princeton University Press.

Corballis, M. C. (2003). From mouth to hand: Gesture, speech, and the evolution of right-handedness. *Behavioral Brain Science, 26*, 198–208.

Corballis, M. C. (2014). Left brain, right brain: Facts and fantasies. *PLoS Biology, 12*, e1001767. https://doi.org/10.1371/journal.pbio.1001767

Corballis, M. C. (2017a). The evolution of lateralized brain circuits. *Frontiers in Psychology, 8*, 1021. https://doi.org/10.3389/fpsyg.2017.01021

Corballis, M. C. (2017b). A word in the hand: The gestural origins of language. In M. Mody (Ed.), *Neural mechanisms of language: Innovations in cognitive neuroscience* (pp. 199–218). New York: Springer SBM.

Corbetta, D. (2003). Right-handedness may have come first: Evidence from studies in human infants and nonhuman primates. *Behavioral and Brain Sciences, 26*, 217–218. https://doi.org/10.1017/S0140525X03320060

Duistermars, B. J., Chow, D. M., & Frye, M. A. (2009). Flies require bilateral sensory input to track odor gradients in flight. *Current Biology, 19*, 1301–1307. https://doi.org/10.1016/j.cub.2009.06.022

Durston, A. J., Peres, J., & Cohen, M. H. (2018). Spiral waves and vertebrate embryonic handedness. *Journal of Biosciences, 43*, 375–390. https://doi.org/10.1007/s12038-018-9756-3

Enrici, I., Adenzato, M., Cappa, S., Bara, B. G., & Tettamanti, M. (2011). Intention processing in communication: A common brain network for language and gestures. *Journal of Cognitive Neuroscience, 23*, 2415–2431. https://doi.org/10.1162/jocn.2010.21594

Fagot, J., & Bard, K. A. (1995). Asymmetric grasping response in neonate chimpanzees (Pan troglodytes). *Infant Behavior and Development, 18*, 253–255. https://doi.org/10.1016/0163-6383(95)90054-3

Fagot, J., & Vauclair, J. (1991). Manual laterality in non-human primates: A distinction between handedness and manual specialization. *Psychological Bulletin, 109*, 76–89.

Faurie, C., & Raymond, M. (2005). Handedness, homicide and negative frequency-dependent selection. *Proceedings of the Royal Society B: Biological Sciences, 272*, 25–28. https://doi.org/10.1098/rspb.2004.2926

Forrester, G., Rawlings, B., & Davila Ross, M. (2016). An analysis of bimanual actions in natural feeding of semi-wild chimpanzees. *American Journal of Physical Anthropology, 159*, 85–92. https://doi.org/10.1002/ajpa.22845

Forrester, G. H. (2017). Hand, limb, and other motor preferences. In L. J. Rogers & G. Vallortigara (Eds.), *Lateralized brain functions: Methods in human and non-human species* (pp. 121–152). New York: Springer SBM.

Forrester, G. S., Leavens, D. A., Quaresmini, C., & Vallortigara, G. (2011). Target animacy influences gorilla handedness. *Animal Cognition, 14*, 903–907. https://doi.org/10.1007/s10071-011-0413-6

Forrester, G. S., & Quaresmini, C. (2013). The right hand man: Manual laterality and language. In L. Regolin & D. Csermely (Eds.), *Behavioral lateralization in vertebrates: Two sides of the same coin* (pp. 125–141). Berlin, Germany: Springer.

Forrester, G. S., Quaresmini, C., Leavens, D. A., Mareschal, D., & Thomas, M. S. C. (2013). Human handedness: An inherited evolutionary trait. *Behavioural Brain Research, 237*, 200–206. https://doi.org/10.1016/j.bbr.2012.09.037

Forrester, G. S., Quaresmini, C., Leavens, D. A., Speizio, C., & Vallortigara, G. (2012). Target animacy influences chimpanzee handedness. *Animal Cognition, 15*, 1121–1127. https://doi.org/10.1007/s10071-012-0536-4

Frasnelli, E. (2017). Lateralization in invertebrates. In L. J. Rogers & G. Vallortigara (Eds.), *Lateralized brain functions* (pp. 153–208). New York: Springer SBM.

Frayer, D. W. (2016). OH-65: The earliest evidence for right-handedness in the fossil record. *Journal of Human Evolution, 100*, 65–72. https://doi.org/10.1016/j.jhevol.2016.07.002

Gebauer, D., Fink, A., Kargl, R., Reishofer, G., Koschutnig, K., Purgstaller, C., et al. (2012). Differences in brain function and changes with intervention in children with poor spelling and reading abilities. *PLoS One, 7*, e38201. https://doi.org/10.1371/journal.pone.0038201

Gentilucci, M., & Dalla Volta, R. (2007). The motor system and the relationships between speech and gesture. *Gesture, 7*, 159–177. https://doi.org/10.1075/gest.7.2.03gen

Giummarra, M. J., Poudel, G., Niu, A., Nicholls, M. E. R., Fielding, J., Verdejo-Garcia, A., et al. (2017). Emotion processing in persons who response vicariously towards others in pain: Disinhibited left-lateralized neural activity for threatening expressions. *Laterality: Asymmetries of Body, Brain, and Cognition*. https://doi.org/10.1080/1357650X.2017.1349781

Gould, S. J. (1977). *Ontogeny and phylogeny*. Cambridge, MA: Belknapp.

Güntürkün, O., & Ocklenburg, S. (2017). Ontogenesis of lateralization. *Neuron, 94*, 249–263. https://doi.org/10.1016/j.neuron.2017.02.045

Häberling, I. S., Corballis, P. M., & Corballis, M. C. (2016). Language, gesture, and handedness: Evidence for independent lateralized networks. *Cortex, 82*, 72–85. https://doi.org/10.1016/j.cortex.2016.06.003

Harris, L. J., Cárdenas, R. A., Stewart, N. D., & Almerigi, J. B. (2018). Are only infants held more often on the left? If so, why? Testing the attention-emotion hypothesis with an infant, a vase, and two chimeric tests, one "emotional," one not. *Laterality: Asymmetries of Body, Brain, and Cognition*. https://doi.org/10.1080/1357650X.2018.1475482

Hauser, M. D., Chomsky, N., & Fitch, W. T. (2002). The faculty of language: What is it, who has it, and how did it evolve? *Science, 298*, 1569–1579. https://doi.org/10.1126/science.298.5598.1569

Hews, D. K., & Worthington, R. A. (2001). Fighting from the right side of the brain: Left visual field preference during aggression in free-ranging male lizards (Urosaurus ornatus). *Brain, Behavior and Evolution, 58*, 356–361. https://doi.org/10.1159/000057576

Higuchi, S., Chaminadeb, T., Imamizua, H., & Kawato, M. (2009). Shared neural correlates for language and tool use in Broca's area. *Neuroreport, 20*, 1376–1381. https://doi.org/10.1097/WNR.0b013e3283315570

Hopkins, D. W. D., Meguerditchian, A., Coulon, O., Misiura, M., Pope, S., Mareno, M. C., et al. (2017). Motor skill for tool-use is associated with asymmetries in Broca's area and the motor hand area of the precentral gyrus in chimpanzees (Pan troglodytes). *Behavioral Brain Research, 318*, 71–81. https://doi.org/10.1016/j.bbr.2016.10.048

Hopkins, D. W. D., Russell, J., Cantalupo, C., Freeman, H., & Schapiro, S. (2005). Factors influencing the prevalence and handedness of throwing in captive chimpanzees (Pan troglodytes). *Journal of Comparative Psychology, 119*, 363–370. https://doi.org/10.1037/0735-7036.119.4.363

Hopkins, D. W. D., Russell, J., Freeman, H., Buehler, N., Reynolds, E., & Schapiro, S. J. (2005). The distribution and development of handedness for manual gestures in captive chimpanzees (Pan troglodytes). *Psychological Science, 16*, 487–493. https://doi.org/10.1111/j.0956-7976.2005.01561.x

Hopkins, W. D. (2006). Comparative and familial analysis of handedness in great apes. *Psychological Bulletin, 132*, 538–559. https://doi.org/10.1037/0033-2909.132.4.538

Hopkins, W. D. (2007). *Evolution of hemispheric specialization in primates*. Oxford, UK: Academic Press.

Hopkins, W. D., & Bard, K. A. (1993). Hemispheric specialization in infant chimpanzees (*pan troglodytes*): Evidence for a relation with gender and arousal. *Developmental Psychobiology, 26*, 219–235.

Hopkins, W. D., & Bard, K. A. (2000). A longitudinal study of laterality in chimpanzees (Pan troglodytes). *Developmental Psychobiology, 36*, 292–300.

Hopkins, W. D., Bard, K. A., & Griner, K. M. (1997). Locomotor adaptation and leading limb asymmetries in neonatal chimpanzees (Pan troglodytes). *International Journal of Primatology, 18*, 104–114.

Hopkins, W. D., & Cantero, M. (2003). From hand to mouth in the evolution of language: The influence of vocal behaviour on lateralized hand use in manual gestures by chimpanzees. *Developmental Science, 6*, 55–61. https://doi.org/10.1111/1467-7687.00254

Hopkins, W. D., & Fernandez-Carriba, S. (2002). Laterality in communicative behaviors in non-human primates: A critical analysis. In L. Rogers & R. Andrew (Eds.), *Comparative vertebrate lateralization* (pp. 445–479). Oxford, UK: Oxford University Press.

Hopkins, W. D., Phillips, K. A., Bania, A., Calcutt, S. F., Gardner, M., Russell, J., et al. (2011). Hand preferences for coordinated manual actions in 777 great apes: Implications for the evolution of handedness in hominins. *Journal of Human Evolution, 60*, 605–611. https://doi.org/10.1016/j.jhevol.2010.12.008

Hopkins, W. D., Pika, S., Liebal, K., Gardner, M. J., Meguerditchian, A., & Schapiro, S. J. (2012). Meta analysis of gesture handedness. In S. Pika & K. Liebal (Eds.), *Developments in primate gesture research* (pp. 93–112). Amsterdam: Benjamins.

Hopkins, W. D., Russell, J., & Cantalupo, C. (2007). Neuroanatomical correlates of handedness for tool use in chimpanzees (*Pan troglodytes*): Implication for the evolution of language. *Psychological Science, 18*, 971–977. https://doi.org/10.1111/j.1467-9280.2007.02011.x

Hopkins, W. D., Russell, J. L., & Schaeffer, J. A. (2012). The neural and cognitive correlates of aimed throwing in chimpanzees: A magnetic resonance image and behavioral study on a unique form of social tool use. *Philosophical Transactions of the Royal Society B, 367*, 37–47. https://doi.org/10.1098/rstb.2011.0195

Hori, M., Nakajima, M., Hata, H., Yasugi, M., Takahashi, S., Nakae, M., et al. (2017). Laterality is universal among fishes but increasingly cryptic among derived groups. *Zoological Science, 34*, 267–274. https://doi.org/10.2108/zs160196

Jacquet, A. Y., Esseily, R., Rider, D., & Fagard, J. (2012). Handedness for grasping objects and declarative pointing: A longitudinal study. *Developmental Psychobiology, 54*, 36–46. https://doi.org/10.1002/dev.20572

Juan, T., Géminard, C., Coutelis, J.-B., Cerezo, D., Polès, S., Noselli, S., et al. (2018). Myosin1D is an evolutionary conserved regulator of animal left-right asymmetry. *Nature Communications, 9*, 1942. https://doi.org/10.1038/s41467-018-04284-8

Karenina, K., Giljov, A., Baranov, V., Osipova, L., Krasnova, V., & Malashichev, Y. (2010). Visual laterality of calf-mother interactions in wild whales. *PLoS One, 5*, e13787. https://doi.org/10.1371/journal.pone.0013787

Koboroff, A., Kaplan, G., & Rogers, L. J. (2008). Hemispheric specialization in Australian magpies (*Gymnorhina tibicen*) shown as eye preferences during response to a predator. *Brain Research Bulletin, 76*, 304–306. https://doi.org/10.1016/j.brainresbull.2008.02.015

Laland, K. N. (2008). Exploring gene-culture interactions: Insights from handedness, sexual selection and niche-construction case studies. *Philosophical Transactions of the Royal Society B: Biological Sciences, 363*, 3577–3589. https://doi.org/10.1098/rstb.2008.0132

Leroy, F., Cai, Q., Bogart, S. L., Dubois, J., Coulon, O., Monzalvo, K., et al. (2015). New human-specific brain landmark: The depth asymmetry of superior temporal sulcus. *Proceedings of the National Academy of Sciences of the United States of America, 112*, 1208–1213. https://doi.org/10.1073/pnas.1412389112

Levy, J. (1977). The mammalian brain and the adaptive advantage of cerebral asymmetry. *Annals of the New York Academy of Sciences, 299*, 264–272. https://doi.org/10.1111/j.1749-6632.1977.tb41913.x

Lindell, A. K. (2013). Continuities in emotion lateralization in human and non-human primates. *Frontiers in Human Neuroscience, 7*, 464. https://doi.org/10.3389/fnhum.2013.00464

Lippolis, G., Bisazza, A., Rogers, L. J., & Vallortigara, G. (2002). Lateralisation of predator avoidance responses in three species of toads. *Laterality: Asymmetries of Body, Brain and Cognition, 7*, 163–183. https://doi.org/10.1080/13576500143000221

Lippolis, G., Westman, W., McAllan, B. M., & Rogers, L. J. (2005). Lateralisation of escape responses in the stripe-faced dunnart, Sminthopsis macroura (Dasyuridae: Marsupialia). *Laterality: Asymmetries of Body, Brain and Cognition, 10*, 457–470. https://doi.org/10.1080/13576500442000210

Liu, H., Stufflebeam, S. M., Sepulcrea, J., Heddena, T., & Buckner, R. L. (2009). Evidence from intrinsic activity that asymmetry of the human brain is controlled by multiple factors. *Proceedings of the National Academy of Sciences of the United States of America, 26*, 198–208. https://doi.org/10.1073/pnas.0908073106

Lonsdorf, E. V., & Hopkins, W. D. (2005). Wild chimpanzees show population-level handedness for tool use. *Proceedings of the National Academy of Sciences of the United States of America, 102*, 12634–12638. https://doi.org/10.1073/pnas.0505806102

Lozano, M., Estalrrich, A., Bondioli, L., Fiore, I., Bermúdez de Castro, J. M., Arsuaga, J. L., et al. (2017). Right-handed fossil humans. *Evolutionary Anthropology, 26*, 313–324. https://doi.org/10.1002/evan.21554

MacNeilage, P. F. (2007). Present status of the postural origins theory. *Special Topics in Primatology, 5*, 58–91. https://doi.org/10.1016/S1936-8526(07)05003-8

MacNeilage, P. F. (2014). Evolution of the strongest vertebrate rightward action asymmetries: Marine mammal sidedness and human handedness. *Psychological Bulletin, 140*, 587–609. https://doi.org/10.1037/a0034298

MacNeilage, P. F., Rogers, L. J., & Vallortigara, G. (2009). Origins of the left and right brain. *Scientific American, 301*, 60–67. https://doi.org/10.1038/scientificamerican0709-60

MacNeilage, P. F., Studdert-Kennedy, M. G., & Lindblom, B. (1987). Primate handedness reconsidered. *Behavioral and Brain Sciences, 10*, 247–263.

Maguire, E. A., Woollett, K., & Spiers, H. J. (2006). London taxi drivers and bus drivers: A structural MRI and neuropsychological analysis. *Hippocampus, 16*, 1091–1101. https://doi.org/10.1002/hipo.20233

Mangalam, M., Desai, N., & Singh, M. (2016). Division of labor: A democratic approach towards understanding manual asymmetries in non-human primates. *Current Science, 110*, 1630–1638.

Marchant, L. F., & McGrew, W. C. (2013). Handedness is more than laterality: Lessons from chimpanzees. *Annals of the New York Academy of Sciences, 1288*, 1–8. https://doi.org/10.1111/nyas.12062

Marie, D., Roth, M., Lacoste, R., Nazarian, B., Bertello, A., Anton, J.-L., et al. (2018). Left brain asymmetry of the planum temporale in a nonhominid primate: Redefining the origin of brain specialization for language. *Cerebral Cortex, 28*, 1808–1815. https://doi.org/10.1093/cercor/bhx096

Masataka, N. (2008). The gestural theory of and the vocal theory of language origins are not incompatible with one another. In N. Masataka (Ed.), *The origins of language: Unraveling evolutionary forces* (pp. 1–10). Heidelberg, Germany: Springer.

McGrew, W. C., & Marchant, L. F. (1997). On the other hand: Current issues in and meta-analysis of the behavioral laterality of hand function in non-human primates. *American Journal of Physical Anthropology, 104*, 201–232.

McManus, I. C., Sik, G., Cole, D. R., Mellon, A. F., Wong, J., & Kloss, J. (1988). The development of handedness in children. *British Journal of Developmental Psychology, 6*, 257–273.

Meguerditchian, A., Phillips, K. A., Chapelain, A., Mahovetz, L. M., Milne, S., Stoinski, T., et al. (2015). Handedness for unimanual grasping in 564 great apes: The effect on grip morphology and a comparison with hand use for a bimanual coordinated task. *Frontiers in Psychology, 6*, 1794. https://doi.org/10.3389/fpsyg.2015.01794

Meguerditchian, A., Vauclair, J., & Hopkins, W. D. (2010). Captive chimpanzees use their right hand to communicate with each other: Implications for the origins of the cerebral substrate for language. *Cortex, 46*, 40–48. https://doi.org/10.1016/j.cortex.2009.02.013

Meguerditchian, A., Vauclair, J., & Hopkins, W. D. (2013). On the origins of human handedness and language: A comparative review of hand preferences for bimanual coordinated actions and gestural communication in nonhuman primates. *Developmental Psychobiology, 55*, 637–650. https://doi.org/10.1002/dev.21150

Meunier, H., Vauclair, J., & Fagard, J. (2012). Human infants and baboons show the same pattern of handedness for a communicative gesture. *PLoS One, 7*, e33959. https://doi.org/10.1371/journal.pone.0033959

Nelson, E. L., & Kendall, G. A. (2018). Goal-directed tail use in colombian spider monkeys (ateles fusciceps rufiventris) is highly lateralized. *Journal of Comparative Psychology, 132*, 40–47. https://doi.org/10.1037/com0000094

Neufuss, J., Humle, T., Cremaschi, A., & Kivell, T. L. (2016). Nut-cracking behaviour in wild-born, rehabilitated bonobos (Pan paniscus): A comprehensive study of hand-preference hand grips and efficiency. *American Journal of Primatology, 79*, e22589. https://doi.org/10.1002/ajp.22589

Nora, A., Karvonen, L., Renvall, H., Parviainen, T., Kim, J.-Y., Service, E., et al. (2017). Children show right-lateralized effects of spoken word-form learning. *PLoS One, 12*, e0171034. https://doi.org/10.1371/journal.pone.0171034

Paracchini, S., & Scerri, T. (2017). Genetics of human handedness and laterality. In L. J. Rogers & G. Vallortigara (Eds.), *Lateralized brain functions: Methods in human and non-human species* (pp. 523–552). New York: Springer SBM.

Prieur, J., Pika, S., Barbu, S., & Blois-Heulin, C. (2017). Intraspecific gestural laterality in chimpanzees and gorillas and the impact of social propensities. *Brain Research, 1670*, 52–67. https://doi.org/10.1016/j.brainres.2017.05.033

Quaresmini, C., Forrester, G. S., Speizio, C., & Vallortigara, G. (2014). Social environment elicits lateralized behaviours in gorillas and chimpanzees. *Journal of Comparative Psychology, 128*, 276–284. https://doi.org/10.1037/a0036355

Regaiolli, B., Spiezo, C., & Hopkins, W. D. (2018). Asymmetries in mother-infant behaviour in Barbary macaques (Macaca sylvanus). *PeerJ, 6*, e4736. https://doi.org/10.7717/peerj.4736

Rogers, L. J. (2002). Lateralization in vertebrates: Its early evolution, general pattern and development. *Advances in the Study of Behavior, 31*, 107–162. https://doi.org/10.1016/S0065-3454(02)80007-9

Rogers, L. J., & Vallortigara, G. (2008). From antenna to antenna: Lateral shift of olfactory memory recall by honey bees. *PLoS One, 3*, e2340. https://doi.org/10.1371/journal.pone.0002340

Rogers, L. J., & Vallortigara, G. (2017). *Lateralized brain functions: Methods in human and non-human species*. New York: Springer SBM.

Rogers, L. J., Vallortigara, G., & Andrew, R. J. (2013). *Divided brains: The biology and behaviour of brain asymmetries*. Cambridge, MA: Cambridge University Press.

Rutledge, R., & Hunt, G. R. (2004). Lateralized tool use in wild New Caledonian crows. *Animal Behavior, 67*, 327–332. https://doi.org/10.1016/j.anbehav.2003.07.002

Sainburg, R. L. (2014). Convergent models of handedness and brain lateralization. *Frontiers in Psychology, 5*, 1092. https://doi.org/10.3389/fpsyg.2014.01092

Salmi, R., Rahman, U., & Doran-Sheehy, D. M. (2016). Hand preference for a novel bimanual coordinated task during termite feeding in wild western gorillas (Gorilla gorilla gorilla). *International Journal of Primatology, 37*, 200–212. https://doi.org/10.1007/s10764-016-9894-0

Shipton, O. A., El-Gaby, M., Apergis-Schoute, J., Deisseroth, K., Bannerman, D. M., Paulsen, O., et al. (2014). Left-right dissociation of hippocampal memory processes in mice. *Proceedings of the National Academy of Sciences, USA, 111*, 15238–15243. https://doi.org/10.1073/pnas.1405648111

Steele, J., & Uomini, N. (2009). Can the archaeology of manual specialization tell us anything about language evolution? A survey of the state of play. *Cambridge Archaeological Journal, 19*, 97–110. https://doi.org/10.1017/S0959774309000067

Suzuki, H., Thiele, T. R., Faumont, S., Ezcurra, M., Lockery, S. R., & Schafer, W. R. (2008). Functional asymmetry in Caenorhabditis elegans taste neurons and its computational role in chemotaxis. *Nature, 454*, 114–117. https://doi.org/10.1038/nature06927

Tommasi, L., Gagliardo, A., Andrew, R. J., & Vallortigara, G. (2003). Separate processing mechanisms for encoding of geometric and landmark information in the avian hippocampus. *European Journal of Neuroscience, 17*, 1695–1702.

Vallortigara, G. (2000). Comparative neuropsychology of the dual brain: A stroll through animals' left and right perceptual worlds. *Brain and Language, 73*, 189–219. https://doi.org/10.1006/brln.2000.2303

Vallortigara, G., & Rogers, L. J. (2005). Survival with an asymmetrical brain: Advantages and disadvantages of cerebral lateralization. *Behavioral and Brain Sciences, 28*, 575–589. https://doi.org/10.1017/S0140525X05000105

Vallortigara, G., Rogers, L. J., & Bisazza, A. (1999). Possible evolutionary origins of cognitive brain lateralization. *Brain Research Reviews, 30*, 164–175.

Vallortigara, G., Rogers, L. J., Bisazza, A., Lippolis, G., & Robins, A. (1998). Complementary right and left hemified use for predatory and agonistic behaviour in toads. *Neuroreport, 9*, 3341–3344.

Vallortigara, G., & Versace, E. (2017). Laterality at the neural, cognitive, and behavioral levels. In J. Call, G. M. Burghardt, I. M. Pepperberg, C. T. Snowdon, & T. Zentall (Eds.), *APA handbook of comparative psychology: Basic concepts, methods, neural substrate, and behavior* (Vol. 1, pp. 557–577). Washington, DC: American Psychological Association.

Vauclair, J., & Cochet, H. (2013). Hand preference for pointing and language development in toddlers. *Developmental Psychobiology, 55*, 757–765. https://doi.org/10.1002/dev.21073

Vauclair, J., & Imbault, J. (2009). Relationship between manual preferences for object manipulation and pointing gestures in infants and toddlers. *Developmental Science, 12*, 1060–1069. https://doi.org/10.1111/j.1467-7687.2009.00850.x

Versace, E., & Vallortigara, G. (2015). Forelimb preferences in human beings and other species: Multiple models for testing hypotheses on lateralization. *Frontiers in Psychology, 6*, 233. https://doi.org/10.3389/fpsyg.2015.00233

Willems, R. M., & Hagoort, P. (2007). Neural evidence for the interplay between language, gesture and action: A review. *Brain and Language, 101*, 278–298. https://doi.org/10.1016/j.bandl.2007.03.004

Wiper, M. L. (2017). Evolutionary and mechanistic drivers of laterality: A review and new synthesis. *Laterality: Asymmetries of Body, Brain and Cognition, 22*, 740–770. https://doi.org/10.1080/1357650X.2017.1291658

Xiao, Y., Brauer, J., Lauckner, M., Zhai, H., Jia, F., Margulies, D. S., et al. (2016). Development of the intrinsic language network in preschool children from ages 3 to 5 years. *PLoS One, 11*, e0165802. https://doi.org/10.1371/journal.pone.0165802

Xu, J., Gannon, P. J., Emmorey, K., Smith, J. F., & Braun, A. R. (2009). Symbolic gestures and spoken language are processed by a common neural system. *Proceedings of the National Academy of Sciences of the United States of America, 106*, 20664–20669.

Young, G. (2011). *Development and causality: Neo-Piagetian perspectives*. New York: Springer Science + Business Media.

Young, G. (2016). *Unifying causality and psychology: Being, brain and behavior*. Cham, Switzerland: Springer International Publishing.

Young, G., Bowman, J. G., Methot, C., Finlayson, M., Quintal, J., & Boissonneault, P. (1983). Hemispheric specialization development: What (inhibition) and how (parents). In G. Young, S. J. Segalowitz, C. M. Corter, & S. E. Trehub (Eds.), *Manual specialization and the developing brain* (pp. 119–140). New York: Academic Press.

Young, G., Corter, C. M., Segalowitz, S. J., & Trehub, S. E. (1983). Manual specialization and the developing brain: An overview. In G. Young, S. J. Segalowitz, C. M. Corter, & S. E. Trehub (Eds.), *Manual specialization and the developing brain* (pp. 3–12). New York: Academic Press.

Chapter 8
Standard Laterality Models

Abstract The last two chapters of the first part of the book on lateralization development and its causation explore further the range of the author's models on the question. First, it considers in depth once more the concept of activation-inhibition coordination, but less from a developmental point of view and more in terms of adult research and models based on that research. It begins with some developmental research and focuses on research on inhibition. The adult research also examines the inhibitory function in the left and right hemispheres. For example, the research shows that simpler inhibitory activities are localized in the right hemisphere, which is consistent with Young's hypothesis that the left hemisphere is specialized for more complex inhibitory skills, that is, in terms of activation-inhibition coordination. The chapter also examines the generalized role of activation-inhibition coordination, that is, independent of laterality/lateralization, in orchestrating both behavior and brain function. For example, it examines research on neuronal activity fitting an excitation-inhibition dynamic. Also, it examines research on difficulties in inhibition found in certain disorders, such as attention deficit hyperactivity disorder (ADHD). The chapter continues by exploring other models in relation to laterality, especially network ones. It then turns to my own work on networked causality and different hierarchical levels in systems, illustrating how such modeling might help in laterality conceptualization, for example, by complementing the activation-inhibition coordination model. The chapter terminates by examining more closely the biopsychosocial model and how it might relate to lateralization.

Models, Discussion, Implications, Conclusions

Models

Introduction

This last part of the first portion of the book presents elaborations of innovative ideas relevant to understanding the phenomenology and causation of brain-behavior relations, generally, and lateralized functions and structures, specifically. It begins

G. Young, *Causality and Development*,
https://doi.org/10.1007/978-3-030-02493-2_8

with the concept of activation-inhibition coordination, which has been underscored to the present juncture of the book as a viable general model of brain-behavior relations. Then, it presents more innovative ideas related to networks/yoking, the biopsychosocial model, and generic change processes.

The goal of the present work is not only to examine lateralization from novel perspectives but also to buttress the concept of activation-inhibition coordination as central to it. This section helps toward realizing that goal by even examining brain and behavior generally that fits this concept (not just in terms of lateralization). Therefore, the upcoming portion of the present work asks the reader to broaden perspectives and consider development, generally, as per Young (2016), in order to bring in innovative perspectives on handedness, manual specialization, and hemispheric specialization. For example, these aspects of brain and behavior lend themselves to study from the perspective of attractors, but little contemporary work examines the relationship between lateralization and attractors. Also, inhibition is a common concept in the study of behavior and brain, and so examination of non-lateralized conceptualization and research can only help in understanding the application of the activation-inhibition coordination model to differential left and right manual and hemispheric specialization and related lateralizations.

Activation-Inhibition Coordination

This section of the book presents further approaches to the concept of activation-inhibition coordination in brain and behavior. The first part discusses the concept with respect to developmental lateralization research and the second with respect to its generalized application to the causality of the lateralization in brain and behavior, including in evolution.

Lateralization

Introduction

Young (1990a, 1990b, 2011, 2016) and colleagues (Young, Bowman, et al., 1983; Young & Gagnon, 1990; Young, Segalowitz, Misek, Alp, & Boulet, 1983) argued that hemispheric specialization development reflects coordination of activation and inhibition in behavior and in the brain. For example, the right hand reaches better early in life because it can better activate and inhibit the muscles and movements involved. Also, the left brain even early in life has the skill to better coordinate subtle and refined sequences, such as in information processing and behavior organization. The right hemisphere also has inhibitory skills, but these are for less refined sequences or for full-scale inhibitory action. Thus, the model presented indicates that one can equally represent both behavioral and brain organization with the concept of dynamic and ongoing activation-inhibition coordination and that the left hemisphere excels in these regards, including in coordinating the right hemisphere through this process, including from early in life and onward (see Table 5.1).

The concept of activation-inhibition coordination is a novel one. Although not ideal, one manner of verifying this conjecture is to conduct searches of the term on scientific search engines. A PsycINFO and all related ProQuest database searches, conducted on August 27, 2017, revealed not one publication with this or an equivalent term, nor did a Google Scholar one. A Google search yielded almost exclusively Young's book publications (Young, 1997, 2011, 2016) on the topic, with isolated research on motor control, as well. The concept of activation-inhibition coordination is noteworthy, because generally it reflects the nature of behavioral expression control and restraint and, also, its underlying structural and functional neuronal and cerebral architecture and organization. Moreover, it affords ways of differentiating abnormal from normal behavior and brain organization, individual differences in normal and abnormal behavior and related brain organization, and general questions related to behavior and brain, such as in evolution.

Development

Similar dynamic models have been applied to understanding the differences between hemispheres. Streri and de Hevia (2015) argued that there are models in these regards related to which type of information each hemisphere deals with and, also, how each hemisphere processes information consistent with its specialization. They noted that Caplan and Kinsbourne (1976) underscored that the left hemisphere might be specialized for a different type of inhibition than the right hemisphere, with the left hemisphere inhibiting the right hemisphere when they are both activated at the same time or when they are competing on the same task.

Along the same lines, on a midline-reaching task, among others, D'Souza, Cowie, Karmiloff-Smith, and Bremner (2017) found that infants in the first year of life gradually decrease extraneous movements in nonacting limbs during unimanual actions. For example, there was less spatiotemporal coupling in the movements of the acting and nonacting arms. Examples of extraneous movements included clenching, wiggling, twisting, and jerking. This reflects an increased inhibitory control in manual behavior, although the study did not refer to lateralized findings.

At the motor level, Barral, De Pretto, Debû, and Hauert (2010) referred to activation and inhibition in control of developmental bimanual movements. They noted that activation could involve the release of inhibition. Note that this type of reasoning is consistent with neuronal models, for instance, of pain (Melzack & Wall, 1965), in which inhibition of inhibition leads to activation. Also, Watanabe, Homae, and Taga (2011) studied developmental changes in inhibitory control in body movements from 2 to 3 months.

There are developmental models that place inhibition as a primary function in growth, in general. It is worth reviewing this approach as a prelude to further discussion of the activation-inhibition coordination model. For example, Bardikoff and Sabbagh (2017) supported the view that inhibition is one of the three primary executive functions (EF) both in children and adults, the other two concerning set shifting flexibly and updating in working memory. Research with preschoolers generally support a unitary factor that includes these three aspects, and then it splits in middle childhood into updating and inhibition/shifting, with differentiation of the latter taking place in early adolescence. Already developmentally, the inhibition function in the executive function model is associated with regions of the right hemisphere (Collette et al., 2005), while EF generally is specialized in frontal regions the left hemisphere (e.g., Darki & Klingberg, 2015). Similarly, Houdé and Borst (2015) reported that right hemisphere inhibition (in the right inferior frontal gyrus, IFG, among other regions) facilitated number conservation problems in 7-year-olds (Houdé & Borst, 2014), while inhibitory skills generally facilitate cognitive developmental transitions from one Piagetian developmental stage to the next and the left IFG is involved in overcoming intuitive forms of thinking in adults.

In this regard, Arsalidou and Pascual-Leone (2016) argued that engaging in problem-solving within one's limit (of attention) facilitates left hemisphere activation. Also, they cited research by Gilsbach et al. (2012) that supported an activation/inhibition capacity in the left frontal gyrus of children performing an attention task. Specifically, in an fMRI study, children lacking the dopamine D4 receptor gene (*DRD4*) with the 7-repeat allele, which is related to attentional inhibition, compared to those who had the allele, expressed lower neural activation.

Adults

Models There are models of hemispheric differences in inhibitory skills that are reviewed below. Typically, the research supports a superior right hemisphere inhibitory skill relative to the left hemisphere. However newer models are approaching the general tone and specifics of the activation-inhibition coordination model that has been proposed by Young and colleagues.

For example, more recent models might not refer to left hemisphere inhibitory skills directly, but they might be implied. In this regard, as reviewed in Tops, Quirin, Boksem, and Koole (2017), Rogers, Vallortigara, and Andrew (2013) referred to the left hemisphere as being better for sustaining responses by shielding from distractors. The behaviors are selected in light of stimuli, goals are selected, and responses persist because of this ability.

Dien (2008) referred to the left hemisphere as "proactive" and the right hemisphere as "reactive." Tops, Boksem, Quirin, and Koole (2014) differentiated the proactive-active model of hemispheric specialization into its dorsal and ventral components. Further, Tops et al. (2017) referred to the left hemisphere as being more "active" in the skill of coping than the right hemisphere.

Note that characterization of the left hemisphere as being more proactive and better in coping is consistent with the activation-inhibition coordination model because the planning, strategizing, problem-solving, and goal selection, guidance, and implementation that are involved would require refined activation processes in concert with ongoing suppression of interference, distraction, and the like.

Research As for adult research, Reid and Serrien (2012) found that, on a bimanual task, right handers showed increased inhibitory processing consistent with left hemisphere control, and intra- and inter-hemispheric inhibitory asymmetries, that is, enhanced within- and cross-hemispheric processing (also see Tzourio-Mazoyer, Perrone-Bertolotti, Jobard, Mazoyer, & Baciu, 2017, in this regard). Kurth, Mayer, Toga, Thompson, and Luders (2013) found that better right-hand pegboard task performance was associated with greater callosal (isthmus and posterior mid-body) thickness. The authors concluded that the left hemisphere has more of a role to play in inter-hemispheric inhibition than the right hemisphere. Generally, the left hemisphere appears better at trans-callosal inhibition than the right hemisphere (Genç, Ocklenburg, Singer, & Güntürkün, 2015).

Gallea et al. (2013) elaborated this notion in a study of *RAD51* haplo-insufficiency patients expressing excessive congenital/mirror movements. They found deficiencies in inter-hemispheric inhibition and bilateral cortical activation of primary motor areas during intended unimanual movement. They related their results to a lack of inhibition from abnormal input to receptive inter-neurons. Along these lines, in a mouse study, Talpalar et al. (2013) investigated the role of both excitatory and commissural neurons that appear involved in right-left motor coordination.

Also, Dambacher et al. (2014) found different associations across certain inhibitory skills and certain brain regions, such that inhibitory skills are varied and, as well, their locations in the left and right hemispheres are varied. Specifically, using fMRI, among other findings, they found that action "restraint" was associated with right anterior insula (AI) and right superior frontal gyrus activation. Also, action "cancelation" was associated with the right AI and with the right MFG. Note that the research needs further elaboration. For example, Serrien and Sovijärvi-Spapé (2013), using EEG coherence, found that the left hemisphere and not the right appeared specialized for the inhibitory functions related to response selection and response withholding. However, the atlas of human cognition project in relation to large-scale probabilistic function/anatomy allowed for flexible decoding of whole brain images (Rubin et al., 2017), and the topic of inhibitory control was related to the right ventral AI, as per the findings of Aron, Robbins, and Poldrack (2004).

Some workers contend that the right inferior frontal cortex (IFC) is more associated with attention than inhibition (per Shallice & Cipolotti, 2018; citing Hampshire, Chamberlain, Monti, Duncan, & Owen, 2010; Picton et al., 2007; Shallice, Stuss, Picton, Alexander, & Gillingham, 2007; Tsuchida & Fellows, 2013). However, recent research points to a role for the right IFC in action suppression, supporting the Aron team model, or at least a variant of it. Specifically, van Campen, Kunert, van den Wildenberg, and Ridderinkhof (2017) used repetitive transcranial magnetic stimulation over the IFC to show that this procedure impairs the suppression of conflicting action impulses during conflict situations in the Simon task in order that the correct response alternative is expressed. Generally, according to van Campen et al. (2017), the selective suppression on this type of task reflects a sub-process of a more generic suppression of action, or action override, in the right IFC (citing Aron, 2011; Levy & Wagner, 2011; Verbruggen, Aron, Stevens, & Chambers, 2010).

Other research by Aron and co-workers is differentiating intra-right hemisphere inhibitory skills. Specifically, Bartoli, Aron, and Tandon (2018) related the right inferior frontal cortex (IFC) to outright stopping, while the right anterior insula (AI) is engaged in more general processes, such as arousal, saliency determination, and adjusting behavior. These researchers used stereo-electro-encephalography (SEEG) to measure broadband gamma activity (BGA) in a stop signal paradigm measuring stop signal reaction time (SSRT). Ocklenburg et al. (2017) found similar results in measuring the P3 phase of the event-related potential (ERP) to left and right visual field tachistoscopically presented stimuli in the No Go portion of a Go-No Go task.

The study by D'Alberto, Funnell, Potter, and Garavan (2017) might help clarify the contradictory results in these latter studies. They noted that the right hemisphere might be specialized for inhibitory function, as revealed by superior inhibitory skills (accuracy) in a patient with corpus callosum agenesis according to performance on three inhibitory tasks (Go-No Go, Single Choice Stop Signal, Forced Choice Stop Signal). However, in their literature review, D'Alberto et al. (2017) noted that, although the research generally supports the right hemisphere as the seat of inhibition (and the right inferior central gyrus (IFG) area, in particular in this regard), the literature also supports at least a supplementary contribution of the left hemisphere in inhibitory control (as argued in Hirose et al., 2012, and for the left IFG, in particular), with the left hemisphere even playing a more critical role than the right in inhibition as task complexity increases (Swick, Ashley, & Turken, 2008).

In this regard, Vallence, Smalley, Drummond, and Hammond (2017) found that long-interval intra-cortical inhibition circuits within the primary motor cortex are more sensitive and powerful of primary motor cortex output in the dominant hemisphere in young adults (although the specialization is lost in older adults). This type of inhibition allows for better selectivity of motor activity during movements requiring dexterity. The process includes surround inhibition, which controls for excitation of muscles that would interfere with the required muscle activity. It is facilitated by the mediation of and inhibitory inter-neurons and $GABA_B$ (gamma-aminobutyric acid) receptor activity. [For further research on the role of GABA in inhibition and its relationship to glutamate in activation in neuronal function, see below.]

Moreover, other research being published further differentiates right hemisphere inhibitory skills and right versus left inhibitory skills. Floegel and Kell (2017) studied differential planning and manual control processes during avatar movements involving unimanual control of a visual cursor by grip force. Specifically, over experimental conditions that varied task demands temporally, spatially, etc., the participants, who were lying in an fMRI scanner, could control online the spatial position of the cursor on a reference trajectory by altering grip force. The researchers measured fMRI in their healthy participants while they completed the task.

The results of the Floegel and Kell (2017) investigation revealed a relative advantage for each hemisphere in the behavior elicited. When planning processes related to sensory information were predominant in the task completed, for spatial planning, the right hemisphere was more activated. This occurred in the temporo-parietal junction according to the fMRI. In temporal planning, in contrast, the left hemisphere was more activated. Specifically, left hemisphere specialization was evident for temporal processing of the sensory information, for example, in the middle temporal gyrus (MTG). As for the online motor phase of the task completed, the left hemisphere was more activated, especially in the intra-parietal sulcus (IPS) region. Generally, then, the left hemisphere excelled in the spatial task involved, and the authors attributed the findings to the left hemisphere's local versus global processing advantage.

As for other research differentiating left and right hemisphere inhibitory control, Zhang, Geng, and Lee (2017) conducted a meta-analysis of 225 fMRI studies on neural correlates related to cognitively-mediated response inhibition. They approached the review from the perspective of finding large-scale neural network correlates rather than regional specializations. The three types of inhibition reviewed related to interference resolution, action withholding, and action cancelation. All three tasks involve suppression of an inappropriate behavior while initiating/executing a better one in the context at hand. Generally, across tasks, the right hemisphere held an advantage, with this taking place in the inferior frontal gyrus, which extended into the insula, medial cingulate, paracingulate gyri, and superior parietal gyrus.

As for the core neural systems involved across these regions, they appeared to involve the fronto-parietal network and the ventral attention network. Interestingly, the associations for the three response inhibition tasks differed, and even by hemisphere. For example, the three tasks appear to function in steps in processing, with the interference resolution one first. The regions associated with it are in the left hemisphere, not the right (the pre-supplementary motor area (pre-SMA) and superior parietal gyrus). These latter two left hemisphere regions are associated with the ventral attention network; the other two response inhibition tasks are associated with regions concerning fronto-striatal circuitry.

Recent Inhibitory Modeling Finally, in this fast-developing field, in contemporary research, the right hemisphere is associated more with inhibition and related processes, such as regulation, relative to prior conceptions of it in terms of withdrawal or avoidance motivation. This research spans trans-cranial stimulation research (Kelley, Hortensius, Schutter, & Harmon-Jones, 2017; Kelley & Schmeichel, 2016), revised BIS questionnaire research (Gable, Neal, & Threadgill, 2017; Neal & Gable, 2017), and BIS questionnaire and goal conflict situations (Wacker, Chavanon, Leue, & Stemmler, 2008, 2010; Wacker, Heldmann, & Stemmler, 2003). Note that the cranial stimulation research as described in the review by Kelley et al. (2017) has the advantage of approaching causality because the stimulation can activate or suppress activity in the hemispheres, depending on whether it is cathodal or anodal, respectively. Also, note that the BIS-BAS model referred to by these latter research groups concerns the revised one, as presented in Gray and McNaughton (2000).

The extensive literature review conducted by Gable et al. (2017) in support of a right hemisphere frontal region inhibition specialization included both motoric studies (e.g., Stramaccia et al., 2015) and others related to behavioral characteristics, such as impulsivity, positive urgency, lack of premeditation, sensation seeking, and lack of perseverance, self-control, and error monitoring (e.g., Gable, Mechin, Hicks, & Adams, 2015; Mechin, Gable, & Hicks, 2016; Schmeichel, Crowell, & Harmon-Jones, 2016). [However, recent research does not always clearly support the model proposed by Gable et al. (2017). For example, the left hemisphere (in the amygdala) has been associated with adaptive emotional skills (Frühholz, Schlegel, & Grandjean, 2017); and mixed results were reported for impulsivity relative to hemispheric differentiation (although with the right hemisphere predominant, Hirjak et al., 2017); but see Wacker (2018) associating extraversion to the right hemisphere.]

Comment The various newer inhibitory models of the left and right hemispheres rarely attribute differential inhibitory skills to the hemispheres, unlike the case for Young's activation-inhibition coordination model of differential left and right hemispheric functioning. For example, Wacker and colleagues refer to the sensitivity to inhibition in the right hemisphere, Gable and colleagues to the regulatory capacities of the right hemisphere, and Kelley and colleagues to the superior inhibitory skills of the right hemisphere. These models of cerebral asymmetries are general ones that collectively refer to emotional, motivational, and behavioral (approach-withdrawal) processes, as well, and others like them refer to information processing aspects, such as inhibition of distractors (Grimshaw & Carmel, 2014). So they cover much psychological ground in attempting to find generalized inhibitory skills related to hemispheric functioning. Further they might specify particular regions of the right hemisphere that are specialized for inhibitory functions, and other models of differences in cerebral lateralization refer to larger entities and their properties that differ across the hemispheres, such as in network models and their local versus global, and small-world, tight versus more diffuse organizational capacities (see above, e.g., Tzourio-Mazoyer et al., 2017).

Moreover, there is antecedent work related to hemispheric specialization in terms of inhibition, for example, Jasper and Raney (1937), as reviewed in Young's work (Young, Bowman, et al., 1983), and antecedent work related to the role of inhibition in differential left-right frontal asymmetry models of motivation/emotional valence, as reviewed in Grimshaw and Carmel (2014, e.g., Jackson, Mueller, Dolski, Dalton, Nitschke, Urry, Rosenkranz, Ryff, Singer, & Davidson, 2003, Terzian, 1964).

That said, the Grimshaw and Carmel (2014) model of hemispheric specialization is the only one of the newer ones that approximates that of Young's activation-inhibition coordination model by ascribing to the two hemispheres different yet complementary roles to the hemispheres. Yet, in Grimshaw and Carmel (2014) model, the inhibition quality remains the same, that of inhibiting distractors. This is another valence model, this time in relation to the quality of the distractors inhibited differentially in the hemispheres. To remind, in their model, the frontal cortex of the left hemisphere inhibits negative distractors and the right frontal cortex inhibits positive ones, with respective examples when hemispheric activity is "low," involving left hemisphere difficulty in disengaging attention from negative stimuli, as happens in depression, and right hemisphere difficulty in inhibiting positive distractions, as happens in addiction.

As much as the Grimshaw and Carmel (2014) model appears applicable to the question at hand of differentiating the cerebral hemispheres in terms of underlying inhibitory differences, it does not include the activity component found in the Young model. Behavior and related processes, as in information processing, are not merely the outcomes of or involve unique inhibitory factors because there are primary activation or excitatory ones, as well, along with their coordination in adaptive functioning. Moreover, distractors and distractions might be too specific in terms of what is inhibited, although, granted, the Grimshaw and Carmel (2014) model addresses executive functioning, in particular. Generally, inhibitory function aims at removing or controlling interfering effects of any aspect of behavior and related processes, such as in overflow motor movements, and not just executive-related complications.

As for the other more recent models under discussion, the one by Wacker and colleagues relates a right hemisphere inhibitory specialization to a left hemisphere activation one, so indirectly concerns both activation and inhibition in coordination. However, the Young model links activation and inhibition in coordination in both hemispheres, but with a better skill set in this regard in the left hemisphere (and with a better inhibitory stopping in the right hemisphere, for example). In terms of the Gable and Neal approach to the question of the right hemisphere inhibitory advantage, they relate their results to core right hemisphere personality attributes, which places inhibition front and center in these regards. However, a more complete model would specify how activation-inhibition coordination skills are different in the two hemispheres and come to influence the full range of behaviors, moods, emotions, affects, motivations, and response tendencies/preferences and styles to the point that a more left hemisphere or more right hemisphere preference or proclivity might characterize any one individual.

Moreover, a comprehensive model of the left and right hemisphere asymmetry differences would be able to translate, reinterpret, or otherwise transpose in its terms findings in the field seemingly unrelated to the underlying dimension that it posits for the differentiation. In this regard, for the present proposal of an activation-inhibition coordination model of differential left and right hemisphere specialization, consider the study by Fujino et al. (2017). They conducted a social-conflict vignette and a resting state fMRI (RS-fMRI) study using intrinsic fractional amplitude of low frequency fluctuations (fALFF). They administered a Cognitive Flexibility Scale (CFS; Martin & Rubin, 1995) and an Implicit Association Test (IAT; Greenwald, McGhee, & Schwartz, 1998) to measure explicit and implicit cognitive flexibility, respectively. These styles have been related to rational and experiential thinking styles, respectively, which were measured by the Rational-Experiential Inventory (REI; Pacini & Epstein, 1999). As per their Fig. 8.3, they found that the level of explicit cognitive flexibility and implicit cognitive flexibility were not only associated with thinking style, as hypothesized, but also with fALFF-determined spontaneous neural activity. Specifically, the former was associated with more neural activity in the left lateral prefrontal cortex (LPFC) and the latter with activity in the right cerebellum.

The results in the Fujino et al. (2017) study could be related to a more explicit flexible and rational cognitive style in the left hemisphere, or even an attitudinal, affective style, as in the left hemisphere being more positive, approach-related, etc. However, it could also be that the underlying foundation to the left hemisphere advantage in this flexible and rational style relates to activation-inhibition coordination. In this regard, navigating socially conflicted situations equitably would seem to require the fine-tuned and rapid adjustments in adaptation that would be facilitated by a hemisphere specialized for proper activation while controlling for interfering, distracting, or otherwise prejudicial and undermining behavior for the required thinking, behaving, and problem-solving at hand. In this sense, having a hemisphere that can engage in this type of coordination, while keeping at bay any interference from the other hemisphere's less refined skills in these regards, while allowing it to apply its outright inhibitory skills, when required, would seem advantageous both in the online sense and evolutionarily.

Further, an adequate model that cuts across other models, explaining well their findings, also points out their inconsistencies while explaining them, and it makes predictions that helps support it relative to other models. In these two regards, the activation-inhibition coordination model of differential left and right hemisphere skill sets stands apart. For example, it is the only model that can explain in its terms all other models both in development and in evolution for handedness, manual specialization, and hemispheric specialization. Also, it leads to strong predictions of what the left and right sides of the body and brain should be doing differently, and even for domains difficult to integrate in the literature, such as left-right hemisphere differences in social behavior. Specifically for the latter, it is not that the left hemisphere mediates positive emotions, approach, or other constructive aspects of other renditions of the valence and related models. Rather, I maintain that its skills are used in complex social situations, even if negative, when refined, subtle, and more than momentary activation-inhibition coordinations are called for, such as in real-life social conflict situations in which the goal is to somehow navigate the dispute and continue on socially.

Thus, we can translate the explicit flexible and rational cognitive or social conflict style evident in the results of Fujino et al. (2017) for the left hemisphere as one that can better enable continuation of the social interaction in the longer term through its better coping strategies compared to the style associated with the right hemisphere of implicit (unconscious) and experiential coping. That is, if the goal is the one just enunciated, to work through the social conflict and move on in one way or the other, the left hemisphere should be the one engaged given its activation-inhibition coordination skills and part of the reason for that is that it is conducive to rational and flexible adaptation to any difficult situations at hand through its foundational skill set. Also, when the goal of the social interaction is not for a longer-term interaction, or it does not require the subtle activation-inhibition coordination that seems evident in more complex social behavior, then the right hemisphere might be the one called upon for its inhibitory-related skills, for example, a rapid activation-inhibition coordination or an outright social suppression, termination, or inhibition. The difficulty with this general type of hypothesis is to determine the threshold for transition from complex and continual social interaction requiring left hemisphere skills and less complex interaction requiring right hemisphere skills. However, there should be much individual variation in this regard, rendering explicit predictions difficult to operationalize but not impossible.

General (Nonlateralized)

From Neuron to Brain to Behavior

Neuron Activation and inhibition are paired behavioral and neuronal processes that need to function in balance for effective functioning. The concept applies even to the molecular level of neuronal function, although the terminology used at that level refers to excitation instead of activation. Consider that axonal firing involves dynamically coordinated spikes of excitation and inhibitory processes. In this regard, Xue, Atallah, and Scanziani (2014) referred to the equalization of excitatory and inhibitory ratios in visual cortical neurons. Singer (2013) described the sequencing required over neuronal firing as involving critical inhibitory functions.

Also see Havlicek, Ivanov, Roebroeck, and Uludağ (2017) on excitatory-inhibitory balance in neural populations; the imbalance that is involved relates to neurotransmitters such as activatory glutamate and inhibitory GABA, for example (e.g., Cheng, Niddam, Hsu, Liu, & Tsai, 2017; Eichler & Meier, 2008; Gatto & Broadie, 2010; Jung, Williams, Nezhad, & Ralph, 2017; Yizhar et al., 2011). Also, see Um (2017) on how glial cells shape activatory and inhibitory synapses and neural circuits.

Circuits Rubin, Abbott, and Sompolinsky (2017) considered that optimal learning in face of output noise is facilitated by a balanced neuronal firing regime of excitation and inhibition. Moreover, the balance emerges by virtue of successful learning. Further, it inheres in connected neuronal networks and not only in individual neuronal firings. Finally, the authors proposed that the emergence and self-maintenance of excitation-inhibition balance in neuronal connectivity facilitates synaptic plasticity.

According to Kirst, Modes, and Magnasco (2017), neuronal circuits express dynamic synchronies and asynchronies, with the latter more associated with flexibility and the former psychopathology. Kirst et al. (2017) related asynchronous dynamics in neural circuitry to excitation and inhibition balancing or homeostasis. Asynchronies in neuronal circuit dynamics allow for self-organized reconfigurations that keep the circuits at the cusp of continual adaptivity to context ("poised at the edge") and optimal response to system perturbation.

When neuronal and central dynamics go awry, resultant psychopathology might include disorders such as autism spectrum disorder (ASD; Padmanabhan, Lynch, Schaer, & Menon, 2017). Rabinovich, Simmons, and Varona (2015) referred to dynamics in excitatory and inhibitory connections among cognitive modes (stable cognitive network patterns), with mode inhibition key, leading, or crucial in stabilizing excitation or controlling cognition. Menon (2013) argued similarly – the physiological basis for aberrant functional brain networking resides in imbalancing in excitation and inhibition throughout development that impacts local circuitry as well as large-scale connectivity.

Brain Rabinovitch et al. (2015) also referred to excitatory brain activity as being activated. They argued that cognitive dynamics are controlled by the inhibition of cognitive processes, or asymmetrical inhibition relative to excitation in connectivity, as in their "winnerless competition" model (Rabinovich, Huerta, & Laurent, 2008). Similarly, in an article on the sampling or Bayesian brain, Sanborn and Chater (2017) referred to dynamical networking of excitation and inhibition neurons that work through advanced sampling algorithms (e.g., Aitchison & Lengyel, 2016; also, see Navlakha, Bar-Joseph, & Barth, 2018).

Dysfunction In terms of psychopathology, the proposed general *p* factor might reflect inhibitory deficits, as per Carver, Johnson, and Timpano (2017). The fear response appears governed by an activation-inhibition coordination, as suggested in the research by Dejean, Courtin, Karalis, Chaudun, Wurtz, Bienvenu, and Herry (2016). They studied prefrontal cortical neuronal assemblies in relation to fear behavior in mice. Specifically, they found phase-specific coding mechanisms that dynamically regulate the formation of dorsal medial prefrontal cortex (dmPFC) neuronal cell assemblies, first involving activations and then inhibitions.

Aside from the fear response, disorders related to fear, such as PTSD and dissociation, appear governed by activation and inhibition coordination dynamics gone awry. Specifically, models have been proposed in which there is an over-activation in PTSD in critical circuitry and over-inhibition in dissociation in other circuitry. The implication is that normal cerebral activity is in balance in these regards, or that, the case of resilience to a traumatic stressor elicits a more balanced response in these regards. Note that the concepts of over-activation and over-inhibition have been referred to as under-modulation and over-modulation, respectively.

That is, Lanius et al. (2014) described that in PTSD under-modulation takes place involving dysfunction of top-down prefrontal cortico-limbic inhibition. Because of this failure, the PTSD responses include psychophysiological hyperarousal (e.g., in the amygdala) and also reduced neural activation (in the medial prefrontal cortex and rostral anterior cingulate cortex, in particular, with effects, as well, involving rostral anterior cingulate reactivity). As for dissociation, for example, in the minority of PTSD patients with the dissociative subtype, emotional over-modulation takes place; it implicates excessive cortico-limbic inhibition, resulting in little psychophysiological responsiveness.

For temperament, Jonason and Jackson (2016) investigated the "dark triad" trait complex and found that narcissism was related to the Behavioral Activation and Behavioral Inhibition systems (BIS and BAS, respectively; Gray, 1982). They measured these systems using the BIS/BAS Scales (Carver & White, 1994). Moreover, all three aspects of the dark triad of traits (narcissism, psychopathy, and Machiavellianism) appeared related to dysfunctional impulsivity, in general.

ASD Padmanabhan et al. (2017) elaborated the dysfunctions in the default mode network (DFN) in ASD and in this regard referred to an "imbalance in excitatory-inhibitory circuits." They reviewed research that indicated hyper-connected DMN links in ASD, with consequences for poorer development of long-range intra-network neuronal pathways and cross-network or inter-network connectivity. This results in increased within-network connectivity and increased local connectivity within DMN nodes, as well as decreased DMN node – non DMN connectivity. The overall developmental result is a shift from the aberrant hyper- to the depleted hypo-connectivity in DM networking, with network "isolation" a defining feature in ASD. Padmanabhan et al. (2017) concluded that ASD is typified by an excitatory/inhibitory "imbalancing" of neural circuits, taking place in the DMN, in particular (Rubinstein, 2010; Testa-Silva et al., 2012; Vattikuti & Chow, 2010; Zikopoulos & Barbas, 2013).

Furthermore, the excitatory-inhibitory imbalance in ASD appears to extend to the neurotransmitter GABA, which is associated with inhibition. That is, atypical expression of or altered signaling in inhibitory inter-neurons that are modulated by GABA appears to be a mechanism in the excitation/inhibition imbalance in ASD (Baroncelli et al., 2011; Pizzarelli & Cherubini, 2011; Thatcher et al., 2009).

Conclusion Thus, from molecule (GABA), to neuron, to circuit, to brain region (e.g., posterior cingulate cortex; PCC), and to full-brain (e.g., long range neuronal pathways), inhibitory processes in conjunction with activation ones, but also often leading activation ones, appear critical to optimal developmental brain function, such as in the DMN. Moreover, when the activation and inhibition coordination dynamic is out of balance, developmental psychopathology is potentiated, such as in ASD.

Other Models

One research group has especially investigated the role of inhibition in psychopathology, and its head is Joel Nigg. Their team has particularly studied inhibition in Attention Deficit Hyperactivity Disorder (ADHD; e.g., Kamradt, Nigg, Friderici, & Nikolas, 2017), as well as substance abuse, basing themselves on Nigg's seminal papers (Nigg, 2000, 2001).

Nigg is expanding his work by relating inhibition-disinhibition to self-regulation, self-control, impulsivity, and the like to developmental psychopathology (Nigg, 2017). He proposed an integrative bottom-up, top-down, hierarchical model to self-(intrinsic) regulation (as distinct from extrinsic regulation). Bottom-up processes include immediate reactive inhibition/behavioral inhibition and longer-term impulsivity. Top-down processes include cognitive control/low-level executive function, such as in response suppression, and high-level executive function, longer-term response inhibition, aside from appropriate strategies and planning, and so on. Relatedly, Eisenberg (2017) maintained that flexible self-regulation or effortful control involves a deliberate turning on or off, depending on the situation, and that this facility is affected by over-control, thereby promoting developmental difficulties.

Martel, Levinson, Langer, and Nigg (2016) have expanded the inhibitory approach to differentiating ADHD symptom expressions and subtypes to a network model. They found that the symptoms of being easily distracted and sustaining attention with difficulty were the core symptoms as ADHD changed with age in symptom expression. Their approach stems from the work of Borsboom and Cramer (2014), who have promoted a symptom network approach to psychopathology instead of the traditional latent variable approach (e.g., depression symptomatology is caused by an underlying dimension of major depression).

Back to Laterality Nigg has applied his model of inhibition in behavior not only to ADHD but also to addictions, and in doing so he found left-right brain differences. In this regard, Heitzeg et al. (2014) found that substance abuse in the early teenage period, or an increased risk for substance abuse disorder (SUD), might be related to blunted left middle frontal gyrus (MFG) activation that is required for inhibitory self-control. Also, see Zorlu et al. (2017), who conducted a diffusion tensor imaging study, and related alcohol dependence to weaker right hemisphere connectivity, especially from the putamen and hippocampus to other brain regions.

Also, Cerutti (2013) found that stimulating the left PFC using anodal stimulation improved performance on a verbal task that had memory load EF demand. In contrast, cathodal stimulation in the homotopic region to the right improved performance on a verbal task involving semantic organization. The authors noted that the results show how facilitatory and inhibitory links function in inter- and intraregional neuronal connectivity in the hemispheres.

Gingras and Braun (2017) referred to focal lesion in the cortex causing imbalances in inhibitory/excitatory weightings in the commissural system. This reminds of Young's concept that different dysfunctions will be expressed by different activation-inhibition coordinations and including differentially in the left and right hemispheres.

New Models: Networks, Causality, and Biopsychosocial Influences

Networks

Model

Introduction Urban, Osgood, Okamoto, Mabry, and Lich (2014) presented a series of definitions about network concepts. They elaborate those of Sporns (2011, 2012), and are presented in Table 8.1. Bernstein, Heeren, and McNally (2017) also presented critical network concept definitions. Nodes are fundamental units in a system and edges relate node pairs.

Table 8.1 Networks and definitions

Network	Definition
Centrality	A measure on the relative importance that a node or edge occupies within a network architecture (e.g., degree, betweenness, closeness)
Connectivity	The set of node connections
Connector hubs	Function to link nodes over modules
Core	A coherent, highly and mutually interconnected node set or group, facilitating resistance to perturbation
Density	The proportion of pairs of nodes that have ties of a given type (existing ties in a network/all possible ones in the network)
Diameter	Paths between two nodes, and to its longest path
Distance	The shortest topological path in a node pair
Edge	Connections or associations between pairs of nodes; their relationship, interaction, or dependency; refers to categorical existence present or the dimensional strength
Global efficiency	A distance measure
Hub	A node that is influentially important, or central to network interconnectivity; a high-degree network node displaying diverse connectivities over modules
Modules	Communities of strongly or densely interconnected nodes, that is, having a large number of mutual connections with few connections outside these links
Motif	A reduced subset of network nodes and edges, or a subgraph
Network	The links (edges) among nodes in a system, including possible emergent phenomena that arise from the interaction causally of the nodes. The nodes are observed, measurable variables, and each variable is considered as its own entity with the variables explored for their relationships (Bernstein et al., 2017)
Node (vertex)	A fundamental element of a system (e.g., a neuron, a person)
Node degree	Its number of incoming and outgoing edges
Node neighbors	A node's set of connected links
Path	An ordered sequence of unique edges and intermediate nodes; the shortest path between two nodes indicates the minimal number of links for two applicable nodes
Provincial hubs	High-degree network node linking constituent nodes within its module
Random network	Its edges between nodes are random
Reciprocity	Network measure concerns the proportion of all directional ties that are reciprocated
Rich club	A set of high-degree nodes with well-connected nodes connecting to each other; the interconnections are greater than expected relative to applicable node degree measures
Small world network	Most nodes in the circuit can be reached from every other node by a reduced number of moves even though they are not direct neighbors; the node clustering is more than random yet the average shortest path length equates with what is found in random networks

Adapted from Sporns (2011, 2012); van den Heuval and Sporns (2013)

According to Kaiser (2017), nodes possess, as well, connected synergies, and groups of network nodes are termed modules. Nodes that are highly connected are considered hubs, and strongly connected hubs are considered to form "rich clubs." They facilitate information integration and synchronization. At the same time, they can be imbalanced. Most neural interconnections are local, not long distance.

Terms At the individual level of analysis, degree centrality in network measures concerns the total number of nodes and edges. Indegree refers to incoming ones, and outdegree refers to outgoing ones. The betweenness centrality network measure concerns the network concept of edges that could lie between or connects two nodes that would not otherwise be connected; and its extent in these regards. In other words, it refers to the number of times that nodes lie on the shortest length between pairs of other nodes. Closeness centrality refers to nodes that could be close to all other nodes in the network, and to its extent. In other words, closeness refers to the average distance of nodes from other nodes in a network. Node strength refers to the sum of the weights of links in a network that are attached to a node. In-strength refers to the total of the directed edge weights that originate from other nodes and end at a specific node. In contrast, out-strength is the total of the directed edge weights that originate from a specific node and end at other nodes.

At the group or subgroup level of analysis, the network measure of modularity refers to a network that could divide into modules. High modularity means a network has dense connections between the nodes within modules but sparse connections between nodes in different modules. Another network measure is clique, which has every individual node directly tied to every other one in a subgroup. Transitivity network measure refers to two nodes that could be connected to a same third node and, also, connected to each other, and to its extent.

At the network level of analysis, centralization refers to how many nodes does a network revolve around, and to its extent. Clustering refers to networks having clumps (small subgroups within the network with close ties to each other), and to its extent.

Note that the work on networks is increasing exponentially, including in new concepts and empirical procedures. For example, Haslbeck and Fried (2017) developed a measure of predictability of nodes, which concerns the degree to which a particular node can be predicted by all of the other nodes in its network. Also, Wig (2017) emphasized architecture of large-scale brain networks as consisting of multiple segregated and interacting subnetworks. Reimann et al. (2017) referred to cliques of neurons that are bound into cavities. It is beyond the scope of the present paper to consider these new directions in network science.

Applications Bernstein et al. (2017) specified that network perspectives are complementary, and they described three major ones in their innovative model. They used a regularized partial correlation procedure via the graphical LASSO (Least Absolute Shrinkage and Selection Operator) method. This method eliminates spurious associations or edges, and it removes potential "false positive" associations or edges. A second statistical approach that they used was to compute the relative importance network (Heeren & McNally, 2016). This statistic controls for multicollinearity; thus, allowing for the determination of a relative importance metric for each edge or association. Third, Bernstein et al. (2017) computed directed acyclic graphs (DAG) to help determine the network causal structure (Pearl, Glymour, & Jewell, 2016). This approach determines which edges or associations are essential to the network using the Bayesian Information Criterion (BIC). By using three different models and statistics to determine the principle nodes in a system, Bernstein et al. (2017) felt more confident in their results. Their specific study concerned rumination in relation to various executive functions and moods. Note that Guloksuz, Pries, and van Os (2017) cautioned about pitfalls in applying network methods to explaining mental disorder, as did Forbes, Wright, Markon, and Krueger (2017); but see Saxe et al. (2016) for another group of authors relating to networks and psychiatry. The work of Forbes et al. (2017) noted that the replicability crisis common to psychology is evident in psychological network resarch, as well, and they advocated both for better methods and modeling (e.g., Young, 2015).

Network models can be applied developmentally (e.g., Kaiser, 2017). Neurons form circuits with spatial and temporal factors at the level of paired neurons, as well as fiber tracts between brain regions, and circuits within sub-cortical and cortical regions. These networked properties of neuron and brain create networked connectivities that are dynamically responsive both to immediate context and long-term developmental change.

Comment

Table 5.1 has specified the inhibitory specializations that seem evident in the behaviors and functions associated with the left and right cerebral hemispheres. Generally, all these terms can be translated into network terminology. Moreover, network terms can lead to new understandings of the concept of activation-inhibition coordination.

Generally, it could be argued that the left hemisphere compared to the right contains functional properties in intra-hemispheric networked connectivities that allow for better activation-inhibition coordination in the sense described. Moreover, the left hemisphere appears better at inter-hemispheric inhibition, which allows it to orchestrate left and right hemisphere cooperation, and so intra-hemispheric network connectivity, as it functions.

It would be interesting to increasingly determine how different left-right hemisphere differences in network connectivities that have been found developmentally, as per the first portion of the paper, such as for hubs, "small worlds," short- and long-range connections, and so on, for different functions relate to this hypothesis. One could ask to what degree the left hemisphere manifests better network centrality, such as "betweenness," closeness, and strength (Bernstein et al., 2017), and to what extent these different concepts of networks converge in suggesting a left hemisphere advantage in activation-inhibition coordination. Moreover, how would these recently applied concepts relate to the approach that the left hemisphere is organized more as small world compared to the right hemisphere, allowing for better efficiency, information transmission, and so on, and so fostering, once more, a better activation-inhibition coordination specialization. It makes sense that the right hemisphere has a more dispersed and less small or focal network organization because it has a relative advantage in visuospatial and related skills, which are more global.

This type of conceptualization should help to further demonstrate that the development of laterality in behavior and brain is central to understanding human psychology and also its evolution, given that network theory and research is burgeoning. Handedness might not be considered an important direct index of brain function; however, it is part of a complex lateralized activity related to behavior and the brain that marks both human uniqueness and its common evolutionary origins in the earliest life forms. In this regard, studying the development of handedness, manual specialization, and hemispheric specialization from the point of view of network concepts contributes to the general understanding of the behavior and the brain and their evolutionary origins.

The next part of the book presents a novel concept related to networks and activation-inhibition coordination constructed with the goal to integrate the various theoretical avenues being proposed to understand the development and evolution of behavior, including in its lateralization. As explained in what follows, the model is based on the work of Young (2015, 2016). It involves two figures based on that work (see Figs. 8.1 and 8.2).

Networked Causality

Model McNally et al. (2015) have applied this network approach to PTSD. Young (2015, 2016) has developed a bottom-up/top-down approach to PTSD that incorporates both the network and construct approaches to psychopathology. That is, disordered behavior is neither the product of upper-level constructs acting down on the behavioral expression of lower-order symptoms nor defined by bottom-up influences on the behavioral expression of the higher-order psychopathology involved. Moreover, there could be intermediate levels between these bottom-up and top-down processes in any one patient's presentation of symptoms and disorder, especially in terms of appraisals.

The first figure (Fig. 8.1) indicates the various ways lower-order behaviors, symptoms, and their clustering can interact. Core items in these regards drive the causality of the person's psychological symptom (e.g., sleep deprivation) and are individualized. Alternately, behaviors/symptoms and their network clustering might not be causally linked to each other and in individual ways, but reflect the top-down influence of an underlying variable (construct), also expressed individually, such as described by the DSM psychiatric disorders (e.g., major depression). These categor-

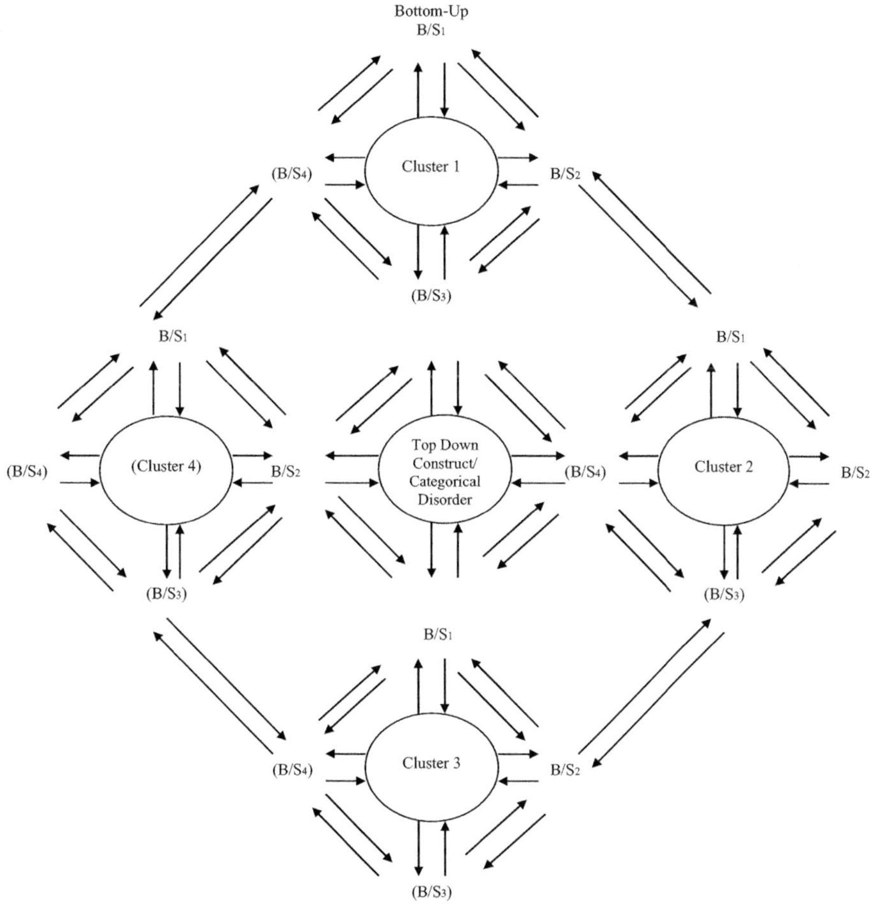

Fig. 8.1 Hybrid behavior/symptom (B/S) network/construct model. The figure depicts the relationship between lower-order behavioral/symptom (B/S) expressions (complexes, networks, their development/abnormality) and higher-order clusters/constructs/disorders (C) as being dynamically reciprocal in causation. The individual behaviors/symptoms could interact causally among themselves (e.g., think the exacerbatory role of sleep disturbance on other symptoms) without any reference to a higher-order construct, such as depression or PTSD. The latter are examples of traditionally conceived top-down integrations of behaviors/symptoms. But Borsboom and colleagues (e.g., Borsboom, Cramer, & Kalis, 2018) have argued that these constructs are not genuinely present phenomenologically nor causal in behavior/symptom expression. The present model suggests a middle, balanced, or hybrid course. In this model, the top-down construct level constitutes an underlying, higher-order level in the person's behavior, while the bottom-up behavior/symptom level interacts with the top-down levels of the system, with both the top-down and bottom-up influences dynamically influencing each other in context and over time. Note. The parentheses indicate that any behavioral/symptom complex under discussion will have differing amounts of clusters, and a cluster will have variable behaviors/symptoms (items). Of the clusters in any mental disorder or in any behavioral complex, for their items, it would be beneficial to specify which are core/primary. For the model presented in the figure, these could be the first clusters or items that are specified. In terms of activation-inhibition coordination, one example might be that cluster 1 involves activation-inhibition coordination, or perhaps clusters 2 and 3 show this (or one or the other) with cluster 4, constituting a variation in these regards. (Adapted from Young, 2015, 2016)

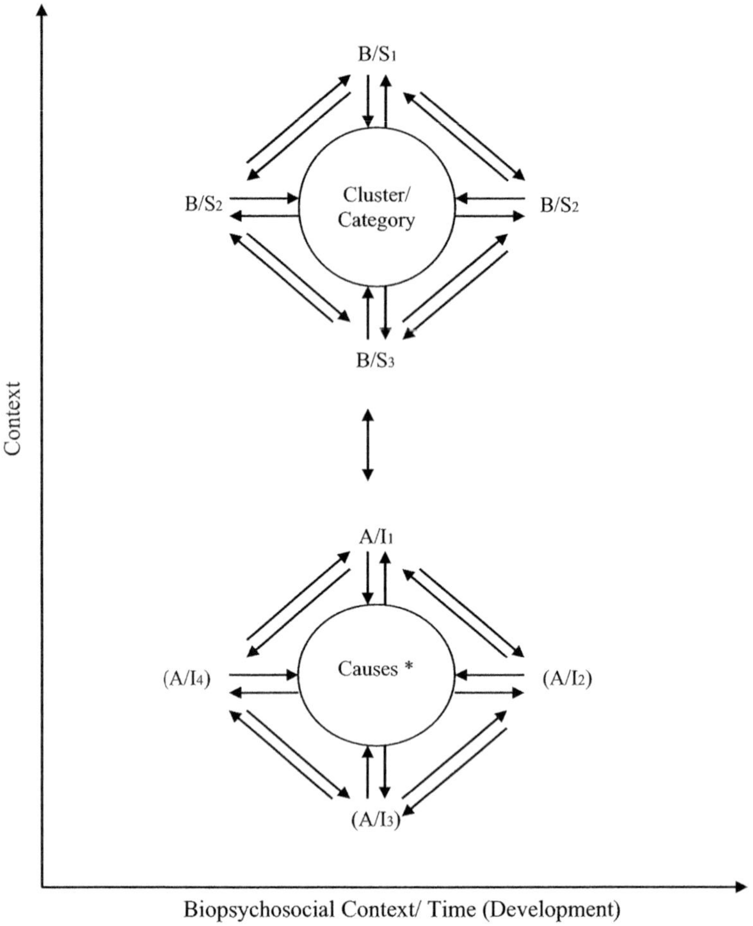

Fig. 8.2 An integrative (bottom-up, top-down) behavior/symptom and cause network/construct model. The figure illustrates how behaviors/symptoms (B/S) and their causes might interact. The behaviors/symptoms might have clusters or even categorical disorders (C); and the causes are shown as activation/inhibition (A/I) coordinations. The behaviors/symptoms form networked connectivities that might reflect activation/inhibition coordinations (e.g., in movements) as well as reflecting such coordinations in neural circuitry. The networked connectivities are liable to emergence at higher levels of organization, for example, in bootstrapping development of depression. Or the behavior/symptom complexes involved might be temporary, e.g., to solve a problem at hand

ical entities might reflect etiological influences that cause them and lead to the expression of the behavior/symptom networks associated with them. Combined models could emphasize one of behavior/symptom networks or constructs as being more primary in causation, or both reciprocally, which is what would be expected in a genuine hybrid model (Young, 2015, 2016).

The second figure (Fig. 8.2) that modifies the causality model presented in Young (2015, 2016) depicts how behaviors/symptoms and their causes might interact. The behaviors/symptoms are shown to form networked connectivities indicative of activation/inhibition coordinations, as are their causes, for instance, in neural circuitry.

Figures 8.1 and 8.2 thus modify the original causal model in Young (2015, 2016) that had been applied to PTSD in order that it applies generally to behavior and brain. In addition, it can apply to any behavior in which there are both specific (or lower-level, bottom-up behavior) and more general (construct, super-ordinate emergent, higher-level, top-down) processes. In this sense, it could even apply to understanding behavioral development and its activation-inhibition coordination, setting the basis for its application to evolution.

For example, according to the model in Figs. 8.1 and 8.2 that integrates bottom-up and top-down causation across levels of a system (Young, 2015), "causality resides in the rich dynamical systematic interactions and reciprocal influences amongst the various levels of a system and their nexus nodes, elements (sub)sets, constructs, and other aspects inherent in them, such as symptom and disorder" (Young, 2016, p. 908). In this sense, the lower-order behavior/symptom, and higher-order construct/disorder levels of a system, and any intermediate levels, as well as the causal factors related to them, can be described both in terms of network dynamics and the underlying activation-inhibition coordination dynamic that might underlie them.

Borsboom (2017) has developed a similar extended network model for mental disorder. He presented propositions that symptoms in psychopathology are connected causally. His model differs in this regard from models of causality that lie in the influence of an overarching construct, such as depression. The causes of mental disorder reside in wider factors, as well – biological, psychological, and societal ones. Symptoms connections are influenced by an external field, which behaviorally might include non-symptoms. Jones, Heeren, and McNally (2017) extended the idea of external non-symptoms that can influence symptom networks to include biological, cognitive, and social variables. Both the articles appear to advocate for a network approach to mental disorder, generally, while respecting wider biopsychosocial influences, which is consistent with the approach of the present work.

Guyon, Falissard, and Kop (2017) adopted an approach similar to Young's (2015, 2016) on the question of whether the latent variable and network approaches can coexist in a combined or complementary model of psychological attributes and psychopathology. For them, psychological constructs emerge dynamically de novo as attractors in the complex systems of behavior and social embeddedness.

Network research can inform the validity of diagnostic categories in the DSM-5, such as PTSD (Fried et al., 2018). For example, Fried et al. (2018) conducted a study of network generality in four trauma-exposed samples. Sleep problems emerged as the most severe symptom, with psychological reactivity, intrusive traumatic memories, detachment, and activity disinterest among the most central. The most central symptoms were not just those uniquely associated with trauma, in that others also were comorbid with depression (e.g., disinterest, concentration problems). The findings speak to the high comorbidity findings of PTSD and depression. Symptoms in both disorders can be considered "bridge" ones.

Bringmann and Eronen (2018) argued that opposition between the latent variable/construct model and the network model is not as sharp as has been proposed. For example, interactive or networked symptoms might have fuzzy boundaries between symptoms, can be represented mathematically in ways similar to those for latent variables, and can be combined with latent variable models (by adding a latent variable model to each network node). Also, unlike what their critics maintain, latent variable models of psychopathology might not reflect either underlying mental disorder constructs or common causation. Also, symptoms could still interact in these models; further, the constructs involved might not be distinct conceptually from their symptoms. That said, network models afford dynamical, time-dependent analyses of changes in symptom dependencies and give new ways of looking at data (e.g., centrality measures).

Note that although Bringmann and Eronen (2018) argued that latent variable and network models are not as distinct as presented in the literature, they do not suggest the type of combined model for psychopathology suggested here, of a hybrid construct/network approach involving individualized emergence of higher-order levels. In this regard, they focused more on statistical commonalities among models and how different approaches are consistent with one approach or the other (e.g., VAR, vector auto regressive models are essentially dynamical).

Comment The present network model has the advantage of applying to normal behavior as much as disordered behavior and is explicitly inclusive of the biopsychosocial influences on behavior. Behavioral causality is multi-factorial (Young, 2016) and includes different levels embedded in a systemic biopsychosocial matrix. Symptom (and behavioral) networks develop and emerge in this context. The model also has the advantage of including nonlinear factors that can promote swift, deep change in a system and its behavior/symptom nodes, networks, and clusters. At the same time, it allows for fixed, non-changing symptom complexes that rigidly resist change, as in psychopathology.

Future research on brain and behavior relationships should continue to specify their underpinning as activation-inhibition coordinations and how they can go awry in these regards. Moreover, given the central role for the left hemisphere as the seat of the most advanced types of such coordinations, including inter-hemispherically, and notwithstanding that the right hemisphere possesses its own inhibitory skills, the study of behavioral and brain lateralities and their development should remain a critical focus in research. That network models are complementary to activation-inhibition coordination ones in these regards adds to the value and validity of both.

That said, the specific relations between types of networked neuronal activity and behavior needs to be better established in terms of activation-inhibition coordinations. For example, most neural connections are excitatory (Kaiser, 2017), but do they form excitatory neural linkages, given that there are cells that are also inhibitory? How does the same question play at the level of larger networked linkages, such as in hubs, modules, small worlds, and subcortical and cortical regions, and in terms of proximal and distal linkages, including inter-hemispherically? What is the role of neurotransmitters in these regards, glial cells, and so on, as well as genes expressed in the relevant neural tissues and any epigenetic gene silencing (environmentally induced) that might obtain?

Exactly how do the different hemispheres develop their functional differences as defined by underlying activation-inhibition coordination (if the research shows that they exist) and the neuronal networks and connectivities involved, and do they differ in the left and right hemispheres, at different developmental periods, or when the environment is adverse compared to expected, and so on? Does the neuronal networking allow for the functions to develop in a reductionist fashion, or are there emergent and feedback properties that create larger behavioral and neuronal-networked wholes or systems through the activation-inhibition coordinations involved? How do the latter emerge in development? Which laboratory tasks can best elicit or represent them at each age? And what facilitates both their emergence and improvement after their disruption when under biological and/or environmental duress?

To conclude the discussion and extension of the study of development of manual behavior and related lateralities that has been undertaken in the present work, it fits into the broader thrust in contemporary study of network connectivities in brain and behavior. Moreover, it is consistent with the model of activation-inhibition coordination in behavior and brain, which provides an economical, elegant model that applies to understanding both components in brain-behavior relationships.

Finally, the cohering glue to all these ideas lies in its original impetus in the study of the reaching infant and the efforts of the developing child as she or he strains to attain desired objects. What can these fundamental early behaviors tell us about behavior and brain generally and their development and evolution? We need to examine the most general of models in psychology to obtain even better answers to this question. As such, the next section considers the biopsychosocial model in relation to lateralization.

Biopsychosocial

Model The different approaches to the role of epigenesis and culture as environmental contributions to genetic influences on the development of handedness and related cerebral asymmetries speak to the need of broad models that integrate all causal factors in their development. Moreover, any integrative model on the development of handedness and related lateralities should consider Laland's (2008) conceptualization of an active reciprocal interaction between genes and culture for development, in general (and its evolution). In this regard, he mentioned the active role that parents play in shaping the handedness of their offspring. One should add that youngsters already play an active role in their development, generally, and are not just passive recipients of biological or experiential influences, as per Piaget's constructivist model (Young, 2011, 2016). One model that incorporates biological and environmental factors while respecting the active contribution of the individual to her or his own development is the biopsychosocial one (e.g., Melchert, 2015; Rath & Elliott, 2012; Young, 2011, 2016; see Fig. 8.3). The biopsychosocial model

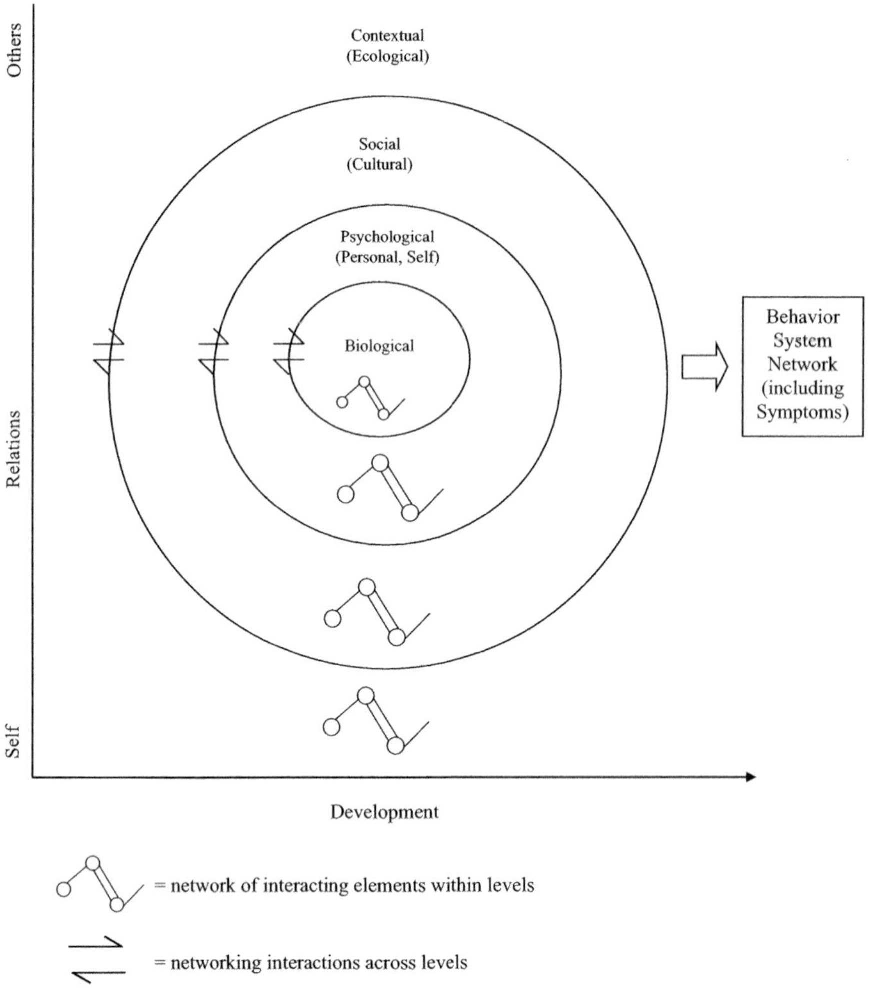

Fig. 8.3 Developmental, systemic/networking biopsychosocial (behavioral) model (including psychiatric symptoms). Behavioral causality goes beyond reaction to lower-order levels, such as genes and stimuli producing passive response. Instead, behavior is actively emergent in a system, with self-related forces involved psychologically as causal factors. The biopsychosocial nexus includes "ourselves" as primary determinants of our behavior, beyond biology and environment especially as we develop. Therefore, to understand the ecological, contextual, cultural, social, and experiential influences on behavior and how it can get disturbed and even disordered psychiatrically, we need to consider the impacts on the developing brain, physiology, and general biology of the individual, but as filtered, causally altered, mediated, moderated, influenced, and otherwise transformed by the individual's appraisals, buffering and coping skills, temperament and personality, intelligence and motivation, reactions to social supports, self-control/regulation, autonomy, independence, resilience, and so on. (Adapted from Young, 2016 [Fig. 17.4])

can be applied to the development of handedness, especially if a component of active contribution by the person to handedness development (or any related development) could be indicated.

Comment However, what would be an appropriate personal, self, or psychological factor that could influence handedness development? In this regard, Young (2016) referred to factors such as coping and a belief in free will. Clearly, these types of influences on behavior and choice do not apply easily to handedness. Thus, what might this type of active contribution by the person to his or her own handedness and related lateralized development look like? Perhaps the answer can be found in the concept of hemisphericity, which has mostly disappeared from scientific consideration and investigation, as outlined above. However, personal preference for or consistent use of one hemispheric use or the other, everything else being equal, could reflect a personal proclivity at one point in development that could stand as an intermediary force in relating to context beyond biology or environment. This is another reason to resurrect the hemisphericity concept; it could help give a fuller biopsychosocial picture of the development of lateralizations, generally, thereby helping to place it within a mainstream conception in psychology.

Lateralized manual behavior and brain structure and function are the products of multiple influences, including biological (e.g., genetic, brain) ones and cultural/environmental ones. This multi-factorial causality found in laterality is consistent with more general causal models of behavior (e.g., biopsychosocial models), although more work is needed in specifying the psychological part of the model, as indicated.

Conclusions

The review of models in development that can apply to laterality development finishes with the broad one of the biopsychosocial model. It illustrates the values of considering new models for the area. Also, it underscores the value of works that emphasize broad perspectives in understanding causality, as per Young (2016). The network perspective has been criticized for not being explanatory, only re-describing, and not providing mechanism (e.g., van Eck, 2018; Zednik, 2018). However, consistent with Young (2016) especially when considered dynamically, the network perspective provides a level of explanation at the organizational level. Multi-scale dynamics involving different time scales over people allow for "mutual emergent meaning" (Dale & Kello, 2018). Dynamic systems allow for such emergence through self-organization, e.g., self-cultivation in terms of conscious building (Sherblom, 2018). Combined network and dynamic approaches can help explain clinical phenomena (e.g., shifting state of the network at the tipping point, Hofmann & Curtiss, 2018). Free will does not have a good case against it through determinism (Bergner, 2018), and should be seen as an emergent, causal factor in behavior.

The next section on new ways of laterality modeling focuses on the author's specific contributions in these regards, with some modeling admittedly being more speculative.

References

Aitchison, L., & Lengyel, M. (2016). The Hamiltonian brain: Efficient probabilistic inference with excitatory-inhibitory neural circuit dynamics. *PLoS Computational Biology*. https://doi.org/10.1371/journal.pcbi.1005186

Aron, A. R. (2011). From reactive to proactive and selective control: Developing a richer model for stopping inappropriate responses. *Biological Psychiatry, 69*, e55–e68. https://doi.org/10.1016/j.biopsych.2010.07.024

Aron, A. R., Robbins, T. W., & Poldrack, R. A. (2004). Inhibition and the right inferior frontal cortex. *Trends in Cognitive Science, 8*, 170–177. https://doi.org/10.1016/j.tics.2004.02.010

Arsalidou, M., & Pascual-Leone, J. (2016). Constructivist developmental theory is needed in developmental neuroscience. *Science of Learning, 1*, 16016. https://doi.org/10.1038/npjscilearn.2016.16

Bardikoff, N., & Sabbagh, M. (2017). The differentiation of executive functioning across development: Insights from developmental cognitive neuroscience. In N. Budwig, E. Turiel, & D. Zelazo (Eds.), *New perspectives on human development* (pp. 47–66). Cambridge, UK: Cambridge University Press.

Baroncelli, L., Braschi, C., Spolidoro, M., Begenisic, T., Maffei, L., & Sale, A. (2011). Brain plasticity and disease: A matter of inhibition. *Neural Plasticity, 2011*, 286073. https://doi.org/10.1155/2011/286073

Barral, J., De Pretto, M., Debû, B., & Hauert, C.-A. (2010). Activation and inhibition of bimanual movements in school-aged children. *Human Physiology, 36*, 47–57. https://doi.org/10.1134/S0362119710010068

Bartoli, E., Aron, A. R., & Tandon, N. (2018). Topography and timing of activity in right inferior frontal cortex and anterior insula for stopping movement. *Human Brain Mapping, 39*, 189–203. https://doi.org/10.1002/hbm.23835

Bergner, R. M. (2018). The case against the case against free will. *Journal of Theoretical and Philosophical Psychology, 38*, 123–139.

Bernstein, E. E., Heeren, A., & McNally, R. J. (2017). Unpacking rumination and executive control: A network perspective. *Clinical Psychological Science, 5*, 816–826. https://doi.org/10.1177/2167702617702717

Borsboom, D. (2017). A network theory of mental disorders. *World Psychiatry, 6*, 5–13. https://doi.org/10.1002/wps.20375

Borsboom, D., Cramer, A., & Kalis, A. (2018). Brain disorders? Not really… Why network structures block reductionism in psychopathology research. *Behavioral and Brain Sciences* https://doi-org.ezproxy.library.yorku.ca/10.1017/S0140525X17002266

Borsboom, D., & Cramer, A. O. J. (2014). Network analysis: An integrative approach to the structure of psychopathology. *Annual Review of Clinical Psychology, 9*, 91–121. https://doi.org/10.1146/annurev-clinpsy-050212-185608

Bringmann, L. F., & Eronen, M. I. (2018). Don't blame the model: Reconsidering the network approach to psychopathology. *Psychological Review, 125*, 606–615.

Caplan, P. J., & Kinsbourne, M. (1976). Baby drops the rattle: Asymmetry of duration of grasp by infants. *Child Development, 2*, 532–534. https://doi.org/10.2307/1128815

Carver, C. S., Johnson, S. L., & Timpano, K. R. (2017). Toward a functional view of the p factor in psychopathology. *Clinical Psychological Science, 5*, 800–889. https://doi.org/10.1177/2167702617710037

Carver, C. S., & White, T. L. (1994). Behavioral inhibition, behavioral activation, and affective responses to impending reward and punishment: The BIS/BAS scales. *Journal of Personality and Social Psychology, 67*, 319–333. https://doi.org/10.1037/0022-3514.67.2.319

Cerutti, C. (2013). Building a functional multiple intelligence theory to advance educational neuroscience. *Frontiers in Psychology, 4*, 950. https://doi.org/10.3389/fpsyg.2013.00950

Cheng, C.-H., Niddam, D. M., Hsu, S.-C., Liu, C.-Y., & Tsai, S.-Y. (2017). Resting GABA concentration predicts inhibitory control during an auditory go-nogo task. *Experimental Brain Research, 235*, 3833–3841. https://doi.org/10.1007/s00221-017-5101-6

Collette, F., Van der Linden, M., Laureys, S., Delfiore, G., Degueldre, C., Luxen, A., et al. (2005). Exploring the unity and diversity of the neural substrates of executive functioning. *Human Brain Mapping, 25*, 409–423. https://doi.org/10.1002/hbm.20118

D'Alberto, N., Funnell, M., Potter, A., & Garavan, H. (2017). A split-brain case study on the hemispheric lateralization of inhibitory control. *Neuropsychologia, 99*, 24–29. https://doi.org/10.1016/j.neuropsychologia.2017.02.017

D'Souza, H., Cowie, D., Karmiloff-Smith, A., & Bremner, A. J. (2017). Specialization of the motor system in infancy: From broad tuning to selectively specialized purposeful actions. *Developmental Science, 20*, e12409. https://doi.org/10.1111/desc.12409

Dale, R., & Kello, C. T. (2018). "How do humans make sense?" Multiscale dynamics and emergent meaning. *New Ideas in Psychology, 50*, 61–72.

Dambacher, F., Sack, A. T., Lobbestael, J., Arntz, A., Brugmann, S., & Schuhmann, T. (2014). The role of right prefrontal and medial cortex in response inhibition: Interfering with action restraint and action cancellation using transcranial magnetic brain stimulation. *Journal of Cognitive Neuroscience, 26*, 1775–1784. https://doi.org/10.1162/jocn_a_00595

Darki, F., & Klingberg, T. (2015). The role of fronto-parietal and fronto-striatal networks in the development of working memory: A longitudinal study. *Cerebral Cortex, 25*, 1587–1595. https://doi.org/10.1093/cercor/bht352

Dejean, C., Courtin, J., Karalis, N., Chaudun, F., Wurtz, H., Bienvenu, T. C. M., et al. (2016). Prefrontal neuronal assemblies temporally control fear behaviour. *Nature, 535*, 420–424. https://doi.org/10.1038/nature18630

Dien, J. (2008). Looking both ways through time: The Janus model of lateralized cognition. *Brain and Cognition, 67*, 292–323. https://doi.org/10.1016/j.bandc.2008.02.007

Eichler, S. A., & Meier, J. C. (2008). E-I imbalance and human diseases – From molecules to networking. *Frontiers of Molecular Neuroscience, 1*, 2. https://doi.org/10.3389/neuro.02.002.2008

Eisenberg, N. (2017). Commentary: What's in a word (or words) – On the relations among self-regulation, self-control, executive functioning, effortful control, cognitive control, impulsivity, risk-taking, and inhibition for developmental psychology – Reflections on Nigg (2017). *Journal of Child Psychology and Psychiatry, 58*, 384–386. https://doi.org/10.1111/jcpp.12707

Floegel, M., & Kell, C. A. (2017). Functional hemispheric asymmetries during the planning and manual control of virtual avatar movements. *PLoS One, 12*, e0185152. https://doi.org/10.1371/journal.pone.0185152

Forbes, M. K., Wright, A. G. C., Markon, K. E., & Krueger, R. F. (2017). Evidence that psychopathology symptom networks have limited replicability. *Journal of Abnormal Psychology, 126*, 969–988.

Fried, E. I., Eidhof, M. B., Palic, S., Costantini, G., Huisman-van Dijk, H. M., Bockting, C. L. H., et al. (2018). Replicability and generalizability of posttraumatic stress disorder (PTSD) networks: A cross-cultural multisite study of PTSD symptoms in four trauma patient samples. *Clinical Psychological Science, 6*, 335–351. https://doi.org/10.1177/2167702617745092

Frühholz, S., Schlegel, K., & Grandjean, D. (2017). Amygdala structure and core dimensions of the affective personality. *Brain Structure and Function, 222*, 3915–3925. https://doi.org/10.1007/s00429-017-1444-9

Fujino, J., Tei, S., Jankowski, K. F., Kawada, R., Murai, T., & Takahashi, H. (2017). Role of spontaneous brain activity in explicit and implicit aspects of cognitive flexibility under socially conflicting situations: A resting-state fMRI study using fractional amplitude of low-frequency fluctuations. *Neuroscience, 367*, 60–71. https://doi.org/10.1016/j.neuroscience.2017.10.025

Gable, P. A., Mechin, N. C., Hicks, J. A., & Adams, D. L. (2015). Supervisory control system and frontal asymmetry: Neurophysiological traits of emotion-based impulsivity. *Social, Cognitive, and Affective Neuroscience, 10*, 1310–1315. https://doi.org/10.1093/scan/nsv017

Gable, P. A., Neal, L. B., & Threadgill, A. H. (2017). Regulatory behavior and frontal activity: Considering the role of revised-BIS in relative right frontal asymmetry. *Psychophysiology*. https://doi.org/10.1111/psyp.12910

Gallea, C., Popa, T., Hubsch, C., Valabregue, R., Brochard, V., Kundu, P., et al. (2013). RAD51 deficiency disrupts the corticospinal lateralization of motor control. *Brain, 136*, 3333–3346. https://doi.org/10.1093/brain/awt258

Gatto, C. L., & Broadie, K. (2010). Genetic controls balancing excitatory and inhibitory synaptogenesis in neurodevelopmental disorder models. *Frontiers of Synaptic Neuroscience, 2*, 4. https://doi.org/10.3389/fnsyn.2010.00004

Genç, E., Ocklenburg, S., Singer, W., & Güntürkün, O. (2015). Abnormal interhemispheric motor interactions in patients with callosal agenesis. *Behavioural Brain Research, 293*, 1–9. https://doi.org/10.1016/j.bbr.2015.07.016

Gilsbach, S., Neufang, S., Scherag, S., Vloet, T. D., Fink, G. R., Herpertz-Dahlmann, B., et al. (2012). Effects of the DRD4 genotype on neural networks associated with executive functions in children and adolescents. *Developmental Cognitive Neuroscience, 2*, 417–427. https://doi.org/10.1016/j.dcn.2012.05.001

Gingras, B., & Braun, C. M. J. (2017). Development of "material-specific" hemispheric specialization from beginning to end. *Laterality: Asymmetries of Body, Brain and Cognition*. https://doi.org/10.1080/1357650X.2017.1373780

Gray, J. A. (1982). *The neuropsychology of anxiety: An enquiry into the functions of the septohippocampal system*. Oxford, UK: Oxford University Press.

Gray, J. A., & McNaughton, N. (2000). *The neuropsychology of anxiety: An enquiry in to the functions of the septo-hippocampal system* (2nd ed.). Oxford, UK: Oxford University Press.

Greenwald, A. G., McGhee, D. E., & Schwartz, J. L. (1998). Measuring individual differences in implicit cognition: The implicit association test. *Journal of Personality and Social Psychology, 74*, 1464–1480. https://doi.org/10.1037/0022-3514.74.6.1464

Grimshaw, G. M., & Carmel, D. (2014). An asymmetric inhibition model of hemispheric differences in emotional processing. *Frontiers in Psychology, 5*, 489. https://doi.org/10.3389/fpsyg.2014.00489

Guloksuz, S., Pries, L.-K., & van Os, J. (2017). Application of network methods for understanding mental disorders: Pitfalls and promise. *Psychological Medicine, 47*, 2743–2752. https://doi.org/10.1017/S0033291717001350

Guyon, H., Falissard, B., & Kop, J.-L. (2017). Modeling psychological attributes in psychology – An epistemological discussion: Network analysis vs. latent variables. *Frontiers in Psychology, 8*. https://doi.org/10.3389/fpsyg.2017.00798

Hampshire, A., Chamberlain, S. R., Monti, M. M., Duncan, J., & Owen, A. M. (2010). The role of the right inferior frontal gyrus: Inhibition and attentional control. *NeuroImage, 50*, 1313–1319. https://doi.org/10.1016/j.neuroimage.2009.12.109

Haslbeck, J. M. B., & Fried, E. I. (2017). How predictable are symptoms in psychopathological networks? A reanalysis of 18 published datasets. *Psychological Medicine, 47*, 2767–2776. https://doi.org/10.1017/S0033291717001258

Havlicek, M., Ivanov, D., Roebroeck, A., & Uludağ, K. (2017). Determining excitatory and inhibitory neuronal activity from multimodal fMRI data using a generative hemodynamic model. *Frontiers in Neuroscience, 11*, 616. https://doi.org/10.3389/fnins.2017.00616

Heeren, A., & McNally, R. J. (2016). An integrative network approach to social anxiety disorder: The complex dynamic interplay among attentional bias for threat, attentional control, and symptoms. *Journal of Anxiety Disorders, 42*, 95–104. https://doi.org/10.1016/j.janxdis.2016.06.009

Heitzeg, M. M., Nigg, J. T., Hardee, J. E., Soules, M., Steinberg, D., Zubieta, J.-K., et al. (2014). Left middle frontal gyrus response to inhibitory errors in children prospectively predicts early problem substance use. *Drug and Alcohol Dependence, 141*, 51–57. https://doi.org/10.1016/j.drugalcdep.2014.05.002

Hirjak, D., Thomann, A. K., Kubera, K. M., Wolf, R. C., Jeung, H., Maier-Hein, K. H., et al. (2017). Cortical folding patterns are associated with impulsivity in healthy young adults. *Brain Imaging and Behavior, 11*, 1592–1603. https://doi.org/10.1007/s11682-016-9618-2

Hirose, S., Chikazoe, J., Watanabe, T., Linura, J., Kunimatsu, A., Abe, O., et al. (2012). Efficiency of go/no-go task performance implemented in the left hemisphere. *Journal of Neuroscience, 32*, 9059–9065. https://doi.org/10.1523/JNEUROSCI.0540-12.2012

Hofmann, S. G., & Curtiss, J. (2018). A complex network perspective on clinical science. *European Journal of Clinical Investigation, 48*, e12986. https://doi.org/10.1111/eci.12986

Houdé, O., & Borst, G. (2014). Measuring inhibitory control in children and adults. *Frontiers in Psychology, 5*, 616. https://doi.org/10.3389/fpsyg.2014.00616

Houdé, O., & Borst, G. (2015). Evidence for an inhibitory-control theory of the reasoning brain. *Frontiers in Human Neuroscience, 9*, 148. https://doi.org/10.3389/fnhum.2015.00148

Jackson, D. C., Mueller, C. J., Dolski, I., Dalton, K. M., Nitschke, J. B., Urry, H. L., et al. (2003). Now you feel it, now you don't frontal brain electrical asymmetry and individual differences in emotion regulation. *Psychological Science, 14*, 612–617. https://doi.org/10.1046/j.0956-7976.2003.psci_1473.x

Jasper, H. H., & Raney, E. T. (1937). The physiology of lateral cerebral dominance: Review of literature and evaluation of the test of simultaneous bilateral movement. *Psychological Bulletin, 34*, 151–165.

Jonason, P. K., & Jackson, C. J. (2016). The dark triad traits through the lens of reinforcement sensitivity theory. *Personality and Individual Differences, 90*, 273–277. https://doi.org/10.1016/j.paid.2015.11.023

Jones, P. J., Heeren, A., & McNally, R. J. (2017). Commentary: A network theory of mental disorders. *Frontiers in Psychology, 8*, 1305. https://doi.org/10.3389/fpsyg.2017.01305

Jung, J., Williams, S. R., Nezhad, F. S., & Ralph, M. A. L. (2017). GABA concentrations in the anterior temporal lobe predict human semantic processing. *Scientific Reports, 7*, 15748. https://doi.org/10.1038/s41598-017-15981-7

Kaiser, M. (2017). Mechanisms of connectome development. *Trends in Cognitive Sciences, 21*, 703–717. https://doi.org/10.1016/j.tics.2017.05.010

Kamradt, J. M., Nigg, J. T., Friderici, K. H., & Nikolas, M. A. (2017). Neuropsychological performance measures as intermediate phenotypes for attention-deficit/hyperactivity disorder: A multiple mediation analysis. *Development and Psychopathology, 29*, 259–272. https://doi.org/10.1017/S0954579416000195

Kelley, N. J., Hortensius, R., Schutter, D. J. L. G., & Harmon-Jones, E. (2017). The relationship of approach/avoidance motivation and asymmetric frontal cortical activity: A review of studies manipulating frontal asymmetry. *International Journal of Psychophysiology, 119*, 19–30. https://doi.org/10.1016/j.ijpsycho.2017.03.001

Kelley, N. J., & Schmeichel, B. J. J. (2016). Noninvasive stimulation over the dorsolateral prefrontal cortex facilitates the inhibition of motivated responding. *Journal of Experimental Psychology: General, 145*, 1702–1712.

Kirst, C., Modes, C. D., & Magnasco, M. O. (2017). Shifting attention to dynamics: Self-reconfiguration of neural networks. *Current Opinions in Systems Biology, 3*, 132–140. https://doi.org/10.1016/j.coisb.2017.04.006

Kurth, F., Mayer, E. A., Toga, A. W., Thompson, P. M., & Luders, E. (2013). The right inhibition? Callosal correlates of hand performance in healthy children and adolescents callosal correlates of hand performance. *Human Brain Mapping, 34*, 2259–2265. https://doi.org/10.1002/hbm.22060

Laland, K. N. (2008). Exploring gene-culture interactions: Insights from handedness, sexual selection and niche-construction case studies. *Philosophical Transactions of the Royal Society B: Biological Sciences, 363*, 3577–3589. https://doi.org/10.1098/rstb.2008.0132

Lanius, R. A., Wolf, E. J., Miller, M. W., Frewen, P. A., Vermetten, E., Brand, B., et al. (2014). The dissociative subtype of PTSD. In M. J. Friedman, T. M. Keane, & P. A. Resick (Eds.), *Handbook of PTSD: Science and practice* (2nd ed., pp. 251–274). New York: Guilford Press.

Levy, B. J., & Wagner, A. D. (2011). Cognitive control and right ventrolateral prefrontal cortex: Reflexive reorienting, motor inhibition, and action updating. *Annals of the New York Academy of Sciences, 1224*, 40–62. https://doi.org/10.1111/j.1749-6632.2011.05958.x

Martel, M. M., Levinson, C. A., Langer, J. K., & Nigg, J. T. (2016). A network analysis of developmental change in ADHD symptom structure from preschool to adulthood. *Clinical Psychological Science, 4*, 988–1001. https://doi.org/10.1177/2167702615618664

Martin, M. M., & Rubin, R. B. (1995). A new measure of cognitive flexibility. *Psychological Reports, 76*, 623–626. https://doi.org/10.2466/pr0.1995.76.2.623

McNally, R. J., Robinaugh, D. J., Wu, G. W. Y., Wang, L., Deserno, M. K., & Borsboom, D. (2015). Mental disorders as causal systems: A network approach to posttraumatic stress disorder. *Clinical Psychological Science, 3*, 836–849. https://doi.org/10.1177/2167702614553230

Mechin, N., Gable, P. A., & Hicks, J. A. (2016). Frontal asymmetry and alcohol cue reactivity: Influence of core personality systems. *Psychophysiology, 53*, 1224–1231. https://doi.org/10.1111/psyp.12659

Melchert, T. P. (2015). *Biopsychosocial practice: A science-based framework for behavioral health care*. Washington, DC: American Psychological Association.

Melzack, R., & Wall, P. D. (1965). Pain mechanisms: A new theory. *Science, 150*, 971–979.

Menon, V. (2013). Developmental pathways to functional brain networks: Emerging principles. *Trends in Cognitive Sciences, 17*, 627–640. https://doi.org/10.1016/j.tics.2013.09.015

Navlakha, S., Bar-Joseph, Z., & Barth, A. L. (2018). Network design and the brain. *Trends in Cognitive Sciences, 22*, 64–78. https://doi.org/10.1016/j.tics.2017.09.012

Neal, L. B., & Gable, P. A. (2017). Regulatory control and impulsivity relate to resting frontal activity. *Social Cognitive and Affective Neuroscience, 12*, 1377–1383. https://doi.org/10.1093/scan/nsx080

Nigg, J. T. (2000). On inhibition/disinhibition in developmental psychopathology: Views from cognitive and personality psychology and a working inhibition taxonomy. *Psychological Bulletin, 126*, 220–246.

Nigg, J. T. (2001). Is ADHD a disinhibitory disorder? *Psychological Bulletin, 127*, 571–598.

Nigg, J. T. (2017). Annual research review: On the relations among self-regulation, self-control, executive functioning, effortful control, cognitive control, impulsivity, risk-taking, and inhibition for developmental psychopathology. *Journal of Child Psychology and Psychiatry, 58*, 361–383. https://doi.org/10.1111/jcpp.12675

Ocklenburg, S., Peterburs, J., Mertzen, J., Schmitz, J., Güntürkün, O., & Grimshaw, G. M. (2017). Effects of emotional valence on hemispheric asymmetries in response inhibition. *Symmetry, 9*, 145. https://doi.org/10.3390/sym9080145

Pacini, R., & Epstein, S. (1999). The relation of rational and experiential information processing styles to personality, basic beliefs, and the ratio-bias phenomenon. *Journal of Personality and Social Psychology, 76*, 972–987. https://doi.org/10.1037/0022-3514.76.6.972

Padmanabhan, A., Lynch, C. J., Schaer, M., & Menon, V. (2017). The default mode network in autism. *Biological Psychiatry: Cognitive Neuroscience and Neuroimaging, 2*, 476–486. https://doi.org/10.1016/j.bpsc.2017.04.004

Pearl, J., Glymour, M., & Jewell, N. P. (2016). *Causal inference in statistics: A primer*. Chichester, England: Wiley.

Picton, T. W., Stuss, D. T., Alexander, M. P., Shallice, T., Binns, M. A., & Gillingham, S. (2007). Effects of focal frontal lesions on response inhibition. *Cerebral Cortex, 17*, 826–838. https://doi.org/10.1093/cercor/bhk031

Pizzarelli, R., & Cherubini, E. (2011). Alterations of GABAergic signaling in autism spectrum disorders. *Neural Plasticity, 2011*, 297153. https://doi.org/10.1155/2011/297153

Rabinovich, M., Huerta, R., & Laurent, G. (2008). Transient dynamics for neural processing. *Science, 321*, 48–50. https://doi.org/10.1126/science.1155564

Rabinovich, M. I., Simmons, A. N., & Varona, P. (2015). Dynamical bridge between brain and mind. *Trends in Cognitive Sciences, 19*, 453–461. https://doi.org/10.1016/j.tics.2015.06.005

Rath, J. F., & Elliott, T. R. (2012). Psychological models in rehabilitation psychology. In P. Kennedy (Ed.), *The Oxford handbook of rehabilitation psychology* (pp. 32–48). New York: Oxford University Press.

Reid, C. S., & Serrien, D. J. (2012). Handedness and the excitability of cortical inhibitory circuits. *Behavioral Brain Research, 230*, 144–148. https://doi.org/10.1016/j.bbr.2012.02.008

Reimann, M. W., Nolte, M., Scolamiero, M., Turner, K., Perin, P., Chindemi, G., et al. (2017). Cliques of neurons bound into cavities provide a missing link between structure and function. *Frontiers in Computational Neuroscience, 11*, 48. https://doi.org/10.3389/fncom.2017.00048

Rogers, L. J., Vallortigara, G., & Andrew, R. J. (2013). *Divided brains: The biology and behaviour of brain asymmetries*. Cambridge, MA: Cambridge University Press.

Rubin, R., Abbott, L. F., & Sompolinsky, H. (2017). Balanced excitation and inhibition are required for high-capacity, noise-robust neural selectivity. *Proceedings of the National Academy of Sciences, PNAS, 144*(44), E9366–E9375. https://doi.org/10.1073/pnas.1705841114

Rubin, T. N., Koyejo, O., Gorgolewski, K. J., Jones, M. N., Poldrack, R. A., & Yarkoni, T. (2017). Decoding brain activity using a large-scale probabilistic functional-anatomical atlas of human cognition. *PLoS Computational Biology, 13*, e1005649. https://doi.org/10.1371/journal.pcbi.1005649

Rubinstein, J. L. (2010). Three hypotheses for developmental defects that may underlie some forms of autism spectrum disorder. *Current Opinion in Neurology, 23*, 118–123. https://doi.org/10.1097/WCO.0b013e328336eb13

Sanborn, A. N., & Chater, N. (2017). The sampling brain. *Trends in Cognitive Sciences, 21*, 492–493. https://doi.org/10.1016/j.tics.2017.04.009

Saxe, G. N., Statnikov, A., Fenyo, D., Ren, J., Li, Z., Prasad, M., et al. (2016). A complex systems approach to causal discovery in psychiatry. *PLoS One, 11*, 1–20. https://doi.org/10.1371/journal.pone.0151174

Schmeichel, B. J., Crowell, A., & Harmon-Jones, E. (2016). Exercising self-control increases relative left frontal cortical activation. *Social, Cognitive, and Affective Neuroscience, 11*, 282–288. https://doi.org/10.1093/scan/nsv112

Serrien, D. J., & Sovijärvi-Spapé, M. M. (2013). Cognitive control of response inhibition and switching: Hemispheric lateralization and hand preference. *Brain and Cognition, 82*, 283–290. https://doi.org/10.1016/j.bandc.2013.04.013

Shallice, T., & Cipolotti, L. (2018). The prefrontal cortex and neurological impairments of active thought. *Annual Review of Psychology, 69*, 157–180. https://doi.org/10.1146/annurev-psych-010416-044123

Shallice, T., Stuss, D. T., Picton, T. W., Alexander, M. P., & Gillingham, S. (2007). Multiple effects of prefrontal lesions on task-switching. *Frontiers in Human Neuroscience, 1*, 2. https://doi.org/10.3389/neuro.09.002.2007

Sherblom, S. A. (2017). Complexity-thinking and social science: Self-organization involving human consciousness. *New Ideas in Psychology, 47*, 10–15.

Singer, W. (2013). Cortical dynamics revisited. *Trends in Cognitive Sciences, 17*, 616–626. https://doi.org/10.1016/j.tics.2013.09.006

Sporns, O. (2011). *Networks of the brain*. Cambridge, MA: MIT Press.

Sporns, O. (2012). *Discovering the human connectome*. Cambridge, MA: MIT Press.

Stramaccia, D. F., Penolazzi, B., Sartori, G., Braga, M., Mondini, S., & Galfano, G. (2015). Assessing the effects of tDCS over a delayed response inhibition task by targeting the right inferior frontal gyrus and right dorsolateral prefrontal cortex. *Experimental Brain Research, 233*, 2283–2290. https://doi.org/10.1007/s00221-015-4297-6

Streri, A., & de Hevia, M. (2015). Manual lateralization in infancy. *Frontiers in Psychology, 5*, 1575. https://doi.org/10.3389/fpsyg.2014.01575

Swick, D., Ashley, V., & Turken, A. U. (2008). Left inferior frontal gyrus is critical for response inhibition. *BMC Neuroscience, 9*. https://doi.org/10.1186/1471-2202-9-102

Talpalar, A. E., Bouvier, J., Borgius, L., Fortin, G., Pierani, A., & Kiehn, O. (2013). Dual-mode operation of neuronal networks involved in left-right alternation. *Nature, 500*, 85–88. https://doi.org/10.1038/nature12286

Terzian, H. (1964). Behavioural and EEG effects of intracarotid sodium amytal injection. *Acta Neurochirugica, 12*, 230–239. https://doi.org/10.1007/BF01402095

Testa-Silva, G., Loebel, A., Giugliano, M., de Kock, C. P. J., Mansvelder, H. D., & Meredith, R. M. (2012). Hyperconnectivity and slow synapses during early development of medial prefrontal cortex in a mouse model for mental retardation and autism. *Cerebral Cortex, 22*, 1333–1342. https://doi.org/10.1093/cercor/bhr224

Thatcher, R. W., North, D. M., Neubrander, J., Biver, C. J., Cutler, S., & DeFina, P. (2009). Autism and EEG phase reset: Deficient GABA mediated inhibition in thalamo-cortical circuits. *Developmental Neuropsychology, 34*, 780–800. https://doi.org/10.1080/87565640903265178

Tops, M., Boksem, M. A. S., Quirin, M., & Koole, S. L. (2014). Internally-directed cognition and mindfulness: An integrative perspective derived from predictive and reactive control systems theory. *Frontiers in Psychology, 5*, 429. https://doi.org/10.3389/fpsyg.2014.00429

Tops, M., Quirin, M., Boksem, M. A. S., & Koole, S. L. (2017). Large-scale neural networks and the lateralization of motivation and emotion. *International Journal of Psychophysiology, 119*, 41–49. https://doi.org/10.1016/j.ijpsycho.2017.02.004

Tsuchida, A., & Fellows, L. K. (2013). Are core component processes of executive function dissociable within the frontal lobes? Evidence from humans with focal prefrontal damage. *Cortex, 49*, 1790–1800. https://doi.org/10.1016/j.cortex.2012.10.014

Tzourio-Mazoyer, N., Perrone-Bertolotti, M., Jobard, G., Mazoyer, B., & Baciu, M. (2017). Multi-factorial modulation of hemispheric specialization and plasticity for language in healthy and pathological conditions: A review. *Cortex, 86*, 314–339. https://doi.org/10.1016/j.cortex.2016.05.013

Um, J. W. (2017). Roles of glial cells in sculpting inhibitory synapses and neural circuits. *Frontiers in Molecular Neuroscience, 10*, 381. https://doi.org/10.3389/fnmol.2017.00381

Urban, J. B., Osgood, N., Okamoto, J., Mabry, P., & Lich, K. H. (2014). Developmental systems science: Extending developmental science with systems science methodologies. In M. Molenaar, R. M. Lerner, & K. M. Newell (Eds.), *Handbook of developmental systems theory and methodology* (pp. 95–127). New York: Guildford Press.

Vallence, A.-M., Smalley, E., Drummond, P. D., & Hammond, G. R. (2017). Long-interval intracortical inhibition is asymmetric in young but not older adults. *Journal of Neurophysiology, 118*, 1581–1590. https://doi.org/10.1152/jn.00794.2016

van Campen, A. D., Kunert, R., van den Wildenberg, W. P. M., & Ridderinkhof, K. R. (2017). Repetitive transcranial magnetic stimulation over inferior frontal cortex impairs the suppression (but not expression) of action impulses during action conflict. *Psychophysiology*. https://doi.org/10.1111/psyp.13003

van den Heuvel, M. P., & Sporns, O. (2013). Network hubs in the human brain. *Trends in Cognitive Sciences, 17*, 683–696. https://doi.org/10.1016/j.tics.2013.09.012

van Eck, D. (2018). Rethinking the explanatory power of dynamical models in cognitive science. *Philosophical Psychology, 31*, 1131–1161.

Vattikuti, S., & Chow, C. C. (2010). A computational model for cerebral cortical dysfunction in autism spectrum disorders. *Biological Psychiatry, 67*, 672–678. https://doi.org/10.1016/j.biopsych.2009.09.008

Verbruggen, F., Aron, A. R., Stevens, M. A., & Chambers, C. D. (2010). Theta burst stimulation dissociates attention and action updating in human inferior frontal cortex. *Proceedings of the National Academy of Sciences of the United States of America, 107*, 13966–13971. https://doi.org/10.1038/35036239

Wacker, J. (2018). Effects of positive emotion, extraversion, and dopamine on cognitive stability-flexibility and frontal EEG asymmetry. *Psychophysiology, 55*, e12727. https://doi.org/10.1111/psyp.12727

Wacker, J., Chavanon, M.-L., Leue, A., & Stemmler, G. (2008). Is running away right? The behavioral activation-behavioral inhibition model of anterior asymmetry. *Emotion, 8*, 232–249. https://doi.org/10.1037/1528-3542.8.2.232

Wacker, J., Chavanon, M.-L., Leue, A., & Stemmler, G. (2010). Trait BIS predicts alpha asymmetry and P300 in a go/ no go task. *European Journal of Personality, 24*, 85–105. https://doi.org/10.1002/per.740

Wacker, J., Heldmann, M., & Stemmler, G. (2003). Separating emotion and motivational direction in fear and anger: Effects on frontal asymmetry. *Emotion, 3*, 167–193. https://doi.org/10.1037/1528-3542.3.2.167

Watanabe, H., Homae, F., & Taga, G. (2011). Developmental emergence of self-referential and inhibition mechanisms of body movements underlying felicitous behaviors. *Journal of Experimental Psychology: Human Perception and Performance, 37*, 1157–1173. https://doi.org/10.1037/a0021936

Wig, G. S. (2017). Segregated systems of human brain networks. *Trends in Cognitive Science, 21*, 981–996. https://doi.org/10.1016/j.tics.2017.09.006

Xue, M., Atallah, B. V., & Scanziani, M. (2014). Equalizing excitation-inhibition rations across visual cortical neurons. *Nature, 511*, 596–600. https://doi.org/10.1038/nature13321

Yizhar, O., Fenno, L. E., Prigge, M., Schneider, F., Davidson, T. J., O'Shea, D. J., et al. (2011). Neocortical excitation/inhibition balance in information processing and social dysfunction. *Nature, 477*, 171–178. https://doi.org/10.1038/nature10360

Young, G. (1990a). The development of hemispheric and manual specialization. In G. Hammond (Ed.), *The cerebral control of speech and limb movements* (pp. 79–139). Amsterdam: North Holland.

Young, G. (1990b). Early neuropsychological development: Lateralization of functions – Hemispheric specialization. In C.-A. Hauert (Ed.), *Developmental psychology: Cognitive, perceptuo-motor and neuropsychological perspectives* (pp. 113–181). Amsterdam: North Holland.

Young, G. (1997). *Adult development, therapy, and culture: A postmodern synthesis*. New York: Plenum Press.

Young, G. (2011). *Development and causality: Neo-Piagetian perspectives*. New York: Springer Science + Business Media.

Young, G. (2015). Causality in psychiatry: A hybrid symptom network construct model. *Frontiers in Psychiatry, 6*, 164. https://doi.org/10.3389/fpsyt.2015.00164

Young, G. (2016). *Unifying causality and psychology: Being, brain and behavior*. Cham, Switzerland: Springer International Publishing.

Young, G., Bowman, J. G., Methot, C., Finlayson, M., Quintal, J., & Boissonneault, P. (1983). Hemispheric specialization development: What (inhibition) and how (parents). In G. Young, S. J. Segalowitz, C. M. Corter, & S. E. Trehub (Eds.), *Manual specialization and the developing brain* (pp. 119–140). New York: Academic Press.

Young, G., & Gagnon, M. (1990). Neonatal laterality, birth stress, familial sinistrality, and left brain inhibition. *Developmental Neuropsychology, 6*, 127–150.

Young, G., Segalowitz, S. J., Misek, P., Alp, I. E., & Boulet, R. (1983). Is early reaching left-handed? Review of manual specialization research. In G. Young, S. J. Segalowitz, C. M. Corter, & S. E. Trehub (Eds.), *Manual specialization and the developing brain* (pp. 13–32). New York: Academic Press.

Zednik, C. (2018). Models and mechanisms in network neuroscience. *Philosophical Psychology*. https://doi.org/10.1080/09515089.2018.1512090

Zhang, R., Geng, X., & Lee, T. M. C. (2017). Large-scale functional neural network correlates of response inhibition: An fMRI meta-analysis. *Brain Structure and Function, 222*, 3973–3990. https://doi.org/10.1007/s00429-017-1443-x

Zikopoulos, B., & Barbas, H. (2013). Altered neural connectivity in excitatory and inhibitory cortical circuits in autism. *Frontiers in Human Neuroscience, 7*, 609. https://doi.org/10.3389/fnhum.2012.00609

Zorlu, N., Çapraz, N., Oztekin, E., Bagci, B., Di Biase, M. A., Zalesky, A., et al. (2017). Rich club and reward network connectivity as endophenotypes for alcohol dependence: A diffusion tensor imaging study. *Addiction Biology*. https://doi.org/10.1111/adbh.12599

Chapter 9
New Laterality Models

Abstract The last chapter of the book on lateralization continues to explore modeling. First, it gives some of the author's conceptualizations on laterality that are more speculative, including on the stages in the evolution of lateralization and steps in change related to that model. Most of the chapter reviews the host of models that have been highlighted in the prior chapters on laterality and its development and evolution. These include the combined invariant-progressive model, which is my integrative one for the opposing equipotential and invariant ones. That is, early laterality might follow the adult pattern, but is still quite variable, unstable, susceptible to environment effects, etc. The developmental cascade model is an influential one, and I indicate the nature of the progressive transfers involved. The chapter reviews the environmental and genetic ones, among others. Some newer models that also might contribute to understanding laterality include ones for embodiment, nonlinear dynamic systems theory and attractors, and networks. The chapter reflects on the evolution of laterality, as well. It concludes with a compendium of areas that have been researched that are beyond the scope of the present work, and thus offers potential future research directions. Finally, it emphasizes, once more, the value of the activation-inhibition coordination hypothesis of lateralization. This chapter concludes the portion of the book on Causality, and it emphasizes the multi-factorial nature of causality in behavioral expression, as well as the author's own work as possible helping in understanding the development of causality in one area (laterality) in a way consistent with a more general approach to understanding causality in psychology, as per Young (Unifying causality and psychology: being, brain and behavior. Springer International Publishing, Cham, 2016).

G. Young, *Causality and Development*,
https://doi.org/10.1007/978-3-030-02493-2_9

Conclusions

Reaching in New Directions

Introduction

The final section of the article extends further the author's work on development generally for the study of lateralization and its development and evolution. Also, it extends the activation-inhibition coordination model in these regards.

Table 9.1 indicates how the steps in lateralization might proceed in development and inform evolution (not that ontogeny recapitulates phylogeny). The model shows a five-step sequence that repeats in five phases (a five sub-stage × five stage model), one created to help understand Neo-Piagetian cognitive development and Neo-Eriksonian socio-emotional/affective development (Young, 1990a, 1990b, 1997, 2011, 2012, 2016).

The three figures (Figs. 9.1, 9.2 and 9.3) further elaborate the Neo-Piagetian/Neo-Eriksonian (sub)stage model. They allow for continued differentiation of the relationship between development, evolution, and handedness and related lateralizations.

Activation-Inhibition Coordination

To date, the paper has emphasized the value of the activation-inhibition coordination model of behavior and brain, generally, and manual and hemispheric specialization, particularly. In this vein, Young (1990a, 1990b, 2011 (Table 26.1–5); 2016 (Table 31.2–6)) developed a model of the development of hemispheric specialization in terms of stages involving increasing left hemisphere activation-inhibition coordination, co-option, and control that presaged contemporary emphasis on network models, as well (see Table 9.1). The table illustrates that the concept of activation-inhibition coordination might help explain the steps in the evolution of lateralization. Also, it illustrates how concepts from network theory can translate this approach into its language.

Stages of Change and in Development

The first figure of the three in this section expands the stage model of Young (e.g., 2011, 2016). The figure indicates the parallels between the stages of change model of Prochaska, Norcross, and DiClemente (1994) and Young's five-stage developmental model. The former model consists of five stages after precontemplation. It begins with contemplation of change, proceeding through to implementation and finally to resolution. Young indicated that the five steps involved can be translated into the language of attractors and complex adaptive systems (CAS). This opens up

Table 9.1 Hypothesized evolution of behavior and brain networking in terms of activation-inhibition coordinations

	Evolutionary Period				
Sub-stages	Reptilian	Paleo-mammalian	Hominin	Homo Sapiens	Modern humans
Coordination [Different nodes in the circuitry involved related over edges to form juxtaposed relations in circuitry]	At first, reflex centers mature without stimulus-sensitive activating mechanisms; nevertheless, they discharge, and this occurs even in pairs through lateral activation-inhibition interplay	By recruitment processes similar to the one in step (reptilian integration) 5, larger neuronal clusters form. They require intra-cluster activation-inhibition synchrony so that corresponding movement sequence is controlled for fine interference by perseverations and by intruding similar movements	The process in level 10 (paleo-mammalian integration) radiates across the hemisphere, permitting cross zone-areas to begin to form inter-linked pairs	The process is level 15 (hominin integration) expands to integration of major anterior (frontal) areas. Welsh and Pennington (1988) describe how these may emerge	To this point, I have emphasized macro processes in activation-inhibition coordination in the brain relating to increasing intra- and inter-zone/region integrations. However, throughout the process of hemispheric specialization and of brain growth, in general, micro processes are taking place related to synaptogenesis, dendritic arborization, synaptic pruning, and sculpting. In a certain sense, circuitry formation and synaptic pruning/reorganization involve neuronal activation and inhibition coordination processes at the micro level that complement the processes at the macro level. To arrive at any of the post-formal cognitive stages in brain function and specializations, the macro- and micro-processes should be working in a complete, optimal balance
Hierarchization [The circuitry established in the prior phase achieves higher-order properties, e.g., become directional hubs]	Fixed order established in reflex pairs by one-way inhibitory suppression of direction in their functional linkage. Also, full stimulus-provoked reflex arcs develop through control by inhibition-disinhibition timing	Neuronal cluster interdigitation goes one step beyond, as pairs form a hierarchy with one subsumed to another by activation-inhibition regulation. The fine interference control described above (paleo-mammalian coordination) also applies here	Zone-areas in the same hemisphere form inhibition barriers between them to better control interference during their interrelating and simultaneous functioning	Inter-hemispheric integration (controlled in the left hemisphere) occurs by optimal synchronization of activation-inhibition coordination. Several phases may occur, and in the last one the integration may include inhibition of major self-reinforcing systems	

(continued)

Table 9.1 (continued)

	Evolutionary Period				
Sub-stages	Reptilian	Paleo-mammalian	Hominin	Homo Sapiens	Modern humans
Systematization [The hubs of the prior phase might evolve into tighter or more flexible higher-order circuits, such as rich or small world ones]	Above process (reptilian hierarchization) expands to include other components at second or both phases of movement. This may involve coupling with other reflexes and/ or interdigitation with extra-reflex neuronal centers primarily sensory-perceptual in nature	Above process (paleo-mammalian hierarchization) expands to permit larger zone-area mobilization. Neuronal cluster hierarchies are synchronized to permit inhibitory control of gross interference at outset and throughout unrelated neuronal clusters	Inter-hemispheric communication collaboration (controlled in left hemisphere) by commissural (corpus callosum) activation-inhibition coordination allows brain-wide mobilization. Several phases probably occur, involving intrahemispheric incorporation of emerging anterior areas into the process. The frontal regions, for example, are known for inhibition of action to allow for evaluation		
Multiplication [The systematized nodes of the prior stage increasingly characterize the evolving system]	Level 3 (reptilian systematization) units coordinated sequentially in time by activation-inhibition balancing	Widespread expansion into extra zone-area surround is a major step, ensuring that the gross interference control described above (hominin systematization) comes to include multiple surround neuronal clusters			

Integration [The system fully takes on the characteristics of the evolving networking system, attaining an organization ready for further coupling with other systems (the next coordination)]	Movement becomes partly reflex-free, as neuronal clusters incorporate via own activation-inhibition balancing extra-reflex neuronal centers involved in control of spatio-temporal changes	The range of interference control now extends cross zone-area, i.e., intra-hemispherically to some extent			

Adapted from Young (1990a)

Based on the work of MacNeilage, Studdert-Kennedy, and Lindblom (1987, 1988) and Corballis (1989, 1991, 1992) in the evolution of human laterality and related behavior, the best-fitting sequence in primate and hominid evolution follows: paleo-mammalian, early prosimian, ancestral monkey, ancestral ape, Australopithecus afarensis, Homo habilis, Homo erectus, Archaic homo sapiens, Homo sapiens sapiens, Cromagnon people, and contemporary people. The 25 steps in the model presented in the Table incorporate and add to this progression

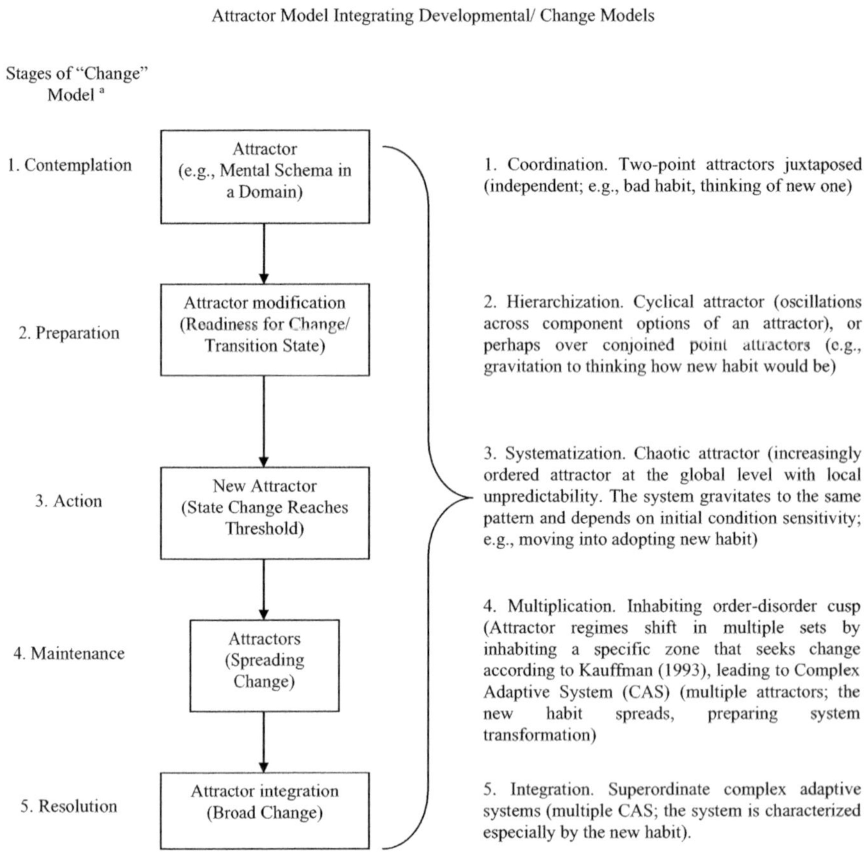

Fig. 9.1 An attractor/complexity developmental model
The figure presents a five-step model of development involving the elaboration of attractors and complex adaptive systems (Young, 2011, 2016). The five-step change model is a generic one applicable to behavioral change processes (Prochaska et al., 1994). Thus, two independent models of behavioral change, one developmental and one on stages in change, both involve five steps
Note. (a) Young (1997) showed the parallel between the Prochaska et al. stage model (1994) of change and the present model of stages in development. Specifically, in terms of their stage of contemplating change, the individual can be considered as coordinating the phases involving present condition and future possibility. With respect to attractor modeling, the future better habit is juxtaposed with the existing poorer one
(b) In the next step of preparing/deciding/determining in transitions in therapy, the individual can be considered as hierarchically organizing commitment and planning as primary in working toward goals. The new habit begins to take precedence (e.g., its attractor)
(c) In the stage of deliberate action, systematization can be considered to characterize organization, given that deliberate action implies a systemic plan into action. In terms of attractors, this means that a "chaotic" attractor has formed, which is essentially not chaotic at all in its organization
(d) Next, the maintenance phase reflects the spreading out or propagation of gains that have been made into wider regions of the system, resembling what I would call multiplication. In attractor terms, the chaotic attractor morphs into a bifurcating multiple attractor dynamic or complex adaptive system (CAS)
(e) Finally, the step of problem resolution indicates that the system is in dynamic integration. Here, the CAS becomes "superordinate"
[a] Adapted from Prochaska et al. (1994), Maddox (1995)

Person (P)/ Organism (O) (e.g., skills, resources)	Existing cognitive/ language/ motor (manual) executive (including inhibition, planning, processing speed, working memory), problem solving, social, emotional, motivational, and coping/ resource allocation skills in conjunction with appraisals of social support/ buffering compared to environmental adversity (past and present)
	X
Environment (E)/ Ecological Niche	Ongoing adaptation to cognitive, social, emotional contextual/ task demands and problem-solving demands for the problem/ domain at issue in conjunction with actual social support/ buffering compared to environmental adversity (past and present)
	=
Networked Behavior/ Symptom (B/S)-Skill/ Resource Yoking	Depending on P/O x E and the context/ problem at hand, the P/O yokes or networks dynamically the skills/ resources required toward adaptation and possible resolution (e.g., as cognitive conceptual control structure or equivalent), leading to feedback into extant skills/ resources and potentiating change (improvement or deterioration). The dynamically organized adapting system involved might reach a sufficiently perturbed state to self-organize at a higher level (e.g., new (sub)stage)

Fig. 9.2 Networked behavior (symptom) yoking model
The figure illustrates a broad (P × E) model of behavior and its development (B) that includes when it gets disturbed (in symptoms, S). It translates the task of ongoing adaptation into the concepts of networks and yoking, which involve shifting dynamical adjustments to the task/domain/context/ problem at hand. The dynamic might include self-organized systematic emergence of higher-order system functioning (e.g., a new (sub)stage). The types of behaviors/skills/resources involved are both personal (organismic) and social/environmental or their self-appraisals. They include motor, language, social, emotional and related ones, and not just cognitive/executive ones. Typically, the whole person solves the problem at hand and the schemes/operations involved are integrated cognitive, emotional, and social ones; for example, (sub)stages can emerge when the perturbations in the system reach thresholds or cusps of change that lead to radical readjustments in system quality to new levels (e.g., sensori-motor to representational levels for a specific behavioral/skill/resource configuration for a task/domain/problem being tackled online). Finally, the concept of activation-inhibition coordination affords a model that can help explain how P/O, E, and B/S networking or yoking can transform to higher levels
The network/yoking model being proposed to help understand behavioral (and symptom) expression and their underpinning bases informs modeling of hemispheric (and manual) specialization. The context/task adjustment process or problem solving in a specific domain, whether cognitive, emotional, or otherwise, requires hemispheric specialization for optimal information processing, neural functioning, resource management, and the like, such that the hemispheres divide well the responses to the demands at hand and engage in shared cooperativity in these regards, as well. Yoking concerns a rapid, dynamic, ongoing, online processing of applicable modules and strategies to the issue at hand, and the left hemisphere excels in the analytic sequencing required in these terms, for example, while the right hemisphere is more holistic, integrative, for example.
(*caption continued on p. 188*)

Fig. 9.2 (continued) Both types of skills, which also relate to the corresponding manual behaviors associated with the hemispheres, can be translated into the language of activation-inhibition coordination (see Table 5.1), giving a generic language applicable to both brain and behavioral function. Moreover, the distinct functions of the left and right hemispheres (and corresponding manual lateralizations) develop from the fetal period onward, such that specialization development can be described in terms of the differential activation-inhibition coordinations of the right and left sides, and their superordinate coordinations
Moreover, in general, development can be described in these terms, both in general brain development and general behavioral development. Development can proceed linearly and gradually or with punctuated step, phase, or sub(stage) acquisitions, e.g., through self-organizing emergence. In this sense, the present model can help to translate any stage/sub-stage and related models in terms of network yoking, activation-inhibition coordination, and related processes. Therefore, at the heart of development and its individual differences, one might find an essential role for left and right hemisphere (and related manual) specializations, along with their differential skills, in terms of a common metric related to networked yoking, activation-inhibition coordination, and so on. In terms of (sub)stages that might develop, the states of the system as expressed in networked yoking and activation-inhibition coordination become more deeply ingrained with age, and are deployed as massive modules, yet decomposed as required for the task at hand to varying degrees to facilitate the adaptive, online problem solving required, but with individual differences in efficacy in these regards

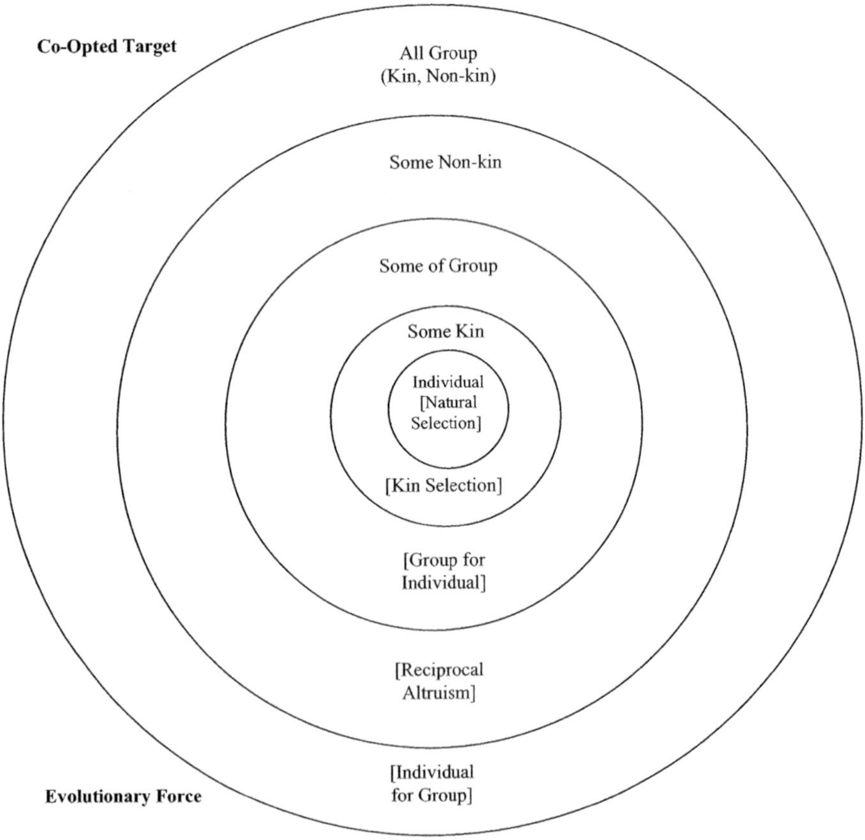

Fig. 9.3 Degree of gene co-opting fostered by different levels of multilevel selection

(*caption continued on p. 189*)

Fig. 9.3 (continued) The figure depicts five evolutionary forces that have acted in selecting human behavior for adaptive fitness. The order given for the forces reflects their order of primacy in the growing person's developmental levels, especially social and cognitive. The caption elaborates especially the last three levels, noting that the third had been formulated originally by Young (1997, 2011). It contrasts with the typical understanding of group selection, as in the fifth level. All the four levels after the first one can be viewed facilitating behavior that attempts to (a) increasingly co-opt phenotypes of others (and their underlying genes, which would be related to some degree to the individual organism) to help in personal survival and reproduction or (b) contribute more indirectly to genetic survival and reproduction through helping related others, even if distantly so

Natural Selection. This is the standard evolutionary force described by Darwin (1859), e.g., related to survival of the fittest. It refers to competitive selection in the adaptation to ecological niche through the hereditary units (now understood as genes) that underlie the adaptive traits involved

Kin Selection. Hamilton (1964) added that individuals might behave to optimize the survival and reproduction of kin who share their inherited units

Group-for-Individual Selection. As described by Young (1997, 2011), in the next level in the present model, children have developed behaviors that allow them to take advantage of group-selected teaching traits. In this sense, the range of genetic resources to which the individual has access for survival and reproductive needs expands to members of the group, whether kin or non-kin, who are acting to create social and institutional structures that facilitate obtaining the survival and reproductive advantages for the children. Generalized teaching strategies have been selected for in adults partly because of the downstream adaptive advantages for one's own offspring or those of kin, as much as for children in general

The cognitive level promoted by the level of Group-for-Individual behavior concerns Piagetian representational structures, which allow for symbolic thought, language use, and so on, through pre-operations and concrete operations. Specifically, the latter cognitive capacity permits logical thought to be expressed in the physical contexts that the child encounters, such as in the particular school subjects to which school-age children are exposed

Note that in the case of children profiting from learning and educational structures, one cannot speak of immediate reproductive advantages. However, the social and cognitive skills developed in the teaching and learning that takes place in educational and instructional settings, as well as the inter-peer social interactions and links promoted, serve these goals in the long run. That is, the resource networking involved in children attending school and otherwise profiting from learning opportunities created by the group might not be perceived easily, because the information and knowledge-base acquired in the educational learning situations, as well as the social connections, might reveal their adaptive advantages only later in development

Reciprocity. Next, as per Trivers (1971), reciprocal altruism or selection acts to increase the scope of gene pools aiding individuals' survival and reproduction by capturing non-kin in expanded peer and social interaction, mutually beneficial social exchanges, alliances and pacts, the tracking of resource donation and receipt, the monitoring of cooperation and free loading, and so on. This helps enhance resource networking access, acquisition, management, and replenishment, all necessary for survival, reproduction, adaptedness, and fitness

Individual-for-Group Selection. Finally, classical group selection (Sober, 1984), or Individual-for-Group selection, acts to increase the array of actors contributing to an individual's fitness, whether kin or non-kin. This acts to increase the extent of resource networking and accrual available to the individual for survival and reproduction. Also, the behavior allows the group to increase its resource access, acquisition, management, and replenishment [think of brainstorming at work], thereby profiting all individuals in the group who are creating the collective product, and others who are indirectly involved [e.g., the profitability of the whole company increases]. Granted, the behavior expressed by the individual may be self-sacrificial, but this need not be the case. Moreover, even if it is, the activity is oriented to increasing group competitiveness, so functions to ensure survival and reproduction of all its members, on the average, whether self or other, or whether kin or non-kin

Adapted from Young (1997, 2011)

the model to wider generality, because attractor/CAS modeling can be applied to both living and nonliving systems (Young, 2011, 2016). Young attempted to find a common language to model the five-step change process that he described for development, and that is consistent with other behavioral change phenomena, such as in the stages of change. In this sense, he described the various stages, whether developmental or otherwise, that he and others have found as ones involving: coordination, hierarchization, systematization, multiplication, and integration.

How general is the five-phase sequence of development/changes and its underlying attractor dynamic, and how might it inform evolution? The second figure of the three constructed to conclude the article presents Young's (1997) model of the five evolutionary forces in development, which includes the classic ones of natural selection, kin selection, and reciprocity, as well as group selection, while adding a new one to the field on the group acting for individuals, especially children. This latter evolutionary force relates to the unique human behavior of teaching, as discussed above, and the corresponding childhood ability to learn intensively from teaching, such as in formal schools. The figure does not show the hypothesis that, in terms of the evolution of human behavior, the five evolutionary forces acted in sequence to promote qualitatively distinct cognitive stages in development, such as described by the Neo-Piagetians. In this sense, the evolutionary force of group for individual had acted to confer adaptive advantage in teaching, for example, given the cognitive skills permitted through the Piagetian acquisitions that corresponded to this capacity.

P × E = B

The third of the three figures in the series constructed to conclude the article and to tie in development, evolution, and handedness presents a Person × Environment model of behavior, but one that includes attractors, activation-inhibition coordination, the specialization of the hemispheres, and so on. The figure illustrates that there are two types of adaptation, one evolutionarily, or in macro time, as in conferring adaptive advantage in evolution, and one in real micro time, as in ongoing adaptation to the context.

Young (2011, 2016) has described how stages and sub-stages persist in development, as mentioned, both for Neo-Eriksonian development and for the Neo-Piagetian. For example, in solving problems, if sensori-motor skills are required, we yoke them to other skills in other (sub) stages that are fitted to the problem-solving strategies and skills required. This figure posits that the same yoking can take place in any type of behavior as we problem solve, and that yoking involves activation-inhibition coordination.

Therefore, we end up with a developmental model in which yoking is critical and networking would be an analogous term. Moreover, the rapid yoking process online can alter, dissolve, reappear, and so on, and improve with time in content quality, in skill and speed, and so on. This immediately adaptive process being described could help to understand how stages and sub-stages could develop and change.

Given the parallels sought over development and evolution, yoking models, for example, in how behavioral networking takes place in problem solving and can be explained as activation-coordination processes, could very well inform evolution. That is, evolution might take place through analogous processes as development. For example, more so than finding any particular behavioral or modular change in evolution, we might emerge with a model of evolution that emphasizes generic adaptive networked yoking taking place phenotypically and enabling species' change and evolution.

Summary, Models, and Implications

Introduction

As a summary, the first portion of this book consists of three parts, with the first concentrating on the development of handedness, manual lateralization, and cerebral lateralization in humans, especially fetally and in the first few years. The second focuses on multi-factorial causality and animal research and evolution. The third focuses on models that might apply to the question of early lateralizations, especially new ones such as the activation-inhibition coordination model. This summary focuses especially on the various models mentioned in the book and how they are complementary, rather than reviewing the empirical findings themselves.

Combined Invariant-Progressive Model

The review of the recent research on early lateralizations in the first part of the article highlights that handedness and manual lateralization differ, with the former concerning preference on daily and simpler tasks and the latter on more demanding and complex tasks. Handedness exhibits a right-hand bias from early in life, but only after several years of development is it stable. Manual specialization reflects the early differential functioning of the hemispheres, and is best evidenced by tasks that are considered complex for the age period at hand.

Thus, reaching at 1 month of age concerns manual specialization as much as constituting a precursor to later reaching and handedness preference. Hemispheric specialization appears to manifest even fetally, and the neonate already is expressing precursors of the adult model in which the left hemisphere typically is specialized for verbal and related skills and the right hemisphere for visuo-spatial and related skills. The model that represents these types of empirical findings is termed the invariant lateralization model, because it is presumed that although the behaviors and skills expressed by one hemisphere or the other might change with development, the underlying common function is the same or similar and already present early in life. There is no need to assume that any aspect of the competing model – equi-potential and progressive lateralization – bears on the early empirical findings related to lateralized behavior and brain. However, the invariant lateralization model cannot fully explain the developmental data on handedness, manual specialization, and hemispheric specialization in that progressive changes are found and transfers from one type of lateralization to another takes place in development. The adult pattern evident in the neonatal lateralization undergoes stabilization that is not complete for years. In this sense, a combined invariant-progressive model of lateralization best fits the data that has been gathered on lateralization early in life.

Cascades

Another model concerning the early development of lateralization involves cascades or progressive transfers from one developmental acquisition to the next. Crucial evidence in development derives from longitudinal research, but the findings are not necessarily linear – for example, instead of finding that an early right head turning bias to the right side predicts later right-side head turning, it is more informative to ascertain whether an early right heading turning, which is an appropriate early behavior to examine for laterality, but does not concern handedness, per se, relates to later handedness. If it does, what would be the mechanisms that allow for the relationship between early head turning and later handedness to develop and have early head turning direction of the head actually influence later laterality of the hand? In this regard, head turning facilitates visual regard of the hand on the side of the head turn so that visual directed reaching is facilitated on that side, as well, which promotes the eventual development of later manual behavior and handedness on the side preferred by the early head turning (as per the research and cascade modeling of Michel and colleagues, e.g., Campbell, Marcinowski, Babik, & Michel, 2015; Michel, 2018).

Experience

This example illustrates that experience plays a critical role in early hand use, laterality, handedness, manual specialization, and hemispheric specialization. The infant's interaction with the objects and people in the environment serve to reinforce and entrench lateralization tendencies. Experience might be intrinsically generated, as in the example, or extrinsically generated, as in parents holding objects to one side in order to reach and grasp or otherwise encouraging a sidedness preference, as in traditional or agricultural societies shaping a conforming universal right handedness. The example also illustrates that cascades might be along the same track or domain, as in the manual one, or to a different track or domain, as in the longitudinal research showing that early lateralized manual behavior predicts verbal skills.

Hemisphericity

The latter example illustrates that there are both micro- and macroenvironmental influences on development, as in parental influence and cultural influence, respectively. However, for the area of handedness development and related lateralizations, one needs to enquire how the person contributes to his or her own development, for example, so that it is considered a biopsychosocial and not just a bio-experiential phenomenon. In this regard, the concept of hemisphericity might need to be resurrected and updated into a new form. For example, it could refer to hemispheric activation as much as preference, as in priming research. In one way or another, both intrinsic and extrinsic factors should be examined for any hemispheric preferences that arise individually such that the person deviates from implementing the normative skills of the hemispheres for the problem at hand, the context, and so on, the specific differential hemisphere-related skills already expressed, and so on. The historical research on the topic has not considered development sufficiently. It could be that early preferences are hemisphere skill dependent, then there is increasing skewness toward one hemisphere or the other through various intrinsic and extrinsic factors, and then the person develops the preference to the point that the skill sets that are consciously chosen in problem solving lean to the skill sets of one hemisphere or the other.

Combined Model Again

Returning to the question of whether early hemispheric specialization reflects an invariant lateralization or an equi-potential and then progressive lateralization, the work showing experiential, parental, cultural, and other environmental and social influences on developing laterality, as well as the cascade model that can help explain experiential influences and transfers in laterality development, serves to illustrate that neither the invariant nor equi-potential-progressive models of lateralization development suffice to explain it in full. It appears that what works consists of the combined invariant and progressive developmental model of early lateralizations. The research has revealed both early plasticity of the hemispheres and their skill sets and later ingrained, stable patterns in development, while respecting the equivalence or similarity of neonatal and early lateralities with the adult model when the right tasks are used.

Nonlinear Model

The nonlinear dynamical systems model (NLDS) speaks to handedness development and related asymmetries in behavior and brain. NLDS is systemic or inclusive of variables that might impact the development of a behavior or in the brain.

However, as its name would imply, instead of focusing uniquely on linear relations among variables and averages in development, it seeks to understand variability and "noise." Therefore, it adds to the study of development, the nonlinear aspects of self-organization, stability at far from equilibrium, bifurcation at the cusp of stretched perturbations, and difficulty in maintaining equilibrium, criticality, chaos, attractor dynamics, emergence, hierarchical organization of levels of the system, top-down and bottom-up influences on the system, yet with no central governing program organizing the system, local variability yet global coherence, gravitating to the cusp of stability or change to facilitate change and development, sensitivity to initial conditions (the so called butterfly effect), and ultimately the system whole being greater than the sum of the parts. As for attractors, they concern regions in the state space of the system at issue to which its dynamics gravitate, as with illness versus health attractors or (and à propos to the present article) right-hand predispositions and use versus left-hand predisposition and use. Metaphorically, the deeper the well representing one attractor or the other that might be predominant, the harder it is to escape its pull and gravitate to a different attractor. Attractor models might include one point only, but for laterality two opposing ones are required. The system might move beyond a dual attractor landscape into a chaotic regime or even a more complex adaptive system, with living organisms providing a good example of multiple attractor complexity. For further description of attractor and complexity theory, refer to Young (2016), for example.

Attractors

Returning to the example of right and left laterality attractors, the model could apply to left and right hemisphere lateralization or to left- and right-hand use on either complex or simpler tasks, as in manual specialization and handedness, respectively. Hand use is not rigidly stable, and it changes in expressed preference; many factors can affect the directionality and derail an otherwise consistent sidedness. Attractor modeling and NLDS approaches can help explain the minutiae of micro changes in asymmetric patterning of brain and behavior and the macro changes that accompany long-term stability developments. This approach applies both to understanding online, adaptive organization to the task, problem, matter, or context at hand, because it concerns de novo reorganizations as required for the overall system structure at hand, yet can help explain overrides to impetuses system change despite invitations to change by ongoing system adjustments and dynamics. It can relate to the noise in the system and the overwhelming nature of variability in behavior and brain that invites attractor instability, or relate to resistance to change and inertia, encouraging system stability and equilibrium despite perturbations, even if extreme. Or, it could relate to abrupt shifts that might appear otherwise inexplicable, even at the smallest system changes, for example, at the cusp of change, given the optimization of system function that gravitating to this position in the system permits.

Other than addressing well the details of the measurable changes in manual and brain functioning, attractor modeling and NLDS help avoid simple models of causality in behavior and brain functioning. For example, they do not consider genetic influences as linearly causal, nor do they consider environmental ones, for a behavior or brain function at hand, but examine their causal reciprocities and synergies without giving any one influence much priority. They admit to any variable that might be of influence in understanding causality, and in this regard, they would not deny that hemisphericity is a factor that could be involved in lateralization development. For example, genetic and environmental influences might be crucial determinants of laterality along these lines, but individual asymmetry differences in preference, use, or activation might develop in the brain as much as for the hand, as in handedness. Perhaps the hierarchical component of the systems model might help understand how the concept of hemisphericity does not contradict recent models on hemispheric specialization and use. Perhaps lower-order system elements organize into attractors that favor one side or the other, for instance, through the initial biasing effects of genes and environment, but the ultimate expression of asymmetries in brain and behavior that stabilize later in development are influenced by an intermediate level concerning personal preferences that are promoted, either passively by parents and the like or actively by the self and through personal factors that are consistent with the specific skills present in the person and what works for the person as she or he applies those skills.

Embodiment

One developmental model that has not been mentioned to date in the present article, but is influential in the developmental literature, concerns embodiment (Young, 2016). It has been applied to development in multiple ways, and given that the newborn starts life sensori-motorically and the use of the hands as in laterality, handedness, reaching, bimanual coordination, and so on is exquisitely an embodied experience, the embodiment model would seem to apply quite well to lateralization, although this has yet to be done, as far as is known (however, in a study of cultural influences on children's drawing and turning tendencies, Portex, Foulin, and Troadec (2017) referred to "cultural embodiment," for example, through active writing/manipulatory practice).

The embodiment approach to lateralization can be explained as in the following. Consider that there are two major avenues in lateralized behavior, manual and verbal, and both involve kinesthetic and proprioceptive feedback, multimodal perception and coordination, and forming integrated schemas relating body movements/actions and outcomes. That is, the lateralization function generally is about embodied behavior and resides in coordination of body, brain, context, behavior, and outcome, with feedback looping to further refine the behavior involved and efficiency, accuracy, and coordinative structuring in peripheral and central dynamics related to it. Tool use begins with sensori-motor dynamics in infancy, and must have begun the same way in the evolution of the behavior millions of years ago in our ancestors. As adults, we apply it with planning and even abstract thought, but developmentally it is a sensori-motor, embodied experience. That tool use is predisposed to lateralization and differential hand coordination speaks to the centrality in evolution and in development of lateralization as an embodied experience. Indeed, lateralization extends back billions of years to the earliest species (evolution will be discussed more below) and it extends back to the earliest periods after conception, such as when the central nervous system begins to develop, and in both cases embodiment must be central to organism functioning as much as any lateralization.

Genes

Genetic models of behavior typically begin by establishing heritability, which concerns the amount of variation of a behavior or trait in the population at issue explained by hereditary factors. As demonstrated in the genetics section of the present work in the above, the heritability of handedness is minimal, essentially because there are so many factors to consider in the biological influence on behavior other than genes. Genes provide instructions through DNA and RNA for protein construction, but the environment can influence handedness development, for example, through parenting and culture, as we have seen. Also, genes can be silenced (e.g., by methylation of the promotor region) in the process of epigenesis, for example, through maternal prenatal stress (e.g., Meaney, 2010). Aside from gene-environment interactions generally, as in compounding influences on behavior, there can be gene by environment interactions (G × E), as in cases when risk factors for both components must be present to elicit a behavioral disturbance. The case of correlated gene-environment interactions complicates the matter further, as in passive, active, and evocative effects of genes on the environment (Young, 2016). Genes themselves interact as in epistasis. Consequently, there is rarely a clear effect of candidate genes on behavior, and, if found, the results are often not replicated. Researchers have turned to genome wide association studies (GWAS), and might survey hundreds of thousands of genes that could be related to a phenomenon, with statistical p values that are astronomically small to avoid Type I error. In these cases, a general effect might be found for a poly-genomic suite of genes related to the behavior at issue, but with no one specific gene explaining much of the variance involved and often new ones found that had not been considered in candidate gene studies. As for handedness itself, few genes have stood out in any way, and although a few are mentioned in the literature review above, it is best not to emphasize them and think poly-genomically and system wide for understanding genetic influences on handedness. Mendelian genetics just might not work straightforwardly in handedness and related lateralities, including for one or two gene side-shifting models.

Activation-Inhibition Coordination

The present book has emphasized the common factor of activation-inhibition coordination for translating behavioral and brain asymmetries into a common metric and for facilitating understanding their relationship. For example, the reaching infant must not only activate the muscles of the arm and hand in relation to the target to achieve an accurate outcome but also must inhibit any interferences either in the moving limb or in other body parts, such as the contralateral limb or anything that would compromise postural support. The activation-inhibition coordination involved in this early reaching or in later vocal behavior is refined, continual, object-oriented, and so on and will succeed in preferred outcome only with supportive peripheral and central processes, such as left hemisphere specialization that supports activation-inhibition coordination. The various skills of the left hemisphere lend themselves to re-transcription in terms of activation-inhibition coordination. Also, effective behavioral adaptation would require the complementary activation-inhibition skills of the right hemisphere and the coordination of the two hemispheres for their skills. For example, the right hemisphere might be specialized for lesser qualities of activation-inhibition coordinations, as well as inhibitory functions generally without activations, and so on. This proposed difference in manual lateralization and in hemispheric specialization in terms of activation-inhibition coordination is generic enough to apply without considering lateralization to development, evolution, behavior, brain, and even neurons and molecular relations in the nervous system. For example, evolution of behavior could concern increasing efficiency in activation-inhibition coordination, generally, and concurrent evolutionary advances in hemispheric specialization might involve similar processes.

Networks

The network model is another one that can re-transcribe or translate the standard ways of describing lateralizations into more nuanced terms that, at the same time, afford new ways of understanding the phenomena. For example, the left hemisphere is described in network terms as more "small world" or tighter in organization and, even from the neonatal period on this way, such that it is better and more efficient in information processing. This is consistent with models of the evolution of lateralization that refer to increased neural efficiency permitted. These types of models of left hemisphere skills speak to earlier models that the left hemisphere is better at sequencing and analysis, compared to the right hemisphere skills of engaging in holistic and synthetic processing (consistent with its spatial advantage relative to the left hemisphere's verbal skills). The network model includes concepts such as nodes, edges, hubs, and other ways that nodes are linked. The model can be applied to understanding both central tendencies in lateralized skills, whether behavioral or hemispheric, and individual differences in these regards. For example, in disturbances in development, such as in ASD, there appears to be hyper-connectivities in left hemisphere brain networking, which serves to promote rigidities in behavioral repetitions, problems in communication and lack of social cognition, and so on.

I have argued that the network model can be applied to any type of behavioral or symptom linking, such as in the individualized development and deployment of cognitive strategies needed on tasks, to solve problems, and so on. In this regard, Epskamp et al. (2018) have argued that network statistics can be used to elucidate personalized or intraindividual network patterns in behaviors, symptoms, and psychopathology. Similarly, the network concept can be applied to the individualized central conceptual structures that might develop in any of the Piagetian (and Neo-Piagetian) cognitive (sub)stages, which I have referred to as conceptual or sub(stage) yoking. Also, elsewhere, I have applied the yoking model to the individualized socioemotional skill sets (or lack of such skills) that develop and are deployed in the social tasks we participate in, as in Neo-Eriksonian development and its disturbances (Young, 2016).

Evolution

This penultimate summary of the models in the article on lateralizations and their explication for the development of lateralizations has covered most major developmental theories, which reinforces the focus on early lateralizations as crucial for understanding behavior and its evolution generally. The following elaborates further the evolutionary implications of the present work. First, study and comprehension of the evolutionary process in general is dynamically shifting, and newer concepts such as group selection and epigenesis are now part of the evolutionary lexicon. Second, as applied to the evolution of lateralization, the evidence indicates that it is as ancient as life itself, or almost so, as it confers advantages, such as in lateral turning tendencies in the earliest life forms and neurons in relation to predator pursuit and prey escape from predators. Third, because the behaviors involved in phylogenesis of lateralization vary extensively, workers have attempted to understand the common advantage that cuts across different phylogenetic epochs, notwithstanding the punctuated phylogenetic and perhaps analogous rather than homologous sweeps in this regard in evolution. For example, concepts related to information processing, neural efficiency, motor planning, and the like, have been used to explain commonalities over evolution in lateralization.

However, the book has proposed options related to activation-inhibition coordination, networking or yoking, systems theory, such as attractors, and so on, in these regards. If these options make sense conceptually and empirically, it might lead to evolutionary models of lateralization that involve phylogenetic continuities more than has been hypothesized. Another track in the evolution of lateralization concerns whether the forces responsible for it were manual first, communication or language first, or social first and which of these factors continued to be primary in evolution generally. Once more, the types of common models that are being proposed would apply to these types of behaviors. The models, such as activation-inhibition coordination, are super-ordinate to the behavioral ones, such as in sociality, because they can explain any content area of behavior (and the brain) in these terms. For example, reaching for and bimanually coordinating to retrieve hidden objects in tubes can be readily translated in terms of activation-inhibition coordination. And communicating gesturally with another non-human primate can be translated in these terms, as well.

The Author's Models

Tables 5.1 and 9.1 and Figs. 8.1 and 8.2 provide more details on the current conceptualization of activation-inhibition coordination in relation to brain, behavior, and lateralization. Table 5.1 documents the proposed activation-inhibition coordination skills deemed as specialized in the left and right hemispheres. Table 9.1 extends the work to what might have happened in evolution in these regards, and extends the model into network concepts. Also, it introduces a five-step generic model of change – coordination, hierarchization, systematization, multiplication, and integration. It has been applied not only to stages in development (Neo-Piagetian, Neo-Eriksonian, e.g., Young, 2012) but also to other aspects of behavior, such as the development of chronic pain, and to parallels in steps in change, even in nonliving systems (Young, 2011, 2016). Figures 8.1 and 8.2 indicate a network model of behavior and the relations of the behaviors to activation-inhibition coordination. Other figures developed for the paper concern a networked biopsychosocial model (Fig. 8.3), a model showing the equivalence of the stages in change model and a generic change model, all in attractor terms (see Fig. 9.1), a Person × Environment model of behavior (see Fig. 9.2), and a diagram illustrating five evolutionary forces that have acted on behavior, including one novel in Young's work, that of group for individual selection processes, such as in child teaching (and the corresponding child social learning; see Fig. 9.3). Together these visuals aid in presenting the innovative ideas in the book and offer succinct figure captions to further capture central contributions of the book.

Overall Integration

This first portion of the present book has attempted to examine the development of handedness, manual specialization, and hemispheric specialization through multiple models, ranging from the biological and environmental to the evolutionary and common function approaches. To this point, the book has emphasized the complementarity of the models without arguing too much that one might be foundational. However, of all the models presented, only one has the potential to re-transcribe or to translate the various skills, contents, domains, tasks, networks, and individual differences in these regards into a common metric related to the brain and behavior. That is, the concept of activation-inhibition coordination helps to specify the differential functioning of both the left and right hands and the left and right hemispheres, as well as in lower-order aspects, such as neurons. The critical task, then, becomes to map the developmental trajectories in activation-inhibition coordination dynamics in development, whether human or animal and whether in behavior or brain (and lower-order aspects such as neurons), leading to further work in applying the concept to evolution. In this regard, consider the concept that evolutionarily early species developed turning tendencies to either pursue prey or to avoid being victims of predators. This type of behavior could be translated easily into activation-inhibition coordination routines that are exquisitely refined for survival (and reproduction). That is, it is not just the reaching hand of the baby that can be translated into activation-inhibition coordination terms but also any behavior that possesses the requisite characteristics.

Implications for Understanding the Nature of Development and of Evolution

Generally, here, development has been considered a dynamic factorial process with multiple expressions and multiple causalities that interact. It becomes increasingly complex yet is accompanied by restructuring that elegantly simplifies, as well, in a twin process akin to activation and inhibition in coordination. The growth of neural networks both structurally and functionally illustrates well this principle (Menon, 2013). Buckner and Kreinen (2013) argued that more plastic neuronal networks (densely connected, widely-spanning, late maturing) typify the evolutionary process, as well. Both the developmental and evolutionary process appear marked by plasticity in neuronal networks that move away from modular to more generalized function (e.g., salience, executive, default), thereby allowing better ongoing adaptation to current context or evolutionary niche, as the case may be. Given the differential functionings of the left and right hemispheres that have been proposed and studied empirically, and the network interpretation of these differences, it would appear that laterality is a critical component in both the developmental and evolutionary trajectories that mark our species. Also, given how I have underscored the value of the concept of activation-inhibition coordination in helping to understand the fundamentals in both trajectories, this skill and its lateralization appears to stand as a primary focus in elaborating the nature of brain-behavior relationships in humans and in our ancestors, perhaps right into the earliest life forms on our planet.

Limitations and Future Directions

The present review and integration consists of a literature review and analysis leading to conceptual innovations in the areas of the development and evolution of lateralizations. They can be tested and new directions in testing them might follow, as well.

At the same time, the book has not analyzed in depth any of the research on basic factors related to lateralization. These include sex differences in handedness and its relations, including in brain development/hemispheric asymmetry (Etchell et al., 2018; Gur & Gur, 2017; Hirnstein, Hugdahl, & Hausmann, 2018; Papadatou-Pastou, Martin, Munafò, & Jones, 2008, 2017; Reber & Tranel, 2017; Sivagnanasunderam et al., 2015); lateralization in older children/teenagers and older adults (Kann, Zhang, Manza, Leung, & Li, 2016; McDowell, Felton, Vazquez, & Chiarello, 2015; Mitchell, Martin, & Adamo, 2017; Sebastjan, Skrzek, Ignasiak, & Sławińska, 2017); left handedness, ambidexterity, and mixed handedness (Denny & Zhang, 2017; Hiraoka et al., 2018; Hodgson & Hudson, 2017; Joliot, Tzourio-Mazoyer, & Mazoyer, 2016; McGrath & Kantak, 2016; O'Regan & Serrien, 2018; Papadatou-Pastou, 2018; Suitner, Maass, Bettinsoli, Carraro, & Kumar, 2017; Woodley of Menie, Fernandes, Kanazawa, & Dutton, 2018; Zago et al., 2016); crossed and non-manual indicators of preference (e.g., Ferrero, West, & Vadillo, 2017); familial sinistrality (Grey, Tanner, & van Hell, 2017; Young & Gagnon, 1990); and strength or consistency of laterality as opposed to its direction (Anderson et al., 2017; Kourtis & Vingerhoets, 2016).

The topics needing investigation are manifold in areas beyond healthy participants and regular lateralization. This includes the need for further research on depression, anxiety, and mood, generally, and central lateralization (e.g., Bruder, Stewart, & McGrath, 2017), individual variations in typical lateralizations or research showing their lack (e.g., Biduła, Pryzbylski, Pawlak, & Króliczak, 2017; Cazzoli & Chechlacz, 2017; Ouerchefani, Ouerchefani, Allain, Ben Rejeb, & Le Gall, 2017), split-brain/corpus callosum agenesis research (Chilosi et al., 2017; Ocklenburg, Ball, Wolf, Genç, & Güntürkün, 2015; Okajima, Futamura, Honma, Kawamura, & Yotsumoto, 2017), research on hemispherectomy (Ivanova et al., 2017; Save-Pédebos et al., 2016), and research on stroke (Buchmann & Randerath, 2017).

Furthermore, other topics that are dealt with in the book with a degree of specification need much more elaboration, for example, cerebral lateralization in adults (e.g., Dieterich & Brandt, 2018; Guadalupe et al., 2017; Lowe, Manocchio, Safati, & Hall, 2018; Savopoulos & Lindell, 2018; Wende et al., 2017). This applies as well developmentally, for example, abnormalities in development and their effects on lateralization or their causation in lateralization, e.g., in ADHD (Gu et al., 2017), in autism spectrum disorder (ASD) (Paquet, Golse, Girard, Olliac, & Vaivre-Douret, 2017; Reiter, Mash, Linke, Fong, Fishman, & Müller, 2018), in dyslexia/language disorder (Verly et al., 2018; Waldie, Wilson, Roberts, & Moreau, 2017; Wilson & Bishop, 2018), and for very low birth weight children (van Ettinger-Veenstra et al., 2017).

Research related to lateralization abnormalities in adult disorders needs to continue, for example, for depression (Cantisani et al., 2016; Lai, Wu, & Hou, 2017; Sankar, Melin, Lorenzetti, Horton, Costafreda, & Fu, 2018) and for schizophrenia (Olejarczyk & Jernajczyk, 2017; Walton et al., 2018).

The continuing research on frontal hemispheric asymmetry for affect needs to be integrated and investigated (Adolph, von Glischinski, Wannamüller, & Margraf, 2017; Nelson, Kessel, Klein, & Shankman, 2018; Nusslock et al., 2018; Ocklenburg, Friedrich, Schmitz, Schlüter, Genc, Güntürkün, Peterburs, & Grimshaw, 2018; Propper, Dodd, Christman, & Brunyé, 2017; Prete, Capotosto, Zappasodi, & Tommasi, 2018; Smith, Cavanagh, & Allen, 2018; Wyczesany, Capotosto, Zappasodi, & Prete, 2018). Also, see other research on findings for emotions and related social processes not involving the frontal lobe (Dasdemir, Yildirim, & Yildirim, 2017; Duke et al., 2018; Ladouceur, Schlund, & Segreti, 2018; Liu, Saito, Lin, & Saito, 2017; Tang et al., 2017; van Elk, Duizer, Sligte, & van Schie, 2017) or frontal affect studies that are in the beta EEG range and not alpha (e.g., Wagner, Wessel, Ghahremani, & Aron, 2017).

Indeed, these different topics intersect and, in this regard, the most current research on dichotic listening is informative, for example (Oltedal & Hugdahl, 2017). The latter have found that laterality results depend on modality (auditory, visual). Other areas of study also have found much variability in results, such that it is difficult to maintain the classic view of left hemisphere dominance for language and right hemisphere dominance for spatial functions (e.g., Bradshaw, Thompson, Wilson, Bishop, & Woodhead, 2017; Dieterich & Brandt, 2018, respectively). Hand activation and selection affects and is affected by higher-order skill, cognition, integration/control, and processing (Andersen & Siebner, 2018; Heck & Mohr, 2017; Howells et al., 2018; Liang, Wilkinson, & Sainburg, 2018; Rugani, Betti, Ceccarini, & Sartori, 2017).

A similar overturning of classic and straightforward modeling is taking place for the biological bases of lateralization. For example, the genes and epigenetic influences might even relate to those involved in ciliogenesis as much as ontogenesis of functional hemispheric asymmetries (Beste et al., 2017; Schmitz, Lor, Klose, Güntürkün, & Ocklenburg, 2017).

Research on activation and inhibition coordination should take place in diverse areas, both generally for brain and behavior (e.g., in mild traumatic brain injury, mTBI; as in Xu et al., 2017) and also specifically related to lateralization of function and over multiple levels, such as synaptic and neuronal function in relation to critical left-hemisphere and right hemisphere associated behavior [For example, applying the work of Shepherd and Rowe (2017), which refers to feedback, feed forward, and lateral excitation and inhibition in the lamination of basic circuit modules in the neocortex; they can serve as a foundation for all cortical structures, their lamination, function, etc., as well as the basis for their evolution (Haberly & Shepherd, 1973; Shepherd, 1974)].

Despite lacking examination in depth of these critical issues in the field, the present manuscript offers the foundations for further review and conceptualization in these areas related to handedness, manual specialization, and hemispheric specialization. The reaching hand of newborns proved the starting point of the present work and, as always, the complexities of their behavior stretches deeply into development and evolution.

This elaboration of Young's description of the activation-inhibition coordination model and the evidence he has cited to date in its support speaks to its generalized potential and how other models, such as networking ones, could map onto it. Moreover, it suggests ways that the model could be tested empirically. Referring to the network model in this regard, to what extent does the description of network concepts on centrality and small worlds that appear to fit the left hemisphere advantage translate into activation-inhibition terms? For example, does the small world network hypothesis of the left hemisphere advantage lead to confirming research with variables in behavior or performance on laboratory tasks that have activation-inhibitory coordination components? Do measures of centrality that might help describe the left hemisphere advantage, such as betweenness, closeness, and strength, converge in showing a left hemisphere advantage? Do the links in both cases over nodes include inhibitory ones as much as activating ones, and their coordinations? Has the concept of network node linking being quite activatory hindered conceptualizations that include, as well, inhibitory links in behavior and brain and the links over nodes, for example, as emphasized in the present case?

As for hypotheses related to network modeling of behavioral lateralization, and their potential retranscription into the language of activation-inhibition coordination, the concept can be applied to the behavioral system of the hands as they manage manual tasks. For example, does the right hand compared to the left one early in life reach and grasp better because it has more central nodes in movement dynamics that create efficiencies in behavior and arriving at the target? Do the subcomponents of the movements and orientations to the target reflect a more cohesive betweenness, centrality, or strength for the right hand? In terms of later development, do the various manual behaviors used by the child arrange systemically into adapted wholes, for example, using unimanual and then bimanual organizational strategies, as required, with overflow movements controlled and with the system better on the right side or governed from that side, as revealed in networks indicating the core hand and its dynamics? Finally, can the system manually come to include associated behaviors and functions, such as inhibitory ones and executive self-control, as found in laboratory tasks, or cognitive development, as measured by assessment procedures, and what are the causal drivers in the links involved? For example, does the use of the right hand as core relate to better cross-behavior integrations within the left hemisphere's purview, or are there some aspects related to activation-inhibition coordination that constitute the essential drivers in this regard, to which other elements of the network causally depend for their functioning, quality, and extent of use, and so on?

Finally, in terms of how top-down levels in systems form and then influence lower-order levels for which they might derive, it could happen through emergence processes such as in nonlinear dynamical theories of systems (NLDST). Also, aside from considering activation-inhibition dynamics, Young's (2011, 2016) model of five steps in the emergence of higher-order systems (as described previously, from coordination and hierarchization to systematization and multiplication, before arriving at integration) might be productively examined in this regard. It could be, for example, that handedness or other lateralizations entrench developmentally as integrations to the left or right side by passing through these five dynamical steps.

Summary

The development of handedness concerns preference on daily tasks and differs from the development of specialized manual function, which involves skill on complex tasks. Both might be right-side lateralized, generally, but they follow different developmental trajectories. Handedness becomes more stable in development into the preschool years, but can manifest earlier. Manual specialization can be demonstrated by using the appropriate skill tasks for any one particular age period, including in neonates. The direction of the asymmetry involved issues from the hemispheric specialization underlying it, for example, in terms of the left hemisphere's superior fine motor and language skills and the right hemisphere's superior spatial skills. In this sense, the developmental data do not support an early equi-potential and then a progressive lateralization model of the development of manual lateralization or hemispheric specialization. Rather, the research is in line with the invariant model, in that from early in life, and even prenatally, the two hemispheres exhibit the properties of hemispheric specialization in the adult and the manual behaviors evident in the research align with the corresponding asymmetric hemispheric differentiations found even at this age period. That said, the critical examination of the research undertaken indicates that in the early years, the development of handedness, manual specialization, and hemispheric specialization supports the validity of both the equi-potential and invariant models, working in complementary ways. Moreover, the review supports a far-ranging model – a common function in activation-inhibition coordination can help describe relative left-right differences in both manual and hemispheric specialization.

The research to date traces the developmental pathways for both lateralized behavior and brain structure and function from one age period to the next (prenatal to preschool), generally finding asymmetries that are consistent with these conclusions, while illustrating the dynamic process in the development of lateralized handedness, manual behavior, and brain structure and function. The research also underscores the value of connectivity and network models in offering different explanations of left-right differences in brain and behavior, which ties into the proposed activation-inhibition coordination model. Laterality in behavior and brain reflects both biological and environmental influences, including genetically and culturally, but much work is needed to update these notions due to the critical and conceptual innovations offered. Moreover, to obtain a better biopsychosocial understanding of development of handedness and related concepts, more work is required on hemisphericity and how it develops.

The present review also deals extensively with manual and brain lateralities in great ape non-human primates toward understanding the evolution of lateralization of brain and behavior. Multiple models have been offered for the underlying factors in the evolution of lateralization, but there may be punctuated sweeps in its phylogenesis, although common mechanisms might underlie the particular differences in functions found, such as in tool use and gestural communication.

Finally, the book presents several models developed by the author that can help to understand generally the development and evolution of behavior and brain. Study of the hands of the reaching child has been shown to have expansive implications in this work.

References

Adolph, D., von Glischinski, M., Wannamüller, A., & Margraf, J. (2017). The influence of frontal alpha-asymmetry on the processing of approach- and withdrawal-related stimuli—A multichannel psychophysiology study. *Psychophysiology, 54*, 1295–1310. https://doi.org/10.1111/psyp.12878

Andersen, K. W., & Siebner, H. R. (2018). Mapping dexterity and handedness: Recent insights and future challenges. *Current Opinion in Behavioral Sciences, 20*, 123–129. https://doi.org/10.1016/j.cobenha.2017.12.020

Anderson, A. A., Smith, E., Chowdhry, F. A., Thurm, A., Condy, E., Swineford, L., et al. (2017). Prefrontal hemodynamics in toddlers at rest: A pilot study of developmental variability. *Frontiers in Neuroscience, 11*. https://doi.org/10.3389/fnins.2017.00300

Beste, C., Arning, L., Gerding, W. M., Epplen, J. T., Mertins, A., Röder, M. C., et al. (2017). Cognitive control processes and functional cerebral asymmetries: Association with variation in the handedness-associated gene *LRRTM1*. *Molecular Neurobiology*. https://doi.org/10.1007/s12035-017-0485-7

Biduła, S. P., Pryzbylski, L., Pawlak, M. A., & Króliczak, G. (2017). Unique neural characteristics of atypical lateralization of language in healthy individuals. *Frontiers in Neuroscience, 11*, 525. https://doi.org/10.3389/fnins.2017.00525

Bradshaw, A. R., Thompson, P. A., Wilson, A. C., Bishop, D. V. M., & Woodhead, Z. V. J. (2017). Measuring language lateralisation with different language tasks: A systematic review. *PeerJ, 5*, e3929. https://doi.org/10.7717/peerj.3929

Bruder, G. E., Stewart, J. W., & McGrath, P. J. (2017). Right brain, left brain in depressive disorders: Clinical and theoretical implications of behavioral, electrophysiological, and neuroimaging findings. *Neuroscience and Biobehavioral Reviews, 78*, 178–191. https://doi.org/10.1016/j.neubiorev.2017.04.021

Buchmann, I., & Randerath, J. (2017). Selection and application of familiar and novel tools in patients with left and right hemispheric stroke: Psychometrics and normative data. *Cortex, 94*, 49–62. https://doi.org/10.1016/j.cortex.2017.06.001

Buckner, R. L., & Kreinen, F. M. (2013). The evolution of distributed association networks in the human brain. *Trends in Cognitive Sciences, 17*, 648–665. https://doi.org/10.1016/j.tics.2013.09.017

Campbell, J. M., Marcinowski, E. C., Babik, I., & Michel, G. F. (2015). The influence of a hand preference for acquiring objects on the development of a hand preference for unimanual manipulation from 6 to 14 months. *Infant Behavior and Development, 39*, 107–117. https://doi.org/10.1016/j.infbeh.2015.02.013

Cantisani, A., Koenig, T., Stegmayer, K., Federspiel, A., Horn, H., Müller, T. J., et al. (2016). EEG marker of inhibitory brain activity correlates with resting-state cerebral blood flood in the reward system in major depression. *European Archives of Psychiatry and Clinical Neuroscience, 266*, 755–764. https://doi.org/10.1007/s00406-015-0652-7

Cazzoli, D., & Chechlacz, M. (2017). A matter of hand: Causal links between hand dominance, structural organization of fronto-parietal attention networks, and variability in behavioural responses to transcranial magnetic stimulation. *Cortex, 86*, 230–246. https://doi.org/10.1016/j.cortex.2016.06.015

Chilosi, A. M., Bulgheroni, S., Turi, M., Cristofani, P., Biagi, L., Erbetta, A., et al. (2017). Hemispheric language organization after congenital left brain lesions: A comparison between functional transcranial Doppler and functional MRI. *Journal of Neuropsychology*. https://doi.org/10.1111/jnp.12128

Corballis, M. C. (1989). Laterality and human evolution. *Psychological Review, 96*, 492–505.

Corballis, M. C. (1991). *The lopsided ape: Evolution of the generative mind*. New York: Oxford University Press.

Corballis, M. C. (1992). On the evolution of language and generativity. *Cognition, 44*, 197–226.

Darwin, C. (1859). *On origin of species: By means of natural selection, on the preservation of favored races in the struggle for life*. London: John Murray.

Dasdemir, Y., Yildirim, E., & Yildirim, S. (2017). Analysis of functional brain connections for positive-negative emotions using phase locking value. *Cognitive Neurodynamics, 11*, 487–500. https://doi.org/10.1007/s11571-017-9447-z

Denny, K., & Zhang, W. (2017). In praise of ambidexterity: How a continuum of handedness predicts social adjustment. *Laterality: Asymmetries of Body, Brain and Cognition, 22*, 181–194. https://doi.org/10.1080/1357650X.2016.1153107

Dieterich, M., & Brandt, T. (2018). Global orientation in space and the lateralization of brain functions. *Current Opinion in Neurology, 31*, 96–104. https://doi.org/10.1097/WCO.0000000000000516

Duke, E., Schnuerch, R., Heeren, G., Reuter, M., Montag, C., & Markett, S. (2018). Cortical alpha asymmetry at central and posterior – But not anterior – Sites is associated with individual differences in behavioural loss aversion. *Personality and Individual Differences, 121*, 206–212. https://doi.org/10.1016/j.paid.2017.04.056

Epskamp, S., van Borkulo, C. D., van der Veen, D. C., Servaas, M. N., Isvoranu, A.-M., Riese, H., et al. (2018). Personalized network modeling in psychopathology: The importance of contemporaneous and temporal connections. *Clinical Psychological Science, 6*, 416–427.

Etchell, A., Adhikari, A., Weinberg, L. S., Choo, A. L., Garnett, E. O., Chow, H. M., et al. (2018). A systematic literature review of sex differences in childhood language and brain development. *Neuropsychologia, 114*, 19–31.

Ferrero, M., West, G., & Vadillo, M. A. (2017). Is crossed-laterality associated with academic achievement and intelligence? A systematic review and meta-analysis. *PLoS One, 12*, e01183618. https://doi.org/10.1371/journal.pone.0183618

Grey, S., Tanner, D., & van Hell, J. G. (2017). How right is left? Handedness modulates neural responses during morphosyntactic processing. *Brain Research, 1669*, 27–43. https://doi.org/10.1016/j.brainres.2017.05.024

Gu, Y., Miao, S., Han, J., Zeng, K., Ouyang, G., Yang, J., et al. (2017). Complexity analysis of fNIRS signals in ADHD children during working memory task. *Scientific Reports, 7*, 829. https://doi.org/10.1038/s41598-017-00965-4

Guadalupe, T., Mathias, S. R., vanErp, T. G. M., Whelan, C. D., Zwiers, M. P., Abe, Y., et al. (2017). Human subcortical brain asymmetries in 15,847 people worldwide reveal effects of age and sex. *Brain Imaging and Behaviour, 11*, 1497–1514. https://doi.org/10.1007/s11682-016-9629-z

Gur, R. C., & Gur, R. E. (2017). Complementarity of sex differences in brain and behavior: From laterality to multimodal imaging. *Journal of Neuroscience Research, 95*, 189–199. https://doi.org/10.1002/jnr.23830

Haberly, L. B., & Shepherd, G. M. (1973). Current-density analysis of summed evoked potentials in opossum prepyriform cortex. *Journal of Neurophysiology, 36*, 789–802.

Hamilton, W. D. (1964). The genetical evolution of social behavior I and II. *Journal of Theoretical Biology, 7*, 1–52.

Heck, N., & Mohr, B. (2017). Response hand differentially affects action word processing. *Frontiers in Psychology, 8*, 2223. https://doi.org/10.3389/fpsyg.2017.02223

Hiraoka, K., Igawa, K., Kashiwagi, M., Nakahara, C., Oshima, Y., & Takakura, Y. (2018). The laterality of stop and go processes of the motor response in left-handed and right-handed individuals. *Laterality: Asymmetries of Body, Brain, and Cognition, 23*, 51–66. https://doi.org/10.1080/1357650X.2017.1311906

Hirnstein, M., Hugdahl, K., & Hausmann, M. (2018). Cognitive sex differences and hemispheric asymmetry: A critical review of 40 years of research. *Laterality: Asymmetries of Body, Brain, and Cognition*. https://doi.org/10.1080/1357650X.2018.1497044

Hodgson, J. C., & Hudson, J. M. (2017). Measurement reliability of atypical language lateralization assessed using functional transcranial Doppler ultrasound. *Biological Psychology, 125*, 173–176. https://doi.org/10.1016/j.biopsycho.2017.03.008

Howells, H., de Schotten, M. T., Dell'Acqua, F., Beyh, A., Zappalà, G., Leslie, A., et al. (2018). Frontoparietal tracts linked to lateralized hand preference and manual specialization. *Cerebral Cortex*. https://doi.org/10.1093/cercor/bhy040

Ivanova, A., Zaidel, E., Salamon, N., Bookheimer, S., Uddin, L. Q., & de Bode, S. (2017). Intrinsic functional organization of putative language networks in the brain following left cerebral hemispherectomy. *Brain Structure and Function, 222*, 3795–3805. https://doi.org/10.1007/s00429-017-1434-y

Joliot, M., Tzourio-Mazoyer, N., & Mazoyer, B. (2016). Intra-hemispheric intrinsic connectivity asymmetry and its relationships with handedness and language lateralization. *Neuropsychologia, 93*, 437–447. https://doi.org/10.1016/j.neuropsychologia.2016.03.013

Kann, S., Zhang, S., Manza, P., Leung, H.-C., & Li, C.-S. (2016). Hemispheric lateralization of resting-state functional connectivity of the anterior insula: Association with age, gender, and a novelty-seeking trait. *Brain Connectivity, 6*, 724–734. https://doi.org/10.1089/brain.2016.0443

Kauffman, S. (1993). *The origins of order: Self-organization and selection in evolution*. New York: Oxford University Press.

Kourtis, D., & Vingerhoets, G. (2016). Evidence for dissociable effects of handedness and consistency of hand preference in allocation of attention and movement planning: An EEG investigation. *Neuropsychologia, 93*, 493–500. https://doi.org/10.1016/j.neuropsychologia.2016.01.023

Ladouceur, C. D., Schlund, M. W., & Segreti, A.-M. (2018). Positive reinforcement modulates fronto-limbic systems subserving emotional interference in adolescents. *Behavioural Brain Research, 338*, 109–117. https://doi.org/10.1016/j.bbr.2017.10.019

Lai, C.-H., Wu, Y.-T., & Hou, Y.-M. (2017). Functional network-based statistics in depression: Theory of mind subnetwork and importance of parietal region. *Journal of Affective Disorders, 217*, 132–137. https://doi.org/10.1016/j.jad.2017.03.073

Liang, J., Wilkinson, K., & Sainburg, R. L. (2018). Is hand selection modulated by cognitive-perceptual load? *Neuroscience, 369*, 362–373. https://doi.org/10.1016/j.neuroscience.2017.11.005

Liu, T., Saito, G., Lin, C., & Saito, H. (2017). Inter-brain network underlying turn-based cooperation and competition: A hyperscanning study using near-infrared spectroscopy. *Scientific Reports, 7*, 8684. https://doi.org/10.1038/s41598-017-09226-w

Lowe, C. J., Manocchio, F., Safati, A. B., & Hall, P. A. (2018). The effects of theta burst stimulation (TBS) targeting the prefrontal cortex on executive functioning: A systematic review and meta-analysis. *Neuropsychologia, 111*, 344–359. https://doi.org/10.1016/j.nuropsychologia.2018.02.004

MacNeilage, P. F., Studdert-Kennedy, M. G., & Lindblom, B. (1987). Primate handedness reconsidered. *Behavioral and Brain Sciences, 10*, 247–263.

MacNeilage, P. F., Studdert-Kennedy, M. G., & Lindblom, B. (1988). Primate handedness: A foot in the door. *Behavioral and Brain Sciences, 11*, 737–746.

Maddox, J. E. (1995). Yes, people can change, but can psychotherapists? *Contemporary Psychology, 40*, 1047–1048.

McDowell, A., Felton, A., Vazquez, D., & Chiarello, C. (2015). Neurostructural correlates of consistent and weak handedness. *Laterality: Asymmetries of Body, Brain and Cognition, 21*, 348–370.

McGrath, R. L., & Kantak, S. S. (2016). Reduced asymmetry in motor skill learning in left-handed compared to right-handed individuals. *Human Movement Science, 45*, 130–141. https://doi.org/10.1016/j.humov.2015.11.012

Meaney, M. J. (2010). Epigenetics and the biological definition of gene x environment interactions. *Child Development, 81*, 41–79. https://doi.org/10.1111/j.1467-8624.2009.01381.x

Menon, V. (2013). Developmental pathways to functional brain networks: Emerging principles. *Trends in Cognitive Sciences, 17*, 627–640. https://doi.org/10.1016/j.tics.2013.09.015

Michel, G. F. (2018). How might the relation of the development of hand preferences to the development of cognitive functions be examined during infancy: A sketch? *Frontiers in Neuroscience, 11*, 739. https://doi.org/10.3389/fnins.2017.00739

Mitchell, M., Martin, B. J., & Adamo, D. E. (2017). Upper limb asymmetry in the sense of effort is dependent on force level. *Frontiers in Psychology, 8*, 643. https://doi.org/10.3389/psyg.2017.00643

Nelson, B. D., Kessel, E. M., Klein, D. N., & Shankman, S. A. (2018). Depression symptom dimensions and asymmetrical frontal cortical activity while anticipating reward. *Psychophysiology, 55*, e12892. https://doi.org/10.1111/psyp.12892

Nusslock, R., Shackman, A. J., McMenamin, B. W., Greischar, L. L., Davidson, R. J., & Kovacs, M. (2018). Comorbid anxiety moderates the relationship between depression history and prefrontal EEG asymmetry. *Psychophysiology, 55*, e12953. https://doi.org/10.1111/psyp.12953

O'Regan, L., & Serrien, D. J. (2018). Individual differences and hemispheric asymmetries for language and spatial attention. *Frontiers in Human Neuroscience, 12*, 380. https://doi.org/10.3389/fnhum.2018.00380

Ocklenburg, S., Ball, A., Wolf, C. C., Genç, E., & Güntürkün, O. (2015). Functional cerebral lateralization and interhemispheric interaction in patients with callosal agenesis. *Neuropsychology, 29*, 806–815. https://doi.org/10.1037/neu0000193

Ocklenburg, S., Friedrich, P., Schmitz, J., Schlüter, Genc, E., Güntürkün, O., Peterburs, J., & Grimshaw, G. (2018). Beyond frontal alpha: Investigating hemispheric asymmetries over the EEG frequency spectrum as a function of sex and handedness. *Laterality: Asymmetries of Body, Brain and Cognition*. https://doi.org/10.1080/1357650X.2018.1543314

Okajima, M., Futamura, A., Honma, M., Kawamura, M., & Yotsumoto, Y. (2017). Interhemispheric cortical connections and time perception: A case study with agenesis of the corpus callosum. *Brain & Cognition, 117*, 12–16. https://doi.org/10.1016/j.bandc.2017.07.005

Olejarczyk, E., & Jernajczyk, W. (2017). Graph-based analysis of brain connectivity in schizophrenia. *PLoS ONE, 12*, e0188629. https://doi.org/10.1371/journal.pone.0188629

Oltedal, L., & Hugdahl, K. (2017). Opposite brain laterality in analogous auditory and visual tests. *Laterality: Asymmetries of Body, Brain and Cognition, 22*, 690–702. https://doi.org/10.1080/1357650X.2016.1269335

Ouerchefani, R., Ouerchefani, N., Allain, P., Ben Rejeb, M. R., & Le Gall, D. (2017). Contribution of different regions of the prefrontal cortex and lesion laterality to deficit of decision-making on the Iowa Gambling Task. *Brain and Language, 111*, 73–85. https://doi.org/10.1016/j.bandc.2016.06.010

Papadatou-Pastou, M. (2018). Chapter 7 - Handedness and cognitive ability: Using meta-analysis to make sense of the data. *Progress in Brain Research, 238*, 179–206.

Papadatou-Pastou, M., Martin, M., Munafò, M. R., & Jones, G. V. (2008). Sex differences in left-handedness: A meta-analysis of 144 studies. *Psychological Bulletin, 134*, 677–699.

Papadatou-Pastou, M., Martin, M., Munafò, M. R., & Jones, G. V. (2017). Sex difference in left-handedness: A meta-analysis of 144 studies: Correction to Papadatou-Pastou et al. (2008). *Psychological Bulletin, 143*, 1115. https://doi.org/10.1037/bul0000121

Paquet, A., Golse, B., Girard, M., Olliac, B., & Vaivre-Douret, L. (2017). Laterality and lateralization in autism spectrum disorder, using a standardized neuro-psychomotor assessment. *Developmental Neuropsychology, 42*, 39–54. https://doi.org/10.1080/87565641.2016.1274317

Portex, M., Foulin, J.-N., & Troadec, B. (2017). Cultural influence on directional tendencies in children's drawing. *Laterality: Asymmetries of Body, Brain and Cognition, 22*, 621–640. https://doi.org/10.1080/1357650X.2016.1266363

Prete, G., Capotosto, P., Zappasodi, F., & Tommasi, L. (2018). Contrasting hemispheric asymmetries for emotional processing from event-related potentials and behavioral responses. *Neuropsychology, 32*, 317–328. https://doi.org/10.1037/neu0000443

Prochaska, J. O., Norcross, J. C., & DiClemente, C. C. (1994). *Changing for good: The revolutionary program that explains the six stages of change and teaches you how to free yourself from bad habits*. New York: Morrow.

Propper, R. E., Dodd, K., Christman, S. D., & Brunyé, T. T. (2017). Relationship between sustained unilateral hand clench, emotional state, line bisection performance, and prefrontal cortical activity: A functional near-infrared spectroscopy copy. *Laterality: Asymmetries of Body, Brain, and Cognition, 22*, 671–689. https://doi.org/10.1080/1357650X.2016.1268148

Reber, J., & Tranel, D. (2017). Sex differences in the functional lateralization of emotion and decision making in the human brain. *Journal of Neuroscience Research, 95*, 270–278. https://doi.org/10.1002/jnr.23829

Reiter, M. A., Mash, L. E., Linke, A. C., Fong, C. H., Fishman, I., & Müller, R-A. (2018). Distinct patterns of atypical functional connectivity in lower-functioning autism. *Archival Report*. https://doi.org/10.1016/j.bpsc.2018.08.009

Rugani, R., Betti, S., Ceccarini, F., & Sartori, L. (2017). Act on numbers: Numerical magnitude influences selection and kinematics of finger movement. *Frontiers in Psychology, 8*, 1481. https://doi.org/10.3389/fpsyg.2017.01481

Sankar, A., Melin, A., Lorenzetti, V., Horton, P., Costafreda, S. G., & Fu, C. H. Y. (2018). A systematic review and meta-analysis of the neural correlates of psychological therapies in major depression. *Psychiatry Research: Neuroimaging, 279*, 31–39.

Save-Pédebos, J., Pinabiaux, C., Dorfmuller, G., Sorbets, S. F., Delalande, O., Jambaqué, I., et al. (2016). The development of pragmatic skills in children after hemispherotomy: Contribution from left and right hemispheres. *Epilepsy & Behavior, 55*, 139–145. https://doi.org/10.1016/j.yebeh.2015.12.013

Savopoulos, P., & Lindell, A. K. (2018). Repetition priming reveals hemispheric differences in compound word processing. *Journal of Cognitive Psychology, 30*, 63–76. https://doi.org/10.1018/20445911.2017.1391269

Schmitz, J., Lor, S., Klose, R., Güntürkün, O., & Ocklenburg, S. (2017). The functional genetics of handedness and language lateralization: Insights from gene ontology, pathway, and disease association analyses. *Frontiers in Psychology, 8*, 1144. https://doi.org/10.3389/fpsychg.2017.01144

Sebastjan, A., Skrzek, A., Ignasiak, Z., & Sławińska, T. (2017). Age-related changes in hand dominance and functional asymmetry in older adults. *PLoS ONE, 12*, e0177845. https://doi.org/10.1371/journal.pone.0177845

Shepherd, G. M. (1974). *The synaptic organization of the brain*. New York: Oxford University Press.

Shepherd, G. M., & Rowe, T. B. (2017). Neocortical lamination: Insights from neuron types and evolutionary precursors. *Frontiers in Neuroanatomy, 11*, 100. https://doi.org/10.3389/fnana.2017.00100

Sivagnanasunderam, M., Gonzalez, D. A., Bryden, P. J., Young, G., Forsyth, A., & Roy, E. A. (2015). Handedness throughout the lifespan: Cross-sectional view on sex differences as asymmetries change. *Frontiers in Psychology, 5*, 1556. https://doi.org/10.3389/fpsyg.2014.01556

Smith, E. E., Cavanagh, J. F., & Allen, J. J. B. (2018). Intracranial source activity (eLORETA) related to scalp-level asymmetry scores and depression status. *Psychophysiology, 55*, e13019. https://doi.org/10.1111/psyp.13019

Sober, E. (1984). *The nature of selection: Evolutionary theory in philosophical focus*. Cambridge, MA: Bradford/MIT.

Suitner, C., Maass, A., Bettinsoli, M. L., Carraro, L., & Kumar, S. (2017). Left-handers' struggle in a rightward wor(l)d: The relation between horizontal spatial bias and effort in directed movements. *Laterality: Asymmetries of Body, Brain, and Cognition, 22*, 60–89. https://doi.org/10.1080/1357650X.2015.1118112

Tang, H., Ye, P., Wang, S., Zhu, R., Su, S., Tong, L., et al. (2017). Stimulating the right temporoparietal junction with tDSC decreases deception in moral hypocrisy and unfairness. *Frontiers of Psychology, 8*, 2033. https://doi.org/10.3389/fpsychg.2017.02033

Trivers, R. L. (1971). The evolution of reciprocal altruism. *Quarterly Review of Biology, 46*, 35–57.

van Elk, M., Duizer, M., Sligte, I., & van Schie, H. (2017). Transcranial direct current stimulation of the right temporoparietal junction impairs third-person perspective taking. *Cognitive, Affective, & Behavioral Neuroscience, 17*, 9–23. https://doi.org/10.3758/s13415-016-0462-z

van Ettinger-Veenstra, H., Widén, C., Engström, M., Karlsson, T., Leijon, I., & Nelson, N. (2017). Neuroimaging of decoding and language comprehension in young very low birth weight (VLBW) adolescents: Indications for compensatory mechanisms. *PLoS ONE, 12*, e0185571. https://doi.org/10.1371/journal.pone.0185571

Verly, M., Gerrits, R., Sleurs, C., Lagae, L., Sunaert, S., Zink, I., et al. (2018). The mis-wired language network in children with developmental language disorder: Insights from DTI tractography. *Brain Imaging and Behavior*. https://doi.org/10.1007/s11682-018-9903-3

Wagner, J., Wessel, J. R., Ghahremani, A., & Aron, A. R. (2017). Establishing a right frontal beta signature for stopping action in scalp EEG: Implications for testing inhibitory control in other task contexts. *Journal of Cognitive Neuroscience, 30*, 107–118. https://doi.org/10.1162/jocn_a_01183

Waldie, K. E., Wilson, A. J., Roberts, R. P., & Moreau, D. (2017). Reading network in dyslexia: Similar, yet different. *Brain & Language, 174*, 29–41. https://doi.org/10.1016/j.bandl.2017.07.004

Walton, E., Hibar, D. P., van Erp, T. G. M., Potkin, S. G., Roiz-Santiañez, R., Crespo-Facorro, B., et al. (2018). Prefrontal cortical thinning links to negative symptoms in schizophrenia via the ENIGMA consortium. *Psychological Medicine, 48*, 82–94. https://doi.org/10.1017/S0033291717001283

Welsh, M., & Pennington, B. (1988). Assessing frontal lobe functioning in children: Views from developmental psychology. *Developmental Psychology, 4*, 199–230.

Wende, K. C., Thiel, C., Sommer, J., Paulus, F. M., Krach, S., & Jansen, A. (2017). Mechanisms of hemispheric lateralization: A replication study. *Cortex, 94*, 182–192. https://doi.org/10.1016/j.cortex.2017.04.013

Wilson, A. C., & Bishop, D. V. M. (2018). Resounding failure to replicate links between developmental language disorder and cerebral lateralisation. *PeerJ, 6*, e4217. https://doi.org/10.7717/peerj.4217

Woodley of Menie, M. A., Fernandes, H. B. F., Kanazawa, S., & Dutton, E. (2018). Sinistrality is associated with (slightly) lower general intelligence: A data synthesis and consideration of the secular trend in handedness. *HOMO - Journal of Comparative Human Biology, 69*, 118–126.

Wyczesany, M., Capotosto, P., Zappasodi, F., & Prete, G. (2018). Hemispheric asymmetries and emotions from effective connectivity. *Neruopsychologia*. https://doi.org/10.1016/j.neuropsychologia.2018.10.007

Xu, B., Sandrini, M., Levy, S., Volochayev, R., Awosika, O., Butman, J. A., et al. (2017). Lasting deficit in inhibitory control with mild traumatic brain injury. *Scientific Reports, 7*, 14902. https://doi.org/10.1038/s41598-017-14867-y

Young, G. (1990a). The development of hemispheric and manual specialization. In G. Hammond (Ed.), *The cerebral control of speech and limb movements* (pp. 79–139). Amsterdam: North Holland.

Young, G. (1990b). Early neuropsychological development: Lateralization of functions – Hemispheric specialization. In C.-A. Hauert (Ed.), *Developmental psychology: Cognitive, perceptuo-motor and neuropsychological perspectives* (pp. 113–181). Amsterdam: North Holland.

Young, G. (1997). *Adult development, therapy, and culture: A postmodern synthesis*. New York: Plenum Press.

Young, G. (2011). *Development and causality: Neo-Piagetian perspectives*. New York: Springer Science + Business Media.

Young, G. (2012). A unitary Neo-Piagetian/Neo-Eriksonian model of development: Fundamental assumptions and meta-issues. *New Ideas in Psychology, 30*, 241–249. https://doi.org/10.1016/j.newideapsych.2011.11.002

Young, G. (2016). *Unifying causality and psychology: Being, brain and behavior*. Cham, Switzerland: Springer International Publishing.

Young, G., & Gagnon, M. (1990). Neonatal laterality, birth stress, familial sinistrality, and left brain inhibition. *Developmental Neuropsychology, 6*, 127–150.

Zago, L., Petit, L., Mellet, E., Jobard, G., Crivello, F., Joliot, M., et al. (2016). The association between hemispheric specialization for language production and for spatial attention depends on left-hand preference strength. *Neuropsychologia, 93*, 394–406. https://doi.org/10.1016/j.neuropsychologia.2015.11.018

Part II
Development

A 25-step Neo-Piagetian/Neo-Eriksonian Model: Elaborating the Neo-Eriksonian Model and Therapeutic Practice

Chapter 10
Stage and Sub-stage Models

Abstract This first chapter on the second portion of the book – on a 25-step Neo-Eriksonian stage/sub-stage model – first describes the empirical (replication) crisis in psychology and argues that grand theories, such as Erikson's, could provide an axis to inform the crisis and help toward resolving it beyond the measures in the field currently being taken. The chapter reviews the author's Neo-Piagetian/Neo-Eriksonian model in order to illustrate its utility in these regards. Then, it reviews the current literature on both Piaget and Erikson. That literature is sparse compared to the research in the past on the stage theories involved, but there are some areas still being quite studied. For Piaget, this concerns the intermediaries in and mechanisms of change, such as executive function, although this literature is not reviewed here. For Erikson, it concerns the identity period in adolescence, which has a vast and ongoing literature, including in test construction and use. The chapter turns to stage concepts in both the Piagetian and Eriksonian traditions, and part of the difficulty with these stage theories is that their stage conceptions are outdated. The chapter describes one attempt to improve stage modeling in developmental psychology related to micro-genetic approaches and waves in development. However, this approach has some limits in its turn. The chapter concludes with presentation and comments on some other Neo-Piagetian theories (e.g., Case, Fischer, Commons), but finds them inconsistent or wanting.

Thesis

Psychology is a science that advances on the waves of curiosity, conceptualization, theory, research design, data acquisition, and interpretation, which guide its testing, empirical exploration, and prediction. Here, I argue that psychology appears to be losing focus on the theoretical side of its science in its quest for empirical publication. Necessarily, data-driven articles are based on restrained hypothesis testing; larger theoretical constructions that have marked the discipline might be losing their place in the rush, with negative consequences for the empirical side of the discipline. For example, grand theories have been put aside except for adherents to the schools of thought involved, and there is little cross-fertilization over them.

G. Young, *Causality and Development*,
https://doi.org/10.1007/978-3-030-02493-2_10

Granted, these theories evolve, but still they do not capture a valued place in the empirical marketplace in psychology. Also, efforts to unify psychology are few and have little impact. This part of the book presents Young's Neo-Piagetian/Neo-Eriksonian stage model as one axis in the ongoing project of unifying psychology, as well as other models related to networks, in particular. In addition, it examines causality as a central axis in the unification project, including of the mechanism of activation/inhibition coordination.

The replication crisis in psychology resides in the very nature of psychology as it is researched and practiced in today's scientific climate. For the most part, it eschews grand theories, overarching perspectives, and efforts at unification for the option of discipline parcellation, subdisciplinary specialization, and siloed dispersion. Paradoxically, at times, the more psychology seeks focal reliable results and evidence-supported practice, the less confident are the public, researchers, and practitioners in what is offered by the research as findings and conclusions. Although at times the findings in contemporary psychological research are fascinating and thought provoking, the results might not be replicated or they might be subject to a welter of withering criticisms attacking their approach, methodology, and conclusions.

Partly, the rush for research grants drives the research enterprise; and scientific prestige is based on funding more than acknowledged excellence in the science and theory behind it. There is little room for reflection and integration beyond mini-reviews and theories, except in isolated cases. Granted, science needs to build from the ground up with reliable empirical findings based on validly derived hypotheses that reflect the existing concepts and research in the field at issue. At the same time, it could better consider those overarching paradigms that inform the field and address critical super-ordinate questions related to the ultimate human nature and what drives it, as is often the topic of these overarching modeling efforts.

Psychology is in midst of a replication crisis that could be stemmed, in part, by better integration of grand theories into its enterprise; they could serve to provide incremental validity to typically constrained or narrowed research hypotheses and empirical data. Grand theories evolve and, moreover, new overarching perspectives arise and, either way, pertinent theory or models could infuse research investigation with novel procedures and hypotheses or predictions for testing. An example of the former concerns Neo-Piagetian theories and an example of the latter concerns network theories.

Moreover, grand or overarching theories can help toward integrating psychology across its subdisciplines. Psychology is a vast enterprise that inevitably leads it to be dispersed and studied in isolated pockets to a degree, at the sacrifice of integrative efforts that might allow it to be more cohesive and expressing more unity. It needs a common language that cuts across its various subdisciplines. Also, it needs to better grasp the common mechanisms that underlie behavior no matter the subdiscipline. In this regard, here, it is argued that the quest for the causal origins of behavior can stand as a unifying axis on which psychology can move forward toward overcoming its siloed dispersion and also in providing matters of import to study in its replication crisis.

Unifying Psychology and Causality: Emergence, Stages, and Connectivity in Development and Psychopathology

Grand Crises

Psychology is experiencing a crisis in confidence about its statistics, replicability, and empirical basis (Lilienfeld, 2017; Nosek & Lakens, 2014), in that hyper-specialization is discouraging deep thinking. For more recent work on the replication crisis in psychology, see Nelson, Simmons, and Simonsohn (2018), Rubin (2017), and Shrout and Rodgers (2018). Science is based on sound empirical prediction and testing, both of which are derived from viable hypotheses, models, and theories. Also, the predictions could be extensions of the research accumulated at the time that any one study is undertaken that serves to inform it. Granted, the focus on improving the empirical research that helps provide the data in the discipline constitutes one of the foundations of the discipline.

However, just as important, the conceptual underpinnings to the science of psychology needs to be progressively differentiated and refined so that the empirical investigations derived from them are optimally reliable and valid toward the overall goal of understanding human nature and scientifically testing predictions about it. In this sense, psychology needs a second crisis of confidence, or one related to its conceptualizing and theorizing, to match the one on its empirical side.

Grand Narratives

Moreover, the focus of this theoretical renewal should seek theories with grand narratives that help integrate the field. In this sense, one course is to create new theories that have an overarching reach, but the type of conceptualizations in this regard often focus on neuroscience, genetics, epigenetics, and the biological bases to behavior generally.

There is a source of theorizing that has attempted broad integrations and could be relevant to the proposal to create acceptable, current grand theories. That is, past theories that have attempted to do so should be reinvigorated and studied in their contemporary guises rather than being dismissed as secondary.

Without such an enterprise of reinvesting in the pursuit of valid overarching theory, or its grand theoretical side, psychology risks lapsing into very restrained hypothesis testing with little generalization beyond the specific focus in any one study. Admittedly, psychology needs to retrench into reliable and valid empirical science; but, as well, it needs to engage in outreach to broader inclusive theory that speaks to the general thrust of psychology to help understand the human condition and how to improve it. Without such an effort, the risks are palpable. Scholars have emphasized how psychology is a science of silos that barely communicate with each other (Perfors, 2016).

Moreover, by seeking broad and valid conceptual and theoretical underpinnings to its scientific study, psychology will cohere better and allow for more cross-domain and cross-disciplinary work. Generally, some decry that psychology lacks unity (e.g., Henriques, 2011; Tryon, 2014; Young, 2016). It was born in vast theoretical enterprises, such as the Freudian/psychodynamic and behavioral/learning theories, and incorporated others of this type, such as the Darwinian and medical models. The theoretical oppositions that have marked the beginnings of psychology, as well as their historical trajectories, speak to the major divergences in the themes that are queried continuously in psychology about human nature. That is, the difficulty in unifying psychology lies not so much in its inability to cohere but in the complex nature of its subject matter, that of behavior and its explanation.

Unifying Psychology: Queries and Quandaries

Efforts to create core unifying, concepts in psychology have not met with critical acclaim. For example, Henriques (2011) attempted such an integration, but Goertzen (2013) referred to it as the blind leading the blind. Young's (2016) integrative effort was considered just a start at best (Evans, 2016, 2017; but see Young, 2017). Staats (1983, 1991) attempted the first major book-length effort to unify psychology through the concept of psychological behaviorism, but it has spawned little follow-up (Tryon, 2014). The area involving the unification of psychology has few adherents and much work is required to fulfill the mission; however, workers query if it is even possible or advisable or just partially so (e.g., Green, 2015; Stam, 2015).

My own approach to the question begins with a philosophical integration, in the concept of neo-reductio-constructionism (Young, 2016). This view is consistent with other similar philosophical integrations or oppositions, such as pragmatic realism (Guyon, Falissard, & Kop, 2017) and realism versus instrumentalism/pluralism/anti-realism, as described in Beni (2018). In addition, the pragmatic, constructivist aspect of the combined model allows for emergence of higher-order levels in hierarchical models of behavior and its organization, as in system modeling of self-organization and circular causality (Young, 2011, 2016). That is, behavior cannot be reduced to neuronal activity and physiology because it can include concepts such as mind, consciousness, and belief in free will, which emanate from lower-order phenomena and then feedback to influence the elements involved.

That said, hard core proponents of a strict reductionism will deny any place in psychology for conceptions such as these, including any grand narrative theories that include and promote them. For example, Freudian thought is anathema to them. However, perhaps more recent Eriksonian work, which ultimately is founded in the

Freudian model, should not be rejected outright, as in contemporary research on identity.

Grand Questions

The Freudian/psychodynamic and behavioral/learning theories that were formulated at the outset of the scientific study of psychology stood as diametrically opposed on critical issues, such as whether all behavior is the product of learning and its consequences or whether there are hereditary, genetic, and biological influences that need consideration (the nature vs. nurture debate). Also, these theories contemplated other controversial topics, such as whether mind and the unconscious exist or are just reductionist expressions that only give the appearance of being independent of their biological bases, but are not in reality.

Another major issue in the origins of psychology concerned whether there are stages in development, such as in the Freudian model, and as developed further in the Piagetian and Eriksonian models for cognition and socio-affectivity, respectively (e.g., McLean & Syed, 2015; Müller, Ten Eycke, & Baker, 2015). Stage models are represented as linear steps that change abruptly, but they are far more differentiated than this simplistic presentation, as will be shown throughout.

Grand Solutions

The questions of the mind and the unconscious and the one of nature vs. nurture in the causation of behavior remain vital issues in psychology. For example, Young (2016) has broached both topics by having an inclusive account of causality that considers belief in free will, epigenetics, and so on, to the point that the process of "emergence" has been proposed as a factor beyond the reductionist process in explicating the nature of behavior and brain, including in the development of mind. About the third issue that bedeviled early psychology, as described above, the question of whether there are stages in development is much less debated contemporaneously.

However, I will be arguing that, by leaving aside grand theories related to stages in development other than considering them convenient heuristics in teaching and discussing psychology, the field of psychology is undervaluing an axis on which its integration can be forged better, including in relation to causality. To ascertain if behavior is more biological and hereditary or experiential and plastic, for example, requires integrative models that do not dwell at the extremes in the opinions offered, and the stage models can help in this regard.

Modeling

Stage Models

Although some of the grand models in psychology only have historical significance, the stage models address an approach to psychological understanding that still has merit because they have evolved to keep up with contemporary concepts. For example, the Neo-Piagetian and Neo-Eriksonian models that have been developed have changed not only the stage and sub-stage structure of the original models but also the mechanisms of change that have been posited to foster movement through the (sub)stages as development proceeds.

The Piagetian enterprise involved describing the stages and sub-stages of development, or the "what" of development, and elucidating the "why," as well, for example, through the concept of "constructivism" in which the child is actively involved in creating the schemas and operations that comprise the stages. The Eriksonian approach is different, focusing on stages that consist of positive and negative poles in experience and for which the environment more than the child plays a critical role in negotiating the crises that might arise in a stage.

Piaget and Erikson

Piaget That said, the Piagetian and Eriksonian models are still relatively ignored. The Piagetian model (e.g., Piaget, 1923, 1970/1983, 1974/1980, 1975/1985) had its heyday in the latter half of the twentieth century, including with the development of the Neo-Piagetian models of Case (e.g., Case, 1985, 1987, 1992; Case et al., 1996) and Fischer (e.g., Fischer, 1980; Fischer & Bidell, 2006; Mascolo & Fischer, 2015) that modified the four Piagetian stages involved and also added sub-stages to them (or levels, tiers, depending on the terms chosen).

Even Piaget did not have a uniform model of the stages in development, as shown in Young (2011), although the field has settled on the sequence of four stages in cognitive development – the sensori-motor, pre-operational, concrete operational, and formal operational stages (also, Piaget especially developed sub-stages for the sensori-motor period, describing six of them that emerge in sequence over the first 2 years of life).

Erikson In Erikson's stage theory, there are eight stages over the lifespan and no sub-stages. The Eriksonian model (e.g., Erikson, 1950, 1958, 1959, 1968; Erikson, Erikson, & Kivnick, 1986) has been modified for the identity portion, in particular (e.g., Cieciuch & Topolewska, 2017; Crocetti, 2017; Marcia, 1966, 1980, 1993; Schwartz, Zamboanga, Luyckx, Meca, & Ritchie, 2016), but with little change to the original eight-stage sequence and no additions of sub-stages, although there are limited exceptions (e.g., Blatt & Blass, 1996; Bugajska, 2017; Erikson et al., 1986;

Robinson, 2016). In this regard, Blatt and Blass added a stage of cooperativity in childhood; Bujaska, and Robinson reworked the generativity stage; and Erikson et al. added a stage after generativity.

Young's (2011, 2016) Combined Neo-Piagetian/Neo-Eriksonian Model

Neo-Piagetian The development of Young's model of the Neo-Piagetian stages and sub-stages in lifespan development (Young, 1990a, 1990b, 1997, 2011, 2012, 2016) began with a careful literature review of extant models (i.e., Case, 1992, and Fischer, 1980, as well as Mounoud, 1976, 1986). He constructed a table that compared them (see Table 10.1). Both Case and Fischer have described a three-step cyclic recursion of sub-stages in development; however, they differed in conceptualizing the sub-stages and about which stages recycle within them. Fischer's model compared to Case's model stayed closer to Piaget's model in the stage portion of the efforts. Mounoud had a model of five sub-stages that recurred, and his sequence of stages was quite different from Piaget's. The combination of stages and sub-stages were the tightest in Case, in that he did not skip age periods that Piaget had considered important, for example, unlike the case of Fischer.

In the end, in constructing his model, Young used (a) a five-sub-stage model (also see Mounoud, 1976, 1986), as justified below, (b) as well as Fischer's 1980 notion of five stages, (c) while examining carefully Case's age separations of the various stages and sub-stages in his model. Young's model, therefore, was a logically derived one and a unified one.

Young adopted a five-step sub-stage approach by basing himself on Piaget's six-step sub-stage sequence in the infancy sensori-motor stage, which Young considered exceptional in its observational base. However, he removed the first reflexive stage in the six-step series by having it end the newly-created reflexive stage prior to the sensori-motor one. Young then had the task of determining the correct label for the five remaining sub-stages because they had labels applicable only to the infancy period and he wanted labels that could generalize to the post-infancy stages.

To determine the fundamental psychological acquisition at each of the sub-stages described by Piaget for the sensori-motor period beyond the labels Piaget had given them so that the sequence made sense as a recycling, recurring set for stages beyond the infancy one and into adulthood, Young examined the terms used by Case and Fischer in their three-step sub-stage sequences, but considered other factors, as well, including the nature of the acquisitions in the subsequent stages. He argued that Case and Fischer worked backward from their research with children to determine the sub-stages in the infancy period, but this approach did not consider the integrity of Piaget's six-sub-stage model in the infant sensori-motor stage.

Using this logical procedure, Young arrived at the sub-stage sequence of: coordination, hierarchization (of the elements coordinated), systematization, multiplica-

Table 10.1 Neo-Piagetian models of cognitive development that include stages and sub-stages over the lifespan

Fischer (e.g., 1980)			Case (e.g., 1985)			Mounoud (e.g., 1986)			Biggs (e.g., 1992)		
Stage	Sub-stage	Age	Stage	Sub-stage	Age	Stage	Sub-stage	Age	Stage	Sub-stage	Age
Reflex	Set	1 month									
	Map	2-									
	System	3-									
Sensori-motor	Set	4-	Orienting (also called sensori-motor pre-coordination)	Elaborated co-ordination	0 month	Perceptual	Global	0 month	Sensori-motor	Uni-structural	0 month
	Map	8-		Uni-focal co-ordination	4-		Application	1-		Multi-structural	
	System	12-		Bi-focal co-ordination	8-		Related	4-		Relational	
				Elaborated co-ordination	12-		Analysis	8-			
							Synthesis	12-			
Representational	Set	2 years	Inter-relational	Uni-focal co-ordination	18-	Conceptual	Global	18-	Ikonic	Uni-structural	1½ year
	Map	5-		Bi-focal co-ordination	2 years-		Application	3 year-		Multi-structural	
	System	7-		Elaborated co-ordination	3.5-		Related	5-		Relational	
							Analysis	7-			
							Synthesis	9-			
			Dimensional	Uni-focal co-ordination	5-						
				Bi-focal co-ordination	7-						

				Elaborated co-ordination	9-						
Abstract (formal operational)	Set	12-	Abstract	Uni-focal co-ordination	11-	Semiotic	Global	10-	Concrete-symbolic	Uni-structural	6
										Multi-structural	
										Relational	
	Map	16-		Bi-focal co-ordination	13-		Application	11-	Formal	Uni-structural	14
										Multi-structural	
										Relational	
	System	20-		Elaborated co-ordination	16–19		Related	13-			
	System of systems	26+					Analysis	15-			
							Synthesis	16–18			
									Post-formal	Uni-structural	21
										Multi-structural	
										Relational	

Adapted from Young (1990a, 1990b, 2011)

Note: Global = Global code; Application = Code applied; Related = Codes related tion (of a system once acquired), and integration. He then applied the series to ages beyond infancy to end up with his five-sub-stage/five-stage model of lifespan Neo-Piagetian cognitive development. Another factor to consider in the labels used was whether the proposed five-step sequence could apply beyond individual development to other change processes, such as the model of stages (steps) in the readiness to change (see Table 11.7).

Along with the other changes made to the stages in Piaget's four-step series (adding an initial reflexive stage, as mentioned, and an ending post-formal stage, in particular), Young's model constituted the only one among the ones examined that respected all of Piaget's steps in his model as well as the age periods that he attributed to them. In addition, Young's model has quite a few more steps in its 25-step lifespan sequence than each of the competing models. Further, it readily incorporates the other Neo-Piagetian sequences. He showed where the other models were similar to his own and, given its vaster scope compared to the others, where their sequences were missing steps. As well, Young showed how the data in support of the other models support at times even better his own model compared to theirs, for example, in that some data putatively supportive of a specific sub-stage in their modeling might show the presence of two sub-stages, not one, and so justify how Young had two sub-stages in his sequence for the age period at issue, and not just the one as found in the other models (see Young, 2011, 2016).

To conclude, Young's Neo-Piagetian model constitutes the only one among the Neo-Piagetian that is fully lifespan, through its comprehensive 25-step lifespan sequence. Further, to repeat, Young showed that the briefer sequences in the competing models were missing steps. As well, Young showed how the data in support of the other models, at times, in reality better supported his own model.

Demetriou and colleagues have developed the most recent Neo-Piagetian stage theory that has sub-stages (Demetriou et al., 2018; Demetriou & Spanoudis, 2018). They referred to the model as especially Piagetian (Piaget, 1970/1983), but with influence of Neo-Piagetians. Thus, their Neo-Piagetian model involves four stages – episodic representations, realistic mental representations, rule-based representations, and principle-based representations. The age of onset of the stages occur at birth, 2 years, 6 years, and 11 years, respectively. The sub-stages involve (a) emergence of a stage, and (b) its integration. Note that other Neo-Piagetian theories have three or more sub-stages in their sub-stage recursion modeling (e.g., Case, Fischer, and Young). Feldman (2004) developed a model similar to Demetriou et al., with four stages and two sub-stages that reoccur in them (more initial, advanced).

Neo-Eriksonian Beyond that, the model that Young developed allowed the opportunity to create a revised Eriksonian (Neo-Eriksonian) model. However, in this case, the change was so radical (becoming 25 steps instead of the original 8 in Erikson's model), and the extant literature so conservative in making any changes to Erikson's original 8 stages in his model, the final product depended much less on comparing other Neo-Eriksonian models and, instead, was basically created by extrapolating from the 25-step Neo-Piagetian one. That said, it was relatively easy to place the original eight stages in the Erikson model of socio-affectivity in correspondence with their correct spot in the Neo-Piagetian series and then create the 17 missing steps.

Coincidentally, for each of the last four stages of the five in Young's Neo-Piagetian model, two of the eight original Eriksonian stages seemed to fit within them. Moreover, the pattern that made sense for each of the four stages in this fitting process was that the two Eriksonian stages that fit in the stage at issue did so in the second and fourth of the five sub-stage slots in the model. It was as if Erikson had anticipated the same key points in the five-step sequence in each stage that Young ended up positing, but not the initial, middle, and last ones of the five involved and, instead, only the second and fourth ones.

The reader should reexamine Table 10.1 to see the relationship between the 25-step Neo-Piagetian series in cognitive development and the parallel 25 steps in socio-affective development. Notice, as well, that Young created labels for the Neo-Eriksonian stages for each five sub-stage grouping (Young, 2012), so that the two series (Neo-Piagetian, Neo-Eriksonian) end up with the same structure (five stages X five sub-stages). In this sense, the model is even more radical relative to the original Eriksonian model on which it is based, because that eight-stage sequence might have covered the lifespan, but only with stages and without sub-stages, and certainly not with names for overarching groupings of steps as Young had done with his own five stages in the model. Therefore, the present Neo-Eriksonian model has greatly modified Erikson's stage conception, the number (5, not 8), their labels, their placement in terms of age period, and so on, aside from the number of steps involved when its 25 steps (stages X sub-stages) are juxtaposed to the original 8.

Comment

The modeling section above has presented the elements of the three major theories under review, those of Piaget, Erikson, and Young. The literature review that follows especially deals with conceptualization and research related to Piaget and Erikson. Specification of Young's model continues after that.

Literature Review

Piaget and Erikson

Piaget Any Google search by decade indicates the downward course given to these types of stage models. Moreover, current work that considers itself Piagetian or Neo-Piagetian barely considers the stage component in his oeuvre, focusing more on factors such as executive control, working memory, attentional processes, neural circuits, etc., that might be associated with cognitive development generally. For example, the most recent book on Piaget and his contributions (Budwig, Turiel, & Zelazo, 2017) barely mentions Piaget's stages and sub-stages. Oesterdiekhoff (2016) considered Piaget as having made contributions rivaling those of Freud, but he did not spend much time describing Piaget's stages. Bolton and Hattie (2018) related the classic four Piagetian stages to the development of executive function and in the prefrontal cortex. Girgis, Lee, Goodarzi, and Ditterich (2018) related post-formal adult development to dynamical modeling, including activation/inhibition processes, which were discussed in the first part of the present book. Börnert-Ringleb and Wilbert (2018) examined the mental operations used in solving concrete operational tasks. Klimstra and Denissen (2017) applied both Piagetian and Eriksonian concepts to their model of identity in psychopathology, but not stage aspects beyond the one on identity in Erikson.

MacNeill, Ram, Bell, Fox, and Pérez-Edgar (2018) have conducted a Piagetian study that supports Piaget's nonlinear developmental model of sensori-motor development (Piaget, 1954). The concept of object permanence refers to the existence of objects as distinct entities outside of the infant's own actions. Piaget studied the concept in the first year using objects hidden partially or fully behind screens after he had initiated interest in the object. A second hiding place is introduced, and eventually the object is hidden there instead of the first hiding place, which is used consistently over trials until the switch to the second one.

The particular task is referred to as the A-not-B task (A-(not-B)). A represents the first hiding spot and B the second one. The A-not-B error refers to the infant seeking the hidden object at point A despite its switch to point B and having perceived its placement at B. That is, the infant is expressing a perservative-type error, and the error has been attributed to not having the concept of object permanence. Also, it has been attributed to being deficient in executive function/working memory/inhibiting a prepotent response/flexibility in cognition. Research has demonstrated much interindividual and even intraindividual variability in infant performance on the task, including if the methods include a delay between seeing the last hiding place and when search can begin.

In the study, MacNeill et al. (2018) examined longitudinally 28 infants monthly from 6 to 12 months of age, when the A-not-B error typically occurs. The A-(not)B task used a box with two wells. A cloth was used to hide the desired toy in the well for a trial. The delay varied from 0 to 6 seconds, with clapping used to break attention and the parent's holding the infant's hands to prevent reaching. The study also examined occipital lobe EEG, using a composite measure of baseline power values. As for the results, the authors maintained that they supported Piaget's theory of qualitative reorganization of infant's sensori-motor object permanence behavior. The study employed nonlinear logistic growth curve modeling statistics, which allowed for nonlinear "S-shaped" sigmoidal curves to best fit the data, if applicable. The A-not-B error was evident at 6 months, the error reduced between 7 and 11 months, including due to delay, and flattened again at 12 months. The authors related their results to changes in trajectories of EEG power occipitally.

Other step models of psychological growth of maturity in adulthood have been formulated. Fossas (2018) related that Kegan (1982, 1994) referred to the adult passing through the stages of socialized, self-authoring, and self-transforming mind, while referring to Piaget's theory as providing a cognitive basis for this development. The lifespan model begins at birth and continues into the elderly period. It consists of six stages total, with three more applicable to infants and children. It includes 20 steps, 4 at each of the first five stages, with the last one constituting the sixth stage. The 20-step sequence is evaluated using an interview procedure (Lahey, Souvaine, Kegan, Goodman, & Felix, 1988). Fossas (2018) found that participants with a self-authorizing mind were most happy, and that different forms of happiness were related to each of the three adult steps in development.

Further work is needed to validate Kegan's model and compare it to my own Neo-Piagetian/Neo-Eriksonian model across the lifespan. A major difference conceptuality is that the socio-affective steps in Kegan's model need further work to render them clinically relevant, unlike in the present case. That being said, Kegan's approach to development of the adult mind is consistent with my own that multiple steps are needed, which is not necessarily evident in the other major Neo-Piagetian models (e.g., Case, 1985; Fischer, 1980).

Erikson Work on identity development, the crux of Erikson's work, barely mentions Erikson's stages (e.g., in the special issue edited by Galliher, Rivas-Drake, & Dubow, 2017; Kaufman & Crowell, 2018). That said, other research investigating identity confirms the place of identity as a stage in adolescence relative to other Eriksonian stage acquisitions (Beyers & Seiffge-Krenke, 2010). The research on identity in adolescence, moreover, continues with adolescent samples (Hatano, Sugimura, & Schwartz, 2018; Nelson, Kling, Wängqvist, Frisén, & Syed, 2018; Pfeifer & Berkman, 2018). Further, the research finds that all dimensions in identity are developing early in adolescence. This result is partially inconsistent with models indicating that the search for identity is taking place later than Erikson had posited, as emerging adulthood models have maintained (Arnett, 2015; Markovitch, Luyckx, Klimstra, Abramson, & Knafo-Noam, 2017; Pfeifer & Berkman, 2018). Overall, the salience of identity both in the Eriksonian model and for adolescents generally cannot be denied. Furthermore, contemporary research supports Erikson's approach to identity in adolescence (Becht et al., 2017), although with variations in his approach to identity evident, as per the original formulations of Marcia (1966).

Pfeifer and Berkman (2018) extended identity research on adolescence by considering neuroimaging studies in self-evaluation. Their review found that, in self-evaluation, early adolescence especially "use" midline structures, such as the ventromedial prefrontal cortex and the rostral/perigenual anterior cingulate cortex (respectively, vmPFC and r/p ACC). Other regions include the dorsal medial PFC and the temporal-parietal junction (respectively, dmPFC and TPJ). The authors emphasized the evaluation process in the development of emerging identities in adolescents, as facilitated by activity in these various regions. I note that the model is consistent with a biopsychosocial one, e.g., the authors argue that the self "can be harnessed" in self-regulation/motivated behavior. Kroger (2018) examined identity issues in case life stories of three participants, who were 34, 50, and 70 years old. She concluded that identity development is an epigenetic process.

Identity is being studied with newer questionnaires. For research on the Utrecht-Management of Identity Commitments Scale (U-MICS; Meeus, 2001), see van Doeselaar, Klimstra, Denissen, Branje, and Meeus (2018) and Piotrowski (2018). For research on the Measures of Psychosocial Development (MPD; Hawley, 1988), see Robino and Foster (2018). For research on the Dimensions of Identity Development (DIDS) developed by Luyckx, Schwartz, Berzonsky, Soenens, Vansteenkiste, Smits, and Goossens (2008), see Hartman and Anderson (2018), and Mastrotheodoros and Motti-Stefanidi (2017). For work with the Dutch Self-Concept and Identity Measure (SCIM; Kaufman, Cundiff, & Crowell, 2015), see Bogaerts et al. (2018). For research on the Identity Style Inventory-4 (ISI-4; Smits, Berzonsky, Soenens, Luyckx, Goossens, Kunnen, & Bosma, 2008), see Piotrowski and Brzezińska (2018). For a general Eriksonian developmental questionnaire, see Darling-Fisher (2018) on the MEPSI (Modified Erikson Psychosocial Stage Inventory; Darling-Fisher & Leidy, 1988, 2015). For research on the Erikson Psychosocial Stage Inventory (EPSI; Rosenthal, Gurney, & Moore, 1981), see Dimitrova, Hatano, Sugimura, and Ferrer-Wreder (2018), Hatano et al. (2018), and Niiyama, Kontkanen, Paavilainen, and Kamibeppu (2018). Waterman (2015) wrote a methodological critique of identity questionnaires that readers should consult.

Similarly, the work on Erikson's eighth stage of generativity generally supports his model (e.g., Ardelt, Gerlach, & Vaillant, 2018; Lawford, Doyle, & Markiewicz, 2018; Mackinnon, De Pasquale, & Pratt, 2016; Malone, Liu, Vaillant, Rentz, & Waldinger, 2016). The concepts of wholeness and self-determination have been applied to this age-period, which are Eriksonian concepts (Kroger, 2015; Ryan & Deci, 2017). Also, the concept of wholeness in Erikson is supported by research on a general factor of psychosocial development (GFPD) that pervades the stages (Dunkel & Harbke, 2017). These types of Eriksonian studies remind that, for Piaget, the age of acquisition of the stages and sub-stages that he describes are secondary to the invariant order in the developmental sequence that the model prescribes (Bickhard, 2016).

A special issue in 2018 in the academic journal "Identity: An International Journal of Theory and Research" is devoted to showing the value of and insights in Erikson's approach to identity for contemporary questions about identity relevant to society (Schachter & Galliher, 2018). Syed and Fish (2018) showed how Erikson considered the psychosocial context, as in the influence of culture, race, and ethnicity on development. Alberts and Durrheim (2018) considered that his work can apply to political struggle. Rogers (2018) viewed Erikson's psychosocial model as transactional. Schachter (2018) considered Erikson's developmental model as integrating biological, psychological, and social influences. Kerpelman and Pittman (2018) proposed studying identity development in terms of attachment theory, which makes it an interface acquisition (also see Lawford et al. (2018) and

Weisskirch (2018) on the relationship between attachment and Eriksonian stage measures in adolescence and emerging adults). The development of identity can go wrong, of course, and negative identity might develop (Hihara, Sugimura, & Syed, 2018). There could be mental health crises that Erikson's model could help address (Coté, 2018). In the end, unconscious processes including "sinister" ones would be involved (Schachter, 2018).

There are several points common to the special issue edited by Schachter and Galliher (2018) on Eriksonian development and my own, but also several differences of note. First, the special issue articles take a broad perspective on Erikson's model and its applications, both in terms of causes and applications, Also, it begins to offer a lifespan investigation, as with Kerpelman and Pittman's (2018) article on attachment theory in relation to identity. Nevertheless, most of the special issue focuses exclusively on identity, unlike the present approach. Also, the present approach delves especially deeply into the psychotherapeutic process that stems from a Neo-Eriksonian perspective, including over the lifespan. This makes the two approaches - the 2018 special issue on Erikson and the present book - quite complementary and constituting potential catalysts to much Neo-Eriksonian work on lifespan development, its crises, and precise psychotherapy.

Others

A counter aspect to the devaluing of the stage component in stage theorizing is that the models that have been developed that do not include stages have a much greater influence in psychology today. They include ones related to informational processing (e.g., Siegler, 2016), cognitive psychology and cognitive behavioral therapy (Leahy, 2017; Wenzel, 2017), as well as ones related to networks (Borsboom, 2008, 2017), neurosciences (Sporns, 2011, 2012), neuropsychology and related disciplines (Gur & Gur, 2017), the medical (psychiatric) model (Insel et al., 2010), and evolutionary psychology (Belsky & Pluess, 2009).

Also, any newer theoretical and modeling approaches that are attempting theoretical integrations, such as systems theory (Thelen & Smith, 1994), the biopsychosocial model (Melchert, 2015), and embodiment approaches (e.g., Marshall, 2016), are more at the fringes of psychology relative to the multiple publications that are more empirical, on the brain, etc. These newer models have not penetrated to a sufficient degree into the ethos of psychology and, indeed, the atmosphere in the field is that these types of integrative models are more heuristic than scientifically functional, having little empirical relevance. That said, some models are making more headway in integrating psychology, for example, in development, the probabilistic learning/Bayesian predictive models (Gopnik & Wellman, 2012); however, in many ways they build on Piaget's model rather than outrightly replacing it (Tourmen, 2016).

Comment

To conclude this portion of the present work, psychology is a field that has increasingly underscored its objective and empirical nature, while battling with the factors that undermine that foundation. However, not giving due to the integrative theorizing in the field that also has been its hallmark might be counterproductive for its mission in the long run.

Moreover, exploring the value of grand theories that could help direct the discipline would aid in improving the scope, empirical investigation, and practice of psychology and its appreciation in wide audiences outside the discipline. Further, the promotion of and improvement in stage theorizing could be especially helpful in this regard. In the following, I indicate some factors why this type of thinking has been devalued in psychology; also, I suggest ways to resurrect the utility and application of stage theorizing.

Stage Conceptions

Piaget

Part of the reason for the "abandonment" of use and investigation of the Piagetian stage concept is that even its definition and conceptualization changes. For example, Barrouillet (2015) pointed out that the stage concept has become more domain-specific and local rather than cross-cutting generalized mental capacities that change abruptly from one developmental epoch to the next. Carey, Zaitchik, and Bascandziev (2015) maintained that the concept of stages and their description by Piaget are here to stay, but their review focused more on the mechanisms of change than the actual stages themselves. Moreover, the evidence in support of the stage model has been inconsistent right from its initial publications in the pre-WWII period (Beins, 2016). Piaget himself might be one of the factors in the current de-emphasis on stages in development because he was less interested in the developmental process, per se, than in the epistemology of "genetic" change.

The question of whether stages even exist has been posed in the literature (Lourenço, 2016). The answer that this scholar provided is affirmative. For example, for Lourenço (2016), some of the criticisms of the concept are unfounded; the "received" view of Piaget's model is not the one that he espoused. Consider the concept of décalage, in which acquisitions for a domain vary with the complexity of related tasks in the domain. Rather than being a factor that undermines the Piagetian concept of stages, it shows that it is sensitive to context and to individual differences, despite the general emphasis on the universal map of cognitive acquisitions that Piaget preferred to emphasize.

According to Lourenço (2016), stages can be defined as:

(a) Hierarchical structures acquired in an invariant order.
(b) They “integrate,” or “overcome” and “transcend,” the stage immediate prior to their appearance. [This aspect of the definition of stages is the one that I dispute the most, see below.]
(c) Stages consolidate or exhibit transitions in which aspects of the prior stage and the developing one can coexist.
(d) Stages manifest an organization (“structuration”) referred to as *structures d’ensemble* (overarching structures of the whole; Piaget, 1970/1983). This refers to their formal and logical properties.

Piaget did not believe that stages and their properties are intervening variables in cognitive processes. Rather, these properties help describe them better. It is the schemes and operations of any one stage that serve as the cognitive mediators in problem-solving, acting on the world, etc., and that the child uses in his/her active constructionism. Moreover, Piaget might have created formalisms of logico-mathematical structures for specific stages, but Piaget especially referred to the logic of “meanings” that the individual articulates in encountering and acting upon the world rather than adhering to a strict formalism (Piaget & Garcia, 1983).

Lourenço (2016) continued that (e) stages exist in equilibrium. They resist perturbations and balance assimilations and accommodations. Assimilation refers to applying schemes or operations. Accommodation refers to changing them to more advanced levels when the applications no longer work effectively.

Note that not all people develop through each of the various stages described by Piaget. For example, in societies without formal schooling, the upper stages might not be realized (Oesterdiekhoff, 2016).

Erikson

Compared to Piaget, stages have a very different meaning in the stage theory of Erikson, who was primarily concerned with socio-affective development. For Erikson, stages were described as tensions between oppositional poles involving new acquisitions that emerge, such as Trust vs. Mistrust (Syed & McLean, 2018, in press). The person confronts novel crises, conflicts, or issues related to the developmental tasks that emerge, which serve as types of organizing structures in the development of the person. If Piaget referred to consolidation of *structures d’ensemble* into interconnected wholes of schemas or operations, which move from one qualitatively distinct structure to the next one that is more advanced, the pattern for socio-affective stages is much more individualized and diverse, and even with fixations and regressions possible. Moreover, each of the stages is qualified by each of the major attributes of other stages in Erikson’s model, and not just its own, although each stage does have one principle issue, such as identity in the adolescent stage.

Micro-Genetic Approaches

Piaget's stage model is taken to be macro-genetic, expressing major shifts in cognitive development several years apart, and happening abruptly and discontinuously, although with transitions, too (e.g., Crossland, 2017). In contrast, micro-genetic approaches to developing cognition investigate the actual strategies used by children in real time. The diversity of problem-solving approaches used by children speaks to a different way of understanding their development (Siegler, 2016). The Sieglerian approach to cognitive development is grounded in what children do in problem-solving and does not superimpose an abstract theoretical model in how children should be thinking, so it is appealing.

However, we need to recall that Piaget's active and constructive approach to cognitive development also has micro-genetic components, so that information processing and related approaches are not as diametrically opposite to Piaget's or stage approaches as one might maintain. For example, Piaget's theory involves perturbations in the child's problem-solving attempts that promote cognitive development (Tourmen, 2016). When assimilation is ineffective as an approach in problem-solving strategy, the child will experience emotional surprise, a disturbance, and enter a phase of confusion and contradiction, which might resolve assuming the required accommodation takes place. Also, children better enter this transitional phase when it includes peer consultation and discovery learning more than instruction and "expert" or adult input (e.g., Lourenço, 2012).

Siegler (1996, 2016) argued that a micro-genetic approach to studying cognitive development supports a model termed the "overlapping waves" theory. For example, when preschoolers solve mathematical problems, already they are using multiple strategies – they could use their finger to add when sums are a total of 10 or less; they could just display their fingers without using them; they could retrieve the answer from memory; and so on. Research has revealed this multiple strategy approach in many cognitive domains and equally for different ages, albeit with more advanced strategies for more advanced ages and problems.

Therefore, Siegler (2016) proposed that several ways of acting and thinking can "coexist" in the child and compete in problem-solving, with the process over time leading to different strategies emerging as the preferred one. In the figure presenting the model in Siegler, at a younger age, three strategies are used, and they emerge successively as predominant. Later in development, two more strategies emerge and the second one emerges as predominant while the first one drops out after a while and never replaces any of the others as predominant.

Comment

Although the Siegler model fits the data that he has derived from empirical work and it springs from his initial interest in Piaget, it is not a Neo-Piagetian model of cognitive development. That is, the overlapping waves of strategies referred to for any one domain do not reflect a general pattern across domains. Moreover, the strategies are so individualized that no sequence that can generalize across children could be evident. Furthermore, by themselves, strategies that crop up to solve specific problems and that are not related to some general cognitive construct do not have inherent in them a stage aspect. Neo-Piagetians would adhere more closely to Piaget's constructivist and structural approach to cognitive development than what the wave model implies, and Siegler would not disagree with that statement.

Neo-Piagetians

Pascual-Leone

The Neo-Piagetians began their work with dissatisfaction with the way Piaget had proposed how children move from one (sub)stage to the next. Piaget emphasized maturational processes, some room for experiential ones, conflicts between efforts to assimilate or apply schemes/operations to problems, the failings that result, the accommodations that ensue, and so on. The Neo-Piagetians grounded their explanations more in cognitive processes such as attention, executive function, and their underlying neuro-circuitry. The area of developmental EF study is still trying to establish correct terminology and measures (Morra, Panesi, Traverso, & Usai, 2017; Podjarny, Kamawar, & Andrews, 2017, 2018).

However, the first Neo-Piagetians did not tackle the question of whether Piaget's proposed sequence of stages was valid, for example, accepting his four-stage cognitive stage model or some variant. This was the approach of the very first Neo-Piagetian (Pascual-Leone, 1970; Pascual-Leone & Johnson, 2017). He focused on adding elements related to the mechanisms of change, e.g., attentional/mental capacity and neural circuitry (Arsalidou & Pascual-Leone, 2016), rather than changing the nature of the Piagetian stages themselves.

Case and Fischer

Other Neo-Piagetians have been more radical and have modified not only Piaget's stage conception but also the stages themselves that mark cognitive development (e.g., Case, 1985; Fischer, 1980). In Young (2011), I reviewed these various Neo-Piagetian models, in a compare-contrast process that led to my own Neo-Piagetian model (as discussed above). I had limited myself in covering models that were lifespan and included sub-stages within each stage, which meant especially comparing Case and Fischer, preparatory to constructing my own model. To review, both Fischer and Case had a reduced set of stages like Piaget. Also, they did add adult steps in development, like other Piagetians. Further, they each had a three-step sub-stage sequence that repeated over stages, although with different labels, characteristics, and so on and even at times different ages when the sub-stages applied for a particular stage/sub-stage combination.

Others

Others also have compared the different Neo-Piagetian models, but not necessarily limiting themselves to lifespan ones or ones with sub-stages throughout. For example, Mascolo (2015) compared the Neo-Piagetian models of Case and Fischer to those of Halford (1993) and Demetriou and colleagues (e.g., Demetriou, Spanoudis, & Mouyi, 2010), both of whom do not have a cyclical sub-stage component to their models. Commons (2016) constructed two tables that compared his own Neo-Piagetian model (Commons & Richards, 1984) with many others, including that of Piaget (Inhelder & Piaget, 1958). Commons' model originally concerned the post-formal period and later was applied across the lifespan. It does not have sub-stages, per se; and instead of referring to stages generally, mostly he referred to "orders."

However, although Commons' first table on the stages that development from birth to early childhood compared his model (and that of Piaget) to that of Fischer (1980), it is especially missing the crucial Neo-Piagetian model of Case (1985, 1992), as well as others, including my own. Also, the Piagetian sequence provided in the first table includes six sub-stages for the sensori-motor stage; but they are partly misaligned with the relevant age periods to which they correspond, might not be numbered, might be incorrectly numbered, etc. Furthermore, it is well known that Piaget's pre-operational stage begins by about age 2 years, but in the table, Commons indicated that Piaget did not have a new step developing at age 2 years; that is, there is a "missing" step in Piaget's model according to Commons at this age! Furthermore, some of the equivalences in the steps in Commons' model to those of Piaget appear misnomers, e.g., referring to the newborn as computational and the 2- to 4-month-old as sensory *or* motor. As for the second table in Commons (2016), it is quite comprehensive in comparing his stage sequence to those of 24 other models. He concluded that his model is the only one that covers the full age span from childhood to adulthood.

Comment

However, in Young (2011), I noted some inconsistencies in Commons' model relative to my own. I even noticed a step missing in his adult series of steps in development when compared to my own model. We can conclude that a valid Neo-Piagetian model in terms of stages and sub-stages should be a lifespan one, should be consistent with Piaget's theory but add steps as per the data and conceptualization in the field, and should take into account the major models that have been proposed to reformulate it, including those of both Case and Fischer. As shown previously, the Young model meets these criteria; and I can add that have not encountered any other that does so. The next section of the present work delves more deeply into the Young model.

References

Ardelt, M., Gerlach, K. R., & Vaillant, G. E. (2018). Early and midlife predictors of wisdom and subjective well-being in old age. *Journal of Gerontology: Social Sciences, 73*, 1514–1525.

Arnett, J. J. (2015). Identity development from adolescence to emerging adulthood: What we know and (especially) don't know. In K. C. McLean & M. Syed (Eds.), *The Oxford handbook of identity development* (pp. 53–64). New York: Oxford University Press.

Arsalidou, M., & Pascual-Leone, J. (2016). Constructivist developmental theory is needed in developmental neuroscience. *NPJ: Science of Learning, 1*, 16016. https://doi.org/10.1038/npjscilearn.2016.16

Barrouillet, P. (2015). Theories of cognitive development: From Piaget to today. *Developmental Review, 38*, 1–12.

Becht, A. I., Nelemans, S. A., Branje, S. J. T., Vollebergh, W. A. M., Koot, H. M., & Meeus, W. H. J. (2017). Identity uncertainty and commitment making across adolescence: Five-year within-person associations using daily identity reports. *Developmental Psychology, 53*, 2103–2112.

Beins, B. C. (2016). Early tests of Piagetian theory through World War II. *The Journal of Genetic Psychology, 177*, 252–264.

Belsky, J., & Pluess, M. (2009). The nature (and nurture?) of plasticity in early human development. *Perspectives in Psychological Science, 4*, 345–351. https://doi.org/10.1111/j.1745-6924.2009.01136.x

Beni, M. D. (2018). The reward of unification: A realist reading of the predictive processing theory. *New Ideas in Psychology, 48*, 21–26. https://doi.org/10.1016/j.newideapsych.2017.10.001

Beyers, W., & Seiffge-Krenke, I. (2010). Does identity precede intimacy? Testing Erikson's theory on romantic development in emerging adults of the 21st century. *Journal of Adolescent Research, 25*, 387–415.

Bickhard, M. H. (2016). Probabilities over what? *Human Development, 59*, 34–36.

Biggs, J. B. (1992). Modes of learning, forms of knowing, and ways of schooling. In A. Demetriou, M. Shayer, & A. Efklides (Eds.), *Neo-Piagetian theories of cognitive development: Implications and applications for education* (pp. 31–51). London: Routledge.

Blatt, S. J., & Blass, R. B. (1996). Relatedness and self-definition: A dialectic model of personality development. In G. G. Noam & K. W. Fischer (Eds.), *Development and vulnerability in close relationships* (pp. 309–338). Mahwah, NJ: Erlbaum.

Bogaerts, A., Claes, L., Verschueren, M., Bastiaens, T., Kaufman, E. A., Smits, D., et al. (2018). The Dutch Self-Concept and Identity Measure (SCIM): Factor structure and associations with identity dimensions and psychopathology. *Personality and Individual Differences, 123*, 56–64. https://doi.org/10.1016/j.paid.2017.11.007

Bolton, S., & Hattie, J. (2017). Cognitive and brain development: Executive function, Piaget, and the prefrontal cortex. *Archives of Psychology, 1*, 1–36.

Börnert-Ringleb, M., & Wilbert, J. (2018). The association of strategy use and concrete-operational thinking in primary school. *Frontiers in Education, 3*, 38. https://doi.org/10.3389/feduc.2018.00038

Borsboom, D. (2008). Psychometric perspectives on diagnostic systems. *Journal of Clinical Psychology, 64*, 1089–1108. https://doi.org/10.1002/jclp.20503

Borsboom, D. (2017). A network theory of mental disorders. *World Psychiatry, 6*, 5–13. https://doi.org/10.1002/wps.20375

Budwig, N., Turiel, E., & Zelazo, P. D. (Eds.). (2017). *New perspectives on human development*. Cambridge, UK: Cambridge University Press.

Bugajska, B. E. (2017). The ninth stage in the cycle of life – Reflections on E. H. Erikson's theory. *Ageing & Society, 37*, 1095–1110.

Carey, S., Zaitchik, D., & Bascandziev, I. (2015). Theories of development: In dialog with Jean Piaget. *Developmental Review, 38*, 36–54.

Case, R. (1985). *Intellectual development: Birth to adulthood*. New York: Academic Press.

Case, R. (1987). Neo-Piagetian theory: Retrospect and prospect. *International Journal of Psychology, 22*, 773–791.

Case, R. (1992). *The mind's staircase: Exploring the conceptual underpinnings of children's thought and knowledge*. Hillsdale, NJ: Erlbaum.

Case, R., Okamato, Y., Griffin, S., McKeough, A., Bleiker, C., Henderson, B., et al. (1996). The role of central conceptual structures in the development of children's thought. *Monographs of the Society for Research in Child Development, 61*, 246. https://doi.org/10.2307/1166077

Cieciuch, J., & Topolewska, E. (2017). Circumplex of identity formation modes: A proposal for the integration of identity constructs developed in the Erikson-Marcia tradition. *Self and Identity, 16*, 37–61.

Commons, M. L. (2016). The fundamental issues with behavioral development. *Behavioral Development Bulletin, 21*, 1–12.

Commons, M. L., & Richards, F. A. (1984). A general model of stage theory. In M. L. Commons, F. A. Richards, & C. Armon (Eds.), *Beyond formal operations: Later adolescent and adult cognitive development* (Vol. 1, pp. 120–140). New York: Praeger.

Crocetti, E. (2017). Identity formation in adolescence: The dynamic of forming and consolidating identity commitments. *Child Development Perspectives, 11*, 145–150.

Crossland, J. (2017). Optimal learning in schools – Theoretical evidence: Part 2 updating Piaget. *School Science Review, 364*, 77–83.

Darling-Fisher, C. S. (2018). Application of the Modified Erikson Psychosocial Stage Inventory: 25 years in review. *Western Journal of Nursing Research*. https://doi.org/10.1177/0193945918770457

Darling-Fisher, C. S., & Leidy, N. K. (1988). Measuring Eriksonian development in the adult: The modified Erikson psychosocial stage inventory. *Psychological Report, 62*, 747–754.

Darling-Fisher, C. S., & Leidy, N. K. (2015). *The modified Erikson psychosocial stage inventory*. University of Michigan Library. Retrieved from http://hdl.handle.net/2027.42/111746

Demetriou, A., Makris, N., Spanoudis, G., Kazi, S., Shayer, M., & Kazali, E. (2018). Mapping the dimensions of general intelligence: An integrated differential-developmental theory. *Human Development, 61*, 4–42. https://doi.org/10.1159/000484450

Demetriou, A., & Spanoudis, G. (2018). *Growing minds: A developmental theory of intelligence, brain, and education*. New York: Routledge.

Demetriou, A., Spanoudis, G., & Mouyi, A. (2010). The development of mental processing. In W. F. Overton & R. M. Lerner (Eds.), *The handbook of life-span development, cognition, biology, and methods* (Vol. 1, pp. 306–345). Hoboken, NJ: Wiley.

Dimitrova, R., Hatano, K., Sugimura, K., & Ferrer-Wreder, L. (2018). The Erikson psychosocial stage inventory in adolescent samples: Factorial validity and equivalence of identity as measured from the United States and Japan. *European Journal of Psychological Assessment*. https://doi.org/10.1027/1015-5759/a000456

Dunkel, C. S., & Harbke, C. (2017). A review of measures of Erikson's stages of psychosocial development: Evidence for a general factor. *Journal of Adult Development, 24*, 58–76.

Erikson, E. H. (1950). *Childhood and society*. New York: Norton.

Erikson, E. H. (1958). *Young man Luther*. New York: Norton.

Erikson, E. H. (1959). Identity and the life cycle: Selected papers. *Psychological Issues, 1*, 5–165.

Erikson, E. H. (1968). *Identity: Youth and crisis*. New York: Norton.

Erikson, E. H., Erikson, J. M., & Kivnick, H. Q. (1986). *Vital involvements in old age*. New York: Norton.

Evans, I. M. (2016). A review of Unifying causality and psychology: Being, brain, and behavior. *PsycCritiques, 61*. https://doi.org/10.1037/a0040558

Evans, I. M. (2017). Response to Evans's (2016) review of Unifying causality and psychology: Being, brain, and behavior: Response to Young. *PsycCritiques, 62*. https://doi.org/10.1037/a0040679

Feldman, D. H. (2004). Piaget's stages: The unfinished symphony of cognitive development. *New Ideas in Psychology, 22*, 175–231.

Fischer, K. W. (1980). A theory of cognitive development: The control and construction of hierarchies of skills. *Psychological Review, 87*, 477–531.

Fischer, K. W., & Bidell, T. R. (2006). Dynamic development of action and thought. In W. Damon & R. M. Lerner (Eds.), *Handbook of child psychology: Vol. 1. Theoretical models of human development* (6th ed., pp. 313–399). New York: Wiley.

Fossas, A. (2018). Psychological maturity predicts different forms of happiness. *Journal of Happiness Studies*. https://doi.org/10.1007/s10902-018-0033-9

Galliher, R. V., Rivas-Drake, D., & Dubow, E. F. (2017). Identity development process and content: Toward an integrated and contextualized science of identity. *Developmental Psychology, 53*, 2009–2010. https://doi.org/10.1037/dev0000452

Girgis, F., Lee, D. J., Goodarzi, A., & Ditterich, J. (2018). Toward a neuroscience of adult cognitive development theory. *Frontiers in Neuroscience, 12*, 1–10. https://doi.org/10.3389/fnins.2018.00004

Goertzen, J. R. (2013). The blind leading the blind? *Theory & Psychology, 23*, 693–694. https://doi.org/10.1177/0959354313483380

Gopnik, A., & Wellman, H. M. (2012). Reconstructing constructivism: Causal models, Bayesian learning mechanisms, and the theory. *Psychological Bulletin, 138*, 1085–1108.

Green, C. D. (2015). Why psychology isn't unified, and probably never will be. *Review of General Psychology, 19*, 207–214. https://doi.org/10.1037/gpr0000051

Gur, R. C., & Gur, R. E. (2017). Complementarity of sex differences in brain and behavior: From laterality to multimodal imaging. *Journal of Neuroscience Research, 95*, 189–199. https://doi.org/10.1002/jnr.23830

Guyon, H., Falissard, B., & Kop, J.-L. (2017). Modeling psychological attributes in psychology – An epistemological discussion: Network analysis vs. latent variables. *Frontiers in Psychology, 8*, 798. https://doi.org/10.3389/fpsyg.2017.00798

Halford, G. S. (1993). *Children's understanding: The development of mental models*. New York: Erlbaum.

Hartman, C. L., & Anderson, D. M. (2018). Psychosocial identity development and perception of free time among college-attending emerging adults. *Leisure Sciences*. https://doi.org/10.1080/01490400.2018.1483850

Hatano, K., Sugimura, K., & Schwartz, S. J. (2018). Longitudinal links between identity consolidation and psychosocial problems in adolescence: Using bi-factor latent change and cross-lagged effect models. *Journal of Youth and Adolescence, 47*, 717–730. https://doi.org/10.1007/s10964-017-0785-2

Hawley, G. A. (1988). *Measures of psychosocial development: Professional manual*. Lutz, FL: Psychological Assessment Resources.

Henriques, G. (2011). *A new unified theory of psychology*. New York: Springer Science + Business Media.

Inhelder, B., & Piaget, J. (1958). *The growth of logical thinking from childhood to adolescence: An essay on the construction of formal operational structures*. New York: Basic Books.

Insel, T. R., Cuthbert, B. N., Garvey, M. A., Heinssen, R. K., Pine, D. S., Quinn, K. J., et al. (2010). Research domain criteria (RDoC): Toward a new classification framework for research on mental disorders. *American Journal of Psychiatry, 167*, 748–751.

Kaufman, E. A., Cundiff, J. M., & Crowell, S. E. (2015). The development, factor structure, and validation of the self-concept and identity measure (SCIM): A self-report assessment of clinical identity disturbance. *Journal of Psychopathology and Behavioral Assessment, 37*, 122–133.

Kaufman, E. A., & Crowell, S. E. (2018). Biological and behavioral mechanisms of identity pathology development: An integrative review. *Review of General Psychology, 22*, 245–263.
Kegan, R. (1982). *The evolving self.* Cambridge, MA: Harvard University Press.
Kegan, R. (1994). *In over our heads: The mental demands of modern life*. Cambridge, MA: Harvard University Press.
Klimstra, T. A., & Denissen, J. J. A. (2017). A theoretical framework for the associations between identity and psychopathology. *Developmental Psychology, 53*, 2052–2065.
Kroger, J. (2015). Identity development through adulthood: The move toward "wholeness". In K. C. McLean & M. Syed (Eds.), *The Oxford handbook of identity development* (pp. 65–80). New York: Oxford University Press.
Kroger, J. (2018). The epigenesis of identity - What does it mean? *Identity: An International Journal of Theory and Research, 18*, 334–342. https://doi.org/10.1080/15283488.2018.1523730
Lahey, L., Souvaine, E., Kegan, R., Goodman, R., & Felix, S. (1988). *A guide to the subject-object interview: Its administration and analysis*. Cambridge, MA: Harvard University Graduate School of Education.
Lawford, H. L., Doyle, A-B., & Markiewicz, D. (2018). Associations of attachment orientation with early generative concern across adolescence. *Journal of Personality, 86*, 726–737.
Leahy, R. L. (2017). *Cognitive therapy techniques: A practitioner's guide* (2nd ed.). New York: The Guilford Press.
Lilienfeld, S. O. (2017). Psychology's replication crisis and the grant culture: Righting the ship. *Perspectives on Psychological Science, 12*, 660–664.
Lourenço, O. (2012). Piaget and Vygotsky: Many resemblances, and a crucial difference. *New Ideas in Psychology, 30*, 281–295.
Lourenço, O. (2016). Developmental stages, Piagetian stage in particular: A critical review. *New Ideas in Psychology, 40*, 123–137.
Luyckx, K., Schwartz, S. J., Berzonsky, M. D., Soenens, B., Vansteenkiste, M., Smits, I., & Goossens, L. (2008). Capturing ruminative exploration: Extending the four-dimensional model of identity formation in late adolescence. *Journal of Research in Personality, 42*, 58-82.
Mackinnon, S. P., De Pasquale, D., & Pratt, M. W. (2016). Predicting generative concern in young adulthood from narrative intimacy: A 5-year follow up. *Journal of Adult Development, 23*, 27–35.
MacNeill, L. A., Ram, N., Bell, M. A., Fox, N. A., & Pérez-Edgar, K. (2018). Trajectories of infants' biobehavioral development: Timing and rate of A-not-B performance gains and EEG maturation. *Child Development, 89*, 711–724. https://doi.org/10.1111/cdev.13022
Malone, J. C., Liu, S. R., Vaillant, G. E., Rentz, D. M., & Waldinger, R. J. (2016). Midlife Eriksonian psychosocial development: Setting the stage for late-life cognitive and emotional health. *Developmental Psychology, 52*, 496–508.
Marcia, J. E. (1966). Development and validation of ego identity status. *Journal of Personality and Social Psychology, 3*, 551–558.
Marcia, J. E. (1980). Identity in adolescence. In J. Adleson (Ed.), *Handbook of adolescent psychology* (pp. 159–187). New York: Wiley.
Marcia, J. E. (1993). The ego identity status approach to ego identity. In J. E. Marcia, A. S. Waterman, D. R. Matteson, S. L. Archer, & J. L. Orlofsky (Eds.), *Ego identity: A handbook for psychosocial research* (pp. 3–21). New York: Springer Science + Business Media.
Markovitch, N., Luyckx, K., Klimstra, T., Abramson, L., & Knafo-Noam, A. (2017). Identity exploration and commitment in early adolescence: Genetic and environmental contributions. *Developmental Psychology, 53*, 2092–2102.
Marshall, P. J. (2016). Embodiment and human development. *Child Development Perspectives, 10*, 245–250.
Mascolo, M. F. (2015). Neo-Piagetian theories of cognitive development. In J. Wright (Ed.), *International encyclopedia of the social & behavioral sciences* (2nd ed., pp. 501–510). Amsterdam: Elsevier.

Mascolo, M. F., & Fischer, K. W. (2015). The dynamic development of thinking, feeling and acting. In R. Lerner (Series Ed.) & W. Overton (Vol. Ed.), *Handbook of child development and developmental science: Vol. 1 – Theory and method* (pp. 113–161). New York: John Wiley.

Mastrotheodoros, S., & Motti-Stefanidi, F. (2017). Dimensions of identity development scale (DIDS): A test of longitudinal measurement invariance in Greek adolescents. *European Journal of Developmental Psychology, 14*, 605–617.

McLean, K. C., & Syed, M. (Eds.). (2015). *The Oxford handbook of identity development*. New York: Oxford University Press.

Meeus, W. (2001). *A three-dimensional measure of identity: The Utrecht-Management of Identity Commitments Scale (U-MICS)*. Unpublished manuscript, Research Centre Adolescent Development, Utrecht University, The Netherlands.

Melchert, T. P. (2015). *Biopsychosocial practice: A science-based framework for behavioral health care*. Washington, DC: American Psychological Association.

Morra, S., Panesi, S., Traverso, L., & Usai, M. C. (2017). Which tasks measure what? Reflections on executive function development and a commentary on Podjarny, Kamawar, and Andrews (2017). *Journal of Experimental Child Psychology, 167*, 246–258.

Mounoud, P. (1976). Les revolutions psychologiques de l'enfant [Psychological revolutions in the child]. *Archives de Psychologie, 44*, 103–114.

Mounoud, P. (1986). Similarities between developmental sequences at different age periods. In I. Levin (Ed.), *Stage and structure: Reopening the debate* (pp. 40–58). Norwood, NJ: Ablex.

Müller, U., Ten Eycke, K., & Baker, L. (2015). Piaget's theory of intelligence. In S. Goldstein, D. Princiotta, & J. Naglieri (Eds.), *Handbook of intelligence* (pp. 137–151). New York: Springer Science + Business Media.

Nelson, L. D., Simmons, J., & Simonsohn, U. (2018). Psychology's renaissance. *Annual Review of Psychology, 69*, 511–534. https://doi.org/10.1146/annurev-pysch-122216-011836

Nelson, S. C., Kling, J., Wängqvist, M., Frisén, A., & Syed, M. (2018). Identity and the body: Trajectories of body esteem from adolescence to emerging adulthood. *Developmental Psychology, 54*, 1159–1171. https://doi.org/10.1037/dev0000435

Niiyama, H., Kontkanen, I., Paavilainen, E., & Kamibeppu, K. (2018). A comparison of personality maturity among Japanese youth and Finnish young adult students: A cross-sectional study using Erikson psychosocial stage inventory and sense of coherence scale. *International Journal of Adolescence and Youth*. https://doi.org/10.1080/02673843.2018.1435418

Nosek, B. A., & Lakens, D. (2014). Registered reports: A method to increase credibility of published results. *Social Psychology, 45*, 137–141. https://doi.org/10.1027/1864-9335/a000192

Oesterdiekhoff, G. W. (2016). Is a forgotten subject central to the future development of sciences? Jean Piaget on the interrelationship between ontogeny and history. *Personality and Individual Differences, 98*, 118–126.

Pascual-Leone, J. (1970). A mathematical model for the transition rule in Piaget's developmental stages. *Acta Psychologica, 32*, 301–345.

Pascual-Leone, J., & Johnson, J. (2017). Organismic-causal models "from within" clarify developmental change and stages. In N. Budwig, E. Turiel, & D. Zelazo (Eds.), *New perspectives on human development* (pp. 67–87). Cambridge, UK: Cambridge University Press.

Perfors, A. (2016). Piaget, probability, causality, and contradiction: Commentary on Tourmen. *Human Development, 59*, 26–33.

Pfeifer, J. H., & Berkman, E. T. (2018). The development of self and identity in adolescence: Neural evidence and implications for a value-based choice perspective on motivated behavior. *Child Development Perspectives, 12*, 158–164.

Piaget, J. (1923). *Le langage et la pensée chez l'enfant* [The language and thought of the child]. Neuchâtel, Switzerland: Delachaux et Niestlé.

Piaget, J. (1954). *The construction of reality in the child*. New York: Basic Books.

Piaget, J. (1980). *Adaptation and intelligence: Organic selection and phenocopy*. Chicago: University of Chicago Press. (Original work published 1974).

Piaget, J. (1983). Piaget's theory. In P. H. Mussen (Ed.), *Handbook of child psychology* (Vol. 1, pp. 103–128). New York: Wiley. (Original work published in 1970).

Piaget, J. (1985). *The equilibration of cognitive structures: The central problem in intellectual development* (T. Brown & K. J. Thampy, Trans.). Chicago, IL: University of Chicago Press. (Original work published in 1975).

Piaget, J., & Garcia, R. (1983). *Psychogenèse et histoire des sciences* [Psychogenesis and the history of science]. Paris: Flammarion.

Piotrowski, K. (2018). Adaptation of the Utrecht-Management of Identity Commitments Scale (U-MICS) to the measurement of the parental identity domain. *Scandinavian Journal of Psychology, 59*, 157–166. https://doi.org/10.1111/sjop.12416

Piotrowski, K., & Brzezińska, A. I. (2018). A cluster-analytic approach to identity style classification: Four seems to be better than three. *European Journal of Developmental Psychology*. https://doi.org/10.1080/17405629.2018.1467755

Podjarny, G., Kamawar, D., & Andrews, K. (2017). The multidimensional card selection task: A new way to measure concurrent cognitive flexibility in preschoolers. *Journal of Experimental Child Psychology, 159*, 199–218.

Podjarny, G., Kamawar, D., & Andrews, K. (2018). Measuring on the go: Response to Morra, Panesi, Traverso, and Usai. *Journal of Experimental Child Psychology, 171*, 131–137. https://doi.org/10.1016/j.jecp.2018.02.002

Robinson, O. (2016). Emerging adulthood, early adulthood, and quarter-life crisis: Updating Erikson for the twenty-first century. In R. Žukauskienė (Ed.), *Emerging adulthood in European context* (pp. 17–30). New York: Routledge.

Robino, A., & Foster, T. (2018). Psychosocial predictors of wellness in college students. *Adult Span Journal, 17*, 3–13. https://doi.org/10.1002/adsp.12049

Rosenthal, D. A., Gurney, R. M., & Moore, S. M. (1981). From trust to intimacy: A new inventory for examining Erikson's stages of psychosocial development. *Journal of Youth and Adolescence, 10*, 525–537.

Rubin, M. (2017). When does HARKing hurt? Identifying when different types of undisclosed post hoc hypothesizing harm scientific progress. *Review of General Psychology, 21*, 308–320. https://doi.org/10.1037/gpr0000128

Ryan, R. M., & Deci, E. L. (Eds.). (2017). *Self-determination theory: Basic psychological needs in motivation, development, and wellness*. New York: The Guilford Press.

Schwartz, S. J., Zamboanga, B. L., Luyckx, K., Meca, A., & Ritchie, R. (2016). Identity in emerging adulthood: Reviewing the field and looking forward. In J. J. Arnett (Ed.), *The Oxford handbook of emerging adulthood* (pp. 401–420). New York: Oxford University Press.

Shrout, P. E., & Rodgers, J. L. (2018). Psychology, science, and knowledge construction: Broadening perspectives from the replication crisis. *Annual Review of Psychology, 69*, 487–510. https://doi.org/10.1146/annurev-psych-122216-011845

Siegler, R. S. (1996). *Emerging minds: The process of change in children's thinking*. New York: Oxford University Press.

Siegler, R. S. (2016). Continuity and change in the field of cognitive development and in the perspectives of one cognitive developmentalist. *Child Development Perspectives, 10*, 128–133.

Smits, I., Berzonsky, M. D., Soenens, B., Luyckx, K., Goossens, L., Kunnen, S., & Bosma, H. (2008). *The Identity Style Inventory-4: Internal research report*. Leuven, Belgium: Catholic University Leuven.

Sporns, O. (2011). *Networks of the brain*. Cambridge, MA: MIT Press.

Sporns, O. (2012). *Discovering the human connectome*. Cambridge, MA: MIT Press.

Staats, A. W. (1983). *Psychology's crisis of disunity: Philosophy and method for a unified science*. New York: Praeger.

Staats, A. W. (1991). Unified positivism and unification psychology. *American Psychologist, 46*, 899–912. https://doi.org/10.1037/0003-066X.46.9.899

Stam, H. J. (2015). The neurosciences and the search for a unified psychology: The science and esthetics of a single framework. *Frontiers in Psychology, 6*, 1467. https://doi.org/10.3389/fpsyg.2015.01467

Syed, M., & McLean, K. C. (2018). Erikson's theory of psychosocial development. In. E. Braaten & B. Willoughby (Eds.), *The SAGE encyclopedia of intellectual and developmental disorders* (pp. 577–581). Thousands Oak, CA: SAGE.
Thelen, E., & Smith, L. B. (1994). *A dynamic systems approach to the development of cognition and action*. Cambridge, MA: MIT Press.
Tourmen, C. (2016). With or beyond Piaget? A dialogue between new probabilistic models of learning and the theories of Jean Piaget. *Human Development, 59*, 4–25.
Tryon, W. W. (2014). *Cognitive neuroscience and psychotherapy: Network principles for a unified theory*. New York: Academic Press.
van Doeselaar, L., Klimstra, T. A., Denissen, J. J. A., Branje, S., & Meeus, W. (2018). The role of identity commitments in depressive symptoms and stressful life events in adolescence and young adulthood. *Developmental Psychology, 54*, 950–962. https://doi.org/10.1037/dev0000479.supp
Waterman, A. S. (2015). What does it mean to engage in identity exploration and to hold identity commitments? A methodological critique of multidimensional measures for the study of identity processes. *Identity: An International Journal of Theory and Research, 15*, 309–349.
Weisskirch, R. S. (2018). Psychosocial intimacy, relationships with parents, and well-being among emerging adults. *Journal of Child and Family Studies, 27*, 3497–3505.
Wenzel, A. (2017). Basic strategies of cognitive behavioral therapy. *Psychiatric Clinics of North America, 40*, 597–609.
Young, G. (1990a). The development of hemispheric and manual specialization. In G. Hammond (Ed.), *The cerebral control of speech and limb movements* (pp. 79–139). Amsterdam: North Holland.
Young, G. (1990b). Early neuropsychological development: Lateralization of functions – Hemispheric specialization. In C. A. Hauert (Ed.), *Developmental psychology: Cognitive, perceptuo-motor and neuropsychological perspectives* (pp. 113–181). Amsterdam: North Holland.
Young, G. (1997). *Adult development, therapy, and culture: A postmodern synthesis*. New York: Plenum Press.
Young, G. (2011). *Development and causality: Neo-Piagetian perspectives*. New York: Springer Science + Business Media.
Young, G. (2012). A unitary Neo-Piagetian/ Neo-Eriksonian model of development: Fundamental assumptions and meta-issues. *New Ideas in Psychology, 30*, 241–249. https://doi.org/10.1016/j.newideapsych.2011.11.002
Young, G. (2016). *Unifying causality and psychology: Being, brain and behavior*. Cham, Switzerland: Springer.
Young, G. (2017). Response to Evans's (2016) review of Unifying causality and psychology: Being, brain, and behaviour. *PsycCritiques, 62*. https://doi.org/10.1037/a0040680

Chapter 11
Neo-models, Neo-stages, Networks

Abstract This chapter presents in depth the 25-step Neo-Piagetian/Neo-Eriksonian model in tabular format, focusing on the Neo-Piagetian portion in preparation for the elaboration of the Neo-Eriksonian one in ensuing chapters. The 25-step model is a lifespan one. The five Neo-Piagetian stages involved hew to Piaget's four-stage model, and the cyclic recursion of sub-stages is based on Piaget's infancy sub-stages. The chapter continues by examining recent research on Fischer's model, and it points out inconsistencies therein relative to my own model. The next part of the chapter presents the concept of Neo-stage. The concept is based heavily on network models, making the stage concept more contemporary and testable. I offer my own innovations in network modeling, as well. The chapter includes aspects of micro-genetic changes as part of the concept of neo-stage. The chapter concludes with a revised approach to the stage concept in the Neo-Eriksonian tradition. The overall conclusions for this chapter and the last one prepare the way for an in-depth presentation of the current Neo-Eriksonian model. The concept of neo-stage presents a more refined and testable model of stages, for example, by including network concepts, so that the upshot of this chapter is that the present Neo-Piagetian/Neo-Eriksonian model of 25 steps in development has moved the original theories on which they are based into a contemporary frame that is more valid, more testable, and more useful clinically. The present model is not a throwback to grand imperial theories, and one that blindly defends them, but it constitutes a forward-looking, flexible theory open to revision and research.

A Neo-Piagetian/Neo-Eriksonian Model

Stage by Stage

Tables 11.1, 11.2, 11.3, 11.4, and 11.5 give the specifics of Young's (e.g., 1990a, 1990b, 1997, 2011, 2012, 2016) Neo-Piagetian/Neo-Eriksonian five-stage × five sub-stage model of development. The five sub-stages of the model are critical to it, because they are based on Piaget's excellent observations of his children as they grew through the infancy sensori-motor stage. The five Piagetian stages derive

G. Young, *Causality and Development*,
https://doi.org/10.1007/978-3-030-02493-2_11

Table 11.1 Stage 1 of Neo-Piagetian cognitive development and Neo-Eriksonian social-affective development

Neo-Piagetian stage	Neo-Piagetian sub-stage	Age range	Neo-Eriksonian stage	Neo-Eriksonian sub-stage	Self-development
Reflexive (pre-sensori-motor)[a]	Coordination	Earlier fetal life	Non-participatory reflexive socio-emotions[b]	Distance acts vs. no acts	Non-self
	Hierarchization	Fairly premature		Nursing vs. rootless acts	Reflexive pre-self
	Systematization	Somewhat premature		Outcome vs. outcast acts	Corporal proto-self
	Multiplication	Full-term newborn		Care-giving vs. careless giving acts	Perceptual intermodal self
	Integration	0–1 mo		Emotional vs. mal-emotional acts	Primary emotional self

Adapted from Young (2012) [Table 2, Page 244]; with the last column taken from Young (2011) [Table 13.11, Page 307–308], original from Young (1997) [Table 3.7, Page 83]
[a]Not in Piaget's original stage model
[b]Not in Erikson's original stage model

Table 11.2 Stage 2 of Neo-Piagetian cognitive development and Neo-Eriksonian social-affective development

Neo-Piagetian stage	Neo-Piagetian sub-stage	Age range	Neo-Eriksonian stage	Neo-Eriksonian sub-stage	Self-development
Sensori-motor[a]	Coordination[b]	1–4 mo	Pre-participatory socio-affects	Dyadic vs. dys-dyadic acts	Inter-coordinated incipient social self
	Hierarchization[b]	4–8 mo		Trust vs. mistrust acts[c]	End-focused trusting self
	Systematization[b]	8–12 mo		Sociability vs. un-sociability acts	Permanent inter-subjective self
	Multiplication[b]	12–18 mo		Autonomy vs. doubt acts[c]	Independent autonomous self
	Integration[b]	18–24 mo		Inter-digitational vs. de-digitational acts	Interior implicative self

Adapted from Young (2012) [Table 2, Page 244]; with the last column taken from Young (2011) [Table 13.11, Page 307–308], original from Young (1997) [Table 3.7, Page 83]
[a]Piaget's original stage model
[b]Reworking of last five of six of Piaget's sensori-motor sub-stages, with the first one being the last one in the sequence of sub-stages in the prior stage
[c]Erikson's original stage model

Table 11.3 Stage 3 of Neo-Piagetian cognitive development and Neo-Eriksonian social-affective development

Neo-Piagetian stage	Neo-Piagetian sub-stage	Age range	Neo-Eriksonian stage	Neo-Eriksonian sub-stage	Self development
Peri-operational (pre-operational/concrete operational)[a]	Coordination	2–3.5 yr	Peri-participatory social cognition	Super-ordinate vs. dis-coordinate acts (quasi-participatory)	Coupling egocentric/centrated self
	Hierarchization	3.5–5 yr		Initiative vs. guilt acts[b]	Hierarchizing initiative self
	Systematization	5–7 yr		Identification and gender vs. problematic identification and gender acts[c]	Systematizing primary-perspective self
	Multiplication	7–9 yr		Industry vs. inferiority acts (participatory)[b]	Concrete operational secondary-perspective self
	Integration	9–11 yr		Role/personality tryout vs. role/personality tryout confusion acts[d]	Projecting tertiary-perspective self

Adapted from Young (2012) [Table 2, Page 244]; with the last column taken from Young (2011) [Table 13.11, Page 307–308], original from Young (1997) [Table 3.7, Page 83]

[a]Piaget's original stage model

[b]Erikson's original stage model

[c]Young (2011) referred to the 5–7 year Neo-Eriksonian sub-stage either in terms of Identification or Gender Acts. Here, the table combines the terms

[d]Young (2011) referred to the 9–11 year Neo-Eriskonian sub-stage in terms of Roles. Here, table adds Personality Tryout

especially from Piaget, with the reflexive stage and a post-formal stage added. His pre-operational and concrete operational stages are included in one representational (peri-operational) stage, akin to what Piaget also had proposed at times.

The Young model was developed in 1990 (Young, 1990a, 1990b) by especially comparing the other major Neo-Piagetian stage × sub-stage lifespan developmental models at the time (Case, Fischer, Mounoud; e.g., Case, 1985; Fischer, 1980; Mounoud, 1976, 1986). Biggs and Collis (1982) had developed a similar model, but it was not consulted then (it is added to the table). The tables also illustrate how the Young model allows for a lifespan stage X sub-stage (25-step) model of "self" development based on it (Young, 1997). The self model is consistent with stage models of development at the time the model was created in 1997 (based especially on the work Sroufe, 1990; Selman, 1980; Loevinger, 1976, respectively). Their self-development stage models fitted seamlessly together into a coherent 25-step sequence that fitted the Young model. This 25-step lifespan model of self-development is the most comprehensive in the literature and illustrates the value of the Young model.

Table 11.4 Stage 4 of Neo-Piagetian cognitive development and Neo-Eriksonian social-affective development

Neo-Piagetian stage	Neo-Piagetian sub-stage	Age range	Neo-Eriksonian Stage	Neo-Eriksonian sub-stage	Self development
Abstract (formal operational)[a]	Coordination	11–13 yr	Hyper-participatory social mutuality	Conscious vs. contra-conscious acts	Abstractly aware conscious self
	Hierarchization	13–16 yr		Identity vs. identity diffusion acts[b]	Identity-seeking self
	Systematization	16–19 yr		Nurturing vs. Mis-nurturing acts	Maturing conscientious self
	Multiplication	19–22 yr		Intimacy vs. isolation acts[b]	Mutual relativistic self
	Integration	22–25 yr		Universal vs. self-singular acts	Accepting universal self

Adapted from Young (2012) [Table 2, Page 244]; with the last column taken from Young (2011) [Table 13.11, Page 307–308], original from Young (1997) [Table 3.7, Page 83]
[a]Piaget's original stage model
[b]Erikson's original stage model

Table 11.5 Stage 5 of Neo-Piagetian cognitive development and Neo-Eriksonian social-affective development

Neo-Piagetian stage	Neo-Piagetian sub-stage	Age range	Neo-Eriksonian stage	Neo-Eriksonian sub-stage	Self development
Collective intelligence (post-formal)[a]	Coordination	25–28 yr	Super-ordinate participatory collective sociality	Meta-collecting vs. disillusionment acts	Holistic meta-self
	Hierarchization	28–39 yr		Generativity vs. self-absorption acts[b]	Activating generative self
	Systematization	39–50 yr		Catalytic vs. midlife crisis acts	Catalytic midlife self
	Multiplication	50–61 yr		Ego integrity vs. despair acts[b]	Satisfied ego integrity self
	Integration	61 - yr		Cathartic vs. abandonment acts	Purified integrated self

Adapted from Young (2012) [Table 2, Page 244]; with the last column taken from Young (2011) [Table 13.11, Page 307–308], original from Young (1997) [Table 3.7, Page 83]
[a]not in Piaget's original stage model
[b]Erikson's original stage model

Table 11.6 Examples of application of the Neo-Piagetian/Neo-Eriksonian five-stage model

	Example		
Stage	Maslow (1943)	Marital steps (Young, 1997)	Management style (work, home) (Young, 1997)
Reflexive	Physiological	Attraction	Negate
Sensori-motor	Security	Attachment	Dominate
Peri-operational	Love (affection, belongingness)	Commitment	Relegate
Abstract (formal)	Self-esteem	Growth	Delegate
Collective intelligence	Self-actualization	Mutuality	Integrate

Table 11.7 Examples of application of the Neo-Piagetian/Neo-Eriksonian sub-stage model

	Application		
Sub-stage	Stages of change[a,b]	Steps in relational (psychological) co-regulation	Nonlinear dynamical system transitions[b,c]
Coordination	Contemplation	Participatory interactor (social, non-social) juxtaposed with self	Point attractors (2)
Hierarchization	Preparation	Knowledge/social acquisition set within into existing structure	Cyclical attractor (over the 2 points)
Systematization	Action	Existing structure (e.g., co-scheme) altered systemically	Chaotic attractor
Multiplication	Maintenance	New acquisition spreads	Complex adaptive system processes (inhabiting cusp between order and disorder)
Integration	Resolution	System wholly transformed in the relational co-regulatory process	Super-ordinate complex adaptive system processes

[a]Adapted from Norcross, Krebs, and Prochaska (2011); original conceptualization of the model by Maddox (1995) and Prochaska et al. (1994)
[b]Adopted with permission of Springer International Publishing. Young (2016); with kind permission from Springer International Publishing. [Second column from Table 33.3, Pages 810–811; Last column from Table 30.3, Page 749]
[c]Adopted with permission of Springer Science + Business Media. Young (2011); with kind permission from Springer Science + Business Media B. V. [Table 28.1, Page 647; slightly modified; see Figure 30.4, too]

Elaborations

Tables 11.6 and 11.7 present further elaborations, additions, and applications of Young's model, as presented in his past publications, although with one new one. Table 11.6 illustrates how Maslow's (1943) model of five hierarchical needs, which was also considered developmental, maps onto Young's five-stage model.

Also, the table shows how Young has applied his model to create five-stage models of the development of relationships and of management styles. Table 11.7 shows ways that Young's five-step sub-stage model can be applied to psychological growth. For example, the stages of change model (Maddox, 1995; Prochaska, Norcross, & DiClemente, 1994) maps onto Young's five sub-stage model. Also, the table indicates how psychological or relational co-regulation (Young, 2017) can develop through five steps according to the model. Psychological or relational co-regulation is a concept akin to the one of co-regulation in Mascolo and Fischer (2015, and references therein, e.g., Fischer, 1980) but broader because it refers to participatory interaction, whether social or nonsocial (e.g., learning from an ethics text).

Comment

Mascolo and Fischer (2015) reviewed the vast scope of the Fischerian Neo-Piagetian model, including its stages and sub-stages. They gave several examples applying the model to critical developmental acquisitions that, at once, illustrate the advantages and disadvantages of the model. Specifically, for the infancy period, they examined how the model can be applied to the steps in the development of reaching. To my knowledge, this is the first time that the Fischerian model includes a step of "complex" sensori-motor actions, which is inserted between the first and second sensori-motor sub-stages, thereby yielding a four-step rather than a three-step sub-stage sequence. That is, the sub-stage sequence is modified to fit the developmental data, which never happens in any of the other stage X sub-stage Neo-Piagetian theories. If there are extra steps in development relative to any series in a Neo-Piagetian model, as suggested by data, it might be advisable to formulate sub-steps in this regard rather then new (sub)stages (for example, I have referred to fractalization processes in this regard, e.g., micro-genetic sequences at one level of a cognitive system being found at lower-order levels, as well).

Also, as mentioned above, the sequence in the Fischerian Neo-Piagetian theory is missing a step in the age period beginning at 2 years. Mascolo and Fischer (2015) provide another example of this lacuna in Fig. 4.8 on steps in the development of moral action.

Overall, then, there is good reason to consider Case's work, and that of Young, as well, as the Neo-Piagetians who have the most complete Neo-Piagetian stage/sub-stage models over the lifespan, and neither model should be excluded in Neo-Piagetian model comparisons. However, as the review of the literature shows, these models might be ignored, and this is to the detriment of obtaining a complete and valid picture of the Neo-Piagetian field of conceptualization and the study of stages and their sub-stages.

Interim Conclusions

This part of the book has several central assumptions that have been addressed in the literature review. Mostly, the assumptions have been supported. The paper will now move on to new ideas that can help the field. But first, the paper reviews those assumptions as an interim conclusion.

(a) First, although the concept of stages in development have been questioned, if the appropriate approach to defining and studying stages is adopted, they will be shown to be valid (e.g., MacNeill, Ram, Bell, Fox, & Pérez-Edgar. 2018). (b) Second, there are misconceptions in understanding Piaget that have contributed to prematurely dismissing the relevance of his stage modeling (Lourenço, 2016). (c) Third, comparison of the different Neo-Piagetian models of stages and sub-stages reveal which ones are more integrative, account for more of the data, fill in missing gaps, lead to better testing of their validity, and facilitate making predictions that work (Young, 2011). (d) Fourth, as argued throughout this present book, cognitive stage models provide the cognitive foundations for advances in equivalent socio-affective stages, as in the Eriksonian tradition. The Piagetian and Eriksonian stage models can be revised to allow for stages along two axes, one cognitive and one socio-affective, which are parallel over development.

The next section of the paper leaves the literature review undertaken and turns to novel suggestions to improve work on stages. It hopes to make models emanating from this tradition more salient for contemporary theorizing in psychology and helpful in empirical investigation in psychology.

Neo-stage

Introduction

This present book maintains that the developmental stage models should not be discounted, discarded, ignored, or considered heuristic, at best, and no longer relevant, at worst. Rather, the traditional concept of stages should be what is discarded. The concept of stages should be revamped so that it considers the individualized variability in cognitive development while respecting the generalized trajectory in that development that appears to indicate universal stages. In order that this notion is accepted, I propose that it be given the rubric of "neo-stage." Just as Neo-Piagetians are revising the stage and sub-stage sequences in Piaget's model and just as they are revising the mechanisms that appear to act in that development, including in underlying cognitive processes, so should they revise the stage concept itself. The literature is replete with how the traditional stage concept needs revision, for example, into a "soft" format compared to the traditional "hard" one, as defined by Piaget (1970/1983). However, I am calling for a revised stage concept that is quite removed from any hard or soft stage model.

Defined

Cognitive As defined presently, cognitively, the revised conception of stages (neo-stages) refers to individualized collections of developing schemes (and operations for the older child) that are micro-genetically recruited for dealing with problems and tasks in a domain or sub-domain and related cognitive challenges at hand.

Whether cognitively or socio-affectively, the adaptive recruitment of extant schemes or operations is local, ongoing, continuous, and rapid. Unproductive ones are dropped. New ones might be added to the repertoire used, as required. Generally, ones in the repertoire are subject to change to fit the parameters of the problem/task/challenge confronted.

Stages If universal patterns over individuals are evident in scheme/operation organization, it is not because of some sort of maturational necessity. Rather, it is because external factors have elicited common solutions in the scheme/operation and problem-solving strategy recruitment involved. Stages might appear universal, but each collection of schemes/operations and problem-solving strategies used by a person in context are derived individually and for the individual problem/task/challenge being confronted.

Non-stages Given these states of affairs, it might even be possible that a qualitative acquisition that heralds the arrival of a new stage is short-circuited by context and individual factors. One might find in a person preference for using the skills associated with an earlier stage instead of a new one. This might produce a situation that appears to support the overlapping waves model (Siegler, 2016), where developing strategies have fuzzy boundaries and some of them might even drop out. The issue here is the dialectic between micro-genetic and macro-genetic acquisitions in development, and below I consider the potential contribution of network theory to address this conundrum.

Erikson Any neo-stage model needs to apply to the Eriksonian track as much as the Piagetian. For example, fixations and regressions are more likely in the former type of stage. Eriksonians refer to the tensions in the developmental task associated with a stage, and they can lead to crises when the negative pole of the continuum is too accentuated relative to the positive one. To generalize this new neo-stage conception of stages in the Piagetian/Neo-Piagetian tradition to the Eriksonian/Neo-Eriksonian one, and to Young's model, socio-affectively, the schemes/operations and problem-solving strategies in the Neo-Piagetian stage(s) associated with a Neo-Eriksonian stage(s) at issue also would be similarly recruited micro-genetically but with impediments (e.g., fixation, regression) likely if abuse/neglect or any serious disturbance in mutuality had been experienced. Or, new schemes/operations and problem-solving strategies specific to the socio-affective issue at hand could be created.

In this sense, it is best to conceive of Eriksonian stages in the same way as the cognitive stages in this regard – there are strategies for socio-affective problem solving that could be elicited, and this happens in individual ways in context micro-genetically, which might lead to habitual patterns that are consistent with the labels given to the stages (e.g., Trust vs. Mistrust).

That said, once more, it is not that there is a universal progression in stages that everyone must navigate. A universal pattern in Eriksonian models appear evident only because of the common solutions (or their lack) that appear at specific ages, and that are buttressed by their cognitive underpinnings (e.g., Neo-Piagetian in the present case).

Yoking Further, skills associated with different stages can be yoked together in combination, if this procedure would be adaptive in the micro-genetic online problem solving in which the developing person is engaged. That is, skills for problem solving that are associated with one stage or the other never disappear through the mechanism of being integrated, transformed, or otherwise altered by new stages that come along. Rather, they are available throughout the lifespan in problem solving, for example, cognitively, even if they are sensori-motor in nature and the person is in the adult age period and is abstract in thinking.

Stage Transitioning Further, the collection of schemes/operations at any one point of time, either available or applied to a problem, task, or challenge at hand, could express a new qualitative attribute. The stage involved could develop to the point that it stands at the cusp of change and bifurcates into a more advanced one as well as the other one remaining. As the collection of skills/strategies systematizes, spreads, and integrates as the schemes/operations available are used and applied, juxtaposed, and related to each other, the system involved can self-organize to a more complex regime. That is, emergence of a qualitatively different scheme or operation can take place through active application, dissonance, reflection, and construction, but with limits set by the underlying neuro-circuitry, executive functioning (e.g., mental attention), and so on, of the person.

The qualitative emergence of a new distinct skill first happens in one of the schemes/operations involved. The process takes place through self-organization of the community of schemes/operations, perhaps through circular processes that bootstrap extant schemes/operations. As the new acquisition is applied, it generalizes and forms higher-order levels distinct from extant ones that feedback and create a hierarchical organization of schemes/operations. This process facilitates ground-up or bottom-up micro-genetic applications in interaction with top-down or superordinate regulation by the more integrated, generalized, and more advanced skill.

How can networks change to a degree sufficient to move from one level of complexity in a system to another? This type of question applies especially to cognitive development and socio-affective development, but also it could apply to stages of change in any system, such as one related to therapy. The next figure illustrates how behaviors/symptoms/clusters could change as development proceeds from one sub-stage to the next (Young, 2016). As per Young (2016), Fig. 11.1 illustrates how change

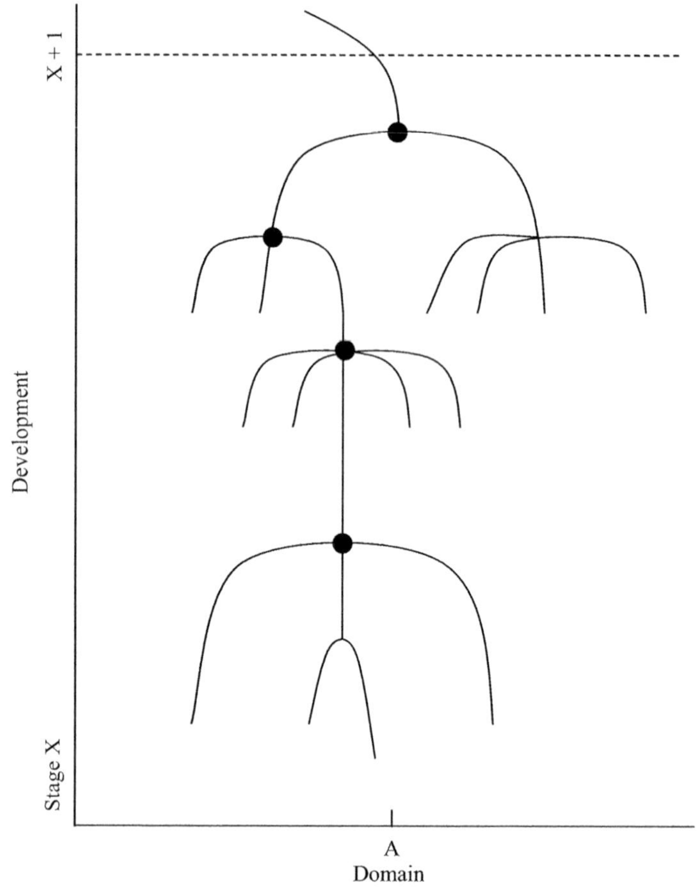

Fig. 11.1 How cognitive structures grow within a sub-stage and into a more complex one following it. The figure illustrates how cognitive structures (e.g., central conceptual structures) grow within a sub-stage, and then into a higher-order one, too (in the part of the figure to the left, at the top). Cognitive structures apply to particular domains or sub-domains (which are task collections; e.g., quantitative, social, narrative). By following the figure from top to bottom, it shows that they might develop from lower-order schemas into second-order consolidations (or more, depending on the complexity involved). They could end with super-ordinate upper-level integrations, such as mathematical rules, ordered social skill sets, or narrative plot structure knowledge. The figure indicates that domain/task development within a sub-stage can traverse the threshold boundary for the skills involved to those related to the one following it developmentally. The figure can be applied to show how behaviors/symptoms/clusters networking grow within a sub-stage, or perhaps into a higher-order one, too. (Note: Adapted from Young (2016) – Figure 37.6)

can take place within a sub-stage from the point of view of developmental stages. The development is online, local, continuous, task-by-task, or strategy-by-strategy. The scheme involved is applied perhaps with minor adjustment. It happens repeatedly, though, creating storage and organization issues. All told, the growth is horizontal rather than vertical. The generalization is lateral rather than emergent to a new level.

The figure also illustrates that development could be toward increasing complexity. For example, a schema reaches threshold for a rule or operation. This takes place because the system is pushed to the edge of ongoing system configuration and to dissolution/reorganization, through the perturbations involved, leading to emergence of a different configuration. In this case, the change is vertical rather than horizontal. The emergence of new levels of complexity in a system reflects self-organization dynamics that equilibrate the perturbations in the system that have become too disequilibrated, unstable, and untenable.

Dale and Kello (2018) took an approach similar to mine with respect to developmental emergence. They referred to dynamic integration, in particular, as promoters of emergence for sense-making, which is related to the present cognitive model. They referred to temporal and spatial (multimodal) integration in this regard, which yields constitutive integration through self-organization.

Multiple Modeling The individualized yoking of schemes and operations that takes place in problem-solving strategies, with different skills recruited from the repertoire in different stages, suggests a model of multiple cognitive intelligences. That is, instead of distinct intelligences, such as more academic or more creative ones, which is the traditional model of multiple cognitive intelligences (Sternberg, 2015), a stage-based conceptualization of multiple cognitive intelligences would consider how different stage skills are present throughout development and are recruited together and work together even if they are associated with stages of different developmental complexity. This concept is quite unlike anything of the standard models of Gardner and Sternberg (Sternberg, 2015), but allows for the integration of the Piagetian/Neo-Piagetian tradition into that type of modeling. Moreover, the same type of modeling can be used to create a model of *multiple emotional intelligences* in the socio-affective track (Eriksonian/Neo-Eriksonian; Young, 2016).

Networking Network theory has been applied to neuro-circuitry, but can be applied to the concept of stages to help further elucidate their topography. For example, system models that refer to self-assembly in spontaneous self-organization of a system once it reaches a critical state of perturbation either due to internal forces, external ones, or both, lack concepts how individual elements of the system relate to each other. Mostly, systems theory concerns macro changes, such as to new attractor basins or their coupling. In contrast, the concept of network circuits, with their nodes and edges, and the central properties that they might express, such as centrality, connectivity, hub organization, small worlds, efficiency, locality/globality, etc. (e.g., van den Heuvel & Sporns, 2013), add a new perspective for understanding the organization of the contents of each level of a system and the hierarchical levels of a system.

For example, perhaps the super-ordinate, top-down level in any one developing aspect of a system is differentiated from the bottom-up level by being more connected and global, with small world and dispersed properties compared to more tightly organized ones in the bottom-up level. Or, perhaps one child exhibits the same loose organization overall compared to another, and generally he excels in one type of problem/task/(sub)domain compared to another because such an organization helps for it. In contrast, another child would have a different strength that is consistent with her tighter network organization.

Micro-development/Macro-development Coordination

Table 11.8 presents a concept that further elaborates the concept of neo-stage and, as with the neo-stage concept itself, it is new to the field. The following clarifies the content and meaning of each of the terms involved in the concept, and its value for understanding development generally and the concept of neo-stage specifically.

Micro-development concerns the online, local adaptation to tasks, problems, stressors, crises, or situations generally that the developing person is facing, embedded in, or otherwise dealing with, and, in some senses, it is equivalent to learning. It happens both automatically and consciously, reactively and actively, and takes place

Table 11.8 Micro-development/macro-development coordination

Concept and factors to consider
Micro-development
Local, online, immediately adaptive changes in behavior (and including in any underlying schemes, operations, skills, strategies, etc.), for example, in problem-solving, dealing with a task, confronting a stressor, in a crisis
Can take place life-long; development is lifespan
Macro-development
Global, re-organization of system involved; neither abrupt nor immediate for the most part; can be to qualitatively different level, concept (e.g., first abstract thought); but that does not imply a new stage, per se
Refers to ontogenesis, generally, in contrast to micro-development, which refers to learning, adjusting in an ongoing context
Coordination
Both micro-development and macro-development have been described in the literature, but not their coordination as a central mechanism in development.
Coordination refers to the extent to which micro-developments lead to macro-developments and the balance between the two tracks
Effective micro-development/macro-development coordination requires: Flexibility; stability yet plasticity; experience-dependent responsivity yet resistance to perturbation; inhabiting the cusp of change yet maintaining equilibrium; and possible self-organizing to higher developmental levels through bootstrapping, emergence, circular causality, and so on, at least if all the components needed for the change are available and amenable to it, including cognitively, emotionally, and socially
Micro-development/macro-development coordination can become dysregulated, too rigid/tight or too disturbed, psychopathological, chaotic/loose, and so on, leading to psychiatric/psychological maladaptive behavior difficulty, dysfunctionality, problems, disorders, and mental disorder diagnoses, as well as impediments to normative, healthy, or otherwise non-problematic development
The concept of micro-development/macro-development coordination should not be taken to inform how stages develop, either cognitively or socio-affectively; but the concept does inform the deep processes that lead to stages and their growth

relentlessly and often throughout the course of one's day. It allows for the gradual accretions in knowledge, skills, problem-solving capacities, etc., leading to widening of the scope, capacity, and quality of the underlying schemes/operations, executive functions, and strategies/skills involved.

Macro-development concerns the long-term developmental changes that take place in ontogenesis, to which the micro-developments contribute (as do maturational, cultural, and other generalized factors). Macro-developments are more global than local, and might include qualitative shifts in the system involved in development (e.g., the first appearance of an abstract thought), whether cognitive or socio-affective, but do not necessarily implicate jumps to new stage re-organizations. Macro-developments depend, in part, on micro-developments; however, micro-developments might take place without any effect macro-developmentally.

That said, Vygotsky (e.g., Vygotsky, 1978) had developed a similar model of development in which micro-learning always have an affect on the extant cognitive structure of the child. For Vygotsky, learning takes place at two levels – first to acquire the learned item "inter-psychologically" and second to incorporate and re-organize the new learning into the existing conceptual structure of the person "intra-psychologically" (Tsethlikai, 2015; Wertsch, 1979/2008). Nader-Grosbois (2011) also developed a similar concept to micro-development/macro-development coordination by referring to micro-development and micro-functionality, on the one hand, and macro-development and macro-functionality, on the other hand, in the development of autism spectrum disorder (ASD). Macro-development was taken to refer to developmental level and profile. Interestingly, the domains of study in her research involved Piagetian stage-related tasks, such as object permanence.

The coordination component of the concept of micro-development/macro-development coordination refers to the balance in the two components as development proceeds. Is there sufficient self-regulatory control, the requisite balance, etc., in micro- and macro-development? Or, does one find insufficient self-other regulation (dysregulation), any indications of imbalance in the coordinations involved, such as over-rigidity, inflexibility, inability to adjust and adapt, or otherwise compromised learning and development, as in ASD, etc.?

The concept of neo-stage is a novel one, and the concept of micro-development/macro-development coordination appears a critical one to explain it. However, this type of coordination does not necessarily lead to new stages in development, because so many factors are involved in that process. Nevertheless, the concept might reflect a powerful mechanism in learning and development that contributes to stage development and transitioning, as well as how that process can go awry.

Comment

The concept of neo-stage derives from the criticisms of the traditional stage concept inherent in Piaget's work. The presentation of its central elements above speaks to a nuanced concept that still needs work. Partly, it stems from a desire to create a generalized stage concept that could apply to Erikson's stage modeling as well as Piaget's. The following sections expand the presentation of both networks and applications to Eriksonian modeling, as preliminarily introduced above.

Networks

Introduction

Aside from what has been discussed in the above, network theory is being applied to developing new perspectives on psychopathology (e.g., Borsboom, 2017; Borsboom & Cramer, 2014; Young, 2015). Instead of considering depression as a top-down construct that influences symptom expression, the network approach emphasizes that symptoms arrange in network configurations and mutually influence each other, with some being more core this way. According to this view, there is no need to invoke a generalized construct such as major depression to explain the individualized array of mutually causal symptoms in a depressed patient, a traumatized patient, etc. In the network concept view, causality inheres in the symptoms themselves as they interact, and some are more of drivers than others in this regard (e.g., poor sleep).

Models

I prepared three figures to help explicit the network behavior/symptom model and the relation of behaviors/symptoms to their causal influences. The first figure (Fig. 11.2) modifies the causality model presented in Young (2015, 2016). It illustrates that the classic construct model and the newer network model to explain symptom relations and their causality are not mutually exclusive. Systems do develop higher-order levels that influence the lower-order ones from which they emanate or emerge. Therefore, the figure shows lower-order behaviors/symptoms and higher-order clusters/constructs/disorders and how they can dynamically relate causally in context and over time.

Fig. 11.2 (continued) network (N) model only (e.g., individualized expression of depression). (**c**) Hybrid model with higher-order C more influential (>) than B/S N. (**d**) Hybrid model with lower-order B/S N > C. (**e**) Genuine hybrid model between evolving behavior/symptom network (N) and emerging higher-order construct (C). The figure depicts the relationship between lower-order behavioral/symptom network expressions (or their clustering) (their development/abnormality) and higher-order constructs/disorders as being dynamically reciprocal in causation. The top-down construct level constitutes an underlying higher-order level in the person's behavior that emerges from the lower-order interactions, while the bottom-up behavior/symptom level interacts with the top-down level of the system, with both the top-down and bottom-up influences dynamically influencing each other in context and over time. (Adapted from Young (2015, 2016). Refer to Chap. 8 and Fig. 8.1 in the present book)

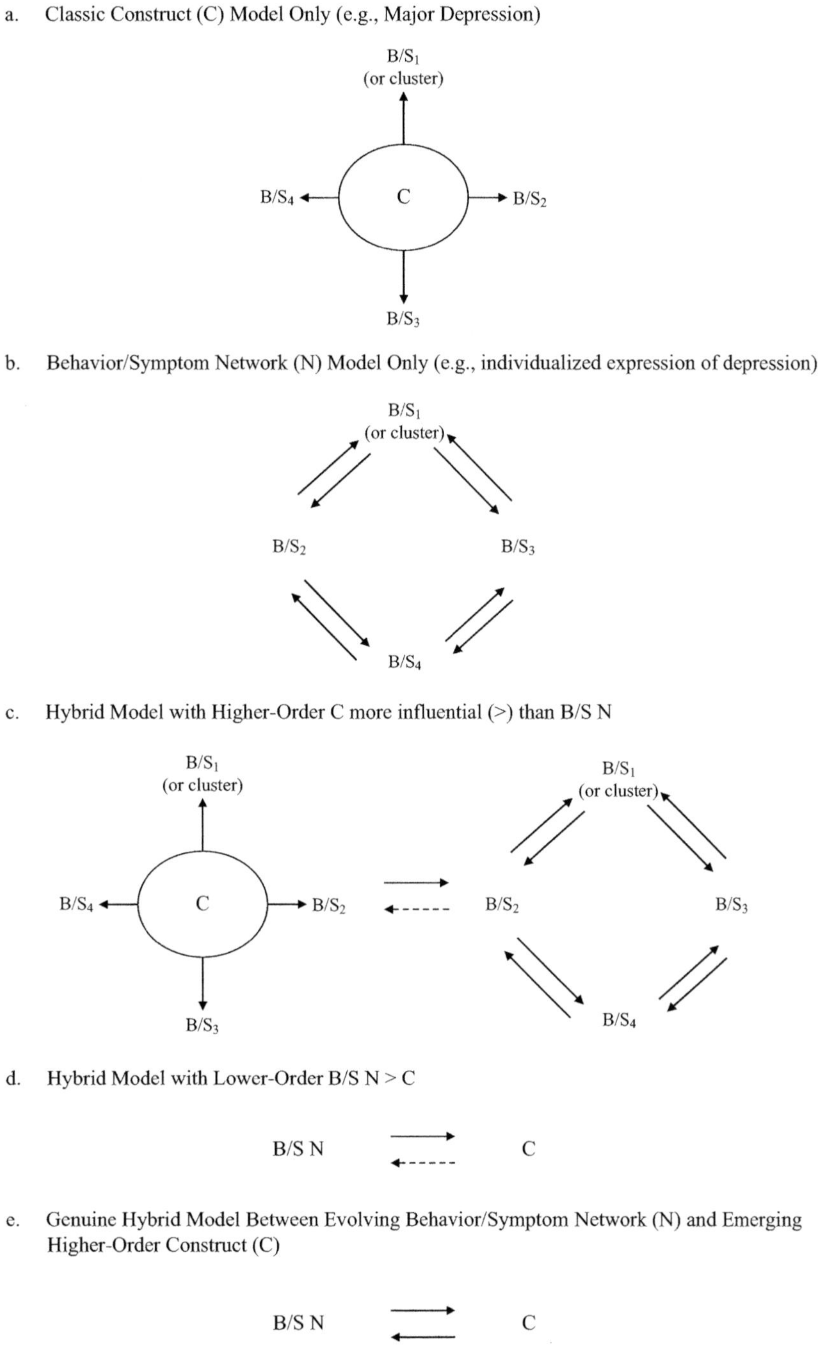

Fig. 11.2 Hybrid behavior/symptom (B/S) network (N)/construct (C) model compared to simpler models. (**a**) Classic construct (C) model only (e.g., major depression). (**b**) Behavior/symptom

(continued)

Note that the present approach to hybrid construct-network models of behaviors/symptoms differs from the approach espoused by network researchers, such as Fried and Cramer (2017). For them, at the psychopathological level, a hybrid approach to networks and constructs situates an external cause or trigger, such as a traumatic event or loss of a loved one, as a first factor that leads to a set of symptoms (or elements). Then, the networks elicited have the symptoms interacting with each other to maintain or re-activate the symptoms, especially by core ones, such as insomnia in the examples provided.

The Fried and Cramer (2017) approach to hybrid construct and network modeling in psychopathology differs from the present, which does not deal with external triggers as causes, at least in this type of modeling. Rather, the present approach examines the processes in symptom interaction and expression after the external causes have been triggered. In this regard, it emphasizes bottom-up symptom interaction in causative networking and, then, further interactions with the top-down hierarchical levels created by the bottom-up interactions through emergence, such as major depression-type profiles or ones related to posttraumatic stress disorder (PTSD) that might emerge. To conclude a strong argument is that other, hybrid network-construct models of psychopathology are not really hybrid in the sense that they do not deal with constructs in the way I have but only external causes that elicit the networks in the first place. In this regard, they still emphasize networks as being causal only in the sense of maintaining and re-activating symptoms and their connections, with nothing higher-order related to constructs such as depression and PTSD, unlike the case for the hybrid model that I have created (Young, 2015). To repeat, other hybrid network models that essentially focus on lower-order networks only are limited compared to my emergentic approach, which includes higher-order levels that feed back to influence the lower-order symptoms/networks.

The second figure (Fig. 11.3) that modifies the causality model presented in Young (2015) is more explicit in how behaviors/symptoms and their causes might interact. It emphasizes the relationship between network organization and the causal influence of the dynamic of activation-inhibition coordination. Specifically, Young has emphasized the general role of activation-inhibition coordination in brain and behavior (e.g., Young, 1990a, 1990b, 2011, 2016). For example, the reaching infant hand must activate the correct movements in sequence while inhibiting interfering ones to be successful and reach the end-goal state. Generally, behavior, then, forms interrelated clusters of networked behavioral connectivities through activation-inhibition coordination. The same happens in the brain, e.g., in neural circuitry, and the links between brain and behavior express the same coordination.

Also, the model in the figures can apply to any behavior in which there are both specific (or lower-level, bottom-up behavior) and more general (construct, superordinate emergent, higher-level, top-down) processes. In this sense, it could even apply to understanding mental disorder and psychopathology. We need to move beyond simplistic nosologies of psychiatric disorder and their psychotherapeutic

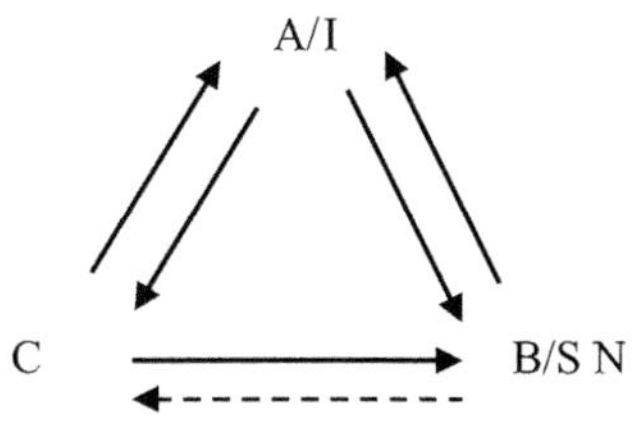

Fig. 11.3 Activation/inhibition coordination as a driver of lower-order behavior/symptom networks and emerging top-down constructs. The figure illustrates how behaviors/symptoms and their causes might interact. The figure illustrates that lower-order behavior/symptom/clusters form networks. They can interact with each other and core ones will be drivers of others. Behavior/symptom/clusters also are influenced by top-down factors, such as emergent higher-order factors (e.g., depression). Systems can develop higher-order levels that influence the lower-order ones from which they emerge. Therefore, the figure illustrates how networked lower-order behaviors/symptoms relate to higher-order constructs/disorders and how they can dynamically interact causally in context and over time. A key driver of both networks and constructs might relate to activation/inhibition coordination of the behaviors/symptoms and their emerging constructs. The behavior/symptom/clusters and the higher-order factors can causally interact and they might be influence by activation inhibition (A/I) coordinations. That is, behaviors/symptoms/clusters form networked connectivities that might reflect activation/inhibition coordinations (e.g., in movements) as well as reflecting such coordinations in neural circuitry. The activation-inhibition coordinations might also influence top-down influences on the behaviors/symptoms/clusters. (Note: Refer to Chap. 8 and Fig. 8.2 in the present book)

treatment to componential and trans-diagnostic, cross-cutting approaches, such as afforded by networked connection models. That is, although network models have been applied to symptom organization, and putative hybrid models have been constructed, they do not really include higher-order levels with disorder involved. However, the present modeling based on Young (2015) affords a combined or hybrid approach in which DSM-type constructs can be included interactively and causally.

As noted in the first portion of the present book, "in this sense, the lower-order behavior/symptom, and higher-order construct/disorder levels of a system, and any intermediate levels, as well as the causal factors related to them, can be described both in terms of network dynamics as well as the underlying activation-inhibition coordination dynamic that might underlie them."

Figure 11.4 further specifies that the nodes and edges in a network (behavior/symptoms and their linkages) could vary from individual to individual – in content, the actual behaviors/symptoms, the actual linkages, their strength, which ones are core, which are causal, and so on. For example, let's assume that the figure represents, for one person at one age in one context, how social conflict is a core symptom in psychopathology (or a general feeling of being overwhelmed, saddened, etc.) and drives the network to stronger, deeper, and more resistant connectivities. If this core connectivity network of symptoms would be mapped in psychotherapy, the therapist will have a better insight as to how to proceed in therapy.

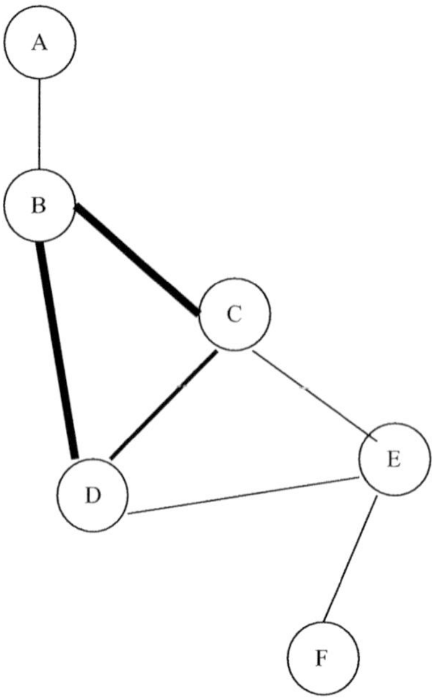

Fig. 11.4 A network of behaviors/symptoms. Nodes represent behaviors/symptoms. Edges represent the links between behaviors/symptoms. Letters for nodes refer to specific behaviors/symptoms. A thicker and darker edge represents a stronger link. The figure indicates which symptoms are core; in this case, B would be one core symptom. Also, the figure indicates how the symptoms mutually influence each other as causal drivers, and especially so for core ones. (Adapted from Schmittmann et al., 2013 based on Epskamp, Cramer, Waldorp, Schmittmann, & Borsboom 2011. Very modified from Young (2016) [Figure 7.9, Page 172])

Comment

My only concern with this type of modeling is that further work is needed how higher-order levels in symptom networks, such as an overriding feeling of depression, consistent with major depressive disorder, are emergently formed in context and can influence in their turn lower-order symptom levels, in a reciprocal feedback process. Moreover, intermediate levels might be formed that mediate between higher-order and lower-order levels, such as individually determined appraisals of context and its salience. In this regard, in Young (2015, 2016), appraisals related to the traumatic event at issue were considered relevant in mediating higher-order posttraumatic stress disorder (PTSD) and lower-order symptom networking and the latter's intra-symptom interactive causality. The causes of PTSD were not seen to reside solely at any of the three levels involved, but in their inter-level interaction along with any intra-level interactions.

To this point, this section of the present book has focused on the Piagetian and Eriksonian enterprises, with newer conceptions related to stages and networks offered, as well. The Eriksonian project is quite applicable to psychopathology as much is the network approach. In the following, I examine further the Neo-Eriksonian stage concept from this perspective.

Neo-Eriksonian Stage Concept

The Concept

The present work mostly reviews and justifies the Neo-Piagetian/Neo-Eriksonian 25-step model of development as proposed in Young (1990a, 1990b, 2011, 2012, 2016) and how it can contribute to psychology. But also, it has contributed a novel idea of referring to the new conception of stage being proposed as "neo-stage." In the following, the chapter examines another novel aspect of the model that has not been considered before this publication, this time on the nature of the proposed Neo-Eriksonian stages in view of the neo-stage concept.

The neo-stage concept suggests that there should not be much difference in how stages develop and work, whether cognitive or socio-affective. As has been shown, the traditional Piagetian concept of stages is quite rigid, with a universal sequence in development of rather abruptly transitioning stages (or sub-stages). Moreover, aside from the question of décalages, the schemes/operations in a stage form relatively integrated structures.

However, the concept of stage in Erikson's model bears little resemblance to this Piagetian way of thinking about stages because, in Erikson's model, each stage consists of an opposition or tension in polarity (e.g., Trust vs. Mistrust) related to developmental tasks that is quite determined in quality by the mutuality with the environment, or its lack. Moreover, which of any two poles dominate in any one stage (positive, negative) is never an absolute, nor should it be in that some frustration is adaptive in development. The Piagetian stages concept does not contain this type of opposition within them. There are conflicts, of course, but that is found in applying extant schemes/operations, as in assimilation, and witnessing that they no longer are helpful. When this happens in the individual, first, it leads to discordance, disequilibrium, etc., and, second, it might lead to progressive accommodative change to the scheme/operation involved. Accommodations might even lead to schema/operational change to the point of attaining a new level of qualitative organization.

The Eriksonian stage concept lies in the polar tension between positive and negative developments related to the new acquisition at each stage. Thus, the advent of an Eriksonian stage could contain enough problems for the development of the person that the stage is poorly navigated. In consequence, fixation, regression, and other after-effects could obtain as the stage at issue is navigated. The causes of difficulties in this regard are socio-affective, such as in personal conflicts with caregivers, poor parenting, and abuse. If there are difficulties in the development in the Piagetian series, which is a cognitive (sub)stage sequence, more than likely, it is from a lack of schooling that hampers the development of later stages, and it is not from negative socio-emotional experiences, per se, being the factors.

Revising the Concept

Just as the stage concept has needed revision for Piaget's understanding of them, leading to the neo-stage concept, so does it need revision in terms of Erikson's understanding of them. For example, in keeping with the Neo-Piagetian basis for the concept of a neo-stage, Neo-Eriksonian stages should be considered as a collection of individualized schemes/operations that serve adaptive, online problem/task/challenge resolution. As with the concept that, for Neo-Piagetian (sub)stages, skills from different (sub)stages can coexist and be recruited together to solve a problem, skills associated with several Neo-Eriksonian (sub)stages might be recruited together and coexist to confront the problems inherent in these types of stages (socio-affective).

Instead of dealing with tasks that relate to object permanence, causality, seriation, classification, mathematics, spatial navigation, and so on, as in the cognitive domain, the developmental tasks in the socio-affective domain, relate to engaging with the other, establishing mutuality, satisfying basic needs, creating independence and autonomy, etc. Despite their surface differences with cognitive problems typically encountered, these socio-affective tasks still require the recruitment of adaptive schemes/operations and the executive and attentional functions necessary to help them apply effectively for the task at hand.

In the end, Erikson considered developing identity as a cardinal task at all stages. Others have similar models. For example, the fundamental developmental task might be either self-definitional or about social relatedness (e.g., Blatt, 2008). Attachment theory has a similar approach in its concept of internal working models related self and other and secure vs. insecure attachment (Cassidy & Shaver, 2008). That is, although the person might be solving socio-affective problems online micro-genetically (or not), there are also grand (or higher-order) narratives macro-genetically developing about the self and other and, according to the present model, they would be conditioned by the Neo-Eriksonian (sub)stage that the person is presently navigating.

That is, the schemes/operations and skills involved in Neo-Eriksonian developmental tasks should form integrated structures in an online and ever-changing fashion for the individual. The process would depend on the social and emotional dynamics involved, as Eriksonians contend. However, the product should be more than forming tendencies toward one pole or the other in the dialectic between them because the specifics will resemble the schemes and operations in the Neo-Piagetian sequence.

Carrying this argument one step further, to this point, I have referred to parallel Neo-Piagetian and Neo-Eriksonian (sub)stages. However, aside from the cognitive base afforded by the Neo-Piagetian series for the Neo-Eriksonian one, the two sequences have been treated as independent. This is far from the case, though, in that cognition and socio-affectivity are not independent developmental processes, but are intimately entwined. For example, there should be integrated cognitive/socio-affective schemes and operations more than or perhaps instead of separate ones for each of the two domains. Finally, the assimilative-accommodative process that leads to the evolution of cognitive schemes/operations in Piaget would appear to be applicable to similar schemes/operations socio-affectively. That is, the mechanisms of change in the Piagetian series, and how it has been modified by Neo-Piagetians, should apply equally well to the Eriksonian/Neo-Eriksonian series. Similarly, network concepts of how behaviors/symptoms, and so on, interrelate, and in a causal way at that, should apply equally well to the Eriksonian/Neo-Eriksonian as the Piagetian/Neo-Piagetian sequences that are involved. Moreover, the concept of activation-inhibition coordination (Young, 2011, 2016), proposed as a common metric to help explain brain, behavior, mind, psychopathology, etc., should apply as part of the mechanisms in Eriksonian/Neo-Eriksonian development as much as anywhere else.

Interim Conclusion

The concept of neo-stage has led to new ways of thinking about Neo-Eriksonian stage models as much as Neo-Piagetian ones. The approach taken in Young (2011, 2016) further articulates an integrated Neo-Piagetian/Neo-Eriksonian stage model that applies over the lifespan. This work illustrates the value of grand theories in psychology, including the generally devalued specific stage models of Piaget and Erikson and their Neo-Piagetian/Neo-Eriksonian variations. Finally, the role of theorizing generally appears devalued in the rush to empirical investigation and dealing with the replicability crisis in psychology. Appropriate grand theories might help re-establish the respect psychology deserves as a science, allow better integration of theory and data in the field, lead to more diversity and less siloing in the science, and generally present a more holistic understanding of human nature, its development, and its evolution.

Implications

Staging

1. Here, I argue that devaluing grand theorizing is counterproductive for the goal of increasing the reliability, validity, and replicability of research in psychology. Without the top-down influence of integrative theories, psychological research risks becoming too siloed and conservative.

2. A major approach to theory in psychology lies in stage theories, such as the Freudian, Eriksonian, Piagetian, and even Maslovian (Maslow, 1943; Young, 2016). However, these theories have less importance today because they were framed with antiquated conceptions of stage. By revising stage understanding to fit contemporary science, as in the concept of neo-stages, stage theories can be appropriately revised and resurrected in importance.
3. The Neo-Piagetian and Neo-Eriksonian scholarship being conducted today does not deal much with revising the stage models in the original theories, despite elaborate attempts to revise the Piagetian stage sequence in the latter part of the last century (e.g., Case, Fischer).

The Present Model

4. Young (1990a, 1990b, 1997, 2011, 2012, 2016) has developed a stage and sub-stage Neo-Piagetian model of five stages and five cyclically recurring sub-stages within each stage (25 steps). Moreover, the model includes parallel stages that are Neo-Eriksonian. Further, the model respects the revised conceptions of stage that are being developed in the field.
5. Young's model constitutes the only Neo-Piagetian stage-sub-stage model that:

   (i) Covers the full age range from the prenatal period to the elderly period.
   (ii) Does not skip a relevant age period or stage/sub-stage, unlike what is found in other major Neo-Piagetian theories.
   (iii) Can explain data that do not fit well with its competing theories, with critical examples provided in Young (2011, 2016).
   (iv) Helps modify other Neo-Piagetian theories by suggesting how missing (sub)stages in their theories can be added to them based on the sequence Young's model describes.
   (v) Makes valid predictions of what research will find as it investigates age periods and (sub)stages not given due weight in other theories.

6. Young's model far surpasses any Neo-Eriksonian model in its scope by:

   (i) Adding many steps to Erikson's original eight-stage sequence, that is, adding 17 steps to them; other revisions of Erikson's model deal with, at most, one of the eight stages, and there has not been one Neo-Eriksonian model with more than nine stages.
   (ii) Showing parallels with the 25-step Neo-Piagetian model; neither Erikson nor Neo-Eriksonians attempted to relate Erikson/Eriksonian stages to cognitive equivalents or underpinnings, such as in Piaget's.
   (iii) Revising the understanding of the organization of Eriksonian stages in that the newer conception of Piagetian stages were shown to inform the specifics of how Eriksonian stages might be organized.
   (iv) As with the Neo-Piagetian model, the Neo-Eriksonian model is testable, and it makes predictions (among others, of what will be found in the new 17 steps added to the model).

(v) Having a psychotherapeutic potential; it has applied aspects because of its roots in psychodynamic theory and psychotherapy (e.g., see Knight, 2017).

Causality

7. Psychology has attempted to unify under various rubrics, including those of Staats (1983, 1999) and Henriques (2011). However, Young (2016) has taken a different course and written a comprehensive work on why causality should be the integrating factor in psychology. Psychology needs to integrate causation study as much as integrating itself conceptually.
8. Causality serves as an appropriate axis on which to view the commonalities over sub-disciplines in psychology, as well as its cross-disciplinary links, because the task of any science is both to describe the phenomenon under investigation and to explain the origins of the phenomenon.
9. In Young (2011, 2016), my approach to the question of causality in psychology was that its study should be more than simply listing in a compendium all its influences; rather, its study should show how these multi-factorial influences co-act together.

Networks

10. Network theory provides a means of generating common ground in the study of psychological development, neuroscience, psychopathology, etc. Network concepts include those of nodes, edges, hubs among nodes, and core nodes as causal, for example, in symptom networks, etc.
11. The concept of networks should be integrated with systems models. For example, networks might apply best to lower-order levels in a system and system dynamics might allow for higher-order levels to emerge through node interactions at lower levels.
12. The concept of activation-inhibition coordination might help in this regard. For example, the way nodes inter-coordinate might concern activatory processes, inhibitory processes, and their inter-coordination in linkages.

Yoking and Multiple Intelligences

13. Part of the approach advocated for understanding stages views their constituent schemes/operations and skills/problem-solving strategies as soft and adaptive online, such that the person recruits micro-genetically what is needed to deal with the matter at hand. The solutions are individually constructed by the person in each matter at hand, with some combinations becoming networked

together more often than others, depending on utility, success, etc., and becoming modal patterns.

14. In this regard, residual earlier developing schemas, operations, and skills, even sensori-motor in nature, can be used if helpful and yoke to higher-order schemas and skills.
15. In this sense, multiple intelligences (Sternberg, 2015) might refer to the range of schemas, operations, and skills that can be brought forth and combined to deal with problems at hand. Similarly, emotional intelligence is a worthy concept; it should refer to socio-affective coordinations of social and affective schemas, operations, and skills related to the Neo-Eriksonian portion of the present model.

New Concepts

16. The present work has proposed a concept of stages termed "neo-stage." It represents a novel variant of the traditional stage concept. It can help give the maligned stage approach in psychology a re-invigoration. The concept has been phrased generally enough to apply to both the Neo-Piagetian and Neo-Eriksonian models of stages.
17. The concept of psychological or relational co-regulation (Young, 2017) speaks to similar ones, such as cognitive or emotional regulation, or self-control, but is more encompassing. It affords another way of viewing behavior and brain as coordinative activities both within the person and socially in all the multifaceted interactions and relations involved. In a certain sense, the concept of psychological or relational co-regulation fits well with the mechanisms of cognitive development proposed by Piaget (e.g., resolving conflict internally and externally in dialogue with peers as problems are confronted) and Erikson (mutuality in negotiating the trajectory developmental tasks and crises in stages).
18. Young's (2011, 2016) modeling allows for understanding human uniqueness. The penultimate stages and sub-stages of human growth (and the causes underlying them), both cognitively and socio-affectively, speak to characteristics of the species not present in any others. Similarly, Young refers to our species as representing *Homo Causa* in that we are very causal organisms, both in trying to understand behavioral causation and being proactive in ourselves (e.g., believing in free will) as one factor in the causation of behavior (beyond nature and nurture).

Micro-development/Macro-development Coordination

19. An important component of the neo-stage concept is the one of micro-development/macro-development coordination. Micro-developments take place regularly in one's day and they might be factors contributing to macro-developments.

20. Macro-developments might involve qualitative acquisitions, like a first abstract thought.
21. However, each new qualitative acquisition does not mean that a stage, per se, has developed. The overall structural configuration of the schemes/operations, and so on, that qualifies as a new distinct stage goes beyond cumulative micro-development and any one macro-development, unless otherwise proven the case.

Overall

22. To conclude, the Young (2011, 2016) approach to integrating stage models in the cognitive and socio-affective realms not only helps describe the behaviors in the human life course, but also gives a scaffold to understand how the multifactorial causality underlying behavior (e.g., genes, epigenetics, the brain and neuro-circuits, the environment and stress) can be unified.
23. In both cases – describing behavior and giving its causes – the projects are ongoing and ever-differentiating. But Young's work, as well as grand theorizing generally, gives it some coherence relative to the dispersion and siloing that is taking place in the field of psychology and jeopardizing it.
24. Saving psychology might mean saving its grand theories, including the stage ones, if their contemporary versions are up to the task.
25. Empirical study needs guiding global theories as much as valid local hypotheses, and the present work has provided directions toward this end.

Finally, Young (2017) proposed the novel concept of relational or psychological co-regulation to represent not only inter-subjective social interaction and relationships but also how we relate to the world, generally, including to written material and ethics codes. We learn from and mutually regulate each other in this mutuality. It can be argued that relational co-regulation constitutes both a behavioral/mental acquisition as well as a means to control and shape behavior and mentalizing, and equally in the self and other. Further, the skills involved might develop according to the steps in the developmental model proposed by Young. Additionally, the principle underlying mechanism in the growth of relational co-regulation might require optimal synchrony in activation-inhibition coordination so that the regulation achieves continual adaptive efficacy. Here, we have an example of how the integrative causal and psychological model proposed by Young is an ongoing dynamic project that can offer new concepts that expands it and subjects it to further critical thought and testing. This view is consistent with the general message of the book about unifying psychology and causality – it argues for continued conceptualization and research related to a growth in psychology toward its unification and also it underscores the value of considering causality as a central axis in this project while arguing for an equivalent ongoing unification effort for causality itself in psychology and the unification of both these aspects in a grand and ever-evolving theory.

Conclusions

Psychology is more dispersed and siloed than coherent and unified. Understanding causality, which is multi-factorial, biopsychosocial, systemic, and self-organizing, could constitute a unifying theme in psychology; however causality itself is disparately studied. Also, there is little agreement on what constitutes unification in psychology and whether it can even be achieved.

Here, it is argued that a proper integration of psychology should remain a constant focus of the discipline, but one that is an ongoing dynamically evolving project, as is the subject of psychology itself, the behavior of the changing person. Also, efforts to integrate causality should be an ongoing project, recognizing the burgeoning study of genetics, epigenetics, neuroscience, early environmental adversity, etc., and more important how these factors interrelate in behavioral expression, both in the typical or normal case and when it is disturbed. The search for common causal principles in psychology will facilitate exchange across its sub-disciplines and integration with other disciplines.

One aspect of causality that could bridge its divide relates to connectivity and networks, as in the Connectome in neuro-circuity (e.g., Sporns, 2011, 2012) and in symptom networks in psychopathology (e.g., Borsboom, 2008, 2017). This relatively new approach in neuroscience and psychology is based on the concept of core nodes and their interlinked connections in edges, such as in fMRI research on neural networks or social networking research. Moreover, the field of network science is interdisciplinary and it incorporates other recent modeling approaches, such as complexity science and nonlinear dynamic theory. Other contemporary models include Bayesian formulations on probability estimation and prediction with network and related modeling concepts, such as free energy and its control (e.g., Butz, 2016).

However, there is little on the development of such networks/circuits; the present focus on stages and sub-stages in development provides an integrative way of approaching this issue. Piaget has provided the quintessential stage model in cognitive development and Erikson has done likewise in socio-affective development. Neo-Piagetians, such as Case and Fischer, have created Neo-Piagetian models, but these have not evolved since their inception at the end of the last century. As for revisions of grand theories that might be pertinent to contemporary research and hypothesis testing, Young (2011, 2012, 2016) has provided an integrative model of causality and psychology that incorporates recent advances in the study of causality (e.g., including the effect of belief in free will) along with traditional integrative approaches related to schools of thought, such as the evolutionary and the Piagetian. His lifespan model describes Neo-Piagetian stages and equivalent Neo-Eriksonian ones (5 stages × 5 sub-stages). The model is embedded in other approaches that can help unify psychology, such as the systems approach. Finally, Young emphasized the concept of activation-inhibition coordination as underlying both for the adequate description of behavior and also for explicating its causation. Here, it is applied to another integrating concept that Young has developed, on relational or psychological co-regulation.

This section of the book has shown how the present Neo-Eriksonian model could inform current developmental and psychopathological science, especially when its (sub)stages are framed as behavioral connectivities that emerge in individual ways hierarchically over development. The integrated (sub)stage model (Neo-Piagetian/Neo-Eriksonian) speaks to the nature of multiple cognitive and emotional intelligences, through the individual ways that (sub)stages are yoked in confronting stressors and in problem solving, whether cognitively or emotionally. The present work proposes the concept of "Neo-stages," which includes the concept of micro-genetic/macro-genetic coordination, to facilitate conceptual and empirical work on stages. It concludes that an integrative model of causality should be an ongoing project and can inform the integration of psychology, including through the cohering concept of psychological co-regulation.

References

Biggs, J. B., & Collis, K. F. (1982). *Evaluating the quality of learning: The SOLO taxonomy (structured of the observed learning outcome)*. New York: Academic.

Blatt, S. J. (2008). *Polarities of experience: Relatedness and self-definition in personality development, psychopathology, and the therapeutic process*. Washington, DC: American Psychological Association.

Borsboom, D. (2008). Psychometric perspectives on diagnostic systems. *Journal of Clinical Psychology, 64*, 1089–1108. https://doi.org/10.1002/jclp.20503

Borsboom, D. (2017). A network theory of mental disorders. *World Psychiatry, 6*, 5–13. https://doi.org/10.1002/wps.20375

Borsboom, D., & Cramer, A. O. J. (2014). Network analysis: An integrative approach to the structure of psychopathology. *Annual Review of Clinical Psychology, 9*, 91–121. https://doi.org/10.1146/annurev-clinpsy-050212-185608

Butz, M. V. (2016). Toward a unified sub-symbolic computational theory of cognition. *Frontiers in Psychology, 7*, 925. https://doi.org/10.3389/fpsyg.2016.00925

Case, R. (1985). *Intellectual development: Birth to adulthood*. New York: Academic.

Cassidy, J., & Shaver, P. R. (2008). *Evolution and human behavior: Darwinian perspective on human nature* (2nd ed.). Cambridge, MA: MIT Press.

Dale, R., & Kello, C. T. (2018). "How do humans make sense?" Multiscale dynamics and emergent meaning. *New Ideas in Psychology, 50*, 61–72.

Epskamp, S., Cramer, A. O. J., Waldorp, L. J., Schmittmann, V. D., & Borsboom, D. (2011). *Qgraph: Network representations of relationships in data*. R package version 0.4.10. Available from http://CRAN.R-project.org/package=qgraph

Fischer, K. W. (1980). A theory of cognitive development: The control and construction of hierarchies of skills. *Psychological Review, 87*, 477–531.

Fried, E. I., & Cramer, A. O. J. (2017). Moving forward: Challenges and directions for psychopathological network theory and methodology. *Perspectives on Psychological Science, 12*, 999–1020.

Henriques, G. (2011). *A new unified theory of psychology*. New York: Springer Science + Business Media.

Knight, Z. G. (2017). A proposed model of psychodynamic psychotherapy linked to Erik Erikson's eight stages of psychosocial development. *Clinical Psychology & Psychotherapy, 24*, 1047–1058.

Loevinger, J. (1976). *Ego development: Conceptions and theories*. San Francisco: Jossey-Bass.

Lourenço, O. (2016). Developmental stages, Piagetian stage in particular: A critical review. *New Ideas in Psychology, 40*, 123–137.
MacNeill, L. A., Ram, N., Bell, M. A., Fox, N. A., & Pérez-Edgar, K. (2018). Trajectories of infants' biobehavioral development: Timing and rate of A-not-B performance gains and EEG maturation. *Child Development, 89*, 711–724. https://doi.org/10.1111/cdev.13022
Maddox, J. E. (1995). Yes, people can change, but can psychotherapists? *Contemporary Psychology, 40*, 1047–1048.
Mascolo, M. F., & Fischer, K. W. (2015). The dynamic development of thinking, feeling and acting. In R. Lerner (Series Ed.) & W. Overton (Vol. Ed.), *Handbook of child development and developmental science: Vol. 1 – Theory and Method* (pp. 113–161). New York: Wiley.
Maslow, A. H. (1943). A theory of human motivation. *Psychological Review, 50*, 370–396.
Mounoud, P. (1976). Les revolutions psychologiques de l'enfant [Psychological revolutions in the child]. *Archives de Psychologie, 44*, 103–114.
Mounoud, P. (1986). Similarities between developmental sequences at different age periods. In I. Levin (Ed.), *Stage and structure: Reopening the debate* (pp. 40–58). Norwood, NJ: Ablex.
Nader-Grosbois, N. (2011). Self-regulation, dysregulation, emotion regulation and their impact on cognitive and socio-emotional abilities in children and adolescents with autism spectrum disorders. In T. Williams (Ed.), *Autism spectrum disorders: From genes to environment*, Rijeka, Croatia: InTech. doi: https://doi.org/10.5772/20070. Retrieved from: https://www.intechopen.com/books/autism-spectrum-disorders-from-genes-to-environment/self-regulation-dysregulation-emotion-regulation-and-their-impact-on-cognitive-and-socio-emotional-a
Norcross, J. C., Krebs, P. M., & Prochaska, J. O. (2011). Stages of change. In J. C. Norcross (Ed.), *Psychotherapy relationships that work: Evidence-based responsiveness* (2nd ed., pp. 279–300). New York: Oxford University Press.
Piaget, J. (1983). Piaget's theory. In P. H. Mussen (Ed.), *Handbook of child psychology* (Vol. 1, pp. 103–128). New York: Wiley. (Original work published in 1970).
Prochaska, J. O., Norcross, J. C., & DiClemente, C. C. (1994). *Changing for good: The revolutionary program that explains the six stages of change and teaches you how to free yourself from bad habits*. New York: Morrow.
Schmittmann, V. D., Cramer, A. O. J., Waldorp, L. J., Epskamp, S., Kievit, R. A., & Borsboom, D. (2013). Deconstructing the construct: A network perspective on psychological phenomena. *New Ideas in Psychology, 31*, 43–53.
Selman, R. L. (1980). *The growth of interpersonal understanding: Developmental and clinical analyses*. New York: Academic.
Siegler, R. S. (2016). Continuity and change in the field of cognitive development and in the perspectives of one cognitive developmentalist. *Child Development Perspectives, 10*, 128–133.
Sporns, O. (2011). *Networks of the brain*. Cambridge, MA: MIT Press.
Sporns, O. (2012). *Discovering the human connectome*. Cambridge, MA: MIT Press.
Sroufe, L. A. (1990). An organizational perspective on the self. In D. Cicchetti & M. Beeghly (Eds.), *The self in transition: Infancy to childhood* (pp. 281–207). Chicago: University of Chicago Press.
Staats, A. W. (1983). *Psychology's crisis of disunity: Philosophy and method for a unified science*. New York: Praeger.
Staats, A. W. (1999). Unifying psychology requires new infrastructure, theory, method, and a research agenda. *Review of General Psychology, 3*, 3–13.
Sternberg, R. J. (2015). Multiple intelligences in the new age of thinking. In S. Goldstein, D. Princiotta, & J. Naglieri (Eds.), *Handbook of intelligence* (pp. 229–241). New York: Springer Science + Business Media.
Tsethlikai, M. (2015). The cultural patterning of cognitive development: Commentary on Allen and Lalonde. *Human Development, 58*, 97–102.
van den Heuvel, M. P., & Sporns, O. (2013). Network hubs in the human brain. *Trends in Cognitive Sciences, 17*, 683–696.

Vygotsky, L. (1978). *Mind and society: The development of higher mental processes*. Cambridge, MA: Harvard University Press.

Wertsch, J. V. (2008). From social interaction to higher psychological processes: A clarification and application of Vygotsky's theory. *Human Development, 51*, 66–79. (Original work published in 1979).

Young, G. (1990a). The development of hemispheric and manual specialization. In G. Hammond (Ed.), *The cerebral control of speech and limb movements* (pp. 79–139). Amsterdam: North Holland.

Young, G. (1990b). Early neuropsychological development: Lateralization of functions – Hemispheric specialization. In C. A. Hauert (Ed.), *Developmental psychology: Cognitive, perceptuo-motor and neuropsychological perspectives* (pp. 113–181). Amsterdam: North Holland.

Young, G. (1997). *Adult development, therapy, and culture: A postmodern synthesis*. New York: Plenum Press.

Young, G. (2011). *Development and causality: Neo-Piagetian perspectives*. New York: Springer Science + Business Media.

Young, G. (2012). A unitary Neo-Piagetian/Neo-Eriksonian model of development: Fundamental assumptions and meta-issues. *New Ideas in Psychology, 30*, 241–249. https://doi.org/10.1016/j.newideapsych.2011.11.002

Young, G. (2015). Causality in psychiatry: A hybrid symptom network construct model. *Frontiers in Psychiatry, 6*, 164. https://doi.org/10.3389/fpsyt.2015.00164

Young, G. (2016). *Unifying causality and psychology: Being, brain and behavior*. Cham, Switzerland: Springer International Publishing.

Young, G. (2017). *Revising the APA ethics code*. Cham, Switzerland: Springer International Publishing.

Chapter 12
Introducing the 25-Step Neo-Eriksonian Model

Abstract The Neo-Eriksonian portion of the present lifespan Neo-Piagetian/Neo-Eriksonian model required a full introductory chapter to explain the approach undertaken. The ensuing chapters that describe the stages and sub-stages involved follow a common format. First, they present past work that I have undertaken related to the Neo-Eriksonian portion of the model, which is minimal. Then, they provide an interim summary that elaborates the past work. The next portions of the model that needed elaboration before therapeutic implications are considered are described. For example, Eriksonian-type stages include oppositions, such as Trust vs. Mistrust, and to this point in my publications on the Neo-Eriksonian portion of the model, I have not presented descriptions of the positive pole of each step, but this is rectified in the chapters after this one. The major portions of the chapters that follow give new work in helping to understand patients and how to treat them therapeutically. The problems that might arise at each of the 25 steps of the present model are described, for example, if the environment is not supportive at a sub-stage being discussed. Also, the therapeutic strategies needed to help with the difficulties that arise for patients in these regards are presented. The longest chapters on the sub-stages in the present Neo-Eriksonian model and their therapeutic applications concern childhood-adolescence and adult development into the late 20s. However, the most critical problems that could arise in development relate to the infancy period, e.g., in terms of early abuse and its consequences. Also, the post-20 age period is considered critical, as in undertaking generativity or experiencing a mid-life crisis. This chapter notes that the 25-step Neo-Eriksonian model described was developed by extrapolation from the 25-step Neo-Piagetian sequence with which it is associated. Moreover, Erikson's eight stages were inserted into that sequence based on a fit with the appropriate age periods involved. The other 17 steps in the Neo-Eriksonian sequence were created by examining their corresponding Neo-Piagetian sub-stage and also the Erikson stages both before and after them, as required.

G. Young, *Causality and Development*,
https://doi.org/10.1007/978-3-030-02493-2_12

Introduction to the Neo-Eriksonian Model

The prior literature review examines recent approaches to stage modeling in both the cognitive (Piagetian, Neo-Piagetian) and socio-affective (Erikson, Neo-Eriksonian) realms. It presents the concept of neo-stage, which provides a novel approach to understanding networked and related approaches as applied to (sub) stage modeling. The concept of stage has been considered too general and lacking in testability, but by importing approaches to the organization of (sub)stages that allow for testability, the neo-stage approach facilitates more contemporary modeling of the schema/operation organization within the (sub)stages that can underwrite qualitative advances in (sub)stage organization.

The neo-stage concept applies to the cognitive level, which so far has been represented best by Case's concept of conceptual control structure (Case, 1992; Young, 2011). That concept is embedded in the traditional statistical approach to testing skill relations, i.e., correlation-based. However, the concept of networks takes a more complete approach in its concepts of nodes and edges (links), as does the similar approach of non-linear dynamical systems theory (NLDST).

Beyond the issue of justifying the scientific testability of any stage model, we need to address the question of its reliability/validity and its usefulness/utility. The theory needs to help us understand human behavior and lead to predictions that can be empirically verifiable. Further, any measure derived from the model should possess adequate reliability, or consistency in the measure, and adequate reliability, or meeting the threshold of measuring what it is supposed to. Moreover, the theory should have some practical value, e.g., on the normative course of development if it is about children and on helping with patients if it is clinical.

The quest for a scientifically sound and a clinical useful concept/measure in psychology/psychiatry might be in opposition, as has been found with various psychiatric diagnostic manuals. The categories of disorder in the manuals might be clinically useful, but perhaps unclear empirically supported evidence. Perhaps the categories are not related to etiological causes that lead to the indicated symptoms, nor might they suggest possible therapeutic techniques that can help (or cure). That is, the research might not support the validity of a particular disorder from a scientific point of view, but its clinical utility might be a factor that overrides the research issues and so it is kept in the diagnostic psychiatric manuals (Young, 2016).

The present Neo-Eriksonian model is built on some major premises that are not research-derived, nor have the suggested 25 steps in the model been supported empirically as a sequence of qualitatively distinct levels as maintained by the model. Moreover, the behaviors/symptoms that mark any one (sub)stage of the model are so heterogeneous that, as yet, they have not been reduced to a manageable list that easily can be empirically supported, so that the model does not lend itself efficiently to empirical testing within any one (sub)stage let alone across them (over time). Finally, the concept of yoking suggests that (sub)stages can coexist simultaneously not only cognitively but also socio-affectively, so that any one clinical presentation is bound to be of a mixed type and not easy to disentangle. In this sense, the 25 profiles of socio-affective expression associated with the 25 steps of the model and the difficulties that patients could face that are consistent with the model present challenges to any clinician who would try to use the model. Theoretically, the model gives ideal prototypes of what patients might present with if they had only one main issue and it was clearly related to one step or another in the model. However, practically, patients present in far more complex ways than having difficulty only with one developmental phase and the repercussion that result.

The same format is used to present each of the 25 steps in the model (except for the last one, which gives only a brief summary). The format for presentation of each step in the model consists of four major sections: (a) prior work; (b) new work, theoretical elaborations; (c) patients and therapy; and (d) the other and change. Each of these sections has about four sub-topics; for example, for patients and therapy, the four topics are (a) patient presentation, (b) mental scanning, (c) therapeutic implications, and (d) stress-trauma resilience/coping.

Neo-Eriksonian Model Premises

The premises that underwrite the present Neo-Eriksonian (sub)stage model include the following:

1. The value of a (sub)stage model of lifespan development is found in the succession of qualitatively distinct steps in development that can serve as heuristic markers of the developmental process, inform difficulties/problems that might emerge at the psychological/psychiatric level at each sub-stage, and guide the clinician to appropriate therapeutic stances and strategies.
2. The particular Neo-Eriksonian sub-stage model is much more differentiated than prior models in the area, giving it a more refined conceptual base. Its 25 steps afford it a tighter organization with more narrow age ranges for any one step in the model compared to prior models. The Freudian model originated the theoretical stage approach to psychological development, and his model consisted of five stages; Erikson expanded the last Freudian stage and emerged with an eight-stage model. There has not really been much change in the socio-affective stage modeling enterprise for 60 years, with perhaps a nine-stage model being proposed here and there (e.g., Blatt, 2008). In contrast, the present model consists of 25 Neo-Eriksonian steps in development over the lifespan.
3. The 25 steps in the present model consist of five stages, each with five sub-stages. This is the first socio-affective stage model to include sub-stages.
4. The stages and sub-stages of the present model are conditioned by the corresponding cognitive (sub)stages with which they are associated. The cognitive portion of the model is Neo-Piagetian (five stages × five cyclically recurring sub-stages). The Neo-Erikson (sub)stage equivalents might develop in the same time frame of the corresponding (Neo-Piagetian) cognitive (sub)stages, but a lack of proper social supports or other negative impacts can jeopardize the Neo-

Eriksonian socio-affective developmental course such that the person is not at the same (sub)stage cognitively and socio-affectively. The person might develop normal cognitive acquisitions but have problematic socio-affective ones in the parallel socio-affective sub-stage at issue. As emphasized in Chap. 1, cognitive development is not driven by problem-solving on contexts and objects and their physical properties. Rather, consistent with Bjorklund (2018), the present modeling approach to cognitive development considers that its material or "aliments" is as much social as situational and object-related.

5. The Neo-Piagetian cognitive sub-stage sequence that provides the framework for the Neo-Eriksonian sequence has extensive scientific evidence in its support, and it is research-based through the evidence it describes in its support (Young, 2011). Also, it was carefully constructed on the basis of well-known, extensively cited Neo-Piagetian theories (Case, Fischer), although ones having less stages and sub-stages. In Young (2011), I showed how the comparison of Case's and Fisher's model showed missing stages/sub-stages and that the evidence gathered in support of their models often fit better my more differentiated one.

The research support for my model according to this analysis gives it a solid empirical support as much as the theoretical one it has through the compare-contrast process undertaken. Further, clear evidence in support of the model derives from Piaget's initial observations of his children's development in the first 2 years of life in terms of the six-sub-stage sequence posited for the sensori-motor period. I built the sub-stage portion of my model based on that sequence, although I removed the first sub-stage of reflex exercise and placed it at the end of the pre-sensori-motor stage of reflexes. The resultant five-step sensori-motor sequence deriving from this empirically supported theoretical maneuver led to the recursive five-sub-stage model in the present stage/sub-stage model. The point is that the research basis for the cognitive portion of the present model gives legitimacy to the parallel socio-affective model that was elaborated from it.

Socio-affectivity

6. The 25 Neo-Eriksonian sub-stages that have been described represent prototypes of what develops at the sub-stage in the age period concerned and how it can go awry. The descriptions are normative, and do not take into account individual differences, possible gender differences, the potential effect of difficulties traversing well prior to sub-stages in development that could influence positively passing through well any particular sub-stage after it, and so on.
7. The problems presented at any one sub-stage might be related to a lack of support or to negative impacts from the environment at a particular sub-stage. However, as development proceeds into later developmental sub-stages, it would be more difficult to relate problematic passage through a sub-stage to

environmental factors; more than likely, it would be related to difficulties inherent to the sub-stage itself, e.g., generativity is demanding even with environmental support.

8. The 25 prototypes that have been described for lifespan socio-affective development according to the present model present possible development problems at each phase of life, but the reality of disturbances in development is that effects of developmental difficulties accumulate and carry forward over time. For example, in these regards, profound early adversity can have long-term carry-over effects that compromise the development in terms of the sub-stages of the model even without new environmental support issues related to them. Moreover, developmental problems are often cumulative over time for a variety of reasons, and difficulties traversing several consecutive early sub-stages can seriously affect the development of later sub-stages. This proviso would apply not only to early sub-stages but any sequence of consecutive sub-stages that have been difficult to negotiate.
9. Given that patients will present with complex combinations of problems stemming from multiple, compromised developmental sub-stages, for example, through continued environmental insults over successive (early) sub-stages, it will be difficult for the therapist to disentangle the inter-layered issues in the developmental progression for the patient, and how the patient's presentation relates to them. The therapist becomes a clinical archaeologist of past embedded psychological issues related to the sub-stages at issue and how they leave sequelae that interact in the ongoing patient dynamic. This assessment style will require ongoing modifications of central hypotheses as the session takes place. The therapist will need a multilevel, systemic approach, tackling on presenting problems for what they are, using empirically supported techniques, and continuing the psychology archaeology to uncover their psycho-affective sources and (poor) environmental support as well as any other matters that might apply.
10. A major roadblock in these regards would be to determine how the socio-affective problems in different sub-stages lead to problematic sequelae that are yoked together, and catalytically interact to compound and exacerbate symptoms. If early sub-stages, for example, appear to be the seat of a patient's problems in therapy, how do they interact and mutually multiply in their effects on the person, and what is the best strategy to defuse this complication? What are the behaviors and problem-solving strategies used in relation to any one sub-stage and how do they aggravate issues rather than minimize them? Or, a patient might have cognitive filters to view the world based on non-consecutive past sub-stages that had been poorly negotiated for whatever reason, and these filters coalesce to create quite confining filters that tailor behavioral response in their image, e.g., hostility attributions and multiply evident poor self-esteem. Or, the strategies used to try to solve socio-emotional and socio-affective difficulties are yoked, failed ones that the patient keeps applying without success.

Décalage

11. The present model describes parallels in cognitive and socio-affective development, and how the cognitive acquisition in any one sub-stage provides the groundwork for the corresponding socio-affective acquisition in any one sub-stage. This process does not imply that, once a particular cognitive acquisition begins to manifest, the corresponding socio-affective one appears simultaneously. Rather, often people are more advanced cognitively than socio-affectively because of the various environmental impacts alluded to. The person might have developed advanced adult cognitive skills but still might be struggling with socio-affective deficits related to early adversity (and so early sub-stages and their characteristics), for example.
12. This presents both advantages and disadvantages to the therapist. On the one hand, the therapist might avail herself of the advanced cognitive skills of the patient who is dealing with psychological/issues whose origins relate to quite early environmental impacts and associated characteristics or skills of early sub-stages. On the other hand, those same skills might have created cognitive schemas/operations rife with the very issues at hand and further exacerbate the negative adaptive measures deployed deriving from them.
13. There might be multiple décalages or delay in this regard, complicating the therapeutic challenge. For example, a young child may have had a difficult time with an isolated early adversity, moved on with support, but then had the problem re-appear in full force because of later developmental issues, as might take place in adolescence. The therapist might find normative cognitive and socio-emotional/socio-affective development taking place up to early adolescence, but with residue of early trauma at two distinct developmental epochs being brought out in the adolescent as the teen years moved on. The cognitive filters involved might be affecting the teen in two different and somewhat independent ways.
14. Psychological problems originating in the earliest periods of life often have the most profound developmental impact. Early childhood abuse, torture, etc., could present the worst psychological consequences. But the therapist might find that the child is resilient, for example, by receiving good environmental support afterwards. In the same vein, later developmental issues might present with quite serious consequences, such as might manifest in adolescence.
15. The therapist will need to use developmentally appropriate interventions/treatment. Techniques applicable at one sub-stage of life might not apply to others. Moreover, techniques need to match the cognitive and socio-affective acquisitions at each stage, being informed by their characteristics and skills.

Neo-stages and Networks

16. The concept of stages in development is not uncontested. The dominant empirical, reductionist, neuro-scientific point of view opts more for a linear ((sub) stage) approach to development rather than one with qualitatively distinct non-

linear punctuations. Part of the doubt about the validity of the concept of stages in development stems from the lack of operationalization of the concept, and the use of terms that some might consider jargon. Also, the concept of stages in development does not lend itself readily to empirical investigation to begin with, given the broad-ranging nature of the concept of stages in development. However, there are approaches, such as nonlinear dynamical systems theory (NLDST), that lend themselves to concepts like stages in development. They refer to emergent phenomena/self-organization, catastrophic inversions, non-directed local re-organizations, bifurcation in attractor fields, complexification, hierarchical levels in a system, and so on. These approaches to development are heavily mathematical and take a different approach to testing developmental findings. They do not jettison variability as noise in the system but consider it the essence of what statistics should be studying in systems of behavior.

17. The most recent advances in conceptualization of brain and behavior dynamics relate to the concept of networks in behavior and in brain organization. The concept originates in the neurosciences. It seeks to determine synchronous firing patterns and sequential ones, as well as functional associations through fMRI (functional magnetic resonance imaging) and other brain scanning techniques, while using a variety of behavioral tasks and areas of the brain measured. Nodes are hub points of activation in the patterns, and edges are the linkages with these central firing markers. The concept has its own extensive catalogue of terminology, but some relate to whether linkages are local or global, for example, small worlds. The fundamental assumption of the present work is that concepts such as these can be applied to configuring the pattern of relations among cognitive task performances, which nodes are key, and how they are linked. Does the cause of the pattern of linkages inhere in the self-organization among the nodes, and do they help explain any referral to putative central, higher-order organizers, such as schemas and operations? Do the particular task performances for any one child, especially if they are well-executed and central, preferred ones, constitute drivers in how other task performances are undertaken? Ideas such as these can explain how evolution to new cognitive (sub)stages in development can take place through bootstrapping advanced nodes that emerge in the cognitive architecture of the person, and causally propagate in the system to dynamically re-arrange any sub-stage to a higher integrative level.
18. The same type of mechanism could help explain the behavioral re-organization at each new sub-stage of socio-affective development. A key acquisition stemming from the underlying cognitive advance in the parallel cognitive sub-stage becomes a lead driver in re-organizing the full complement of behaviors in the sub-stage. There is no recourse needed to refer to a central plan, or independent mechanism driving the change in behavior, because it is inherent to the network of behavioral nodes and their linkages. Altering one by advancing it to a new qualitatively distinct level serves to infiltrate the rest of the network involved and dynamically bootstrap its change through the causal linkages and drivers involved.

19. Although there are similarities in how parallel cognitive and socio-affective sub-stages in development might unfold, especially through common mechanisms in this novel way of understanding (sub)stages and their node/edge dynamics (which I refer to as a neo-stage concept), there are other factors to consider in relating the two parallel acquisitions. First, cognition and socio-emotions/socio-affectivity are never truly distinct, following separate but coordinated development. The underlying cognitive schemes/operations or networks involved cannot divorce one domain from the other in practical application. Second, the problems in development that might take place socio-affectively could lead to aberrant inter-behavioral linkages, despite an apparently normally developing cognitive sub-stage networking/organization. This is not to say that there could be deficient cognitive structuring in any one sub-stage, e.g., related to attention deficit hyperactivity disorder (ADHD), learning disability, or psychotic derangement.
20. These kinds of network modeling and statistics/applications to the concept of (sub)stages go far beyond standard statistical techniques, such as analysis of variance and multiple regressions, and go far beyond statistical techniques applied to whether a child has advanced through one sub-stage to another in a coherent fashion (e.g., Rasch modeling). These older statistical techniques are bound to correlations among task performance at any one age, which masks individual differences/variability as targets of statistical/analysis, and also are bound to whether all children have arrived at a sub-stage in the proper sequence by looking at mean performance indicators, which also is a limited statistical approach. If network and related concepts are not used to determine inter-behavioral linkages instead of correlations, means, and the like, the nature of the linkages hypothesized will miss out on central aspects relevant to (sub)stage conceptualization.

Testing the Model

21. Given the complexity of the Neo-Piagetian/Neo-Eriksonian model proposed, it is impossible to conduct simple empirical verification of its postulates and predictions. It will require a nuanced approach that considers, among others, the concept of neo-stage, yoking of sub-stages, cross cognitive and socio-affective linkages, and so on. Even the network approach being supported is not standard because it is a hybrid network/system theory model, with embedded emerging layers of different complexity in top-down and bottom-up relationships in reciprocal balance (top down example – emerging depression; bottom-up example – exacerbating causal networks related to insomnia).
22. There will be complications in testing the present model created by its vast hypothetical base, the inevitable uncertainties/inconsistencies in describing it, the lack of full rigorous operationalization at this stage in the development of the model, and so on. The model inevitably will undergo revision and better

precision, and so direct testing of some of its present aspects might be premature or miss the mark. The clinical application of the model will help refine and improve it.

23. Hypothesis generation and testing take place in multiple ways and the present model fits a clinical direction in these regards. To what extent does the model help the clinician, can the clinician perceive some of the networks involved by graphing them, can the clinician give direction to the experimentalist by suggesting operational measures/questionnaires, etc.? For example, Erikson's concept of identity is studied extensively through classically structured questionnaires based on Marcia's revision of the concept, among others. Can questionnaires be developed that are applicable to the new 17 steps of the 25 steps in the model?
24. The concept of activation-inhibition coordination might be useful in explaining networked relations with sub-stage nodes, given my hypothesis that this concept can explain much about behavior and brain. Further in this sense, the concept applies to neuro-scientific investigation and offers a linkage among cognitive development, socio-affective development, and associated networks in brain function.
25. The ultimate utility of the present model will lie in evidence that effective therapy has transformed some core network linkages of crucial nodes at the base of aberrant, disordered behavior toward a better equilibrium. Moreover, the therapy should also initiate a more economical, elegant, node/edge structure in associated brain regions/structures. By showing the relationship of cognitive and socio-affective development, behavior and brain relationships, and therapy and changes in these dynamics, the value of the present model will be highlighted and help promote its use to help people.

Conclusions

The prelude of propositions preceding the presentation of the 25 steps in the current Neo-Eriksonian model gives sufficient conceptual basis to bolster their description. The following gives some pragmatic considerations. First, the prior work that had been done on the model is cursory, at best, although the basic sub-stage headings are sufficiently accurate as presented in the appendices accompanying the chapters.

Some of the aspects of the prior work on the model are presented in ways that are too general, incomplete, and even not quite applicable. However, the interim summary provided after presentation of the prior work for each sub-stage of the model fleshes out and regulates these lacunae. It also provides a preliminary glance of therapeutic approaches that could be applied in each sub-stage, at least to a degree, a topic that is elaborated as each sub-stage description proceeds after the interim summary of each sub-stage. Also, each sub-stage hints at the extremes that can develop at each sub-stage in a socio-affective sense, and also possible feedback/rebound effects. For example, a teenager having difficulty with identity might adopt a hypo-identificatory approach or, to the contrary, a pseudo and hyper-identificatory approach. Moreover, the former might include socialized identities not deeply felt/incorporated, and the latter might include anti-identities that include negative emotions, such as rejection of others/peers/societal rules/regulations. The last part of each sub-stage description ends on a more positive note of how positive passage through the sub-stage might help move the person forward to psychological maturity.

The reader will notice some redundancies from one section to the next after the interim summary for each sub-stage. For example, the section that follows the interim summary is on the cognitive (mis)perception of the other, and usually it gives a short introduction to major developments in the sub-stage before addressing the issue at hand. The reader will also notice that beginning review summaries in sections after the interim summary might not only repeat the major themes in the interim summary but also at times phrase them in new ways, or add new refinements or material, thereby adding to the original summaries in the interim sections. Instead of placing any new material in these sections into the interim summaries, I left them in the sections in which I had created them, given their consistency with the rest of the material in the sections.

One way of reading the text on the 25 steps in development in the present model other than reading them one after the other would be to read any one section, such as on the cognitive misperception of the other or on therapeutic implications, from one sub-stage to the next. In doing so, the reader will note that there is a consistency of style and content from one sub-stage to the next for the particular section, but the consistency does not necessarily last. This proved especially true when I arrived at the adolescent and adult sub-stages relative to the infant and child sub-stages.

Note that the adolescent and adult stages into the 30s were the ones most elaborated in the present model. This does not diminish the importance of the earlier or later sub-stages in the model; for example, they concern being treated as if one only is a bag of infant reflexes and so worthy of the worst kind of abuse, or they concern the midlife crises in the 40s.

Some material repeats in different forms from one sub-stage to the next, given the themes of the sections involved, e.g., on working schemas, mental scanning, and dealing with trauma/abuse. Also, critical themes re-appear, such as those related to the surround (environments, parents, etc.) not being supportive of the normative development in a sub-stage.

Moreover, matters related to self and other often are dealt with multiply over the sections describing each sub-stage. This type of redundancy is effective in having each section give the basics required to what follows. Moreover, dealing with central topics such as self and other in different ways from one section to the next following the interim summary gives the text conceptual differentiation.

The reader will note that some sub-stages resemble each other socio-affectively, such as those related to trust and attachment in infancy and ones dealing with the other generally and then as other peoples later in the development. Nevertheless, in describing these similar sub-stages, I take care to avoid ambiguities about them and, therefore, any confusion.

The validity of the Neo-Piagetian/Neo-Eriksonian model of 25 lifespan steps in development that has been proposed depends both on the integrity of the 25-step Neo-Piagetian sub-stage sequence and the corresponding Neo-Eriksonian one. The former is built on other models (Case, Fischer, in particular) and has empirical support and conceptual consistency through the compare-contrast format used and the research on the other models shown to better fit my own. The resultant five-step cycle of sub-stages that repeats over the stages involved sets the conceptual base for the Neo-Eriksonian sub-stages, and seem to work in the sense that these latter sub-stages both fit the language of the corresponding cognitive sub-stages and allow proper placement of Erikson's original eight-stage model within the 25-step sequence.

Finally, as I created the terms to specify the 17 new steps in the 25-step Neo-Eriksonian sequence, not only did I consider the nature of the cognitive sub-stage with which each is associated, but also I considered the logical sequence of sub-stages that seemed required to fill in the gaps between the extant Eriksonian stages. For example, does it not make sense that a nurturing sub-stage should precede the intimacy one? Also, in placing the eight Eriksonian stages with their matching Neo-Piagetian sub-stages, I described them not necessarily in the original Eriksonian terms but, rather, in a way that reflected the corresponding cognitive sub-stage associated with them and also the apparent sub-stages in the 25-step sequence that both preceded and followed them. That is, even the original eight Eriksonian stages as positioned within the present Neo-Eriksonian model were fitted or sculpted to fit the overall 25-step sequence and, therefore, in some sense are as original as the totally novel 17 new ones.

References

Bjorklund, D. F. (2018). A metatheory for cognitive development (or "Piaget is dead" revisited). *Child Development, 89*, 2288–2302.

Blatt, S. J. (2008). *Polarities of experience: Relatedness and self-definition in personality development, psychopathology, and the therapeutic process*. Washington, DC: American Psychological Association.

Case, R. (1992). *The mind's staircase: Exploring the conceptual underpinnings of children's thought and knowledge*. Hillsdale, NJ: Erlbaum.

Young, G. (2011). *Development and causality: Neo-Piagetian perspectives*. New York: Springer Science + Business Media.

Young, G. (2016). *Unifying causality and psychology: Being, brain and behavior*. Cham, Switzerland: Springer.

Chapter 13
The Reflex-Based Sub-stages: Nonparticipatory Reflexive Socio-emotions

Abstract The first stage in Young's 25-step Neo-Piagetian/Neo-Eriksonian model concerns Neo-Piagetian reflexive activity from the prenatal period into the first month of life. The five sub-stages of the stage concern coordination, hierarchization, systematization, multiplication, and integration. The Neo-Eriksonian stage equivalent to the Neo-Piagetian one is called Non-participatory reflexive socio-emotions. The person who lives at this level despite being more advanced cognitively, for example, due to extreme abuse, has her/his existence considered inconsequential. The person might react with silence or chaotic nihilism, but not with organized revolt. The therapeutic challenge will be immense for patients who present like this. The chapter describes the five sub-stages in the Neo-Eriksonian sequence related to this stage. None involve an original Eriksonian stage. For each sub-stage, after presentation of prior work on the sub-stage and an interim summary that elaborates that prior work and prepares the way for new additions to the sub-stage, the sub-stage is expanded in its description to allow for therapeutic application. The topics in the chapter in these regards include self-response to the cognitive (mis)perception of the other; positive pole in Eriksonian development; negative social self-working schema; patient presentation; therapeutic implications; mental scanning; relational co-regulation; stress/trauma resilience/coping; horizontal change; vertical change/constructing new stories; and matters related to consciousness, responsibility, etc.

The Reflex Stage Sub-stage of Coordination (Earlier Fetal Life): Sub-stage 1

Self and Relational Development [Initial Theoretical Elaborations]

By way of introduction, the following presents a very brief description of the present step in Young's 25-step Neo-Eriksonian developmental model. It is presented again at the end of Chap. 18 along with the other 24 steps in the model, to help give a collective overview of the 25 steps in the model.

G. Young, *Causality and Development*,
https://doi.org/10.1007/978-3-030-02493-2_13

Distance acts vs. no (lifeless) acts (early fetal life). Even from very early on, people could be rejected a lot, and even severely abused. Their life is at risk (any torture fits here). If this happened to you, you could react by wanting to kill yourself and behaving to hurt yourself. In general, your behavior is very reflexive not directed well or on target toward its goal. It is disorganized in its movement, even with the wrong distance to targets. Perhaps you feel it's hard to move and feel lifeless.

Appendix 1.1 gives the brief amount of work already done in prior publications related to the task of developing in depth the Neo-Eriksonian (sub)stage model. The next section of the chapter gives an interim summary that elaborates the contents of Appendix 1.1 with respect to the present sub-stage being considered, of the sub-stage of Reflex Stage Sub-stage of Coordination.

Interim Summary

Before delving into the relationship between cognitive sub-stage in development and implications for corresponding socio-affective development, the manner in which I present the cognitive acquisitions of each sub-stage needs clarification. Keeping in mind that these sub-stages are Piagetian-based but have been updated into more contemporary language and include five sub-stages within each of the five stages, which is a much more complex model than Piaget's original one, I should not resort to using Piaget's concepts, such as concrete operations, as if they were existing cognitive structures within the child's cognitive mapping that govern cognitive activity through their filter and deployment. Piaget did not consider these concepts in this way. That said, for me, they constitute short-hands to represent the panoply of cognitive schemes/operations/plans available at any one sub-stage in the present model and, therefore, often I refer to them as separate activatory entities in cognition.

Also note that, before beginning describing the first sub-stage in the present model, it is important to examine the concept of the cognitive (mis)perception of the other, which provides a metric for understanding the nature of the environmental support or its lack for the needs of the child/person. Each sub-stage in the current model indicates in this regard what would happen if the environment was unsupportive at the level of the sub-stage and what would happen if people were treated in the way indicated despite being more advanced cognitively than the sub-stage indicates socio-affectively. Therefore, the lower/earlier the (sub)stage involved in the (mis)perception, the worse the environmental support. As an example, if people are treated as if they were a bag of reflexes, at best, the environment would be abusive and even murderous.

The cognitive (mis)perception of the other changes accordingly to the stage in which it becomes an issue. If treated poorly when people are infants, the environment would be dominatory and repressive. If treated this way as children, the environment would be pacificatory and channeling, and so on.[1]

[1]Note that in moving from one sub-stage to the next within any one stage in the model, the environment becomes less negative in terms of the cognitive (mis)perception of the other (e.g.,

The following gives a more detailed view of the environment in terms of the cognitive (mis)perception of the other when the environment functions as if the person is a bag of reflexes, and nothing more, including in the early born. That is, if perceived as a reflexive entity, at best, with not even the right to live, the person will be exposed to an entirely abusive social environment to the point of torture (and, collectively, even genocide), and can feel obliterated as a result. The person would be subject to the worst abuse, even death (and without remorse of the perpetrator(s)). The impulse that would develop in the person subject to this obliterating regime would be not wanting to live. The child living this regime might not have the capacity to resist suicidal and self-injurious behavior. The cognitive and socio-emotional skills available to the developing person in this sub-stage are the most minimally reflexive, with no real self-development taking place. The person subject to this regime might have experienced it right from birth and have grown cognitively in some senses, but the corresponding socio-affective development will resonate more with the reflexive stage properties than any later developing cognitive properties.

The individual might be living at this most basic level for a number of reasons. The same reasons are applicable to living at any level in the model that is below the one of the actual cognitive sub-stage that should be evident in all domains of life. First, the individual might be developing normally, but the environment is unsupportive, as described. That is, for the present case, the type of worst abuse being discussed could begin right with the birth. As for other people who might regress to this level, fixate on it, and not grow further, this will happen when their environments change significantly for the worse – the state reduced to could be quite far from the previously attained socio-affective sub-stage state.

Note that, generally, people facing extreme environmental stressors that serve to defile, abolish, or otherwise greatly limit their psychological functioning do not live exactly at the first sub-stage level indicated in the present model. On the one hand, even if they are living this level, they still could be in a positive growth process to some extent if there is some positive support. More than the person who had always lived such a tortuous regime, they might develop new ways of coping, resisting, and accommodating. That said, any positive growth process will be minimal and distorted, and will be affected by the severity of deprivation and abuse experienced in the environment.

Further, any progress toward new sub-stage acquisitions after the extreme abuse will be influenced, altered, and deformed by the severe challenges, crises, and dangers involved. Moreover, for most anyone, each sub-stage traversed over the course of life before being put into these types of extreme environments will carry their own risks – even in the best of environments, there might be developmental difficulties associated with one to several sub-stages, and the effects involved

attitude, discourse quality). Also, in describing the cognitive (mis)perception through the sub-stages within any one stage of the model, this means that the qualitatively better environmental regime associated with the next stage is beginning to manifest, too. In this regard, that new regime should be somewhat evident by the last sub-stage in any set of five sub-stages in any one stage of the model.

would be cumulative multipliers, as negative cascades in development or even vicious circles accrue.

Finally, in the present modeling, sub-stages do not get integrated and disappear as higher-order ones develop. Rather, they might exist in parallel and might be called forth to function simultaneously (yoking), depending on the matter at hand. So the individual might express variations in sub-stage skill combinations independent of variations in the individualized configuration of skills of any one sub-stage in the person. Not only can sub-stages, at least their major means of functioning, be yoked together in individual ways, but also which one might be the primary axis in the yoking could vary from one context to the next, such that sub-stage yoking might not necessarily involve the most advanced central, core one as predominant.

As noted, every (sub)stage in development brings with it challenges even if the environment is perfectly supportive, responsive, matched, contingent, sensitive, warm, appropriately limit-setting, facilitative of self-control and interactional regulation, instigatory of exploration, curiosity, etc. For example, each developmental acquisition offers new potentials that need to be activated, attempted, tested, and refined based on feedback/outcome. Each new acquisition might be applied initially in over-exuberant, poorly fitting, disorganized ways. But only through these preliminary attempts at adaptivity can new acquisitions be honed and tailored to become properly fitting adjustments.

One classic example in this regard concerns the cognitive egocentrism of the preschooler. This acquisition is not conducive to taking the perspective of the other. However, as the self solidifies through its newly acquired representational base at this age, it can expand to coordinate with, first, the representation of the other and, after that, the differential needs and wants of the other. That is, only through cognitive egocentrism, and even the "selfishness" it leads to, can the development of sensitivity to the concerns of the other develop (perspective-taking, mind reading, theory of mind).

Any newly developed (sub)stage presents challenges to the person in any Eriksonian-related model and might present difficulties psychologically even in a fully-supportive environment. Turning to what this means for the reflex coordination sub-stage of the present model, the reflex coordinations afforded by the sub-stage will develop with exuberance, but often will be misguided in fitting to context. However, only through that over-exuberance can they eventually acquire better organization, target-fitting, and adaptivity in context, along with their narrowing down/pruning to facilitate these adaptive outcomes.

Also, note that, in cases of a non-supportive environment, the socio-affective characteristics typical of a sub-stage might be pushed to the negative extreme. The classic example resides with the Eriksonian stage of Trust vs. Mistrust. However, Mistrust is not the only possibility in this regard. The developing infant might develop a generalized Trust to any person present, with insufficient wariness and monitoring of the parent. Or, to the contrary, no matter the person, for the infant

Mistrust will always prevail. The parent might not give indications to be wary in ambiguous situations to the infant in the former case or might be so unsupportive that any Trust is precluded in the latter case. As with any sub-stage in the present model, a balance in parental/environmental behavior (and outcome) is required.

In this regard, with respect to the first lifespan sub-stage in the present model, which applies both to the extremely at risk premature fetus developing reflexes and the people treated as if they were only reflexes and not even worth keeping alive, the extreme reactions in this regard, at least for the latter adult, clearly would involve, at one extreme, not wanting to live/suicide attempts that are more than a cry for help and that are with genuine intent. At the other extreme, the person might want to try to keep alive no matter what, even to the point of justifying extreme abuse/murder in her/his turn.

Finally, note that in the interim summaries of the 25 steps in development of the current model, the goal is to prepare the way for understanding how it could be applied to the therapeutic context from a Neo-Eriksonian perspective. In this regard, the interim summaries will sometimes include material not given sufficient work-up in prior material. In this regard, the two sub-stages involving the preschooler come to mind, e.g., in terms of the implications of cognitive egocentrism and the implications of repression into unconsciousness, respectively, which were not really dealt with in my prior work but which are dealt with in depth in this book. Also, the interim summaries will add material on appropriate interventions for the developing infant/child/youth/adult facing difficulties for a sub-stage at issue. For example, the individual living at the level of this first sub-stage is treated so abusively and without concern for even survival that fearing murder, or reacting with murderous frustration might be real possibilities that have to be dealt with therapeutically. The interim summaries for the sub-stages often will refer to therapy, but this theme will be elaborated more fully as each sub-stage description unfolds after the interim summaries, as is clear with the present sub-stage in the material that follows.

Self-Response to Cognitive (Mis)perception of the Other

The individual living a regime of being treated reflexively, and fully so, such that any other way of being treated is dismissed, rejected, undermined, or not even acknowledged as possible, is obliterated into silence, or annihilated in psychological, cultural, or even personal (bodily) murder. Dehumanizing genocide and torture are classic examples. The person might react, but with so little power, resources, and skill available that the response is chaotic, disorganized, or nihilistic. The person could feel lifeless, listless, unmotivated to even move, not be capable of any activity that involves navigating distance in an organized way to any target toward a desired goal. At this level of the response (reflexive coordination), at best, alternate views are juxtaposed or perhaps compared, but with too few personal and social capacities to envision which options as better and preferred.

Positive Pole in Eriksonian Development

When development is proceeding well, even in the first fetal stages, preparations toward the development for an integrated nervous system and behavior are unfolding well. The earliest fetal movements are directed toward bodily areas, such as the mouth or the uterine wall. The reflex pairs involved, and any chaining, reflect appropriate distance reduction to the target, and with appropriate slowing toward bodily regions, too (Parma, Brasselet, Zoia, Bulgheroni, & Castiello, 2017). However, when behavior resides indefinitely at this level for whatever reason, such as due to abuse, or even if it is muted, development is delayed, fixated, regressed, or otherwise is not properly balanced and gravitates more to the negative pole of the sub-stage at issue, which, in this case, refers to obliteration or otherwise an imbalancing in the extreme inappropriate distance acts.

Negative Social-Self Working Schema

If the social-self working schema becomes fixated at this level, it will be pervasively negative. The sense of other will be obliterated in a suicidal fog. Links in social behavior, as well as social links to others, will be little more than unorganized reflexively-mediated pairings or chains of pairings. The internal working model (or schematization of self and other) will not be close to being representational, malleable, and flexible. Behavior will be poorly organized to any target, and not taking place from any sense of security or secure base. Self-destructiveness will be associated with any schema related to the other.

Attachment, Neo-Eriksonian Development, and Therapeutic Implications [Patients and Therapy]

Patient Presentation

In this aspect of the current work, patient presentation is not offered as a list of specific symptoms or as DSM diagnoses. Rather, patient presentation refers to a general description akin to a prototypical description. There are too many variables, including age, contextual, relational, and cultural factors, to be more specific (aside from any role of genetics, neurobiology, epigenetics, etc.). In this sense, the patient exhibiting psychological disturbances with a focus on the underpinning schemas and dynamics in the step of Neo-Piagetian Reflex Coordination/Eriksonian Distance vs. No Distance Acts will present as especially devastated, distraught, disjointed, annihilated, hopeless, suicidal/self-injurious, without direction, without any hint of awareness or thinking constructively, and especially reactive, either with utter resignation or with a lot of irritability. Suicidality would be a predominate theme. The person might present with the same behaviors that she/he had been subjected to, i.e., intense hate, murderous intentions, and extreme abuse of the other.

Behavioral/Symptom Mental Scanning

Bodily scanning refers to focusing on the various body zones head to toe in order to evaluate the presence of or degree of pain, discomfort, tightness, etc. Mental scanning is an analogous psychological process that involves the person conducting a psychological exploration and investigation of ongoing behavior, thought, feeling, and relations, in order to seek out: bad habits; maladaptive habits; problems in omission or commission in these regards; inappropriate, hurtful, and harmful expressions (to self, to other); immature, displaced, or otherwise non-constructive tendencies and actions, and so on, all with the goal of controlling them, blocking them, altering them, replacing them, growing beyond them, and so on.

The difficulty for those who have experienced the worse abuses is that their psychological resources are limited to reflexive reactivity, at best, with a feeling of being overwhelmed and without the ability to establish any direction. There might be much repression into unconsciousness, dazed behavior, dissociation, etc. Therefore, the person might strike out chaotically, self-silence, be incapable of self-understanding or speaking out, and so on. In short, any mental scanning undertaken might be limited in results, show a poverty of insight, and confront deeply ingrained and powerful defense mechanisms that protect against the overbearing harm experienced. The mental aspect of the scanning will be quite limited to isolated, basic behavioral and emotional perceptions, with little connectivity, and without giving any associated cognitive rationales or without any rational accuracy.

Therapeutic Implications

For any patient whose primary problems relate to this sub-stage, or indeed to any sub-stage in the model, generally, the patient needs to be ready for change and the therapist needs to be attuned to that readiness, working toward creating it if it is absent. Also the therapist should be working at the level of behaviors/symptoms of the predominant sub-stage that the person is experiencing, or the set involved, and focus therapeutic facilitations and strategies to fit this (these) assessed level(s). The therapist should be at or just slightly above the indicated level(s), bootstrapping to a degree the process of intra-individual change, whether horizontal within a level or vertical to help move beyond it. Recall that there are five stages in the current model – from the reflexive, sensori-motor, and peri-operational (pre-operational, concrete operational) stages to the more advanced abstract and collective intelligence stages. These five stages are akin to a progression in development from the physical, emotional, and cognitive levels to the conscious and existential ones, respectively, and therapy should be tailored accordingly (e.g., using behavioral techniques, emotional regulation, cognitive, narrative, and spiritual approaches, respectively).

The patient who experiences psychological devastations even partly at this level of reflex coordinations will need extensive support. The person subject to this type of abusive regime being discussed would have developed only the most primitive reflexive, reactive and self-destructive responses that could lead to harm of self and harm of others (e.g., intergenerational transmission of abuse). Suicide prevention will be a major concern. The typical need to create excellent rapport will be accentuated. Part of the therapeutic task will be to help the patient work through, accept, and move on from the deep hurts experienced and the paucity of skills developed, but very little progress can be expected in relation to better developing a sense of self and a modicum of respect for the other. The social-cognitive filters will be quite destructive and new appraisals will be required. The self will be undifferentiated and reflexively responsive, while the other will be greatly misperceived. Both self and other as target of any behavior, thought, and emotion will require the gradual shaping of new, more constructive stories or narratives, with only small steps in this regard possible. Basic behavioral strategies will help. The therapist teaches breathing exercises or other behavioral strategies that increase relaxation and that moderate hyper- or hypo-arousal. Generally, the patient will be unreachable, totally chaotic, disengaged, and at the edge of suicide or even murderous intentions.

Stress/Trauma Resilience/Coping

Stress/trauma resilience/coping refers to the capacity to resist, moderate, alleviate, rebound from, or otherwise adapt to stressors, whether internal, external, or both, including of an intrusive, external traumatic nature. The stress could be a general adversity or a specific traumatic experience. Resilience refers to avoiding the degeneration that could potentially occur, at least to some degree, and coping refers to using means and deploying resources to deal with the aftermath. In both cases, personal resources are taxed, and perhaps to the extreme.

For people living at the equivalent of this first sub-stage of life, should adversity arise either at its inception or later on through extreme environmental deprivation/degradation, stress/trauma resilience and coping mechanisms will be nonexistent or totally ineffective. If exposed to this type of regime, the most the person can expect to do is to randomly strike out in behavior at self or other, using a reactive, reflexive orientation without control, organization, or planning (reflexively; there will be two links at a time, at best, and only of the most primitive behaviors). Suicidality or even murderous intentions will constitute a constant background in sessions, and any stress/trauma resistance/coping will be very fragile, crumble, or even be nonexistent.

Therapeutic Strategies [the Other and Change]

Relational Co-regulation

When developing normally, we can track the growth of relational co-regulation right from conception because it is a concept that applies to any species, including single-celled organisms living in a bio-matrix. For multi-cellular organisms, it refers to the inter-communication among interrelated cells in tissues or cell aggregates. For more advanced animals and humans, it refers to the inter-participatory activity of mutual co-regulation in relations, and the strategies used in managing the joint activities involved, including of a psychological nature. The concept differs from related ones, such as self-control, emotional regulation, etc., because it can also include inter-relations with non-living material, e.g., from texts, media sources, etc., and the growth engendered by reading, learning, etc., e.g., of ethics texts.

In this regard, for reflexive coordinations at the beginning of life, at this level, co-regulatory skills are extremely primitive and related to intercellular coordination in the genesis of critical central nervous system precursors in the neural cleft. If movements are present in the reflex pairings involved, they are barely target-oriented, and not coordinated in a constant, adaptive, fixed order. The pairs themselves might chain haphazardly and asynchronously. Cell proliferation, migration, and connectivity are responsive to local cues in a stochastic process, but not much more.

When later relational co-regulatory skills fixate or regress to this type of reflexive pairing in behavior, it is disorganized, contextually insensitive, reactive, and essentially immediately expressed without reflection, while being rooted in the most primitive of social behaviors without self-control. The other is treated as the self and as a reflexive entity. Suicidality is predominant, with either crying out for help or genuine suicide attempts taking place. Murderous intentions might emerge.

Behavior/Symptom Network/Connectivity Change (Horizontal)

Understanding and dealing with clinical symptoms, disorders, and impairments involve understanding behavior in context. There are two major levels in the system of behavior – one that is ongoing, immediate, and contextually focused and one that is broader, longer term, and super-ordinate or hierarchically removed from immediate behavior, e.g., developmental growth, consciousness, self, and intelligence. The first level concerns actions, thoughts, feelings, and relationships that can be changed for the better without changing the overall developing growth function or other higher-order function. This concerns making lateral change in how behaviors or symptoms are organized, brought to the fore, utilized, and altered for the better. Behaviors/symptoms form local and global networks/connectivities as they self-organize systematically. Some are more core, pertinent, salient, or used more frequently as fall-back strategies. Some are secondary this way. Others are linked to the core ones, and pulled into their expressive orbit. Clustering or grouping within one's set of behaviors/symptoms takes place. This happens in individual ways and in context-sensitive ways for each of us. Some are more entrenched, resistant to change. Some are more maladaptive, negative, inappropriate, etc. Each of us can improve upon bad habits, for example, and the core behaviors that are part of them, as well as their drivers, both external and the internal ones that are part of the behavior/symptom networks, themselves, e.g., poor sleep.

Behavior/symptom network connectivities are highly individualized for multiple reasons. They concern which behaviors/symptoms (nodes) in a network relate to each other, for example, activating synchronously together, arranging sequentially, one predisposing the other, one predicting the other, and so on. The core ones are more crucial for symptom expression. The nodes connect in links (edges). The links potentially represent causal factors in eliciting behaviors/symptoms. There is no need to refer to higher-order (latent) constructs/variables to explain the linkages among behaviors/symptoms and which ones are core.

However, hybrid models (e.g., Young, 2015) acknowledge the causal facilitation not only in the linkages of symptoms but also in higher-order systemic integrations that emerge or emanate from the lower-order behavior/symptom interactions and serve, in turn, to influence the expression and linkages in the lower-order behavior/symptom level. Behavior/symptom expression, their change, and their causal linkage are multi-factorially determined, including with respect to the higher-order more generic level that functions in a top-down way on the lower-order behavior/system interactions, which function in a bottom-up way.

Consider the case of clinical depression, by which I refer to the complex of depression-related symptoms that an individual might express and not necessarily the list of symptoms in the DSM diagnosis of Major Depression. Because of the changing landscape of individual growth, context, culture/family, past psychopathology or psychological/vulnerability, neurobiology/physiology, neural architecture/networking, brain organization/disturbance, and so on, that an individual might have experienced, not only will the particular behavior/symptom complex for any one individual at any one (developmental) time differ from one time frame to the next for the person (intra-individually) and from one person to the next (inter-individually), so will the nature and subtlety of the emergent high-order mood, affectivity, and emotion related to depression, sadness, etc.

Note that the change process, whether horizontal or vertical, involves not only possible changes in behaviors/symptoms and their higher-order manifestations but also in other related psychological attributes, such as emotions and cognitions. For the latter, the cognitive schema/concept and its linkages also will be individually expressed. For the former, the emotional color and associations associated with the cognitions will vary immensely because of the multiple factors that influence emotions and their expression. Recall that the higher-order factors being discussed in the context of behavior/symptom networked connectivity, such as an overriding sense of depression, are different from the one of long-term growth and the like. Instead, in this case of change, it refers to immediate system reconfiguration at higher-order levels as part of the self-organizing wholes that vary online as the behavior/symptom interactions in context continue and alter.

Another level in behavior/symptom organization, or disorganization, as the case may be, relates to intermediate levels between the immediate ongoing one to context and the emerging higher-order ones related to mental disorder, mental function, etc. This middle level is a powerful one in behavior/symptom expression because it involves appraisals, for example, of one's skills, coping, personality, and resources, including socially, in family, etc., and those of others, e.g., are they supportive/non-supportive, helpful/harmful, etc. These appraisals could be simple cognitive schemas, or more general social-cognitive filters to perceive the world, or even more representational and wide-ranging narratives or stories about the self and world.

How do these various concepts and qualifications play out for the present sub-stage under discussion, of reflex coordinations? How does someone who has lived a regime of extreme abuse that leaves this sub-stage as the primary one experienced, even if some advances beyond it are possible, e.g., cognitively, move out of the worst consequences of having lived at this sub-stage? That growth must begin with horizontal or lateral changes from the worst behaviors/habits (e.g., suicidality) to better ones.

Will the person having lived such an abhorrent regime be too constrained and influenced by extremely counterproductive habits, appraisals, and views of the self and world? In meeting people like this in therapy, it can be expected that their appraisals will be very narrow, express suicidality, and even hostile intent at every junction encountered in their life, given the lived history of abuse or related regimes. Extreme irritability, anger, etc., might be easily induced or, to the contrary, the person will be deflated, flat, unable to react at all even to the worst experiences, be numb and dissociated, and express suicidal, self-injurious intent, and be extremely depressed. The core behaviors/symptoms will revolve around hopelessness, helplessness, worthlessness, and extreme dis-empowerment. The growth process will be severely compromised and essentially curtained and absent.

In this scenario, the therapist will focus on establishing the most basic of constructive connectivities. The core symptoms that drive behavior will be especially dysfunctional, disconnected, involving unprovoked lashing out, or turning off everything, and so on. Through proper therapeutic rapport building, presenting simple alternatives, and so on, new options in reflexive reactivity might build slowly, but without insight, change in schema structure beyond the minimal, and so on.

Behavior/Symptom Growth, Deep Change (Vertical)/Constructing a More Positive Life Story

The change process in development can involve advancement to a qualitatively superior sub-stage developmentally. The change in this sense, from one sub-stage to the next in the present model, in a vertical or upward direction, does not take place abruptly. Rather, vertical change will take place in steps within a sub-stage, which will involve four to five steps. These steps are referred to as sub-steps. They will proceed from initial implementation to final coherence. These sub-steps somewhat parallel the ones in the sub-stage sequence, from coordination to integration, as in a fractalization process. The sub-steps refer to and can be labeled as: (a) Tentative Beginning, (b) Clear Initiation, (c) Improved Application, (d) Spreading Maturation, and (e) Systemic Synthesis, perhaps with the last one overlapping with the first one of the next sequence.

How can people grow through the worst consequences of abuse, in which they function like a bag of reflexes, or as an expression of reflex coordinations? There are reasons other than severe abuse that might move the person into this most basic psychological state, one that is devoid of anything but the most basic reflex coordinations. There might be terrible malnutrition, severe brain damage, severe psychiatric morbidity, or other pervasive neuro-developmental insults and distortions in development. Whatever, the cause, the type of vertical change possible would be toward constructing options in immediate, reflexive reactivities that might temporarily hold sway.

Vertical change will take place with less difficulty in cases in which development had proceeded normally and there had been an abrupt regression due to overwhelming external circumstances and the like. For example, the person might have experienced a terrible traumatic or abusive incident that had reduced the person psychologically to a point that is well below prior adaptive psychological functioning. In the right corrective context, with proper emotional and social support and targeted psychotherapy, good progress can be made toward returning the individual to improved and optimal functioning.

Note that change processes, whether horizontal or vertical, alter the general sub-stage level at which the person is functioning. The changes in nodes and links in any one domain have the potential to alter the overall sub-stage configuration of symptoms/behaviors and their emergent, higher-order states, such as feeling depressed. In the present case of reflex coordinations that are changing in the vertical direction, the person would be moving away from suicidality/homicidality as core driving symptoms/behaviors and toward a less dangerous presentation.

Importantly, sub-stages and their changes are being presented as functioning predominantly at one sub-stage at a time, but this is far from the adaptive case for each individual. To the contrary, people live at multiple sub-stage levels, and coalesce or yoke them as needed to solve adaptive problems at hand. This procedure is highly individualized, of course, and any changes within one sub-stage has the potential to alter the multiple sub-stage coalescing/yoking and deployment of the skills involved in problem-solving that is part of coping, resilience, and stress and trauma management.

Finally, individual factors in sub-stage construction, change, and use include so many variables related to context, past, and problem-solving factors, such as personality, motivation, and culture. For example, there might be good proclivities to act, take charge, see options, and so on, relative to behaving with passivity, resignation, and determinism. But the opposite might be evident, as well.

The concept that the skills in sub-stages can coexist/alter in their interdigitation according to adaptive needs, and in individual ways, with the sub-stages already being individually organized and constructed, speaks to the complexity in the organization of behaviors, symptoms, higher-order constructs such as depression, and their top-down/bottom-up interaction. When the skills of sub-stages are deployed this way in cognitive problem-solving, each sub-stage represents a type of intelligence, and, as aggregated individually, they represent "multiple cognitive intelligences." When the sub-stages involved are more Neo-Eriksonian rather than Neo-Piagetian, as per the present developmental model of stages and sub-stages, we can speak of "multiple emotional intelligences."

Change, therefore, takes place in the components of multiple cognitive/emotional intelligences represented by individualized sub-stage skill co-action in the present model. This change can be quantitative, as in horizontal change within sub-stages, and more qualitative, as in vertical change in any one sub-stage or their multiple, co-actional configuration.

The therapist, therefore, is left with the difficult task of deciphering not only the primary sub-stage being expressed at any one time, through its expressed behaviors/symptoms (nodes) and their linkages (edges) but also the manner in which they are adaptively combined or aggregated in socio-emotional (affective) problem-solving. In both cases, whether working with the predominant sub-stage being expressed at any one time or how they are combined, the therapist will confront a dynamically changing clinical field. Some cases will be highly resilient to shifting sub-stage, creating new sub-stage expression combinations, changing any of the difficulties experienced even horizontally, and so on, which will make treatment harder.

The therapist needs to adopt the attitude of being a tuned psychiatric/psychological strata detector/investigator and horizontal/vertical change facilitator. The therapist needs to decipher the primary sub-stage that is driving the symptoms/behaviors being presented and any sub-stage combinations that are involved. The task would appear almost impossible, given the proposed 25 strata (sub-stages) in the present Neo-Piagetian/Neo-Eriksonian model. But, as with other psychiatric/psychological models, the behavior/symptom signs, their expressions and leakages, and constant sensitive awareness can facilitate the task. Moreover, I have described the 25 sub-stages in sufficient depth so that they are clearly differentiated. Each can serve as a template, prototype, or focused example of what to expect generally at each strata (sub-stage).

Given this evaluation task that the therapist faces through the present sub-stage model, the therapist can be viewed as a behavior/symptom archeologist/sleuth. For each individual, the developmental strata (sub-stages) leave individualized residue as they develop and dynamically alter (they never disappear, are not integrated into higher-order sub-stages) and return to predominant use for whatever reason. Their history of concatenation, yoking, assembling, collecting, or otherwise multiple arrangements online to solve individual problems, whether cognitive, socio-affective, or both, also leaves individualized residues. The effort to reconstruct how the residues arrived to their present state will be a demanding process and an ongoing one, but is necessary for better therapeutic outcome, depending on the goals set by the therapist and patient.

With severe abuse associated with the first sub-stage in development, the best that can be expected is slight change in automatic negative reaction, with some self-control deriving from that. At the initial stages of therapy, the patient's personal narrative of self and life will not change. Only with time, as the person moves out of the automaticity of this sub-stage can small gains be made in these regards. Part of it would include acceptance, working through, trying to start over in a new direction, etc., instead of wholesale change, creating brand new narratives, etc. However, despite including these basics in therapy, they will not have much impact. Instead, at best, some change in the worst habits, suicidality, etc., can be obtained.

The therapist might facilitate a new way of looking at the past as something terrible that happened, and that can't change, but is not continuing, so that there is an opening to live life and see the world differently. That would include examining whether critical core negative behaviors/symptoms are still required in the present. Emphasis would be placed on the value of life and of resisting suicidal impulses, having some self-control and appreciating that, contributing as best as one can in relationships, and being able to find some relax time, happiness, and joy, and otherwise being more present and participatory in the moment.

The life story that the therapist can help the patient reconstruct could be focused on perceptions of events in time, creating acceptance and future orientation, and facilitating taking charge and responsibility in self-healing and creating some connection to the other, at least to the degree possible. Although some happiness will develop as much as it can with a more constructive story, the deep processes involved in story reconstruction at this level should focus primarily toward getting some control in life, developing some aspects of a sense of a positive self and being a decent person, and integrating positively to the degree possible in some relationships, although safely.

Any person still living an abusive, annihilating regime or otherwise severely developmentally compromised, will find it almost impossible to move into a more constructive story about one's self and life beyond the one that suicide is the best option and things will not change in the future. The therapist would search for changes in these regards and act to promote them, but will also explore all avenues to help the patient through extra-psychological services, such as in law, the police, and social services, at least to the degree possible. Avoiding murderous intention would also be a focus.

Consciousness, Theory of Mind, Selves, and Responsibility

The concluding portion describing the first sub-stages of the new work on the present Neo-Piagetian/Neo-Eriksonian 25-step model of development and its application to the therapeutic context examines some higher-order concepts that I have developed in relation to the model. Table 13.1 [e.g., on Consciousness, Self, Other] presents the areas under discussion, and it is noted that in my prior work on them I did not develop five sub-stages for each of them, but just presented the five stages involved. The following attempts to provide therapeutic implications

Table 13.1 Consciousness, self, and other

Stage	Consciousness[a]	Cognition-emotion-body of the other	Self-definitional Neo-Maslovian needs	Relatedness self Neo-Maslovian needs	Foundational moral motives (positive poles[b])	Responsibility[c]
Reflexive	Non-consciousness	Nascent intersubjectivity	Generativity self-actualization (meaning) [family, work education-instruction, community, culture, collective, planet]	Generativity self-actualization (meaning) [family, work education-instruction, community, culture, collective, planet]	Sanctity/humanizing	Responsive
Sensori-motor	Preconsciousness	Embodied mentalization/intentionality	Self-esteem identity (me-identity) [individualism]	Self-esteem we-dentity (us-identity) [collectivism]	Conscious identification/application	Response-able
Peri-operational	Unconsciousness	Representational theory of mind First-order (false belief) Second-order (eyes tasks)	Initiative-education, love (affection) affiliation	Initiative-education, love (belonging) affiliation	Reciprocity/respect	Responsibility
Abstract	Conscious	Third-order theory of mind (abstract)	Safety/trust/security/care	Safety/trust/security/care	Care/linking	Re-responsibility
Collective intelligence	Supra-conscious	Post-formal theory of mind (collective intelligence)	Immediate physiological needs [e.g., nursing]/survival	Immediate physiological needs [e.g., sex]/reproduction	Life preservation	Re-responsibilities

Adopted with permission of Springer Science + Business Media. Young (2011); with kind permission from Springer Science + Business Media B. V. [Second and Seventh column from Table 35.2, Page 813, its third and fifth column; Third column: Table 15.1, Page 350, its second column; Fourth and Fifth column: Figure 19.4, Page 454; Text Extract (285 words), Page 813–814]

Adopted with permission of Springer International Publishing. Young (2016); with kind permission from Springer International Publishing. [Sixth column from Table 34.5, Page 844, its fourth column]

Note: For each stage, five sub-stages apply (coordination, hierarchization, systematization, multiplication, integration) various footnotes

Note: Haidt (e.g., Graham & Haidt, 2012; see Young, 2016, p. 838) had elaborated five foundational moral motives, which are: Harm/Nurturance; Fairness/Justice; In group/Loyalty; Authority/Respect; and Chastity/Atheism. Young (2016) had organized them according to his revised Neo-Maslovian model, which has five levels like

(continued)

Table 13.1 (continued)

the original and also in his model. Also, Young's model has two core aspects at each level, whether concerning self-definition and relatedness (following Blatt, 2008). Young (2016) differentiated Haidt's original list of five moral motives by organizing them according to the self-definitional and relatedness component of his Neo-Maslovian model. The present table provides integrated terminology for the dual foundational moral motives at each of the five levels of Young's revised Neo-Maslovian model. The terms selected respect both Young's reworking of Haidt's terminology for the five foundational moral motives and Young's terminology for the five levels in his Neo-Maslovian model. Thus, they stretch from life preservation and care/linking to conscious identification/application and sanctity humanizing, with the middle level involving Reciprocity/respect. As with Maslov's original model the present Neo-Maslovian and Neo-Haidtian ones constitute developmental progressions as much as needs/motives complexities

The particular higher-order aspects of the person's developing cognition and socio-affectivity relate to consciousness, the nature of the self, foundational morality, and a sense of responsibility, which together indicate apex psychological completeness or maturity. However, inevitably the prenatal fetus has a lack at these levels (non-conscious, are responsible, no self, no concept of any aspect of other, no morals, no meaning or sense of value, etc.). Glimmers along these lines will develop slowly, with the preliminary phases involving reflex growth and nothing more. However, at this first juncture even basic physiological needs and survival are threatened by a host of possible insults

The person forced to live at this level because of extreme abuse, torture, locking up, or otherwise experiencing life threatening or murderous intentions will not be able to reach beyond the experience except through hope perhaps. Of course, these growth parameters (consciousness, sense of self, sense of other, responsibility, morality) could develop full-fledged before catastrophic events obliterate them, and so hope can be the vanguard of other developmental acquisitions that could re-invigorate and rehabilitate them once the extremely abusive regime is destroyed or otherwise lifted

The person might be partially able to move out of the suicidality ideation/intention orbit, and the therapist should construct this a first step in the slow walk toward further growth

[a](a) In terms of degree of consciousness, the fetal period should be considered one of non-consciousness
(b) One can place the preconscious in the infancy period
(c) The childhood period is one famously marked by the development of the unconscious, as per Freud's psychodynamic model
(d) One classic hallmark of the adolescent period is that it is the beginning of consciousness
(e) Finally, just as the adult could develop a collective intelligence that seems one step above the teenage stage of abstract thought, so the adult could develop a supra-consciousness that is one step above the stage of the opening of consciousness

[b]Negative pole in each case = lack, behaving oppositely, disrupting (purposely)

[c](a) In terms of the five principal stages of the present model, the reflexive period is considered one where the fetus is responsive but not initiatory
(b) In the sensori-motor stage, the infant is more active and agentic, as well as voluntary and selective to some degree. The infant can be considered "response-able"
(c) As for the child, Piagetian logic develops and the child is capable of undertaking responsibility but is limited in how much can be handled
(d) The adolescent is capable of dedicating the self to a cause in a fanatical way, and could commit to one over and over, in a process of constant rededication to the responsibility (although parents would be happy with rededication to the simpler tasks of life at home and at school). In this regard, I refer to the process as involving re-responsibility
(e) Finally, the adult who arrives at the level of advanced psychological maturity that might accompany the stage of collective intelligence can have the sense of re-responsibility flourish and become multiple and varied, in a process which I term one of re-responsibilities

and applications for these concepts not just in terms of the stages but also in terms of their sub-stages. In this regard, with respect to the first sub-stage of life on reflexive coordinations, there is little that can be said about consciousness, responsibility, and ultimate psychological growth, except that the seeds are laid from conception onward and they begin to be expressed in fetal life as the nervous system develops.

The study of consciousness is burgeoning (e.g., Chambliss, 2018; Friston, 2018), and from very different perspectives (philosophy, brain modeling, respectively). However, the present approach consists of a differentiated sub-stage approach, which, to my knowledge, has not been attempted in the modeling to date that has been undertaken.

The Reflex Stage Sub-stage of Hierarchization (Quite Premature): Sub-stage 2

Self and Relational Development [Initial Theoretical Elaborations]

A very brief description of the present step in Young's 25-step Neo-Eriksonian developmental model follows. It is presented again in Chap. 18, to help give a collective overview of the 25 steps in the modeling.

Nursing acts vs. rootless acts (fairly premature). As you grew, starting in the early nursing period, you experienced major abuse and your self was denied or not allowed to grow. You grew feeling that you had no anchor, or were missing roots. You felt helpless and hopeless. Also, you did not feel like caring for yourself. This might have led you to not care for anybody. You felt the same way even when you became a parent (or will feel that way when you have children one day).

Appendix 1.2 gives the brief amount of work already done in prior publications related to the task of developing in depth the Neo-Eriksonian (sub)stage model. The next section of the chapter gives an interim summary that elaborates the contents of Appendix 1.2 with respect to the present sub-stage being considered, of the sub-stage of Reflex Stage Sub-stage of Hierarchization.

Interim Summary

The person who has lived a regime that reduces her- or himself to socio-affective function at the reflex hierarchization level will have experienced abuse and denial of self that precludes even the most basic advances socio-affectively. These consequences might coexist with other less harmful attitudes associated with other sub-stages, but the latter do not predominate when the person has lived a regime such as this. Behavior is rootless, without anchor. The impulse is not to want at all to take care of the self. If the person is a newborn, even nursing is compromised. If a child lives this hopeless lifestyle, she or he will be helpless, ignore caring for the self, and not come close to developing a sense of self. The person living at, regressing to, or fixated at this sub-stage of development will have developed very minimal constructive emotional and social capacities. Generally, in behavior, given the cognitive architecture in the corresponding Neo-Piagetian sub-stage, there might be reflexive-type behavior in pairs having a fixed-order, or with one being super-ordinate, but the skills are primitive such that there is no hint of self-organization other than the beginnings of related reflexes serving particular corporal ends.

The extreme dangers of this sub-stage relate to its lack of self-care/abandonment of self-care. At one extreme, the adults living at this level will abandon totally any self-care and expose themselves to death by neglect, malnutrition, etc. At the other extreme, the person might over-react and consider only taking care of the self no matter what the consequences for the other, including that the other is at risk of abandoned care, neglect, and death in her/his turn.

Self-Response to Cognitive (Mis)perception of the Other

The individual who is subject to a degree of cognitive (mis)perception of the other that is inherently abusive, potentially murderous, etc., but with at least some other more positive perceptions contemplated or possible, is essentially suppressed, and even has her/his life in danger. But relative to the extreme abuse associated with the prior sub-stage, the possibility of experiencing a different regime opens some sense of reacting more than in disorganized silence and self-annihilation. At times, the non-targeted chaotic reaction, could take on a semblance of a more directed, structured response. This sub-stage is about reflexive hierarchization, so that one finds the experience of feeling totally abused being predominant, but with some leeway given. A glimmer of reaching out to different ways of being might obtain, but still would be reactive, reflexive, and without much hope.

The primary tendency to self-annihilate, engage in suicidality, and so on, are somewhat muted when the person living this regime does not have to confront totally abusive and murderous intentions. But the potential for a lack of or absence of self-care and concern can lapse easily into addictive behaviors. The person will be highly at risk for eating related and self-sustenance (eating) disorder, addiction (substance use/abuse) disorder, etc.

Positive Pole in Eriksonian Development

In normal development, basic reflex survival mechanisms can be paired, ordered, and related to each other in a dominant-subordinate relationship, as required, such that, for example, nursing is well-orchestrated. [The person who is forced to develop a reactive reflexive entity, under a regime of terrible abuse, but with some alternate, less destructive experiences, as well, can develop some self-care tendencies. Behavior has some direction and sustenance/maintenance, but not much more. The balance of a more positive compared to negative pole expression in an Eriksonian sense in this sub-stage is upset. Indeed, the danger of slipping into aimless and self-destructive behavior is increased, with an increased risk for self-harm, self-annihilation, and suicide thought (and action).]

Negative Social-Self Working Schema

Social-self working schemas that functions at this level will have the most primitive organization in terms of dominant-subordinate reflex pairings. Just as nursing will, at this level, subsume other reflexes to sucking, the social organization allowed by these most primitive schemas will arrange to subsume secondary aspects to primary internal and context-selected end-points. When the schemas are negative, such as in the very at-risk early preterm infant suffering either internal biological vulnerabilities, environmental deprivations/insults/abuse, or both, the ability to deploy socially happens just in the most basic ways, and even at that it is unresponsive, maladaptive, disorganized (incorrectly organized), and not on target functionally. The person who has been exposed to the negative regime associated with this level will be highly at risk to the point that she/he will express no or little self-care, thereby endangering both body and mind through eating disorder, addictions, etc., and generally having no base to serve as a secure point, with rootlessness prevalent. The other might be perceived only as a tool to gratify self-destructive tendencies, including addictions.

Attachment, Neo-Eriksonian Development, and Therapeutic Implications [Patients and Therapy]

Patient Presentation

Patients presenting at this level of psychological disturbance will be almost as radically devastated as the patients at the prior level, but they will be somewhat more coherence, albeit, without changing much the generally chaotic picture. One might find the most primitive anchors (e.g., addictions) serving as generally futile safety nets, ones with only the most basic reflexive linkages [Recall that the sub-stage involved is underpinned by reflexive hierarchizations]. The person is still immersed in suicidal thoughts, but there might be hints at self-care and self-protection. Struggles in soliciting, accepting, and being thankful for alimentation, whether physical or psychological, will stand at center stage.

Behavioral/Symptom Mental Scanning

A person who has lived an abusive regime that allows for minimal organization of behavior in pockets of reflexive adaptations that govern maladaptive habits might be able to detect bad habits related to suicidality, self-care destructiveness, and other-person destructiveness. However, the scanning process will be limited, not enduring, and undermined by the excesses in poorly adaptive behaviors that have been adopted, including in over-use of food and substance as coping mechanisms. At best, these habits mask, hide, or otherwise avoid the issues behind the habits, which cannot be properly scanned, analyzed, and dealt with.

Therapeutic Implications

Although there might be some easing in the imminent threat of suicide, and actual attempts, at this level, the potential for active suicidal ideation will still be marked. The therapist will have to emphasize basic self-care, in that even self-regulation of bodily functions, let alone psychological ones, will be compromised. The self will be constituted by isolated islands of reflexive skills built with a top-down/bottom-up arrangement, but with few constructive elements in the subordinate role. For example, the person will reflexively acquiesce to the environment's unreasonable, self-destructive demands and impositions due to poorly constructed reflex-type self-images. The other will be conceived as an overwhelming force, and the other's demands and impositions will be awaited passively and with trepidation. The likelihood of finding severe eating disordered behavior, self-injurious behavior, risk taking behavior, addictions, suicidality, etc., will be high. The therapist will need to insert into this self-dialogue by teaching self-calming behavioral relaxation exercises and functioning as an alternatively acting role model, while building up counter, more positive stories, all in an arduous process of therapeutic engagement with much accompanying patient retreat, vacillation, and rejection.

Stress/Trauma Resilience/Coping

Stress/trauma resilience/coping might include the simplest of reflexive-type coping mechanisms as predominant over self- and other-destructive ones. These mechanisms will be physically/corporeally based, such as in food indulgence or substance use and overuse. Generally, the strategies will not succeed to deal with the stress/trauma at issue, and merely mask it, avoid it, hide from it, and so on. Indeed, there will be no information processing of the stress/trauma and it will be taken as an overriding force, which cannot be dealt with other than through these maladaptive escape/avoidance procedures, with eating disorders and addictions primary as trauma/stress control behavior.

Therapeutic Strategies [the Other and Change]

Relational Co-regulation

At this level of reflex hierarchization, and its undifferentiated, rootless (even in breast-feeding) acts, the self and other engage in dialogue in a broken haphazard way that splinters, ignores, or might not even recognize basic human survival needs. The self appears only briefly as a present entity, while being aimless and fixated on destructive patterns in health maintenance (corporal, psychological). The other is held as a poor source of social support, dangerous even, and generally excluded as a help for the person or unable to help the person. There might be some self-care expressed, but only in the most basic and physical ways. More likely, social relations will be primitive and focused on self-harming behaviors, such as eating disorder and addictions. The therapist will need to provide the required supportive base, as well as having skills to deal with self-destructive behavior, including extreme eating disorders and addictions.

Behavior/Symptom Network/Connectivity Change (Horizontal)

The person living at the level of reflexive hierarchization can barely organize constructively pairs of the simplest behaviors, such as with simple coping or braking mechanisms controlling deep suicidality or enraged lashing out. The person can barely care for the self, and is mostly negligent in this regard, with only sporadic good habits. The worst bad habits that might be expressed include substance addictions. Perhaps through the simplest resilience mechanisms or removal of the deleterious environment in which the individual abides, the person can begin to get some control of the maladaptive behavior at issue, but only ephemerally, tentatively, and with attempts easily abandoned. There will be (almost) no schema construction of the mediating context, and defenses will be set up. Bad habits will be engaged in, and poor ways applied to better control them. But fleeting intuitions along better lines might glimmer. The core symptoms will move away from all vestiges of self-construction, care, and growth into areas of nihilistic thrashing about, with interspersions of trying to alter this primary condition. The therapist should attune to any such efforts and actively seek to promote them, knowing the severe weight of the addictions and other disturbed behaviors that will predominate. The therapist should take stock of any efforts along these lines and help create new narratives about caring for the body as a first step in growth of a more positive and adaptive psychology. Much behavioral work should be implemented on self-care, addiction control, and a healthy lifestyle, including in healthy eating and nutrient intake.

Behavior/Symptom Growth, Deep Change (Vertical)/Constructing a More Positive Life Story

The person surviving at the level of reflex hierarchization is barely capable of using constructive coping mechanisms. These mechanisms will be of the most primitive, corporal-focused nature, with little resistance to or efficacy in dealing with any type of stress. However, as the person concretizes better coping skills, she/he will be able to expand the range of their application or the duration of their use. This will potentiate some movement toward a more systemic use of the coping mechanisms, e.g., in dealing with the stress or the bad habits that had accompanied it, such as addiction.

That said, the person who is living barely beyond a total annihilating, abusive, if not murderous regime nonetheless will be living a life of misery, lack of care, and rootlessness. The most basic survival mechanisms possible in this context will be concerned with placing life before death, trying to live instead of wishing to die, engaging in basic self-care instead of letting go all care, seeking some stability in light of the chaos, and trying to control the worst bad habits, such as suicidality and addictions. At best, some respect for the body and hope for its sustenance, both through self-actions and external support, should be a primary theme in therapy narrative reconstruction.

Consciousness, Theory of Mind, Selves, and Responsibility

The youngest prematures are living in a world immersed with reflex coordinations, at best. Even basic survival functions like suckling/nursing are fraught with poor equilibrative control and outcome, as well as physiological need inefficiencies and survival risks. There are no advanced cognitive skills, or even sensori-motor ones, which can permit any growth in self/other awareness/consciousness, taking control/being agentic and responsible, and appraising meaning/maturity requirements, and so on. At least, the process toward these critical ultimate human end points will have started.

As for the person forced to live at an equivalent of this sub-stage, she/he will have only the slightest opening to move from reflex coordinations to hierarchizations. The latter might include some optimal arrangements with more positive elements in a dominant relationship to negative elements, but nothing approaching the types of ulterior developments of which we are describing. There will be no consciousness/awareness (self/other), responsibility/control by the self, meaning making/maturity, and expressions of morality that are possible. Harboring hope along these lines might develop, depending on the age that the abusive regime involved had started, its duration, intensity, and so on, and on the resilience/coping (vestiges) of the person. The person might be able to imagine some self-care and accepting care. The therapist should work toward promulgating these therapeutic advances as part of a growth process, potentially leading to more mature outcomes for the self and for dealing with others and the world.

The Reflex Stage Sub-stage of Systematization (Somewhat Premature): Sub-stage 3

Self and Relational Development [Initial Theoretical Elaborations]

A very brief description of the present step in Young's 25-step Neo-Eriksonian developmental model follows. It is presented again in Chap. 18, to help give a collective overview of the 25 steps in the modeling.

Outcome acts vs. outcast acts (that excluded you) (somewhat premature). From early in life, you developed simple goals, and tried to reach them. They got you what you wanted. But maybe the environment (parent) did not even support this basic activity and you were disregarded and not allowed to have any goals. You were treated like an outcast, or not belonging to anything, and were not allowed to speak or be what you wanted. Maybe you became the same way, and greatly ignored all people and ignored yourself.

Appendix 1.3 gives the brief amount of work already done in prior publications related to the task of developing in depth the Neo-Eriksonian (sub)stage model. The next section of the chapter gives an interim summary that elaborates the contents of Appendix 1.3 with respect to the present sub-stage being considered, of the sub-stage of Reflex Stage Sub-stage of Systematization.

Interim Summary

Reflex systems characterize this sub-stage. They form organized entities of dominant-subordinate paired reflexes that have added elements to assure contextual adaptation, and so are flexible to a minimal degree. The somewhat premature newborn expresses behavior through these primitive control schemas. The socio-emotional behaviors expressed are reflexively organized but relatively isolated, sporadic, and primitively social compared to how the term social is used normally. Goals for the behavior exist, which constitutes a major advance, but difficulties could lie with a lack of optimal support to allow for goal orientation success. The goals that might be present allow for nascent bodily based self-schemas to emerge, such that we can refer to a "proto-self." The self-schemas include sensitivity to the target of the reflex complexes used effectively. However, without proper social support, as is evidenced in the negative cognitive (mis)perception of the other associated with this cognitive sub-stage, the goal structure in behavior normally evident in this sub-stage in the appropriate context is not realized. Especially for the adult living a regime like the one under discussion, instead of supported outcome-seeking in behavior, one finds unsupported, rejecting, and even abusive "outcast" generating behavior, with consequent disregard and possible rejection by the person involved in her/his turn. Being treated like an outcast fosters an attitude of not belonging to anything, and not being allowed to speak or be what the person might want for her/himself. The palpable danger of this sub-stage, for example, in terms of the cognitive (mis)perception of the other, is notable – dismissal/disregard/disrespect for the life of the person, not even acknowledging/ignoring the person.

The other(s) in the life of the person is left to fend for themselves, even with the possibility of death by negligence. At the other extreme, the person over-acknowledges the other, lives only for the other, and exhibits self-abnegation to the point of placing oneself in mortal danger through personal neglect.

Self-Response to Cognitive (Mis)perception of the Other

Alternate responses to a sense of self-annihilation, suicidality, addiction, and other extreme responses to the abusive regime experienced become increasingly possible, in that more organized systemic reaction complexes formulate. Also, the abusive regime does give some leeway, and reflex systems can emerge that are goal-directed, context-appropriate, and allow for simple coping. The pervasive suppression and death potential evident if living according to the prior sub stages apply less, and the person can organize more adaptive filters that keep in view basic goals and possible positive outcomes. Some sense of corporal self-efficacy might develop, with adaptive primitive control schemas keeping an attentional focus, albeit often toward dangers in the surround.

The quality of these primitive self-constructions will depend on the degree of environmental support, which generally will be dismissive, ignoring, negligent, and even rejecting. The person risks expressing corresponding negative reactions in consequence, focusing on behaviors that are self-destructive and reflect lack of self-growth, including self-obliteration. The nascent corporal proto-self will be undercut and disintegrate in such circumstances. Indeed, the risk for suicidality, addictions, etc., remains as constant possibilities. These risks might arise through the psychiatric/psychological dynamics in this particular sub-stage despite the more primitive and earlier-developed fixated reflexive sub-stages with which these auto-destructive behaviors are associated.

Positive Pole in Eriksonian Development

The somewhat premature newborn faces multiple challenges in navigating the world, but does have some adaptive reflex complexes to help her/him, with target-oriented ones subsuming others in context-appropriate ways. Because behavior can be targeted effectively, it can help in the discernment of the generalized stimulus attributes of the target, leading to more integrated perceptual wholes. The baby slips into a relaxed, accepting state co-relationally with the target, and the beginnings of corporal self-schema construction begins co-relationally.

Negative Social-Self Working Schema

The person living at the negative level of psychological function in this sub-stage will express a quite negative view of the social other, who will be perceived as overbearing, negligent, and worthy of rejection. The underlying working schema will be reflex-based, but consolidated systematically to allow for minimal target-related organization. In the negative social support context, in which the behavior experienced will be non-supportive if not overtly damaging, the other will be perceived as simmering with rejection and potential violence, such that a guarded distance will be kept. The self of the other will be viewed as an amalgam of reactive, negative reflex-like behaviors.

Attachment, Neo-Eriksonian Development, and Therapeutic Implications [Patients and Therapy]

Patient Presentation

There might be indications of suicidality control and addiction control, but the predominant, core symptoms in the patient living at this level will relate to a diffuse, absent, or otherwise minimally built and poorly adaptive self. The self will be viewed as consisting of separate pockets of possible coping adaptations in context, but ones that are ephemeral, generally ineffective, or excessively rigid. Emotions will be all over the place and regulated only piecemeal, at best. Cognitions will be disorganized. Self-control will be deficient, tangential, and expressing denial of a separate intact self. The person with this type of presentation will be seen as reactive and reflexive. The person will need basic therapy through practice, exercise, role play, modeling, finding appropriate strategies, behavioral techniques/skill building, and pleasant event scheduling, for example.

Behavioral/Symptom Mental Scanning

The person who attempts obtaining insight at this level of function will be limited to apperceiving sequences of reflexive reactions with some coping mechanisms involved, especially behavioral. The person might become slightly aware of her/his undercutting of self-construction and of self-sabotage in the minimal corporal proto-self schemas that the person is constructing. It will be easier for the person to apperceive the risks of and needed control of ongoing suicidality and of any addictions. But implementing successful control of these impulses with cognitive strategies will fail, because the extent the habits will be deeply ingrained and intransigent, which will preclude much of any success, especially in the short term, unless the therapeutic focus is related especially to the person's corporal survival and physical integrity.

Therapeutic Implications

The therapist in co-relation with a patient who is living the described regime will require good self-building skills. The corporal proto-self of the patient will be founded in primitive reflex systematization control schemes that are organized but isolated. There will be much work to stitch together a more inclusive self-image that can cope better with stress, trauma, negligence, abuse, etc., which, has resulted in expressing negativity and subversion of an independent self. The image of the other as suppressing, rejecting, and negligent will comprise the dominant cognitive social filter in social cognition. The patient will waiver in achieving minimal constructive outcomes, including in self-construction at the level of a coherent body to be protected. The patient also will have difficulty in construction of others as people who can act independently of her/himself without evident malice. The risk is that the self in the patient as much as the perceived other in the patient are construed as outcasts, worthy of rejection, and requiring of rejection.

Stress/Trauma Resilience/Coping

Relative to the last sub-stage considered, in the present sub-stage, one will find a slight increase in resilience and coping capacities in cases of stress and trauma. Whereas prior resilience/coping to stress/trauma reactions might have involved suicidality, addictions, and other signs of having no control and engaging self-destructiveness, in the present case, some basic, constructive target-oriented behavior is possible, albeit at the reflexive, corporal level, perhaps, for example, through physical exercise. The risk is that the person is incapable of any coping successfully because of the nature of the environment, as she/he lapses into self-destructive behavior, giving up on the self, adapting bad habits that harm the body, etc.

Therapeutic Strategies [the Other and Change]

Relational Co-regulation

The social interdigitational networking involving self and other, with mutual interactive control, does not proceed in any way that is reciprocal, normal, and self- and other-sensitive. The person behaving at this level is still especially reflexive in behavior, even if more advanced cognitively relative to prior sub-stage manifestations, and acts with systemic reflex complexes that adjust to the environment, but not much more. The self is developed at a level that is minimal, corporal-oriented, and atrophied, while the other is perceived as a dominant, impairing entity, who is abusive, negligent, not caring, and rejecting. Social relations will be guarded, at best, avoided, or rejected, in a vicious circle of exclusion, withdrawal, and neglect of both self-construction and other-respect. These types of deficits will not be cognitively based, but will be limited by the nature of the cognition involved.

Behavior/Symptom Network/Connectivity Change (Horizontal)

Bad habit countering and control at this level will be limited by the underlying cognitive base of systematized reflex complexes. The ability to stay on target by using very basic behavioral sequences might be evident in resisting bad habits, altering them, or controlling them, but only to a small degree and without much generalization. There will be no sense of self-efficacy or self-esteem to ramp up self-control, and bad habits will constantly reappear/reinvigorate and test/detract from any gains. The other will not be sensed in any way as a coherent self but only as a disparate sequence of controlling behavior that dismisses/rejects the person. Getting some control of reactive rejection and aggression via therapists in therapy sessions will help, as long as some external social support is involved. However, assuming the person is still living the destructive regime at issue, more likely, the environment will continue its non-supportive role and/or disintegrate into effortful undermining of gains as its controlling regimen is challenged.

Behavior/Symptom Growth, Deep Change (Vertical)/Constructing a More Positive Life Story

With appropriate proto-self construction and external support, the person can begin to move forward to solidify and expand the basic coping mechanisms and more positive self- and other-construction profiles being formulated, although any of these gains will be only the most basic and behavioral without cognitive reflection. The potential for generalization will grow, and core self- and other- control mechanisms might become more resistant to perturbation and loss.

The therapist will attempt to facilitate growth in the person living at this level by using basic behavioral strategies that reinforce primitive corporal self-construction. Taking care of the body will be accentuated as a first step in this regard. The therapist will work on understanding the self and its relationship to the other and the environment, even if these entities are rather primitively conceived, because achieving some progress toward such goals will allow constructing a more positive self-image with some basic control in life. Fostering good personal habits allows the person to not only acknowledge the nascent self but also the nascent other as a separate corporal, behavioral and perhaps somewhat psychological entity. The person can learn to stay focused on basic targets in behavior, even if only reflexively-mediated, apperceive the other as a separate person to a degree, and act *for* the self and not just against the other. This will have a positive cycling effect in persistence in effort by the self, helping toward achieving desired outcomes even if very basic, and creating some social integration rather than just having the person functioning at the margins as an outcast.

Consciousness, Theory of Mind, Selves, and Responsibility

The premature infant who is out of the survival danger zone might have more systematized reflexes with more target-oriented behavior that succeeds more smoothly in obtaining programmed outcomes. The person forced to live at this level will be exposed to an abusive regime that gives only minimal leeway. There will be no room for expression of higher-order consciousness, responsibility, morality, and self-other growth. The therapist should attune to and encourage any growth impulses along these lines, which will start with primitive awareness of self and other, but one that is quite corporal- (physiological, physical) based and without cognitive reflection and emotional empathy.

The Reflex Stage Sub-stage of Multiplication (Full-Term Newborn): Sub-stage 4

Self and Relational Development [Initial Theoretical Elaborations]

A very brief description of the present step in Young's 25-step Neo-Eriksonian developmental model follows. It is presented again in Chap. 18, to help give a collective overview of the 25 steps in the modeling.

Care-giving Acts vs. careless giving acts (full term newborn). Normally, right from birth, newborns develop a beginning self based on the body and actions, like grasping a finger. But the environment (parent) might not treat the baby well — being negligent and even abusive sometimes. Perhaps the environment (your parent) was uncaring or gave you poor care because of this. So, as you grew, you began to not care for yourself. Or, maybe you went the other way by constantly trying to seek care, but without knowing how.

Appendix 1.4 gives the brief amount of work already done in prior publications related to the task of developing in depth the Neo-Eriksonian (sub)stage model. The next section of the chapter gives an interim summary that elaborates the contents of Appendix 1.4 with respect to the present sub-stage being considered, of the sub-stage of Reflex Stage Sub-stage of Multiplication.

Interim Summary

The full-term newborn has already developed in the prenatal period basic reflexive cognitive-related capacities governed by primitive schemas of systematized reflex pairings that function well in context. With birth, the newborn develops the capacity to effect patterned behavior through full-scale schemas. The schemas that had developed in the prior sub-stage can be applied beyond their original targets in the particular domains that had been addressed prenatally to the wider world post-birth, even if inexactly. The developing nascent self of the baby can move beyond a primitive corporal-based proto-self into a more environmentally-responsive and even cross-modal or inter-modal perceptual self. The self is psychologically emergent at this juncture, as is the neonate from the prenatal matrix. The newborn is in a position to accept positive care given from care-givers and to thrive accordingly.

However, problems in these regards can arise in several ways. The child might have problems related to eliciting care-giving for whatever reason, not being able to activate the ability to receive care, thrive, and optimize life. The child may be born into an environment that is at least partially haphazard, negligent, rejecting, abusive to a degree, or otherwise offering careless care-giving, care, and giving, at best. Early interventions, if required, should target parental matching to the needs of the greatly vulnerable infant. If a person is forced to live this regime, the dangers are that she/he will live struggles related to self-care and shrivel psychologically, or care will be rejected and the person will lapse into deep psychological pain and manifest abandonment of any concern for personal health. Or, to the contrary, all the person will do is endlessly solicit care, and express over-dependence to the point of denial of any possibility of self growth.

Self-Response to Cognitive (Mis)perception of the Other

The regime experienced by people forced to live at this level is marked especially more by negligence, a lack of concern, and a lack of care. They will experience less extreme forms of abuse than if they had been living according to prior sub-stages, although the abuse might be found at least partially. Normally, people are open to receiving care-giving, care, and giving, but this capacity could be compromised and even annulled if one is forced to live in this regime. If the person is not overtly rejecting already, vicious circles in lack of responsiveness, ignoring, and rejecting could develop, leading the person to create distance, reject, and refuse receiving/giving care, as the case may be. The other who might be involved with the person and be exposed to her/his behavior (not as the original abuser) could respond similarly to the person. The nascent aspects of the perceiving self in the person could become asphyxiated, just like the brain of the baby in birthing with anoxia.

Positive Pole in Eriksonian Development

The newborn enters the world with the challenge of promoting and receiving care-giving, caring, and giving. In optimal circumstances, this aspect of the present Neo-Eriksonian sub-stage of Care-giving vs. Careless giving Acts is negotiated well in that the baby is born with a behavioral repertoire honed by evolutionary, Darwinian natural selection to elicit the sensitive, contingent, and warm parental response needed for her/his survival. And the care-giver similarly possesses the required skill and motivation to bond and to create the conditions for optimal care-giving and security in attachment. The newborn suckles, relaxes in skin-to-skin contact, and perceptually opens to the world.

Negative Social-Self Working Schema

Experiencing a contrary type of negative environment will act to undermine the ability to receive care from the other, who, especially for the adult subject to this type of regime, will be perceived as uncaring, unable to give, abandoning, and not worthy of accepting. The rejection cycle between self and other could magnify into entering into a silent world of unresponsiveness or, in contrast, the person's world could consist of thrashing about and undirected hostility. The social self-working schema will be reflex-based, but patterned, generalizing, and with perceptions of negativity and no care(giving) rather than positivity and care(giving) being received.

Attachment, Neo-Eriksonian Development, and Therapeutic Implications [Patients and Therapy]

Patient Presentation

The full-term newborn having difficulty at this sub-stage will tend to have difficulty with the receiving of care-giving, care, and giving. The person entered therapy with a predominant focus on these lines will present with the same difficulty, and even with rejecting behaviors. A person like this will be seen as having primitive appraisals, at best, yielding outlooks conditioned by them. The person will be limited to using the most basic sensory-perceptual schemes, which will be of a generalized reflexive nature. This will encourage reactive responses to the other, such that they will be lacking in any kind of reciprocal sociality, consideration of the other, and positive affectivity/emotionality. The self will be blocked in development at all levels, having isolated pockets of targeted behavioral plans, but not of a constructive nature. There will be an absence of caring, giving, and care-giving toward the other and a similar absence of efforts by others to provide the same, with no or few additions to the social support network. The therapist, will be met with disinterest, denial, and even outright rejection. The therapist will have to present as totally and unconditionally accepting and unperturbed by these rebuffs, while promoting some self- and other-positive regard through behavioral interventions and strategies.

Behavioral/Symptom Mental Scanning

Efforts to ascertain foci of mental/psychiatric/psychological disturbance and their origins will be hampered by the lack of ability to deploy cognitively sophisticated strategies in this regard. Inhabiting a mental space akin to the full-term newborn because of an oppressive environmental regime that precludes much growth will limit the cognitive level to the equivalent of patterned reflex activity in context with some generalization possible from core reflex systems. The person's emerging self will not be able to ascertain how behaviors/symptoms and bad habits/disorders can be traced to the deleterious environment lived. But some detection of one's lack in self-care, self-caring, and self-giving might be evident to the person, as well as the corresponding lacunae in the environment.

Therapeutic Implications

The major task of the therapist will be to serve as a constant axis of support as the patient moves from a stance of rejecting care to accepting it. The therapist functions like a surrogate care-giver manifesting caring, giving, and care-giving in the therapeutic encounter. Engagement will be difficult but possible as the nascent, emerging self develops a sense of increasing positive perceptions of the world. The patient will have become used to uncaring, abusive, neglecting, dismissive, rejecting, and even harmful discourse, at least in part, but will have had spheres with less malignant experience from which the self can perceive the world differently and generalize some positives. The organizing reflexive schemas of the patient can lead to targeted social behavior and images of the other that contain some positive elements.

Stress/Trauma Resilience/Coping

The person forced to live at the level equivalent to the full-term newborn will attempt to cope through reflexive sequences of behavior in context, but will not be able to elicit sufficiently well enough any effective caring from the environment (stress/trauma buffering and management). The nascent self will be extremely ineffective in marshalling any personal or social resources, and the other will deny, diminish, devalue, ignore, and so on, the person, even defying the person to prove claimed stress/trauma or responding with statements like "Just deal with it," while rejecting the person. The saving grace will be that the patient can engage in some caring of the self and reach out with some helping behavior to others, although always with an underlying tension and potential for retraction.

Therapeutic Strategies [the Other and Change]

Relational Co-regulation

The full-term newborn appears to enter a phase of intersubjectivity in which the experiences of body and surround are shared, and are mutually interactive and communicative. The patient who had lived an unsupportive regime at this level, and entering a therapeutic relationship, has the potential to engage similarly despite the history of psychiatric/psychological difficulties experienced. The struggle between accepting and rejecting care-giving, care, and giving from the other against the backdrop of rejecting these options offered by the other will be replayed in therapeutic session. The emerging self will have been buffeted and tested at least in part by a rejecting, dismissive, negligent, and even abusive environment, and the therapist will be caught between the tendency toward genuine interactive experience with the patient and her/his withdrawal from and rejection of same. The underlying cognitive architecture associated with these behavioral patterns concern reflex multiplication, or expanding acquired reflexive systems beyond their original context and with additions attached to them that facilitate the generalizations. Socio-affectively, the process of behaving from this cognitive framework translates into creating schemas for patterned behavior that normally adapt to different people, e.g., in infant face perception or expressing attachment-related behaviors, such as crying to solicit help. However, in patients having problems even at this level, the synchronization of reflexes, action tendencies, behaviors, socio-emotions, and physiological/arousal control mechanisms toward adaptation in context could be sufficiently compromised such that establishing any type of interactive subjectivity will be severely impaired.

Behavior/Symptom Network/Connectivity Change (Horizontal)

Some control, alteration, and even removal of unwanted behaviors/symptoms and bad habits/impairments might be possible and accrue in a positive therapeutic milieu. The person's external corrosive environment will not be total, and openings to positive change would be possible. The self is a nascent one with some room for the multi-layered, emergent, generalizing schemata organizing in its construction to adapt adequately in context, including socio-affectively. However, the nature of any gains in this regard will be limited: (a) by the reflexive nature of the self/schemata and the psychological tension about accepting/rejecting care/care-giving/giving; and (b) by whether sufficient care(giving) behavior compared to their lack has been and is being provided in the environment and any felt apperceptions that they engender about their quality.

Behavior/Symptom Growth, Deep Change (Vertical)/Constructing a More Positive Life Story

The person living issues related to getting/accepting vs. not getting/rejecting care-giving, care, and giving needs to generalize any gains along these lines toward developing a more positive integration of self-perception and other-perception. However, the environment will not be especially supportive toward this end and will be rejecting, careless, and expressing often enough a "taking" attitude more than a giving one, such that the growth initiative is curtailed. The challenge for the therapist, in the absence of evidence that the environment will change, is to foster at least some growth, nonetheless. The person might be able to move toward some positive directions with a more supportive and sensitive attitude by the therapist.

The most important aspect of the new narrative that a person who has lived at this level can aspire to relates to rebirthing. Despite the terrible experiences lived, the person is ready to entertain that life can offer something different and more positive. The self can start a growth process outside of the negative environment, and the schemas involved in self- and other-apperception can include the person needing care and beginning to accept that need. Rejecting this need, being careless about it, and being incapable of giving care, care-giving, and giving, in turn, will be part of old narratives that the person is learning to rewrite, rescript, and replace.

Consciousness, Theory of Mind, Selves, and Responsibility

The newborn solidifies developmental acquisitions and multiplies out reflex-based systems into more generalized applications. The underlying schemas are getting quite independent, but limits prevail, nonetheless. The issues confronted by the baby at this life phase relate to accepting care-giving, caring, and giving, and growing in self-components. The environment should be supportive and responsive in these regards. However, a person living negatively at this level (even if well beyond it cognitively) will be exposed to lack of care-giving, care, and giving, if not worse. There will be little room for thriving or even living with any type of sense of growth imperative. There will be a paucity of development toward higher-order functions related to consciousness, self-other differentiation, morality, and responsibility. The therapist can take advantage of any signs of growth in higher-order functions to amplify them, such as the patient expressing a will to develop one's sense of self, receive care, give care, and so on. The themes of responsibility, morality, and consciousness could be introduced as part of growth trajectories.

The Reflex Stage Sub-stage of Integration (0–1 mo): Sub-stage 5

Self and Relational Development [Initial Theoretical Elaborations]

A very brief description of the present step in Young's 25-step Neo-Eriksonian developmental model follows. It is presented again in Chap. 18, to help give a collective overview of the 25 steps in the modeling.

Emotional acts vs. mal-emotional or negative emotional acts (0 – 1 month). Early in life, babies often are emotionally content. But from early on, you were very emotional, frustrated, unhappy, and even were in rage, fear, or both. The environment (parent) was not supportive, and did not deal well with your emotions, leading you to have further emotional turmoil or trouble. As you grew, you continued to express a lot of negative emotions, or perhaps you went in the opposite direction, showing no emotions and feeling detached.

Appendix 1.5 gives the brief amount of work already done in prior publications related to the task of developing in depth the Neo-Eriksonian (sub)stage model. The next section of the chapter gives an interim summary that elaborates the contents of Appendix 1.5 with respect to the present sub-stage being considered, of the sub-stage of Reflex Stage Sub-stage of Integration.

Interim Summary

The newborn moves beyond the birthing period into an emotional world of need satisfaction or frustration. In the first month, relatively independent schemata form that can organize some targeted, context-sensitive, and adjustable patterns in behavior. They are reflexive, nonetheless, but they help organize patterns in behavior that are flexible to some extent. As they succeed in the environment to acquire targeted items, the activities so organized lead to emotional contentment/satisfaction/relief/calm. However, at the opposite extreme, frustrated efforts in activity can lead to discontentment/distress, basic agitation/rage responses, and perhaps survival-accentuating fear-type responses. The marking of targeted behavior by the nature of the primary emotions elicited suggests that the independent schema-based self of the newborn in the first month of the life is a primary emotional one, with emotions either appropriate or inappropriate in the supportive context (mal-emotional, in the non-supportive one). If intervention is required at this age, it should focus on the basic needs of the infant at the physical and socio-emotional levels.

The extreme reactions possible in the adult who has been forced to live an equivalent regime will involve either extreme emotional expression, especially of emotions related to distress/dissatisfaction and fear/rage. The person would be judged to be too heavily invested in inappropriate emotional expressions, and they would be expressed in most every moment of her/his reality. Conversely, the person might be totally devoid of emotions, behave robotically, and be considered quite detached from reality.

Self-Response to Cognitive (Mis)perception of the Other

The newborn develops basic emotions related to satisfaction/frustration, and they can be adaptive/appropriate or maladaptive/inappropriate. Part of the emotionality expressed relates to the care-giver's behavior, e.g., good sensitivity, managing the baby's emotions. However, the person forced to live in an emotional cauldron because of the inconsistent/negative dismissing/negligent, and even abusive/rejecting regime she/he might be exposed to, at least partially, for example, when the social environment is not listening/communicating, will lead to negative (e.g., frustrative) reactions. The self will express primary negative emotions overtly and haphazardly, but perhaps somewhat directed to the source of frustration in the environment.

Positive Pole in Eriksonian Development

The newborn in the first month of life expresses basic emotions related to need satisfaction/frustration. The emotions are appropriate (or not) in context, and adaptive (or maladaptive). The positive side of this challenge is expressed with emotions of quiescence/contentment and relief/relaxation of need. Continual satisfaction along these lines leads to a generally contented baby (e.g., in nursing, having other basic physiological/corporal needs attended to). This appropriate environmental (parental) behavior includes appropriate context-sensitive and contingent optimal stimulation that is neither over- nor under-stimulation. The care-giving figure continually provides warmth, appropriate care-giving, and positive development-promoting behaviors.

Negative Social-Self Working Schema

Context-responsive yet relatively independent schemata (reflex integration based) suffused with emotions in integrated patterns can be positive or negative (adaptive/appropriate vs. maladaptive/mal-emotional/inappropriate). The baby experiencing more the negative pole than the positive one in this regard will experience the social environment that is responsible for the affective distress, at least at times, as inconsistent/disquieting and even rejecting/rage-worthy. Should this regime continue, the appraisals of the other that will develop could include inappropriate (narrowly focused) rejecting and hostile attributions that merit, in turn, rejecting and hostile responses. The alternate option is to perceive the other as unsatisfying and lacking in responsivity, which will facilitate withdrawal and apathy.

Attachment, Neo-Eriksonian Development, and Therapeutic Implications [Patients and Therapy]

Patient Presentation

The newborn in the first month of life not being satisfied in basic physiological and related needs will be dissatisfied, discontented, distressed, and even frustrated/enraged. The patient who lives this type of regime on an ongoing basis will express similar sentiments, and target many people around her/him using generalized rejecting responses and with related hostile attributions. Or, the person might present as very depressed, withdrawn, and isolated. Or, the patient might gravitate between these externalizing and internalizing tendencies. Perhaps the patient will have little insight beyond that she/he is emotional, in general, or the people around him/her deserve the negative emotions expressed because of their attitudes, which might potentiate vicious circles. Note that the rejection associated with this sub-stage is different from those of earlier ones, being part and parcel of behaviors associated with extreme emotions rather than being uniquely associated with a response to apperceived abuse, lack of care, etc.

Behavioral/Symptom Mental Scanning

The patient in therapy having experienced life from the perspective of the equivalent of the newborn in the first month of life will be conditioned by the emotional turmoil accompanying that period when frustrations of basic needs dominate satisfactions in this regard. The person will be able to pick out the dominant maladaptive emotions organizing her/his life, but not understand how to change them. If conjecturing about the self, the person will see a confused morass of un-satisfactions, frustrations, blockages, unmet needs, and either emotional riot or emotional emptiness.

Therapeutic Implications

The patient at this level needs to be guided toward expressing more positive, constructive, appropriate, and adaptive emotions consistent with satisfaction, calm, relief, and a type of inner acceptance without externalized lashing out. The therapist needs to model this type of behavior her/himself as the patient gravitates to extreme emotional negativity, thereby helping to defuse, deflate, canalize, re-orient, reconstruct, and help with even the negative emotions as well as creating more positive ones. The therapist functions as an emotional regulator of sorts, using acceptance/behavioral strategies to dampen/soothe negative emotions and heighten/build positive ones.

The patient's sense of self will be packed with unruly emotional expressions governed by basic schemata integrated on the negative side of the emotional continuum. And so the therapist must work with the patient through acknowledgment/validation, listening and communicating, and pointing to different possibilities emotionally. The latter will have to be worked into the existing negative emotion-laden, socio-affective repertoire of the person. The concept of the other, at least for others who had not been part of the problem to begin with, i.e., unsupportive parents, needs to be reworked into a less volatile image without embroiled emotions. People can be viewed as emotionally stable, appropriate, contained, and constructive, rather than as rejecting/enraged or distant/withdrawn.

Stress/Trauma Resilience/Coping

The individual living at the sub-stage equivalent of reflex integration, and so with needs, emotions, nascent self, and co-regulation with others greatly jeopardized, will have difficulty in deploying any adaptive resilience and coping strategies to stress/trauma. The social environment around the person will not have been solely destructive, abusive, etc., as with prior sub-stages, in that space for listening/communicating will have been allowed, but there will not have been any fostering of independent thinking. The schemata governing behavior of the infant at this level will not have been totally reflex-controlled and will have been partially independent of reflexes, such that some flexibility in behavior will have been evident. The same will apply to the patient living the type of negative regime associated with this level, but it will be with emotions that are highly unruly/frustrated, only partly focused, and with a sense of being overwhelmed, overlooked, and without resources. The self that will be evident will seem overtaken by malfunctioning emotions, either malevolent ones or muffled ones.

Therapeutic Strategies [the Other and Change]

Relational Co-regulation

The full-term newborn begins life in a reflex, action-laden movement dynamic that is accompanied by basic satisfaction/frustrative emotions. Schemata develop that are increasingly less reliant on isolated reflexes and are patterned and targeted. In this sense, the emotions expressed and shared with the other could reflect positive or negative experiences with need satisfaction. The same applies to people as they develop, but the patient entering therapy could have a lifetime of experiences of unsatisfied needs and consequent associated negative emotional expressions. The emotions shared in this sense will not be adaptive, mutually interactive, quiescent/calming, and indicative of satisfaction. Rather, frustration will be the hallmark of expressed emotions, and will act to curtail any reciprocity in interaction. The person will be both defensive and defending against hurt. The relational co-regulation will express either an over-control in order to contain/try to regain control, or an under-control in withdrawal, isolation, and self-damping.

Behavior/Symptom Network/Connectivity Change (Horizontal)

The patient embroiled in the emotional quagmire of this sub-stage or the equivalent will express emotions reflexively, but in patterns that have somewhat of a target focus and independence from basic reflexes. The person in therapy having lived this type of regime associated with this level, but who is now better supported, might be able to make lateral gains away from a frustrated milling inchoate/rampage to a smoothing out/regulating of the emotions, at least to a degree, e.g., with some tamping down/abeyance, and even need satisfaction/resolution. There might be minimal gains toward promoting alternate emotional reactions to frustration/stress/trauma. That the environment had not been uniformly abusive and rejecting will help. The therapist can help create alternate scenarios for the patient, but needs to work especially on frustration control and means of need satisfaction. The self can be constructed as one involving primary positive, sustained, connecting emotions instead of negative ones that instill rejection, fear, dismissal, and so on.

Behavior/Symptom Growth, Deep Change (Vertical)/Constructing a More Positive Life Story

As always, the therapist needs to be aware of the patient's current psychological state, its deep injuries, and what is needed not only for horizontal change away from present behavioral (and emotional) patterns but also toward qualitatively improved actions, appraisals, and problem solving strategies. The person living in a life equivalent to the sub-stage of reflex coordinations will have independent schemata and associated emotions to work with, and they can be facilitated toward upgrading and transforming to sensori-motor type schemata coordinations. This might allow, for example, some juxtaposition of frustration and satisfaction in emotional reactions, with growth eventually resulting through their comparison and view of their differential advantages and disadvantages. The negative emotional saturation evident in people forced to live at in this sub-stage because of regimes experienced might thus gravitate to more adaptive emotions and prepare further growth beyond emotionality.

The patient who is living an emotional life of frustration and need dissatisfaction can learn to tell an alternate story about the self that one's emotions can be more positive/constructive, indicative of satisfaction/contentment, and facilitative of interactions with others on a more controlled emotional plane. Emotions do not have to be seething, scalding, scathing, simmering, out of context, maladaptive, and so on, but can be appropriate, adaptive, showing contextual flexibility (even if that can be constrained by the basic schema structure underlying the emotions), and serving personally helpful social ends (to the limited degree possible at this level).

Consciousness, Theory of Mind, Selves, and Responsibility

The newborn births into an emotional world, and satisfaction relative to frustration should express her/his benchmark experience. The full-term newborn self begins as a primary emotional one, with underlying independent schemes permitting adaptive, context-appropriate emotions. However, a person forced to live at this level will be emotionally charged and will retreat into expressive anger or into withdrawn depression, among other related emotions. The self will have difficulty growing beyond these bounds, with the sense of other similarly constrained. There will be little room for any realistic awareness/consciousness and acting constructively for self and other at the level of morality/responsibility. The therapist can encourage moving out of the emotional morass into some semblance of emotional regulation, toward improving the patient's personal life, sense of self, and adaptive actions in the world. This attitude might help foster acting outside of the most primitive emotions and increase minimally apperceptions of self and other outside of images of roiling or frozen/absent emotions, whether internally- or externally-directed.

References

Blatt, S. J. (2008). *Polarities of experience: Relatedness and self-definition in personality development, psychopathology, and the therapeutic process*. Washington, DC: American Psychological Association.

Chambliss, B. (2018). The mind-body problem. *WIREs Cognitive Science*, e1463. https://doi.org/10.1002/wcs.1463

Friston, K. (2018). Am I self-conscious? (Or does self-organization entail self-consciousness?). *Frontiers in Psychology, 9*, 579. https://doi.org/10.1189/fpsyg.2018.00579

Graham, J., & Haidt, J. (2012). Sacred values and evil adversaries: A moral foundations approach. In M. Mikulincer & P. R. Shaver (Eds.), *The social psychology of morality: Exploring the causes of good and evil* (pp. 11–31). Washington, DC: American Psychological Association.

Parma, V., Brasselet, R., Zoia, S., Bulgheroni, M., & Castiello, U. (2017). The origin of human handedness and its role in pre-birth motor control. *Scientific Reports, 7*, 16804. https://doi.org/10.1038/s41598-017-16827-y

Young, G. (2011). *Development and causality: Neo-Piagetian perspectives*. New York: Springer Science + Business Media.

Young, G. (2015). Causality in psychiatry: A hybrid symptom network construct model. *Frontiers in Psychiatry, 6*, 164. https://doi.org/10.3389/fpsyt.2015.00164

Young, G. (2016). *Unifying causality and psychology: Being, brain and behavior*. Cham, Switzerland: Springer.

Chapter 14
The Sensori-motor-Based Sub-stages: Pre-participatory Socio-affects

Abstract The second of the five stages in the current Neo-Piagetian/Neo-Eriksonian model concerns the infancy period. Development in this stage requires much care-giver support, and the first year of the period has been described by Erikson as involving Trust vs. Mistrust. Also, the second year was described by him as involving the development of Autonomy vs. Doubt. The present model consists of five sub-stages within each stage, and the task was to place the two Eriksonian stages in infancy at the appropriate level or sub-stage of the current model. The trust phase seemed a good fit with the second sub-stage, which covers 4 to 8 months. The Autonomy phase appeared consistent with the characteristics of the fourth sub-stage among the five in this stage, or the one at 12 to 18 months. This left the author with the task of creating three new Neo-Eriksonian sub-stages for the infancy period. Considering the Neo-Piagetian sub-stages with which each is deemed associated, and taking into account their characteristics, the first, third, and fifth sub-stages in the present model for the infancy period were considered to involve dyadic, sociability, and interdigitational acts, respectively, as well as their corresponding negative poles. The three added sub-stages fit into the trust/autonomy sequence but add research-based sub-stages to complement them. Note that the three sub-stages involved denote increasing social interactive skills. It is noteworthy that placement of the active attachment process in the sub-stage at 8 to 12 months follows the one of Trust vs. Mistrust. That is, in the present model, the trust and attachment constructs are not synonymous. Also, note the pattern of the two Eriksonian stages fitting in sub-stages 2 and 4 of the five sub-stages, with the three new sub-stages that are involved fitting in sub-stages 1, 3, and 5. The same pattern is found for the subsequent four stages. It would appear that, intuitively, Erikson had emphasized only two of the five sub-stages within each of the stages of the current model, and they always concerned the second and fourth of the five sub-stages involved in each stage.

G. Young, *Causality and Development*,
https://doi.org/10.1007/978-3-030-02493-2_14

The Sensori-motor Stage Sub-stage of Coordination (1–4 Months): Sub-stage 6

Self and Relational Development [Initial Theoretical Elaborations]

By way of introduction, the following presents a very brief description of the present step in Young's 25-step Neo-Eriksonian developmental model. It is presented again at the end of Chap. 18 along with the other 24 steps in the model, to help give a collective overview of the 25 steps in the model.

Dyadic acts vs. dys-dyadic or poor interaction acts (1–4 months). Normally, the growing infant is learning how to interact the right way with people. But even then you experienced a non-supportive environment (parent). It involved too much control, domination, and manipulation. The result was that, as you grew, you did not learn to interact with people the right way. You were not warm or sensitive. Instead, you were clumsy and confused socially, and could withdraw in silence. Or, perhaps you were angry and rejected people.

Appendix 2.1 gives the brief amount of work already done in prior publications related to the task of developing in depth the Neo-Eriksonian (sub)stage model. The next section of the chapter gives an interim summary that elaborates the contents of Appendix 2.1 with respect to the present sub-stage being considered, of the sub-stage of Sensori-motor Stage Sub-stage of Coordination.

Interim Summary

The infant who develops into the first and fourth month of life has survived the most difficult prenatal, birth, and early postnatal periods. The infant of this age moves out of behavior conditioned only by reflex and reflex patterns, what Piaget referred to as the sub-stage of Reflex Exercises, into a clear sensori-motor stage. The schemas developed after birth that were mostly reflex-based, albeit quite context-sensitive, adjusting, and flexible, with target orientation success possible, now begin to coordinate, with the classic example being visually directed reaching. The reflex-base in behavior begins to acquire reflex independence to the point that the coordinative schemas can flexibly reconfigure, as required. However, there are limits in the sense that the schemes lack a clear primary/secondary or dominant/subordinate relationship, especially as the sub-stage initiates, e.g., visually directed reaching lacks the required smoothness and target success.

The person forced to live at the equivalent of this sub-stage due to environmental forces will suffer extensive psychological repercussions, although not as severe as the associations with living abuse, torture, etc., as in the prior sub-stages. The person exposed to a regime akin to not being allowed to grow psychologically beyond the early infancy period will experience domination, subjugation, control, manipulation, authoritarianism, repression, and so on, with little room for any adaptive response in the silencing/sterilization that the regime is meant to encourage. However, as with other sub-stages, as we have seen, there could be an externalizing response aside from an internalizing one, and in this case there might be some organization to it, so that it can be called revolution instead of haphazard rejection or rage. That said, the internalizing response should be a major outcome, for example, in passively receiving an external monologue instead of engaging in active dialogue and in passively expressing a dis-coordinated social interaction instead of an active reciprocity in dyadic interaction.

The underlying cognitive acquisition facilitative of developmental progress in the very young infant involves independent schema coordinations and, therefore, at the social level, the very young infant can coordinate simple back and forth social exchanges with the care-giver. The smiling cooing infant at this age creates joy in any recipient and appears to experience an internal joy that is communicated to the other, creating positive or virtuous cycles of dyadic exchange. The schema coordinations are not completely organized, being juxtapositions that are partially organized through the holding frame of the adult involved. Nevertheless, the growing self can now be conceived as an interacting, socially coordinative one, although only at an initial level of complexity that can readily dissolve into poor synchrony in social exchanges that are lacking contingency, warmth, etc., and that seem clumsy and confused, while retreating into silence, too.

In terms of the person forced to live at this level, the social dialogue with the other will be similarly dysfunctional, prematurely aborted, filled with poor coordination, be confused and create confusion, and so on. The control by the other of the person could involve competition/imposition instead of outright dominance/subjugation/repression/sterilization, and the silence or revolution potentiated in reaction will characterize or echo in any of the dyadic interactions involved.

The emergence of sensori-motor skills, as in the coordinations of this sub-stage, is accompanied by the typical over-exuberance in the application of newly acquired capacities as development proceeds. In this case, the incipient social impulses might be more dys-dyadic and poorly fitting in context even with a sound environmental support. The coordinations might be uncoordinated attempts. However, with a supportive environment modulating the infant's initial social impulses, the trials attempted will be refined as development proceeds and they will end up better adapted.

Per usual, without the heady energy of applying newly developing skills of any sort, the honing and improvement in the skills will not take place as well as could happen. Should the infant not receive adequate support as she/he develops in the first months of life, timely intervention will help. The intervention with the caregiver should focus on providing basic care, being sensitive, contingent, affectionate, and so on, given the importance of this period in establishing care-giving behavior throughout the first year of life that promotes secure attachment and all that this acquisition portends in the positive sense for development.

Self-Response to Cognitive (Mis)perception of the Other

As the newborn moves out of the birthing period, she/he is adding to the emotional repertoire that is developing an increasing dyadic social interaction/dialogue skill. The very young infant becomes more adept in co-relational interactive synchrony, based on developing schema coordination underpinnings applied socially. The danger in this age period relates to receiving inadequate dyadic responsivity and dyadic facilitation, to the point of dominance, wanton disregard, and total asynchrony. The same danger applies to individuals forced to live a regime equivalent to this sub-stage level. Due to the undercutting in the growth of the self (referred to as the incipient interactive, inter-coordinative, and social self in the case of the very young infant), the self of the maltreated person at this level responds with trying to absorb the dis-coordinate, controlling messages in the environment, but the person cannot do much more and wilts in any attempt to do so. The externalizing pole in this reaction will involve a self saturated in anger and revolution to the degree possible in the circumstances.

Positive Pole in Eriksonian Development

The very young infant is underwritten by sensori-motor schemas that can coordinate to allow for dyadic interchange. Interaction reaches a point that it is synchronous, inter-coordinated, and mutually engaging, but with the adult functioning as a guiding frame. The danger of dys-dyadic interactions that are uncoordinated is alleviated by attentive, responsive, contingent, and warm care-giving. The very young infant expresses positive emotions at the core and a social exchange immersed in positive emotions (e.g., joy, delight).

Negative Social-Self Working Schema

The very young infant confronted by an environment that does not respond adequately to her/his need for socially coordinative interaction will entrain a pattern of social responsiveness that is inconsistent, uncertain, asynchronous, and stressful. The behavior of the care-giving adult will lead to creation of sensori-motor schemas of the other at this level that include dis-coordinating, insecuring behavior specific to the person, with a strong potential to generalize. Social behavior will be networked cognitively in the sensori-motor schemas as monological, or disjoined dyadically, and lacking in smooth, dyadic communication, so expressing dys-dyadic upheavals in functioning. There is no room for self-agency allowed by the other, through the constant control strategies used by the other. The domination experienced leads to a self replete with dis-coordinated expressions and linkages in inefficient interactive communication procedures.

Attachment, Neo-Eriksonian Development, and Therapeutic Implications [Patients and Therapy]

Patient Presentation

Patients encumbered by relational difficulties at this level will have difficulties involving independent sensori-motor schemas. They will experience difficulties in establishing consistent exchanges in social interaction and will revert either to social isolation and one-way communications or to constantly disrupted maladroit attempts at continued social dialogue. The social self will appear stunted and stifled, and will manifest social disengagement strategies alternating with futile engagement strategies. This will lead to either social exasperation and failure to engage or to hypersociality but in an unregulated, spatially, and temporally misplaced way. The other will be confusing to the person, and so the other might elicit social wariness/avoidance in the person. The person will have lived a dominating, sterilizing, subjugating regime, and might try to create some semblance of social normalcy using strategies that, ironically, repeat the rejected experience. However, others will reject this approach, unless their social agenda is similar for their own reasons, leading to asocial asynchrony to the extreme.

Behavioral/Symptom Mental Scanning

The person who has lived a regime equivalent to the one of the very young infant in the sensori-motor coordination sub-stage will search adaptive social skills that might have developed, but will find a paucity of them, or impoverished ones. People at this level will feel either that they have been abandoned socially because of how the other reacts to their insufficient social efforts or that the other reacts with controlling efforts, taking advantage of them, and so on. The person will be blind to the proximal reasons for her/his social behavior, i.e., the specific social skills involved are lacking, but she/he might have a diffuse understanding of the social regime lived and its general effects, e.g., being dominated and not knowing how to function socially.

Therapeutic Implications

The therapist working with patients who express behavior consistent with this level needs to keep in focus the nature of the sub-stage involved – it concerns the development of smooth social dyadic exchanges that are dialogical, interactive, coordinative, synchronized, and primarily with social intentions to social objects. However, as yet, it does not concern social means and ends as secondary to cognitive (sensori-motor) ones; that is, the cognitive base for this sub-stage that gives it its social characteristics does not yet include purposive intent right from the start of an action. Normally, the self is incipiently social, while the other is socially facilitative and framing, or as much as a genuine reciprocal social partner that can be permitted at this level of sophistication. The person in therapy might be far removed from this ideal social presentation and embedded in a social manifold that is devoid of genuine dialogue, avoidant or incapable of such, and replete with opposite tendencies of overruling the other, speaking with only wanting to be listened to and expecting total control while psychologically blanking out of the other and without any or much joy in the interaction being expressed in either party (self and other). The therapist will assume the worst in the regime lived by the person, starting from early in life, with excessive parental control/domination, subjugation/repression, and self-sabotage being quite marked. The therapist will function as an appropriate, normative, and sensitive social other who will indicate different social skills that could work in obtained desired social goals. The therapist will try to create a sense of the other that is not objectified as a person distant and out there but that, rather, has some subjective status as an independent party with her/his own social goals and needs that need respect. The theme of dominance will emerge continually in session, as either a major aspect of the patient's social function or through the contrary one of submission.

Stress/Trauma Resilience/Coping

The sub-stage of sensori-motor coordination that is typical of the well-developing young infant brings advantages relative to the prior reflex-based sub-stages with respect to stress/trauma resilience/coping. Whereas the person living a regime equivalent to any reflex-based sub-stage in the present model will have very limited resilience and stress/trauma coping mechanisms, the person living a regime that is more like the present one and not an infant's initial sensori-motor ones will have some potential stress/trauma adaptation. The environment might have been a dominating one that sterilizes/controls, but the person still can find some dyadic and general social resource strategies by adapting to that regime, accepting it while trying to otherwise move forward, and learning basic social skills even if warped by the environmental subjugation/oppression. That said, more likely than not, social skills and social resource recruitment will be highly limited in effectiveness, and the person will flounder socially more than anything else when subject to stress/trauma. The person, therefore, might resort to excessive internalizing/social isolation reactions, denial/indifference to the people who could help with stress/trauma, or open rejection of any social entity, in a backlash/displacement phenomenon. The language used might be the one often heard, e.g., "You'd better…".

Therapeutic Strategies [the Other and Change]

Relational Co-regulation

The newborn in the first months of life normally spends time in interactive co-regulation with the care-giver, although the care-giver serves as a major scaffolding element in this regard. Coordinated social dances might take place at fractional second intervals, with physiologies somewhat interlocked and mutually entrained. The coordinative sensori-motor schemas involved underlie an increasing dialogic socializing, but with the process being parentally monitored and directed. But the newborn can shape the parent, too, to some extent, through social "invitations" in behavior, although with limits in the behavior and required accommodations called for from the adult. However, the young infant who is incapable of this level of social sophistication will have her/his incipient social self quite curtailed, negatively canalized, and increasingly disorganized toward either excessive internalizing or externalizing reactions and associated insecure-related sentiments, as well.

The patient who enters the office with a presentation analogous to this one will have lived a regime not unlike the one suggested for the infant at this age. The environment will be oppressive/repressive, asynchronous with the person, and control-focused. The person generally will relate to the social environment not unlike the way the very young infant relates to her/his equivalent one. In any way examined, the social orientation of the patient will be considered clumsy, dysfunctional, and lacking in interactive skills.

Behavior/Symptom Network/Connectivity Change (Horizontal)

The patient with deficient social skills, even in terms of creating basic chains of dialogical, interactive, coordinated social dyadic communication, and reciprocity, will experience social frustration, insecurity, rejection, and the response of submission, with the countering, protective response of domination, in turn, also possible. The person will be working with basic sensori-motor processes that have become the focus of social interaction, so social efforts will be deficient in integrating verbal and nonverbal communication in effective goal-oriented chaining, and so on. The person will gravitate to more primitive social behaviors in any move to improve socially, with the sensori-motor base crucial in this regard. Therefore, interactions that are coordinated will be possible, but they will be more physical than linguistically or abstractly communicative. Depending on the ultimate socio-affective level attained despite early, lifelong, or later regimes detrimental to the person, in terms of social skill facilitation, the social skills that could improve at this level will be organized sensori-motorically with words as subsidiary accompaniments to the social goals established. The therapist can promote this type of social engagement, and with more advanced social skills distantly in the offing. The person at this level can make lateral moves to control some adverse social habits and replace them with more productive ones, but they will be social chain/dyadic interchange bouts of a short duration with little end-goal focus.

Behavior/Symptom Growth, Deep Change (Vertical)/Constructing a More Positive Life Story

A person living a regime of poor social exchange skills will be able to learn some social skills through effective therapy. The person will be oriented to develop practical sequences in basic social skills in conjunction with the other's social behavior. The person will learn about the dyadic complementarity of social relations and how to control dys-dyadic, dysfunctional, and anti-dialogical social behavior. However, this will happen ever so slowly and it will require much therapeutic patience. Moreover, it will be greatly compromised, if not annulled, should the person still be living in a regime of domination and subjugation. The therapist can aim for consolidation of some of the learned skills to negotiate better the social quagmires and traps, and the person might then grow toward gravitating to the learned skills while inhibiting the ones used previously that had been the expression of the negatively framed incipient social self.

The patient living at the level of maladaptive dyadic interchanges in social coordinations will have learned to devalue the social component of the self, be despondent or irritable, in turn, and be quite confused how to change, assuming that that is even an objective. The therapist can take advantage of the basic social coordinations possible by way of the underpinning cognitive (sensori-motor) coordinations in the behavior of the person to help transform the story told by the person to being capable of basic social coordinations instead of having only poor or absent social coordinations.

Consciousness, Theory of Mind, Selves, and Responsibility

The very young infant entering the first sensori-motor sub-stage goes beyond the reflex-predominant lifestyle that she/he had been living into one in which cognitive schemas are fully reflex independent, coordinated (e.g., allowing self/other dyadic/dialogic social interchange), and incipient social in a positive and joyful sense, assuming the environment is conducive toward promoting these outcomes. The level of consciousness shifts out of the nonconscious to the preconscious (think attentional focus). The theory of mind of the infant does not yet exist in the framework of the representational skills of the child yet is intersubjective because the cognitive apparatus of the infant allows for the growth of sensori-motor-driven purposeful behavior, even socially. Hence, some perspective taking is possible in terms of bodily mediated activity.

In terms of the first sub-stage of the sensori-motor period, this means that these advanced human attributions have taken on a new foothold in which some initiating capacities and skills in these regards can be coordinated either among themselves or in conjunction with the other. This is most clear in the research on early developing morality even in the first few months of life, as demonstrated by young babies preferring helpful characters relative to others (Bloom, 2016). The self-definitional self transforms from one uniquely physiologically (need-)based to one that relates to safety/care, etc. The self in its relatedness guises has the same foci. Morality cannot develop so early in any overt altruistic sense, but there are relevant precursors, and the foundational moral motives also concern care and social linking. As for the issue of developing the penultimate human characteristic – that of responsibilities, or taking on multiple responsibilities at each second of our lives, without complaint, relapse, or otherwise abdicating our responsibilities – the very young infant is developing recursively a response-able to the responsivity of the social other (and so is being responsible).

The person forced to live at this level will be experiencing a dominating/subjugating controlling regime that attempts to sterilize it or create an emptiness in which the controlling entities involved can dictate their terms onto the psyche of the person. There will be no room for helpful social connections to form with the other and her/his activities. The cognitive apparatus will be lacking in these regards, anyway (i.e., about embodied mentalizing/intentionality). Therefore, the social skills needed for social engagement that would help will be severely compromised. Thus, there will be little place for anything more than minimal survival-related awareness/attention, consciousness, and goal-oriented and embodied mentalization. There will be an absence of considering safety as primary and care as natural and, as well, moral altruism or taking any responsibility. However, the sensitive and tuned therapist will undertake to generate positive movements toward these ends by attaching them to more basic social skills being learned as possible long-term, desired additions socially. The opening to that development will close repeatedly as the patient advances and retreats developmentally through the sessions. Psychological maturity or completeness could be emphasized as the birthright of all humans, no matter what their beginnings or current psychological state.

The Sensori-motor Stage Sub-stage of Hierarchization (4–8 Months): Sub-stage 7

Self and Relational Development [Initial Theoretical Elaborations]

A very brief description of the present step in Young's 25-step Neo-Eriksonian developmental model follows. It is presented again in Chap. 18, to help give a collective overview of the 25 steps in the modeling.

Trust acts vs. mistrust acts (4–8 months). In the first year of life, normally the infant develops a sense of trust or confidence in people. But if the environment (parent) is not supportive, the person might not be able to trust people and create any close relationships. If this happened to you, also you might feel down and without purpose, and be passive or suspicious. Perhaps you became angry inside, too. Or, instead perhaps you trusted blindly anybody else (and were taken advantage of by them).

Appendix 2.2 gives the brief amount of work already done in prior publications related to the task of developing in depth the Neo-Eriksonian (sub)stage model. The next section of the chapter gives an interim summary that elaborates the contents of Appendix 2.2 with respect to the present sub-stage being considered, of the sub-stage of Sensori-motor Stage Sub-stage of Hierarchization.

Interim Summary

The present Neo-Piagetian/Neo-Eriksonian stage/sub-stage lifespan developmental model consists of 25 steps in each of the cognitive and socio-affective sequences involved. The Neo-Piagetian sequence in the present model sticks quite closely to Piaget's original formulation of the stages in cognitive development and the sub-stages evident in them, at least for the first sensori-motor stage (he did not describe much of sub-stages in the other stages). In contrast to the present model hewing relatively closely to Piaget's vision of cognitive development stages and sub-stages in the infancy period, the same cannot be said for the Neo-Eriksonian component of the present model as it pertains to the original Eriksonian model. For example, Erikson never described sub-stages but they are included in the present Neo-Eriksonian model as extrapolations from the parallel cognitive Neo-Piagetian model. Erikson gave an 8-stage sequence in his approach to lifespan development, whereas the current model consists of 25 (5 stages x 5 sub-stages) steps. Therefore, the current Neo-Eriksonian model has added 17 steps to the original eight Eriksonian steps in development. Moreover, in describing them, I added many different types of topics so that the model is very expansive, given the present goal of wanting to apply the model therapeutically. Thus, I asked, where in the 25-step Neo-Eriksonian sequence being proposed do the original 8 Erikson stages fit and, further, should the original 8 stages be described in the present model exactly as Erikson had described them?

About the question of the developmental epoch in which each of Erikson's 8 stages fit in the current 25-step Neo-Eriksonian sequence, so far, I have described 6 early developmental steps in which Erikson's original 8 stages do not fit. But now, in the seventh one of the current model, I arrive at placing Erikson's first stage of Trust vs. Mistrust within its ambit. This illustrates both the comprehensive nature of the current model, and the lacunae in Erikson's. There are 17 missing steps in Erikson's model relative to my own after considering his eight stages, and the first of his eight stages fits only the seventh step in the current model. To conclude, a fulsome account of the socio-affective side of development was started beautifully by Erikson. However, the current model has greatly amplified it, with many more steps, in particular, including even before the first one in his series is even considered.

About the particular sub-stage at the seventh level in the current model, it is built on the cognitive acquisition of sensori-motor schema hierarchizations. As with all the steps of the current 25-step model, the understanding of the socio-affective acquisitions involved is conditioned by examination of and extrapolation from the cognitive acquisition at its base. The placement of Trust vs. Mistrust at this present juncture fits here because the cognitive foundation for this socio-affective acquisition can be found in sensori-motor hierarchizations, as explained next.

The developmental age of the acquisition of Eriksonian Trust vs. Mistrust is keyed to the first year of life, in particular. The qualities of this first stage of life in Erikson's model speak to the qualities of the sensori-motor hierarchization sub-stage in the present Neo-Piagetian model. Whereas the latter cognitive sub-stage is conditioned by reflex-independent schemas that can coordinate in a dominant-subordinate relationship, as in rattle shaking to elicit a cacophony of sound, the Eriksonian stage of Trust vs. Mistrust bears the same qualities associated with this cognitive sub-stage. For example, developing a sense of trust in the care-giver entails coordinating self and other sensori-motor embodiments into a hierarchical relationship in which the self in relation to the other is established as dominant in need satisfaction, emotional regulation, dyadic interaction and providing constant and reliable warmth/comfort. The other becomes a source of confidence and mutual (co)regulation in all these regards.

The sensori-motor hierarchical schemas at work in this sub-stage allow for purposeful, agentic, context-relevant, coordinated activity by the infant, but only once a goal is discovered accidentally in the context. This illustrates that the care-giver functions as the primary interstitial glue to the coordinated trust that develops and also the infant-care-giver trust-creation process.

At the same time, a sense of trust might not develop in the infant, for example, due to the care-giver not be able or even wanting to create mutuality at this level. The coordination between the infant and care-giver will not include delight-inducing and delight-responsive behaviors; rather, the infant will be let down in initiatives having these emotional adjuncts and experience a sense of failure in the effort undertaken and a sense of mistrust (lack of faith) in the lack of social reciprocity and the undermining of trust/confidence/faith by the other. The infant might not be able to trust anyone or create close relationships. As the child grows, she/he will be socially lethargic/passive or paranoid/suspicious, and angry, too. Trust could go the other way and be blindly given (setting the stage for being taken advantage of).

The infants' sense of agency will be ridden with doubt, uncertainty in taking initiative, purposeless behavior, and disturbances in having confidence that any initiative in end-focused, goal activities will achieve the desired outcomes. The infant at this age is expanding the possible range of emotional responses to these frustrations, and they will vary across types of fretting, feeling low, fear, and crankiness/irritability. The infant might appear to be accelerating attempts to gain control of inconsistent or negative reactions or, to the contrary, resign from any such attempts, ceding control and not engaging in any efforts to gain it, in a passivity reaction.

The older person subject to a type of social regime that approximates that of the young infant confronting mistrust rather than trust will be exposed to the other behaving with manipulation, subversion, undermining, and over-control in an attempt to counter, contradict, compete, and otherwise discourage a constructive trust-building relationship. The person might react with the range of emotions indicated above, and direct them into haphazard revolutionary reactions that could transfigure into directed ones.

Note that the account of the stage of Trust vs. Mistrust in Erikson's model is truncated in its present adoption. In Erikson's model, the age span for which the stage of Trust vs. Mistrust is included involves the whole infancy period. However, in the present model, Trust vs. Mistrust is placed in a much narrower time frame of the midyear of the first year of life (i.e., approx. 4–8 months), given the goal of the present work to fill in missing steps in development both before and after the placement of any one of the original 8 stages of Erikson's model in the 25 steps of the present model.

Note that even the normally developing infant in a supportive environment might have issues with Trust vs. Mistrust. Erikson had maintained that each of the stages in his model represent an opposition that presents a continual dialectic between the poles of the stage involved for any growing person, no matter what the environment. For example, in the present case, developing too much trust without any countervailing mistrust will be counterproductive. The infant might indiscriminately enter any relationship with a trusting attitude, e.g., to overindulgent, imposing strangers. The parent must buffer the child and shape appropriate attitudes to different people, as might be required by the particular person and context. Interventions that might be required in this phase of the life of the infant and parent should be aimed at building trust in the infant through teaching trust-eliciting behaviors in the parent.

The extreme dangers related to trust that might develop in the adult who has lived a regime related to mistrust could swing toward being too trustful or too mistrustful; that is, the person might have indiscriminate trust in anyone, even to the point of placing herself/himself in danger, being taken advantage of sexually abused, etc. Or, to the contrary, the person might never trust anyone, even if no danger is evident. The person might be always on guard, suspicious, paranoid, etc., in relation to any other.

Self-Response to Cognitive (Mis)perception of the Other

The infant in the midyear period enters the primary Eriksonian stage of Trust vs. Mistrust; and the social self that is developing is agentic, initiatory, and goal-focused (at least for accidentally discovered end points that are repeated for their "spectacles," as in repeated rattle shaking, which takes the form of delightful games with the tuned care-giver). The independent schema hierarchies formed in this embodied (sensori-motor) interplay assure continuity in the mutual regulation afforded, thereby breeding trust/happiness more so than distrust/no trust.

Care-givers could breed the opposite reactions, engendering profound mistrust instead of trust. They will entertain the care of the child with personal agendas rather than being able to partake in genuine reciprocity (and with their role being predominant in the exchanges toward this end). The person who has lived a lack of support akin to what the midyear infant lives in negative contexts will develop deep inabilities to relate to others with trust/confidence, will interact with personal agendas, and so on. Distrust/mistrust/no trust will predominate. The self will have a core that lacks in initiative, lacks in purpose, expresses goals that are not mutually regulative/reciprocal and that are without joy/delight/faith. The person will be prone to engage in the type of behavior received – manipulative control, undermining of the self, sabotage/countering/contradiction, and so on – with resultant emotions being either internalizing (sad, dissociated, not trusting) or externalizing (irritable, reactive/revolution).

Positive Pole in Eriksonian Development

The infant at midyear in the first year of life reaches an apex, arriving at the Eriksonian socio-affective stage referred to as Trust vs. Mistrust. Trust is encouraged by a care-giver who supplies a constant supportive presence that caters to all the physiological, emotional, and cognitive/curiosity needs of the growing infant. This type of care-giver serves to develop a generalized confidence/faith in the environment, and a similar socio-affective resonance with the care-giver. The infant immersed in this trust-promoting care becomes more personally agentic, happy, socially inter-coordinated, and socially contextually responsive.

Negative Social-Self Working Schema

The infant in the midyear of the first year who is exposed to care-giving that is the opposite of being constantly positive/responsive and reliable, with associated warmth/trust-promoting behaviors, etc., will develop a social-self working schema that veers away from the positive to the negative. The social self at this age should be quite social in initiations/agency and goal focus/context sensitivity. However, insensitive and inconsistent care-giving will inhibit social initiative in behavior, serve in the reduction of a positive sense of personal agency, create social goal abandonment, and instill a general fear/mistrust. The hierarchized sensori-motor schemas at the basis of the cognitive and social-affective acquisitions at this sub-stage will lack constant, reliable positive social elements as dominant over associated negative ones, leading to social disjunction/mistrust.

Attachment, Neo-Eriksonian Development, and Therapeutic Implications [Patients and Therapy]

Patient Presentation

The person living a regime in which basic trusting processes in the social other have been compromised to the point of the person becoming very distrustful will have difficulties generally in social engagement. The other will seem a distant object that is unattainable or a rejecting one that removes the possibility of any social engagement. The person will either retreat into a shell protecting against the hurt of mistrust/social removal/rejection or will adopt a harsh, bristling shell as a preengagement defense in any social engagements that might materialize. At worst, the person will be extremely paranoid about any social engagement, the reasons the other might have in wanting them, and the possible outcomes of any social engagement entered into. The person might be either over- or under-initiatory socially, being hyper-controlling in initiations or hyper-avoidant of them. Either way, instead of mutuality in self-other engagements arranged in an optimal hierarchization of self-other behavior, the goal attitude of the self (e.g., hyper-control socially) or the attitude toward other (e.g., hyper-abandonment socially) will express a deviant dominant-subordinate (submission) relationship.

Behavioral/Symptom Mental Scanning

The person who has lived a regime devoid of trust will be aware of the psychic void or psychological emptiness that she/he is feeling and, if the person has created a socially opposite attitude of mistrusting people, will be aware of the effort to maintain a protective social distance from others. However, as with the infant who is not aware of trust, per se, because of developing in an unhealthy social environment in the midpoint of the first year of life, the adult might not be able to pinpoint the issue of Trust vs. Mistrust as the crux of the empty personal feelings and protective social-distance maintaining behaviors. As for the damaging effects of social controls that have been harshly visited on the person, manipulations, etc., the person might understand these pernicious behaviors in the other. However, the person might not be capable of self-analyzing the same behaviors in herself/himself if they had been adopted. It will be easier for the person to see her/his social passivity, if that is what had been adopted by the person.

Therapeutic Implications

The patient who is expressing symptoms at this level of Trust vs. Mistrust will be mistrustful and have little faith in social relations, generally, and in specific relationships that might be involved, as well. There might be a morbid fear of attempting social initiative and search for social reciprocity because of past failures in this regard stretching back a long way, and perhaps even to the care-giving environment in the first year of life. Issues of seeking and giving constant and reliable social support and receiving the same will predominate. The social self will be withered and riven with social apathy or misdirected and misunderstood social initiative, with part of the difficulties therein relating to a lack of clear social goals. The major negative emotions (internalizing, externalizing ones) will be evident. Typically, the social encounter will be brief, irregular, and with alterations in dominance and submission, eventually gravitating more to one of dominance/externalizing emotions (e.g., hyper-control, anger, hyper-engaging socially) or submissive/internalizing ones (e.g., abandoning control, low mood, succumbing socially). The therapist needs to consider the underlying cognitive control structure involved of hierarchical sensori-motor schemas (or their equivalent for the adult expressing mistrust). That is, at the base, the behavior being expressed will be incapable of moving out of some sort of dominance/over-control or submission/under-control dynamic because of the experiences lived through that had been reflective of an absence of social and emotional stability/trust promotion.

Stress/Trauma Resilience/Coping

A person incapable of establishing trust will have her/his resilience and coping mechanisms to stress/trauma severely compromised. This will happen because the required social skills, sense of security engendered by having established trusting relationships, and the reciprocal mutuality in social initiating and letting social initiating take place will not manifest. The mistrustful axis in the trust/mistrust opposition will predominate, as happens with young infants facing similar trust-denying regimes. The behaviors encountered will be controlling, subverting, and contradictory to the normal social interweaving that should be taking place through hierarchized schema organization.

In this social environment, and given its cognitive underpinnings at this level, the individual, whether in the first year of life and living a poor trust-building period or for the older person who has had that growth potential paralyzed by an equivalent regime, will not have the personal or social skills/resources to deal effectively with stress/trauma. There will be either internalizing or externalizing behavioral/emotional reactions, or both, for example, in confused and confusing alteration in stress/trauma response, such as social abhorrence then social aggression.

Therapeutic Strategies [the Other and Change]

Relational Co-regulation

The young infant in the Trust vs. Mistrust phase normally develops a sense of confidence in the relationship with the care-giver, having experienced constant, reliable, and supportive care. The hierarchical sensori-motor schemas allow for organization of self and other in mutually regulated interactions, with both leading/

dominating and engaging/enjoying in the "game." However, in care-giving environments that discourage this type of social reciprocity, the social self has little faith, mistrusts, recedes from social initiation, or otherwise disengages, as in fear or anger. Comparable to the infant, the adult forced to live a regime like this one fails to develop social trust and does not become socially trustworthy. The fertile ground for shared engrossment in social activity is rendered barren. Social agency is expressed for personal ends rather than mutual ones.

The social environment will have been and/or will continue to be manipulative/controlling or undermining/subverting. The relational co-regulation will be profoundly disturbed not by the initiatory self of the person but by the disturbed initiations or their absence in the other. Without proper relational co-regulation, interaction frequencies will evaporate if not dissipate, leaving a social void that the person might be desperately seeking to fill. The therapist will have to start by laying the seeds of building trust.

Behavior/Symptom Network/Connectivity Change (Horizontal)

The patient at this level of confronting basic trust issues will behave with a panoply of nonproductive social behaviors inimical to creating social confidence in the other and to eliciting trust-creation behaviors from the other. The lack in trust/confidence/faith will be marked by mistrust in the other, who will be seen as someone who is not dependable/reliable, except perhaps momentarily for personal/selfish ends. The other will be negatively characterized in the center of a social schema as a nonaccepting, manipulative entity whose social initiations cannot be read at face value. The person's social self will always be apprehensive about the other and leery, losing spontaneous initiative and also the opportunity to create social reciprocity/mutuality underwritten by knowledge of having constant social support from the other. However, the tendency for unbridled, non-contingent, and rapidly dissipated over-intrusive smothering from the other will remain palpable. In this chaotic regime, the therapist can act to create trust especially by creating a trusting environment in sessions and giving "homework" for working through mistrust outside of sessions. The in-office attitude should be one of constant, responsive presence, and acceptance, as would be the goals for extra-office homework. Trust doesn't switch on instantaneously, and the gains made will be slow and arduous. This message applies both to the in-office attitude of the person and the effect of social confidence building outside the office. Eventually, some sense of social trust could develop and solidify through more appropriate social skill development and use.

Behavior/Symptom Growth, Deep Change (Vertical)/Constructing a More Positive Life Story

The person immersed in a social envelope without trust of the other will have a most difficult time bursting out of the frame to a more trusting self and its associated social behavior. Once some positive growth is made in removing the shackles of a social world without trust and using trust-building social skills, not only will mistrust take a secondary position and be better controlled, but also the dynamics of social relations will be more personally initiated, focused, goal-oriented, and positive emotionally. The underlying cognitive structure to the mistrust having developed would involve hierarchized sensori-motor coordinations, everything else being equal, but these can take on more constructive elements in therapy. This will allow freedom to grow into higher-order levels in socio-affectivity involving sensori-motor systems organized constructively in context.

The person who is exposed to a mistrust-creating environment will be struggling with the controlling, manipulative, inconsistent, and even subverting/sabotaging behavior of the other, who will evoke leeriness and little confidence/faith. However, as the therapist helps the person work through the past toward a more adaptive present such that the future seems more hopeful, the basic requirement of having trust in the process will be augmented by developing a sense of trust in the growing self and in the attitude toward the other that might be developing slowly. The therapist can complement and accentuate any narrative themes about trust embedding in social relations and about behaviors associated with mistrust being replaced by more constructive behaviors.

Consciousness, Theory of Mind, Selves, and Responsibility

The infant facing the challenge of building trust or mistrust will be doing so in a sensori-motor sub-stage involving hierarchical coordinations. The mutual regulation entailed will be context-sensitive, yet with social goals and initiatory behavior expressed by the infant, too. The trusting, agentic self will grow in social contexts that are non-controlling and constantly supportive, in a balance of self-other reciprocal interchange. The sensori-motor base of the behaviors involved precludes the development of anything beyond the preconscious and embodied social intentionality/linkaging. But the hierarchized coordination at this sub-stage of development will allow for some gains in these and related regards through the primary/secondary coordinations permitted, e.g., in self-other goal-related behavior, assuming the environment has been trust-promoting. The therapist can further the transitioning of a person who has lived a mistrustful social regime by placing at the apex of developing constructs of the self and other the self as worthy of trust and the other as trustworthy. This will provide the foundational elements to ulterior long-term growth of dependable social relations and to self-mediated growth for being continually responsible, morally focused, and psychologically mature/complete. Once the pathway to these ends is laid, the person at least is given the option of laboriously following it toward its meaningful ends, even if it takes a lifetime.

The Sensori-motor Stage Sub-stage of Systematization (8–12 Months): Sub-stage 8

Self and Relational Development [Initial Theoretical Elaborations]

A very brief description of the present step in Young's 25-step Neo-Eriksonian developmental model follows. It is presented again in Chap. 18, to help give a collective overview of the 25 steps in the modeling.

Sociability acts vs. un-sociability or poor sociability acts (8–12 months). Normally, the growing person develops social behavior that helps create positive relationships. This starts in infancy, including in positive attachment to the parent. However, without good parental/care-giver support, a person could develop insecure attachments and not be good socially even after. Social behavior becomes avoidant, fearful, rejecting, or ambivalent. If this happened to you, perhaps you attached to anybody without being careful about it. Or, perhaps you totally avoided any relations, being super wary and isolated.

Appendix 2.3 gives the brief amount of work already done in prior publications related to the task of developing in depth the Neo-Eriksonian (sub)stage model. The next section of the chapter gives an interim summary that elaborates the contents of Appendix 2.3 with respect to the present sub-stage being considered, of the Sensori-motor Stage Sub-stage of Systematization.

Interim Summary

In the latter half of the first year of life, the infant enters the critical phase of developing attachment to the care-giver. Attachment quality can be secure or insecure, with the latter involving ambivalent/resistant or avoidant/anxious attachment, in particular, or even the D profile (disorganized, dazed, disoriented) associated with abuse (Young, 2011). The development of attachment is accompanied by internal working models (IWMs), which I have referred to as social-self working schemata. Typically, in the secure attachment type, internal working models involve feelings of being loved and of being worthy of love (behavior of other and sense of self-worth, respectively). The cognitive foundation to this critical attachment behavior resides in the infant's acquisition of systematized sensori-motor coordinations.

This systematization acquisition in this sub-stage allows sensori-motor coordinations to relate in a hierarchical way, as in the prior sub-stage, but it includes refinements related to each of their elements and their better inter-coordination systemically. For example, the infant can reach around a screen, or push it aside, to get at a desired hidden object, coordinating means-ends relationships in purposeful behavior right from the start of a movement. The infant's behavior in these types of tasks is facilitated by the coordinated, hierarchized sensori-motor system that is involved, being capable of representing the hidden object before reaching for it.

However, behavior such as this is still greatly sensori-motor and not genuinely representational in terms of symbols standing for objects, such as in language/speech or pretend play. Also, the sensori-motor base of the image is indicated by the infant needing to have obtained the desired object or had interest evoked about it either when it was not hidden or half hidden before it was placed in view behind the screen in the task. All this to indicate that even if primitive images of objects can be established by infants and guide them in their search for objects when they are hidden, the objects are not divorced from the sensori-motor actions related to them, e.g., in their exploration/manipulation search and goal resolution and then retrieval and re-exploration/manipulation.

Given that the cognitive bases involved in this sub-stage at this juncture in development concern sensori-motor systems, and in which images of sought objects can develop, as described, it makes sense that the parallel socio-affective acquisition in this sub-stage concerns attachment to the care-giver. The quality of the latter is established empirically in the care-giver reunion situation after a series of 2 min situations in the laboratory, beginning with the care-giver serving as a secure base of exploration of toys in the observed room. Once the attachment figure leaves the infant alone and returns, we query whether the infant's reaction is one of wanting to get up in the care-givers' arms, reaching out for her/him, or otherwise. The infant might cuddle and then return to toy play, even if she/he had fretted during the care-giver absence episode. These secure infants react differently than insecure ones, who might be ambivalent, e.g., wanting to get up in the arms but not wanting to stay, or who might be avoidant, e.g., not wanting to get up in the arms at all (aside from those manifesting the D profile, who are like deer frozen in headlights). The secure infant, in particular, might manifest a great amount of positive social behavior, although there might be temperamental differences (e.g., socially inhibited infants) involved, too. The self-image will include relatively permanent images of shared, intersubjective social chains in interactions achieving positive social endpoints and a sense of comfort. The image of the other will be one of a person providing securing affection aside from satisfying other basic needs, care-giving needs, and being capable of entertaining social dialogues. The interactional quality of the dyad will involve reciprocal sharing, as in the care-giver serving as a secure base for exploration.

The Eriksonian opposition at this stage involves more than the issue of Trust vs. Mistrust, because it moves into attachment-securing behavior undergirded by positive images of the care-giver, so that much sociability in the interaction between the infant and care-giver obtains, even if temporarily interrupted. The opposite pole of unsociability is possible, but does not often predominate.

The adult involved in a regime akin to the insecurity-promoting one might be dismissive, unconcerned, inconsistent, continually saying "no" without giving explanation, non-contingent, insensitive, lacking in affection/caring, and even rejecting/abusive, which will activate the insecure types of attachment. These insecure attachment types are characterized differently in the adult compared to the infant but still might be related to them longitudinally.

These three attachment qualities would seem to be variants of the standard stress response of fight, flight, or freeze, i.e., respectively, resistance/ambivalence, avoidance/anxious, and D (dazed, disoriented, etc.). The concomitant negative emotional states or processes associated with these three attachment qualities, respectively, would be anger/worry, wariness/fear, and dissociation/dislike/abhorrence/terror, among others.

The person who has lived a social reality that has created attachment difficulties, disturbances in a sense of security, and so on, will have difficulty in engaging in security-promoting behavior and in receiving it well from the other. There might be predator-prey type of interactions, with security-promoting efforts dismissed/undercut by both parties. The negative social world of the self and other will become one of insecurity rather than security promotion.

The attachment qualities of a secure or insecure nature that had developed in infancy are carried forward into later social relations, through the role played by internal working models. The relationship between early and later attachment styles is not direct, because internal working models become more abstractly representational as the child grows and, as well, intermediate experiences between the infancy and youth/adult periods are involved. Nevertheless, the quality of early care-giver/infant interactions in terms of warmth, sensitivity, contingency, and so on, have long-term repercussions socio-affectively in the core attribute of feeling secure socially or not (and in the different insecure ways indicated). As with other sub-stages in the current model, unqualified application of new acquisitions always present challenges, and this is valid even for supportive environments. For the present sub-stage, this would refer to indiscriminate attachment behaviors to any adult. The attachment figure who behaves appropriately will contour the child's energetic attachment behavior outreach to safe significant others. The sub-stage does not concern a broader indiscriminate social attachment, in that it involves a more focused search for a secure attachment figure no matter who is the other.

As for early interventions that might be required for infant-parent pairs, clearly they should focus on how the parent could build secure attachment and how to deal with signs of insecure attachment. Due to their own psychological difficulties, parents might reject the child because of cognitive filters applied when secure attachment behaviors are not manifested, or when the child expresses insecure types. Or, they might misperceive the positive nature of secure attachment behaviors, and reject the child anyway.

The extreme dangers of this stage for the adult exposed to an unsupportive, insecure-promoting regime are that the other is indiscriminately attached to without any self-protective concerns, and so the person is placed in risky situations. The opposite reaction might be that the person is totally incapable of any secure attachment relationships, shirks from/avoids them, and so on.

Self-Response to Cognitive (Mis)perception of the Other

The infant proceeding into the latter months of the first year of life normally is developing a secure attachment and develops a sociability that elicits secure attachments. The underlying primitive image/internal working model of the care-giver can be evoked even if she/he is absent and, therefore, serves to complement the security felt in her/his presence. That primitive image capability lies in the ability of the infant at this age to systematize sensori-motor scheme coordinations or add elements to the components and their coordinative contexts, as in reaching behind a screen to get a desired object with purpose right from the start of the behavior. The self-schema and associated behavior developing are integrated with those of the other in a reciprocal social mutuality of sharing, trust promotion/reception, and so on. The cognitive acquisition in this stage includes object permanence, which makes the primitive image of the attachment figure like a permanent imagined object, as required by the context. The other still is socially linked and sensori-motorically activated, so the other is a subjective or intersubjective cognitive entity. Infants in this age period who are experiencing promotion of insecurity rather than insecurity will be incapable of eliciting security and making the other feel secure.

The adult who lives in a social environment not unlike that of the insecure infant toward the end of the first year of life will develop a sense of self analogous to the one being discussed for the infant, which will be pervaded by a sense of insecurity and which will be underwritten by social behaviors incapable of eliciting security and providing security to the other. The images guiding the behavior will not be positive ones about a securing figure but will be negative ones about insecuring figure(s). Social behavior will be replete with negatives, curt "No's" that cut communication, and falling into communicative disorganization. The emotional reactions could be either internalizing dislike/worry/escape or externalizing aggression.

Positive Pole in Eriksonian Development

The infant in the last quarter of the first year of life who has developed a secure attachment will evidence sociability behaviors of increasing context sensitivity and ability to prolong interactions. The infant will display genuine affection, liking, and enjoyment in reciprocity with the attachment figure. The infant will be capable of using the attachment figure as a secure base, exploring toys, interacting with appropriately behaved strangers, referencing the mother, and reacting positively to appropriate signals in ambiguous situations, including social ones, and otherwise accepting secure-promoting behavior and enjoining in same, although not with intentionally at the outset of all behaviors.

Negative Social-Self Working Schema

The infant at the end of the first year of life who is not developing secure attachments, positive images/internal working models of the care-giver, sociability interactions skills, social goal establishment in mutually positive social exchanges, and affection and the like in social encounters with the care-giver will develop social-self working schemas that are marked by undergirding insecurity-facilitation behaviors that carry forward in all social interactions. The self that develops with this beginning will be marred by an absence of a subjective sense of secure attachment and associated sociability acts and will be characterized by insecurity, poorly developed intersubjectivity, little sharing/affection/sociability, and behaviors that inhibit reciprocal social relations with others, such as refusing social invitations and displaying dislike and aggression. The cognitive filters deployed socially will include negative images of the other that will color all social interactions.

Attachment, Neo-Eriksonian Development, and Therapeutic Implications [Patients and Therapy]

Patient Presentation

The patient without a positive, secure attachment will present with a negative, insecure one, such as being resistant of attachment, ambivalent about it, or disoriented/dazed or "frozen" about it. Intersubjectivity, sociability, sharing, affection, allowing mutual regulation, and having social intentions and social maintenance behaviors to realize desired social goals will be compromised. The primitively represented image/internal working model of the other will be one involving insecurity promotion, inability to create or accept security, and social skill deficits, generally. Indeed, the patient will mirror this impression of the other. Proximity seeking, contact, warmth, comfort, friendliness, and other social interlinking behaviors will be absent or sporadic, or otherwise one will find ineffective social behavior will include giving orders, denying the other, cutting off communication, and not serving as the equivalent of a secure base. Internalizing emotions will include dislike of the other, avoiding reactions, or worry about the social world of the person. Externalizing ones will include petulance/aggression affectivities.

Behavioral/Symptom Mental Scanning

The person who has lived in an environment that has fostered insecure as opposed to secure attachment will have an underlying negative image of the social other replete with insecurity-promoting behaviors. This other image/internal working model of the other will have a reciprocal self-image/internal working model, and the person will visualize social interactions as incomplete, stuttering, without clear goals, and generally insensitive, non-contingent, and lacking in mutual regulation. The person will be seeking security, or rejecting it and, therefore, live in a listless, confined social world. The person will understand this and either attempt impulsive security-promotion or, to the contrary, withdraw into security avoidance (or alternate in these styles, with standing in the social headlights and being frozen socially possible, too, depending on the quality of attachment). The person will be able to link internalizing and externalizing emotions to the lack of sense of attachment. Discerning which quality of attachment is at issue, or whether it is their admixture, will be more difficult, as will be the required security-promoting behaviors needed that would help. Similarly, pointing out the required discourse/communication skills in this regard, as well as the ones needing replacement, might be difficult for the patient.

Therapeutic Implications

The patient who is living with a history of an insecure attachment profile will have extensive social interaction problems related to insecurity in other relationships. Both the cognitive schema/internal working model of the self and of the other will be distorted and difficult to change because of their embedding in primitive images of self and other having permanent attributes involving insecurity and difficulties in security promotion. Social behavior will not be organized systematically with self or other as alternately leading in the interaction or with the second party reciprocally accepting and preparing to lead in her/his turn. Social behavior will seem stunted, without direction or aimless, deficient in sharing and sociability, and indifferent about establishing proximity/contact, or with anxiety about it or rejection of it possible, as well. Giving orders and negations will abound in social discourse. Emotions will involve ambivalence, fleeing, unfriendliness, rejection, or disorientation.

The therapist will be tasked with working on basic secure attachment behaviors and social skills that foster continuity in social interactions, such as more openness, allowing oneself to give comfort or solace, using advice and problem solving strategies, and giving sensitive presence in social support. The therapist will need to work in basic communication functions in role alternation (listening/validating, turn taking, how to speak to the other verbally and nonverbally). The therapist will focus on reworking the negative or insensitive image the patient has of the social other that has been conditioned by past experiences and the corresponding image of the self as insecure/unsociable, incapable of chained intersubjectivity, lacking in relevant positive emotions, and deficient in proximity/contact/security seeking/promoting/acceptance. Discourse will have to change to facilitate social sharing/dialogue, chaining, goal establishment, maintenance, and fulfillment, and a more positive impression of self and other.

Stress/Trauma Resilience/Coping

The person with an absence of secure attachment will use insecure attachment-related resilience/coping mechanisms to stress/trauma. The infant facing an insecure attachment promoting regime still tries to maintain attachment but uses avoidance (yet monitoring), ambivalence (including avoidance), or dazed/frozen responses. The adult might engage in similar resilience/coping strategies when confronting stress/trauma if the person has not developed securely attached relations. The generalized social other might be represented by a basic image/internal working model of being insensitive, unresponsive, insecurity-promoting, and so on, and so will not be counted upon as a social resource, except perhaps in cases for which having someone of this type is considered better than having no one. The self will be constructed as lacking in effective resilience/coping mechanisms and will have difficulty maintaining positive sociality/sociability when confronted by stress/trauma. The communicative/discourse style will not be conducive to eliciting social support.

Therapeutic Strategies [the Other and Change]

Relational Co-regulation

The infant reaching the end of the first year of life normally will have developed a secure attachment to a sensitive, contingent, responsive care-giver and use the care-giver as a secure base for object/people exploration. The image/internal working model of the secure-giving care-giver will guide the infant in her/his social engagements, allowing for the working toward/establishment of social goals, for example, to obtain desired outcomes in context. The self will be secure in attachment focus. The infant experiencing insecure attachment will lack the ability to engage in the social role alterations that characterize social interaction/intersubjectivity at this age and will have mixed if not dispirited social interactivity with both care-givers and others. The social co-regulation afforded by the care-giver will be equally mixed and dispirited. Instead of highly social and rewarding interactions, the infant will experience unrewarding ones and displace from/replace the social interactions involved.

The adult forced to live a regime akin to this one will lapse into behaviors associated with insecure attachment and unsociability, such that relational co-regulation will be non-securing. The negative image of the self and of the other will lead to social goals that are not conducive to maintaining social interactions and achieving some sort of mutuality in the exchange. In fact, individuals with insecure attachment will either avoid interactions, "freeze" in them, reject them, or be quite ambivalent and ambiguous about them. The co-regulation will suffer, in turn.

The therapist should focus on building secure attachment-related social skills and fostering the creation of secure attachments, even in the therapeutic context. However, the patient might lapse excessively into pre-existing insecurity-promoting behavior and the images/internal working models associated with them.

Behavior/Symptom Network/Connectivity Change (Horizontal)

The patient who is insecure in attachment will have a social profile marked by insecurity, uncertainty, lack of continuity, lack of appropriate social skills, poor discourse skills, random social goals, and negative impressions of others (as unfriendly, non-sharing, unsociable, self-concerned, and with either ambivalent, rejecting, or even abusive behavior/attachments). The therapist should function as a secure base to help the patient construct a more positive image of the other, more positive social skills, and movement toward the capacity to desire and create secure attachments. The underlying cognitive acquisition in the sub-stage associated with this level involves sensori-motor coordinated systems/primitive representational images/internal working models, so that the therapist can use this base and serve as an axis of sensitivity, reciprocity, and stability toward effecting positive change, that is, through invoking representation of the other as having positive coordinated elements in the cognitive system involved.

Behavior/Symptom Growth, Deep Change (Vertical)/Constructing a More Positive Life Story

The person making lateral gains in moving from poor quality attachment (insecurity) to positive quality attachment (security) will be in a position to generalize from the particular attachment figure involved (even if that is therapist) to others. Also, the self-image/internal working model will be more positive and includes security acceptance and security promotion attributes as parts of the self. The primitive representational images of the self and other will move toward more malleability and generalizability. The images at this level are primitively representational in the sense of involving coordinated sensori-motor schemes in systematized entities. They will grow in the next sub-stage to more generalized, applied entities for multiple domains, others, and relations. The moving toward and into attachment security behaviors and relations in this sub-stage will goad development forward toward the next one.

The individual without a sense of attachment to a specific other and generalized others will be either seeking attachment inappropriately and ineffectively or withdraw/flee/freeze in the process. The emotions experienced will be analogous ones or affectionless and internalizing/externalizing. As the person develops toward more constructive images of self and other, e.g., as being capable of "love"/security and accepting of it, with the other being capable of giving it and receiving it, too, the underlying cognitive base of the behavior (coordinated sensori-motor systems, primitive representations/images, IWMs) will undergird narratives with novel elements related to security, positive attachments, and better social skills, and with the other reciprocally responsive and attachment promoting in these regards, too.

Consciousness, Theory of Mind, Selves, and Responsibility

Developments in these super-ordinate areas of growth will take place slowly in the developing infant, even in optimal environmental circumstances. In the present sub-stage under discussion, the critical acquisition of secure attachments will have long-term implications for social relationships, generally and, as well, for associated specific behaviors, such as morality/altruism, consciousness, perception of the self and other, and taking responsibility. The course of development can take many paths, but starting on the positive slope in such a crucial developmental period will optimize growth toward long-term maturity and psychological completeness, everything else being equal (e.g., continuity in the optimal environmental circumstances).

The Sensori-motor Stage Sub-stage of Multiplication (12–18 Months): Sub-stage 9

Self and Relational Development [Initial Theoretical Elaborations]

A very brief description of the present step in Young's 25-step Neo-Eriksonian developmental model follows. It is presented again in Chap. 18, to help give a collective overview of the 25 steps in the modeling.

Autonomy (independence) acts vs. doubt (dependence) acts (12–18 months). Normally, like the toddler, we become eager and act for ourselves, feel confident in exploration, and feel satisfied in social behavior. But perhaps your environment (parent) did not give you good support of your independent activity, and you ended up feeling dependent and not confident. You found it hard to take initiative and explore. You become inward and dissatisfied. You even felt dominated. Or, you went the other way; and you became defiant, argumentative, and not cooperative.

Appendix 2.4 gives the brief amount of work already done in prior publications related to the task of developing in depth the Neo-Eriksonian (sub)stage model. The next section of the chapter gives an interim summary that elaborates the contents of Appendix 2.4 with respect to the present sub-stage being considered, of the sub-stage of Sensori-motor Stage Sub-stage of Multiplication.

Interim Summary

The 1-year-old infant progressing through the first half of the second year of life is making major cognitive and socio-affective gains. Motorically, the infant enters the walking phase, which affords liberty of action. Language-wise, the infant's capacity grows in increasing vocabulary and shared focus on object naming in joint attention. The active phase of attachment continues, with increasing exploration from a secure base. The cognitive underpinnings to these developments refer to structured chaining of systematic schema pairs (sensori-motor multiplication), allowing complex combinations, embeddings, subprograms, linear plans established in context, trial-and-error exploration, and variations in existing means-end relationships through exploratory rearrangement of the ends for existing means and trying new means for established ends. The infant at this age has the motor capacity, cognitive capacity, and social basis to enter a phase of independent action, search, goal attainment, and exploratory eagerness. Erikson qualified this time period in the life of the infant as one of facing the challenge of Autonomy or Independence vs. Self-Doubt or dependence. The nature of the general acquisitions in this period of life justify referring to it as the age of establishment of autonomy/independence. At the same time, the environment needs to be supportive to reach these acquisitions successfully.

In the latter half of the first year of life, the young infant has developed both a sense of trust and a secure attachment to the care-giver, assuming the environment had been supportive. These acquisitions do not guarantee that the adaptive support of the environment continues. The concept of fit indicates that the environment might be functionally supportive up to a certain point but not after, for example, in the present case if the walking infant creates too much supervisory stress for the care-giver. Of course, the problems in the environment might be carry-forward ones from prior phases, such as not being supported in the development of Trust vs. Mistrust or Secure Attachment vs. Insecure Attachment.

The cognitive (mis)perception of the other associated with the end portions of the sensori-motor sub-stage involves domination of the person, although the extent of the domination is less an issue. However, the inability of the environment to engage in optimal support of the infant's exploratory independence would be consistent with imposing a degree of domination that would impede this motoric, cognitive, and socio-affective drive.

Should the environment be supportive of the infant at this age, as the infant explores the environment, the infant's burgeoning language skills would help it maintain a psychological closeness to the care-giver/adult despite the increasing physical distance that might be involved. The looking back to monitoring of and joint attention with the mother, for example, will facilitate and cycle positively to promote increasing exploratory independence while fostering continued psychological trust and security. The language of the adult, both in terms of indicating safety concerns (e.g., "watch out") and the naming of objects and things (aside from people and places), normally, would be a supportive adjunct to the infant's exploratory eagerness, and the infant and parent would work in tandem to have the infant engage with the environment in order to satisfy her/his exploratory will. The positive social-self working schema that develops in this action, cognitive, and socio-affective context coordinates self and other in chained sequences of structured, systemic sensori-motor schema coordinations such that the other becomes an intrinsic part of the sensori-motor cognitive organization of the infant's activities and growth in self-construal. The self becomes not only agentic, even if initially with a sensori-motoric characteristic in context, but also understands herself/himself to a degree as an independent agent in this regard (e.g., as if saying, "I can toddle there and let's see how mummy reacts"). Thus, the self is increasingly developing as an independent, autonomous one, at least in action and associated consequences, which is facilitated by the increasing language exchange over distances that accompanies the resultant action-based exploratory and independent forays in the environment.

The infant exposed to an environment that does not positively support her/his independence and autonomous exploration will experience hesitation/inertia, self-doubt/lack of self-confidence, and dependence/lack of use of a secure base to explore independently. The discourse received will at least partially dominate and inhibit the infant. The construal of the self as an independent autonomous agent will not develop as clearly or even majorly as it should this regard.

The Eriksonian stage of Autonomy vs. Self-Doubt will gravitate toward the latter and mark further development. The emotions the child might experience in this regard include dissatisfaction as a more internalizing emotion and defiance as a more externalizing emotion.

The cognitive (mis)perception of the other indicates that living at the level of the equivalent of this sensori-motor sub-stage might elicit sterilization vs. revolution, and the corresponding dissatisfaction vs. defiance emotions, as well. That is, for the adult forced to live at a level equivalent to this infant sub-stage, any sense of independence/autonomy/self-confidence will be dominated by a sense of dependence/self-doubt/inertia hesitation. The self will forever question self, other, and environmental engagement/exploration/curiosity and diminish experiencing emotions of eagerness/satisfaction. The ability to plan social engagement, chaining, and independent harmonious co-creation socially will be hampered/dampened. For the person, neither the self nor other will be considered autonomous agents capable of self-satisfying independent actions freely chosen in context.

As with any sub-stage in development, excesses will take place at the beginning related to new acquisitions as they are enthusiastically tried out. For the present sub-stage, this concerns excessive autonomy acts and behaving too much with a sense of independence. The sensitive care-giver will have to be especially vigilant, given the quick pace of the toddler's exploratory vigor. As more appropriate initiative and feeling is promulgated and sets in, any excessive self-doubt will be minimized.

If the parent cannot handle the increase in autonomy activation, intervention should focus on how to properly deal with this behavior. The parent might be overwhelmed/not care/not watch/under-control, etc., or over-control, be hypervigilant, stifle/strangle, etc., but a fine balance in these regards needs to be instilled.

Self-Response to Cognitive (Mis)perception of the Other

The infant in the first half of the second year of life is developing an increasing exploratory skill, psychological independence, and sense of autonomy. When those acquisitions are jeopardized by a non-supportive environment, self-doubt creeps in, along with behavioral dependence and a lack of autonomy. The potential sequential chaining of coordinated, systematized schemes in linear planning is affected such that exploratory eagerness is compromised. The self normally develops as an autonomous agent capable of minimizing physical and psychological distance to the caregiver through verbal interaction, looking back, monitoring, etc., but this type of means-end coordination is undercut and minimized. The other is viewed as dominant or weakly present or otherwise unavailable/interfering of the desired independence.

The adult living an equivalent regime of the infant in this age period will also have issues related to autonomy/exploration, physical independence, and self-confidence. Even if environmental and social initiatives are undertaken, they might not continue to desired ends as self-doubt/dependence creeps in and predominates. The self will be dependent and non-autonomous more than anything else. The concept of the other associated with this self-image also will be limited in undertakings in autonomy; exploratory, independent ways of behaving will not be viewed as inherent in the other. The other will be viewed as manipulative to a degree, absent/non-supportive psychologically, or both, depending on context.

Positive Pole in Eriksonian Development

The infant in the first half of the second year of life confronts the Eriksonian challenge of establishing a sense of autonomy and independence compared to self-doubt and dependence. When well-supported, the infant will explore autonomously, independently, and with self-confidence and eagerness. The care-giver acts as a psychological secure base as much as a physical one, and through language bridges the physical distance that accompanies exploration. The latter is trial-and-error, given the underlying cognitive bases of coordinated, chained systematized sensori-motor schemes, which allows for "accidental" discovery of new means-ends relationships in context (and without forethought). Further, the promotion of the autonomy/independence that might be fostered by the environment not only has socio-affective repercussions but also cognitive ones, because the associated cognitive solidification, application, and expansion of the cognitive schema in the present sub-stage structure (or operational structure in later sub-stages) will flourish when the socio-affective aspect of the sub-stage flourishes, as well. As with the prior discussion of Trust vs. Mistrust, note that the present approach to describing the Eriksonian stages is conditioned by the particular cognitive sub-stage subsidiary to it.

Negative Social-Self Working Schema

The infant starting the second year of life should be capable of autonomous, exploratory independence filled with eagerness and self-confidence. When the social support is lacking in these regards, the infant will show less of each of the following: exploratory resolve; independent, context-determined exploration; autonomous will; verbally mediated psychological bridging of any physical distance; and co-creation with the supportive other of personal agency. The other will be viewed as manipulative to a degree, absent/uninvolved, and so on, and this will even lead to fear of exploration, taking independent steps, and physical separation. The other will be viewed as a barrier to autonomy promotion, evoking self-doubt, and will be viewed as being incapable of agentic encouragement of the person, etc.

Attachment, Neo-Eriksonian Development, and Therapeutic Implications [Patients and Therapy]

Patient Presentation

The person depleted of a sense of autonomy/independence/self-confidence will be hesitant/express inertia. Each act or thought undertaken will be immersed in self-doubt, and other emotions, such as alarm and fear, might predominate. The social skills of the person will be shorn of self-confidence, as well, and the general impression given will be of extreme caution in actions, thoughts, and socio-affective efforts that are contemplated, planned, or put into expression. The self of the person will not be capable of entertaining purposeful, independent agency, social or otherwise. The other as construed by the person will be viewed as non-supportive of any initiative demonstrated by the patient, and even manipulative and suppressive of any such efforts.

Behavioral/Symptom Mental Scanning

Patients lacking in a sense of autonomy/independence/self-confidence, along with a lack of agentic eagerness to meet desired social goals, might be able to appreciate these deficits, although perhaps not their causes and consequences. They might sense a pervading inability even to act freely without second thoughts, or knowing that correct options in behavior/thought/feelings have been chosen. Their social planning and follow-through skills will be hampered by their self-doubt, which will create reciprocal repercussions in both perceived images of self and other and their relatedness. Patients such as this might not be able to realize the extent of the self-other interconnectedness and what is missing in this regard but might grasp the behaviors underlying the lack (e.g., manipulation to a degree) and perhaps how to change them/improve.

Therapeutic Implications

The patient who is greatly dependent, self-doubtful, non-autonomous, lacking in willful exploration, and agentically inhibited/fearful most likely will have had non-support for independence/autonomy and also neglect/suppression/manipulation, generally. The therapist will have to offer more than rapport building and creating a sense of security in the relationship, because techniques will be needed to elicit self-confidence, independent exploration/autonomy, and the desire to take tentative steps in these regards despite the personal (negative self-images) and social (rejection of exploratory initiatives) failures in these regards.

Stress/Trauma Resilience/Coping

The adult who lacks a sense of autonomy/independence/self-confidence/personal agency will have difficulty both in personally dealing with stress/trauma through resilience/coping and in soliciting/recruiting helpful social/institutional support. Any initiatives taken in this regard will be suffused with self-doubt, not followed through, etc. The person might retreat into an alarm/social avoidance at the internalizing level or, to the contrary, anger/social comparison to/envy of others who cope better than them at the externalizing level. The person might try different problem-solving strategies, but tentatively, incompletely, and pessimistically. The will to autonomous independence in coping efforts will be expressed through trial-and-error, will be trying to the person, and perhaps tumultuous.

Therapeutic Strategies [the Other and Change]

Relational Co-regulation

In the second year, the normally developing infant will enter into a phase of explosive curiosity/exploration, agentic independence, blustery self-confidence, and eager anticipation of the joy in striking out. The parent will develop backaches if totally supportive, leaning over, watching endlessly for the slightest fall, for dangerous table edges, etc. The developing sense of self in the infant will bask in these acquisitions, with self-schemas brimming with positive attributes along these lines. The parent will gladly toddle along with the tiny one, talking, pointing out, advising, prompting, and generally supervising and being one step ahead of the child psychologically if not physically.

The infant who experiences more haphazard care along these lines will suffer more than physical bruising and hurt, for inroads will be made on psychological well-being, as well. Both the view of the self and the view of the other will suffer erosion in the basic attribute of having self-confidence and being open to its promotion. A sense of exploration/independence/autonomy will be limited/devalued/deformed.

The adult who experiences analogous non-supportive/autonomy-depriving environments will also experience intrinsic self-doubt and restriction of autonomous behavior/thought/emotion. The fear of any independence might permeate the patient presentation.

The therapist should understand the cognitive understructure to this type of presentation and try to recreate an independence-seeking assertiveness through interweaving of coordinated chains of social skills and self-other relations from the perspective of linear planning, even if discovered "accidentally" in context. The therapist should aim to be a genuine "co-" in the mutual social regulation toward a shaping of autonomy/independence and an ultimate improved self-confidence.

Behavior/Symptom Network/Connectivity Change (Horizontal)

The patient expressing self-doubt, dependence, non-autonomy, and lack of agency will need to work toward the countervailing attributes. The cognitive structure of the infant with similar attributes involves sensori-motor schemas that will not be coordinated, systematized, and generalizing or spreading out into the myriad social spaces of the infant, unlike the case that would be found for the well-supported infant. The person stuck at this level can be moved toward more positive attributes related to autonomy/self-confidence by appropriate therapeutic matching along these lines, including in homework assigned. The patient might take a long time to develop the desired autonomous and self-efficacy skills. The therapist can co-regulate that growth through being aware of ongoing gains and matching them by being a half-step ahead on an ongoing basis.

Behavior/Symptom Growth, Deep Change (Vertical)/Constructing a More Positive Life Story

As the infant self concretizes in the second year of life into an autonomous, agentic, independent, and confident one, although this will happen only with the appropriate supportive environment, the reciprocal other becomes conceived similarly in these terms and growth toward an interdigital self-other mutuality can proceed apace. Sharing becomes more coordinated, covering more domains (e.g., in toys, socially), and generalizes through increasing malleability and expansion of the undercurrent sensori-motor cognitive acquisitions. Social doubt is cast aside, social relations entertained with more eagerness, and coy-type emotions to elicit and maintain social interest by the other develops. The grounds for movement toward sensori-motor cognitive scheme integration are laid.

The person in therapy moving forward with this type of presentation starting point will need to allow the improving self-confidence in personal agency, independent activity, and autonomous psychology to include social interdigitation, social interest, empathy, and positive affective feelings for the other to translate into growth toward a more coherent, representational self, as befitting the next landmark stage in development concerning pre-(peri-)operations. The patient will prepare for further changes socially through talk therapy, simple bibliotherapy and related electronic therapy, and some active work in sessions, but the patient will work at her/his own speed in discovering what works.

The patient who has experienced a lack of autonomy/independence/self-confidence/personal agency will have developed a sense of self that mirrors these lacks. She/he will be hesitant, lack motivation, express confusion/fear/apathy socially or, at worst, experience frustration/anger/lashing out at people around her/him. People like this will feel as if they are rudderless yet dependent, and linked to others too much but without genuine links, while perhaps expressing bravado and misplaced/displaced courage/recklessness as acts to boost self-confidence.

The therapist will need much more time to have these types of patients working at shifting gears and value a nascent cohesive sense of self that could grow with proper attitude and proper behavior/emotions/thinking. The image or perception of the other might similarly improve, for example, as someone who can accept autonomy and encourage it, while creating valid (and valuable) social links. The therapist will encourage the patient to practice and incorporate new positive elements told to the self both about the self and other and to reevaluate what is possible as the person grows outside bad habits and ongoing self/other perspectives, toward adopting more adaptive, constructive behaviors and stories told. However, there will be limits to how these new narratives are constructed, given the cognitive basis of the sub-stage associated with this type of patient presentation. For example, elements of the new story will be discovered "accidentally" rather than purposely from the outset, as in a trial-and-error process. What the therapist emphasizes will have to be rediscovered by the patients on her/his own, through the efforts encouraged by the therapist.

Consciousness, Theory of Mind, Selves, and Responsibility

Just as positive passage through the prior sub-stages relating to trust and attachment will allow for smoother passage through later sub-stages in growth, thereby facilitating better development in morality/consciousness, self/other construal, and having a sense of responsibility/maturity/psychological completeness, the proper passage through the presently concerned sub-stage of sensori-motor coordinative schema multiplications will facilitate a positive trajectory in these most human traits and aspirations. For example, the cognitive base will allow for trial-and-error explorations of better confidence, autonomy, independence, and self and personal agency, which are all foundational acquisitions toward these higher-order psychological constructs.

The Sensori-motor Stage Sub-stage of Integration (18–24 Months): Sub-stage 10

Self and Relational Development [Initial Theoretical Elaborations]

A very brief description of the present step in Young's 25-step Neo-Eriksonian developmental model follows. It is presented again in Chap. 18, to help give a collective overview of the 25 steps in the modeling.

Interdigitational (give and take) acts vs. de-digitational (give or take) acts (18–24 months). As we grow, we learn to interact with give and take (not just giving or taking). But if you did not receive environmental support (parenting) for this, you might have difficulty in sharing, being concerned for others, and feeling fondness and even love. Instead, you might hate people. As for sense of yourself, you might not feel self-pride and even hate yourself. Maybe you will seek too much power or avoid confrontation, so people manipulate you easily.

Appendix 2.5 gives the brief amount of work already done in prior publications related to the task of developing in depth the Neo-Eriksonian (sub)stage model. The next section of the chapter gives an interim summary that elaborates the contents of Appendix 2.5 with respect to the present sub-stage being considered, of the sub-stage of Sensori-motor Stage Sub-stage of Integration.

Interim Summary

The 18-month-old enters a new window in cognitive development because the infant can use symbol plans to underwrite behavior/thinking. However, the nature of the symbol capacity in the 18- to 24-month age period is misconstrued in the literature. The infant at this age is not representational in the sense of having a symbol that stands independently for an object, thing, person, or place or otherwise symbolically alone and independent of sensori-motor aspects in its behavioral plans and thought sequences. That is, according to Piaget, the infant at this age is still in the sensori-motor stage despite primitive representational advances. The child might be in the sixth infant sub-stage and use symbol plans, but they are still tinged with sensori-motor components. The child might be able to mentally invent new means through mental combinations, and with purpose from the start of the invention (it is no longer accidental, or discovered by accident in context). However, the symbols at this sub-stage are not uniquely representational because of their sensori-motor associations and triggers. For example, one of Piaget's children looked at a small item with a drawer that could open and she only proceeded to open it after opening and closing her mouth. Symbols are sensori-motorically informed at this level and not without sensori-motor concomitants from which they might spring.

Despite the sensori-motor link to the symbolic capacity that develops at this age, the cognitive opening to the social and general environmental world of the infant cannot be underestimated. For example, the infant can make combined, embedded plans, and ones that are reversible, too. The infant is inquisitive, excited, and feels pride in her/his accomplishments. At the socio-affective level, the infant engages in complex social interdigitations, or embedded, reciprocal social exchanges imbued with mutuality and with give-and-take. This lays the seeds for give-and-take sharing, empathy, and deep-seated affection/fondness/appreciation of the other, which is a kind of love.

The self-other dynamic continues its differentiation at this sub-stage. Just as there is cognitive object permanence, with search behind double screens possible by the child for desired objects, so is the self a constant permanent entity that does not depend on context and social responsivity by the other for its permanent status. The interior cognitive abilities help define the self in this regard as much as anything else that is external, even if the latter are crucial for determining the experienced quality (e.g., self-love vs. self-loathing).

The child who excessively interacts socially, trying out new stratagems consistent with preplanned symbolic-type mediation, might generate dys-synchronous social activity, an imbalance in sharing that will be more like taking ("It's mine"), etc., leading to social uncertainty as the other (e.g., another child) responds accordingly. The sensitive caretaker will mediate and create the necessary cautions and give-and-take reciprocity/sharing in the interactions. The repertoire of the child at this age includes a verbal/language explosion in vocabulary, two-word utterances, pragmatic use of language in social context, and reference to the self (using "I" and "Me" in this regard). The child can cognitively infer to a degree and socially engage, that is, implicate cognitively and implicate into the social environment.

The parent might not be fully supportive at these levels, and manipulate the child toward desired ends rather than allow any cognitive activity desired by the child, social interaction preferred, etc. And the child might react with a lack of social interdigitation/give-and-take, with less social skills, e.g., give or take.

If the parent needs intervention in these regards, it should be to explain the value of promoting reciprocity/sharing/give-and-take for the long-term development of the child, and the peace of mind of the parent. Negotiating this phase well will bring to both multiple social dividends. The child could be overpowering this way (taking too much) or, to the contrary, overpowered/submissive, e.g., giving or giving in too much. The concomitant emotions involved here would be opposite to nascent love and nascent empathy, such as loathing/aversion/contempt and social withdrawal/coldness, respectively. Other emotions could include shame/embarrassment instead of pride and even rejection/revolution, e.g., to avoid any manipulation.

The adult living in a social environment akin to this one will have difficulty in sharing, giving and taking, social engagement in complex, planned, reciprocal, interdigitated chains, and giving/receiving deep/strong/intense love/fondness/affection. The adult who has lived an unsupportive regime in these regards might react with the opposite of the rejection of sharing/giving, etc. and lean to indiscriminate sharing/giving, etc. This could severely disadvantage the individual in many ways, e.g., in not engaging in financial self-protection, engaging in indiscriminate sociality no matter what the consequence, etc. The self will be viewed as impermanent and permeable rather than constant and impermeable, or perhaps of a spiteful, rejectable nature instead of an appreciative, giving, empathic one. Social challenges/opposition will not be subtle and allowing for continued dialogue but will chill interactions if not freeze their continuation.

Self-Response to Cognitive (Mis)perception of the Other

The infant entering into the second half of the second year of life will be cognitively and socially engaged, planning means-end reorganizations, chaining behaviors together toward selected goals, experimenting while doing so, and creating pride in accomplishments. Emotions related to affection/love will be evident socially, as well as empathic and sharing behavior. Cognitively, there will be the first signs of mental detours/reversals, and, socially, these will manifest, as well. Symbols will guide these activities, although with sensori-motor vestiges.

The infant who does not experience a supportive environment in these regards will not experience the planned, chaining in behavior either cognitively or socially. Rather than expressing interdigitational cognitive and social organization, the infant will express poorly organized, inefficient, and failed efforts in these regards (de-digitational social exchange in socio-affective terms).

The adult facing the equivalent regime also will be deficient/aberrant in sensori-motor-mediated symbolic activity in cognitive/social organization. The self will not be organized as a constant permanent psychological entity but as a variable, ephemeral, and changing one, perhaps even at the slightest whim or to the most minor perceived slight.

Sharing, empathy, give-and-take in relations, affection/nascent love feelings, role exchanges, and social flexibility in detours/reversals will not be evident in the person, with little room for appreciation/pride and vaunting the self in "I" or "Me" statements. The concept of the other similarly will be divorced from these interdigitational and implicative possibilities. The person might experience deep dislike of others/hate and with social skills restricted to not-so-subtle attempts at manipulation.

Positive Pole in Eriksonian Development

Toddlers in the second half of the second year of life express an exuberance in social interdigitation, sharing, give-and-take, affection/nascent love, empathy, mental and social planning, and detouring/reversing from their symbolic (yet sensori-motor linked) cognitive base. They engage in refined social exchanges, interlink with others, develop a self that is socially in synchrony, constant in characteristics despite variations, and verbally astute (e.g., using the words "I" and "Me"), while expressing pride and presence.

Negative Social-Self Working Schema

Infants in the 18- to 24-month age period normally develop interdigitated sharing, empathy in interaction, give-and-take coordination with the other, pride/nascent love, and social exploration of new means-end linkages right from the start of a behavior through sensori-motor-mediated symbolic constructions/inventions. The self is viewed holistically as cohesive. The other is viewed similarly.

If the environment does not support this positive development, it can sink to discoordinated, non-connected, unplanned social effort with interspersed manipulations, taking and not giving, or too much giving without reciprocity, depending on the context. There will be a sense of shame/embarrassment/guilt and even contempt/hate/feeling over-possession of the other or, to the contrary, feeling rejected/overpowered/subjugated by the other, who seems incapable of proper social dynamics.

Attachment, Neo-Eriksonian Development, and Therapeutic Implications [Patients and Therapy]

Patient Presentation

The patient who has lived this type of psychology will present with basic deficits in social interaction skills related to continuity, alternate role taking, reciprocal exchange, back and forth give-and-take, dealing with minor disruptions whether self- or other-induced in the social dynamic, sharing/empathizing, and feeling affection/fondness, and any hint of love/appreciation of the other/respect for them (e.g., they deserve to feel pride). They might present as either socially overpowered/submissive/subjugated or as overpowering/possessive/subjugating. Their emotions will impede continuity in social interactivity, e.g., too intensely disliking/rejecting or too much shame/rejection being experienced. Typically, the self will be fluid, weakly cohesive, and hyper-alert to any potential social insult or even an appropriate social interruption. People will be criticized for their flimsiness and flightiness.

Behavioral/Symptom Mental Scanning

Patients deficient in chainable, flexible, embedded, reversible, and planned goal-directed purposive social skills right from the start of social behavior interchange, as partially underwritten by symbolic (sensori-motor-related) activity and a cohesive self-image, might have preliminary impressions of what is involved in their presenting problems. They might perceive their impractical social variability in context, their inefficient social continuity-promoting skills, as well as their tendency to express negative emotions/sentiments, such as intense temper tantrums, dislike/hate, rejection, spiteful attitude, uncaring feelings, possessiveness/manipulation, and social aversion/avoidance. They might understand somewhat how their social skill problems and approaches make the other feel uncomfortable and rejecting of the person, in turn, but might not know how to change this other than in hardening one's social stance. There might be glimmers of wanting better and of opening to guided change.

Therapeutic Implications

The patient caught in a web of social weaknesses that preclude facile and flexible social exchanges that are reciprocally satisfying and beneficial to self and other will need to develop the requisite social skills in these regards. The patient will need to balance give-and-take, and dampen tendencies to do one or the other (give or take), while engaging in and allowing more sharing/empathy/affection/appreciation. This will facilitate growth in self pride and, ultimately, in nascent love feelings being possible toward the appropriate social other. The therapist should aim to strengthen the sense of self cohesion and consistency so that it can weather social disruptions, inefficiencies, and even failures with the other. The appropriate other needs to be considered more as a valid entity in her/his own right, who does not merit anything like the typical excessive dislike/contempt/hate/manipulation, overpowering/possessiveness, etc., that might be expressed (or the opposite tendency of feeling overpowered/submissive/subjugated). The therapist needs to appreciate the symbolic basis behind the social filters of the person (even if sensori-motorically influenced).

Stress/Trauma Resilience/Coping

The adult deficient in appropriate social interdigitation skills (and all that goes with them cognitively, socio-affectively, and emotionally) will be incapable of avoiding unplanned/poorly planned, scattered, disjointed, reactive, incomplete, and socially isolated. Unsuccessful stress/trauma resilience/coping attempts. The person will persist in inefficient, inflexible plans with little reflection on possible outcomes/effects and will embark in efforts more or less doomed to failure, leading to resentment, rejection, contempt, hate, etc., as well as embarrassment, shame, guilt, and self-loathing. The internalizing reaction might be accompanied by deep depression and social aversion while the externalizing one might be accompanied by aggressive manipulation and threat.

Therapeutic Strategies [the Other and Change]

Relational Co-regulation

The toddler who is 18 to 24 months old will continue to explore the world cognitively and socio-affectively with increasing skills because of an underlying symbol plan capacity right from the start of an activity, albeit with a sensori-motor origin to it. The linear, embedded plans possible allow the child to create a subtle social interdigitation that includes continuity, online adjustment/handling well any impingements, and so on. The infant can – change tack, retreat, and try something else; purposely try novel social combinations to preferred ends and even create new preferred ends, while using existing social behaviors to realize them; verbally engage with the other as well as socially; and play social games and embed in affectionate/shared/empathic, if not loving, social interplay. The infant will experience a sense of social facility and mastery and pride in these activities. The parent will be the cognitive and social support/facilitator, and even the innovator in all these regards. For example, language/speech skills are burgeoning at this age, and the parent becomes the verbal support/word explainer and pragmatic and contextual foil.

However, the toddler who is not so well-supported in this vein might not develop the interdigitated cognitive, social, and verbal skills required for proper socio-affective functioning at this age. The social fallback will not be dynamic sharing/give-and-take/empathy/affection and more but stunted social planning without purpose from the start of a social exchange and poor execution of the plan in context through ongoing inability at adaptation and adjustment. The lack of flexibility socially will shrink social skills and horizons to short interactions with simple goals often imposed rather than negotiated with any skill. The social stratagems used will spring from an inconstant self-image without an incorporated social role undertaking capacity and the exchange of social roles with the other. Speech will only be about self wants and goals rather than socially mediated and reciprocal ones. The risk of social co-regulation slipping into failed unilateral efforts at the regulation will increase, along with the other engaging similarly (which might have been the case since the outset).

The adult who continues to live in this type of psychological filter of self and other will act in ways not unlike the toddler living this regime, but in more magnified ways. The person will be incapable of normal dynamic socio-affectivity in context, with a give-and-take in social regulation depending on personal goals and plans and those of the other. Sharing will be all but impossible from the perspective of reciprocal exchange for cementing the social relationship. Fond, affectionate feelings for the other (or more) will be absent compared to the opposites of aversion, loathing, contempt, hate, rejection, etc. The self will be brittle, bendable, breakable, and belittled by the person and also the other, everything else being equal.

The therapist working with a patient with this type of presentation needs to accentuate social skill development that breeds flexibility and continuity in social relations without emotions related to disapproval, coldness, social manipulation, rejection, hate, etc. The therapist needs to work on establishing constructive social plans and goals to aim for in social interactions that would encourage a sense of self cohesion and respect for and reciprocity with the other. The person needs to view relational co-regulation not as regulatory efforts to unilaterally manipulate/overpower/possess the other or to be received with this attitude without resistance, but as a conjoint effort to grow in mutually beneficial and regulated directions enjoined in by both parties.

Behavior/Symptom Network/Connectivity Change (Horizontal)

The patient dominated by social skill deficits related to problems in social interdigitation/sharing, empathy/nascent love, give-and-take/social role entwining, and so on will need proper therapeutic support and skill training to develop into a more adept social partner who can experience a cohesive social self, pride, etc. The cognitive support system for the normally developing acquisitions in this regard includes symbol-mediated (although sensori-motorically entrenched) planning, mental combinations, novel social strategies, integration of positive bootstrapping verbal descriptions of the self, and internal embedding/detours/reversibility in planning/execution.

The therapist needs to work at this level, and help the patient develop and use better social habits while relegating old maladaptive ones to subsidiary options typically held under control. The therapist could subtly direct the patient toward this type of self-control by using language such as, "You could realize your social goals by trying the strategies you are learning. We can work through where they succeed and where you have difficulties as you give me feedback." (If there is a partner/significant other involved, a co-learning can be undertaken with that person, too.)

The ultimate goal of the therapeutic intervention would be to facilitate better social responsivity that encourages social adaptiveness, continuity, and goal attainment (of the goals adopted at the outset of the social interaction). Creating social sharing/empathy, fondness/affection, etc. will strengthen the image of the self as a separate yet socially mediated entity, with constant positive attributes to be proud of, share, and use constructively. The goal would be to facilitate a more integrated, cohesive view of the self, and how it relates to the other, who will have the same characteristics, thus facilitating social enjoinment and enjoying.

Behavior/Symptom Growth, Deep Change (Vertical)/Constructing a More Positive Life Story

The infant in the last sensori-motor stage of schema integration is approaching the next stage of peri-operations. The first sub-stage in this regard concerns peri-operational symbol plan coordinations. This sub-stage is equivalent to Piaget's pre-operational stage, or the start of his representational period (pre-operations and concrete operations). The symbols involved in the first peri-operational sub-stage have no sensori-motor linkages (although representational peri-operations and sensori-motor schemas can be linked through yoking in cognitive and socio-affective problem-solving, as required contextually and as fits the individual and her/his predilections). By successfully navigating the interdigitational/sharing challenge at the end of the infancy period, the very young preschooler at 2 years of age takes on a greater challenge of using symbols uniquely and organizing symbol plans in juxtaposed coordinations, which allows for super-ordinate planning (which is more advanced than linear, interdigitated ones). The qualitatively different and more advanced cognitive foundation of this age period allows the 2-year-old to go beyond the cohesion facilitated in the self-construct at the end of infancy to an even more coherent self-image. Instead of just an image of the self as constant and with an overall sense of part-to-part linkages, the overall scheme of the self now appears more indivisible and fully networked. The grounds are laid for a self that is "egocentric" in Piaget's terminology, that is, centrated on the self of the child but without social manipulation or other derogatory attributes involved. The overall positive thrust in cognitive and affective development at the end of the sensori-motor period will allow movement toward the next sub-stage in early childhood, which revolves around cognitive representations that include coordinations in symbol plans and also eventually socio-affective initiatives as defined by Erikson.

The patient having difficulty at the level equivalent to the sub-stage of sensori-motor integration, in the appropriate therapeutic context, will be overcoming difficulties in sharing/empathy, social interdigitation, self-cohesion, and being socially inappropriate in interaction (e.g., too overpowering, too submissive). The stage will be set toward integrating sensori-motor schemas by coordinating the products of those integrations, thereby facilitating genuine representational ability. This will have positive repercussions cognitively, emotionally, and socially. However, one by-product of the initial construction of a representational self will be its egocentric property. This will have negative ramifications if not properly supported and shaped. Therefore, as development continues, movement toward the next sub-stage in the developmental sequence will be compromised, including its progress toward developing Eriksonian initiative.

The patient struggling with deficits in social skills pertaining to sharing/empathy, give-and-take/social interdigitation, and planning/organizing goal-oriented social behavior might approach social interactions in a manipulative/overpowering or helter-skelter submissive/giving in way. The emotions will be cold or rejecting and not conducive to the expected adaptive social interchange and role reciprocity typically found. The images of both the self and other and the behaviors expressive of them will lack cohesion/constancy as well as flexibility/repair capacity.

The therapist will have to approach the patient with an empathic conversational and pragmatic/nonverbal/social discourse that accepts/appreciates efforts made and helps reorient the person cognitively at the social level (e.g., the social filters used, the perception of the other and of one's capacity to deal with the other). As the patient learns to better traverse the dynamics of social interaction and conversational exchange in the office, the therapist can accentuate the presence of sufficiently developing social skills in the patient to apply to the real-life social world of the patient. Too often, the patient will devalue herself/himself and her/his social skills, but by demonstrating their utility in interaction with the therapist, generalization can be encouraged for out-of-office social interactions. This might lead to a better sharing/empathy/concern for the other, at least in part, and better self-regard. If a partner or significant other is involved, appreciation/nascent love can become part of the new story being told by the self to the self (and other).

The therapist might want to point out how dynamic social chaining in behavior involves rapid adjustment, detours, reversals, secondary subunits (topics and plans), embedding, innovations, reciprocity, and role exchanges with the other, pre-established social goals that are flexible, nonetheless, and forming interrelations with the other that include longer, continuous interactions in which the symbolic (sensori-motor-mediated) images of self and other that are involved remain constant even if interactions vary greatly in context (and for individual reasons). This will serve to help the person create narratives about the self as socially competent and capable of engaging in acceptable social dialogue and successful social encounters.

Consciousness, Theory of Mind, Selves, and Responsibility

The infancy period witnesses great strides in cognitive and socio-affective development. By its end, the infant is ready to enter the Representational period and thinking with symbols and their coordination. The social planning in the last sub-stage of the infant sensori-motor stage includes symbol plans, as well, but they are not fully representational due to their sensori-motor linkaging nor are they yet coordinated between them. Nevertheless, the growth that takes place in the cardinal human acquisitions of consciousness/morality, understanding self and other, and behaving responsibly with care toward the other, while acquiring full psychological maturity, is one step further along at this sub-stage that ends infancy. The process is abetted at this sub-stage by the increasing capacity to imagine outcomes from the start of a behavior, that is, to engage in purposeful activity as behavior begins, including socially. Both the self and the other, as well as their reciprocal interdigitation and sharing, together prepare not only empathy and the like but also nascent feelings of love. Surely, these types of socio-affective acquisitions are critical to the ultimate human attributions that will develop as the human journey continues.

References

Bloom, P. (2016). *Against empathy: The case for rational compassion*. New York: Ecco Press.

Young, G. (2011). *Development and causality: Neo-Piagetian perspectives*. New York: Springer Science + Business Media.

Chapter 15
The Peri-operational-Based Sub-stages: Peri-participatory Social Cognition

Abstract This third chapter presents the actual stages of the present Neo-Eriksonian model, and their five sub-stages, which focuses on childhood. It includes two original Eriksonian stages – initiative vs. guilt and industry vs. inferiority – which are placed in the second and fourth sub-stage slots of the current model. The three new sub-stages added involve superordinate, identification, and personality/role acts (including tryouts), respectively. The identification sub-stage hearkens to the Freudian Oedipus/Electra situation/complex resolution. The role/personality tryout acts refer to the preteen's exploratory activities toward teen and adult-like functions. Because childhood is involved, and the original Piagetian stages in this age period concern pre-operations and concrete operations, in the present model, the age period involved (childhood) is referred to as peri-operational. The corresponding Neo-Eriksonian stage is also referred to as a peri-one (peri-participatory). Erikson referred to the mutuality with the environment, and the present model acknowledges this but also refers to participation and relational co-regulation in the developing child. The child moves from a quasi-participation that corresponds to the preoperational stage to a fully participatory one, which corresponds to the concrete operational stage. The child grows through the cognitive egocentrism of the 2-year-old at the beginning of the stage into the capacity to take third-order perspectives of the other at the end of childhood. Despite these normative acquisitions, when the environment is not supportive, the child gravitates to the negative poles of the Neo-Eriksonian oppositions described. They include problematic identifications and personality/role tryout confusions.

G. Young, *Causality and Development*,
https://doi.org/10.1007/978-3-030-02493-2_15

The Peri-operational Stage Sub-stage of Coordination (2–3.5 Years): Sub-stage 11

Self and Relational Development [Initial Theoretical Elaborations]

By way of introduction, the following presents a very brief description of the present step in Young's 25-step Neo-Eriksonian developmental model. It is presented again at the end of Chap. 18 along with the other 24 steps in the model, to help give a collective overview of the 25 steps in the model.

Super-ordinate (well-coordinated) acts vs. dis-coordinate (uncoordinated) acts (2–3.5 years). Normally, we feel "together" (the parts of my self are super coordinated) and do not think that we are in pieces (not coordinated). But if your environment (parent) was not supportive this way (was controlling, for example), you did not develop to feel and felt "in pieces." So you put your personal needs in the middle of everything (being "egocentric," self-centred). Perhaps you were somewhat resistant, too. Or, perhaps you always accepted whatever other people wanted.

Appendix 3.1 gives the brief amount of work already done in prior publications related to the task of developing in depth the Neo-Eriksonian (sub)stage model. The next section of the chapter gives an interim summary that elaborates the contents of Appendix 3.1 with respect to the present sub-stage being considered, of the sub-stage of Peri-operational Stage Sub-stage of Coordination.

Interim Summary

The childhood period spans about 8–10 years, beginning with the 2-year-old and ending with the preteen years. The child develops from a hesitant post-toddler barely being able to speak in sentences, but being playful and initiatory, to a confident exploratory preteen, trying out adult-type roles and personalities, but with a lot of trepidation facing the upcoming teen and adult years. Cognitively, the child moves from a cognitive egocentrism to the border of abstract thought, and the conscious awareness that such an acquisition affords. The environment (parent) needs to support the child throughout the childhood growth period, in that toy and group play in the 2-year-old transforms and extends into major advances in friendships, schooling, peer influence, and socio-affective challenges.

The 2-year-old child begins a monumental shift in development, entering the stage the representations (Piaget, pre-operations; Young, peri-operations) in which symbols are used without any sensori-motor associations. Each symbol stands for a referent, or signifies, indicates, denotes, or otherwise represents the referent (e.g., object, person, place, and thing). In the first sub-stage of any stage in Young's Neo-Piagetian model, an exemplar of the acquisition ending the prior stage (in its last sub-stage) can become coordinated or juxtaposed in pairs, thereby constituting a new cognitive advance, as in peri-operational representations. In the particular sub-stage under discussion, which initiates the peri-operational representational stage, the symbol plans that had developed in the prior ending sub-stage of the sensori-motor stage can be coordinated, thereby broadening cognitive activity. For example, one symbol plan of the two involved in this initial representational stage symbol plan coordination can represent the referent and another can represent the symbol for it, thereby creating a foundation for active symbol proliferation and use in the representation stage. For instance, in imaginative play, one quintessential representational activity, a child can build a toy house with play bricks with some sort of modeling process in mind, refer to the house as the family home, and so on. Language/speech flourishes, as in the child now producing two-word utterance coordinations to create larger units, for instance, three-word utterances. The symbol plan coordinations suggest the beginning of higher-order cognitive structures, relational configurations, and generalizing symbols both for the child's cognitive constructive process and to be communicated to the other, as much as anything else (and going beyond isolated part elements in the higher-order structure).

The cognitive refinement of having paired symbol plans to help organize behavior allows for better goal differentiation, such as trying to enlist the other for personally defined ends. This type of cognitive activity is the source of the characterization of the child at this age as egocentric. Piaget did not use this term in any pejorative sense; rather, it refers only to the inability to take the perspective of the other, or its lack. Theory of mind research confirms that even the 3-year-old, let alone the 2-year-old, has difficulty with this "mind-reading" activity (Young, 2011).

Piaget argued that, because of cognitive egocentrism at this age period, the young child cannot decenter in the cognitive sense. That said, the child ceaselessly juxtaposes her/his goals in context, and with the other present, and so on, in order to attempt to incorporate any and all elements into the plans created such that they can facilitate arriving at personally desired goals. The coordinations being undertaken by the child in this age period, along with the symbol plan basis behind them, can be used to qualify the growing sense of self in this age period. Overall, the self-concept is a product of the different cognitive juxtapositions of symbol plans, and is preliminarily coherent and together as the child tries to enlist the other toward realizing its goals. The self is the cognitive anchor in social intercourse.

One might think that this cognitive egocentrism in the 2-year-old represents a regression relative to the social interdigitational skills that had developed at the end of the second year of life. However, on the one hand, relative to the sensori-motor basis for social interdigitations that develop in the 18–24 months age period, the cognitive egocentrism in the initial representational sub-stage heralds the use of sensori-motor-divorced symbols and their coordination in context toward desired ends, so it represents a developmental cognitive advance. On the other hand, by definition, cognitive egocentrism does not mean social egoism. The environment needs to canalize the young child's representation-based actions in her/his cognitive and socio-affective activity so that the cognitive egocentrism does not evolve into a social egoism.

When this does not happen appropriately, the self might fragment rather than develop a coherence in context, or it might develop isolated, hardened kernels of socio-affectivity as defense mechanisms, with little connectivity and little room for modification and growth. Instead of feeling one is "together" (the parts of the self are greatly coordinated), one might feel that she or he is in pieces (not coordinated). The parent who does not accommodate to the growing child at this age might engage in assimilative efforts to render the child pacified, docile, and compliant. No resistance is allowed, which paradoxically might create resistance. The parent channels the child, uses rewards and other reinforcements in order to reduce the child's child-centered goal formulation ability to preferred parental directions and outcomes. The child can develop contextual goal standards to aim at, but they will be conventional, stilted, and without innovation or surprise for the parent.

The strategies used to neutralize the child's personally derived thinking might include confusing, directing, and even disrupting/disorganizing strategies, or using benign neglect (silence, saying "I don't know"). Rather than higher-order organization evident in the child's behavior through use of symbol plan coordinations, the child appears dis-coordinate, disjointed, dispersed, context-mismatched, and otherwise incoherent. The child's image of the other is similarly fragmented and fractionated.

The adult living in a regime that has created an equivalent psychology will be equally egocentric, confused, controlled, and "not together." The self-centration will be excessive and block social relations involving the other and her/his goals as part of the goal structure constructed. The person might be totally repressed and compliant, or might express some resistance, but perhaps randomly and without focus. The person will communicate with others in a way that mirrors the environment that had induced the self-atrophy and retrenchment into egocentricity. That is, the person will expect compliance, try to control/channel, use tantalization as a strategy to do so, and even proceed to disruptive/disorganization social strategies along with statements inhibiting any efforts to think independently ("You're not thinking right"). It is possible for the person to have the reactive response of becoming so egocentric that it becomes extreme egotistic/egoistic behavior. The ego develops very limited capacities for other relations beyond the ego's needs, and thus social relations suffer accordingly. The person is considered very selfish and disregarding or demeaning of the other, and behaving in this way to preserve self-established needs and goals. Ultimately, it would appear that the seeds of personality disorders related to narcissism are laid by behaving this way, should it happen at a young age.

Self-Response to Cognitive (Mis)Perception of the Other

The young child in the 2- to 3 ½-year-old age period will be developing a self that is based on symbol plan coordinations, so self-image representations can be placed center stage. The self at this age has been termed egocentric, but not in any denigrating way. Rather, this concept refers to a lack in the ability to take the perspective of the other. That said, social engagements can reflect increased complexity relative to the prior sub-stage through even more refined, interdigitated, and reciprocal social sequences. Relational superordinate cognitive structures develop that allow for these coordinations socially. These symbol plan coordinations allow for the development of higher-order cognitive structures in multiple domains, including in pretend play, conversations/stories, and family role arrangements.

Emotionally, the sharing/empathy that had developed in the prior stage along with affection/nascent love feelings will continue to develop, but with an increasing danger of the opposite feelings in an unsupportive environment. Intense dislike/disruption might be evident when desired goals are thwarted. Instead of empathy/compassion, there will be emptiness and chilliness bordering on a harmful attitude. The self will gravitate away from benign cognitive egocentrism to outright dismissal of the other and any claimed/perceived desires/needs. The "terrible twos" indicate difficulty at this age because of the child's surplus of energy and the testing of environmental boundaries and restrictions through egocentric-mediated goal establishment. However, in the unsupported environment, the young child becomes not only "testy" but even truly "terrible."

The adult who will have experienced an environment like that of the unsupported 2-year-old will also develop an egocentric self, but one that transforms into an egotistical, selfish, and demeaning one. Criticism of the other will be constant and color social interaction. The goal will be to create confusion/compliance and disrupt/disorganize any planned social organization that considers the desires/wants of the other as relevant. The other will perceive the person as lacking in social skills, fragmented/dispersed, and even hostile/hateful. Indeed, the self experienced by the person might seem superficially together in its egotistic attitude, but it will be fissured, parcellated, and fragilely knit together, if at all.

The parent having difficulty dealing with the child's blossoming representational skills and their cognitive and socio-affective implications might benefit from interventions that include role play by the therapist in play situations. Feedback can be provided about why the child acts, talks, plays, and emotes in the way she/he did in the circumstances, and their socio-affective implications. The parent can learn to better appreciate the child and act accordingly based on the explanations and examples provided.

The cognitive egocentrism of the child, as well as the potential to be placated by material rewards, could result in a child too focused on rewards. The child might be rewarded to the point of becoming "spoiled." The therapist will need to explain how behavior such as this develops and work toward reorganizing the parent(s)' reward and punishment activities. The dangers of the child becoming coercive of the parents should be explained, and how the child might gravitate to like-minded spoiled, disruptive children in a vicious circle excluding any social association with better-adapted children.

Positive Pole in Eriksonian Development

The 2- to 3 ½-year-old who is well-supported by the environment glistens with an unbridled loving nature. The self is representational, planful, playful, and coherent, with an overarching view of socializing, context, and the other. However, the reciprocal sociality of self-other dovetailing that accentuates in this period does not mean that the self is other-focused. The cognitive limits of egocentrism and centration dictate that the other's views are tethered to that of the self, and not perceived separately and as valid in and of themselves. That said, interactions are intimately joined, functionally adaptive to goals governed by representations, and quite enjoyable to both parties, as they coordinate socially.

Negative Social-Self Working Schema

Normally, the 2-year-old develops quite positive impressions of self and other, although that of the other is limited by the characteristic of egocentrism. The child uses language/speech in which the words "I" and "Me" are front and center in her/his discourse on her/his desires and needs, yet the loving feelings toward the other are powerful inhibitors of uncaring selfishness, as is the tailoring limit-setting that the other offers to the child. The self presents as having it together and coherent with overarching representation-mediated social organization toward desired goals evident. However, in an unsupportive environment, the 2-year-old will fuss and whine, disrupt and disorganize, and punish the parent with howls and wails. Or, the child might distance herself/himself from the parent, dash away, hide, and disjoin/disconnect. The image of the self that is constructed by the child will be negative, as a hider or whiner, among others, and the image of the other will be negative, as well, as a confuser or complainer, among others. The social dynamics will be viewed from the perspective of a selfish self or a self devoid of coherent properties, even of selfishness. The apex emotions will not relate to love experiences but to despising/rejecting/hateful ones, both as a marker in one's actions and as a perceived attribute of the other.

Attachment, Neo-Eriksonian Development, and Therapeutic Implications [Patients and Therapy]

Patient Presentation

The patient who enters the therapeutic relationship with a representational egocentric self that has deviated into egoism/selfishness will be hard-pressed to engage in meaningful, reciprocal exchanges with the other that values in any way the other. The self will seem a unified entity at the surface, impermeable to social rejection and negative reactions to that. However, the interior under the shell will be kernelled islands shorn of feeling and meaning other than isolated structures involving compliance, perhaps due to a fear of shame and humiliation, and will include isolated structures involving resistance, but perhaps without concern for consequences and with strong dislike/rejection/spite, and hate quite possible. Social life will be incoherent, fragmented, dispersed, or negligible, with self-justifications including statements such as, "This is right for me. The other is wrong anyway." The patient might engage in too much self-indulgence, shopping therapy, etc.

Behavioral/Symptom Mental Scanning

The egotistical/selfish patient with an underlying representational capacity that restricts self-perceptions to centration on the self and with other-perceptions only as a tool for self-satisfaction will have little ability to understand how her/his behavior and attitude impact the other and compromise self-development. The patient will not be receptive to the therapist out of selfishness in behavior. The person might, however, grasp that personal goals are not being realized by her/his behavior, and be open to change them, but for egotistical needs of satisfying better self-centered goals. This could open ways to view the other differently, and see better how the other might be open to different social strategies toward helping the person realize her/his goals. Eventually, the image of the self of the person could extend its opening to incorporate a better understanding of the other and her/his needs/goals.

Therapeutic Implications

The patient expressing an overriding sense of ego, entitlement, use of the other for personal goals, planned taking advantage of the other, and otherwise demonstrating excessive and insufferable selfishness will present major challenges to the therapist, who typically enters the therapeutic relationship with a diametrically opposite "together," integrated self. There will be therapeutic confrontations testing the therapist as the egotistic attitude prevails in the patient and she/he attempts to pacify the therapist, rendering the therapist docile and manipulable. Patient like this will rant and rave about how integrated they are, and protect the deep splits in the sense of self that are hidden beneath a protective shell. The other generally will be seen as coupled appendages to the self, anchored to the self inflexibly toward fulfilling purely self-constructed goals without consideration of any other in the construction. The therapist will have to demonstrate supreme patience and not alter in her/his accepting or at least understanding stance, while educating indirectly the patient on the toxic effect on others of how she/he presents. The goal will to have the patient incorporate, coordinate, or couple new perspectives on the self and other into possible opening seams in the otherwise impenetrable staunch and steadfast hardened ego of the self, and create some ability to at least hear the other.

At the other extreme, the self might be so compliant as to lack any self-defense. It will be egoless, splintered, and seeking of immediate rewards, having little self-control. Patients like this will never think for themselves/think that they can think well, and will descend into endless indecision/"I don't know" statements and goalless meandering. The social planning ability of the patient will create the discoordinations that will function as self-fulfilling prophecies, with the person having little ego strength and capacity to match to the other in a dynamic dialogue that is fulfilling.

Stress/Trauma Resilience/Coping

The patient who has lived an environment that has not supported early representation and coherent self-developmental acquisitions will lapse into excessive egocentrism/egotism/selfishness, with little capacity to flexibly adjust to stress/trauma, cope, and express resilience, including through soliciting help from the other. The other will not be viewed as a separate, person with her/his own goals and needs, and the patient will either resign passively to her/his fate in depression or resist and react with frustration before any adaptive efforts in dealing with stress/trauma take place. The social dis-coordination in these regards might lead to social behaviors and other actions that spiral out of control into vicious circles. The therapist will have to act as a buffer and buttress positive change toward long-term personal healing and toward equity between self and other in relational co-regulation.

Therapeutic Strategies [The Other and Change]

Relational Co-regulation

The child between the ages of 2 to 3 ½ will be cognitively representational and egocentric, but will have a social skill repertoire that includes preplanned goals and explorative activity to realize them. Representations take the form of symbol plan coordinations, and so social activity can be of long duration, dynamic in adjustment, and enjoyable in interplay, all this assuming that the environment is supportive. Representations allow for this increased social flexibility, but the egocentric centration also present in this sub-stage of early representations limits the extent of the flexibility to self-determined and self-centered goals. The symbol plan coordinations permit self-presentation as coherent and together to a degree and even constructed with higher and lower levels in organization. The other becomes coupled to the self as part of the plan to realize egocentric goals.

The care-taking other plays an important facilitative role in the development of the child's coherent self, but even if there is social reciprocity due to the support offered, the self and other, as higher-order constructs, are not similarly fully reciprocal because of the self's egocentric attitude. That is, social reciprocity in behavior at this age manifests an increase to a degree in social mutuality, but the cognitive constructs of self and other are limited in this sub-stage because of the child's cognitive egocentric centration. Therefore, there will be a disjoint even in the normally developing case of a goal-establishing and socially mediated activity on the part of the child and a lack in accounting for the possible different goals of the other while doing so. That said, the other constitutes an important source of learning about the social world and the limits of the child's egocentrism, while helping to expand it beyond its self-centrated orbit.

The child at this age who is not well-supported in these regards will not be able to develop the social flexibility in social interactions expected and will not be able to solidify the self as a coherent entity, albeit egocentric cognitively. Indeed, the other might be too challenged by the nascent egocentric exploration of the child and consider it too forward or exploratory to the point of being exploitative. The other will attempt to slow down these exploratory forays in social personal planning/goal setting and placate the child toward following other-centered plans and goals. The strategies used to do so might be implicit or explicit, and involve indirect or direct approaches. The child's efforts will be disrupted/shepherded to a different preferred course and subtly (or perhaps not so subtly) criticized/canalized. The other will expect compliance/adherence without deviation or might react aggressively or by withdrawal/neglect. Needless to say, the child will be learning equivalent social strategies that will be brought into peer play/sibling interactions, and carry them forward for use with others throughout life. A sense of affection for/love of the other will be curtailed or conditioned on acceptance of the canalization, whether speaking of the 2-year-old or the person who had lived an unsupportive regime as described for the 2-year-old. In each case, the self will be decomposable/dis-coordinated, not together, and egocentric to the point of selfishness. It will disregard anything about the other, and the representation of the self and other will not be coordinated into potentially complementary roles. There will be fractures in the image of both, with their connection relegated to the other party being required to serve the self.

The therapist encountering this type of patient will need to "keep it together" in order to help solder together the constituent, fractionated self of the patient. In order to accomplish this therapeutic goal, the therapist will need to be both "heat" (warmth) and metal (limit setting) so that aspects of the other can be viewed by the patient as different from one's self(ish) needs. The patient will need to learn new ways of thinking about the self and other beyond the view of the self as the only entity having needs and the other as only being there to satisfy them. The social skills of the person will need to improve in order to allow for planning and coordinating with the other to a degree, while relating those lower-order social skills to higher-order goals of creating more compatibility in self-other perceptions. The relational co-regulation in the patient and other (e.g., a significant other in the life of the patient) will improve as the relational co-regulation develops toward decreasing selfishness and increasing normal egocentric (not egotistical) attitudes, thereby fostering better self-other mutuality. The goal will be to support the beginnings of unconditional affection and even love feelings by the person for the appropriate other.

Behavior/Symptom Network/Connectivity Change (Horizontal)

The patient who presents as having lived in an environment that does not permit normally developing self-image coherence, permissible selfishness (to a degree, and depending on the context), and interlinked superordinate higher-order coordinations in behavior and attitude (e.g., in self-other relations) will present as deficient socio-affectively. The patient will experience difficulties in social interaction co-regulation, fondness/affection/love feelings for the other, and ability to listen to the other in a balanced way (e.g., neither with over-compliance/no resistance nor with reactive resistance no matter what/ non-compliance). The person will have representational views of the self and other that are disjoined and separate, except in terms of the other being only there to serve the self. The parts of the self and those of the other will be disjoined, dispersed, and fractionated, as well, except for an exterior shell gluing the self together. The psychological welding will not be leak-proof, and leakages will clearly happen in these regards. One example might be the patient adapting the same behaviors experienced to create this type of self shell and this type of perception of the other right from the first encounters with the other.

The therapist working with this type of patient will seek to transform the overly egocentric selfishness of the person toward lesser degrees if not full accommodation to the social realities of the other, what others might expect, and so on. The person might be stuck in the self-centered mode, but still be capable of being less self-centrated and more appreciative of the other. Developing lower-order social skills that could filter up to higher-order self and other representations might help in this regard.

Behavior/Symptom Growth, Deep Change (Vertical)/Constructing a More Positive Life Story

The late infant who enters the early childhood period involving representations (via coordinated integrations of sensori-motor plans) needs to successfully navigate the challenges that develop with respect to an egocentric cognition/self, and this will be difficult even with a supportive environment. At 2 years of age, the self needs to stay a coherent yet socially flexible entity, although the cognitive limits at this age preclude taking the perspective of the other. The superordinate higher-order representational cognitive structure behind the child's socio-affectivity will help the child avoid the potential dis-coordination (cognitive, social) at this sub-stage and keep a positive emotional outlook (e.g., affection/love to the appropriate other).

However, the young child who is not well-supported in these regards will experience social disregard/isolation by either being too egotistic or being too passive and retreating socially. The child could become a reinforcement/reward seeker just to satisfy the egocentric needs that have downgraded to egotistical ones. Or, the child could seek reinforcement/reward in order to keep in tune with parents' coercive and controlling behavior that had tantalized them toward compliance. Or, the parents might give reinforcement/rewards as a way to give in to their child's tantrums/giving up when the reward-seeking behavior starts. Whatever the case, normally the other who is involved will not mirror the young child's outward projection of its inner (egocentric, centrated) needs; that is, the other will react with appropriate accommodating behavior and with concerns to help the child grow through the issue at hand. Therefore, in the appropriate context, the self of the child will not grow into a super egotistical child (spoiled). Or, to the contrary, with inappropriate support, the child might grow to express egotistic/selfish aspects and end up "egoless." The child will avoid self-construction and other interactions from a mutual frame, and both internally and externally end up socially "linkless."

The patient whose psychological presentation is akin to that of the young preschooler (but with all sorts of difficulties stemming from being fixated at that level because of experiences lived) can move vertically to different levels of psychological integrity by fully engaging in the horizontal changes suggested for bad habits, for self and other construction, and for social interaction/superordinate organization. This will prepare the way for the coordinated symbol plans of this sub-stage of development to move toward a more hierarchical and adaptively organized coordination of the symbol plans involved and their emotional, social, and socio-affective consequences (e.g., a more flexible cognitive egocentrism/social selfishness).

The patient telling herself/himself overly self-focused stories about the self will not be able to overcome the cognitively egocentric/socially egotistical basis in her/his social behavior without appropriate social or therapeutic support. The stories told will fixate on the falsely superior qualities of the self, in a narcissistic self-aggrandizement. The other will be banished in all ways as part of the patient's narrative, except as self-aggrandizing enhancements. Or, conversely, the self will be considered as one that is depleted, worth abandoning, and without backbone, given that overcompliance/passivity to the wishes and whims of the other prevail. The story told to the self about the self will be imbued with descriptions of fragmentation, dispersion, and disconnection, both among the parts of the self and in relation to the other. There will be no superordinate, higher-order whole self-images and self-concepts able to resist a sense of incoherence of the self and its weakening. The person might be including descriptions of the self as self-centered, or worse, e.g., selfish.

The therapist will work to ensure the construction of a new narrative about the person that she/he can tell to self and others. The old view of the self, its social skills, its attributes, etc. can be reworked/transformed and revised/revived to include alternate scenarios; for example, self-focus can be revamped as a strength to give an anchor to positive linking to the other. The concept held of the other can be reworked from one of an entity to use for one's purpose to one who has her/his own purposes to consider. The other's perceived attempt to canalize the self toward the other's desired ends can be rewritten as possible openings to creating shared ends. The person can learn to evaluate the self as a "together," coherent "ego" in waiting to enter into mutually beneficial relations with the other in which neither self-egotism nor self-abandonment will take place.

Consciousness, Theory of Mind, Selves, and Responsibility

The advent of representational capacities in the early preschooler marks a major advance in cognitive development and allows for the continued growth toward ultimate human attributes related to consciousness, morality, responsibility, and so on.

The representations of the peri-operational (preoperational) stage take the form of coordinated symbol plans that permit the emergence of qualities such as seeds toward the development of a theory of mind, a sense of responsibility and an initiative-taking self. The child will soon be open to formal education, group peer affiliations, while establishing loving relationships with family and significant others. Social interactions will be imbued with reciprocity, respect, and the beginnings of behaving according to mutually established goals toward ends that serve both self and other. At the same time, this childhood period is marked by the great upheaval of Freud's Oedipus/Electra complexes, and the repression of sexual desires into the unconscious. Erikson's conception of life stages as psychosocial, and not just psychosexual, is consistent with the child (and other) having the resources to deal with these types of crises.

The Peri-operational Stage Sub-stage of Hierarchization (3.5–5 Years): Sub-stage 12

Self and Relational Development [Initial Theoretical Elaborations]

A very brief description of the present step in Young's 25-step Neo-Eriksonian developmental model follows. It is presented again in Chap. 18, to help give a collective overview of the 25 steps in the modeling.

Initiative acts vs. guilt acts (3.5–5 years). The growing person balances being forward (in initiative) and being inward and withdrawing. The person could feel guilty when being too forward. For example, pre-schoolers might have sexual feelings for the parent (of the opposite sex) that are too forward and do not go away, even without you knowing it. If the environment (your parent) does not handle this well, you could develop unconscious (unaware) sexual problems that continue, into adolescence onwards or general problems in initiative (having too much or too little).

Appendix 3.2 gives the brief amount of work already done in prior publications related to the task of developing in depth the Neo-Eriksonian (sub)stage model. The next section of the chapter gives an interim summary that elaborates the contents of Appendix 3.2 with respect to the present sub-stage being considered, of the sub-stage of Peri-operational Stage Sub-stage of Hierarchization.

Interim Summary

The 3 ½- to 5-year-old enters another dramatic phase of life in this age period. If the self had been egocentric to this point, it now takes on an initiating persona, and pushes boundaries even into forbidden territory. The undercurrent representations to this behavior in the cognitive sub-stage concern symbol plan coordinations transforming into dominant/subordinate relations. The coordinations go beyond the juxtapositions of the prior sub-stage, and do not simple place the self's desires as primary (centrated) relative to those of the other due to cognitive egocentrism, because the coordinations can be genuinely hierarchized.

The child at this age level of 3 ½ to 5 years of age rejoices in play, and in play that is more than dyadic, that is, in group play on the playground. There might even be gender differences and segregation in this regard, e.g., more rough and tumble play among boys, while using the play (laugh-like) face. Whatever the context, the play takes on a rule structure, with either preestablished more formalized games used or on-the-spot rule-based ones created. The child's underpinning growing representation skills are responsible for and undergird this play behavior because the representational capacity now involves symbol plan coordinations that are hierarchized into adaptive dominant-subordinate relations. This allows the child to relate to multiple others in the group, create or contribute to rule creation in games, or at least follow them, and otherwise inter-coordinate self and other(s) into relations with some sort of hierarchical structure. The same can be said of the blossoming verbal skills of the child at this age. Clauses can be embedded. Sentences can be sequenced. Sub-events can enter story telling. Emotional complexity at this age takes on the same attributes of hierarchization. For example, affection for the other in playful exchange has more of a chance of being reciprocated and creating a crescendo of laughter in the parties that can spread in the group. Of course, the same can be said for negative emotions of pouting, petulance, etc.

The coordinated hierarchized symbol plan coordinations at this age period of 3 ½ to 5 years underwrite the emergence of a major social cognitive acquisition in the child, that of having a theory of mind of the other. Typically, this happens toward 4 years of age. The child can overcome the cognitive egocentrism of the prior sub-stage by placing the perspective of the other in relation to that of the self, although with one's own as dominant in a dominant/subordinate relationship. A 4-year-old child who is asked what is in a candy box having images of candies on the box will say "Candies." But if shown pencils inside the box instead of candies, she/he will realize that another child who has not seen the pencils (e.g., being outside the room waiting to come in and be asked the same question) cannot appreciate that pencils are in the box. However, even though the 4-year-old can understand what the other child will say is in the box in this scenario, the 3-year-old might maintain a "false belief" and state that another child about to be asked the same question will answer that the box contains pencils. It is only with the development of representational symbol plan hierarchizations in the 3 ½- to 5-year-old period can this "false belief" fall by the way side.

The hierarchical nature of the child's representational cognitive activities has social repercussions. The self and other will be related in one cognitive structure, but the self will be hierarchized as predominant. That is, socially, the child in this age period will be highly initiatory, as befits the hierarchizing nature of the underlying symbol plan coordinations. However, there are limits in the cognitive capacity described; for example, Piaget referred to this age period as involving pre-operations. The child is representational but is using intuitive more than logical thought, more animistic than concrete operational thought, etc. So, the social initiations might not be well thought-out, organized, rule-based to begin with, etc. Moreover, as will be discussed shortly, there are serious ramifications in the child's initiatives when it involves the Freudian Oedipus/Electra situation/complex.

The child at this level will encounter many situations in which initiatives will require sensitive correction by the parent, who will focus on teaching consequences. The 3 ½- to 5-year-old might be seen as someone living the age of overt parental discipline. The parent will use the language of "that behavior is inappropriate," "there are consequences," "you need time out," and so on and attempt to offer some form of explanation. The parent will reinforce acceptable initiatives by saying "good job" and the like. The child supported this way will experience emotions such as self-satisfaction/acceptance and a more likely acceptance of the other. The child who is not given this tolerant yet restricting type of parental behavior could gravitate toward inappropriate/misplaced initiatives or, to the contrary, develop a lack in initiative, as the case may be. Associated feelings will concern not only guilt but also a general sense of one being wrong, as well as self-dissatisfaction and a dissatisfaction with the other.

At the socio-affective level, in terms of the Freudian Oedipus/Electra situation/complex, the self is placed in a dominant relationship to the desired parent, and this leads to inappropriate urges that have to be restrained by the parent(s). According to Freudian theory, the urges are repressed into the unconscious. Otherwise, the preschooler at this age ends up with much energy and persistence in her/his inappropriate sexual impulses without any guilt. Successful navigation of this crisis empowers the development of deeper love feelings toward the parent, setting the stage for later transfer to the selected love object. Also, the stage is set for attending initial formal educational structures, like preschools (although daycares can be great learning environments, as well).

When the child lives a regime that had led her/him to be fixated at this level, the undertaken initiatives might be excessively active without monitoring of the effects on the environment/other (e.g., hyperactivity) or, to the contrary, they might be totally damped and lost in suppressed inhibition. The lack of proper support from the parents/environment will have invalidated the child's initiative, ignored it, or perhaps overtly repressing it, leading to no initiative and inertia. The self will not be a contextually appropriate initiating one, but an unfocused initiatory one or an initiative-repressed one. If the Oedipus/Electra situation/complex becomes disturbed to the point that it persists aberrantly, there might be an accompanying and overbearing sense of guilt, or, to the contrary, the child might act inappropriately without any sense of guilt, although that might be overtly acknowledged or leak out occasionally.

As for the child living in a well-supported environment through her/his initiatives manifest too much uncharted initiative without self-controls, the environment will have to coach the child without unduly damping her/him. The fruits will show in cognitive, emotional, and social behavior. That said, the parent having excessive difficulty coping with a child's initiative will need interventions that are child- as much as parent-oriented. The child will be in a position to engage in preliminary verbal exchanges with the therapist, aside from engaging in play therapy. The parent can watch and learn from the therapist's interactions with the child. Parental education and efforts to change parental behavior by validating her/his concerns, understanding her/his own initiative needs, etc. will help. The family dynamic will need assessment, too.

It should be noted that initiative behavior is endemic at this age period and is an apex index, marker, or "organizer" behavior that characterizes it. Of course, the developing infant and child evidence initiative before this age, but not as an apex marker as is the case here. As well, evidently, initiative takes place at all steps in development after the preschool period. Thus, although initiative is the focus socio-affectively at this age, it is part and parcel in one way or another at all ages developmentally. The same proviso about behaviors predominant at one (sub)stage/phase also being expressed before it (or after) happens throughout Eriksonian socio-affective stage models. In particular, Erikson considered identity the critical socio-affective acquisition in the teen years, but found its expressed in precursors beforehand and also afterward in growth.

Self-Response to Cognitive (Mis)Perception of the Other

The symbol plan coordinations of the 3 ½- to 5-year-old develop a hierarchized dominate-subordinate relationship, which allows for placing self and other needs in better synchrony, but typically with those of the self as primary. This means that the child will be expressing initiative, but without the ability to take the perspective of the other at all, at first, at 3 years of age, and only at 4 years of age becoming capable of placing that perspective of the other as secondary in self-other relations. Play will differentiate into elaborate imaginative scenarios with subthemes; discourse or storytelling will include not only plot but also perhaps an embedded subplot; and social interactions will be able to have sub-interactions on secondary matters without losing the primary train of the interaction. Love feelings will flower if all goes well. Feelings of love for the other can be subordinated to the other's prohibitions without negative effects. The child's self as part of the agentic synergy of the child at this age will express explosive initiative, and it will require monitoring/containment and redirection/displacement.

In the case of a child experiencing a lack of appropriate environmental support for her/his initiatives, the chances increase of an extended curtailing of the child in her/his initiatives leading toward an inward turning. Or, the child could become initiative-saturated and keep initiating in most any context, even if inappropriate. The self would be an endless initiatory one, with the environment reacting with extensive control efforts to have the child give in/give up. Or, the environment, being exasperated, conversely might give up, leading to uncontrolled child initiation. The parent might invalidate/ignore the child, which could lead the child to do the same. Also, efforts to initiate might elicit inappropriate guilt or no guilt, as the case may be.

The adult who has lived in an equivalent regime will be struggling with initiation issues, as well. The self will be initiative-saturated, and uncontrollable or, to the contrary, the self will be initiative-depleted or pacified/too controlled. Guilt will be an overriding emotion experienced. Or, the contrary of feeling guiltless might predominate. Blame will always lie elsewhere, and overt lying about things will be more possible (which would also happen with the guilt-free excessively and uncontrolled initiatory young child). The cognitive apparatus associated with this level of functioning concerns symbol plan hierarchies in the representation involved. In terms of the over- or under-initiatory person, either the self or other, respectively, will be at the apex of a disturbed dominate-subordinate relationship in these regards. Love feelings will be problematic, both of self and other.

Positive Pole in Eriksonian Development

The well-supported 3 ½- to 5-year-old will demonstrate adaptive initiatives, undertaking them with energy and persistence. The environment will not be unduly repressive, so the child will avoid feeling guilty about the initiatives. At the same time, the initiatives in the socio-affective arena will lead to the Oedipus/Electra situations, which are associated with the development of the superego through the parental control/admonishment required. The child continues with full-scale and broad initiatives, but not in the Oedipus/Electra situations, which according to Freudian thought leads to repressions into unconsciousness. This process helps avoid conflicts and allows for rewarding ventures into the multiple cognitive social and related domains in the child's life. Loving feelings toward the parent will magnify, along with increasing respect for parental discipline and family affiliativeness/ sense of belonging.

Negative Social-Self Working Schema

The 3 ½- to 5-year-old who is enjoying an initiative lifestyle with a supportive environment that does not ignore, suppress, or otherwise disrupt it will not be guilt-ridden. The child will neither greatly over-initiate nor engage in excessive under-initiative. The social self will involve positive representations of both the self and other. The self will be invested with symbol plan hierarchizations in which the self is considered as primary, yet with coordination with the other involved, as well. The other will become part of the superordinate cognitive structure of the child, whether the other is physically present or not, through both general positive encouragement of initiatives by the other and also prohibitions on their inappropriate direction or targeting.

However, in unsupportive environments related to initiative, the working schema of the other will involve initiative suppression, ignoring, or confusion. Parents might invalidate self-initiative, redirect the child who tries to initiate only to their own desired initiatives, although perhaps not doing so overtly but with tantalizing rewards. The self will be left in a confused labyrinth of unfulfilled initiatives, suppressed initiatives, or guilt-inducing ones. The other will be perceived as overtly repressive in these regards. Or, the manipulation will be subtle and appear benign, but to the point of succeeding in overmanaging the child's initiatives. The parents might function like a widely active helicopter hovering above the child's living field. Feelings of love for the parents will be diminished, selectively expressed, or even repressed.

Attachment, Neo-Eriksonian Development, and Therapeutic Implications [Patients and Therapy]

Patient Presentation

The adult who has lived a regime in which there are long-standing issues related to initiative will gravitate either to a hyper-initiative or hypo-initiative lifestyle. The first type will not care at all what the other thinks of the initiatives, being in total denial that the other might have a different perspective than the self. The person will be inconsiderate, unappreciative of the other, even mean/absent of loving feelings, and without guilt. The second type will be totally empty of initiative, being supremely passive, guilt-ridden at any attempt at initiative, etc. The person probably will have negatively experienced the Oedipus/Electra complex. In contrast, the first type will consider aberrant sexual impulses related to that complex as normal/acceptable. A third type will go back and forth between these two types, being volatile about them, confused about them, etc. Also, the three types will present with different ego-superego relations. The over-initiative type will have a too powerful ego and be dismissive of evident superego controls. The under-initiative type will have a weak ego with a too strong superego, and be repressed. The third type will alternate confusingly between these extremes.

Behavioral/Symptom Mental Scanning

Patients who have struggled with initiative, either by expressing too much of it in an out-of-control way or too little in an overcontrolled way, might project their initiatory deficits on the other or they might excessively blame the other for their initiatory difficulties. This would be especially true if the Oedipus/Electra complex had developed in the late preschool period because of ineffective parental challenges/control/repression of the psychosexual impulses involved. If the repression had become quite generalized of the behavior of the person at that age, under-initiation would be a major outcome. Or, to the contrary, had there been little repression/suppression/initiatory control at all; the initiatory difficulties would take on overactive and impulsive characteristics that also could reach a point of posing immense challenges. No matter what the course, the greater the initiatory challenges, the greater the patient will have difficulty mentally scanning her/his psychological/psychiatric difficulties. By definition, repression in the Freudian sense means that psychological/psychiatric difficulties are not available to the conscious. The person might be able to self-perceive whether she/he is hypo- or hyper-initiatory but perhaps not know any reason why nor think it aberrant or that it has negative consequences for the other. The person might not be able to appreciate why there are difficulties related to loving feelings. The therapist will have to help the patient develop a balance in initiatory control and also be alert for leaks from the unconscious. Then, the therapist can help the person scan for the behaviors that accompany the unconscious, its repressed matter, and their negative effects, and help in developing a conscious self in equilibrium and capable of love.

Therapeutic Implications

The patient with conflicts centered on initiative will have associated issues that might even include ones concerning the Oedipus/Electra complex. The person will be either overly aggressive in initiative, and unconcerned about consequences, or under-aggressive about initiative and too concerned about consequences. The patient will have experienced aberrant disciplinary strategies, including in receiving inappropriate punishments, ineffective rewards, or attempts at pacification/channeling. The initiatives undertaken in the life of the person might be reckless/self-destructive or they might be safe, bland ones, with no risk-taking. The person might have had the initiative self-aggravated and hyperactivated toward impulsivity or, to the contrary, repressed, neutralized, and rendered nonexistent or compliant. The patient might be chafing at the bit in impatience to break out of the chains holding her/him back, or, to the contrary, not be bothered by them at all, being placated by the regime experienced. The person might want more restraining blinders to keep the unfocussed and uncaring initiatives in check. Or, to the contrary, not be concerned by them in any way, preferring to fulminate against the regime experienced. Also, people like this will need work on the self-imposed punishments and reward systems that they will have placed on themselves, or the ones that they seek out and encourage through their own behavior.

The therapist will need to be aware of the conflictual dominant-subordinate relationships that the patient will have established cognitively, emotionally, and socio-affectively. The equivalent sub-stage at issue in the child concerns symbol plan coordinations in a hierarchical manner and, in terms of self-other relations, this means the self will be aberrantly dominant, or the other might be, depending on whether the person is hypo- or hyperaggressively initiatory. The emotion of guilt or its lack might color/control the emotional background, depending on the initiatory style. Feelings of love will be diminished or repressed. The Oedipus/Electra dynamic might be one of unbounded expressions of morally unacceptable impulses or, to the contrary, their total repression, leading to wider sexual or diminished sexual issues, respectively. The person might express love in this context, but aberrantly.

The therapist will have major work to do at multiple levels for this type of patient. First, the initiatory type and its associations need to be determined. Second, the therapist will function as a de facto positively supportive environment to balance either the over- or under-expression of initiative and its associations. Third, the therapist will help the patient learn more appropriate initiative-related social interactions with the other, in order to bring about feelings of satisfaction and guiltless enjoyment in relations with others, at least when behavior is appropriate. The potential to develop loving appropriate feelings will improve, but will persist as an issue.

Stress/Trauma Resilience/Coping

People who have experienced poorly moderated initiatives in behavior will be either over- or under-initiatory, or perhaps alternate this way. They will be undercontrolled or overcontrolled, respectively, in these regards. They will be less guilt-activatory in their initiatives that go wrong or, to the contrary, too guilt-ridden and express way less initiative than is mentally healthy. They might carry associated baggage related to the Oedipus/Electra situation/complex because of early experiences. Their unconscious might be overly repressed but leak, nevertheless, with psycho-sexual themes, or even many other ones through an overactive repressive-cum-leakage process engendered by the initial repression in the older preschooler period. Self-other relations will be skewed by the initiatory imbalances, whether it leans one way or the other (hyper, hypo). The person might have heard too many environmental curtailments/admonishments to "Stop"/"Don't." Or, the person might have modeled what has been heard and repeat constantly to oneself self-invalidating/ignoring statements. The adults around might have preferred their own initiatives to that of the person, and were subtle in canalizing the initiatives expressed to preferred options. Or, they might have attempted to stamp out the initiatives of the person in less covert and more repressive ways.

The ability of people who have lived regimes like this to deal with exterior stresses/trauma that might add to their psychological burden will be hampered. People like this might engage in supercharged ineffective initiatives, or, to the contrary, they might be incapable of taking any initiative, depending. The associated mood will be one of feeling that one's acting on the stress/trauma is ineffective, and without an ability to stop it. Or, one might feel that the way adopted to act is the most effective course, but with pessimism that the stress/trauma will be under control or stop.

The therapist dealing with a patient like this will need to instill better coping skills, inhibitory capacities, and self-direction in behavior toward effective ends. The therapist might want to teach simple self-talk to help the patient get control of out-of-control impulsive initiations or, to the contrary, to motivate initiatory attempts when the first impulse is to do nothing. Speaking of emerging love feelings that could develop and proceed in wished-for directions could help, but the dangers of poorly directed behavior in these regards should be highlighted.

Therapeutic Strategies [The Other and Change]

Relational Co-regulation

The older preschooler between 3 ½ and 5 years of age will be manifestly initiatory in her/his cognitive, social, and socio-affective activity, with the environment called upon by that activity to impose matching constraints, or at least guide the child toward acceptable ends when she/he strikes out in unacceptable directions. The underlying representational cognitive capacity that develops in this sub-stage to support the various initiatives of the child relates to symbol plan coordination hierarchies, and they allow for self-other coordinations of a dominant-subordinate relationship, including in: group play and structuring conversational content and social interaction; taking into account the perspective of the other; and so on. The social initiatives might be constant, unbounded, and unchecked by the child, in a hyper-initiatory fashion, or quite restrained and hypo-initiatory, depending. The initiatives or their difficulties will represent the essence of the child and stand as the predominant qualification of the child's self attributes. If the initiatives are appropriate, they will evoke in the other facilitatory, encouraging reactions. If they are not, or if the environment is not supportive, they will evoke corrective, canalizing, or inhibiting ones. In a certain sense, the self and other are more mirror-image in attitude and behavior than in prior sub-stages of the present model. On the one hand, the child and adult can engage in reciprocal initiatory activity, and do so in the group context, as well. On the other hand, any lack of controlled, positively directed initiation by the child will need strict parental control. This applies to the Oedipus/Electra situation/complex, to be sure, but also generally to the full scope of the child's cognitive, play, social, group, emotional, and socio-affective initiatory activity.

The child requires a constant vigilance and positive control to her/his initiatory pursuits, and when the environment is incapable of providing it or does so in ways considered as disturbed or inappropriate, the child's initiatory impulse could become exaggerated, mitigated, or stamped out. The parent might react with indirect but effective strategies in this regard, such as ignoring, invalidating, responding tangentially, manipulating toward the parent's own ends the initiatory activities, etc. Or, the control efforts might be quite severe, such as use of punishments, withdrawal of favorite rewards, repressive time-out procedures, conditional love pronouncements, etc. The dangers inherent for the child in these environmental approaches to initiatives could lead to: diminishing initiative; creating a lack of motivation; inducing excessive guilt; and repressing love feelings, or, to the contrary, accentuating initiative but in an out of control fashion; heightening motivation but in an uncontrolled way; suppressing any sense of guilt in these regards; and activating uncontrolled loving feelings. The corollary danger is that the child exports these self and relational characteristics as she/he interacts with any other, e.g., siblings, classmates, and playground buddies. Generally, excessive hyper- or hypoactivity in initiative might be promoted with negative personal and social consequences. The other will be considered as an initiatory foil who has no say in the initiations and should not complain of consequences. Or, in contrast, the other might be expected to start all initiations and the child will not complain no matter what their nature.

As for the therapist who has to deal with patients presenting in equivalent ways to the poorly supported child in the initiative period because they had or still are living a regime like the one described, the therapist will have to know when to suggest controls/restrictions on inappropriate initiations that the patients are describing in relation to others in their life (or even in relation to the therapist). The patients will have to learn about the different mindset/attitude/approach the other might have in relation to their own (as in acquiring a valid theorizing mind about the other/mind reading about the other's mind), which will facilitate more reciprocal, acceptable initiatives by self and other acting in concert socially. The therapist will foster appreciation of the mindset of the other to the point that guilt reactions might prevail over guilt-free reactions in the context of inappropriate initiatives. The therapist will have a major challenge to disentangle the Oedipus/Electra situation/complex that might have developed and work toward its resolution. The ultimate goal will be to help develop and free appropriate love feelings toward the other. Without tackling that issue, the hierarchical structure in the cognitive representational symbol plan hierarchizations that underscore social, emotional, and socio-affective relations at this level will be imbalanced and affect the view of the other.

Overall, the cognitive architecture of the child at this age period under discussion allows for increasingly complexity in and enjoying of, social interactions and relations. However, without initiatory supervision, redirection when needed, and suppression when required, relational co-regulation could be quite impacted, including psychosexually. This would hold true both for the child in the 3 ½- to 5-year-old period and for the adult who had not had appropriate support all the while and is in need of therapy.

Behavior/Symptom Network/Connectivity Change (Horizontal)

The patient who is imbalanced in initiative, either being excessive or minimal in these regards, needs to gravitate toward a more equitable center ground on the matter. The initiatives undertaken need to be controlled, properly directed, not guilt-inducing, and adaptive. The point of view of the other has to be considered continually and effectively. The underlying cognitive basis behind this sub-stage in development concerns representational symbol plan hierarchies, which are conducive to balanced dominant-subordinate, self-other social relations in terms of initiative, responsivity, mutuality, relational co-regulation, and so on. If the social problems at this level are too deeply ingrained, or if there is an associated Oedipus/Electra complex, the patient will be quite imbalanced in initiatory psychosexual impulses. Other repressions, initiatory inhibitions or their lack, or social difficulties related to aberrant superego (parental, environmental) control or its lack will complicate the clinical picture. The therapist treating patients with this presentation should attempt to foster insight into unconscious repressions and effects on loving feelings, but will have much difficulty. The leakages/dreams/slips of the tongue, etc. will help in this regard. The patient might be able to shift to a more balanced initiatory psychological life that is more respectful of the other (and the self!). More than likely, the person will have engaged in improper repression of acceptance of the other's initiatives, and will have to learn to control this social impediment. Also, less outspoken strategies in this regard, such as ignoring/invalidating the other, will need their own checks and replacements.

Behavior/Symptom Growth, Deep Change (Vertical)/Constructing a More Positive Life Story

The child who has navigated successfully the initiatory/guilt/Oedipal/Electra crises of the late preschool period is in a position to move on to proper identification with others, especially with parents and their roles, and to magnify loving feelings. This development takes time and the feedback on the part of the parents/adults/environment on inappropriate initiatives, or over- or under-initiative proclivities, will be essentially to smoothing out the child's unruly, misdirected, or repressed impulses. As cognitive development proceeds toward representational symbol plan coordination systematization, the ability of the child to move toward balanced initiatory behavior and then balanced identification with others and their roles (especially of parents) will improve. The same growth potential applies to patients who are working through improper initiatives, self-other psychological constructions, gender acts, etc. With therapeutic support to help in the initiatory imperative, the person can move on to deal with any difficulties with the ensuing identificatory process.

Patients who have lived with an environment that has dis-equilibrated the person's initiatory outreach will be over- or under-initiatory and have associated guilt feelings and problematic or absent love feelings, depending. The presence of an Oedipus/Electra complex will greatly complexify the clinical presentation. The patient will tell stories about the self as hyper- or hypo-initiatory/impulsive/motivated, and with poor social judgment or discerning abilities. For example, they will be puzzled why their social effervescence is not admired, accommodated, or reciprocated. Or, they will feel that the other has blanketed them with so much control that initiatory activity has drowned or cannot reach the surface. If Oedipally/Electrally contorted, the social initiatory base of the person will have inappropriate psychosexual impulses. There might be great confusion/depression about that or even rage/resistance.

The therapist working with patients like this needs to redirect the patients' stories of the self and other to more balanced views. The self needs to be construed as more appropriately initiatory, and any isolated examples in this regard should be extolled and serve as a basis for generalization. When were there good initiatory controls as required by the circumstances? When were there good initiatory efforts toward positive social goals? How can these efforts be built up and widened in scope? For the Oedipal/Electra conflicts that might be evident, at least to the therapist, the new stories told need to be constructed gradually. Any leakages from the unconscious should be taken as signs sent to others (the therapist) that the person wants to understand the issues involved and to change in order to have a better self impression and social relations (including in love). All guilt associations with the leakages will require sensitive handling and reframing.

Consciousness, Theory of Mind, Selves, and Responsibility

The child who progresses well through the great crises associated with the present sub-stage under discussion, that of representational symbol plan coordination hierarchies, will have traversed a primary threshold period toward psychological maturity. The sub-stage concerns initiative/navigating the Oedipus/Electra situation/complex and developing loving feelings not only to parents but also to family and eventually significant others partners that will come her/his way. Positive developments along these lines will nurture appropriate unconscious development by removing repression and development toward more consciousness, as well as respect for and reciprocity with the other, including in the taking the perspective of the other/theory of mind capacity. The self will be initiatory and better prepared for life's challenges. The other will be considered an appropriate disciplinary partner in this regard and supportive. The person's moral base will move into wanting to satisfy and listen to the other in order to preserve the loving relationship in which the child is living, preparing further developmental advances in these regards. The child's social circle will grow in group interactions and play. The cognitive underpinning will not be muddled or muddied by inappropriate initiations, repressions, overcontrol, undercontrol, impulsivity, mean feelings, and so on. The responsible aspect of the world of the adult will be one that the child can understand to a degree, imitate, and prepare to adopt.

The Peri-operational Stage Sub-stage of Systematization (5–7 Years): Sub-stage 13

Self and Relational Development [Initial Theoretical Elaborations]

A very brief description of the present step in Young's 25-step Neo-Eriksonian developmental model follows. It is presented again in Chap. 18, to help give a collective overview of the 25 steps in the modeling.

Identification and gender acts vs. problematic identification and gender acts (5–7 years). In growing, we identify with, or want to be like people who are around, especially parents. This helps you learn about and act like the gender that you prefer. But your environment (parent) might not be supportive about this. This could create problems for you, including not wanting to be like the parent or becoming opposite to how is the parent. Or, perhaps you do not identify with anyone, and have become narcissistic, uncontrollable, etc.

Appendix 3.3 gives the brief amount of work already done in prior publications related to the task of developing in depth the Neo-Eriksonian (sub)stage model. The next section of the chapter gives an interim summary that elaborates the contents of Appendix 3.3 with respect to the present sub-stage being considered, of the sub-stage of Peri-operational Stage Sub-stage of Systematization.

Interim Summary

A watershed moment in the history of the developing human concerns the acquisition of Piagetian operational conservation. The child who develops concrete operations becomes capable of using a primitive logic in the physical situations involved, including in problem-solving. The child can use reversible planning or mental rerouting by returning to the starting point of thought and taking another path in thought. This allows for multiple logic-related cognitive acquisitions. In the present terminology, concrete operations are allowed because of the development of underlying representation symbol plan systems. The child can develop expansive symbol plan coordinations, hierarchize them, and contextualize them while adding adaptive additions. Thus, for example, one component of the symbol plan systems can represent one avenue in thought, while another can represent another after reversing direction and returning to the starting point.

The conservation task illustrates concrete operations at work, and represents the hallmark task of their development. In conservation, the child understands that there are two dimensions to a task and the child should not focus just on one of them. For example, in this de-centration process as applied to one of the earliest conservation acquisitions – number conservation – the child realizes that if three pennies are aligned in a straight line with spaces between them and a second row is matched to it, spreading out the second row does not mean that there are more coins. This holds because, although the line is longer, there are also larger spaces between the coins, which balance out that increased length. This type of logic is referred to as compensation. Another way that symbol plan systems allows for logical justification in conservation is through the argument of negation, in which the child will argue that even though the row of coins has been made longer, it can be reversed to the original starting point. Or, the child could argue that it is still the same number of coins (identity) despite the transformation or that nothing has been added or taken away. In all these arguments, the child's capacity to view the whole system and its hierarchized coordinations allows that a transformation of one sort or another has not led to substantive material change in the coin amount.

The development of concrete operations/representational symbol plan systems portends not only the acquisition of a precursor physical-based (not abstract) logic in context but also of organized rule systems. The child at this age (5–7 years) can start formal education at institutional schools. The child goes to no end to create complex rules in the play engaged in. Language/speech advances into storytelling, with episodes involving problems to solve and their resolution.

The stage is set for later entry by the 7-year-old (and on) into the Eriksonian stage of industry in applied work at school but, at this level being discussed (in the 5- to 7-year-old), the child enters into the socio-affective sub-stage of Identification and Gender Acts vs. Problematic Identification and Gender Acts. The child had been developing gender roles and constancies in prior development and had passed through the Oedipus/Electra situation/complex. The repression of the desire for a parental target psychosexually has been accomplished with suppression into unconsciousness. But the child completes the process in this sub-stage by identifying with parents, their roles, and their attributes, depending on their sex, the sex of the parent, and the twists and turns in the Oedipus/Electra situation/complex process. Moreover, the child can identify with other significant others in family, at school, and so on.

Identification means that the child incorporates and transforms according to the roles, attitudes, attributes, etc. selected (or imposed) for identification. The characteristics are psychological and the child at this age is transforming into a psychological self rather than one defined especially by external characteristics/clothes/sex, etc.

The representation symbol plan coordination systems of this sub-stage allow for this identification process to take place through the paired plans they permit to evolve and relate. For example, the plan for the self (I) represents psychological attributes. Also, those of the other are similarly psychological. Finally, the child can take the psychological characteristics of the self and other in these symbol plans in these regards and expand the psychological self accordingly through the symbol plan systematization that relates them.

The identification/incorporation process is facilitated when the environment is generally supportive of the organized rule-creation skills of the child as it applies to self-definition and relatedness to the other. The upshot of the process is that the child accepts the parents (or significant others), identifies with them differentially, and increases the relational and emotional bond with them. The potential for rejecting the parents, identifying with negative as opposed to positive characteristics, becoming different from any role model, attitude, or characteristic that they represent in an anti-identification process, or expressing either internalizing or externalizing emotions in the (anti-) identification process are mitigated/minimized.

The identification process in this period continues in later sub-stages to further differentiate the psychological self. The self in this sub-stage takes the perspective of the other and examines her/his roles, attitudes, attributes, or characteristics. However, this procedure is accomplished toward redefining and growing the self, in particular, so it is still subjective, first-person, unilateral, and primarily personally focused in goal. The identification is not a conscious process in these regards, but proceeds with the self seeming the primary target of the process.

Note that identification as defined presently is more than direct imitation, reinforced learning, or otherwise a passive process. The child is active in the cognitive construction of her/his schemes/operations and this is increasingly evident in this sub-stage. The child has an active exploratory bent fueled by curiosity and discovery learning. The child engages others in questions, querying, and establishing and transforming the rule systems that she/he is trying to figure out.

In a certain sense, the same process of identification applies with the child's learning material at school. Learning takes place at two planes – the first is a straightforward rote repetition and the second is an incorporation and transformation of the learned material into the existing cognitive structure (in this case, organized rule systems related to representational symbol plan coordinations that are organized into systems). In this sense, the middle child is ready to learn exponentially and improve rapidly in reading, writing, mathematics, etc.

Equivalently, social learning is subject to the same dynamic of curiosity, mastery, and growth. The playground becomes a vast social learning forum. Social identification includes taking characteristics of classmates into one's own social styles, habits, attitudes, etc. Once more, the potential for negative identifications can emerge, depending on the school, class, and classmate context. The same applies to neighborhood peers and their context.

The parent will need to monitor all these potential influences on self-development. Needless to say, the influence of social media has become a paramount influence on child development at this age, and parents need to be constantly supervising their middle school age children in these regards.

Now consider when parents are not supportive of a positive identification and psychological self-differentiation process. The parent might canalize/cajole/dismiss/or otherwise jeopardize the process, for example, by never giving explanations to the child. Perhaps the parent feels threatened by the child's growing psychological presence. Perhaps the parent fears the outcome of the ongoing gender development taking place. The self of the child might end up more a reaction against than a construction for (i.e., against the parent and not for the self, or constructed positively). The child's siblings, friends, school, and social activities might all deviate from parental expectations, as well.

Even in the best of circumstances, identification processes can be compromised. The parent should persist in putting the best face forward (literally) for identification purposes. The child will gravitate to some negative identifications through some negative role models at school, on TV, etc. The child is exploring these identifications without malicious intent and would need subtle correction.

However, the child who has been quite unsupported developmentally at this age might express especially negative identifications, including in gender acts. The parent might seek professional help. The therapist at this point will develop genograms, or charts of all the parental and social influences on the child, including at school, in the neighborhood, with friends, siblings, and social media. The therapist will establish the goals of the family and consider their values, culture, individual and group differences, etc. The therapist will relate to the child (and family) as a good surrogate identification target through a compassionate non-blaming attitude. The therapist will not be an instrument of parental repression, if that seems to be the parental goal, but act to have the family system dynamically improve through shared efforts. The child should not be scapegoated by the family but boosted in all ways toward developing an adaptive, positively identificatory psychological self in relation to a positive supportive family.

As for an adult who has lived difficulties related to the identification process, in particular, the identifications that will have taken place will either be negative, absent, or otherwise disturbed. Negative identifications could include those related to negative psychological characteristics of others, anti-identifications with respect to others (incorporating opposite characteristics, e.g., opposite to parental psychological characteristics), or otherwise infiltrating the self with twisted, deviant, or reduced identifications, leaving a very negatively identified self or, to the contrary, an impoverished one. The person still will be governed by representational organized rule systems in the form of symbol plan coordinations organized systematically, but their essential characteristic socially might revolve exclusively around the self and its needs (increasing narcissism, as in an absent de-centration in conservation), being subjective at all levels without any objective aspects. Emotionally, this will result in experiencing the emotions that accompany the types of identifications being discussed. The person will be dominated by negative internalization or externalization emotions and experience problems psycho-affectively because of this in terms of gender role/behavior/identification acts. The risks include being unruly, expressing maladaptive social behavior, and gravitating to others like themselves in delinquent or otherwise unruly groups.

It should be noted that the child's capacity for taking the perspective of the other (theory of mind) that had developed in the prior sub-stage becomes more differentiated in this one. It becomes second-order, e.g., inferring mental aspects just from seeing eyes in photos, as opposed to the initial first-order skills in these regards (as in the false-belief task). The child might be capable of making these second-order theory of mind inferences through the precursor logic inherent to this stage.

The implications for the child or even the adult who lives a regime not supportive of proper identifications, including in gender acts, is that the person will not be able to make remote judgments of the mind/thinking of the other, let alone direct ones, and resort to one's own warped cognitive filters of the other in these regards. The other can become an inappropriate target of behaviors that mirror the misperceptions involved.

Self-Response to Cognitive (Mis)Perception of the Other

Normally, the child in the 5- to 7-year-old period is acquired beginning representational cognitive concrete operations, organized rule systems, second-order theory of mind skills, symbol plan coordination systematizations, learning formats at formal educational institutions, transformative identifications incorporated into the self of a psychological nature (e.g., the characteristics of the other), and positive gender acts within the identifications and through them. The self-image takes on aspects of the other that invigorates play, social relations, discourse, and family and parental dealings. The identifications will include ones related to siblings, classmates, neighborhood peers, social media characters, and so on. Normally, they reflect acceptance of key parental attributes, their directions, and the environment they create for the child.

The child having difficulties in identification due to poor social support, especially from the parents, risks developing a psychological self that is imbued with negative psychological characteristics, rejecting images of the parents/anti-identifications, or, to the contrary, impoverished/poorly articulated identifications. These difficulties might generalize to poor mind-reading (theory of mind) skills, as well, and to inappropriate gender acts in the socio-affective developmental context.

The adult who has endured identification difficulties, perhaps stemming from experiences in the age period being discussed, will express similar difficulties, but even more so. The identifications of the types described will be more deeply ingrained and more intransigent to intervention as the seeds of personality difficulties and disorders are laid. Emotions experienced will parallel the identifications, e.g., oppositional, depressive, or impoverished (flat). There might be some insight possible based on the organized rule systems/symbol plan systematizations that had predominated in the age period at issue. But will they be sufficient to help the person engage in reversible thought, see the pathway followed and its reasons, return to a hypothetical starting point with negative repercussions equilibrated, and reengage on a different identificatory courses? The more adaptive natural, self-constructive, and discovering self of the person might have been quiet dampened and quieted. Psychological vestiges of poor identificatory patterns, including those imposed by the parent, might proliferate and characterize the psychological characteristics of the self. The construct of the other might be as much in need of restructuring in the identifications being made as the construct of the self, and the negative psychological presentation of the self to others might lead them to give negative feedback to the person in their turn.

Positive Pole in Eriksonian Development

The major tasks confronting the child in the age period in which formal grade school starts includes identification processes, engaging in gender acts, and otherwise creating a psychological self with positive characteristics related to the parent and other significant others, including of her/his own age peers (e.g., in class). The child will partake gladly in family activities, looking forward to family downtime. The child will listen attentively to and accept family advice and suggestions/ideas, on the one hand, and prohibitions/restraints and narrowing down of overly enthusiastic but inappropriate identifications, on the other hand. This applies especially as the parent tries to keep in balance in the child general identifications, gender identifications, and related gender role/behavior acts.

Negative Social-Self Working Schema

The child who has developed representational concrete operations underwritten by symbol plan coordination systematizations will be creating organized rule systems, including in relation to parental and other psychological characteristics that are in the process of transforming the self of the child through identificatory incorporation. In an accepting mold because of positive parental and related support, the psychological attributes that express the growing self in this way will help the child through establishing appropriate gender acts, e.g., in roles, behaviors, and personal attitudes. However, in a non-supportive environment in these regards, the social schemata of the other that might develop will not be so accepting, positively identificatory, and gender-appropriate. The identification attributes might be rejecting, negative, oppositional, or, to the contrary, minimal, impoverished, etc. The second-order theory of mind skills of the other will be affected, leading to poor understanding of the other. The social interactions of the child will express these psychological characteristics and might lead to comfortable peer interactions only with peers having similar problems, including in gender acts. The parent might have acted with curt nonexplanations/orders and the child will act accordingly or worse, e.g., with rejection/aggressivity. This attitude might carry forward into peer relations, including with the opposite sex later in life, and lead to sexual disrespect, sexual narcissism, and worse, as in sexual objectification/violence.

Attachment, Neo-Eriksonian Development, and Therapeutic Implications [Patients and Therapy]

Patient Presentation

Patients immersed in issues related to identification will manifest problematic directions in the other processes, that is, in those that had appeared since the identification problems had developed in childhood. Normally, the identification with parents and significant others will be positive/create an integrated psychological self, allow for positive resolution of gender act challenges, etc. and be undergirded by cognitive representations that permit their continued positive growth into adulthood (i.e., operations moving from the concrete to the abstract type).

However, the adult who had not been properly supported in these regards, e.g., ignored, dismissed, and guided to inappropriate parental identifications/poor gender acts, will wallow in identificatory and gender act difficulties, as well as poor theory of mind/mind reading skills, such as those related to negative identification/gender acts, oppositional identification/gender acts, or, to the contrary, minimal/impoverished identifications/gender acts. The patient will have friends like him/her, have had school problems, and generally a self with inappropriate self attributes/gender-related issues that affect self-esteem.

Behavioral/Symptom Mental Scanning

The patient stuck at a level equivalent to the one of the 5- to 7-year-old grade school child will face issues in identification and in accepting parental gender acts. The person will have self constructs involving negative attributes, and inabilities in psychologically reading the mind of others. The person might be able to recall very well the behaviors of the parental figures that might have provoked the identification backlash/distortion and the details of the identifications that were involved. However, people like this might be limited in appreciating the identifications as being deeply psychological and intrinsic to their self-image and to their typical psychological habitus/disposition. Also, people like this will have a subjective impression of the self and not be able to analyze it much dispassionately, objectively, and in relation to the other and its influences. So, they will be incapable of doing much of the psychological work in depth in therapy, or to alter the identifications without support and guidance of the therapist. It will be difficult for the patients to parse out positive versus negative identifications, and their source, as well. Or, to the contrary, the patients will not discern the presence of anti/oppositional identifications and their source or poverty in identifications, but perhaps they will discern an intrinsic blandness or an indecisive, directionless approach to life or, to the contrary, a pseudo high energy and improper directions in life.

The therapist can use the cognitive capacities associated with the identifications, even if they had been problematic/distorted, e.g., by using the patient's capacity for reversibility in thought. Also, the problematic gender acts might not be scanned in any way at the beginning of therapy. The therapist will have to work with the logical capacity of the patient, albeit primitive most likely, to point out the risks of problematic identifications and their possible consequences for gender acts, hoping for some self-insight and future corrective measures in the construction of the psychological self of the person.

Therapeutic Implications

The patient with problems related to parental and related identifications, rejecting parents and significant others, engaging in problematic gender acts, and having created a self suffused with negative, rejecting, oppositional emotions or with depressed, withdrawn ones, as the case may be, will need much therapeutic work on the problematic psychological self that had developed. The latter's attributes will be counter to parental/significant other positive ones, if any, while including parental/significant other negative ones; or it will be indecisively thwarted/minimized and reduced to shriveled identifications. Mind reading skills will be problematic. The associated gender acts will reflect the qualities of the identifications, and will be problematic in how one should deal with others psychosexually. The normally active curiosity expressed cognitively, socio-emotionally, and in exploring the psychology of oneself and the psychology of others will be either hyper-expressed, but in negative directions, or hypo-expressed, and yielding a highly passive individual psychologically.

If hyper-expressed, the active but negative curiosity of the person will infuse many relevant activities and relations with people, leading perhaps to diagnoses of psychiatric personality disorders or tendencies. Their direction will depend on the regime experienced in the environment but will verge on the confrontational, externalizing type or, to the contrary, in the hypo-identificatory style, the internalizing depressive, avoidant, dependent type. The former will want to forcefully assimilate the other into her/his psychological world view and the latter will be maladaptively open to the other doing the same to her/him.

To better understand the patient and how she/he might behave in therapy, the therapist should understand the cognitive representations associated with the origins of the identification issues and how they might have changed with time. The psychological reconstruction of the past should show that, in middle childhood (the 5- to 7-year-old age period) when the first concrete operations were developing, the child had access to preliminary logic in physical contexts, a reversibility in the thought process, organized rule systems, and symbol plan coordinations systemically underpinning them. The therapist could use the representational, reversible rule-based thought processes that might have been compromised in the past toward the development of negative/anti-identifications or, to the contrary, to reduced identifications to others, toward creating with more positive identifications that could replace negative/reduced ones once they are managed appropriately. The therapist might say, "What could you do if you went back in time (and saw this bad habit plaguing you today in the midst of developing back then) to change it so that it would not bother you today? How can you implement that change in the present knowing this?" Appropriate therapeutic goals would include: proper self-identifications, more accepting attitudes and emotions, working through problematic gender acts and other mind reading, and otherwise learning more active, positively directed, and support-promoting social skills. The therapeutic process involved will not be short-term, in order that the changes made might be quite positively anchored in the long-term.

The therapeutic stance might be harder to implement in the confrontational/negative identifactory patient because of the associated externalizing emotions and traits. The stance might be easier for the de-identifying/minorly identifying patient, but the accompanying deeply ingrained internalizing depression/withdrawal would need a boost in the active self-reconstruction to turn the corner therapeutically. The overall therapeutic approach should involve a directed conversational style, directed in the sense of knowing the goals that should be realized in terms of identification and related problems, and conversational in the sense of eliciting the preliminary logical and thought reversal processes inherent in the patient at this juncture to eventually promote/provoke the necessary change. In this sense, directed does not mean being directive and providing explicit directions to the patient.

Stress/Trauma Resilience/Coping

People with problematic identifications, acceptance of parents/significant others, gender acts, and theory of mind capacities, as well as overly negative or deviant psychological self-attributes will not be able to be resilient about/cope with stress/trauma as they would otherwise. Normally, they should be able to use the logic afforded by their cognitive operations (concrete and perhaps abstract), organized rule system creation capacities, reversibility in thought, and symbol plan coordination systematizations to problem solve with good success in cases of stress/trauma, at least in cases when the latter are not overwhelming/catastrophic. However, when people have a backlog of difficulties stemming from the identification phase of development, these cognitive skills will be circumvented/set aside in the turmoil of stress/trauma, and less advanced cognitive skills will be used in attempts to solve the problem at hand, e.g., intuitive pre-operations will be used and contradict any logical, operatory ones if they are deployed. The confrontational or withdrawing nature of the person, as the case may be, and as hardening into maladaptive personality traits/disorders/tendencies, will also interfere with the process of dealing with stress/trauma. Resilience will be sapped by wasted energy deployment to maintain the personality structure, leaving less free energy available for stress/trauma resolution/resistance. The person might resort to the type of language heard from the environment in efforts to contain/redirect her/his negative/anti-identifications or, to the contrary, her/his minimized identifications, further interfering in efforts to deal with the stress/trauma at hand.

The therapist helping patients such as this to deal with stress/trauma will notice the inability of the patient to deal with the matter relative to other patients without this type of preexisting psychological vulnerability. If the baggage of the patient includes identificatory issues, they will interfere with the normal rapport building and treatment adherence that should take place in session. The therapist could use the patient's concrete (abstract) operational skills/reversibility capacity to help an otherwise integrated patient who has experienced a recent stress/trauma to retrace/relive the stress/trauma at issue and work through it in normal circumstances. But with a patient quite evidently having identificatory/gender act issues, that ability will be lessened if not neutralized or worsened. The therapist will have to not only teach stress/trauma management techniques but also work on problematic identifications/gender acts through the concrete (abstract) logic and thought reversibility that she/he should aim to elicit as helpful bases to the therapy.

Therapeutic Strategies [The Other and Change]

Relational Co-regulation

The 5- to 7-year-old has developed initial representational concrete operations that afford advances in the cognitive base underlying emotional, social, and psychosocial/psychosexual development. The child's preliminary contextual (not abstract) logic allows for more elaborate, complex social relations, involving more mutual regulatory activity. The child will be identificatory in a positive sense and so possess positive psychological attributes. But the child might also have the capacity to detect, monitor, and even reject identifications that are negative, anti-/oppositional, too active/untamed, or in need of hyper-support.

A major developmental task in this age period concerns the challenge of developing appropriate gender acts relative to problematic ones. This would include appropriate behaviors, roles, attitudes, and identifications, with acceptable organized rule systems governing activity in relating at the gender level to others. The child's ability to self-correct through the reversible cognitive thought trajectories and to start over along new ones would be beneficial in helping to correct inappropriate/unacceptable identificatory and related processes in these regards.

The self-other dynamic can be righted if imbalanced on gender-related issues, and this will be much harder to accomplish if the environment/parent is unsupportive/inappropriately behaving in the case of the child, or if the adult who has faced a similar regime as a child cannot find the right type of support, including therapeutically. The perspective-taking (mind reading) of the other will be seen through the lens of the "I" in either case, and improvement relationally with the other will be difficult. Poor quality or minimal/anomalous identifications take place in unsupported or negative environments, and the therapist working with this type of patient will have to function as a relational co-regulatory agent supporting proper identification in the developing life of the patient, including in terms of her/his gender acts.

Behavior/Symptom Network/Connectivity Change (Horizontal)

The patient with negative anti-, or reduced identifications, and who expresses associated negativity in emotions, and negative feelings about the psychological self and in other through mind reading, along with problematic gender acts, will be capable of slow lateral growth movements to positive identifications, self-other psychological constructions, and equilibrium in gender acts. The person might even resist change if it is too threatening to her/his existing defense mechanisms, personality traits/disorders, or acquired ways of dealing socially with the other. The reactive resistance that might accompany the cognitive misperception of the other could very well generalize to the patient's approach to the therapist and create tension in session. The therapist should not be confrontational in turn and, instead, should offer steadfast support.

Or, the patient might be totally passive, pacified, self and impoverished of positive psychological characteristics. The therapist will have to build in indirect, supportive ways new positive identificatory incorporations and transformations while working toward controlling, inhibiting, and altering negative/anti ones. The person who has associated problematic gender acts will require much support/conversation to promote some insight, etc. in order to effect the beginning of change. The language the patient might have heard to deflect the person's developmental course (Couldn't it be that…; Yes, but another way…) could be used by the therapist to help shift the patient to different perspectives about the patient's self and her/his perspective of the other's psychology, and redirect gender-related difficulties toward positive outcomes.

The child who had experienced a supportive environment all along, but nonetheless is having difficulties with identifications/psychological self and other construals, as well as gender acts, could profit from similar language used constructively. In both cases (patient, child), the cognitive skills associated with the sub-stage at issue will facilitate the horizontal change possible. The adult/child will be able to oppose present and ideal hoped-for images of self and other in terms of identification, gender acts, etc., through the concrete operations (reversibility in thought, etc.) available, and so work toward change, albeit with support required. For the child, the therapeutic limitation will be the child's limited logical abilities. For the adult, the limitations will be the deep entrenchment of the identificatory/gender act and related difficulties.

Behavior/Symptom Growth, Deep Change (Vertical)/Constructing a More Positive Life Story

The person expressing difficulty with identifications, gender acts, self and other psychological constructions, mind reading, and so on can move on through positive participation in therapeutic sessions. Directed, conversational support by the therapist will help. Talk therapy should not simply be opportunities to vent but also be occasions to listen and learn from the therapist, reflect and look back, and so on. The new positive identifications that might develop should be those unique to the patient in her/his symptom constellation and context. As these issues are resolved, growth toward latency/industry in the child, or the equivalent in the adult patient who had experienced an identification-compromised regime, will increase noticeably.

The patient who has identification and related difficulties for gender acts, self-other psychological construction, mind reading, and so on will tell a range of stories about the self or other. If the identifications are negative/anti−/oppositional/rejecting/nonaccepting, these attributes will dominate in the stories told. The "I" will be the major story protagonist, with the other a foil, rejected, and so on, depending, and not described in a balanced way. If the identifications are impoverished/minimized/absent, the stories told by the person about the self will be similarly narrow/brief in duration and so on. If gender issues are especially involved, they might be included in the narratives. New stories that could be constructed should involve new more positive identifications, problematic gender act resolutions, better self-esteem through more positive impressions of a growing positive psychological self, and so on. The patient will have the psychological resources to entertain new possibilities in story construction through the preliminary logic (or more advanced logic) that might be available and the thought reversal process associated with it. The therapist can use a more conversational mode with patients like this and feed ideas toward the patient incorporating them into his/her narrative and self-transforming it as a result.

Consciousness, Theory of Mind, Selves, and Responsibility

The middle school age child who traverses well the questions of positive identifications, gender role acts, psychological self and other construction, acceptance of parents, etc. will have a solid basis for moving toward greater awareness, morality, responsibility, respect for the other, good self-esteem, and so on. The cognitive representational acquisitions of concrete operations/thought reversibility, symbol plan coordination systematizations, organized rule systems, and so on will help the child to be better able to envisage and act upon the ultimate human attributes in question at the level indicated by her/his cognitive sub-stage. The child will be actively curious at school, learning, discovering, and incorporating/transforming the network of cognitive schemas inherent in the higher-order concrete operations present. The child will be home-responsible, listening to parental requests; school-responsible, paying attention in class; play-responsible; enjoying games and chatter with peers; and socially responsible, behaving as expected and with a relative skill, at least to the degree possible. Temper flare-ups will be rare and easily managed. Social affiliations generally will be enjoyed, and love feelings for the parent(s) will be accentuated (and reciprocated when received). Gender acts will be appropriate, preparing the way for the respect of later targeted partners. Generally, the child will be on a positive growth trajectory toward conscious caring for the other, morality, responsibility, and self-growth.

The Peri-operational Stage Sub-stage of Multiplication (7–9 Years): Sub-stage 14

Self and Relational Development [Initial Theoretical Elaborations]

A very brief description of the present step in Young's 25-step Neo-Eriksonian developmental model follows. It is presented again in Chap. 18, to help give a collective overview of the 25 steps in the modeling.

Industry (putting in good effort) acts vs. inferiority acts (7–9 years). In growing, normally we enjoy learning, including at school, feel motivated, and develop peer friendships. However, your environment (parent) could have shown little interest in your learning, manipulated you, created harsh rules, etc. This could have led you to lose interest in school and learning, lose self-confidence, have the wrong friends, feel inferior, and even rebel. Or, perhaps you went the other way, and felt too superior, while you became insensitive and lied as needed.

Appendix 3.4 gives the brief amount of work already done in prior publications related to the task of developing in depth the Neo-Eriksonian (sub)stage model. The next section of the chapter gives an interim summary that elaborates the contents of Appendix 3.4 with respect to the present sub-stage being considered, of the sub-stage of Peri-operational Stage Sub-stage of Multiplication.

Interim Summary

The 7- to 9-year-old child who has entered formal schooling at the grade school level has acquired basic concrete operational skills. These skills will be expanding at this age, including in conservation. The child becomes more adept in using logical reasoning/rule-governed systemic thought in the situations confronting her/him, including by applying reversibility or going back to the starting point in thought. Normally, the child at this age has resolved Oedipus/Electra situations/complexes in a positive direction, as well as gender acts and related appropriate identifications, such that she/he applies herself/himself well to the learning tasks at school. The child appropriates well the contents of the learning, while avoiding inferiority feelings related to self-perception if there are stumbling blocks in this regard. The child revels in industriousness/zealousness, self-confidence, discovery learning, and receiving expert teaching while not reacting negatively to lack of success in her/his endeavors by feeling devalued/inferior in the self.

The undergirding cognitive capacity permitting these acquisitions concern the development of generalized representational symbol plan systems, for example, to new domains, such as new areas of conservation. The advances in symbol plan use permit inter-coordinated, combined, chained, ordered, and alternating/expanding skillful application of the concrete reasoning of the child to socio-emotional as much as intellectual tasks. The child is capable of perceiving not only the mind/intentions of the other but also that the other is similarly evaluating the child, so that a dynamic of mutual evaluation of the self and other takes place as the child interacts with others. The self, then, of the person is a socially reciprocal psychological self capable not only of first-person perspective-taking (theory of mind, mind reading, viewing the perspective of the other) but also of higher-order perspective-taking. Additionally, the child can apply her/his cognitive skills toward logically estimating her/his own psychological characteristics, including whether she/he is trying, likes to learn, knows what she/he knows, and is following rules including in learning and at school.

Of course, children at this age are applying these cognitive gains to analyze social relations, moral actions, and so on and generally consider the logic in the rule systems encountered as primary. Perhaps the children appreciate the mind of the other and that the other is evaluating their mind, but this does not make them more mindful of the inherent rights of the other and that their actions toward the other might violate extant rules and still not violate moral standards. The child will be able to weave more complex stories, such as stories having both major and minor plots and in which both types are resolved in the narrative told. Similarly, the child will carry on social interactions at multiple, simultaneous levels with major and minor goals interweaved, and with efforts to work through all of them. At the same time, the child can engage with significant others with affection/love, affiliation/belonging, and respect/mutual regulation. As for schooling, the same applies – the child is able to learn multiple learning lines in different subjects, juggle them well (e.g., in reading, mathematics, music), etc.

These psychological attributes had been present in the prior sub-stage of peri-operational systematization, but they proliferate in the present sub-stage of peri-operational multiplication. The child needs to engage appropriately with a host of different people in her/his life using the cognitive operations/symbol plan structures available as the cognitive base, and this allows not only for an education-based "industry" but also a "social" one. People can be categorized in multiple ways, e.g., having this role but also that one (classification skills). They can be serially organized (e.g., teacher has most knowledge, then older child, then class-mate). So others can be differentiated psychologically on multiple dimensions and compared and organized along those dimensions. The same ability applies to evaluating one's psychological characteristics. For example, the child might know what she/he excels in, her/his likes, and how she/he rates compared to other children in these regards. These social comparison skills can change with experience, learning, knowledge, etc. (reverse, alter). Nevertheless, they serve as anchors in dealing with others and how others react to the child.

The environment needs to provide the support required for the child to advance on these multiple fronts in the ways indicated. Teachers need to educate appropriately. Parents need to teach and buttress appropriately. Experts in any activity in which the child participates need to guide appropriately. But the child has a significant role to play in the learning and knowledge acquisition taking place. Liking to learn, wanting to try the best, feeling self-confident as the knowledge base grows in the home, at school, and generally all require a motivated, alert child.

If the environment is not supported at these levels, the growing motivation of the child to learn at all these levels can be subverted. The environment might prefer to control the child irrespective of the consequences, and curb curiosity, motivation, etc. The child might be overly canalized/manipulated/directed toward ends uniquely chosen by the environment (and perhaps inappropriate ones, at that) rather than stemming from the natural proclivities of the child or the normative, standard "curriculum" in society expected at school or home. The environment might respond passively to any individualized activity or thought process of the child (e.g., Uh-uh, rather than giving an enthusiastic response), or even use (inappropriate) reinforcements to shape the child in its preferred directions. The environment would be taking advantage of the rule-centric nature of the child at this age period and create the rules it wants the child to adhere to.

Or, the environment might be quite critical, manipulative, etc., to the point that the child does not negotiate well the educational, social, and emotional challenges endemic at this age and create a lack of self-confidence, a sense of inferiority, difficulty in motivation/trying one's best, and a lackadaisical, "lazy" attitude to learning, or even outright resistance/rebellion, depending. The self will be characterized by a sense of inadequacy/failure. The child may react with abandoning the positive "industry" goals she/he could have, lapsing into a sense of having no or little control over her/his life, manifesting maladaptive undercontrol, or, conversely, engaging in overcontrol. The danger is that the self compensates for the sense of inferiority by having a false sense of superiority, attempting too much control, using the other for one's own needs and foregoing any sensitivity to the other/mindreading/trying to understand what the other thinks, etc. The child could sink to using overt manipulation of the other, to promises of rewards to the other that are not psychologically appropriate, and even to deception/lying. The cognitive basis of concrete operations/logical thought and reversibility will be applied for egotistic ends that will rob the ego of any empathy, effective reciprocal social problem-solving, and learning what the other really thinks and taking it into account. The representational symbol plan coordinations that have become systematized and then are proliferating in this sub-stage of development will lead to narratives about the self and other filled with mis-construals, but that will be otherwise adaptive for the child in the circumstances in which she/he finds herself/himself (self-deception in order to get through).

The adult who has been forced to live a regime much like the one being described will have the characteristics of the child as described, but even more so. The adult might find it difficult to escape the sense of inferiority, live a productive "industry," develop reciprocal affectionate/loving relationships, and otherwise use representational concrete logic to solve the multiple cognitive, socio-emotional, and socio-affective problems found in life and the distortions in her/his psychology.

Self-Response to Cognitive (Mis)Perception of the Other

The child functioning well at this level, and with a proper parental/environmental support, will flourish in her/his growing concrete logic and proliferation of representational symbol plan coordination systematizations, growing industriousness in learning and schooling, etc. and will be without a sense of inferiority/failure. The engagement with the other will include attempts to understand how the person thinks, and even in how the person thinks of the child. This will help fashion/formulate the child's sense of self, which, for all intents and purposes, will be a rule-governed one, but with logic capable of structuring organized rule systems that can be altered (even reversed). Socially, friendships can be made/enjoyed, but then they can be reversed/negated, if called for.

In non-supportive environments, the child's cognitive and social industriousness/zealousness might not develop optimally. Instead of trying her/his best, exhibiting industry, optimizing learning, etc., the child might express poor effort/laxity and disturbances or lack of gain in learning. The self will feel inferior/inadequate and rebel/resist. It might react with letting go/under-engagement or with over-effort/over-engagement, depending. It might exploit/manipulate or deceive/lie to the other. The other typically will be channeling/manipulative toward the child or perhaps just disinterested/uninvolved. The child will have those tendencies mirrored in the self.

The adult experiencing a similar regime will develop as just described for the child, but even more so. The sense of inferiority/failure might be pervasive, along with a widespread laxity/de-motivation. Industry will be absent and idle activity prominent, perhaps with idol worshipping of one sort of another (usually promising quick fixes). Logical rationality will be hidden behind illogic, absent thinking will prevail over thinking through and thought reversal in problem-solving, and seeking help from others will be either maximized or minimized, depending on the style involved. The other will be treated with distance or disrespect, as the case may be, instead of closeness and bonding.

Positive Pole in Eriksonian Development

The present sub-stage concerns Eriksonian industry, and that, for Erikson, spans the whole grade school time frame. However, in the present model, it is limited to a 2-year period (7–9 years of age), and so is focused on the initial application of industriousness to formal education. At the same time, the age period applies to other areas of mastery, such as in social activities, leisure activities, and learning generally (e.g., new sports, skills). The child can develop a sense of adequacy/accomplishment and earned pride/contentment as new learning takes place in any area and is acknowledged. The child is especially rule-governed but contributes to rule creation through her/his increasing cognitive logic (concrete operations/proliferating symbol plan coordination systematizations). This contribution by the self feeds the growing sense of mastery cognitively, socially, and emotionally. The child's social world blossoms in affiliation, affection, and strong love feelings for significant others.

Negative Social-Self Working Schema

The child who has developed a positive industriousness will apply it to school, at home, with peers, and generally (e.g., in leisure/sport activities). The child will be keenly logical, organized; rule-oriented; applied, wanting/enjoying the learning, or perhaps just following without complaint the rule/accepting that learning is required; and liking the challenges if not tolerating them. The child will be active in exploration and learning, as well as in discovering actively and in learning from experts/teachers.

If the environment is not supportive in these regards, these various positive characteristics will not develop accordingly. The child might appear lazy, disinterested, and even oppositional, but this attitude will mask a deep crisis in self-confidence and belief in the ability to succeed. The child will exhibit preference for poor effort/laxity as an excuse in not confronting/feeling positive about the challenges involved, and so on. The other will not be construed as an actively interested and involved person in the life of the child but as someone going through the motions, disinterested, and even lazy and only trying to get what she/he wants at the expense of the child. The other will be understood as having negative perceptions of the child, which might exacerbate a sense of inadequacy/not trying, and even induce resistance/rebellion. A compensatory reaction to either not succeeding in tasks undertaken of whatever kind or to the environment devaluing those efforts, could lead the child to develop the opposite of a sense of inferiority (a sense of superiority).

The adult who behaves similarly will have had equivalent attitudes expressed by significant others in her/his life. Their expertise/knowledge will be dismissed and any efforts at learning/knowledge accrual made by the adult might involve study by the person (self-study), if undertaken at all. The sense of inferiority could develop in the person, as described or, conversely, one of superiority could develop.

Attachment, Neo-Eriksonian Development, and Therapeutic Implications [Patients and Therapy]

Patient Presentation

When industry represents a major concern of patients, they display problematic motivation and low self-confidence at multiple levels, for example, in functional role (school, work, care-giving, as the case may be) and in social and family relationships. They will not enjoy doing things, nor apply themselves, etc. They will have a negative image of themselves involving self-depreciation. Their emotions will involve passive resignation/poor engagement in anything or, to the contrary, a too active over-engagement/attempt at control in a belated effort to avoid the demoralization of a sense of inferiority/inadequacy/failure. Their psychological problems might have begun in the grade school age range when logic begins to develop, including through concrete operations and reversal thought processes becoming more prominent. Therefore, these types of patients might have difficulty thinking through things in any task requiring industry, including working at social relations. Normally, people use organized rule structures to navigate the complexity of the world, but these will be deficient, haphazard, illogical, and maladaptive. The symbol plan coordinations that should be systematized and multiplying out will be riddled with inefficiencies and errors that will preclude effective social cognition, including in reading the mind of the other and how the other might be reading the mind of the person. This could lead to extreme passivity/resignation or, conversely, extreme overactivity/overcontrol that inevitably will lead to frustrations all around, social irritability, and lack of consideration (or worse) of the other. A sense of superiority might emerge strongly and discolor images of the self and other.

Behavioral/Symptom Mental Scanning

Patients asked to mentally scan for symptoms, one's psychology, impressions of the self, construals of the other, etc. will be able to use the contextual logic that is associated with the sub-stage at issue (peri-operational multiplication), but with the limits in its development that an unsupportive environment had incurred. These types of patients will know that they are under- or over-industrious, and have associated feelings of negative self-worth (inferiority) or perhaps overly positive self-worth (superiority complex). They might not try their best or, conversely, express an overexuberance in this regard, but in maladaptive ways. They might understand resignation/passivity and undercontrol or, conversely, express reactive frustration/rebelliousness and overcontrol. They will understand that the other perceives faults in them either way, but will they be capable of reacting constructively to them? The underzealous type will automatically agree with all criticisms directed to the person and attribute a total truth value to them, even if unwarranted. Conversely, the overzealous type will automatically reject all criticisms emanating from the other, considering all of them as totally invalid. The self-perception of the person in both cases will be imbalanced, as much as will be the perception of the other.

The person might appreciate the nature of the unsupportive environment at the root of her/his problems with industry/inferiority (superiority). However, without supportive therapy, and understanding the need for it, the person will remain stuck. She/he will have concomitant issues concerning relatedness/sociality, affiliation/belonging, affection/love, and general respect for self and other. The person might lack the insight how to redress relevant imbalances, but all the while might have a clear longing to do so. The dangers in this regard if the wounds/challenges should be left to fester is that reactions like apathy or, conversely, lashing out, will set in and propagate.

Therapeutic Implications

Patients with problems related to industry will express feelings of inferiority, will engage in social relations lacking in considerate understanding of the other and appreciation of the other's view of the patient, and will show poor motivational effort in school/work or other primary roles, as well as in cognitive curiosity and desire to learn with follow-through. The patient will avoid the cognitive effort to think logically about complex school/other roles and social/emotional challenges and will use more primitive cognitive structures if initial attempts at applying logic are made to issues at hand. The patient will test the calm demeanor required of the therapist because effort/motivation/application/trying one's best will be quite compromised if not absent. The patient's self-esteem will be abysmally low. This will impact negatively social reciprocity and fair self-evaluation. The patient will turn too inward in self-protection from the hurt of potential failure. The onus will be placed on the other to unduly help the person compensate for her/his lacks and expend extraordinary efforts in this regard. In unsupportive environments, the other will have her/his own agenda, leading to open conflagration with/deception by the other and consequent passivity/resignation by the patient. The patient presentation in this style might include thinking of herself/himself as having poor effort/lassitude and an "I don't care" attitude.

Or, conversely, in another style, the patient might react with an over-industriousness in all relevant spheres. The person will try hard, but usually still fail in the effort expended, whether cognitively, socially, or emotionally. The other might be co-opted into the extreme industry undertaken. The patient's perceptions of the other will be to minimize/discount/reject the other or even reverse any compliments received. The patient who presents this way warrants a different approach than the first type – to temper, tone down, and reverse/redirect some of the more maladaptive perceptions, feelings, and actions expressed.

In either case, the therapist should aim for moderation in industry and associated cognitions, roles adopted, social and emotional behavior/attitudes, and understanding of the self. The platitude of trying one's best irrespective of the outcome should be used, as well as complementary ones of respecting the other and the other's opinions/attitudes toward the patient while doing so. The underzealous patient might need to be treated as a jealous person who needs to work through blockages/impediments, while the overzealous type might need to be treated as requiring better self-regulation and consideration of the other and her/his views of the patient. The emotions associated with these extreme approaches will reach more of an equilibrium as the zealousness does. This includes balancing the imbalances in feeling inferior/superior.

The therapist could use the patient's increasing logical, operational, organized rule systems and their proliferation, and the story telling skills of the patient to have the patient try to reverse maladaptive thought processes and associated behaviors, emotions, motivational problems, and social difficulties toward different directions. The conversational therapeutic style will be used, but with many suggestions how to implement a balanced industry/zealousness in the multiple domains of daily life (cognition, school/work/care-giving roles, dealing with others, improving the self concept). The therapist will have to work on how the patient can deal with a non-supportive environment, e.g., neglect/not concerned about industry-related matters, or being threatened by them and attempting to deviate them to preferred targets and outcomes). The therapist will aim to improve industry in all relevant spheres – cognition/school, daily role/function, and social/emotional relations, leading to equilibrated social affiliation/belongingness/respect and emotions with affection/acceptance of the other and understanding their views, and with loving feelings, as the case may be. The inferiority (or its converse of a superiority complex or the like) will take a long time to self-correct even with the support and conversation reasoning and suggestions of the therapist.

Stress/Trauma Resilience/Coping

The child who has developed advanced cognitive skills related to logical concrete operations, reversible thought procedures, organized rule structures, symbol plan coordination systematization proliferations, etc. will be in better able to deal with stress/trauma, if the environment is supportive. But the environment will still have to play the crucial role in this regard. The child will be coached on what she/he can do to cope and will apply herself/himself assiduously in this regard, given the industry/strong effort that develops at this time in normal circumstances. The child's self-perception will be shaken by the stress/trauma, but can be buffered and used to advantage.

However, in less supportive environments, the child will be incapable of proceeding so logically, organized, and industriously when stress/trauma encroaches on her/him. Similarly, the adult who has lived a regime in which industry/zealousness has been undercut will have her/his resilience and coping mechanisms to stress/trauma undercut. The process of using contextual logic, trying to return to the starting point before the time that the trauma/stress had taken place and then working through, and using more adaptive resilience/coping techniques will be affected/disturbed. The adult (a) might become excessively lackadaisical/sensing the self as inferior or, to the contrary, (b) might become hyper-industrious, but ineffectively so, while having a false, misplaced sense of superiority. Either way, the person will not apply well extant cognitive, emotional, behavioral, and social skills to deal with the stress/trauma at hand, or ongoing learned ones, as well. In the hypo-industrious former case, the adult might not even try to deal with the stress/trauma, feeling that any effort is doomed to failure. In the hyper-industrious case, the adult might be overly responsive, investing a wide array of energy and strategies to deal with the stress/trauma, but with a lack of clear logic and organization, thereby dooming the effort to failure, as well. In the first case, the sense of inferiority will lead to an underevaluation of the effectiveness of what can be done and, in the second, a sense of superiority will lead to an overevaluation of what can be done. In both cases, social resource recruitment will suffer, by a depressed lack in the first case and a lack of social skills and acceptable way of approaching the other in the second case.

The therapist working with an adult who has stress/trauma issues could take advantage of the contextual logic/cognitive operations available to the person, but these skills might not have propagated sufficiently over cognitive, social, and resilience/coping domains to help the person problem solve effectively. The therapist will have to try to tap into the industriousness/applied nature of the person that might have developed, in part, to have it generalize to working through with support to the stress/trauma at issue.

Therapeutic Strategies [The Other and Change]

Relational Co-regulation

The 7- to 9-year-old enters into new relational structures by virtue of her/his industriousness, motivation, increasing self-confidence, desire to learn, query, absorb, discover, and apply acquired knowledge and ability to accept corrective feedback (e.g., by teachers) and improve in the contextual logic used accordingly. In all domains, the underlying expanding representational concrete operational activity generalizes (with its symbol plan coordination systematization application and proliferation). The child applies the organized logical rule system she/he is creating in context to understand the other, her/his mind, what the other thinks of the child, as well as the self and the relations the child enters into with the other. The child is sociable, affiliative, expressive of the need for sociality, happy in it, and when appropriate, affectionate and loving. The child is willing to respect the other, including the other's opinions and attitudes toward the self, assuming, of course, that they are respectful, in turn. Granted, corrections and shaping will be visited on the child but constructively and without undermining the child's zeal and industriousness. In these optimal circumstances, the relational co-regulation between the child and other approaches increasing equitable reciprocity, although the environment/adult/significant other still is applying and modeling constructively her/his expertise.

The child has the ability to engage in mutuality in the reciprocal regulatory process because of the accompanying reversibility in thought that accompanies her/his concrete operational logic. The child can behave or think one way, understand a corollary or even different way in these regards expressed by the other/parent/teacher/environment, and return to point zero in order to reconstruct a different, more co-regulated trajectory in thought/behavior/sociality/attitude, etc.

The child who lacks adequate support in this grade school age period might have difficulties with industry/zeal, motivation/trying, feeling inferior instead of self-confidence (or overly superior in reaction), and in either being passive and de-motivated or being overly active, but inappropriately so. The other will have difficulty regulating either of these extremes and the child will lapse deeper into the ruts indicated. The same would apply to the adult who has lived an equivalent regime in industry/effort. The person might be excessively diminished in effort/industry/zeal or, conversely, overly applied in these regards, but maladaptively. The self of the person will be under- or over-aggrandized and the other's opinions and perceptions of the other will, in parallel, be either under- or overvalued.

In all cases, whether dealing with the child or the adult living in an unsupportive environment with respect to industry/zeal, the normally increasing equitable self-other mutuality in relational co-regulation will be imbalanced and will descend into aggravation of the imbalances found. The other/parent/significant other/environment might be overtly manipulative/canalizing in efforts to direct or even tamp the industry/effort of the person. Or, rather, the surround will be uninterested or mildly intrusive, leaving the person (child, other) to find her/his own way with respect to industry/role/sociality, etc. That is, in this second style, the lack of equity in the relational co-regulation in these unsupportive circumstances will express more a relative absence than wholesale intrusion by the other.

Behavior/Symptom Network/Connectivity Change (Horizontal)

The patient with issues related to industry/applying oneself, self-confidence, and appreciating what the other thinks of her/him might present an under- or over-industrious/zealous style. The patient will be deeply ensconced in patterns of behavior that proactively resist any constructive effort to learn, solve problems, etc. and will constantly devalue the self, not try, feel sad, etc. Or, conversely, the patient will behave oppositely and have unrestrained but chaotic over-industry/overzeal, with maladaptive consequences, including how the other views the person, the persons' perception of such, and the consequent effects on self-esteem (the defense in this case will be to reject those perceptions and express an unwarranted superiority instead of inferiority feeling).

The patient who expresses either of these industry-related imbalances will need to gravitate toward a more equilibrated approach to industry/zeal/self-confidence. The task will be difficult because of the regime the patient might have experienced to get to this point, e.g., industry-denial/channeling to the environment's ends and devaluation of the self/reducing self-confidence. There will be complications in associated sociality and emotions in either case. For example, for over-industry/overconfidence, the emotions will be related to overblown impressions of one's skills, rebelliousness, sense of superiority, overcontrol, etc., accompanied by devaluing the other, etc. For under-industry/inferiority feelings, the emotions will be the opposite to the point of extreme self-abnegation/denial/put down/sadness.

The therapist working with patients like this will try to foster redress toward balance in industry-related matters and associated impressions of the self and emotions about the self and others. The therapist will not only establish rapport, allow venting, advise/suggest, etc. but also will take advantage of the characteristics of the industry-focused individual by giving stratagems to use in daily roles so that industry becomes reasonable in application, yet constant and thorough. The underlying cognitive base of concrete operations will facilitate this task as the person constructs an organized rule system that covers many aspects of her/his life. The working through will require much time, because the effort itself in reconstructing the (dis) organized rule systems that govern multiple life spheres will depend especially on the degree to which the industry-challenged patients can work industriously/assiduously toward change.

Behavior/Symptom Growth, Deep Change (Vertical)/Constructing a More Positive Life Story

The patient who is resolving issues with industry will be proceeding toward the next grand theme in development according to the present model, which concerns the preteen (and person moving forward) trying out new roles and personalities preparatory toward moving into more defined roles and personalities at later ages. To do so, the person needs the zeal/motivation of a balanced industry phase development, so the person can tryout, evaluate, and modify new roles and personalities in a fastidious, planned, and prudent way, yet with unplanned exploration and innovation also included.

The patient needs to refurbish stories told to the self and other based on the premise that new stories about one's balanced sense of industry are in the making. The new stories should take the tack that the person is applying oneself, enjoying learning, gathering and using knowledge, and improving in all relevant spheres. The person could indicate how a positive self-confidence and a reduction in a sense of inferiority are improving.

However, the patient might have been either too under-industrious or over-industrious in reaction to the regime lived so that the reconstruction process of the stories told will involve different strategies for the two types. The under-industry type will require therapeutic strategies such as finding the exception to the rule, using solution-focused questions, etc.; while doing initial homework assignments applied to various life roles that readily build up a sense of confidence. In the over-industry type, the therapist will need to redirect the zeal to more adaptive ends, consideration of the other, etc. The person in the first case will be reporting that industry, effort, liking to learn, and positive self-evaluation are growing. The person will add that not only the person telling the new story should hear the story but also other people should be told the new message about the person. There should be subplots related to each of the domains (cognitive/learning, social/relational, emotional/affective, etc.) stabilizing and improving. In contrast, the person in the second case will be reporting better focus/outlets in industry behavior, while not losing the associated zeal/self-confidence (but with correction of any sense of superiority taking place, such that there is a balance in self-perception).

Consciousness, Theory of Mind, Selves, and Responsibility

The 7- to 9-year-old will continue movement toward penultimate human development in terms of consciousness, morality, responsibility, self-growth, and other-respect in the way described presented above for the prior age period of 5–7 years of age, because of the common underlying base of a logical/concrete operations/reversibility in thought, etc. These developments will be accentuated by the acquisition of industriousness/zeal and love of learning/growing sense of self confidence that accompanies the sub-stage. The child at this age is approaching the preteen period in which roles and personality types are experimented with, preparatory to adolescence, which children at this age witness all around them. If developing well, children at this age will move into adolescence well-prepared for being socially concerned and helpful. They will be on the path to proper expressions of conscientiousness, morality, responsibility, etc.

The Peri-operational Stage Sub-stage of Integration (9–11 Years): Sub-stage 15

Self and Relational Development [Initial Theoretical Elaborations]

A very brief description of the present step in Young's 25-step Neo-Eriksonian developmental model follows. It is presented again in Chap. 18, to help give a collective overview of the 25 steps in the modeling.

Role/personality tryout acts vs. role/personality confusion acts (9–11 years). The growing person tries out different roles, friends, attitudes, and personalities, both for the challenge and having fun. If you had problems in the environment supporting tryouts such as these, maybe you had a hard time exploring them, or explored them too much but on the surface only. So you became confused in your tryouts, and stopped them. Or, you tried out negative (e.g., anti-social) tryouts in roles/personalities (and you felt different moods, including brooding).

Appendix 3.5 gives the brief amount of work already done in prior publications related to the task of developing in depth the Neo-Eriksonian (sub)stage model. The next section of the chapter gives an interim summary that elaborates the contents of Appendix 3.5 with respect to the present sub-stage being considered, of the sub-stage of Peri-operational Stage Sub-stage of Integration.

Interim Summary

The preteen years are magical ones because the child is capable of safely trying out possible roles/personalities that she/he can imagine, relate to others in imagined and exploratory, innovative ways (in ways divorced from the extant self characteristic configuration), and even take on the view of the other in full in the imagination process. The concrete operational base underpinning this imaginal potential possesses the contextual logic of the prior sub-stages, but the thought reversal underlying the acquisition expands to trying out the said roles/persona in inquisitive if not euphoric/giddy fashion with excited peers.

The cognitive base for this new acquisition involves improvement in the concrete operational logic of the child to include symbol plan coordination systems in integration. This permits the ability to place an imagined novel self in relation to the actual self-perceived one. The symbol plan coordination integrations at the base of the expanded concrete operations allow the preteen not only imagine minor role/personality tryouts but also more complex holistic, integrated ones that cut across more adult-like roles and personality attributes. Because of the integration, parallel navigation of different role and personality options in relation to actual self-perceived ones can take place, with testing of the alternatives imagined through sequential forward and then reversed thought processes and not the only through only one imagined trajectory without reversibility.

The novel roles/personalities imagined and then tried out by the preteen do not have to be incorporated into the extant self structure because the preteen can dismiss them readily as experiments, fun, or whatever, and revert to her/his self-perceived self after each gambit. However, the role/personality tryouts are not uniquely created out of fantasy and fun, because they constitute imaginations of possible roles/personalities as much as anything else. Moreover, they have a social dimension and are shared with peers, for example, who might give relevant feedback.

The persona/attributes imagined this way might stem from copying parents, teachers, peers, heroes in the media, etc. Further, the industry of the prior sub-stage propels the "work" involved, making the imagined roles/personalities more tangible. In the end, the imaginative process involved will lead to alterations in the self of the child. Normally, the preteen is dealing adroitly with the imagined role/personality tryouts in which she/he is engaged, to the point of essential enjoyment in the process/giddiness/shared laughter. Or, it could be imaginings that are quite serious, applied, detailed, and the product of a frenzy in effort. A lot of the roles/personalities imagined will be for pure fun, with no real intention to adopt. But they can be informative to the child, nonetheless. Others will be more practical, and quite indicative of possible future directions. Some will be consistent with parental and normative expectations, while others will be quite different in these regards. Indeed, this innovative explorative process of imagined functional (role) and self (personality) options might be quite adaptive and preparatory to continued positive development. Another adaptive advantage of the process is that the preteen lets go/releases/abandons the ongoing self and personality functions in order to tryout totally different ones. Granted, they might reflect parental/environmental influences/preferences to a degree, but they are not part of the extant make-up of the child, allowing for further self/personality and role differentiation.

At the same time, the other is similarly differentiated. The other provides influences/models, but these might be ignored, quickly tried out/discarded for personal (self) preferences. The other becomes an equal in the mutuality of imagined differences in self/personality/role options, but with these aspects incorporated/rejected to the same degree as is happening with the preteen's own extant self structure and its influences on imagined roles/personalities. The preteen is willing to suspend temporarily all influences/models, including her/his own, in order to jump into unknown options in these regards and apply/carry them out in the safety net of the preteen years. The social mutuality in the engagement will affect the preteen in one way or another, as will the contents of the imagination. What is projected eventually could become introjected and leave traces that grow the preteen in the image involved.

However, for the preteen to fully engage positively in the imaginative process of role/personality tryout, the environment has to be supportive. At a minimum, the environment might point out its preferred alternatives for role playing/personality adoption and give only lip service to the preteen's imaginations in these regards. The environment might impose limitations on the process that mirrors its own limits. The environment might go further and neutralize/pacify the preteen's imaginations, creating lacks in imagination along these lines. Thus, the preteen might express no independent imaginations and adopt fully only those presented/modeled to her/him. Or, to the contrary, the preteen might try to preserve some independence in these regards and select imagined roles/personalities that are the opposite to those preferred by the environment (antiroles, antipersonalities). The chances of the preteen developing conduct-disordered behavior preparatory to later delinquent behavior accentuates in this type of imaginative type. Also, the preteen might flit very quickly from one imagined role/personality tryout to another without committing to tryout any in any consistent way. These different role/personality imagination options reflect the types of oppositions in adaptation found in prior sub-stages (e.g., under-industry vs. over-industry). The self might end up quite confused through these role/personality imagination difficulties and stop creating/testing them altogether (moratorium), for example.

Adults who had been exposed to a similar regime when having been a preteen will find it harder to solidify a positive sense of self with self-accepted roles and personality attributes. They, too, might reflect uncontested acceptance of others' preferred imaginations/models in these regards. Or, conversely, they might have anti-roles/personalities in these regards, and so on. The danger is that these types of reactions become quite extreme. For example, the suppression of imagined options in roles/personalities leaves an impoverished self. Or, conversely, the anti- roles/ personalities are extremely maladaptive. The resultant primary negative emotions will concern brooding or anger and the like, depending, instead of euphoria, while the resultant sociality will be quite absent, or, conversely, perhaps wildly in play but maladaptively so.

Self-Response to Cognitive (Mis)Perception of the Other

The preteen facing difficulties in imagined role/personality tryouts will be confused in the process. The preteen could gravitate to a sparse/absent imagination process in this regard, either foreclosing any activity this way or engaging briefly. Or, there might be an undisciplined overimagination in these regards. Other options are possible, including anti-imaginations, as already discussed.

The cognitive basis for the imaginative activity in this phase still concerns representational concrete operations having associated contextual logic, thought reversals, etc., but the concomitant symbol plan coordination system integrations allow for the extensive role/personality imaginings involved. In the case of problematic role/personality imaginings, the narrated plots by the preteen will include subplots that constitute exasperating if not insoluble complications, which will jeopardize the story of the whole imagined roleplay/personality tryout. Moreover, the normal self-distancing that accompanies the role/personality tryout will be distorted, as will be the relationship to others and their influences/models/suggestions in these regards. Instead of an equitable mutuality in self-other influences/models/suggestions in imagined roles/personality, there will be either a total discounting of the other or a total acceptance of the other, depending on whether the imaginings involved are totally self- or other-determined, as is wont to be the case given the non-supportive context for the preteen.

The self-imagined role/personality tryouts are projected ones emanating from the self and ones that are normally independent of the other to a degree. However, in problematic contexts, the imaginations involved might be wound down/under-imaginative, or haywire/overimaginative, depending. The self might be replete with internal conflicts/emotional agitation, for example, in attempts at putting aside the current self-structure to imagine/explore/test options; in trying them out, nonetheless; and thereby experience a too great cognitive/socio-affective dissonance (e.g., with brooding) between the extant and imagined self structure. Also, the self might mask or even remove the internal conflicts (at least to the degree possible) by total adherence to the perspective of the other's influences/views on the imaginings at issue, with the person becoming socially pliable instead of independently able in these regards. The other may give some credence to the person ("That's different; that's OK), but only if the person is conforming to the wishes/models of the other. Or, conversely, the self might take an anti–/negative/rejecting imagination stance with respect to personality/role tryouts, depending.

Whatever deviant direction taken in imagined role/play personality (under- vs. overreacting), the preteen will be restricted/limited, and going through successive imaginations (or their lack) that make any ameliorative efforts more difficult. The same applies to the adult faced with an imagination-constricted environment with respect to role/personality tryouts, except the confusions will be more marked relative to those of the preteen. The person might end up superconservative and conformist and reflect the other's desired roles/personalities and their influences. Or, to the contrary, the person might end up super flaky and anticonformist, and reflect only her/his own influences/suggestions on imagined roles/personalities, or display rejection/behaving oppositely to those of others, or do both.

Positive Pole in Eriksonian Development

When the preteen is well-supported, the normative advances in development at this age take place with little negative repercussions. The child can engage in unbridled imagination of roles/personalities and try them out both with assiduousness and gleeful anticipation of what others might say (think acting out with peers any such imaginations). Both the self (current structure) and the other (influences/ suggestions) are put aside for constructive imaginings and applications in these regards. The imaginings are not made against any other but are genuinely for the self. They are not driven by internal conflicts but by internal imaginations, in particular, albeit responsive to a degree to the other. They are not maladaptive ideas, but adaptive ones toward self-growth and earning other respect/praise. They might be over-exuberant but can be trimmed back through accommodative efforts either by self or other.

Negative Social-Self Working Schema

The preteen with positive imagined role/personality tryouts will enjoy the experience and will try them out fastidiously, for the most part. The extant self structure will be left aside, allowing for innovative exploration. The others' influence/suggestions in these regards might be duly considered, but an equity will prevail and there will be minimizing self-other influences/suggestions, etc. in the imaginings. The child will need good support to allow and even encourage the tryouts, which will already constitute challenges in some of the options followed.

In the case of the unsupportive environment, the imaginative tryouts will be contaminated by ongoing issues in extant self-construction and in extant relational difficulties with the other. There might be restricted/abandoned imaginative efforts or, conversely, unrestricted/unbounded ones, with no regard to effects on the self or the other. The cognitive basis of the sub-stage involved concerns peri-operational concrete operations, which allow for a reversible contextual logic. This ability helps in the imaginative process in role play/personality tryout, but when compromised by an unsupportive environment, the systemic symbol plan coordination integrations involved will be restricted/less connected, and so will the resultant imaginations.

The other will be conceived as having no ideas/worthless ideas, in these regards, or, conversely, much needed ideas/too powerful ideas that cannot be resisted in the imaginative efforts. The other will be considered as either unimagined/unimaginative or overly influential in her/his imaginations and its contents. The self either will be supplanted by the other, becoming a supplicant, or will be always at odds with any of the imaginings deriving from the other, thereby becoming in the self-evaluative process an unequivocal savior (and perhaps excessively so as a self-attributed hero for society).

Attachment, Neo-Eriksonian Development, and Therapeutic Implications [Patients and Therapy]

Patient Presentation

The patient who has had difficulties in imagining alternate roles/personality attributes and trying them out in the preteen period might have quite similar problems in the adult period, but accentuated. There will be confusions, conflicts, contradictions, compensations, and emotional cauldrons associated with the imagination difficulties, although conversely, perhaps just conservative conformity and imaginative containment/control. In the latter style, the self will be over-anchored in limited roles/personality attributes, with little deviation from them possible or entertained. In the former style, the self could be under-anchored, sprouting in role/personality-type tryouts, but outlandishly so.

These different imaginative styles in the preteen will have different ramifications for the self. The self might be narrowly conceived and with little or few exploratory branches from a constructed trunk (under-anchored). Or, conversely, the self might be scattered, with more than one truck, with multiple obscuring branches, and otherwise seem confused and confusing (over-anchored). The other will be similarly construed, with quite different options of the structure perceived, depending. The restricted over-anchored self type will have a parallel view of the other and consider the other bereft of tryout efforts along the lines indicated. The same applies to an overly exuberant/under-anchored self – the other will be conceived similarly and excessively but superficially trying out roles/personalities. The therapist will need to explore these different dynamics and relate them to the underlying symbol plan coordination systematized integrations for both self and other (and their relation).

Behavioral/Symptom Mental Scanning

The patient who had experienced an environment quite like that of an unsupported preteen will have issues with imagined/tried out roles/personalities, for example, too little/restricted or too much/out of control. The person will be able to perceive the expressed range of roles/personality attributes, but perhaps not the details of their maladaptive nature or with a full understanding of their source. The self will be seen as timid/tepid in imagined role/personality tryouts or, conversely, as roiling/boiling to do so, but without directed conviction/convection. In self-scanning, the person should be able to pick up on her/his confusion/uncertainty and brooding/euphoria/and over-consistency/inconsistency, as the case may be.

The therapist will find a patient who has presenting problems that stem apparently from the earlier-lived preteen phase, but with two quite different styles. The hypo-imaginative type will require therapeutic boot-strapping of imaginative processes in role/personality tryouts that lead to constructive outcomes, so the approach will be to listen/learn and intercede/question constructively as appropriate, to activate/help self-construct new imaginations/coping, etc. The hyper-imaginative type will require controlled stopping of unrestrained/unruly imaginative processes in these regards toward a moderate and adaptive equilibrium. So the approach might require more listening and learning by the therapist toward giving feedback thoughts and having the person change accordingly in any negative imaginatory manifestations. The questioning of the therapist will be aimed at eliciting both self-inhibiting and self-reconstructing questions by the patient of the extant role/personality structure. The therapist can serve as the foil and get the patient to self-reflect, although the logic will not yet be abstract enough, so the therapeutic questions should be guided accordingly.

Therapeutic Implications

The patient experiencing imaginative difficulties related to role adaptation/personality attributes might be either too under-anchored or too over-anchored in imaginative possibilities in these regards, most likely stemming from similar issues experienced from the preteen period onward. The environment might have been supportive to that point, but it will have been tested too much by the testing attitude of the preteen in imaginative role/personality play tryouts and had objected to the testy attitude of the preteen that had resulted once objections to the imaginations were raised. Or, the environment might have otherwise made efforts to dismiss/canalize/shape the preteen's imaginations in different directions.

The poverty-in-imagination type will be highly constricted and constrained, which will diminish self-construction into differently imagined directions. The roles attempted will be conventional, without challenge, and with no upside. The personality attributes that had developed will be similar narrowed, and not treading outside of conventional boundaries. The overimaginative type will express a plethora of imagined roles and personality attributes, but without realistic adaptation or with any consistency, conviction, or staying-power. The person might be considered flighty, having fetishes, and with a fertile rather than a fallow imagination, although the imagination will be perceived as not weeded/pruned and oriented appropriately.

The therapist also will have to deal with the patient's self, social, emotional, and cognitive associations with these two styles. The self of the underimaginative type might be too conventional/contained to imagine any alternatives in role/personality attributes. The therapist will need to give more than homework exercises to try to elicit different imaginings. The therapist will ask the patient many questions instead of giving homework to tryout of the office. The approach is to open the patient to the possibility of new possibilities in imagined role/personality attributes. The questions might be leading, but never directive. They will be open-ended rather closed, and they will aim to find openings in the person's closed self structure or to create openings through the questions toward an inquisitive and possibility-opening nature. In contrast, the self of the overimaginative type will be infused with multiple, coarsely and superficially defined role/personality attribute imaginations. They might be quite negative, anti-, and disruptive, aside from being ephemeral, flimsy, etc. The therapist will also use open-ended questions that are nondirective (but leading). However, they will be aimed at closing some of the improbable/impractical, destructive openings in imagination of role/personality tryouts that had developed. The therapist will try to have the patient choose from among the imaginations made and applied the ones that are more adaptive or have the potential to end up that way if worked, modified, improved, etc. Or, the patient might need to suppress all or most of those and create entirely new directions in her/his fertile but unkempt imaginative process in role/personality tryouts. The therapist will encourage both becoming well-rounded in role/personality tryouts no matter what the type, while remaining open to new possibilities.

In terms of the patient's social life, the therapist will find that the underimaginative type will have underimagined social relations. The person's peers/friends will be much like her/him or perhaps different but with a constrained imaginative profile, nonetheless. In contrast, the overimaginative type will be all over the place socially, will be out of place in many circumstances, and will feel that she/he has no home base or place, feeling unanchored. As for emotions, the under- and overimaginative types, respectively, will be especially outwardly euphoric, heading toward mania, and especially inward/brooding, heading toward depression, respectively. Finally, cognitively, the underimaginative type will be sparsely connected in her/his symbol plan coordination systemic integrations, unlike the overimaginative type, who will be over-connected (but in need of trimming).

Stress/Trauma Resilience/Coping

The preteen with advanced integrated cognitive operations will be able to imagine alternative roles/personalities and try them out, especially if the environment is supportive. This process might facilitate positively dealing with stress/trauma through newly imagined resilience/coping techniques and problem-solving strategies. Typically, the preteen will have help in this regard through the supportive environment, and the preferred option might be to use known resilience/coping strategies, let the environment handle it, and so on.

If the preteen is not supported in these regards, there might be either hypo-imagination of role/personality or hyper-imagination, and, in both cases, the resilience/coping mechanisms of the child facing stress/trauma could be more maladaptive than would otherwise be the case. The hypo type might excessively withdraw, be incapable of any deviation from known techniques/problem-solving strategies, etc. The hyper type might be too rash and brash, and use totally unrealistic techniques/strategies.

The adult having lived an equivalent experience as the preteen in these regards also will be hypo- or hyper-imaginatory, as the case may be, with consequences for resilience/coping to stress/trauma. The first type will evidence no flexibility in approach, with little range in the approaches used. The second type will have an abundance of tools/ideas to resist/cope with stress/trauma but all quite off the required mark. The therapist will need to boost the imagination process as applied to resilience/coping with stress/trauma in the first type and trim/taper the approaches in the second type toward effective approaches. This will require a twofold strategy, one at the general imaginative level and another in terms of specific applications to stress/trauma resilience/coping. The therapist will be aiming for a more integrated, nuanced perspective of self-resilience/coping in relation to the environment, generally, including with respect to stress/trauma. In addition, the therapist will teach resilience/coping techniques that fit the cognitive basis for the sub-stage at issue, e.g., advanced, logical self-talk in approaching problems. The underlying cognitive base for the sub-stage at issue, symbol plan coordination systematizations in integration, will facilitate these types of therapeutic goals. The patient will have a partial ability to view self-other (environment, stress/trauma) as an inter-coordinated, integrated system that she/he can influence through new and more focused imaginings in role play/personality, including in stress/trauma management.

Therapeutic Strategies [The Other and Change]

Relational Co-regulation

The preteen who is engaging in her/his imaginative pursuits of innovations in roles and personality tryouts becomes exceedingly relational. The imaginary outcomes involve roles/personalities that are played out in the social life of the person as much as in imagination, in front of mirrors, etc. The electronic social media outlets available to the preteen compound the opportunities for role/personality play, and the conversational/visual depiction exchanges often will involve imaginary roles/personalities. The imagination involved might be so intense that the preteen's own self-structure is cast aside and the roles/personalities adopted would be quite novel, at least in part, with respect to the extant structure. Similarly, the mind of the other might be read, their evaluations of the self understood and reckoned with, etc.; but the other might become an abstract, absent entity in the mind games of the preteen's imaginative play with respect to role/personality. Therefore, the relational interaction between self and other will be held temporarily in abeyance as the preteen wades into uncharted territories in imagination about roles/personality.

The preteen's social relations become marked by parallels in the novel roles/personality game played, and her/his emotions might reflect an abundant ludic touch. In short, via the underlying expanded reversible, concrete operational skills of the preteen, the imagined possibilities of self-expand accordingly, new roles/personalities can be tried out, laughed at/taken seriously, etc., and then they can be laid to rest so others can be innovated. Normally, preteens are moving in and out of the role/personality imaginative process as they indulge either with engaged peers/others or in delight/seriousness when alone. The self is temporarily side-lined, as might be the other's views of imagined role/personality tryouts, but the regulative interaction between self and other returns when the child reengages with the normal course of the day. Any lack of equity of self-other regulation (e.g., its absence in the imaginative tempest) advances toward a more equitable comanagement of the child's behavior/emotions/sociality, although with the parent quite limiting, as required, when the preteen strays from safe alternatives, ongoing obligations, or both.

The preteen who is not supported in the normal preteen imaginative function related to role/personality tryouts will have the normal relational co-regulatory process altered toward dysfunctionality. The imaginative outcomes will not be innovative and potentially practical, positive tryouts in role/personality but, rather, they will be distorted/destructive or shrunken/dispirited, as the case may be (overimaginative, underimaginative, respectively).

The adult who has experienced an equivalent negative environmental condition to the one described for the preteen's imaginative process will have that imaginative process further affected. It will either be stunted/stagnated/stalled or rampant/runaway/riotous, as the case may be. The repercussions for the person socially/emotionally, for the self and other conceptions, as well as for the cognitive base behind the problematic identifications will compound the relational co-regulatory imbalances and difficulties. The self, in particular, might emerge as a superficial mask of surface personality/role tryouts, with either a meek, mellow, uncertain, or an overly aggressive, volatile role adoption/persona/personality harbored at the core of the self, as the case may be. The other might be construed similarly, with layers of roles/personality attributes, and some that are opposites of others.

The question will arise in both cases, who is the genuine self or the genuine other. In this scenario, the relational co-regulation with the other will be like a cat and mouse game over and across the different levels of the self, with some more core or genuine than the others. The social-emotional life of the person will be equally variable and unstable over levels of self-expression and other conceptualization. The undergirding advanced cognitive conservation operations of the person (and the abstract ones that might have developed, if an adult is involved, e.g., as a patient) will not reflect their integrated potential in these self-other relations, and in the concepts of self and other associated with them.

Behavior/Symptom Network/Connectivity Change (Horizontal)

The patient functioning like the preteen having imaginative role/personality tryout issues will either be hypo-imaginative or hyper-imaginative in these regards, with consequences for social, emotional, cognitive, and self-perception/other-perception.

The person will be confused in role/personality acts, either being maladroitly under-effusive in these regards or over-effusive. The imagination-inhibited type will have difficulty adding to a limited and limiting set of imagined and actualized roles and personality attributes. There will be a confined/conservative person who risks with much temerity any movement outside of a preconstructed role/personality box. The imagination-proliferation type will have multiple imagined and actual role/personality types, but with limited reality-adjustment and ability to select the most adaptive ones for the context at hand. Should the options imagined and concretized had gravitated to externalizing/aggressive/rebellious and conduct-disordered/delinquent/antisocial varieties, the person might prove doubly difficult to deal with, if not intransigent and intractable. The person might sit in therapy with crossed arms, staring aggressively, in representation of a closed mind to the question.

In the first case, the emotions will be placid/flaccid. In the second case, they will be either rambling/ranging widely or perhaps rough/gruff. The affectivity of moodiness or brooding might apply, respectively, in characterizing the cases. Sociality will mirror these emotions, although the other might not react with calm/aplomb, and further exacerbate the emotions/sociality expressed. The self of the hypo-imaginative type will lack imagination in and be controlled in risk taking in roles/personalities. The self of the hyper-imaginative will clearly be the opposite.

The cognitive structure in both cases underlying the landscape of imagination/actual tryouts in roles/personality attributes will be similar at a higher-order level but quite different at a lower-order level. That is, in both cases, the symbol plan coordination systematizations in integration will be present, but aberrant. In the first case, the integrations will be based on poorly and sparsely developed imaginings, with some perhaps quite blocked off to the integrations because of environmental controls and constraints, if not outright deconstructions undertaken with respect to the imaginings involved. In the second case, the integrations will be more expansive, but the symbol plan coordination systematizations involved will consist of poor reality-matched imaginations, confrontational ones, etc.

The therapist working with imaginatively challenged patients like this will need to evaluate whether the hypo- or hyper-imaginative type is involved. Both types will need proper rapport building, psycho-education, etc., but use of questions will be a good adjunct. In the first case, they can be used to induce self-reflection and new constructive imaginative outcomes, with the (concrete) operational thinking style taken into account. The self-reflection might be limited to the preteen cognitive base (contextual rather than abstract logic) at the origin of the imaginative issues. In the second case, the questions will need deconstructive as much as reconstructive/constructive foci, given the plethora of maladaptive role/personality imaginings/actualizations that might be involved. Gradually, the patient will be able to take the questions posed to herself/himself and apply them personally about the self, how the person views and relates to the other, etc. toward improving role/personality tryout functioning.

Behavior/Symptom Growth, Deep Change (Vertical)/Constructing a More Positive Life Story

As the patient moves out of problems related to imaginative/actual role/personality attribute tryouts that had been dysfunctional/debilitating, she/he can imagine new, more constructive possibilities in these regards. The imaginative process will better express itself and the products of imaginative applications will be more reality-oriented and adaptive. The person will create an equilibrium in any hypo- and hyper-imaginative tendencies in role/personality play and equilibrate the most negative emotional, social, and maladaptive self- and other-perceptions. The person will be establishing the basis for moving toward the next great adventure in psychological development, that is, functioning from an uncontaminated fully abstract, logical cognitive capacity with its positive implications for psycho-affective growth.

The patient learning new narratives about the self and how the self relates to the other with respect to imaginative/actual tryouts of roles/personality attributes will tell effervescent stories of curiosity and novel projections of how she/he could be in this regard. The stories will indicate how the person has an elaborate storyline with plots and subplots related to new roles and personality attributes that are being imagined, concretized, tried out, and evaluated, in contexts both when the person is alone or with peers and family. The person will not fear ridicule at misconceived efforts but will take it as a learning experience that has been attempted and then jettisoned as nonproductive, although it might have been fun and socially cohering, nonetheless, which is its own reward. The person will learn to see strengths where none had been noticed before, turn presumed disadvantages into advantages, and so on. For example, through change-inducing questioning, the person will realize that a hypo-imaginative style served as a protective mechanism that had its adaptive time, but new times are opening and new possibilities emerging. The hyper-imaginative style will be understood as the strong basis in imagination that simply has to be tailored and reworked so that desired positive ends (and narratives) are in the offing.

Consciousness, Theory of Mind, Selves, and Responsibility

The preteen might be totally immersed in an imaginary world of role/personality play/tryouts and then getting feedback. Some of the efforts will be sidelines, leading nowhere, except perhaps for the joy and learning experience in the exercise, while others will be quite focused and opening of new possibilities/extensions in being and its outreach. The preteen will be testing the limits of the self, while testing environmental patience, at times too. The peri-operational concrete operations underwriting this imaginative potential into integrated cognitive wholes will permit reversible, contextual logic in the imaginary process at issue and prepare the way for the development of abstract logic/formal operations in the next (sub)stage in development. The growth of consciousness in the sense of awareness of self, other, and their relations to each other and also to the world will grow, allowing for increased reflectivity, morality, responsibility, and identity/self and other growth.

But even in the sub-stage involved here (of peri-operational integration), the basis is set for more concern for the other, her/his opinions, and engaging reciprocally with her/him. The sub-stage holds much promise, too, in these regards when the roles/personalities imaginatively tried out are of the caring, constructive, social, and other-sensitive types.

Reference

Young, G. (2011). *Development and causality: Neo-Piagetian perspectives.* New York: Springer Science + Business Media.

Chapter 16
The Abstract (Formal Operational) Sub-stages: Hyper-Participatory Social Mutuality

Abstract Erikson viewed the adolescent-early adult period as involving the crises of identity and intimacy, respectively. However, the developments in these areas extend to even later in development in contemporary times, at least in more developed societies. That said, certainly, these are major acquisitions, but are they enough to fully characterize the age period? In the present Neo-Eriksonian model, these two stages are placed at the second and fourth sub-stages, and three more are added to complement them – related to consciousness, nurturing, and universal acts. The early adolescent has acquired abstract thinking skills according to Piaget, and this affords a broad awareness by the teen of herself/himself, the surround, including parents/friends/schooling, and the relationship of the self to the surround. In these terms, consciousness refers to an abstract-thought supported reflectivity, and it grows throughout adolescence and adulthood. Another addition to this stage concerns the placement of Nurturing before Intimacy. It would seem that a generalized nurturing is required before a genuine intimacy can develop. Finally, the third sub-stage addition to this stage involves universal acts. The corresponding Piagetian sub-stage involving abstract integration and so the early adult (emerging adult) has the capacity to relate self, surround, and other into broad vistas in which even planet/world might fit. The early adult can imagine worlds beyond the immediate one, which is preparatory to the later-developing generativity, and its application to work, family, etc. Identity is the cardinal acquisition in this age period, but it keeps expanding. Intimacy might lead to early family and work, and attitudes in these regards will transform as generativity evolves.

G. Young, *Causality and Development*,
https://doi.org/10.1007/978-3-030-02493-2_16

The Abstract (Formal) Stage Sub-stage of Coordination (11–13 Years): Sub-stage 16

Self and Relational Development [Initial Theoretical Elaborations]

By way of introduction, the following presents a very brief description of the present step in Young's 25-step Neo-Eriksonian developmental model. It is presented at the end of Chap. 18 along with the other 24 steps in the model, to help give a collective overview of the 25 steps in the model.

Consciousness (being aware) acts vs. contra-conscious (not being aware) acts (11–13 years). Once the thinking of people becomes logical and abstract, such as in the teen years, they can develop an awareness of the self, other people, the environment, society, and their place in the world. If your environment (parent) was not supportive of this type of thinking and opening, you had difficulties in being aware like this. Perhaps you were less conscious and more conforming than normal, or you were conscious but in fanatical or superficial ways.

Appendix 4.1 gives the brief amount of work already done in prior publications related to the task of developing in depth the Neo-Eriksonian (sub)stage model. The next section of the chapter gives an interim summary that elaborates the contents of Appendix 4.1 with respect to the present sub-stage being considered, of the sub-stage of Abstract (Formal) Stage Sub-stage of Coordination.

Interim Summary

Adolescence constitutes a major milestone in development. The age period of 11–13 years is a landmark in physical/psychosexual development. It covers the first sub-stage of the present model's formal operational or cognitive abstract stage, which concerns the coordination of cognitively abstract structures. In the present model, the abstract sub-stages average 3 years in duration, and so the formal abstract stage of the present model reaches the adult age period with the fourth of the five sub-stages involved (that of abstract multiplication), at 19–22 years. The fifth sub-stage in this series concerns the adult stage of emerging adulthood. Thus, in the present stage under discussion (the cognitive abstract one), the person develops from beginning sub-stages involving the early teenage years and puberty into the later sub-stages involving early adulthood. The abstract operations involved cognitively in the formal period are simpler relative to the more complex, super-ordinate abstract structures in the ensuing adult period (collective intelligence; think – solving an algebra problem compared to writing an algebra textbook). Once adolescents can think logically and abstractly, they can develop an awareness of the self, other people, the environment, society, and their place in the world.

The formal operational stage differs from the prior concrete operational stage in terms of not only the quality of the logic involved (physical-based, contextual vs. abstract) but also the age span involved. The earlier stage of the two that includes concrete operations (peri-operations)/representations spans the period from 2 to 11 years, or all of childhood. In contrast, the later stage of the two being discussed spans the age period from 11–25 years, or all of adolescence and also into early adulthood. However, there is a relevant split in the peri-operational stage that makes it somewhat comparable to the age split in the abstract stage. That is, as we have seen, the early peri-operational period concerns pre-operations and the later peri-operational period concerns concrete operations, respectively. These two periods concern the preschooler vs. the school age child, which are ages that constitute quite different cognitive capacities, as is the case for adolescence vs. early adulthood.

If all goes well in adolescence, the advent of abstract, formal operations cognitively and of puberty physically greatly transform the teenager. As parents, we would hope that our adolescents become more mature, but this is not always the case for several reasons. On the one hand, teenage brain development might lag behind in certain areas (e.g., frontally) that are involved in self-control relative to the swifter maturation of more emotional/subcortical areas (Steinberg, 2017). Second, many teenagers enter a phase of storm and stress (Hollenstein & Lougheed, 2013). This does not mean that all teenagers do, but a good percentage will have difficulties in these terms, for example, with discipline (e.g., curfew) issues, moodiness, and increased risk-taking from early to mid to late adolescence, respectively.

The development of abstract cognitive skills takes the form of coordination of streams of logic in the first abstract sub-stage of coordination. The early adolescent can take the imaginative capacity developed in the last sub-stage of the prior peri-operational stage and far surpass the focus on imagining role/personality tryouts. Instead, the young adolescent can now coordinate or juxtapose one logical stream with another. This can apply especially to school subjects, such as learning mathematical functions/algebra, etc., but, as well, it can apply to learning about one's past, seeing how one was raised, juxtaposing this with alternate possibilities, all with a hope for better environment and future, and so on.

The stories told about the self and other are not just ones involving plots/subplots in parallel and perhaps resolved in the end. Rather, they now concern master narratives about the self as has developed in the past and also the self that one aspires to be in the future. Moreover, the early teen is becoming increasingly conscious of the world around him/her in every sense, and might develop an environmental consciousness, or a humanistic one about human (other) suffering, as much as any other that is focused just on the self. The early teen is opening to the world; opening the conscious in the sense of meta-awareness about the world, the self, the other, and all the intricate relations involved; and freeing the self to the degree possible from limited and limiting socio-affective constraints, including what might have been buried in the unconscious about the past, unduly repressed in earlier sub-stages, accommodated to without full acceptance just to get on and keep going, etc. The storm and stress of the age will push up volcanic desires and the early teen will be genitalized/sexualized. But, once more, repression might be unduly harsh, and instead of finding a helpful parenting/environment, sexual issues will rise to the surface in a tempestuous and "uncivilized"/disrespectful manner. That said, normally, the explosive hormonal upswelling will be self- and other controlled/redirected or tempered and tamed, if not partially moderated, so that development in all areas can proceed apace. The early teen's impulses are gentrified/civilized, and the wider development of consciousness can continue, albeit with constant sexual ruminations as a backdrop if not forefront.

The moodiness of the early teen will appear in tonic spurts more than in chronic or phasic irritability, and emotions might bear the mark of agreeableness more than disagreeableness. Parents will develop close relationships with their early teens if all goes well, such that teenage stress will be experienced at a lesser level relative to the teens expressing cooperativity and seeking advice when perplexed. The parent will counsel wisely on morals, how to deal with the preferred romantic peer, the need for study and schooling, keeping out of all kinds of trouble, and so on. The early teen might oppose/rebel, but hopefully briefly, and without extreme negative consequences. The early teen hopefully had been put on a track to "slow" development in this period and not on a "fast" unplanned/improvised and impractical/impertinent development (e.g., teenage pregnancy).

The self of early teens should normally be an equilibrated one, even if an uneven one, as found in their growth rate and its spurts. The early teen self should be a conscious one, to be sure, about one's needs and the environment about, but also a societal one, including being aware of the environment and expressing caring for it. Also, the early teen will be aware of the needs of the other in a relational respect including, for example, what (in)justice means, and so on.

The early teen will be able to have abstract notions along all these lines that she/he can explain. However, the capacity to organize them beyond their isolated frames will be lacking, and the early teen might lapse into extreme simplified ideology or even fanaticism about any new awareness/conscious contents. The same might apply to how the early teen looks at people, including parents. The early teen might become super-critical, excessively judgmental, and overly condemning. Just as the early teen's genitalized/sexualities impulses will require control, so too will other aspects of adolescent mental and muscle flexing.

The early adolescent enters into not only a generalized/sexualized world but also the world of power over self and other, and it can get out of hand. The sexual object can be overpowered/de-powered while the early teen self-empowers in these regards. The early teen might glorify the self, give it too much power, and add that relations to the other are uniquely in the service of self-empowerment through the overpowering of/de-powering of the other.

Certainly, parents/the environment have to be quite vigilant of these power imbalances that might develop sexually or otherwise. The breeding of the conscious in the early teen might become very Machiavellian and manipulative/narcissistic to the extreme. Instead of freeing repressed ideas as consciousness grows, the early teen might begin the process of repressing others and also repressing one's growth of consciousness.

Needless to say, the early teen's social environment becomes especially complex, and peer influence can take nasty turns. There might be innocent experiments with alcohol/street drugs that get out of hand. There might be no forethought given to peers pushing toward shoplifting, and the consequences could be disastrous. Cliques/crowds might form in which preliminary pseudo-identities are established, but they can transform to truancy/delinquent acts. There might be normal amorous intentions, but lustful/lascivious or narcissistic/self-centric peers can take advantage of this and lead to teenage pregnancies. The dangers are endless and constantly present. Parental supervision might not be able to help in any way, despite the closest relationships possible with the early-teen.

However, as mentioned, most early teens have modified storms and stresses, and don't violate expected behavior to any significant degree. They apply their flourishing abstract skills to mathematics, reading, science, music, and so on. They understand the complex rule structure of society and how they fit in. They revel in learning abstractly, in growing, and in the opportunities that they can foresee into the future. They work out difficulties in relational encounters, and respectfully.

Early teens who do not have a supportive environment will not be able to develop an open consciousness, the will to grow in awareness, etc. They will not develop: a respect for the other to the point of wanting to help; the desire to work through understanding the past toward bettering the present and future; the motivation to study hard and tilt toward a responsible future at multiple levels (socially, in work, etc.); and otherwise immerse in the passion and regulated power plays possible in this age period. They will drift toward opposite tendencies, and close up the conscious openings that they might be experiencing. They will act to counter any consciousness imperative. They might even turn off/tune out, and stay out of touch both with interior thoughts and feelings and with trying to understand the same in others.

They will not develop a self that is free to grow untrammeled by the effect of repression, but will cover it up with fear. The self will be fixed/frozen, instead of free/flexible/flowing. It won't rise to the highest common denominator but sink to the lowest one.

The other will be an afterthought, and not an abstract one in any sense, at that. The self will be depreciated in value, as will the other. The early teen will be considered as going through the motions or even "motionless" and lacking in emotions.

The environment that promotes this type of outcome will be disempowering, limiting/repressing of conscious/consciousness development, and reflective of a dissonance in cognitive/socio-affective integration. It will be either too intellectualized or too emotionalized and not in balance in these regards.

The early teen might react in an opposite way to turning off/staying "unconscious." The latter is the hypo-conscious type that might develop in unsupportive environments in the early teen's life. Another possibility is that the early teen develops a hyper-consciousness instead of a hypo one. However, as with any hypo type being discussed in the present work, it will, in reality, be a pseudo type or imbued with a false consciousness. It will not delve into real personal issues, real problems in the environment and world, and motivate practical and consistent effort to succeed and stay out of teenage-associated trouble.

The pseudo-consciousness in the early teen might express surface awareness. The early teen might pontificate about/criticize the other, and be on the verge of being disagreeable, rebellious, or worse. The task of the parent/environment will be to disambiguate all the multi-factorial impacts on the early teen and the myriad of directions detracting from adaptivity. The therapist will have the same goals, depending, and need to engage the early teen in one-to-one respectful relations so that trust and recreation/reframing of the adolescent angst can take place. The therapist will seek more balanced genitalized/sexualized, power/consciousness and free, abstract thinking in the early teen. The therapist will reframe that the ultimate power that the early teen can have is to use the power of the newly developed abstract thought to better understand the self, the other, the world, and all their relations.

Otherwise, a closed, confined, anti- or contra-consciousness will develop. The early teen might become excessively confined, conforming, and conventional or, to the contrary, excessively power-focused in an attempt to mask underlying powerless in being able to deal rationally and equitably with the self and other. This type of reaction in the early teen will be accompanied by being judgmental/fanatical, and otherwise neither in touch internally nor in tune externally.

Self-Response to Cognitive (Mis)Perception of the Other

The early teen who is having difficulties related to developing an active, constructive conscious that turns adaptively both inward and outward will get mired in either an over-repressive, disempowering absence/closure of consciousness or, to the contrary, an under-repression of consciousness, which would be accompanied by a harmful over-empowering/pseudo-consciousness. The view of the other will be dragged into these consciousness problems, leading to a disregard/dismissal/unawareness of the other (ingathering of power) or sacrificing of the self totally to the other (outsourcing/misplacing power).

The cognitive basis for the early teen's development of a conscious, open, aware self who can reflectively evaluate self and other in relationship involves the development of abstract operations in which logic is no longer contextually driven. The teen can think hypothetico-deductively and hold all variables constant in the problem at hand, while varying one at a time in order to see outcome. This way, the teen can assess the present in terms of all the relevant parameters involved, which includes impacts of the past, what problems might have arisen therefrom, and how they might have affected her/him. As the teen becomes more cognizant of the multi-factorial influences on her/his behavior, in conjunction with wanting to deal well with the present and be constructive about the future, this growing consciousness would help the early teen to grasp the full extent of the influences on her/him at the horizon and beyond (hidden from the present horizon, that might have a role in the future, etc.).

The compromised self in the early teen that does not have an open consciousness developing in the way indicated, and through the cognitive processes indicated, will have difficulty in juxtaposing: self and other; past and present; and present and future; while being frozen and not confronting problems while living conventionality, and so on. As mentioned, for the compromised self in the early teen years, the environment does not promote the unmitigated exploration of a liberating unconscious toward having a liberated conscious attitude in thinking about the self and other, family and society, etc., that helps in personal growth. The self will either close its consciousness (be hypo-conscious) or too overly open it, but not realistically or with constructive goals (be hyper-conscious/pseudo-conscious).

The implication for treating the person is that the corresponding nature of the sociality with the other in the open conscious vs. closed/confined/contra-conscious type will be diametrically opposite in deep structure, although perhaps similar in surface structure. The closed conscious type will have an overly restricted limitation in obtaining a realistic view of the mind of the other person, get into that mind, and perceive what the other thinks of her/him, in order to better set aside those opinions/attitudes and move forward in self-other mutually defined growth, and so on. The other will be conceived of as bland and undefined as the teen. The closed type will not even want to get into the other's mind, being unconscious still about one's own mind failing/fearing to discover it, etc. In response, or perhaps because the other is like this as part of the devaluing environment the early teen faces daily, the other could be continually devaluing the teen, e.g., cynically, and the teen might in turn do the same to others.

The person exposed to this type of other could adopt the same attitude about the unconscious/conscious of the other. That is, mind-reading might take place superficially (what is she/he thinking (of me)) and not deeply (e.g., not being able to discern what are the reasons for these opinions in terms of both (my) contributions to them and any distortions that the other might have (e.g., in the unconscious) in formulating them).

The other will not be considered a whole, conscious person who deploys power justly (e.g., authoritative in parenting style), but as an overpowered, unfair one (rightly so or not) (e.g., authoritarian in parenting style) or as an underpowered, neglectful one (perhaps permissive, too, depending). The self of the other will be perceived as a mirror reflection of the self of the teen in its lack of synchronized cognitive-emotional underpinnings, and the other will be seen as disappointing to the teen, either being too intellectual or too emotional. Overall, the teen/self will feel a lack in reciprocal empowerment by the other, and experience a lack in coordinated psychological part-whole relations, as well as limits or blocks in consciousness.

The other might be very subtle in the disempowering process of the teen (e.g., saying, "True, but didn't you forget anything;" "Not quite" and without explaining). The teen might also behave similarly in dealing with other people, i.e., always circumventing the other's conscious reflections out of protection for her/his lack of shame/fear of what might be found, etc. The other might become too judgmental, and the teen, as well. The teen might become too moody as the cognitive and emotional reserve is depleted in trying to manage all the internal and relational conflicts/constrictions/unconscious leakages, etc. The other might approach the teen with an equivalent hyper-moodiness, which might have been one of the instigating factors in the self's conscious closure to begin with.

Adults will have all these tendencies exacerbated, if they had faced an equivalent crisis of consciousness due to an unsupportive environment. Perhaps the most profound effect from having lived in an environment that had been unsupportive of the exploration and freeing of the unconscious into the conscious is the likely development of either hypo-consciousness or hyper-consciousness (but at a pseudo level). The latter type will foment internally yet try to present as placid and peaceful externally. However, leakages and their consequences will be telling and tiring and impede self, cognitive, social, emotional, and socio-affective development.

People experiencing these types of difficulties might be totally pleasant but only toward fulfilling self-defined and narcissistic goals. The smiles will be perceived as counterfeit and expressed for personal instead of genuinely social reasons. People like this, not having a direct link to unconscious processes and their freeing, might behave in ways that they genuinely believe are socially sincere, but they will be totally narcissistic and grandiose. They will believe totally their genuineness. They will deny untoward unconscious influences. They could be very convincing. However, the unconscious leakages will reveal to others the cognitive/unconscious games being played. Granted, some others might be naïve, or want to believe the subterfuge so much that its signs are ignored.

In some senses, the sociality of the unconscious/closed type might approximate that of the conscious/open type, but the underlying deep structure eventually will help uncover the potentially underhanded nature of the behavior. Given the unconscious elements to the behavior of this type of person, the gender issues that might have surfaced in earlier periods will be accentuated (e.g., misdirected sexuality to children) or they might now emerge had they not developed previously. Here is one situation in which the pseudo-conscious of the person might develop, and they will become hyper-moral, proclaiming innocence of any motivations this way, deny any and all personal foibles, find it easy to point out such foibles and personality disturbances in others, etc.

Positive Pole in Eriksonian Development

The early teen who is opening up to the world, constructively allowing previously repressed unconscious contents to free themselves, creating adaptive functioning in the present and looking forward to a better future, will be dealing well with the pubertal/hormonal upheavals and new cognitive abstract skills. The early teen who navigates well the crises associated with this age will be able to deal with any social/emotional and renewed psychological/psychosexual genital/sexual/gender issues that might arise. The environment that is supportive in these regards will have much to do specific to the physical and psychological turmoil in the early teen, such as imposing views on appropriate peer contacts and curfews, helping to manage exploration of alcohol/drug use, instilling appropriate morals/values, encouraging respect of romantic dates/intimate friends, managing well the variability in mood endemic to this age group, mitigating fast-track issues such as risky sex, poor peer choice, truancy, etc., as well as understanding and adjusting to the differential frontal lobe/subcortical growth spurts, unseemly sleep schedules, social media influences/monitoring, etc. The teen will have many questions for the parent, including about past problems, family issues, why certain thoughts are not coming into awareness, and conflicts, both internal and external. If well-managed, the answers can help the teen move forward and make choices that are freely chosen and not determined by other sources, whether in the past or present, whether parental or otherwise, etc.

Negative Social-Self Working Schema

The early teen who is navigating well the upswelling of pubertal hormones, abstract thinking, freeing of unconscious thoughts, renewed relational issues centered on genital/sexual/gender matters, etc. will still require much parental support. However, if the environment had not been supportive as these new physical and psychological growth processes unfold, the teen will not develop a holistic self, or clear positive self images, nor a positive view of the other along with the correct behavior that should be expressed toward the other. The personal working schema of the self normally should be an opening one, freeing up of repressed thoughts into unconscious. The personal working schema should be one in which the maturing I of the self takes its rightful place in the family of selves of the person. The I/self should moderate self exuberance that might take place to the detriment of the other. To the degree possible, the I/self should shore up a sense of equanimity in dealing with the other, reflective of a balance in power. The teen should exude the warmth received from the parent, for example, and respect the limits that had been set (as per the authoritative style).

If experiencing this type of supportive environment, the early teen will apply to the openings in the world the newly developed abstract thought. The hypotheticals imagined will include not only a better self and relations with others but also a better world that one would want to contribute to. And the other will be seen as a partner in this latter constructive enterprise. Whatever the early teen's undertakings, whether at school, at home, or with peers and in society, parents will be valued for their advice, peers who are well-chosen will become important allies, teachers and other important significant others will be supportive adjuncts, etc.

However, when the environment is not supportive, or devalues/undermines/represses the new openings and developing conscious of the teen, the image of the self will not be so positive and the image of the other will suffer accordingly, as well. The self will close up, clutter/cluster with repressed thoughts that are quite negative, sexually inappropriate, even dangerous, etc. The image of the other will be mirrored in the self's view of the self. The other will be considered all powerful and a source of control/repression or totally weak in any effort to moderate the conflicts and leakages that would be manifesting.

The underconscious type will abandon all efforts to think for herself/himself. The person will be highly meek/mild, conflict-avoidant, compliant/conventional, and unable to do or say anything that would keep the powers at hand happy and contained. The hyper (pseudo)-conscious type will deny anything of value said or done by the other and believe totally in the self-manipulations/deceptions in which she/he engages. The other will become an ignorable, without anything genuine to offer as the teen falls into increasing lack of genuineness. As much as the other might have contributed to these problems by disempowering/limiting consciousness, the teen will do the same in a mirror response to other others.

Attachment, Neo-Eriksonian Development, and Therapeutic Implications [Patients and Therapy]

Patient Presentation

The adult presenting with difficulties equivalent to ones that an early teen might express with respect to a closed conscious, repressions in unconsciousness; power imbalances; genitalized/sexualized problems in dealing with the other; disrespecting limits/violating other's rights; moodiness/disagreeableness; low self-esteem (or perhaps reactive grandiosity); a very judgmental attitude; a lack of freedom in thought (frozen); disarticulated cognition/emotion; and a keen conformity/conventionalism (or perhaps a reactive anti-conformity) will be a major therapeutic challenge. The patient might express an over- or under- (un) conscious/repressed style.

The patient might have responded to the conscious limiting/repressing regime experienced by either becoming hypo-conscious or hyper-conscious, depending. The former type will be exceedingly repressed, emasculated or the equivalent, self-controlled/other hyper-vigilant, and so on. The person will confine herself/himself socially, choosing social contacts who are not threatening in any way to the repressions in the unconscious and their liberation/deliberation. The person will be very conventional in what is explored abstractly. The whole self-structure of the person will be a placated one, powerless, and bound to multiple constraints such that any hint of free thought, emotion, and action will not be evident. The past will be a graveyard and not to explore, the present a fallow field not to fill and make fertile, and the future an unimagined/uncontemplated barrier. Emotions will be flat, reflective of feeling totally disempowered and abdicating the self to full control by the other.

The hyper-conscious type will present quite differently but in a pseudo/false way. This type of patient will exhibit empty bravado, misplaced power plays/trips (although they might work, depending), extreme moodiness/disagreeableness/cynicism-ridicule, extreme fanaticism/judgmentalism, and endless rejection of anything about the other in favor of preferred opinions/attitudes deriving from the self. Also, this type of patient will exhibit concomitant extreme defensiveness to any threat that could release powerfully repressed contents in thought/emotions/psychosexual-social affectivity and, as well, all perverse genitalized/sexualized/gender issues related to that. Self-esteem will especially derive from reducing the self of the other, disempowering others/trying to overcontrol/limit them, disenfranchising them from growth opportunities/psychological integration, being fanatical, and the like.

Behavioral/Symptom Mental Scanning

The patient functioning with repressed unconscious issues and consequent genital/sexual/gender issues will present as either under-empowered psychologically, sexually, and socially or, conversely, over-empowered in these regards. The first type will float passively through the mind field of possible repressed thoughts while the second type will skirt them aggressively, adopting pseudo-conscious attitudes. The hypo-conscious type might be able to notice her/his extensive social and sexual passivity and even an accompanying fear of the other, while the hyper-conscious type will think that her/his hyper- and inappropriate sexuality as something that is normal. This type of person will pontificate against moral do-goodness; justify any sexual attitude that is unacceptable to the majority, even if perverse or illegal; and rail against those who do not accept any type of difference in these regards. This person might be able to scan her/his genital/sexual/gender unconventionality to a degree, but, as mentioned, she/he will recoil, retract, and think nothing is wrong. The person might be able to see the hurt caused to others but, in the end, will attribute blame to the other (it's her fault, parents shouldn't dress children like that).

The problem with both types (hypo, hyper) is that the conscious is effectively closed and its contents not open to scanning. This will complicate the process in terms of seeking the deep roots of the difficulties with the repressions into unconsciousness involved. Working with the patient's higher-order abstract logical skills might help uncover more scannable repressed material, but this opening will take time and can only proceed at the pace that the patient's mind is comfortable with, even with therapeutic facilitation and coaxing. Deeply buried repressed material can be brought to the surface and scanned for insight, but there will be regressive forces, too, creating undercurrents that pull them back out of awareness and scannability. Leakages will remain a prime source of therapeutic material.

Therapeutic Implications

Normally, the early teen's conscious should be opening with a controlled, non-problematic release of hitherto repressed thoughts. They would have been well-managed by parental prohibitions at the time of their repression, e.g., with respect to the Oepidal/Electra situation/complex (and also by the child's psychic structure). The pubertal awakening at this age will be a spur to the genital/sexual, psychosocial/psychosexual reawakening in this period. Moreover, the early teen's new abstract thinking skills will help her/him balance all the competing impulses/desires, thoughts/emotions, and genital/sexual/gender-related issues being confronted. The early teen will neither overpower the other in a pursuit of (un)conscious goal satisfaction, e.g., in sexuality, nor underpower the self and become a flaccid, hidden, sexual/psychosexual locus. Cognitively, the early teen's abstract cognitive apparatus will allow basic comparison skills and critical thinking skills applied to perspectives of the past, present, and future. The emotions involved will be variable, as fits this age period, but perhaps more with moderation and agreeableness than moodiness and disagreeableness, should there be appropriate environmental support. Indeed the early teen might be totally enamored with the exponential learning that can take place through formal abstract thought. The I can develop self-esteem both about this learning capacity and the other ways that the early teen is becoming independent, social, and functional.

The early teen having consciousness-opening difficulties will be old enough to have one-to-one therapy sessions with the therapist. The early teen is at an age in which individual counseling can take place, aside from any family counseling. The early teen still needs to give voluntary informed acceptance to the therapy, but it is not a formal consent, only on informal assent. The therapist should establish the ground rules with the parent(s) about sharing information obtained in the individual counseling. All parties might agree that anything can be shared or, to the contrary, that the early teen will be served best by keeping everything confidential from the parent(s), within the limits of the applicable jurisdictional law.

The therapist will face two major patient types, as has been the case with other sub-stages in the present model under discussion. That is, the early teen might be either hypo-conscious or hyper-conscious and in either case not in equilibrium. About the hypo-conscious type in cases in which the early teen has not been well-supported environmentally, the conscious will close, clam up, clamp down, self-confine/repress, and otherwise remain out of awareness of cognitive operativity. The early teen might be so intimidated both by the environmental pressures involved outwardly and the seething nature inwardly of the unconscious forces underneath that the defensive shell used to shield/encase the unconscious creates to render it impenetrable. These forces will be almost totally in control of the contents at issue, with no opportunity to escape/leak out/bubble up to the surface. The weight of the effort to contain radiation from the unconscious will de-energize the early teen, and she/he will present as sapped of energy, de-motivated, with no sexual/relational interest, content to be alone, frozen socially, and unable to express ideas, but perhaps with an ability to parrot those of others. Moreover, the teen might even be quite inhibited and conventional/anti-intellectual.

The other type of early teen that is conscious-challenged will be hyper-conscious, and the teen will present as excessively moral/fanatical/judgmental yet manipulative/deceptive, opportunistic/socially pathological even, and inconstant/variable. The mood/attitude will be disagreeable, power-seeking, and other-disarming. Sociality will involve grandiosity/narcissism, and charming efforts to take advantage of the other. The person will try masking the difficulties with the unconscious and its untoward contents/thoughts/emotions/desires and genital/sexual deformations.

The patient who has lived a regime similar to that of the early teen in the sense of creating unconscious repressions and conflicts will have them accentuated by time and circumstance. The therapist might have more difficulty at this sub-stage than others because of the unmasking of the unconscious that will be required and also in assuring its effective, controlled release. The therapist will use mental opening and closing strategies, as was appropriate in the prior sub-stage of inappropriate role/personality tryouts in imagination. But the unconscious expressions of the problematic repressions involved will make the opening and closing therapeutic process that much harder. At the same time, this increased difficulty could very well be balanced by the patient's access to abstract operations/logic, which can be used to deal better with the past, improve the present, and prepare for the future. The danger is that the patient overintellectualizes the process and is not in touch with or coordinated with the emotions involved. The equilibrium sought must not only be over time (temporal; past, present, future) but also over cognition and emotion together as well as across self and other together.

The opening process for conscious release applies to the hypo-conscious type and the repressions involved need to be worked through and accommodated preparatory to their transformation and inclusion into an integrated psychic structure. The therapist will need to enter the mind-set of the conscious-challenged patient such that the therapist co-participates in the exchange process involved. This will empower the patient to self-facilitate the desired changes and deal with them effectively.

The hyper-conscious type of patient will need consciousness-closing techniques for success in therapy. However, the closing process will be to cap a dysfunctional, superficial, devious, and contra-conscious pseudo-consciousness lacking in any genuine self-understanding and other respect/acceptance. The other will be mistreated/disempowered in relation to the degree the self is overly self-indulgent/inappropriately empowered. The repressions that are not confronted in the unconscious of the patient will lead to equivalent repressions in the image of the other that become part of the influences on the interactions with the other by the patient, or perhaps there will be counter attributes attributed to the other psychologically.

How the other is (mis)treated by the person will be a foil of how much the self needs the treatment, and the two types of patients that might manifest will require different approaches, as well. The therapist might face extreme anger leakages from the shell surrounding the hyper-conscious (pseudo, contra) type, at the risk of violent explosions. The hypo-conscious type will require a slow, careful approach, and much monitoring, as well, but for the sake of controlling extreme internal implosions (suicidality perhaps) rather than external explosions. Either way, the therapist needs to be a bastion of sensitivity/rapport skill/expertise and controlled release of the repressions involved. Schema therapy/cognitive therapy might help as a technique because of the abstract thinking processes that could be tapped in the patient. The therapist should help the patient see the network of behaviors/symptoms and the social networks that have been constructed in order to accommodate to the repression involved, as well.

Stress/Trauma Resilience/Coping

The early teen arrives at the stage of life in which puberty, abstract logic, and the freeing of the repressed unconscious all take place. These could be exhilarating times if all goes well and the environment is supportive. If stress/trauma imposes on the early teen in these developmental circumstances, the increased abstract reasoning that is possible can help the teen to problem solve more effectively. The freedom to think more clearly has many advantages. At the same time, puberty can be upsetting not only physiologically, but also psychologically, and so affect resilience and coping efficacy.

Moreover, the uncapping of the repressed contents of the unconscious might have major repercussions in the kind of situations that the early teen chooses and the thoughts/emotions/actions toward others in the sexual/genital/gender throes unleashed. That is, the stresses involved might be as much internally generated as externally generated, and the situations chosen, because of unsheathed/hidden impulses, might end up being quite traumatic, too.

The environment is crucial in this age period because of all its inherent dangers, and normally it can help buffer stresses/trauma whether internally or externally derived. However, the early teen is struggling with establishing psychological independence from the parents, and might not wish to share everything with them, especially if they are the cause of the teen's stress/trauma. The teen is left in a bind, without sufficient personal resilience/coping mechanisms for major issues that might crop up yet without sufficient desire to include parents to help at every deviation or detour on the road. Sometimes, though, going it alone will only worsen things. The adolescent at this age should keep in mind that personal secrets could end up personal disasters.

When the environment aggravates the early teen's impulses and struggles with dealing with an opening consciousness, the teen might become hypo- or hyperconscious, as mentioned. In the hypo case, the ability to deal with stress/trauma will be severely compromised by the lack of independence in thought, feeling, and action that accompanies the strategy. The self will already be disempowered and so an extra stress/trauma will not activate effective resistance/coping mechanisms.

As for the hyper type, an excess of conscious activation will be superficial/pseudo, scattered/not deep. The early teen will be incapable of thinking, acting, and feeling with clarity and using the full complement of resilience/coping mechanisms to deal with extra stress/trauma when it arrives. The teen will feel overpowered in this regard and energize all tools to throw at or through the stress/trauma, but with poor accuracy.

The adult who has difficulty with repressed unconscious contents, sexual maturation, using abstract logic, etc., will express these latter types of issues in dealing with stress/trauma, but even more so.

The genital/sexual/gender issues might be quite prominent and obfuscate any adaptive efforts in daily life, especially in dealing with others. The stresses/trauma experienced might be quite dramatic when they derive internally from such conflicts, such as hyposexuality/hypersexuality, aberrant sexuality (children), and disrespectful, abusive sexuality (objectification, rape).

The therapist working with patients like this will have to not only teach appropriate stress/trauma management skills and resilience/coping but also will have to deal with underlying, unresolved conscious-related issues, such as blockages in freeing repressed material in the unconscious. For the hypo-conscious type, the therapist could take advantage of the patient's abstract logic skills to accomplish these goals. The hypo-conscious unlocking of repressed material could take place through building rapport using cognitive techniques, and working toward establishing insight. For the hyper-conscious type, the pseudo/superficial nature of apparent conscious issues will be difficult to circumvent, but the same constructive strategies would apply once the pseudo issues are tackled. The nature of the repressed material liberated from the unconscious might be very different in the two types, but whatever the contents, the sexual/genital/gender issues will be paramount and in need of proper therapeutic engagement. The self can have respect only when the other is respected.

Therapeutic Strategies [The Other and Change]

Relational Co-regulation

The early teen absorbed in her/his burgeoning awareness will orient it to the self, other, relations, the environment, and so on. The teen will do this from the vantage point of an inquisitive cognitive structure animated by abstract thought coordinations. They will allow juxtaposition of conscious/liberating unconscious, self/other, impulse satisfaction tendencies/self-control, etc. The teen will have her/his conscious opening process compounded by pubertal development, such that the confluence of the two factors might accentuate both release of previously repressed material in the unconscious and reawakening of genital/sexual/gender issues. The teen will profoundly investigate these matters as they arise and even push that they become personal issues and also issues concerning the other. The self-other relationship will be at the forefront in how the early teen thinks, feels, and behaves. The pubertal awakening guarantees this, as does the active pursuit of school knowledge, knowledge of the self, knowledge of the other, etc., and this will accelerate with the abstract thinking activity.

At the same time, the early teen will be excessively ruminative and wanting to be alone with favorite pass-times including in social media, electronic gaming, the Internet, music, learning all matters of teenage style, etc. The so-called generation gap will accentuate with parents as the teenager self-defines with material distinct from parental preference. That said, for matters of morals/values, the parent can still constitute an important touch point, although peers and their pressures can contribute, as well. The latter types of influence might especially be at the vanguard of influences on the early teen, along with (social) media influence, in cases in which the environment has not been supportive. If the parent feels threatened by the teen's self-exploration, the teen querying how she/he had been raised by the parent, with the parent being concerned about the teen's internal conflicts and leaking/liberating repressed material from the unconscious bothering him/her, etc., then the parent might retreat from any type of support. Or, the parent might even go further and try to manipulate/keep under repression the repressed material in the unconscious. The parent becomes a disempowering agent in limiting conscious awareness to whatever does not threaten the parent. The parent might be very judgmental in doing so, fanatical in opinions offered, and otherwise inhibiting free thought and the ability to follow on the self-chosen course. The parent fixes the child in her/his desired image, repressing any free thought (e.g., "Didn't you forget something;" Didn't you mean to say [read thinking]?)

In the confines of this regime, the early teen will not develop a mind that is free to explore past, present, and future. For the past, whatever had been repressed into the unconscious might continue to remain out of awareness, and even blissfully. However, leakages/links will inevitably arise and create confusion/querying. The early teen might react with hypo- or pseudo hyper-consciousness, depending on the extent and type of parental repression of the repression-freeing impulses. In the hypo type, the typical excitement in exploring new knowledge with the new abstract skills available to the early teen will stultify. The typical excitement in the newly matured pubertal development will be crashed/crushed. The early teen will be left to agree to anything said by the parent, conform to any suggestion made, etc. The society around the teen will be viewed through the prism of a compliant self wishing seclusion instead of exclusion, except if conformity-promoting.

The other type of early teen will be pseudo-conscious, falsely free, and lamely liberated. The gravitational pull of the repressed material in the unconscious will be too strong and the early teen will aim to create counter gravitational pulls in contra (counter) conscious directions, including in unshackling the straight-jacket of genital/sexual/gender constraints and prohibitions.

The early teen who ends up so tight in consciousness development in an unfavorable environment will try to avoid the deep conflicts involved in the unconscious, the repressions, etc., by fleeing the unconscious instead of freeing it. There might be overindulgences in extreme self-satisfactions, addictions, other masking behavior, etc.

There might be disrespectful and risky/harming sexual proclivities sought, as well. The deep satisfaction from resolving conflicts and internal repressions will be replaced by efforts to seek superficial satisfaction in sexual activity, empowering a sexual and disrespectful self, disempowering/disrespecting the other in these regards, and so on. The other becomes not only an objectified outlet but, even more, an outlet of deep sexual unsatisfactions, sexual misconduct ideas if not actions, and so on. In this scenario, the relational co-regulation of self and other takes a nasty, morbid turn, with the other not only related as if the person does not exist independently but also robbed of any physical and psychological independence by improper (and perhaps dangerous) sexual fantasies if not activities.

Behavior/Symptom Network/Connectivity Change (Horizontal)

The patient expressing issues related to repression into unconscious and the inability to free them and deal with them will present major challenges to therapists. The issues normally will have arisen or have been exacerbated in the early teen period when the multiple landscape-changing advances of puberty, the advent of abstract logic, and consciousness opening are exploding. In this regard, the patient might have experienced a repression that had been taking place in the early teen years. The reaction by the patient might be of the hypo type, and a maximal repression into unconscious will pervade all activities, and affect personality, relations with others, etc. Or, the patient might have had a reaction of hyper- but pseudo-consciousness, e.g., hyper-morality/judgmentalism/fanaticism. The first type will have been disempowered at all levels, psychologically, sexually, etc. The second type will have been over-empowered at all levels, but with negative consequences on the other, who will be subject to disempowering techniques in order that the patient achieve hyper-satisfaction. The first type will admit to every wrong-doing of which she/he is unjustly accused, while the second type will admit to none, and even reverse-blame the other through hyper-exaggerated cognitive distortions.

The therapist will aim to open the unconscious of the repressed type, but without opening a Pandora's box. Without controlled release with reflection on and insight about the repressed contents possible, the risk will be for either extreme hurt or extreme re-repression, making the process that much harder to deal with. The therapist will aim to close the pseudo-conscious of the second type, removing all indulgences in these regards so that superficial indulgence in the self is lessened toward finally dealing with the underlying issues. Then, the repressed material might emerge for processing, but the risk of it being too overwhelming or being returned to the unconscious will be just as palpable for this type, if not more.

The therapist will aim to modulate the problematic expressions of genital/sexual/gender issues, by empowering the hypo type, and controlling/"repressing" adaptively the hyper type. The social life of the hypo type will need boosting at the level of respectful advances and dating. The social life of the hyper type will need bursting/busting rather than boosting. The inappropriate advances and dating behavior involved will need to be replaced by a more temperate, respectful attitude. The emotions of the hypo type will be flaccid and hidden, without energy or focus. In contrast, the hyper type will be turned up and on but oppressive in a disrespect/denial of the other, while denying with an insouciant (unconscious, false) smile that she/he had done anything wrong.

As the therapist makes some headway with the patient, the possibility increases that the patient will manage unleashed repressed thoughts/feeling or suppressing pseudo-conscious ones. In order to tackle the genuinely repressed unconscious material, the patient should confront the thoughts/feelings being freed even when they include difficult genital/sexual/gender issues, including of an aberrant/deviant nature, in that any attempts to avoid these central issues, at least in the long-run, will be detrimental. The work will be much harder, but insight will be possible when these concerns are not repressed, at least when signs of readiness for change in these regards appear to manifest. The therapist should take advantage of the patient's abstract logical abilities and freeing emotions to work toward cognitive/emotional integrative structures that allow for better genuine consciousness opening, with the goal of dealing with the unrepressed unconscious contents no matter what their nature. The cognitive restructuring will require advanced cognitive techniques melded with others, as appropriate, e.g., interpersonal.

Behavior/Symptom Growth, Deep Change (Vertical)/Constructing a More Positive Life Story

The patient who had experienced inner turmoil related to a closing of consciousness, blocking the freeing of repressed thoughts/emotions, expressing too little or too much power in relation to the other, depending on whether her/his reaction to the consciousness closing has been a hypo or hyper (pseudo) one, and so on, will resolve some of these issues in a supportive environment, including therapeutically. The patient will be able to resolve associated genital/sexual/gender issues, use her/his abstract logical abilities in a balanced way, be more aware in social relations and be less fixed/conventional, too, while opening the perspectives on the past, present, and future in a positive direction. The patient will be more agreeable/less moody, will not have splits in cognitions (intellectualizing) and emotions (emotionalizing), and will moderate past fanatical/judgmental evaluations. This will prepare the way for dealing with repressed thoughts/feelings as they continue to percolate out of the unconscious. The patient won't have blockages toward moving into the next sub-stage of the current Neo-Eriksonian model – on identity. This latter period is the one for which Erikson is most noted, and the present approach mirrors his as shall be shown, but adds contemporary elements.

The patient learning to deal with problems in conscious awareness due to blockages in releasing repressed/thoughts/emotions can be helped along by learning how to tell better stories about the self and how she/he relates to the other. The differential power relationships will have to be addressed, as well as aberrant/deviant genital/sexual/gender issues no matter how distressing. The pseudo masks adopted in consciousness, e.g., hyper-morality/fanaticism, will have to be addressed, too. The patient can start by using the abstract thinking skills that are available to construct stories with new themes, e.g., of liberation, freeing up, choosing agreeableness. The person can argue that the problems created by the past, no matter how difficult to face, had developed at a time when she/he was a victim. But now the story can change because she/he is a survivor who is finding the right balance as the turbulence flows around. The hypo type will refer to the viscous nature of the turbulence (unconscious) and how hard it is to move through it, but that she/he is making progress. The hyper type will refer to how easy it is to move forward when the medium is so thick that one floats on top of it, but that she/he is making progress toward the release of the murkiness below.

Consciousness, Theory of Mind, Selves, and Responsibility

If all goes well, the entry into conscious awareness in the early teen years is a breakthrough development toward value-based morality, deep appreciation and respect of the other, balanced self-esteem, and agreeableness. The teen can take on responsibilities and discharge them with aplomb and skill. The abstract logic available to the teen helps understand interrelations among past, present, and future, and furthers the goal of being an integrated, mature, loving, and hard-working person at all levels.

These types of thinking skills have the emotional integrations for dealing well with crises/stressors that might arise. They facilitate glimmers into consciousness as possibilities, and their growing liberation. The adult life does not feel forbidding, its fruits forbidden. Its roles and responsibilities are seen as revelations and revitalizations that the teen looks forward to fearlessly, although with some caution.

The Abstract (Formal) Stage Sub-stage of Hierarchization (13–16 Years): Sub-stage 17

Self and Relational Development [Initial Theoretical Elaborations]

A very brief description of the present step in Young's 25-step Neo-Eriksonian developmental model follows. It is presented again in Chap. 18, to help give a collective overview of the 25 steps in the modeling.

Identity acts (positive ones) vs. identity diffusion (or negative identity) acts (13–16 years). The growing person explores different identities, selves, or questions of "Who I am." Your environment (parent) could interfere in creating a positive identity that you like. This could lead you to: (a) confusion in identity; (b) putting off the search for identity; (c) simply adopting identities of other people without thinking about it; (d) adopting negative identities, such as in teenage gangs/ delinquency; or (e) adopting many identities, but all surface, false, or fake ones.

Appendix 4.2 gives the brief amount of work already done in prior publications related to the task of developing in depth the Neo-Eriksonian (sub)stage model. The next section of the chapter gives an interim summary that elaborates the contents of Appendix 4.2 with respect to the present sub-stage being considered, of the sub-stage of Abstract (Formal) Stage Sub-stage of Hierarchization.

Interim Summary

The mid-teen (13–16 years) is caught between asserting independence and identity and adhering to and dealing with the multiple prohibitions and responsibilities that the environment dictates to her/him. Erikson had maintained that the teenage years are especially about establishing identity, and he opposed it to identity diffusion. Marcia had realized that identity revolves around the axes of exploration and commitment, so that diffusion might take the form of foreclosure and moratorium, for example. Other workers have continued to modify Erikson's original model (e.g., see Fig. 16.1, taken from Cieciuch and Topolewska (2017)). The circumplex model in the figure adds socialization and normative factors to exploration and commitment toward understanding the range of identity trajectories in development.

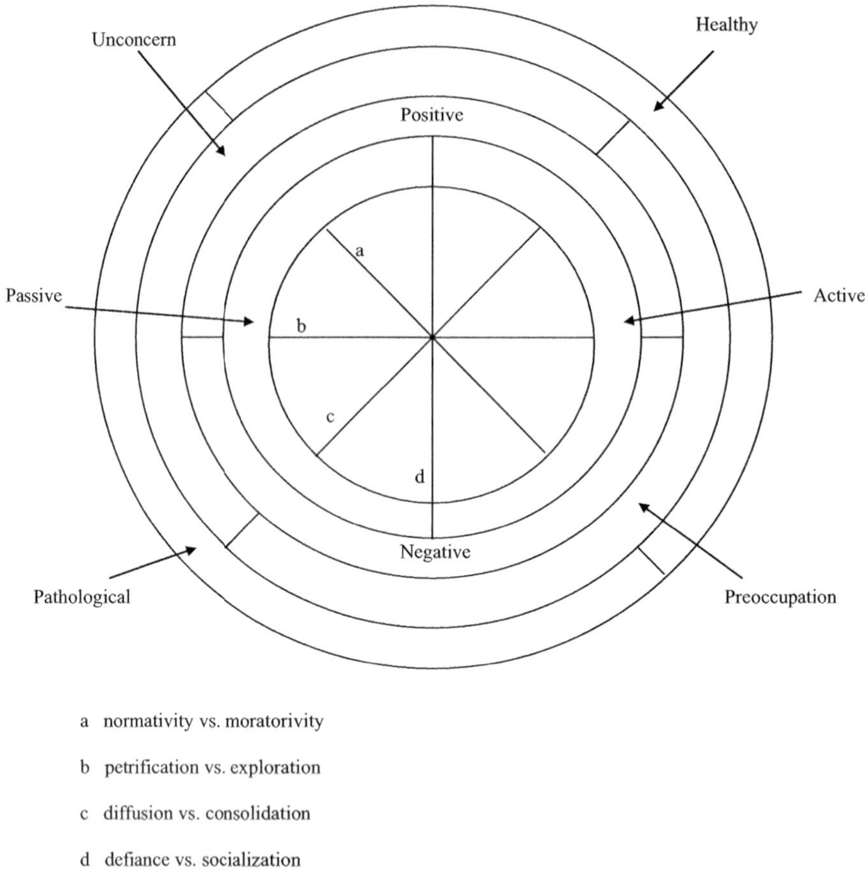

Fig. 16.1 Circumplex of *identity formation modes*. (The figure illustrates the standard dimensions of consolidation and exploration of identity within the perceiver, but includes more social ones (socialization, normativity). The eight poles of the model are characterized as active/passive/positive/negative, being concerned/indifferent, and healthy/pathological; Adopted with permission of Taylor & Francis. Cieciuch and Topolewska (2017), reprinted by permission of the publisher (Taylor & Francis Ltd., http://www.tandfonline.com))

The major contemporary critique of Erikson's identity model is that the age of adolescence is not the primary one marking it as an organizer. Rather, the age period extends into the early 20's, for example, into the university student age (at least in more developed countries). The present approach is consistent with this modern view but still perceives the psychological seeds of identity development as being laid in the mid-adolescent period, e.g., in ideal circumstances.

The general cognitive acquisition that characterizes the mid-teen age period concerns formal Piagetian operations, which involve abstract logic. Moreover, the specific cognitive acquisition in the sub-stage involved concern hierarchized relations in coordinated streams in abstract logical thought. This skill permits the mid-teen to compare perspectives to each other, to more general perspectives, and so on. This allows the teenager at this age, at least in ideal circumstances, to query self-identity and relations to others in terms of abstract psychological attributes and their various manifestations and permutations/combinations in context. The concept of identity is part of the self-construct that teenagers ask themselves about, explore, test, refine, and repeat in a continual process of internal engagement about the issue. However, it cannot take place without external engagement with the other. At this point in development, the concept of the other also involves the identity of the person (or institution, as the case may be). Who are they? What are their core psychological attributes (or attributes that can impact my core psychological attributes?) How do we relate psychologically, or should relate psychologically?

Identity is social as much as anything else, as these types of questions illustrate. The I is really a We and the Me an Us. Yet the other is not simply a foil for the self, a mirror image, because it might test or force issues as much as the self/person. The interaction involved is especially participatory, egalitarian, and reciprocal, with each of the self and other defined and refined by the interaction dynamics. As undercurrent, of course, is the ever-present pubertal/genital/sexual/gender manifold that might encompass the other and the respect (or its lack) of the other that might be involved. In this regard, Table 16.1 gives my point of view on the evolution of respect for the other that normally takes place in development according to the five stages of the present model. I present it here because it fits well in this particular sub-stage, in which heightened sexuality and the risk of objectification are increased.

The construct of identity should be seen in the context of construct of the self, in general. The self is a hierarchically arranged construct with multiple levels at this particular sub-stage. It is a fluid concept that dynamically changes with questions posed about personal identity. The higher-order level in the construct will be superordinate to multiple aspects in lower levels, and there will be feedback between the two tiers. Normally, the top-level tier is a positive core one that animates the others, such as positive psychological characteristics that conjoin into a positive general image of the self. However, the top-tier level of the self-concept might be negative/anti- in identity (defiant, delinquent), foreclosed/placed on hold, perhaps after shifting rapidly, in moratorium, socialized by the other without any real self/person input, etc.

Notice that the self and identity can be described in similar terms, but the identity concept is a more specific one. Recall that, for the sub-stage involving identification, the preteen was described as engaging in imaginary role/personality tryouts. The concept of identity is similar, but the identities established are broader and might include concepts such as essential morals, values, ideology, and duties, with social obligations/contracts primary, as well, and the relation of self-other generally (including over time) involved, too. A key identity domain might accentuate responsibility and the continual need to take and invest in it. The mid-teen might become a paragon of conscientiousness, and with idealism more than blind fanaticism underscoring it. Consequently, the self might seem "truer," more real, more genuine, more personal and individuated, and more adjusted and benevolent at this age compared to prior ones. The self of the other might be similarly conceived, and friend-

Table 16.1 Self-esteem, self-focus, and objectification of the partner in development

Self-esteem		
Stage	Normally developing	Compromised
Reflexive	Roots of self-esteem in the self-efficacy and sense of omnipotence of being able to elicit effectively responsivity in the environment	Obliteration of the roots of self-esteem and being unable to elicit at all any self-sustaining response in the environment
Sensori-motor	Developing of a sense of security due to the security promotion of the environment	Developing of sense of insecurity due the promotion insecurity of the environment
Peri-operational	Sense of competence and confidence as each social and task-based skill develops, through appropriate support from the environment, leading to a generalized poise and sense of self-esteem	Sense of competence and confidence develops with difficulty as social and task-based skills are not appropriately supported, leading to either a maladaptive overconfidence with no foundation or a chronic under confidence, doubt, and shame
Abstract	As part of their positive identity development, a sense of self-efficacy is further cemented by appropriate environmental response. A sense of assurance develops in the adolescent's self-esteem. We end up with an adolescent who is self-assured	As part of their negative identity development, difficulties in a sense of self-efficacy develop by inappropriate environmental response. A sense of uncertainty develops in the adolescent's self-esteem. We end up with an adolescence who has chronic uncertainty
Collective intelligence	The adult's self-esteem develops positively as the adult engages in the environment, and finds environmental support, as well. The self-esteem is communal, because the person values the state of others and their self-esteem. As their generativity is actualized in their collective actions, adults feel integrated and confident in their communal actions (communal confidence)	The adult's self-esteem develops negatively as the adult engages in the environment and/or does not find environmental support. The person feels negative about others and the community (e.g., cynical, rejecting). They could lapse into excessive self-focus and overindulgence

Self-focus		
Stage	Normally developing	Compromised
Reflexive	Omnipotence	Obliteration
Sensori-motor	Security	Insecurity
Peri-operational	Self-confidence allows for acting for the self and showing initiative, yet being sensitive to the other	Difficulties in self-confidence lead to problems in acting for the self, or over activity in acting for the self, which is the beginning of outright narcissism. The child shows too much initiative or too little. There are difficulties and problems in being sensitive to the other (e.g., insensitivity)

(continued)

Table 16.1 (continued)

Self-focus		
Stage	Normally developing	Compromised
Abstract	Positive and constructive self-focus and assurance in the process of developing identity and relationships with others	Negative and distorted self-focus, as well as uncertainty; identity poorly develops and relationships are self-centered in motivation. The adolescent presents as narcissistic, which is having an exaggerated, inflated, and defensive sense of self-esteem (Brummelman, Thomaes, & Sedikides, 2016)
Collective intelligence	The adult expresses a communal sense of self-esteem, relating her development integrally to the development of everyone around her and her context. One manner of describing it is to say the adult has a total integrative consciousness	Narcissism can develop extremely in the adult by being totally self-focused and insensitive, without any concern for the environment and other people and their context. One manner of describing it is to say the adult has a total, integrative narcissism

Objectification		
Stage	Self	Other
Reflexive	The newborn's experience leads it to be totally dominated by her wants and emotions, leading to problematic schemas of the self	The newborn's experience in early parenting is insensitive, leading to the development of problematic schemas of the other
Sensori-motor	The insecurity experienced contains the roots of self-objectification, e.g., denying the self-other relationship	The roots of objectification of the other begins; for example, not being sensitive and empathic to the other
Peri-operational	Self-objectification in the child begins outright, with the child dealing especially with her needs, while behaving such that other people deal with her the same way	Objectification of the other by the male begins to show in his behavior and thinking; for example, they exclude, harass, bully, beat, and demean the other
Abstract	Self-objectification flourishes; the adolescent considers the self as an object and lets other people consider herself as object	Objectification of the other becomes prominent in the adolescent; males view all females as objects for their basest needs, e.g., sex, money
Collective intelligence	Self-objectification in the adult is total with respect to the self and letting others treat the self as object	Objectification of the other in the adult is total; for example, all women are worthy of murder, collective rape, as happens in war, etc.

ships, camaraderie, etc. might take on deep qualities that bind over time and place. Friends become essential parts of both self and identity compositions. Emotionally, best friends are joy-immersing.

Adolescence is a time of upheaval, and so the developmental scenario just described will not go as smoothly as depicted. This will be especially the case when teens are not supported by parents, peers, institutions, etc. The environment might try to stop identity investigation/adoption, channel it to its ends, create confusions in this regard, elicit defiance/anti-identities, etc.

The mid-teen can react with under- or overidentifying, depending. The under-identifying type will cut short/cutoff identity adoption, curtailing exploration/commitment, and perhaps simply adopt socialized identities rather than any self-explored/committed ones. The overidentifying mid-teen will function like the over-(pseudo)-conscious adopting early teen, i.e., with superficial, fast-changing, false identities taken and without much personal exploration/commitment to them. The identities will be frivolous/fringe, etc., or they might be quite negative/anti-/defiant. The latter might become quite resistant to change, e.g., in delinquency. The identities involved will not have been the product of careful, logical, compare-and-contrast procedures in hierarchical abstract thinking, so could be reworked using this potential cognitive underpinning in the right environment.

The patient who has hypo- or hyper-identificatory difficulties will present much like the identity-challenged teen, but with more deeply ingrained difficulties. The person will be diffused/confused in or removed from the pursuit, with anti-identities (e.g., defiance) possible. The identities might be superficial/pseudo, as well. The therapist will want to use the abstract reasoning basis of the patient to help the patient self-investigate the identities and establish their advantages/disadvantages, as well as their consequences socially and emotionally. Invoking the concept of deep positive identities that help define the core self might be one pathway to adopt to help the patient take a more positive path.

Self-Response to Cognitive (Mis)Perception of the Other

The mid-teen who should be developing identity in a supportive environment will have problems in identity formation if the environment is not supportive. Already, the mid-teen years are challenging ones, and forging identity requires persistence and, when required, the ability to reverse misinformed directions. But when the environment complicates this crucial developmental task, the self-construct process of identity could lapse into a lack of psychological effort (hypo-identity) for the task or, conversely, into poorly directed efforts, and only at a superficial if not frantic level (hyper-identity), at that.

The self consists of a multiplicity of selves or components and the essential core ones will contain elements related to identity. The self develops from early in life, but the development of identity only starts in the mid-teen years, so it is only a component of it. At the same time, identity is an overlapping acquisition with the self, with new elements unrelated to prior self acquisitions. Self-esteem had been developing all along, as well as a self concept, quite psychological in characterization at this point in time, and the general question of "Who am I" had been broached. Identity concerns roles, to be sure, e.g., vocational, but also is related to morals/values, etc., and so it's more about the deep self. It too comes in multiplicities of domains and applications, and broadens with time.

The self is necessarily a social concept, like identity. One cannot ask who one is without understanding the interface with the other. The self is relational as much as personal. The same applies to identity, e.g., morals and values are not just about one's stance but how one relates to the other with and through said morals and values. The same relationship between personal self and identity is found in the relationship of the perception of the other's sense of self and identity. The challenge is to focus on and understand the contents of the mind of the other in these regards and relate them to the person's self and identity.

The teenager living in an environment that is not supportive of a search for identity might create a hypo-identificatory style or a hyper-identificatory one. The hypo-identificatory teen will cut off identity searching, or not even start the process of searching, while adopting identifications molded or foisted on her/him by the environment. The hyper-identificatory teen could be quite superficial/pseudo about the process, and adopt even negative/anti-/defiant identities.

The constructed other will be a mirror of these types of identity styles, and might be perceived as acting against the teen's identity formation, or perhaps framing ones for the teen, without malevolence (assuming that the identity issues are the first major ones being experienced in development and the environment had been good enough until this time). The patient living an equivalent regime might also be hypo- or hyper-identificatory, and perceive the self and other in these terms.

The therapist will need to help the patient equilibrate the patient's identity statuses of the self and those perceived in the other. The therapist can take advantage of the patient's abstract logic to build a better identity structure, and place it in the core understanding the person has of the self. Having the person enumerate the advantages and disadvantages of present identity trajectories will help, and documenting their social impacts, too, will help.

Positive Pole in Eriksonian Development

The search for identity might initiate in the mid-teen period, and involve initial formations, but, unlike what Erikson had conjectured, much of identity work takes place in subsequent age periods, including in youth and early adulthood. Identities concern important life domains and personal saliencies. Mid-teens could explore and commit, achieving relevant identities but, as development proceeds, they will change. They will be refined and even discarded as the teen develops, with other ones added. The teen will be influenced socially, so the identities found will reflect self-other interactions and mutualities. The identities will solidify and gravitate to the center/core of being/personhood, defining the teen as much as anything else. The stories told to the self and other about one's identity will be positive stories about high-point identities that mark the person. They will be developed through the abstract reasoning skills of the teen, for example, through hierarchizing self stories about identity to other's stories, and validating them as one's own, with self stories as anchors and other's stories as complements to help elucidate them. Thus, the environment will have a critical role to play in identity formation, and it is a highly social as much as personal act.

Negative Social-Self Working Schema

The mid-teen normally should be engaged toward forming positive identities, including in positive roles, likes, values/morals, ideologies, and what is interesting and worth pursuing. The environment will be supportive and even proactive in these regards. The I of the teen will be self- and other-defined in mutuality, including for identities. The latter will not be permanent as the teen explores options, commits, etc., but they will solidify with time and continued preference, although change, too. The other will be both a contributor to the teen's identity formation process and a recipient as the identities are played out in the teen's world. Identities might be held in the person's inner world, but they are projected into and acted out in the outer world, which gives feedback (both direct and indirect). The teen becomes exquisitely social because of and through her/his identificatory processes, and social embedding helps construct them, too.

However, in unsupportive environments, the working schema the teen has of the social other will not be so positive, shared, and constructive. The person will be viewed as having benignly ignored the teen, leaving her/him to explore alone her/his identity-creation impulses, or, conversely, the teen will criticize the person for subverting/undermining or even stopping/suppressing the process.

The teen can react in two major ways, and each affects negatively the impression of the other. In the hypo-identity style, the teen does not invest in identity formation searching/processes, and lives in a vacuum in this regard, or simply adopts identities shaped by/imposed by the environment. In contrast, the hyper-identity style might involve formation of multiple and rapidly changing identities, but they will be superficial/pseudo and perhaps anti-/defiant in nature. The other as perceived from these perspectives will be quite different. The other in the hypo-identity style might be introjected for her/his identity attributes, while, for the hyper-style, the other might be rejected in terms of any influence on identity.

Either way, the social self working schema of the other will not find a middle ground of being positive, constructive, etc., in a mutual identity-building process. The teen will be either hyper-ignorant of the other, discarding any effort to know her/him, learn from her/him, model her/his identities, etc. Or, the teen will be hyper-invested in the other in terms of identity absorption and construction, such that the teen's own influence in the identity construction process will be minimal to absent.

Attachment, Neo-Eriksonian Development, and Therapeutic Implications [Patients and Therapy]

Patient Presentation

The adult who is facing identity issues, especially if they are related to poor support on the matter in the mid-teen years in which the identity formation process might have initiated, will wallow in confusion/consternation and identity diffusion/cutoff because of the central role identity plays at this age. The self generally will be either too open or too closed to exploratory initiatives (e.g., Need to establish who am I; or, Not important to known who I am), and the identity component of the self also will be correspondingly open or closed to such initiatives (e.g., What are my morals/values? or, Why even worry about having an ideology, being idealistic?).

The patient who is under- or overidentificatory in these regards will express emotions that are associated with the style – the under type will be content, at best, with the adopted/imposed identities she/he has incorporated from the other, but will not have an undercurrent of bristling joy as might be found in the person with well-developed, positive identities. The over type might be superficially joyful, and even extremely so, but not at the core. Moreover, defiance could be the head emotion characterizing the person. The social life accompanying the hypo- and hyper-identity patient profiles will parallel the emotional ones, with social targets affiliated with the hypo case being equally flat. For the hyper style, sociality will include relating to others who are like herself/himself and the resultant social interactions will be superficial/pseudo as much as anything else.

The therapist needs to boost the patient when she/he utilizes the abstract logical skills that could help in the circumstances. These skills concern hierarchization of abstract logical coordinations, which can be applied to self-other relations, identity comparisons and contrasts, etc.

Behavioral/Symptom Mental Scanning

The identity-challenged patient will be able to perceive the absence of a solid sense of self and identity structure, whether of the hypo- or hyper-identity type. Normally, the adult has a rich repertoire of formed identities in all relevant spheres and functions accordingly. They are like scripts or narratives that impregnate the self and its thoughts, feelings, and actions. They constitute core elements of one's sense of personality, and sense of one's core essence. However, when asked to undertake mental scanning, the types of psychological identities that will be noticed by a patient having identity issues will not resemble identities that provide strength to a person. Rather, for the hypo style, they will be weak/of little benefit constructively, or even absent in the scans provided. Perhaps the patient will reflect the hyper- as opposed to the hypo-identity style in this regard, though. Once more, even though multiple identities might be depicted after scanning, they will be maladaptive in being superficial/pseudo and scattered and ephemeral, with one to several possible of the negative/anti-/defiant type. The identity picture will be confused/diffused cutoff/curtailed, etc. The patient might be able to relate the identity profile to an unsupportive environment, such as a suppressing, ignoring, or even malevolent one at a critical time in life when identities could have been explored/committed to. The patient will notice concomitant emotions, such as flatness in the hypo type or with defiant emotions concerning the other who had molded/imposed her/his identities. Or, perhaps for the hyper type, the defiance might be evident to the patient, but it will be justified as normal, and helpful in obtaining desired ends, etc.

Therapeutic Implications

The patient imbalanced in identity formation pursuit might be either hypo- or hyper-identificatory, depending. In both cases, the abstract logical thought processes that typically accompany identity formation in the teen can be tapped to help the patient. The therapist will foster use of the compare-contrast skills involved, as facilitated by the hierarchization aspect in the abstract logical thinking. The hypo-identificatory type will need to be guided toward the challenge of finding genuine identities that can stoke the self and its contentment. The hyper-identificatory one will need preliminary tamping of pseudo/superficial/negative/anti-/defiant-related identities.

Stress/Trauma Resilience/Coping

The mid-teen facing identity issues and setbacks will have less of an ability to deal with stress/trauma compared to peers having no or little difficulties in this regard. The types of identities that develop in the supportive context could help the mid-teen deal better with the rapid physical, cognitive, self, social, and emotional developments taking place. When the environment supports exploring identities in important areas, such as morals/values, ideologies/relating to society, respecting peers/partners, and so on, a solid foundation exists for dealing with both internally generated and externally generated stress/trauma in terms of resilience and coping. However, the unsupported mid-teen, as well as the adult patient expressing identity issues equivalent to that of the mid-teen, will have deficits in identity formation in one of two major ways (hypo-identifying; hyper-identifying). This will reduce the resilience/coping of the mid-teen/patient to stress/trauma because, normally, positive identities help to hyper-connect the components of the self; help tighten/bound the self to sympathetic others; help the person stay calm when confronted by stress/trauma; facilitate the use of abstract logic/comparative thinking/hierarchization in placing the stress/trauma in appropriate personal and social context; and promote good social resource recruitment. The identity-challenged individual will have difficulties in succeeding on all these stress/trauma resilience/coping fronts. Identity provides an axis that can bootstrap self-confidence, for example, in dealing with stress/trauma.

Therapeutic Strategies [The Other and Change]

Relational Co-regulation

The mid-teen experiencing difficulties with normal identificatory processes such that they are restricted or magnified, leading to hypo- or hyper-identification, respectfully, will relate to the other in turn with this marginalized/magnified identificatory prism. The self image will reflect the identificatory challenges/crises of the self and affect the perceived other in its identificatory reflection. The hypo type will express an identification profile devoid of personally chosen identifications, being either more or less empty or hyper-socialized (other-directed/selected) in the choices made (foreclosure; moratorium). The other will be unable to breach the teen's barriers in the former case and will be a dominant force in the latter. The hyper type might express many but superficial/pseudo identities that bear no consistency or depth. The other will be ignored/avoided for any identificatory input in this case. The patient having lived an equivalent identification impasse will have similar identification issues, but more so compared to the teen. The therapist will attempt to help her/him to individualize and develop a more genuine self and identifications.

Behavior/Symptom Network/Connectivity Change (Horizontal)

The patient who needs to move from either a hypo-identity or hyper-identity style to a more balanced constructive identity profile will have to work at multiple levels of the self, sociality, emotions, and so on. The identity-impoverished type might have socialized identities but not personalized ones, with other people overly involved in establishing the identities. The identity-overabundant type might have personalized identities, but they will be false/pseudo/superficial and even anti-, negative, defiant, and rejecting of the other. The therapist will be supportive and support identity exploration by posing "What if" type questions and calling upon the patient's abstract logical/comparative hierarchizing skills. More positive identities can be established with depth, but only after the person ponders and gives self-reflective narrative responses to these types of questions. In addition, the therapist will work toward minimizing the defiance in the pseudo/hyper type.

Behavior/Symptom Growth, Deep Change (Vertical)/Constructing a More Positive Life Story

As identities stabilize in the patient (or mid-teen, depending), the next step in development is broached more positively. It involves nurturing acts, underwritten by abstract logical systems in thought. The absent/minimal and perhaps socialized identities in the hypo-identity style (hypo in the sense of a lack of personally constructed, explored, committed to identities) will give way to more positive personally formed identities that can prepare for positive nurturing. The same would apply to modulation of the hyper-identity style, because more genuine identities would develop in place of pseudo/superficial (and even anti-, negative, opposing) ones.

The patient (mid-teen) struggling with identity can recount new stories of emergence, growth, finding oneself, learning what are the positives in the core of the self, how positive are one's new-found identities, and so on. The hypo type will vaunt the positive constructive stories about identity, including living by deeply held values, respect of the other, etc., but without moralizing and having an air of superiority/

self-justification. If socialized stories of the self had been part of the stories told, they can be reworked toward taking ownership of them or even discarded. The hyper type will discount the negative, anti-, defiant stories and replace them with positive, constructive offerings. The depth and solidity of the stories will need to be emphasized in order to build a sense of self confidence and respect for and by the other.

Consciousness, Theory of Mind, Selves, and Responsibility

The mid-teen developing well her/his positive identity structure will have deeply ingrained morals/values/ideologies/respect of the other, etc., which will serve to move the teen toward an increasing sense of responsibility and self-confidence to ably undertake responsibility. The teen with a self that is buttressed with positive identities will be able to perceive similar positive identities in others and will seek out people like this in a cyclical turn. The self and other will not just be concepts defined as I/Me but also as We/Us. Fanaticism will be controlled and emerge as sensitive appreciation and cognitive inquiry into the world of ideas and the world of people. The teen will be well on the way to adopting behaviors, feelings, and attitudes indicative of an encompassing morality, sense of responsibility, and personal maturity.

The Abstract (Formal) Stage Sub-stage of Systematization (16–19 Years): Sub-stage 18

Self and Relational Development [Initial Theoretical Elaborations]

A very brief description of the present step in Young's 25-step Neo-Eriksonian developmental model follows. It is presented again in Chap. 18, to help give a collective overview of the 25 steps in the modeling.

Nurturing acts vs. mis-nurturing (not nurturing) acts (16–19 years). The growing person engages in caring behavior of other people, to give them support and bring out the best in them. The environment (parent) might not support nurturing, and the person will not nurture or care for people. If this happened to you, this will affect your social relationships. Perhaps you will ignore people, not like them, and so on. Or, perhaps you will nurture people a lot, but only on the surface and without real caring.

Appendix 4.3 gives the brief amount of work already done in prior publications related to the task of developing in depth the Neo-Eriksonian (sub)stage model. The next section of the chapter gives an interim summary that elaborates the contents of Appendix 4.3 with respect to the present sub-stage being considered, of the sub-stage of Abstract (Formal) Stage Sub-stage of Systematization.

Interim Summary

The late teen (16–19 years) will have advanced from the initiation of Identity formation in the prior sub-stage of the current model (abstract hierarchization) to the next sub-stage of abstract systematization. The identity formation process continues into this sub-stage and subsequence ones, including in emerging adulthood. The identities that have been formed can solidify because the hierarchizations of the prior sub-stage systematize. That is, the dominant-subordinate relationship of personal identities being formed in relation to the influence of the other in this regard, for example, can develop as more established when systematized in this sub-stage. They can become more fully personal and embedded in the self-identity matrix. Moreover, new identities can develop in this period of late adolescence and become firmly ensconced in the self-identity matrix in a more complete process had the identity initiated in the prior sub-stage.

Erikson had considered that the stage of Identity is followed by the one of Intimacy. However, the present model has interpolated a step between the Identity and Intimacy ones. It involves Nurturing. This precursor stage to Intimacy makes eminent sense for several reasons. First, the present Neo-Eriksonian model builds its 25 steps based on the parallel Neo-Piagetian one of 25 steps. Therefore, the Neo-Piagetian stage of Abstract Systematization requires a Neo-Eriksonian equivalent and the one of Nurturing makes sense in this regard, as will be explained below. Second, Intimacy itself requires precursors related to Nurturing generally. Intimacy can be considered a specific outgrowth of a more generalized Nurturing. Third, in a certain sense, Nurturing is akin to a more advanced Identity related to respect for the other, being a good moral person, and so on.

As presented, the concept of late-adolescent Nurturing is not just about Nurturing the other and social relationships. Nurturing includes being responsible in multiple adult-type functions. Nurturing concerns engaging in genuine reciprocal social relations. It concerns adopting with care and future perspective adult-type functions (or ones preliminary to that), such as in studying or work. Adult-type functions constitute more than adopting the rules involved. It is not just about performing well in the tasks related to the roles. Rather, it is about being cognizant of all the dynamics in the roles and behaving as an adult might, rather than behaving just to discharge (mechanically) the roles involved. Nurturing is deeply undertaken, involving the core selves/identities holistically, and not just in superficial ways on a seemingly superfluous role.

The late teen behaves conscientiously. The behavior is more than about being aware/conscious. It is about functioning from positive, constructive identities established (or being established) and being enthralled in the engagement in the function at hand. The engagement is as deep as the core self/identities from which it springs and reflects an inherent sense of being good/responsible at all levels, etc.

Nurturing is also a social act because, in relating to others, the late teen functions like an adult. The teen is responsive/sensitive yet active/proactive. There is a mutual reciprocity that speaks to the concept of "intra-action." The baby intra-acts with the other/mother. The concept of interaction does not capture that the relationship in the interaction is more important in understanding it than the components (people) involved in the interaction as well their incoming stances to the relational interaction. As people interact, they are continuously defined and redefined by their participatory engagement in the interaction and leave behind their incoming status/stance into the relationship. Thus, there are never really independent actors in an interaction who conjoin in a relationship unchanged by the interaction. In this sense, two people and their relational exchange are best characterized as an intra-action within a social system in which two elements exchange/relate and are modified by the exchange/relationship (and context). In some senses, intra-action might appear more marked in earlier life stages because the baby is defined and redefined so much by the relational exchanges she/he has with the environment. Although, true, the Nurturing aspect of the present sub-stage of the current model affords the late teen more of an equal contribution to the relational engagement with the other; the intra-action approaches an equitable balance. The late teen is well on the way to becoming an active intra-action active relational contributor when socializing with the other, especially as a romantic partner.

Nurturing, then, is a profoundly dialectical activity, with sensitivity/responsivity and empathy/caring for the other person potentially a part of the process. Best friends might need a lot of support, for example, or a younger sibling, too. The late teen is ready for the task. A gym buddy might need a lot of instruction and the late teen is ready for the task. A classmate might profit from study groups, and the late teen actively creates one and helps. A co-worker might need advice and the late teen is front and center. A partner might want two-way reciprocal sexual frolic, and the teen is there. In short, the late teen is ready to nurture/take care of mind and body of self and other. The other could be family or friend, group or institution, or other(s) in need (e.g., as in civic/volunteer work). The late teen is maturing into the adult function at all levels, preparing for genuine Intimacy.

The late teen is also nurturant cognitively, or engages in nurturance of personal mind. The underlying cognitive basis to the teen's psychology at this age involves abstract systematization. Streams in abstract logic can be coordinated hierarchically, with dominant-subordinate relations, and also they can be connected systemically in context so that they are more adaptive. When cognitive systems coalesce at this sub-stage, they allow for the creation of super-ordinate abstract processes. The prior sub-stage of abstract hierarchization facilitated compare/contrast abstract logic but, when the process systematizes, the person can better reciprocally interrelate the dominant/subordinate abstract logical components in context and undertake valid critical thinking and hypothetico-deductive thought of a more complex nature. The mind develops systemic understanding as a result, and can see how personal and other perspectives relate and coexist for cognitive problems as much as for social and related ones.

The late teen, then, sees a larger whole; develops personally constructed abstract formulations to guide her/him in context, including in relating intra-actively to similar structures in the other; and nurtures a finely adaptive, mutually engaged cognition in context. Because the late teen can obtain understanding of larger wholes, including of how the other thinks/behaves/emotes/relates, the late teen can self-nurture the mind and nurture the mind of the other, as much as acting on the physical self and other. Late teens might try to understand complex social systems that act on the self and other, determine their negative impacts and logically propose solutions, or become part of social movements that act rationally against the harms committed to people, but they will do so without the mid-teen's potential fanaticism/misplaced ideology (or at least that is the hope).

The late teen needs proper support for this development toward adult function/nurturing to unfold well. However, the environment might be totally unequipped to help the teen in this transitioning, or it might even act to undercut it for whatever reason. The late teen might find herself/himself alone, facing an uncaring or hostile world in these regards. The teen might leave home prematurely, get pregnant, get into alcohol/drugs, etc. (and perhaps with less experimentation compared to the younger teen who might do the same), given the imminent adulthood.

The late teen having difficulty with nurturing (as well as the older patient) lapse into a psychology of not wanting to nurture/not caring at all for the other. I have termed these mis-nurturing acts. The late teen cannot envision or engage in adult-type functions. The areas of studying hard, working assiduously, caring for a person, being responsible at multiple levels, and so on, are removed from the person's optics. The abstract systematization that can be used in logical decision making is not entertained at all. The standards developed for behavior/feeling/relating to others are not personally constructed after critical thought. Social life is asymmetric, with the other hardly considered for bidirectional relations. The present is the only time frame that counts, with working and growing toward the future discounted if not demeaned.

The person is not super-ordinately conscientious and nurturing/caring of the other, but super-ordinately contra-conscientious and uncaring of the other. The stories told about the self exclude the other and the stories of the other exclude the self. There is no social sharing and reciprocity, in an adult-like way, and the impression given is that the person is childlike in areas, and will act only for the self. If nurturing appears part of the repertoire, it is superficial/pseudo and transparently clear that it is exhibited only to feel good superficially or for extremely selfish motivations.

The social emotions in the person who can't or won't nurture in a genuine fashion at these levels will include indifference to/ignoring the other, or even loathing of the other, depending. There will be no deep fondness of the other that might otherwise be found. There will be no egalitarian partnering in sociality with the other. Social relations will take place for inappropriate reasons, such as entrapment/ensnaring, instead of positive engagement/equality. The other will be entwined rather than enshrined.

There will be two kinds of problematic nurturing profiles in the late-teen/adult having nurturing imbalances. The hypo-nurturing type will remove herself/himself from any nurturing invitation or opportunity. Nurturing will not be part of the central core that could animate behavior/feelings/sociality. If nurturing is manifested, it is without empathic giving and is a reflection of socialization rather than deeply held convictions. The hyper-nurturing type will engage a lot in behavior that resembles genuine nurturing, but it will be superficial/pseudo, and even contorted/conniving. There might be an underlying loathing of the other as the acts are undertaken, with irrational lambasting of the other also possible.

The therapist working with teens/patients like this will need to work with the nurturing-dismissing attitude of the hypo type and the false nature of the nurturing of the hyper type. The selves/identities in both cases will require work, as will the sociality/emotions involved. The abstract systemic logic that serves as the basis for genuine nurturing could be encouraged and applied to the types of issues being described. To recall, nurturing includes both the physical and mental of both the self and other, and the therapist can help the teen/patient explore the meaning of this concept and its implications.

Self-Response to Cognitive (Mis)Perception of the Other

This sub-stage in the abstract stage of development is the third involving teenagers. The first two concerned identifications and identity, respectively, and implicate self-definitional development, in particular, compared to relational development, although both are involved. Development takes a different tack in the third and last adolescent sub-stage in the current model because it shifts to nurturing/taking care, which automatically includes a heavy emphasis on the other. The teen at this age might have a partner, be sexually active, etc., and even preparing for or already committed to a long-term or life-long relationship. However, typically, the teen will find this type of commitment premature even though possible. The late teen is sexually driven, and potential partners become social behavior recipients. However, if supported well, the late teen will treat the other with respect during dating (and later in intimacy).

The valid nurturing aspect of the late teen's social behavior extends to family, friends, classmates, workmates, etc. The teen could be quite conscientious in responsibilities undertaken, which are adult-like functions, and she/he could be quite aware that they will help in launching into adulthood. The adult-like aspect of the teen's attitude in discharging her/his responsibilities serves to guarantee that at least an element of nurturing will be involved in any function adopted. In one way or another, at this age and in the proper context, nurturing becomes a central focus of behavior. Given all these considerations, in the nurturing aspect of the late teen, everything else being equal, the other becomes an axis in behavior as much as the self and its wants. The relational mutuality inherent in relating to the other with nurturing ensures potentially a deep egalitarian engagement.

The late teen/adult who has not been well-supported in Nurturing, or otherwise has difficulties therein, will not consider the other in the central way as described for the typically developing teen. The other will not be an object of positive nurturing and care. The other might receive mis-nurturing instead, including in neglect/no nurturing by omission and harming/mis-nurturing by commission. Instead of being conscientious toward the other, there might be contra-conscientious co-opting of the other for personal needs or conscious harming for whatever reason. Instead of the good person engaging in nurturing, "bad" behavior might be expressed toward the other. Treating the other from the perspective of behaving from adult-like functions will not materialize, and the person might be childish/petty instead, or even loathing of the other.

The hypo-nurturing type will withdraw into the self even as she/he interacts with the other, or will be seeking unfair advantage. There might be socialized nurturing expressed, but it will not be deeply held and personal. The hyper-nurturing type will be superficial/pseudo in nurturing and also use it toward seeking personal advantage. The other will be seen as an object to entrap in the personal web of desires, needs, and wants, without any reciprocity due to the person. The teen/patient might be capable of socializing only with kindred spirits, such that she/he and the other will be engaging in constant dueling and advantage-seeking behavior. The teen/patient might have access to the abstract logic systems that characterize the sub-stage in which nurturing typically appears, but won't be able to apply them in constructing an other-focused self in which self and other are reciprocally coordinated in a super-ordinate equitable construct. Without external help, the person will not be able to engage in the critical thought required to alter the self-other construct toward including nurturing as part of relating to the other. Personally derived standards referred to in dealing with the other will lack the goodness and taking-care components associated with nurturing.

Positive Pole in Eriksonian Development

The late teen who is well-supported in this critical period before clearly entering the adult period will be able to cope well with issues related to Nurturing and caring for the other. The nurturing will be wide-ranging and not just refer to intimate social relations with a partner. The late teen will be adopting adult-like functions at school/work, as the case may be, with parents/friends and classmates/workmates, etc. The teen will nurture self as much as other, body as much as mind, thinking as much as the social/emotional domain, etc. The extent of the nurturing could reach into concerns for society, minorities, etc., and involve taking a stance on the rights of others. The teen will behave responsibly in all these various arenas of adult-type function and engage reciprocally with the other/surround. The future will be a focus as much as the past and all relational activities, outside the mundane daily type, will be imbued with deep caring. The teen will make use of the underlying abstract systems in thought that she/he can use to construct/create personal and critical standards and expectations of self and other. The other's ability to do the same in an egalitarian mutuality will be appreciated. Nurturing and caring for self and other will be the basis of defining the self and relating to the other and the environment/surround. The teen will be a conscientious actor, an other-sensitive self, and a socially immersed I, with the other being considered as a responsive equal who is coexisting, co-defining, and co-maturing. Crises will be managed well by corelating, and corelating will mark the person rather than unilateral relating.

Negative Social-Self Working Schema

The late teen, when well-supported, will enter into nurturing relationships, for example, with parents, partners, and friends. The late teen will have an impulse to care for the other that will be grounded in a deep corelational process. The late teen will impress in her/his adult-like approach to life and be dynamically engaged in adult-like functions. Each function will elicit a nurturing/caring approach to the degree possible. The other will be the beneficiary of a supportive attitude, with the other being foremost on the mind of the teen. The story told about the other will not be outside the realm of the self, for each will be embedded in the stories about self and about other. This intra-active process will lead to a superstructure of self-other relations involving equity/equality and conscientious application.

However, many late teens will face challenges in nurturing, especially if unsupported in these regards. The other could act to or try to cancel the teen's nurturing/care motivation for personal reasons, such as being too needy and forcing the teen to give her/him help, but without a benevolent attitude. Or, the other could not show interest in eliciting any nurturing behavior in the teen, and she/he will thus struggle in attempts to be nurturing. The other might overtly or covertly channel/train the teen to be nurturant only in restricted and personally relevant (egotistical) ways, such that the teen develops little personally derived and self-enabled nurturance. The other might be quite negative/anti-nurturant and create a negative/anti-, contra-nurturing approach by the teen. Will the teen mock the person genuinely in need, take advantage unscrupulously of the need, and so on? Will the teen (immorally) take advantage of others who show genuine nurturing and resist mutual engagement in these regards?

The other might behave in a way that develops either a hypo-nurturing or hypo-nurturing style in the late teen. The same would apply to the adult exposed to a similar regime. The hypo style will involve the mirror of how the other had behaved in shaping the teen's/adult's approach to nurturing. The style will be dismissive/neglecting or perhaps there will be a certain constructing/restructuring of nurturing practices in the person but of ones that are not deeply held and committed to. In the hyper style, the nurturing will be multiple, scattered, and superficial/pseudo. It might succeed with naïve others, but ones not so naïve will consider the person as fake/dis-genuine, etc. The underlying loathing that the person might have for the other will be evident despite the putative nurturing, and any goodness professed might be doubted/contested.

Attachment, Neo-Eriksonian Development, and Therapeutic Implications [Patients and Therapy]

Patient Presentation

The late teen/adult who is having difficulty with nurturing issues will show a lack of care for the other and engage in mis-nurturing acts. Generally, the person will not take on adult-type functions in a responsible way. The person will be engage in adult-type activities, but just to discharge them, like in studying or work, and not with dynamic engagement. The other will not be an equal partner no matter what the relationship, and this holds for romantic partners, too. Reciprocity will be lacking in social relations, which will be either unilateral toward the self side or the other side, depending. If the other weighs more heavily in this balance, there could be much nurturing expressed, but of a pseudo/superficial/fake type. There might be even anti-/negative nurturing activity in this hyper-nurturing type, e.g., nurturing at the surface, but withdrawing that attitude when really required or turning against the other when more than superficial nurturing is required. The only true care in this approach is egotistically self-directed, in that the person acts only to take care of himself/herself, no matter how much the other requires help, for example. The hyper-nurturing type will not have proper personal standards and think critically about social relations/the other. Nor will the person relate well to the self in these regards. The other will be someone to ignore, take advantage of, try to fool, etc. The thought applied to the other will be uncritical, and with a what's-in-it-for-me attitude. The hypo-nurturing type will have an absence of standards and thinking about the other, having an attitude of nothing-is-in-it for me.

The patient will present as immature rather than mature, without a future-focus and an adult-like demeanor, and not deeply concerned for any other or only superficially so. The therapist will work on narratives about being more adult-like, caring, nurturing, conscientious, and critically self-reflective, while working at the patient having a better critical understanding and appreciation of/engagement with the other, toward repositioning an emerging goodness at the core of the self and relating to others.

Behavioral/Symptom Mental Scanning

The patient either deficient or inappropriately exaggerated in nurturing/caring for the other will be expressing a mis-nurturing/lack of other-care style in relating to the other. The adult-like functions that might be expressed will be immature, self-serving, and so on. The patient might be aware of the social void and sense of personal self-focus that characterizes her/his psychology, but might not be able to relate it to the poverty/absence (or self-centric misdirection) of any nurturing/caring for the other. The person will be pining for genuine relationships but not know how to obtain them. The other will be perceived as a person lacking in nurturing/care for the self, in turn, whether merited or not, because of the misperception of the other. The hypo-nurturer will feel a social void or perhaps will have filled it with socially constructed and not deeply felt nurturing (so lack genuineness in the behavior). The hyper-nurturer will also feel unfulfilled despite engaging in much pseudo-nurturing, or might feel loathing in the nurturing superficiality being maintained.

Patients experiencing problems in nurturing/caring for the other might decry the lack of meaning in their life, but not know how to avoid that feeling. They might use their abstract systematization logic to develop a super-ordinate understanding of the world and their place in it (including for self and other/relationships). But they won't be able to imagine how to increase relational engagement and how nurturing/caring for the other is crucial to stitching it together. So they might be dismissive of the therapist suggesting that the answer lies in opening the self, relating to the other genuinely with everything that that entails, and so on. This therapeutic effort might eventually lead to a more mature, reciprocally responsive individual who develops personal standards, critical thought, and so on. The person could bring some nurturing/caring into relationships, preparing for a more nurturing attitude and potential deeper caring for the other. The patient will also need help to detect self- and other-loathing until improvements are made in controlling mis-nurturing/not caring for the other.

Therapeutic Implications

The therapist working with the late teen or even adult expressing issues related to mis-nurturing/lack of care for the other will find one of two types – either a hypo-nurturer or a hyper-nurturer. The hypo type will be nurturing-deficient, at least from a personally derived, genuine perspective, because there might be only a socialized nurturing that follows the shaping/dictates of the environment. The hyper type will be scattered/enmeshed in nurturing, but superficially/not deep and even pseudo in style. There might be an anti- or harmful nurturing at the core. Either way, the person will be shirking the adoption of a genuinely nurturant attitude to adult-like functions, such as those related to school/work and care for others/sociality. The functions might be adopted and discharged, but without a deep commitment/appreciation stemming from a shared reciprocity with others. The underlying cognitive dynamic in the functions adopted/discharged will lack a basis in a comparative/critical thinking perspective that places the function at the central axis of the person, everything else being equal, unlike what might happen later on in a more balanced approach to life. The function might lack a central meaning to the person, and be only material without anything spiritual (in the broadest sense of the term). The I will not be a socially embedded, participatory one, conscientious and with personal standards but a free-floating one without the anchored core of stability that otherwise might obtain. The self will not be nurtured by the person, just as the other is not being nurtured by the person. Growth will be hit and miss, because without a proper nurturing, the bad habits of self-indulgence or other-negligence, and so on, might predominate.

The therapist can work with patients like these by encouraging internal reorganization of self/core components to place the desire for nurturing/care for others as central/fundamental and as a worthy goal to strive for. The therapist might question any nurturing that is not genuine and self-generated (e.g., is it socially decided; pseudo?). The therapist will use more advanced cognitive and narrative techniques in these regards. As for helping to facilitate better nurturing/caring for the other, interpersonal strategies could be used, even if for role playing to an imaginary audience. The patient might grow into the social, self-other relations being promoted. The therapist can also use the abstract logic/comparative-critical aspect of the person's cognition to underscore the advantages and disadvantages of the growth that would accompany a better nurturing/other-caring attitude, especially with the adult epoch so near and intimacy beckoning (which should not be confused with having a partner). The therapist should flag the inherent goodness of the person, and any way that positive social and emotional experiences reflect that. An inherent sense of goodness will help elicit nurturing and caring for the other, and feed back toward doing the same for the self.

Stress/Trauma Resilience/Coping

The late teen compromised in nurturing/caring for the other will be losing an important source of stress/trauma resilience/coping, as will the patient with similar issues. Nurturing is critical to relating with genuine reciprocity and receiving care, in turn, when it is required. The person lacking in genuine nurturing will have associated difficulties related to conscientiousness/maturity, having an adult-type functioning, personally derived standards, comparative/critical thought, and functioning from a core of deep goodness. These missing attributes will further affect resilience/coping to stress/trauma. The person might appear lost in the quagmire of stress/trauma or, conversely, be overly engaged with others about it but not genuinely. The hypo-nurturing type might reflect the first resilience/coping style and the hyper-nurturing type the second one. The self of the mis-nurturing person will be removed from the social environment to some extent, at least in terms of genuine reciprocity, so that the person will be left to her/his own devices in dealing with stress/trauma. The person might more easily express emotions that negatively impact resilience/coping because of a lack sociality or genuine engagement in nurturing/caring. That is, the person might manifest emotions related to an other-loathing, leading to a listlessness/under-excitability in dealing with stress/trauma or, to the contrary, an agitation/over-excitability.

Therapeutic Strategies [The Other and Change]

Relational Co-regulation

The nurturing late teen ideally taking care of the other from a personal stance of being genuine, conscientious, adult-like, responsible in reciprocal sharing, and mature with critical personal standards appropriate for her/his age will see one's place in the wider social/societal context and the super-ordinate linkages of all involved. In this scenario, the late teen will be relating to the other in genuine self-other inter-participation of a coequal nature. The self will not be seeking advantage from the other/taking advantage. The other will not be viewed as an object/underling, etc., but rather, worthy of nurturing/being taken care of out of a genuine sense of personal goodness.

The teen/patient having issues in these regards will not be able to corelate to the other in this sense of coequality. The regulation of the self, the other, and the relationship will be splintered and induce sharp divides in any core, positive elements related to nurturing/taking care of the other. If a romantic partner is involved, the couple will be fractured in nurturing/taking care of the other, especially if the partner has corresponding nurturing or related issues. The hypo-nurturing/caring-for-other patient will express a paucity of genuine nurturing and related motivations. They might be absent or fronted socially (either way dis-genuine). The hyper-nurturing type will be similarly dis-ingenuine in nurturing, even if pseudo/false presentations in this regard manifest. The patient will experience self-other corelational regulation fissures related to nurturing/caring for the other. In this disconnected self-other map, nurturing/caring for the other will be either pushed aside or "used to obtain advantage."

Behavior/Symptom Network/Connectivity Change (Horizontal)

The late teen/adult exhibiting deficits in nurturing/caring for the other will entrench in mis-nurturing styles and have difficulty in engaging in adult-like functions, generally, at least with a sense of conscientiousness/genuineness. The person will struggle with thinking critically using abstract logic and from deeply held personal standards. Any nurturing undertaken will be constructed by the other or from necessities of circumstance, rather than deriving from a sense of genuine reciprocity/sharing/engagement with the other as a coequal. Therefore, emotions will relate to a self-focus or a pseudo/surface feeling for the other rather than deeply held emotions, except if self- or other-loathing develops. In this context, it will be difficult to escape the hypo- or hyper-nurturing style expressed, behave in genuine adult-type functional activity, etc. Conscientiousness/maturity will develop only through proper environmental support, perhaps through a sensitive romantic partner or a well-versed therapist. The latter will explore the sense of void relative to feeling genuine, the meaning of relationships, and the rewards of nurturing/caring for the other, along with the advantages of seeing the full landscape of life, including what lies beyond the horizon when a hope for reciprocal/mutual nurturing/caring for the other establishes in a person.

Behavior/Symptom Growth, Deep Change (Vertical)/Constructing a More Positive Life Story

The person moving out of a phase of having difficulties with nurturing will be moving toward fulfillment in intimacy. The person will be able to envisage nurturing/caring for the self as a building block for a deeper, loving relationship with a romantic partner. The sense of self will feel more mature and ready for fully mature romantic relationships that might even lead to monogamy, children, caring for children, etc. The person will be developing an internal sense of genuine goodness that can be applied/translate romantically into intimacy rather than isolation.

The late teen/adult making progress in changing toward a nurturing/caring-for-the-other individual will be able to describe the sense of deep internal goodness felt and the conscientious, mature person emerging. The story will be one of growth into adult-like functions, including in relating positively to the other with coequal enjoyment, affection, etc. The person can describe a new narrative in which the other is as much a central character as the self. Life will be more meaningful, more relational, and less about me, myself, and I in favor of her/him and us together.

Consciousness, Theory of Mind, Selves, and Responsibility

The late teen navigating well the sub-stage of abstract systematization in logic, as found in the present model, will express a mature conscientious in nurturing/caring for the other. The cognitive underpinning of the sub-stage will allow for personally constructed standards, comparison/critical thought, and super-ordinate structuring, which will create a field in which the person can place self in relation to others, one's responsibilities, acting with a helpful, moral attitude toward the other, etc., while expressing a sense of responsibility for all adult-like functions. Underlying this attitude will be a deep respect for the other, and a relational reciprocity that imbues all engagement with any other. When living like this, full psychological maturity would be in the offing.

The Abstract (Formal) Stage Sub-stage of Multiplication (19–22 Years): Sub-stage 19

Self and Relational Development [Initial Theoretical Elaborations]

A very brief description of the present step in Young's 25-step Neo-Eriksonian developmental model follows. It is presented again in Chap. 18, to help give a collective overview of the 25 steps in the modeling.

Intimacy acts (with partner) vs. (social) isolation acts (19–22 years). The growing person gives positive effort, including at work or in school, and with any romantic partner and any children. The person feels a deep, long-lasting love for the partner, if any is present, and feels deeply involved in everything done. Without environmental (parental) support (or with past problems), you could reject romance and feel lonely and empty. Or, you could go through the motions and be fake in any relationship with a partner, even behaving roughly.

Appendix 4.4 gives the brief amount of work already done in prior publications related to the task of developing in depth the Neo-Eriksonian (sub)stage model. The next section of the chapter gives an interim summary that elaborates the contents of Appendix 4.4 with respect to the present sub-stage being considered, of the sub-stage of Abstract (Formal) Stage Sub-stage of Multiplication.

Interim Summary

This particular sub-stage in the current model involves abstract multiplications in logic, which refer to propagating abstract systems that develop in the prior sub-stage over multiple domains (and toward their integration in the next sub-stage). This cognitive diversification in abstract thought allows the super-ordinate abstract mental structures formed in the prior sub-stage, and which had allowed a comparative, critical abstract thought, to generalize to varied domains as the skill advances within the person's cognitive architecture. The systems involved are evaluated, applied, differentiated, and adapted contextually toward building coherent multiple cognitive frameworks working in combination.

The I/self that can develop in this cognitive structure will also be one that works toward higher-order combinational levels, such that core elements anchor others. The prior sub-stage involved systems in this regard but, in the present sub-stage, the domains that the I/self applies to expand and differentiate while combining and linking. I had referred to this process as relativistic, which in the present case refers to flexibility in exploring the I/self structure as new areas are added to the structure, such as in identity/values, and senses of responsibility/behaving in adult functioning. The I/self might be called individualistic at this sub-stage in striking out into adult functions with whole-hearted application. However, this concept does not emphasize enough the intense mutuality in social relations at this sub-stage, and the role of the other both in helping the I/self self-define and creating the social context in which that can take place.

The cognitive sophistication inherent in the cognitive underpinning to the sub-stage (abstract multiplication of systems in logic) allows the person to feel both unique and deeply engaged with others. This sets the stage for weighing cognitively larger systems as they differentiate into multiple life domains, which is a critical acquisition in functioning maturely in the world of full-scale responsibilities. People living at this level can envision their role in developing the uniqueness of I/self as they take on the tasks necessary to meet their obligations in the world of responsibilities. They do not shirk them but revel in them (at least to the degree possible), given the growing network of their logical abstract system differentiations and applications. For example, before even considering the world of work, the person at this sub-stage of development is building a sense of general self that allows for testing new ideas, creativities, and individually defined components. The person will not be absolutist in this regard, but flexible, while growing the core I/self.

The person "delves and debates" as the self differentiates, but not just with the person's multiple, relativistic perspectives. Rather the engagement is with the other, too, given the co-mutuality in sociality at this age period. For example, peers cooperate to construct intellectual, social, and societal edifices at this age to the degree that the cognitive basis in the period permits. The other participates in the co-construction involved in prompting reflection, expanding the contents, and considering implications of the cognitive structure reasoning/stance/narrative involved.

At the socio-emotional and socio-affective level, the advances in the sub-stage of abstract system multiplications in logic represent a major threshold in development because they concern engaging in adult functions, generally (the age period here is 19–22 years), and because they concern Eriksonian intimacy, specifically. The prior sub-stage involved acquisition of competencies in nurturing/caring for the other, which prepares intimate partnering, too.

In the present sub-stage, the underlying cognitive acquisition of the sub-stage permits a deeper engagement with the other socially and emotionally, in that the commitment to the other reaches the apex of a potential long-term one, everything else being equal. For abstract systems, which concern the cognitive acquisition in the prior sub-stage, the nurturing that is possible might be limited in the case of romantic partners to a lesser range and depth of feelings/activities/domains relative to what is possible for the present abstract systems in multiplication. The nurturing can expand in the latter to longer-range commitments and ones involving all major adult functions. Study/work, as the case may be, is not undertaken uniquely for self growth but for "we growth," as found in the couple. The adult function is not just individualistic to create a unique person but synergistic to create a unique couple. The person can behave responsibly in the adult functions not just for self-glorification but also for couple creation. The person does not abandon the functions on whims, or willy-nilly, but gives herself/himself to behaving optimally in the functions in order to succeed wholesale in them for the common couple good as much as the individual good.

The late adolescent might profess undying love to the romantic partner and feel deeply in love, but the nature of love in the early adult stage takes on a different aura. Love is not just an emotion; it is a lifestyle. Love is not just a feeling for the other. It is an approach to life with the other. Love can develop as much as any other emotion. The anger of the baby evolves into varied emotions and displays in the adult. The contentment of the baby grows into the excited joy of the adult, and so on. Love has a longing component, and that accentuates, as well, in the adult. To conclude, in the early adult period a new type of love emerges, one that is broader, deeper, and longer, and perceived as elaborate/extensive in all these regards.

The label often given to the age period in this sub-stage concerns "emerging adulthood." Although I question the utility of this term, given that it does not reflect a universal acquisition, I do not discard it for parsimonious reasons, and also because I approach the term in a different way compared to the standard way. In the present approach, emerging adulthood develops as a stage of life not just due to sociocultural reasons, such as society being able to offer young people at this age educational opportunities that allow them to postpone undertaking adult functions, especially vocationally and in generativity. As well, emerging adulthood develops as a stage in life because, like other sub-stages in the present Neo-Eriksonian model, it concerns a developmental period that is permitted by having acquired the relevant cognitive underpinning, as much as anything else.

Emerging is an adjective that suggests a new period of life, especially given its contiguity with the first age period associated with adulthood. However, in the present model, emerging is an adjective that would apply at multiple developmental points, and not just at the start of a new adult cognitive/socio-affective stage or the collective intelligence stage. Nevertheless, emerging is an adjective that applies very well to the 19- to 22-year-old, which is the age that involves the present sub-stage, and the 22- to 25-year-old, which is an age that involves the next one. These ages are associated with undergraduate and graduate/professional education, in particular, which prepare for adult function with energetic headway. That said, keep in mind that the Eriksonian challenge traditionally conceived at this age period of earliest adulthood involves romantic relations.

In emerging adulthood, many people at this age are engaging fully in adult functions, such as in work, but even their studies are engaged in with the same intensity and commitment as any work. More important, for present purposes, the crucial adult function that applies at this age relates to intimacy and the associated emotions of love and longing, as described. That is, emerging adulthood should be considered synonymous with Eriksonian Intimacy, at least in terms of how these concepts are dealt with in the present model.

The type of development described for the 19- to 22-year-old entering early adulthood appears to easily allow the development of Eriksonian intimacy and associated love/longing. However, this presumes that the environment has been and continues to be supportive of the developing person's psychology. Moreover, it presumes that the ideal romantic partner that fits the bill is available and willing. Needless to say, life never is so easy. Moreover, the sub-stage being discussed is about much more than intimacy, because it refers to enthusiastically adopting all of life's major functions with deep commitment, from study/work to partner/children.

When the environment is not supportive of the person's push to engage in the full scope of adult functions with enthusiasm and commitment, difficulties in feeling that the self is an adult/mature and engaging in its apex function of Intimacy will set in. Instead of adult assuredness, relating well to the other as a partner at all levels, including in intimacy for a select one, and otherwise loving that person and life and all its offerings and mysteries, the person lapses into feelings of social isolation, loneliness, and desolation. The I/self does not explore different domains and modalities of self-expression and relating to the other. Rather, the I/self feels selfless in the sense of not being unique and self-defined and also feels an absence of reciprocal relatedness. That is, because the I/self is not properly anchored at its core, the romantic partner, if there is one, will not be, due to the inability to attract more mature, psychologically integrated partners.

The I/self gravitates to constricted, growth-inhibiting absolutes because they are easier and less conflicting, and the person seeks the same in potential romantic partners. The dyadic exploration and growth permitted in a genuinely co-mutual relationship is aborted to begin with, and intimacy is sacrificed for a comfort in familiarity, at best. But the familiarity exists at the plane of a lack of vitality and so the couple will stagnate, although the partners might be ready to accept that and live at that level. Emotionally, instead of love, hate might set in. Potentially, the type of more genuine and intimate love that has been described for the ideal outcome in this age period will be out of reach.

Moreover, the person who has Intimacy issues might react with a hypo-intimacy, or, the contrary, a hyper-intimacy. As with other sub-stages in the present model, the hypo type might express a socialized style in intimacy, but it will be other imposed/molded rather than personally chosen/built. As for the hyper style, it might include pseudo/fake intimacy and even a negative, anti-intimacy. The hypo style will express a lack/avoidance of intimacy, in particular. The person will generally have difficulty with adult function. I'm reminded of some of the seven deadly sins in this regard, e.g., greed, laziness. In terms of relationships with romantic partners, the romance might be quite diluted if it takes place, e.g., following social norms and without genuine feelings. As for the hyper-intimate type, one label for it might be sex addiction. The associated feeling would be lust/lasciviousness instead of love/longing. The person will be obsessed but shallow in the dating game. Partners will be considered "toy mates." Or, the person might have one partner but not know how to treat her/him with equality and magnamity. Rather, the person will be oppressed, depressed and always on the edge of arguments and leaving. The relationship is more like cat and mouse instead of building a strong basis together. If a negative, anti-, contra style develops for intimacy, the person will be rejecting of it, haughtily dismissing any potential partner, or perhaps finding a partner who accepts that the extreme arguments and even verbal or other abuse predominates, that is, with no or little permanent objection and leaving the relationship despite the argumentative undercurrent.

In all these types of cases, couple therapy will help. The person might need an individual-focused therapy, as well, for dealing with the general difficulties in dealing with adult function. The therapist should open dialogue with the person that elicits how personal growth can best take place and with a commitment to grow to be a better partner in a genuine intimacy.

Self-Response to Cognitive (Mis)Perception of the Other

The sub-stage of abstract systems multiplication in logic that marks the first adult time period (19–22 years) sets the basis for adopting adult functions, including in intimacy. The other becomes a main focus, including toward establishing a romantic partnership. If the relationship goes well, the longing and love feelings take on a different color compared to prior sub-stages in the model because of the deep genuine commitment associated with it. Generally, the youthful adult behaves with more responsibility, investing fully the self into the task at hand, and cooperating/collaborating with the other, either directly or indirectly, to establish and achieve mutually satisfying goals (e.g., a deep co-mutual commitment in a romantic relationship). The new adult takes seriously all responsibilities, and can see the romantic relationship and the couple's reciprocal innervation through the multiplying abstract systems developing in its cognitive structure. The abstract period generally allows for a voyage of self discovery, which inevitably means other discovery, as well. The mind of the other includes multiple abstract systems over multiple domains, including socio-emotionally and socio-affectively. The early adult uses her/his equivalent skills in an attempt to decipher the personal cognitive structure that has been built in these regards (and be reciprocally influenced by them). The mind of the other becomes the multiple loci of exploration of the other, as well. Self and other exploration of the two minds involved takes place reciprocally. The co-minds so created are co-formed and co-regulated.

This is especially true for intimate partners for whom one expresses a deep and long-term commitment and love. The other becomes an object of high regard without being placed on a pedestal. The love engendered animates both parties and infuses the self (and self esteem) of each party. Each person can grow, given the foundation that love provides. The growth eventually will become positive in feedback, and reach horizons beyond the two individual growth trajectories of the partners involved before the committed love had taken place and had provided the mutual discovery and co-building process involved.

The early adult who encounters environmental or other circumstances that are not conducive to establishing intimacy and related adult functions might feel a sense of aloneness and isolation even if there is a romantic partner involved. The relationship might founder in incomplete, insincere, clumsy, or contrary attempts at intimacy. The other might evaluate the person as putting on a façade, either hiding an absent/socialized intimacy or a negative/anti- one, something like passive-aggressive behavior, or superficially expressing intimacy but deeply resenting and rejecting it (as well as the other as recipient). The other might elicit deep, hateful feelings instead of loving ones. Longing for the other will be replaced by longing for an end to the relationship or even longing for a second (another) romantic (sexual) partner.

Just as the self will not be individuated yet co-mutual, so will the other not be ascribed a personal uniqueness to respect (and the person will not realize her/his responsibility toward promoting that sense of uniqueness). Just as the person might engage in contra-intimacy acts, so might the person expect or foster the same in the other. The lack of support felt from the other for adult functions attempted, whether perceived or misperceived, will translate into providing a similar lack of support to the other.

The communication between the parties will either be dry and superficial or perhaps hot and pseudo-deep but, in any case, not deeply genuine and functional in the adult sense. The scope of discussion in the couple will exclude anything approaching the products of an inquisitive, shared abstract system multiplication in logic in which this type of logic grows across domains and inter-connects across them. The other will be bereft of co-mutuality intellectually as much as in intimacy, leaving a barren communication and interaction, perhaps punctuated by hot emotions between the cooling exchanges.

The person risks abandoning the other, or otherwise destroying or greatly harming the relationship. The relationship might be so fractured and irreparable that both parties experience loneliness/isolation/desolation even when presumably close to each other, active sexually, etc. The other will be perceived as partly present, at best, for example, in attempting to secure self-interested goals. In the hypo-intimacy type, if there is a romantic partner, these tendencies will be exaggerated. Loneliness will characterize the relationship; liveliness will be absent. As for the hyper-intimacy type, the romantic partner can expect a volatile relationship, constant surface expressions of love, but accompanying signs of hate, too.

Positive Pole in Eriksonian Development

In meeting well the challenges of intimacy, the early adult will be tackling the full range of adult functions that are required. She/he will have a co-mutual, loving relationship with a romantic partner and apply herself/himself with an equal commitment to study/work, as the case may be, and other responsibilities. The person will not feel mired in the multiple adult functions undertaken, but will feel in flow. The person will feel both unique in personal attributes yet united with the other and open to co-growth; with the other's uniqueness respected and encouraged, too. The person will be intimate with self and other, close to deep core positive attributes in both, and facilitative of their growth. The person will use a refined logical assessment of the self, other, and context to help accomplish these goals, and will do so for all undertaken adult functions. When matters outside the control of the person impose/impact her/his life, the person remains calm to the degree possible and engages the situation with the same responsible, committed approach that characterizes all actions undertaken. External stresses are seem as relative to the grand picture, in which intimacy and all domains of adult functioning have provided rich resources to help handle well the issues.

Negative Social-Self Working Schema

The early adult who is in a supportive surround will have the ability to enjoin in intimate relations and bring that approach and feeling into other adult functions, such as engagement in study/work, with family/friends, etc. As a romantic partner, the other will elicit co-love feelings, in which self and other are fused but still preserving their uniqueness that had made them attractive in the first place. Being well-supported in creating an attitude of intimacy toward a romantic partner and an equivalent attitude in other adult functions requires an open mind that shares personal stories and general moralities and values. The supportive partner entertains with good advice and appreciative calm the positive growth of the person in these regards.

When the surround does not behave this way with respect to intimacy, efforts in creating a committed loving relationship will be compromised. The other will be represented as an influence on/the cause of the felt isolation/loneliness, by ignoring/dismissing or even pushing away/rejecting the person. If there is a romantic partner involved, nonetheless, the relationship will be neither romantic nor a partnership in the true sense of the word. The other will not be loved, in that the self will be incapable of expressing love, except perhaps on a superficial level or in a socialized way. Without the self-other duality placed ahead or super-ordinate in a larger system that multiplies out across contexts and domains in the couple, both the subjective sense of self of the person and the perceived other as object of the self will not have associated with it a positive working schema in couplehood. The other might be hated, even, with rebound hate onto the self possible, too.

Rather than individuating in a co-mutuality with an intimate loved one, in a process that generates personal growth and respect for the other, the self will flail in trying to stand out for a personally derived individuality. And the perception of the other, similarly, will not have any stamp of uniqueness, except perhaps in negative terms.

Both the hypo- and hyper-intimacy styles will reflect these negative social self working schemas, but with added properties. The other in the hypo style will be viewed as impossible to attain in any intimate way, a distant figure. The other in the hyper style will be viewed as easy to obtain in intimacy, because of the multiple pseudo/false intimacy-promoting strategies used. The danger is that when the targeted partner sees through the charade, the person will express frustration, anger, and even domestic violence. Of course, the latter could be promoted by difficulties in transitioning positively in any of the prior sub-stages of the present model and even more so.

Attachment, Neo-Eriksonian Development, and Therapeutic Implications [Patients and Therapy]

Patient Presentation

The early adult who has developed normally but finds herself/himself confronting intimacy issues, perhaps due to a poor environmental support at this point in time, or perhaps due to a bad choice for romantic partner, or an inability to find one, might feel a deep loneliness/isolation/desolation. If there is a romantic partner and the problems derive from an unsupportive environment, the general capacity to engage in adult functions (e.g., study work, socially) will be affected negatively. The adult will enter therapy not only feeling quite alone even if she/he has a romantic partner/friends but also quite dissatisfied at school/work. A constant theme will be wanting to end all one's adult functions in relations, including romantic ones, and in other adult functions, including the crucial ones of school/work. The lack of capacity to experience genuine intimacy in romantic relations will generalize to having an inability to genuinely commit to and apply oneself long-term to other domains of adult functions.

The self will not be a content, stable, personalized entity, but a discontented, unstable, and nonindividualized one, without personally constructed, positive, core attributes. The other will be the other side of the same coin of the patient, being a separate, unhappy entity. There will be no genuine love in the couple, if a romantic partner is present, but there will be much ignoring, head games, bickering, side swipes, and even frontal assault/hate possible.

The hypo-intimate type also will bemoan the emptiness even though there are multiple partners in her/his life. The patient will not be able to connect the social dots and other adult function dots, missing the ability to see the grand cognitive, social, and emotional structures that govern her/his life. The paucity of connectivity and, indeed, the paucity of connector sites (domains) to which intimacy/genuine adult functioning has taken hold will fuel the sense of isolation/loneliness/emptiness. The self will reside in isolation from the other in the cognitive structure created to represent them, and the other will be a figure forever distant, or forever fighting and fitful, if present.

Behavioral/Symptom Mental Scanning

The early-adult patient with Intimacy difficulties will feel isolated alone, empty, or desolate. The mental scanning will be able to pick up this sentiment, as well as the lack of intimacy if there is no romantic partner. The person will be asking, "What is wrong with me?" or querying, "What is wrong with people for not wanting me?" If there is a romantic partner, though, the person might deflect questions about self-competence in love relationships to problems residing in the other and her/his inability to connect with the person. The focus will be on the other as intimacy-breaking.

The person will be able to perceive her/his own argumentative style, and even a hateful or love-hate attitude that might derive, but she/he might not attribute it to personal issues and deficits. There will be little or no acknowledgment of maturity issues, problems in adapting other adult functions, etc., but the person will decry the lack of passion in her/his endeavors, and that it feels like she/he is just going through the motions. The person might constantly express wanting to abandon adult functions, and even the present romantic partner, for being unfulfilling and passionless. But the person will not be able to perceive that the type of love they express or want is not of the mature, co-shared type, and blame the emptiness on the other, the institutions involved (e.g., school, work), as the case may be.

The person will not feel unique, an individual who is respected for being her/his own person, but will have little inkling why. The person will state that he/she has all the proper adult goals, so should be respected for that. But the person will offer little discussion of co-respect for the other and why that is important. The cognitive style of the person will be siloed, with separate domains tackled logically but the need for a growing inter-connectedness of the domains will not be grasped.

The hypo-intimate person will have these identity-related tendencies magnified, with the sense of isolation deeper and despairing. The person will be lazy in love, giving up too soon. The hyper-intimate type will be the opposite, greedy in love, but at a superficial/pseudo level, and with disapproval/rejection by the other magnified.

Therapeutic Implications

The early adult with intimacy issues will have general difficulties in engaging genuinely and fully in adult functions. The sense of responsibility that the person should express, the level of maturity evident, and the absence of an individuated yet socially embedded self will require therapeutic sophistication in dealing with the person, such as in narrative reconstruction. If intimacy issues do not preclude getting a romantic partner, the need for couple therapy will inevitably manifest.

The therapist will have to deal with a pervasive sense of isolation/loneliness/emptiness/desolation. This will be expressed both for the hypo-intimacy type and the hyper-intimacy type – the former because of an absence of romantic partner and the latter because of two or even too many, everything else being equal. This reminds me of one case I had in which the fellow came to the first session with his wife and the second with his girlfriend, and then asked me which one he should choose in the third session!

The therapist will need to help the patient construct a grand narrative in which the central role of the other, as well as adult functions, generally, are paramount, including in romantic relations. The other is not just a play thing but a genuine partner in all senses of the word. Couple therapy could reinforce the independence and uniqueness of the other, yet how the couple can collaborate and cooperate to make their partnership grow. Each partner in the relationship can grow to her/his optimal level through the support and love offered by the partner. This will feed back into a positive growth cycle that will affect the growth of the self (individuated yet connected), the emotions involved (e.g., loving and longing instead of loneliness and emptiness), and the concept of the other (lovable, worthy of receiving love from the person).

Intimacy is not just a feeling; it is an act. The person needs to feel the process deeply, engage in it, learn how to do it, and how to maintain it no matter what the disruption and its source. The other needs to be honored in her/his individuality and what she/he brings to the relationship. All adult functions need to be viewed from the same perspective. Genuine intimacy means behaving with passion in all life spheres. It begins with a genuine soul and ends with a shared whole.

The hypo-intimate type will require intimacy skill and motivation-boosting while the hyper-intimate type will require the same, but with an additional tempering of negative relational indulgences. The former type might need to learn that, if socialized intimacy is present, it needs to transform into a personally constructed, genuine style. The latter type might need to learn that pseudo/false/superficial/fake intimacies eventually will be dug out by the other and that the relationship will not survive, everything else being equal. Much discussion will be needed on the nature of love as a mature, long-term commitment and on the nature of hate as a frustrative displacement that needs to be controlled and transformed.

Stress/Trauma Resilience/Coping

The early adult failing to establish genuine intimacy will have a more difficult time coping with/expressing resilience about stresses/traumas that might materialize. Normally, coping includes especially problem-solving skills instead of emotional ones only, and this would be crucial for the early adult who is adopting critical adult functions, generally. However, if the person cannot genuinely engage with co-loving reciprocity with a romantic partner, the same difficulty in confronting stress/trauma might arise, and appropriate problem-solving will be diminished or even displaced by emotionality.

Not having an intimate romantic partner to help deal with the stress/trauma will be another complication in this regard. The person will also have deficits in a buttressed/fortified self that includes elastic/plastic stress/trauma resistance/coping mechanisms. The cognitive apparatus might not deploy the advanced cognitive skills (abstract systems multiplied in logic) that are available, so the grand picture is not perceived. The self will not be individuated/unique, so potentially innovative solutions to problems might be doubted/discarded for more conservative but less helpful solutions. Moreover, the person will feel isolated/lonely/empty even if a romantic partner is available, because the lack of genuine intimacy in the relationship will undo the early magic in the relationship. The hypo-intimate type will have this sentiment compounded while the hyper-intimate type will not be able to mask it even with frantic dating and sexual adventures. To the contrary, the inevitable disappointments and even the hate that might develop will detract from the dispassionate evaluation of stress/trauma and the required solutions.

Therapeutic Strategies [The Other and Change]

Relational Co-regulation

The early adult doing well in terms of intimacy, ideally, will have relational interfusion with the romantic partner, live a co-love, and place couplehood even above personhood, which would be an ethos heightened if children are involved. The person will be able to self-involve with all adult functions and take on the activities with a sense of responsible participation and maturity-enhancing motivation. The I will spread its wings in terms of domains of adult responsibility. The person will engage in learning, reciprocity, and eventual teaching/mentoring in various adult functions. In essence, the same applies to relating with intimacy to the romantic partner. No matter how mature and psychologically intact one feels, each of us grows in and through any social encounter, especially if it is positive and constructive. The romantic other is not just a frame or foil in which positive change might take place but a firebrand of possibility in which positive change will, especially if the attitude adopted reflects genuine intimacy, and magnifies it accordingly. It is a truism that our romantic partners often complement us, but the purpose is to engage in co-complementarity and weld our different components into a shared psychological identity, coupling and growing all the while. Ideally, the early adult doing well in intimacy perceives the grand picture of the multiple life domains in which she/he functions, their interconnectivity, her/his presence as a unique person in the mesh, and yet that it is all relativistic and positively changeable through the mediation of the other in the life exchanges undertaken.

If the person is having difficulty with intimacy, the relational co-regulation even with other life domains might be affected. Instead of a reciprocal harmony and an ability to quell disturbances/stresses in any of the domains, including in attempts at intimacy, turmoil might take precedence and not resolve. The I/self will not grasp the value of dialectical exchange that fosters mutual growth. Rather, the I/self will divide conceptually self and other. The person will converse more with the self than the other, who is not treated as a foil to allow self-reflection and growth but an opaque mirror in which the self sees only what it wants. The self excludes co-regulation from the relationship and is absolutist and one-sided in self-construction, with the other considered unimportant in the process.

The hypo-intimacy style presents further problems along these lines because there will not be a romantic partner for the most part. A sense of isolation/loneliness will predominate. The same applies more or less to the hyper-intimacy style because relations might be multiple, but also will be superficial/pseudo/empty. If there is a socially constructed intimacy instead of a personally constructed genuine one, the intimacy will falter due to its weak foundation. If there is an anti-, negative, or otherwise rejecting relationship with a romantic partner instead of a genuine intimacy, the oppositional nature of the style will lead to a fractious relational co-regulatory style, which would be replete with arguments, anger, and even domestic violence. Then, external relational co-regulatory institutions/mechanisms will intervene.

Behavior/Symptom Network/Connectivity Change (Horizontal)

The early adult struggling with intimacy and adult function, generally, will have a difficult time avoiding a sense of isolation/loneliness/emptiness and will engage in hypo- or hyper-intimacy acts. The person will tell stories about the hole in her/his life because she/he cannot attract a genuine romantic partner and have a fulfilling, loving relationship. The person will be incapable of seeing the self in the context of an increasing network of life domains in which the other has an essential co-mutual role. The person will not feel that she/he can take a personal stance on important issues, and will feel psychologically weak, while perceiving that others have the same view of her/him. There might be a romantic partner involved, but there might be more a desire to leave her/him or, conversely, there will be more disagreements/anger, etc., than anything else. And also there will be a lack of feeling that life with the partner is shared and worth keeping. Abandonment will be a major issue that keeps arising (e.g., leaving the partner, quitting school, quitting the job).

The person presenting psychologically like this will be capable of change toward genuine intimacy, and all that it entails for adult function, love feelings, and so on, with proper social or therapeutic support (e.g., if a patient has a perceptive romantic partner). The person will need to work through the intimacy issues through couple therapy if there is a romantic partner, or to role play romantic relations if there is not one.

If the person has a hyper-intimacy style, the pseudo/superficial (manic, addictive?) nature of the person's dating/intimacy lifestyle will have to be addressed. The person will learn to moderate psychological excesses related to intimacy, either of the hypo- or hyper-variety. Hate, if present, will diminish. Loneliness, which might be present even if a romantic partner is present, will diminish. Fostering intimacy in all adult roles, for example, through genuine, passionate undertaking, will increase. Bad habits, e.g., related to multiple partners/cheating, or sexual addiction/lust, will diminish. The person will perceive the whole of her/his life better and dedicate better to the other and the co-mutual regulation of their romantic relationship and couplehood.

Behavior/Symptom Growth, Deep Change (Vertical)/Constructing a More Positive Life Story

As the person negotiates well crises in intimacy in the early adult period through good social support, therapy, or otherwise, the next sub-stage of the current lifespan model will be traversed more easily. It involves universal charity/genuine concern for any other and empathically creating in them the same concern for the other that is found in the person. Intimacy allows this to develop because there is both a personal plenitude filled with loving feelings for a romantic partner and the positive adoption of adult functions, while seeing the map of their growing connectivity (and feeling that connectivity in the self as the shared co-mutuality with the other grows). The self/I is multiplicative, individualistic, and relativistic, while networking its abstract systems in logic. This allows the person to see the grand picture of her/his life. This prepares movement/acceptance toward an increasing integration in abstract thinking, taking responsibility, life-domain connectivity, universal charity/empathy, self-knowledge/other-knowledge, and their harmonious integration.

The person having difficulties with intimacy can learn to tell, or be facilitated to tell, stories around growing toward genuine intimacy. The challenge of finding co-love and maintaining it by sensitive, mature behavior is one the person will describe as being the new mission of self. The person will preach respect for the other and wanting to build a strong, permanent couple, whether or not there is a romantic partner currently in her/his life. The person will describe a story that rejoices in growth, both of self and other, such that any absence will involve longing yet a sense of security and trust. The person will see the grand picture of her/his life and want to preserve it with constructive actions for which others will be thankful, from romantic partner to work/classmates and to parents/friends. The person will describe how she/he feels unique yet increasingly connected. The person will state knowing what is best for herself/himself and any offspring she/he has with the partner (presently or 1 day). The person will extol the romantic partner and vaunt the new sense of couplehood created.

Consciousness, Theory of Mind, Selves, and Responsibility

The early adult resolving intimacy issues will develop a growing sense of responsibility/morality, spreading awareness and perception of the grand scheme of things, deep commitment to adult function, understanding of the other, a growing self, desire for and nurturing of long-term couplehood with a romantic partner, and so on. The early adult will be in a position to develop improved, integrated abstract system integration skills, which will facilitate these acquisitions. The connectivity of all adult functions will be better appreciated and grow toward a more universal empathy beyond the focus of creating a long-term, genuine couplehood, as befits the early adult age period.

The Abstract (Formal) Stage Sub-stage of Integration (22–25 Years): Sub-stage 20

Self and Relational Development [Initial Theoretical Elaborations]

A very brief description of the present step in Young's 25-step Neo-Eriksonian developmental model follows. It is presented again in Chap. 18, to help give a collective overview of the 25 steps in the modeling.

Universal (general concern for all people) acts vs. self-singular (self-focused) acts (22–25 years). The growing adult is concerned for all people and desires to care for or help anybody in need. This is especially true for family, but could apply to any one, too. There is a basic helping moral value felt about everybody. Without getting good support this way, you could become a person who rejects helping others, family and all people included, or only helps them without feeling (or just to get praise).

Appendix 4.5 gives the brief amount of work already done in prior publications related to the task of developing in depth the Neo-Eriksonian (sub)stage model. The next section of the chapter gives an interim summary that elaborates the contents of Appendix 4.5 with respect to the present sub-stage being considered, of the sub-stage of Abstract (Formal) Stage Sub-stage of Integration.

Interim Summary

The 22- to 25-year-old often is in the process of completing professional or graduate education, in what some have termed emerging adulthood. In the present approach, this age period is not restricted to those still studying and delaying undertaking full adult responsibilities. Rather, the age period, as all others, are underwritten by a new cognitive acquisition according to the current Neo-Piagetian model, and the new cognitive acquisition has socio-emotional and socio-affective consequences (as per the present Neo-Eriksonian model). If the person does not develop into the cognitive sub-stage involved, of abstract integration, or more precisely, Abstract multiplied systems in integration, the corresponding socio-affective Neo-Eriksonian sub-stage cannot develop. This makes sense in terms of the contents of the Neo-Eriksonian sub-stage affiliated with the Neo-Piagetian one at issue, as it is quite sophisticated.

The Neo-Piagetian sub-stage at this level concerns integrating or harmonizing the diverse abstract systems that had developed, creating a unified cognitive structure in which coordinated, hierarchized streams of logic that had systematized propagate in their application to various life domains. This abstract cognitive skill permits the young person to succeed in professional studies/graduate school, for example. The constant studying and learning allow for super-ordinate knowledge assimilation and creation, putting it all together into a coherent knowledge of a field of study. The person is not ready to write a textbook or scholarly book on the subject area, which is more a product of the higher-order abstract thinking in the next cognitive stage of collective intelligence, but still can do quite well in creating a coherent, fulsome understanding of a field for examination purposes. The same cognitive ability applied to study by the young person can help in other life domains and undertaking the responsibilities therein, as well as seeing the integrated whole across the life domains involved without losing track of each domain, as in a differentiating, branching cognitive structure.

In terms of socio-affectivity, the person in the late youthful adulthood period of the mid to late twenties can engage in universal charitable acts, such as expressing empathy/genuine concern for any other or all others, any community, etc. The growing adult is concerned for all people and wishes to care for or help anybody in need. This is especially true for helping family, but could apply to anyone, too. There is a basic helping moral value felt about everybody. The harmonization implicit in the abstract cognitive structure allows for a sense of harmony with any other/all others. The person still focuses on the major life tasks of this age period, such as studying/working, creating intimacy in a romantic partnership/caring for young children, as the case may be. But the scope of felt harmonization with the wider world expands, too. Note the sentiment involved is different from the later sense of generativity that develops in that the present universal concern is underwritten by an abstract integration in thought while the later generativity, at least as how presently defined, is underwritten by super-ordinate abstract structures over hierarchies of integrated abstract structures.

What does the concept of harmonic empathy refer to, or the one of a universal concern for other(s)? Harmonization in this sense involves not only setting up an internal harmonization of self-knowledge and daily responsibilities/relevant adult functions, but also it refers to integration of wishing for and seeking the same integration in the other. In a certain sense, the self at this age and level of maturity cannot exist without any or all others who do not feel safe, secure, developing/mature, etc. Ideally, the self is so interwoven with the other that any suffering or harm to the other is felt personally. Granted, the person cannot act to help everyone, but at least there is a deep commitment to want to do so, as well as the same commitment for the environment/planet and all its fauna and flora. The person might be too young to do much beyond studying/working/caring for immediate significant others, but the person does what she/he can beyond that and aspires for more. Harmony in self exists only in so far as does harmony in others, and disharmony in others hurts the core of the self as much as the core of the other. Charity might begin at home but it ends at the stratosphere (or beyond) in which the other lives. Meaning is not just discovered; it is lived in co-creation with the empathy given the other. In this personal vision of self and other, the person grows into an autonomous self who is not only self-sufficient (at least psychologically) but also grows into a reciprocally relational self who never thinks that any and all others have sufficiently enough when that is not the case.

Moreover, most people lack enough in one way or the other, and the person adopts a genuine ideology of self-sacrifice (but with self-protection, too) in her/his sense of self-sufficiency. Other-growth becomes self-growth, and other-growth fosters self-growth exponentially. Ideally, the self becomes a universal self with the I abandoning any hint of selfishness (but with self-protection, too) in the self and in dealing with the universal other. Practically, daily life places focus on the self, study/work, success, significant others/family, etc., but the ideal is always a backdrop to the practical and animates it with dreams for self and other fulfillment.

How difficult it must be for a person with this ideal to see suffering in the other. It pierces the core; for example, a child's wailing tears at the fabric of being. But the person calls for all the personal and social resources possible for the suffering seen, even if it is on the other side of the world as social media does the trick. If young people have to go to media to defend a cause, they will, but with more nuance and better thought-out strategy compared to the idealistic (and potentially fanatical) teenager. The person accepts the problems faced by the other as her/his own as part of the universal empathy experienced. The person accepts the struggles, conflicts, tragedies, dramas, ambiguities, uncertainties, etc., of the other as issues requiring insight, help, strategizing, etc., within the limits of the person. Worldwide networking might reduce those limits and open up endless resources, as we see constantly in the news with young people.

Moreover, in connecting with others as a sense of universal empathy develops, dialogue/multilogue creates elaborated visions, scaffolded efforts, and collective successes. The universal empathy as a feeling creates a universal empathic activity. The person understands better how the self-impetus to help compounds with similar motivations in others to generate genuine and much appreciated co-helping.

However, the universal empathic feeling might just apply to one person, one child, one institution, one animal, one bit of suffering, and so on. That is, even a universal empathy might be expressed by a single act for one target. Charity might not only begin at home and not leave it, for example, because home responsibilities might be all consuming and nothing is left for anything else. But the person knows that her/his time will come for greater charity, and even helping one person/child from this stance of deep morality and commitment is already an example of the greatest charity possible.

The ultimate way a person can help the other is to build up the other to the point that the other can take charge of helping herself/himself. One can be a beacon of light that shines on people, or a beacon of light that makes other people shine on people. The first option might be a Herculean task to undertake, and necessary in the circumstance at hand, but the second should be evaluated as equally important, especially given the logarithmic fissioning/fusing reactions in helping that it could engender.

The young adult struggling with issues of universal charitable/harmonious acts risks degenerating into a lack of empathy for any other/community and retreating/retrenching into extreme self-focus, self-indulgence, or self-singular acts. The person will have trouble accepting any suffering in the other, and will even resort to blaming the victim. Others will be disparaged, demeaned, devalued, and left to suffer, perhaps with a discourse that they deserve it and it is good for them. There will be a universalized non-empathy/lack of concern for the other, with social coolness/aloofness and possibly even rejection/contempt/disgust of the other.

The person might express a lack of universal empathy in either a hypo-empathic style or a hyper yet pseudo style. The first (hypo) type will be more unconcerned for the other in any way and just take care of personal responsibilities, although the lack of caring for the other will seep into all activities and perspectives. The second (hyper) type will be superficially engaged in multiple empathic activities and/or express continually an empathic concern for others, but the charity entailed will be dis-genuine/superficial and non-credible. The former (hypo) type might be socialized into universal empathy, that is, it would not come from a sense of personal engagement and commitment in the process but a shaped/imposed attitude. The latter (hypo) type might not only simply be overly empathic at the pseudo/false level, but also without the capacity to hide an undercurrent of being anti-empathic/other-rejecting, etc.

The therapist working with these types of individuals will need to help them find an internal balance and accommodation with their past and/or lack of social/environmental support that had fostered the imbalance. The therapist should take advantage of the abstract integration skills associated with this level of adult development, and seek to activate them in the person's search for personal harmony and desire for social harmony.

Self-Response to Cognitive (Mis)Perception of the Other

The young adult in the 22- to 25-year-old period enters a sub-stage cognitively referred to as abstract integration. This cognitive acquisition will have consequences both for self and other perception, especially if the accompanying socio-affective acquisition related to universal empathy is compromised, for example, by a problematic surround/support. Normally, the self at this sub-stage functions toward harmonizing its components and applications to all aspects of adult function, including having, as required or invited by circumstances, to express a universal empathy. The person expresses genuine concern for the other (for all others) and avoids self-focused indulgence/singular concentration on the self. Universal charity is an underlying theme, as is avoiding suffering by the other.

The I takes ownership or responsibility for the other, within the limits of personal and social resources. Personal meaning accrues from the meaning given to the other. Self autonomy devolves around how much the other has autonomy. Problems are shared. The person does not implode into the self, having to search through the shattered shards for slivers of fulfillment, which cannot genuinely exist should universal empathy be declined, jettisoned, or otherwise absent.

The person might be so taken with multiple responsibilities that the universal empathy is masked. However, had development proceeded well before the person's responsibilities overwhelm her/him, the other who had been put on the back-burner could still elicit a hope in the person that in the future the person will help as best she/he can. Universal empathy involves acts, in particular, but they cannot always be undertaken in extant circumstances. The other is not abandoned in these types of circumstances, in that help could be sought for the persons involved through the good auspices of empathic others or relevant institutions.

The person might have had a distorted surround/environment in these regards, fueling/abetting a type of negative reaction to the other. Refusing the mantle of universal empathy, which otherwise would be a natural development had development proceeded smoothly to this point (e.g., the young adult period when professional graduate school might be the focus), would distort the natural perception of the other as needing empathic help if needs/circumstances would require it. This abandonment of the other will negatively impact the self, which will gravitate toward feeling abandoned, in turn, or not worthy of charity/help.

If the person retreats/retrenches into the self and rejects/avoids helping the other, the abstract integration that permits a construct of a whole and wholesome self will be missing empathy for the other and also empathy for the self. The person might reject her/his own self for its empathic limitations and seed self-singular acts to mask the rejection of other empathy. The person might overembellish the self and think of herself/himself as a stalwart in leading-edge life domains, e.g., through success at school/work and even with family/significant others, but the admiration felt from others will never be satisfying enough. The self will have a dark unfulfilled part as long as the other is left unfulfilled in the sense being discussed. Nothing that is self-focused/singular will be able to fill that interior dreariness or vacuum.

As the self engages in empathic concern for the other, and engages the other and the problems at issue accordingly, the self's dark corners will lighten and core positive components will replace them. When the other becomes the lead in the stage production, all the helping hands of the self who are involved receive the applause.

The emotions experienced are not only empathic but also humble. The person is not acting for the self in any degree but for the other in every degree. There is no implicit bias/explicit rejection, or disparaging, demeaning, and devaluing attitude. The intrinsic value of the other is recognized and encouraged. The self can only exist with value when the other has value. Self harmony is limited by a lack of the same harmony in the other. Self and other are always reciprocally integrated/interdependent, especially when a universalizing empathy/charity is at issue. They (self and other) go hand in hand and heart in heart.

The young adult who suspends universal/empathic concern, or who cannot even contemplate feeling and behaving this way, could react with a hypo- or hyper attitude in these regards. The hypo type will reflect a total absence of universal empathy, perhaps to the point of being totally self-indulgent. However, if the person had been socialized to be universally empathic but, nevertheless, not having a deep personal commitment to feel and behave this way, the other will be treated well enough, although only because of the socialization involved (e.g., entrained, imposed). The hyper style will express a pseudo empathy for all others but will be viewed as ersatz/false by careful observers. Hyper types will seek adoration but risk approbation when the veneer of their superficial behavior no longer hides the deep (self-inflating) motivations involved. The other might even be the recipient of anti-, negative universal caring actions, such as in mixed messages ("Here's my help; What do I get in return; it must be more than what I gave"). In this style, the other will be denied in her/his essence, told to do it alone, and otherwise disharmonized from the self, which will only leave deep scars on the self in this vein.

Empathy for the other will take a long time to build. Perhaps receiving unconditional positive regard and empathy despite the rejection/exclusion of the other involved might be one way of building empathy. Perhaps a loving romantic partner will provide the key, a mentor, or even a therapist. The other will become vital for the self only to the degree that the self permits it and the person who is helping tries her/his best to help the person in these regards.

The abstract integration cognitive skills could permit an increase in the type of reflections that could lead to these types of changes in empathy for the other. Otherwise, without clear thinking and good help, the self will never experience the required self-empathy to grow toward interior and exterior harmonization.

Positive Pole in Eriksonian Development

The young adult who engages well in universal empathy despite the varied challenges of daily life will experience not only a deep interior sense of harmonization of self/I but also a strong sense of exterior harmonization with the other and surround. The abstract integration capacity at the cognitive level that underlies this sub-stage of the present model allows for these types of harmonization to develop. The multiple life domains addressed leave their marks on the person, who tries to integrate them into a logic of morality, participation with the other, and even owning the problems of the other. Without this outreach toward the other, the self is incomplete, inward at least, in part, not fulsome/wholesome, etc. Denying the suffering of the other denies the self. By having a universal perspective of helping, the self helps the self grow toward universality. Self autonomy means other sufficiency. The self accepts the other. Within the limits of time and other resources available, the person addresses what the other needs (without having the wool pulled over her/his eyes) and acts accordingly. The help is not given superficially, in the expectation of rewards, with mixed feelings, and so on, for the helping is its own reward, as is seeing the other grow as a result of one's own applied humanity.

Negative Social-Self Working Schema

The young adult who is well-supported life-long socially will develop a positive social self working schema in which the other is perceived as deserving of empathy; the other is considered a plural, a community, as is any other and not just someone known personally or an intimate partner. The underlying cognitive acquisition at this age involves abstract integration, which permits this holistic view of the other. The other is not just an abstraction, an imaginary other, but a deeply relational other with whom one engages personally. The self and other mutually define each other and the universal empathy toward the other defines the extent of one's sense of psychological fullness. The other who is helped toward autonomy fulfills ones sense of autonomy. The other who is helped toward being capable of charity builds one's self-concept to involve being charitable, generally, and being more than a person who distributes isolated simpler acts of charity. Alleviating suffering becomes a moral imperative; the other become's one's meaning. Accepting the harms inflicted on others constitutes the start of having a role in the remediation of the harms. It is understood that helping others only to help the self constitutes a misfocused appication of independence and an approach that impedes the development of a more positively focused interdependence.

However, these ideals and ideology require optimal surrounding support in order to develop. The self could retreat/retrench into self-focus, singularity, indulgences, and cast aside anything to do empathically with the other. Instead of universal empathy, there might be universal disdain for the other. The wider picture is not harmonious of self and other but, to the contrary through the rejection of the other, it is harmful of self as much as other. The only thing owned is a self that is isolating from the other, who is considered unworthy of help in any form. The self is reduced in humanity to the same degree that humanity is rejected.

Non-empathy does not mean no empathy, because there might be in-genuine empathy for the other in the (hypo) socialized type and pseudo-empathy for the other in the (hyper) superficial type. Either way, the other has no real meaning and might be demeaned. Either way, the other is reduced to an image, a cipher of a possible self, while the self of the person reflects that image, becoming a cipher in the real self. Self and other are intertwined at this age, and when the social self working schema is as negative as this, both unravel in the braided cord of their potential unity.

Attachment, Neo-Eriksonian Development, and Therapeutic Implications [Patients and Therapy]

Patient Presentation

The young adult experiencing psychological difficulties related to a lack of universal empathy might express the lack in several different ways. First, the person might be quite empathic, but only to immediate family, romantic partner, etc. However, the lacunae in developing a full-scale generalized empathy might create difficulties in expression of specified ones because there will be lacks in empathy that might filter through even to loved ones. The patient at this level might wonder why she/he cannot feel the same universal concerns for people as some other people that she/he knows. Or, the patient might have a selective empathy for certain communities but not others.

It is hard to have a universal empathy, for there are so many implicit and explicit biases in any culture. However, people can work through and master them, and some patients may find this a difficult task. Perhaps the patient needs sensitivity training, and the person is part of a group undergoing this type of training. Or, the patient might have a generalized empathy, but barriers to its full expression, for example, from past developmental issues, ongoing context, or social surround influences work against its expression. The patient might appear very universally empathic, but not feel it deeply and so think it is superficial.

For whatever reason, the person will need revision of her/his empathy attitudes and actions and insight into the individualized deficits being expressed and of concern to the person. In the simplest cases, the therapist will explore the developmental and social origins of the blockages toward removing them and freeing the genuine universal empathy yearned for. At the other extreme, the patient might be totally non-empathic to any other and need much therapeutic work. The person might be cold/hardened to the generalized other and might not come to the office for therapy on that issue. Rather, other issues will arise, for example, relationally, and the empathy issue will be secondary but perhaps a basic one to tackle.

In all these cases, a sense of a lack of internal harmony or harmonious relations with others, or both, will be evident. Also, the person might complain of an inability to work well with classmates/colleagues or family/significant others due to an inability to relate to them and wanting them to do all the work in the relationship (owning the issues involved). The patient will profess to have autonomy/self-sufficiency, but only because of an extreme self-focus, and any matters related to the other, especially being concerned for them, are problematic and rejected. Or, the person will deny any sense of autonomy/self-sufficiency because of the attitude of the other.

The person might express negative "other" acts, anti-other acts, etc., retreating/retrenching from the other and focusing only on the self and self-indulgences. Instead of being engaged in the world, the patient appears disengaged from it and superficially unsatisfied when some insight hits, but generally okay with this state of affairs. The other is seen as the source of any problems with empathy (they don't deserve it; they deserve what they get), and the person is self-satisfied with her/his disdainful attitude.

The hypo type will have more of a leave-me-alone attitude and the hyper type more of an attitude of leave-no-one-out. However, the former type might self-reverse through socialization (shaped, imposed) and the latter type might express a deep idealism and empathy but really mask a pseudo/false/superficial engagement/empathy, with underlying rejection and disdain related to the other.

Behavioral/Symptom Mental Scanning

The young adult patient who is having empathy-related issues and is asked to pick out by scanning the most salient issues being experienced might not focus on empathy, per se. The patient might decry everything about everybody around her/him, foisting blame on them, instead of understanding the excessive self-focus, self-indulgence, or self-singularity that characterizes her/him. The person might admit to not having any desire to help anyone, except perhaps family members/co-workers (and only if they have to and only in an effort to bring back order and peace into his/her lives). The person might criticize others for being empathic and demean/devalue certain groups who receive largesse of any type from anyone, including nonprofit and government institutions. The person might feel that she/he is the only one saying things like it is, with others being too politically correct/putting on a show/seeking some sort of advantage, etc. The person might have a universal harmonization capacity available as conditioned by an underlying abstract integration, but the cognitive structure constructed in these regards will be riveted with inconsistencies, illogical self-justifications, etc. The person will not be able to see the rifts in the logic, and the islands of confusion created. The person might feel that her/his life has deep meaning she/he takes ownership, is autonomous/independent/self-sufficient, etc. But she/he might not realize that "no man is an island," that the other is half of the self (or more), that adaptive interdependence with the other nourishes the growth to feel autonomous, self-sufficient, etc., and that constructive charity and harmony in engaging to help the other is the best nourishment in these regards.

Therapeutic Implications

The young adult patient having issues with generalized empathy/universal charity will not feel harmonization with the other. There might be impacts on general adult functioning if this is a primary issue for the patient, for example, in study/work or family/friend relations. The inability to feel affinity for the suffering other will rebound onto the self, creating a deflated self and a suffering one, in turn. The person will be hoping for autonomy and self-sufficiency but will be haunted by an inability to find that and perhaps also by a lack of empathy for the other, although that lack might be masked/defused. The patient will want to take ownership for herself/himself and study/work without abandon, but not want to consider taking any responsibilities for the predicaments in which others find themselves. The self will be a falsely or weakly autonomous, independent one, because genuine autonomy springs from genuine other-concern and consequent action. The person gains traction as an individual by inhabiting the universal.

The patient might understand these contradictions but not know how to resolve them. More likely, the patient will feel a personal self-abandonment or personal self-indulgence, with associated emotions of feeling cool to the other and unconcerned for the other. The therapist will have to work through feelings of social disdain and blaming the victim. The other will need to be given a perch in the psychology of the self as the motor that drives self-growth.

The therapist might assign biblio- and film therapy of great people who inspire the public, look for inspiring, caring quotes, etc. The person's sense of spirituality/religiosity should be explored and contrasted with her/his expressed attitudes.

The hypo type might have a socialized empathy, and the therapist would work toward the person owning it genuinely. The hyper type might be multiply empathic, but superficial/pseudo, and the therapist would work for a more genuine attitude.

The anti-empathic type will need more work in controlling the underlying rejection/antipathy toward the other and seeing the effects and limitations of this attitude on the self.

Stress/Trauma Resilience/Coping

The young adult who is non-empathic, generally, will be without proper social resources to help deal with stress/trauma. In addition, the coping style will be one of self-sufficiency, but the strategies available might be compromised by their lack of social building through co-regulatory relational interactions with others. The person might be a success in major adult functions (school/work), but even that won't help in fortifying resilience/buttressing coping mechanisms, because there might be little ability to cope with extraordinary situations involving stress/trauma. Moreover, the perception of stress/trauma will be more subjective, given the lack of generalized empathy. Without a proper sense of harmonization/integration/universal empathy for the generalized other, the person might not feel that a great stress/trauma is something that can be dealt with and that social resources can help. The person might feel super-autonomous, self-sufficient, independent, etc., and so lack the safety net of reciprocal interdependence and participation with the other in helping with the stress/trauma. Indeed, the person might lash out against any helper and even blame her/him for the problem. A vision of the other being empathic to the person when the mind of the person excludes any possibility of helping the other would be too discordant.

The hypo types might be too passive in the face of trauma/stress, because they will be receded into the self and fostering the myth of autonomy and self-sufficiency. The hyper types might seek out many helpers but find rejection/disdain, given the underlying rejection/disdain at the heart of their own empathy. The hypo types will be cool but burned by the trauma/stress and the hyper types will be hot and perhaps even more burned (seared) by it. The hyper types might take advantage of the other under undue stress/trauma, using their resources unjustly for personal ends, etc.

Therapeutic Strategies [The Other and Change]

Relational Co-regulation

The young adult succeeding in engaging in universal empathy will have a harmonious relationship with the generalized other, and express charitable intentions. The person will express a dynamic interdependence with all others or at least enter the relationship with that premise, opening the self to possibility and to possibility for the other, as well, especially if the other needs help. Interfused with the other, the self preserves some sense of autonomy that springs from a self-sufficiency, while surrendering to the needs of the other (but not blindly or naively, and in a self-protective mode, too). The "I" can be called universal (empathically) in its integration of abstract themes and actions in relevant adult functions/life domains, because empathy is not divorced from daily life but intrinsic to it and likely to manifest when any situation arises relevant to it in any daily function. The other is not an ideal but a living partner in life building. Self and other are co-owned, because helping the other helps the self and helping the self allows for better helping of the other.

Empathy is not a catchword but a lifestyle, with adult functions secondary to it. Helping is not an after-thought but a central thought in the core I/self. The other in the core I/self is core to that self, a meaning that defines one's meaning. When I accept you, within self-protective limits, no matter who you are, I accept to grow no matter from what point I am growing.

If the young adult is having difficulties in a universal empathy/harmonization, the relationship with the other will be centrifugal rather than centripetal. The self will always become the self's center and the other will always lie in the marginal zone, at best. Charity might be expressed, but it won't endure because of its lack of genuine character. The suffering of the other might evoke sympathy, but it will retract and be reinvented as blaming the victim and the like, in order to preserve a false and fragile sense of self-integrity.

The other does not exist independently in this framework, but is an appendage to the self-serving self, a temporary self-glorification mechanism, at best. Non-empathy prevails even in the midst of declared empathy and helping. The abstract integration skills associated with the young adult fail in creating an integrated self-other dynamic with reciprocal entwining and self-other defining. Ownership is applied only to one's own perspective and self-aggrandizing approach, which is self-focused, self-singular, and self-indulgent.

The larger picture is missing the most important piece – the other empathically perceived and charitably helped. The other might be criticized for her/his own problems and left to her/his own devices, no matter how primitive and inadequate. There is no attempt at helping in regulation for the other, no co-regulation established, at least positively, and no universality in any sense of the word. The relational co-regulation expressed is limited to a misperceived need to co-regulate one's own self and its parts. The other is excluded in the formula, so that the formula will be limited. Self-determination is never just determination by the self.

As for the hypo style of empathic concern for the other, the description above offers a good understanding of it. There might be a socialized component, though, too, with the person adopting an empathic concern for the other, but through shaping/imposition more than a genuine self-accommodation. Also, to the contrary, there might be a superficial/pseudo generalized empathy and with an undercurrent of rejection/disparagement/disdain of the receiving party at the same time.

Behavior/Symptom Network/Connectivity Change (Horizontal)

The young adult mired in difficulties related to generalized empathy will be incapable of perceiving the suffering of the other, providing charity to the other, feeling an integrated harmony in which self and other reside in mutual need, helping, repair, and gain, and otherwise feeling universally embedded in a co-mutual self-other relational regulation with the other that defines both self and other and promoting their growth. The person will be locked into an I "for me/about me/what's in it for me" attitude instead of an I "being about us/how can I help, how can you grow through my help" attitude. The I becomes the center of the self and the other becomes peripheral, at best. The self might feel autonomous, but that is impossible if the other is segregated into an exclusion zone. The person might sense being trapped in adult functions related to school/work and family friends, yearning for breakaway freedom. But the person will fail to realize that freedom lies in helping the other empathically with their suffering.

Locked in a world in which the person's life situation is prioritized and the other is minimized, the life situation of the person will not really advance, except perhaps materially (or being on a life trajectory to succeed in accumulating material wealth), because of the disharmony in the self. Even then, the material acquisitions will not satisfy the person, who will suffer through not seeing the big picture of life, or they will not provide the satisfaction sought. Excess material earned will be seen as the personal rewards for the self rather than potential sources of help for others in need. The material will be seen as primary rewards instead of helping in dispensing charity and all the rewards that stem from giving to the other to help. The self will be considered a rich field of self-indulgence and the other a burned field of scorched earth. The world will be considered the person's playing field and the other will be considered there uniquely for the person's pleasure and profit. The person will reject universalized empathy even if there is universal misery.

However, the person retreating and leaving the other to their destiny will lose long-term mutual gains – material, spiritual, or otherwise. The other will not be passive in face of being treated this way and the person who behaves this way might feel remorse to a degree for a while. But that will not last and the person will harden in and retreat, leaving the other to sink.

The hypo type will be bereft of a generalized empathy, or not be genuine in expressing a universal empathy. The hyper type will scuttle about trying to express sincere empathy for the other, but leaks of unconcern, disdain, etc. will percolate up and reveal the pseudo/false nature of the expressed empathy.

The person who harbors this kind of attitude about the other will need to see the effects on the inner core self, social relations, and even leakages into study/work. The person will have to understand the ramifications not only for the other but also for the self when she/he behaves this way. Subjective well being might appear positive, but an inner discordance could jeopardize its standing and lead to psychological disarray. All material gains will be placed at risk despite the heavy investment psychologically to get them and maintain the gains in the long-term.

The therapist will be empathic in working with the person and broaden and build a more solid, socially concerned foundation as an underpinning to a solid self that can find positive feelings in helping the other. Any other might elicit the helping motive, but the person cannot be naïve in her/his empathy. The therapist will help the person find balance in these regards and a deep commitment to help the other 1 day, at least if available time, responsibilities, material factors, etc., make the time opportune to engage in the helping. This type of approach might assuage the person and allow the new self (and other) being constructed to emerge slowly but surely.

Behavior/Symptom Growth, Deep Change (Vertical)/Constructing a More Positive Life Story

The person struggling with empathy issues can move forward with proper support, whether by a loving partner, therapist, wise friend, etc. The scope of empathy a person owns will define her/his humanity/harmonization, integrity/integration, self-other co-connection, and enmeshment in self-definition and other relatedness. The person achieving these realizations will be applying her/his abstract integration skills to create a unified story of charity/helping being good both for self and other. Owning less materially might mean owning more spirituality.

The person will be ready to move well into the next major life transition involving collective intelligence and its socio-affective consequences. The person capable of using a second-order abstract intelligence will coalesce together people, heart and mind, applicable experience, etc., to create super-ordinate abstract structures in which the major questions of life are posed and answered satisfactorily. Life becomes more than existing in that it becomes existential. Life becomes more than seeking meaning because meaning becomes life. A life impregnated by spirituality does not mean any orthodox practice; it means encountering life in a godlike way in each moment that we live and spreading that way of living to everyone as best one can.

The person telling stories about the self that denigrates the other, denies the other's suffering, justifies a lack of empathy/helping/charity, etc. can learn to tell a new story that empathy is part of the human condition and, when given carefully so the other does not take advantage of it, actually helps the self grow. Life is a two-way street and feeling concern for the other elicits feelings of concern by the other. The person can indicate that helping the other has positive repercussions for the self as long as it is genuine and done in a self-protective way. This way, it is a win-win rather than lose-lose activity. These types of story lines allow the person some wiggle room in the narratives constructed about her/his sense of empathy for the other because they include a self-protective function and a win-win outcome. The person might want to tell a story of empathy for the other being essential to the being of the person, but it might be expressed well only later in time because of pressing study/work and family/social obligations in the present. Nevertheless, the story told could refer to the embers of empathy for the other having been lit and expressing from time to time, demonstrating their reality to all concerned, including the other so helped.

Consciousness, Theory of Mind, Selves, and Responsibility

Ideally, the young adult is advancing in generalized empathy, universal charity, self-other/dependence/interdependence integration, and harmonization of autonomous self-sufficiency and helping the other in a virtuous circle of positivity. In doing so, the young adult will be growing increasingly toward a supra-consciousness, supra-morality, supra-maturity/sense of psychological completeness, and genuine respect for and reciprocity with all others. The person would be ready for the penultimate ethic of taking re-responsibilities, or rededicating to each responsibility at each second of one's life, including all in which all others are involved.

References

Brummelman, E., Thomaes, S., & Sedikides, C. (2016). Separating narcissism from self-esteem. *Current Directions in Psychological Science, 25*, 8–13.

Cieciuch, J., & Topolewska, E. (2017). Circumplex of identity formation modes: A proposal for the integration of identity constructs developed in the Erikson-Marcia tradition. *Self and Identity, 16*, 37–61.

Hollenstein, T., & Lougheed, J. P. (2013). Beyond storm and stress: Typicality, transactions, timing, and temperament to account for adolescent change. *American Psychologist, 68*, 444–454.

Steinberg, L. (2017). *Adolescence* (11th ed.). New York: McGraw-Hill Education.

Chapter 17
The Post-formal/Collective Intelligence (Super-ordinate Abstract) Sub-stages: Super-ordinate Participatory Collective Sociality

Abstract The last chapter on the present Neo-Eriksonian lifespan model covers the adult years beyond the earliest ones. They cover the passage through setting up one's life in terms of major adult functions (study/work, partner/family) and generatively giving to them and the wider society. As development proceeds, there might be midlife crises and perhaps looking back at life with despair more than with ego integrity. The last phases of life should involve cathartic experiences. The underlying cognitive architecture includes super-ordinate abstractions, which underwrite the broad generativity and sense of re-responsibilities that makes for an adaptive adult life.

The Collective Intelligence Stage Sub-stage of Coordination (25–28 Years): Sub-stage 21

Self and Relational Development [Initial Theoretical Elaborations]

By way of introduction, the following presents a very brief description of the present step in Young's 25-step Neo-Eriksonian developmental model. It is presented again at the end of Chap. 18 along with the other 24 steps in the model, to help give a collective overview of the 25 steps in the model.

Meta-collecting (seeing the big picture) acts vs. disillusionment acts (25–28 years). The young adult could see big picture of the world and all its interconnections at many joined levels. You could develop concern for the growth of all groups of peoples, wanting them capable of helping other peoples. If things go wrong this way, you could ignore or even act against other peoples, detesting them, and feel disillusioned/down. Or, you could help peoples only because you have been taught to, and you do it only superficially.

G. Young, *Causality and Development*,
https://doi.org/10.1007/978-3-030-02493-2_17

Appendix 5.1 gives the brief amount of work already done in prior publications related to the task of developing in depth the Neo-Eriksonian (sub)stage model. The next section of the chapter gives an interim summary that elaborates the contents of Appendix 5.1 with respect to the present sub-stage being considered, of the sub-stage of Collective Intelligence Stage Sub-stage of Coordination.

Interim Summary

The young adult (25–28 years of age) enters a normative age when graduate studies/professional school is terminating or otherwise when adult functions are being undertaken in full or are about to begin. The person at this point in life normatively is developing a cognitive structural base that is post-formal in nature, or second-order abstract, creating super-ordinate abstract structures from the integrated abstract constructs in cognitive structure that had been constructed previously in various domains.

The sub-stage involved that applies to this age period is referred to as collective intelligence coordination. Collective intelligence refers to my version of the post-formal period (Young, 2011). Other post-formal models might refer to dialectical thought and the like, but the concept of post-formal abstract thought involving super-ordinate abstract structures fits other current conceptualization (e.g., Commons). The present version of the model indicates that the super-ordinate abstract structures involved are collective in several senses of the word. First, they "collect" or integrate first-order abstract structures. This refers to, for example, the ability not only to understand well a discipline, such as psychology in graduate school, and do well in studying for it but also to write theses, books, etc., on the topic, further integrating knowledge in it. Second, collective intelligence refers to "collecting" people together in brainstorming. The cognitive product that results reflects a general group intelligence in the work group members rather than a collation of individual intellectual output. Meta-collecting ideas are spirals of contributions from all group members that would not have been created without the transactional process involved. Third, collective intelligence refers to unifying mind and heart, thinking and emotion, etc., because the cognitive structures involved are not created in cognitive laboratories but in real-life contexts in which emotions are as much a part of the calculus as are cognitive factors. Fourth, we can add that the second-order abstract structures created in the post-formal period are products of interactive experience as much as personal reflection. They are not created in a vacuum, an ivory tower of reflection divorced from the real word, but are expressions of dialectical, embodied, visceral exchanges with the environment, the surround, people, etc. and so are living structures that depend on participation with others and reflect the growth in cognition that that participation provides.

The first sub-stage in the collective intelligence stage of the present model concerns coordination. This sub-stage begins a five-sub-stage sequence, as with the four prior stages of the present model. Typically, coordination refers to the juxtaposition of two cognitive acquisitions that had been integrated in the prior sub-stage.

For example, after a cognitive acquisition in a prior sub-stage systematizes, and then spreads out (multiplies) throughout the cognitive architecture, it is ready to integrate over the new domains. In this regard, the integrations of the prior sub-stage that take place before the coordination in an ensuing sub-stage stand as landmarks in cognitive development, and their juxtaposition in the ensuing sub-stage is equally crucial because it allows for a new stage to develop.

In the present context of the stage of post-formal abstract collective intelligence, this means that, in the age period under discussion, the person should be capable of coordinating two integrated abstract structures, or juxtaposing them to allow some sort of super-ordinate process, such as their comparison. This will prepare the way for a super-ordinate abstract structure and, as well, further differentiation (dominate-subordinate relations) and systematization (in context), etc., as other sub-stages in the sequence emerge. Therefore, for example, with respect to psychology, the person would be able to take a second-order view of different perspectives/approaches in the discipline and create a comparative perspective on them, leading toward their further super-ordinate abstract "structuration." Perhaps the person can compare one major theoretical approach to another, one methodological approach to another, and so on. Or, perhaps the points of view of psychology and neuroscience can be compared in a domain, leading toward a common approach/perspective on the topic.

The second-order abstract structures under discussion do not have to concern academic subjects. They might concern areas like creating a complex work manual (think a new computer), company reorganization charting, etc. Many threads would have to be integrated and the integrations juxtaposed in either of these examples. If there are more than two threads, the process of their comparison would involve two at a time, and the resulting super-ordinate abstract structure would complexify to a degree. The second-order abstract structure that is fundamental to the stage of collective intelligence might refer to a meta-theory/overarching principle and can be referred to as abstract meta-intelligence aside from collective intelligence. However, the process of its creation will begin with the types of coordinations being discussed.

The consequence of this new acquisition in cognitive skill in the young adult is that avenues open up not only intellectually but also in self-development, socially, emotionally, socio-affectively, and so on. The young adult could see big picture of the world and all its interconnections at many joined levels. For example, the self of the young adult in this age period, as underwritten by the new abstract collective intelligence coordination skills, will be a more holistic, "collecting" one. The self at this age will reflect the poles of the issue of autonomy/self-sufficiency/independence vs. universal empathy/helping/charity. These threads will be super-ordinately juxtaposed and compared toward creating a wholeness in the web of the self that appreciates both perspectives and allows both to flourish simultaneously without contradiction (dialectically). The self is a meta-self and the I within the self is a meta-I (symbiotic) because neither self nor I is one of a unique entity in focus without the other in focus. The self/I is conceived as a collective (symbiosis) of components that includes empathy to any other as a component while creating a super-ordinate comparison process of all components leading toward their co-actional fusion/integration (symbiosis) with time. This means that the person feels coordinated symbiotically with the generalized other at all levels and can act for the community of peoples (all peoples, humanity) and contexts (society, environment, and planet) at any level.

The feeling accompanying this type of self/I is that of awe and wonder, for it is a worldly feeling that even accepts mystery with a sense of enlightened attitude. There is no disillusionment with the self/I or no gloom/dispirited mood with any other, or with the human and surround context, but only persistent hope and action for the common good against any odds or the aspiration to have this approach to life as time, context, ongoing constraints, etc. permit.

The other, as adduced from this perspective, is a generalized one not just of any community but of all communities collectively. The world becomes the field, and the other all the groups in the field. All peoples need help, but some more than others, and some direly so. The person feels connection with all of them (but does not naively or blindly help anyone asking; there is some self-protection required). And the potential for optimal development of all peoples constitutes the primary focus in any helping (or their environment, the planet, etc., as the case may be but with the self-protection factor involved). The approach is that peoples are collectives, and we have to behave ethically/justly for all of them, and they should develop to the point of doing the same both for their members and the members of other peoples. Ideally, all groups are equal and all deserve full freedom, emancipation, etc. In this view, socializing is not about dyadic exchange, mutual co-regulation, etc., but about people engagement, relational co-regulation with peoples, etc.

The person/self does not self-abnegate nor abrogate her/his own rights, because staying integrated allows the goals at issue to stay in focus and be achieved to the degree possible. Losing the self in the other does not optimally help the other. Fusion of self-other does not mean confusion of self and other. The risk of extending the self too deeply into the helping process can lead to burnout, apathy, etc. and a descent into disillusionment. Taking care of the self helps in taking care of the other.

Needless to say, living this ideal is extremely difficult, and there are so many ongoing constraints in our lives that it cannot be a constant process. Moreover, our surround is never 100% engaged in this ideal, so often we are left to put it into practice at an extreme level of altruism on our own. Furthermore, we might have had environments in which this type of idealism in life had been undercut, subtly or otherwise. The consequences are that the person might experience some desire to think beyond the self and have a positive attitude to others, but perhaps not much if at all. The person might be very involved in working the grindstone, and have no time for the other, at any rate, so the attitude toward the other will be stifled by context more than anything else yet still could be sufficient for purposes of growing well psychologically. The person might be studying/working in the most advanced fields of study, have a family she/he loves and invests in, and so on and not be able to get past the immediate concerns of life to engage a wider vision. However, as long as that vision remains, the person still could be on the correct growth trajectory in these regards.

Whatever the reason, the person might make no or just tentative and futile attempts to coordinate with other peoples; not experience the wonder of feeling community with the world, etc.; and live at the level of ignoring or being disillusioned with all other people(s). The person might proceed even to act against peoples. In this scenario, others are put down, or worse, and considered sources of personal profit one way or another, instead of being considered part of a collective good in which the person can profit from by being part of it. Alt views, left or right, might provide the fodder for such negative personal views of peoples and feed anti-communal perspectives on peoples.

The person might react in hypo or hyper ways to the crisis in communal attitude, for example, ignoring/detesting peoples, as described, or superficially/pseudo engaging them, but without deep genuine commitment. The hypo type might act as if she/he were deeply and genuinely committed to all peoples but only through shaping/imposition by significant others. In this about face, there still would not be any genuine commitment to peoples in the sense described. The hyper type might appear quite genuine, but an underlying detesting attitude will give away the true motivation.

No matter what the pathway taken away from a genuine, committed positive approach to peoples, it will be difficult to put the person on the right track. Therapists will use the examples in the life of the person that show concern for others, e.g., of family members, to broaden and build a better attitude to all others. The therapist will also use the person's advanced post-formal abstract cognitive skills in collective intelligence to query wider, more humanistic visions for all peoples and the planet. The therapist will turn to more nobler therapies, such as engaging in existential therapy, or any therapy that speaks to the grandest of human visions, and the place of the person in the community, planet, and indeed the universe.

Self-Response to Cognitive (Mis)perception of the Other

The young adult in the 25- to 28-year age period is acquiring post-formal abstract (collective intelligence) coordination skills. This acquisition conditions a worldview, through the super-ordinate abstract structures being created. It involves all peoples and their need for respect and for help of their humanity (e.g., free from persecution/discrimination, obtaining justice/living in a just society). The self develops in this cognitive context to have a world vision (or "collective" conscientiousness about all others). If development proceeds normally this way, and the constraints of time, circumstance, etc. are not overwhelming, people like this can engage deeply with whole communities of people, experience the awe of being part of a world worth fighting for and saving at all levels, and live a life of universal ideals/morality/values while still discharging all relevant adult functions, but with the added element of respecting/wanting the best for peoples of any color, creed, etc. that they might encounter in their daily travails. "Symbiotic holism" is a concept that subsumes the types of coordinations under discussion – self with other/self with world; equality/justice and emancipation/liberation; abstract idea with abstract idea (super-ordinate) toward that end; and meta-components subsumed in larger structures, whether cognitive, social-emotional, or otherwise.

The other in this worldview becomes every and all others, including at the peoples level. The self in this worldview includes respect and seeking equality/justice for all peoples, in a mirror of what is hoped for all peoples. Self-other is a collective, a fused and coordinative co-regulatory relational phenomenon in which self still exists even if defined by the relationship with the other. The individual other always exists in her/his subsumed status to peoples, and hopefully more than the surround allows, through the positive attitude/actions of the self.

However, the ideal rarely reaches this plateau of being, given our life circumstances and contexts, aside from any nonsupport from the surround in these regards. There could be one stream in behavior that is generically empathic, but perhaps it will be sporadic and limited. Moreover, it will be unlikely that another stream related to a generalized empathy will be present and coordinate with the first toward creating a super-ordinate structure with a generalized altruistic worldview on which everything depends and all actions follow.

The person might be incapable of any generalized altruism to any people and turn uniquely inward toward the self and its needs. The other will be only "another," someone/some people to put on the back burner or even out of awareness completely. In the worst-case scenarios, the other is denigrated, considered beneath the person, who considers himself/herself as the sole person in need of altruism. The world revolves around her/his pedestal, with the columnar statue of the self having empty bulging eyes as much as any origin Greek statue. The person expresses disillusionment with society, but eventually that could become disillusionment with the self. The person experiences apathy about others but that could turn into apathy about the self. The other is our reflection; we are her/his/their mirror. When we reach for ourselves in the mirror, the hand reaches inward to the image in the mirror, or to ourselves. We are really the other in the psychological world we reflect. In this type of philosophy, when the other is defiled, we are defiled. When we harm the other, we harm ourselves. When the other does not exist, we do not exist.

If we adopt a hypo style in these regards, we leave the other to the surround; we leave the world. If we adopt a hyper style, we think we are worldly, but it is superficial and fools no one. The hypo style might be really hyper in the sense of having an imposed/shaped concern for other peoples through socialization. The hyper style might be really a hypo one because its false concern for peoples is really an empty one. The latter approach might include an anti-/negative view of others, which also will be hard to hide, in that the other is our lie detector.

Positive Pole in Eriksonian Development

The advent of post-formal, collective intelligence in adulthood heralds new socio-emotional/socio-affective acquisitions related to the super-ordinate abstract structures that develop. Two different streams in super-ordinate abstract thinking can be juxtaposed/compared-contrasted, and this ability facilitates moving into a super-ordinate abstract structure that allows coordination of cognitive-emotional constructs of self/society-community of peoples. The person deeply engages people collectively, even the planet/universe, from an interrelated mind-heart unity in self, yielding a feeling of wonderment and awe in the engagement. Humanity is considered a combined entity, and elicits existential questions of our place in the world, and the place of all peoples in the wider ecology that we inhabit. We act for community, being part of it, and inter-coordinate with community, it being part of us. We collect parts of ourselves together, ourselves and others together, and our ideas super-ordinately together (either by ourselves or with others, as in brainstorming). We enlighten and feel enlightened and do not feel disillusionment nor create that in others. We give of ourselves to the other without sacrificing ourselves, and we see the other as people that we should help develop to have the same attitude when they cast their gaze on any other. Apathy is not part of the vocabulary of the person nor in any way do we allow it, at least to the degree possible, to seriously take hold in any other. We believe that the collective of peoples is a unity, a positive force for all others, including ourselves, and act to the degree possible toward having this vision concretize.

Negative Social-Self Working Schema

The youthful adult who develops super-ordinate abstract abilities will use this logic potential to construct higher-order maps of her/his social world and her/his relation to it as much as using it to solve cognitive-related problems, e.g., at school/work. The person will try to map the internal consistencies in her/his concepts of self and other, seek inconsistencies, and resolve them through various juxtapositions/compare-contrasts. The maps will not consist of simple abstract ideas, but will consist of their linkages in overarching ones [e.g., for the self – I am part of a community; that community is part of a people; that people is part of a community of peoples; each person in the community deserves the utmost respect and all the help that she/he needs to grow and develop to partake in and give back fully to the community. My self/I is fused in its parts and fused with the other. I/we are a collective as are you/them, and as are and I/we in relation to you/them. Self is symbiosis with other. Self is other-self. Other is self-other. Wholeness exists in every particle of my life, in that each particle reflects the whole macroscopically and is the whole microscopically. My life story is a web of all life stories in one universal story. My attitude/moral/value is a mirror of yours, reflects yours, informs yours, and becomes yours, just as yours becomes mine. I am a collector of ideas and I relate them into grand structures, just as I relate you and I, we and us, into one quest for equality with emancipation for all individuals and all peoples as a subplot to that story theme. My hope for a better universe of peoples extends to a hope for a better planet for people and beyond. No person should be beyond hope.]

However, as much as this ideal defines the other in a positive way, and creates a social schema that is dynamically proactive for and responsive to peoples, it requires much lifetime support for the youthful adult to actualize. Moreover, if the support is not present in this crucial period of developing a universal concern for all peoples, the person risks abandoning the notion or never even contemplating it. The other is not considered a universal other of peoples and communities but a multiply-split other in which not everyone merits full respect and help, or, the attitude/moral/value could be worse. The person cannot feel coordinated with/integrated into society, because society is not considered fully meritorious of respect/help, and, indeed, the rejection might be worse. The stories heard of the other could be ones passed on from prior generations, e.g., involving racism. The self enters a defensive space of self-protection and an offensive space of striking out against the reviled other.

The post-formal abstract logic available to the youthful adult at this stage of life might be used to create a web of pernicious lies about the other, or some others/peoples, instead of a web of a positive vision of all beings, all others. Or, the person might not be rejecting of the other, but just totally apathetic ("Their fate is not my fate. Their destiny is their own; I do not have to fight it."). The person becomes disillusioned with everything, and it relates back to the apathy felt for the other ("How can I feel the light inside when I don't see it shining anywhere. People are not worth it. I am not worth it. I like collecting things, not people. I don't like trying to see the big picture in any positive way, because it will be always be negative, and people just don't deserve what society gives them, and certainly I don't want to give them anything.").

As with the prior sub-stage in the current model that concerns universal empathy for the other, the present sub-stage might involve people who under- or over-invest in the matter at issue, that is, in terms of feeling unity or symbiosis with all peoples/communities/societies. The underinvested type for this issue will develop a social-self working schema that separates self from other, viewing the other as not worth fully respecting, helping, or worse. The over-invested type will be superficially invested and in a false variety. The former type might be socialized to feel connected to all peoples, but not in a personally held, genuine way. The over-invested type might proclaim many statements in support of all peoples, but with an underlying dismissal/rejection, considering them even beneath her/him, e.g., racially. The other becomes a caricature who is deemed worthy of help, but, in reality, that help is pseudo or even retracted/undermined. The other is viewed as flimsy and not worth being full or fulfilled, which, through reflective mirror processes, is the ultimate image of the self that might come to develop in the conflicted person.

Attachment, Neo-Eriksonian Development, Therapeutic Implications [Patients and Therapy]

Patient Presentation

The youthful adult lacking connectivity to society/community/peoples will not experience the normal symbiotic coordination/integration that might develop with others. The person might be incapable of (using well) the underlying super-ordinate abstract thought pertinent to this communal sense of peoples (and the planet), with the accompanying sense of awe/wonderment. The person, instead, will regret the lack of ability to forge such social links and will descend into disillusionment with society/community/peoples. Rather than having a "meta-collecting" esprit (e.g., higher-order abstract ideas, self-other coordination at this level conceptually, and in practice), the person will be intellectually and socially selective, choosing non-threatening situations in which a comfort zone is possible, although it will be all but impossible to keep the ignored/rejected other beyond the gates. The sense of symbiotic consciousness that might be present to a small degree, or that the person might want to have grown normally, might lead to internal conflicts, which might in turn lead to external manifestations, e.g., giving the cold shoulder to the other without any reason, treating all others coldly, manifesting implicit racial bias, etc. The person will intellectualize the inherent rejecting attitude in her/his social dynamic, using dispassionate yet distorted reasoning to justify the attitude.

Generally, the cognitive structure will not achieve the higher-order connectivity in cognitive concepts, such as in self concepts and, certainly, the one for the other will be twisted. The reflectivity will not appear appropriately formulated and will miss an overarching moral meta-view that informs the thinking. The web of ideas will not be fused/coordinative, and indicative of existential/meta-physical ideas, but will be underdeveloped and peppered with fire walls between pockets of ideas without interconnectivity. The self will not be a meta-concept but a sickly defensive one or an attacking offensive one. The former type will be hypo in nature, showing no concern for the other/peoples. The latter type might mask the underlying animosity for the other with a pseudo-positive attitude that will try to demonstrate people respect and advocacy for helping peoples. The former type might do so due to social convention, but apathy is more likely. The latter type will succumb to the inconsistencies in attitude/action and lash out not only at other peoples but even significant others, who become the pincushion for frustrative expression. Disillusionment will eventually peak in this type as much as the other one.

Behavioral/Symptom Mental Scanning

The youthful adult who enters therapy with issues related to ignoring/rejecting other peoples will be able to recognize the issues but probably obfuscate the causes and cures. The person will maintain that she/he feels connected to the people, the world, etc., but it will not be to all peoples, all the world. There will be selective omissions and perhaps even spiteful statements (errors of commission) or worse. The person will recognize her/his feeling of doom and gloom, disillusionment and lack of enlightenment, and dispirited attitude instead of a pervasive sense of spirituality. However, the person will notice that she/he might be ignorant of the causes involved in this approach to life. Also, the person might not be capable of adopting a more universal acceptance of peoples because of the influences of the past and present environment in these regards.

That is, there could be other reasons behind the attitude under discussion, such as expressing overt racism related to past learning, modeling, etc. There could be problems in development at prior periods of life impeding proper resolution of the challenges in the present period.

The astute therapist will seek out whether the types of problems presented are due to the challenges solely in the immediate period at issue or are more long-standing and different in nature (and more difficult to deal with therapeutically). The person might feel split, unconnected, disjointed, and so on and ask for ways of creating more internal jelling together. The therapist should point out that the self/I is not alone in the world but intrinsically part of it, and the jelling required might include a better contemplation of and opening to the other ("Is there another way of seeing…"). Overall, the person should be incapable of weaving together a better welded self that includes all others/people until she/he can approach in a constructive way these types of questions. The person will be able eventually to scan the existential, spiritual, and holistic areas of her/his psychology to see what is involved and how it might be improved.

Therapeutic Implications

The youthful adult experiencing crises related to feeling at one with all peoples, coordinating symbiotically with all others, and feeling awe/wonder at life in all its guises will need a therapy that evokes deep connectivity to all aspects of life, including by using existential questioning, spirituality mining, and supra-world model building. The first type of therapy will work on the self and one's place in the world, the second on the nature of the world and its unity, and the third on a unified model of the self and world that regulates/resolves inconsistencies, including from developmental and emotional blockages. The goal would be to loosen the restrictions and impediments in building higher-order abstract structures that are inclusive of all relevant ideas and allow for their comparison's contrast/juxtaposition at this point in the life cycle, so leading to an inclusivity in dealing with all other peoples, not just the other in an individual sense or the other in a generalized sense. The therapist will monitor a sense of apathy about the self and other and a sense of disillusionment, as well. The apathy might be about the other, but a mirror apathy about the self inevitably will be evident as walls dividing the self at its core become brittle and fall, causing worse internal connectivity. The disillusionment will be more about the self, and the lack of higher-order meaning/spirituality in life, but will also mask a disillusionment with the other ("Why can't they just leave, get on without our help, etc.," Why is the government helping them so much and not its own people"). The therapist will ask about universal values/morals and try to induce the self to accept an acceptance of other peoples through the person's reflexivity rather than through directed therapeutic techniques. The therapist might start with eliciting the wonder at nature, the awe generated by contemplating the universe, and the surrender to mystery that marks aspects of spirituality.

The symbiotic engagement associated with the first sub-stage in the post-formal collective intelligence stage is an impressive gain developmentally, but it is limited to the coordinative nature of the sub-stage. Higher-order abstract ideas form through juxtaposition/compare-contrast processes at this level, but they cannot include a hierarchical, systematized widespread embedding of the beliefs and feelings involved leading to an integrative concept. Living that development takes the rest of one's lifetime as responsibilities grow and come to include all others/peoples as part of one's world and one's feeling of being at one with the world.

The hypo-invested type can move toward this end slowly but surely through the therapeutic techniques mentioned. The hyper-invested type will need more work toward this end in that the superficial front of universal connectivity must be deconstructed before a more genuine structure in these regards builds. In this section on therapy, there is no need to dwell much on the socialized type or the antitypes, with an underlying rejection being present despite a superficial peoples connectivity. In both cases, the therapist will seek to arrive at the genuine engagement required with others/peoples in order to navigate the crises at issue.

Stress-Trauma Resilience/Coping

A worldview that does not consider all peoples as worthy potentially reduces the stress/trauma resistance/coping abilities of the person. Without a symbiotic web coordinating all peoples into a universal community, the ability of the person to deal with stress/trauma will be weakened by the energetic inefficiency of creating an internal network of concepts about the self and other that is not coordinative, collective, and fused. The risk of apathy/disillusionment with respect to self and other also increases, which would further weaken stress/trauma resilience/coping. The ability to create a super-ordinate abstract structure of personhood, peoplehood, and their relation to each other and the planet/world adds an interior steeling effect to stress/trauma occurrences. Moreover, it affords a wider range of social supports possible for the task. Living in expectation of community with other people allows for expectation that the community will help you in turn when required, even if circumstances happen on the ground to interfere in its accomplishment. The wider web of possibility engendered by seeking coordinated connectivity with all peoples speaks to an internal resolve and forceful character (even if quiet in these regards) that can translate into effectively dealing with stress/trauma. The existential and spiritual issues that accompany such a worldview can only help in these regards.

Therapeutic Strategies [the Other and Change]

Relational Co-regulation

The youthful adult disengaging from the community of others/peoples will not be able to mutually engage in self-other co-regulation toward positive systemic accommodation of the web of meta-ideas, perspectives, and attitudes that form and govern self and other (including peoples, world) understanding. As the universe of the self expands to include all aspects of the other, including in its peoples and all their needs, the symbiotic connectivity felt for the other expands even to the planet that others inhabit and also the universe that the planet inhabits. Connectivity grows along with one's vision of where connectivity should head and exclusion of any collective other in these regards leads to disconnected connectivity in need of welding to evoke the unity possible in social/world connectivity.

A diminished other diminishes the self, and a diminished people doubly diminishes the self. When the other is merely dealt with superficially by the self or otherwise rejected/used, the self is also superficial rather than a psychological sound unity. Having elevated hopes for the suffering other (as people), and acting on them to the degree possible, doubly elevates the self and its interconnectivity, both in terms of self-components/core parts and in expressed relational co-regulation with the other.

If the self deflates in disillusionment after inspecting what seems to be at the core, the difficulty to turn the corner toward behaving with enlightenment toward the other is that much harder. Disillusionment with the self creates disinterest or even rejection of the other as defined as peoples (and their needs). The person will flail at foreground targets in life goals because there will be hurtful holes in the perception of the human background, instead of a healing holism when viewing the other/peoples. Forsaking others is forsaking the self. The excluded other guarantees an excluded self. The disappointment in the self could be pervasive, leading to an ingrained gloom difficult to manage.

The hypo-invested type will have feelings like this but may mask them through socialization. The hyper type might mask them through over-investment along these lines, but the mood masked might be quiet aggressive to the other as much as gloomy in the self. Either way, the other will be misperceived as unworthy of inclusion and so riddling self-other connectivity with unconnected nodes and causing relational dysregulation rather than co-regulation.

Behavior/Symptom Network/Connectivity Change (Horizontal)

The therapist with a patient whose issue is that she/he does not coordinate psychologically to self and all peoples in a symbiotic whole (along with the planet/universe) will need to show pathways to change in which the other is a resource that enriches the self, no matter how impoverished, different, and so on that the other might seem. The global connectivity of self and other creates community, and the person who is not participatory in this outreach will not find the inner peace (and indeed exhilaration) that might come with it as it comes to characterize the essential self and is acted upon to the degree possible.

The person who entrenches the self in fortresses that exclude encounter and communication with other peoples and their troubles will find that the walls are weak, they can be porous and perforated, and the person will not be able to maintain the charade of self above all. We seek global security and must realize that it is dependent on each of us helping out to the degree possible. The other's suffering can spread like a virus into our own mentation and our group psychology, and the barriers that we create to prevent this invasion cannot last.

The patient wishing to escape feelings of disillusionment, apathy, and so on needs to ask the origins of the feelings. Disillusionment/apathy reveal something about the core self that is missing. The therapist will probe to determine how to reorient the person toward self-building processes, which inevitably must include more beneficence toward the other/all others/all peoples and beyond. Universality is a mantra that accompanies entry into this age period of being a youthful adult, given the underlying post-formal abstract cognition that develops at this period.

The problem simply could be that the person is so engrossed in daily responsibilities (study/work/family) that there is not much room for anything else and the person yearns for more but cannot specify exactly what that is. The therapist will use an existential/spiritual approach, among others, to encourage the person to engage the other more deeply and widely, including all peoples as part of one's concerns. The therapist will try to create in the person a web of connectivities along these lines in the super-ordinate abstract structures about the self/responsibilities/world created. The therapist will encourage exploration in knowledge/professional domains, artistic/creative ones, etc., and their integration into a unity of responsibility such that the sense of responsibility can extend to other peoples. Wonder and awe in an extended sense stem from a holistic, collective approach to living and being.

Behavior/Symptom Growth, Deep Change (Vertical)/Constructing a More Positive Life Story

The person making progress in moving toward self and social connectivity that includes all peoples can begin to develop toward a fulfilling sense of generativity of the self-acting in society (e.g., in studies, work, family, toward any other). The person will not be in the throes of self-absorption and stagnation as she/he moves toward a considerate and applied attitude toward all her/his responsibilities. The person will leave behind any vestiges of disillusionment/apathy as the barriers dividing self from the full other are brought down/modified. The person will be required to maintain a self-protective stance in doing so, not being naïve, and checking for reciprocity by groups of others in order to avoid being taken advantage of. Group work does not mean that there is an absence of self-interest, but it is moderated and focused constructively at this level.

The youthful adult learning to be more other-group oriented will open pores in the self that have been closed to integrative exchange with other peoples. The narrative told in this regard might be just an opening to possibility given the realities of daily life. The person might tell herself/himself and others that she/he was too busy before to see how the self fits in the wider world, but now that this theme is being explored, it feels wonderful. There used to be a reflexive closure to the outside groups in the life of the person but now there is a welcoming hope for their betterment and the possibility of helping toward that goal. The person might indicate how she/he is a better person because her/his worldview now includes all peoples. We live on a planet with limited resources and beautiful faun and flora, and they must be protected. We live in a planet with many groups, and many suffer, but the person might ask what she/he can do to help, even minimally. When the other is seen as part of your community, the collective that you form in your mind includes a more peaceful and pleasant you. When you can extend that to helpful actions, those feelings percolate through your core self and animate your life. The person might tell exciting stories along these lines as the new view of the other solidifies.

Consciousness, Theory of Mind, Selves, Responsibility

The youthful adult now in possession of super-ordinate abstract logic cognitive skills can construct second-order abstract ideas, such as those related to a whole discipline rather than piecemeal. These post-formal, collective intelligence skills open whole new vistas not only in cognition but also in many aspects of daily life, including socio-emotionally and socio-affectively. The person can construct generic cross-domain theories, meta-theories, supra-principles, second-order abstract reasoning, and pan-vision webbed integrations related to self-other/groups and their harmonic coordination. The person at this age and with this attitude "meta-collects" ideas, people, cognitive-emotional links, experiences, etc. to form symbiotic wholes that help relate self-other, different groups, and so on into a unity of coordinations/juxtapositions.

When applied to critical questions of what makes us human, this post-formal abstract thought process allows for a supra-consciousness that hovers over all things and ideas or a broad and deep awareness of self, other, and their multi-varied relationships. The person views all others in this worldview, all peoples, and this does not distract from the sense of re-responsibility that accompanies this age. Each (sub) domain of responsibility is undertaken with grace and acceptance and rededicated at each second with humbleness and thankfulness. Adult maturity has been defined in terms of self-actualization, generativity, self-determination, psychological completeness, etc., and all these concepts inform the growth process in the youthful adult arriving at the post-formal stage of collective intelligence. By expressing sanctity for all life and for the planet/universe, by humanizing every other and all peoples, by being their sanctuary, in part, and by living a life of meaningful meaning for the self and all others, not only will the self (and family) grow optimally but also the other in which we are mutually embedded will do the same and (eventually) help us do the same. Life is a circle, and it englobes all of us, including our precarious globe in need of our help as much as the life living on it.

The Collective Intelligence Stage Sub-stage of Hierarchization (28–39 Years): Sub-stage 22

Self and Relational Development [Initial Theoretical Elaborations]

A very brief description of the present step in Young's 25-step Neo-Eriksonian developmental model follows. It is presented again in Chap. 18, to help give a collective overview of the 25 steps in the modeling.

Generativity (generating) acts vs. self-absorption (no responsibility) acts (28–39 years). Growing adults give their best to their responsibilities, from family and relationships, to work and study, to society. The conscious, identity, relating, and helping attitudes of the prior steps in life become real in all activities. If problems come up for whatever reason, you could let go your responsibilities, feel empty, focus only on yourself, and not grow. Or, you might try hard to take your responsibilities, but just on the surface or because of your training.

Appendix 5.2 gives the brief amount of work already done in prior publications related to the task of developing in depth the Neo-Eriksonian (sub)stage model. The next section of the chapter gives an interim summary that elaborates the contents of Appendix 5.2 with respect to the present sub-stage being considered, of the sub-stage of Collective Intelligence Stage Sub-stage of Hierarchization.

Interim Summary

In Western society, the adult in the late 20s often begins the epoch journey of undertaking multiple responsibilities for work and family, with the process continuing into the 30s. According to the present Neo-Eriksonian model, the socio-affective acquisition that encompasses these activities is referred to as generativity, which, for Erikson, involved a concern for the next generation. Thus, in the present context, work refers to functioning adaptively in order to provide the material resources for family or any generative activity that captivates the person, such as volunteering for a nonprofit, mentoring someone at work, or contributing to one's denominational institution. The generative nature of the person at this age indicates that the self could be deemed a generative one. The very nature of generative activity implies that it is meant to activate the receiver into progress toward optimal outcome/development. The child should be cared for optimally; the work situation should be dealt with optimally, as would any continuing graduate/professional studies; any societal work also should aim for optimal outcome; as would dealing with the environment/planet and its life forms, generally. The person does not undertake all these different types of generative acts herself/himself but absorbs into familial/institutional activities that have the same goals. The collective is a powerful medium for positive change along these lines. Moreover, the person hopes that others in the family/society circle absorb the role modeling/demonstration of generative activity. In short, growing adults give their best to their responsibilities, whether family and relationships, work and study, or society. The conscious, identity, relating, and helping attitudes of the prior steps in life become applied in all daily activities.

The underlying cognitive acquisition that permits generativity is the ability to form higher-order abstract structures involving hierarchization (dominant-subordinate relations) of coordinated juxtapositions in super-ordinate abstract logical structures. The person might grasp the abstract complexity in one (sub)domain or another in her/his life and can do so for several of them. The person can then place them in relation, e.g., with cognitive structure for family (or future family, as the case may be) dominant, and the one for work (or study) is linked to it but subordinately. These kind of hierarchical arrangements about the abstract cognitive structures concerning major life domains allows for generativity, in general, as a dominant theme in the various combinations of (sub)domains considered. Generativity acts are meant to empower the other but, in doing that, they empower the self. At the same time, the emotions experienced are not power-focused or self-enhancing ones. Rather, they are ones related to experiencing self-fulfillment.

The contrasting emotions when generativity stagnates refer to emptiness/stagnation/self-absorption. The person might experience self-inflation as a reactive protective mechanism or already be so imbued by the self in this age period that genuine generativity is all but impossible. Being humble and having humility are more conducive to generativity than seeking self-empowerment as a goal of the activity. The more the self is the focus of the investment in the other, the more not only is the other deactivated/disempowered but also the self is, as well, at least in the genuine sense and in the long-term.

As with other sub-stages in the current model, one can describe a hypo and hyper type, which in the present sub-stage refers to hypo- and hyper-generativity. The former refers to the self-absorption/stagnation outcome and the latter to being very engaged in generativity but in a pseudo/false way. The hypo type might evidence a supra-engagement in generativity, though, through socialization and not genuine commitment. The hyper type might have an undercurrent of rejection of the other, making it quite complex.

As with the other sub-stage challenges that the person might experience, the therapist will seek to instill a positive, genuine attitude for the issue at hand. This means, in the present case, having a focus on the concept of re-responsibilities and feeling sublimely at peace in doing so – the rewards in generating optimal outcomes in the (sub)domains in adult function that are being discussed are much more advantageous than any of their drawbacks. Another issue to consider therapeutically is how de-powering the other de-powers the self.

Self-Response to Cognitive (Mis)Perception of the Other

The adult in the late 20s and 30s typically is in a generative phase of taking multiple responsibilities and undertaking them with full awareness of how difficult, yet rewarding, they might be. The adult at this time of life is applying herself/himself diligently to school/work, family/friends, society/communities, and the wider world, including in environmental concerns/activism. The self is a generative one, with a cognitive structure of super-ordinate abstract dominant-subordinate relations of self in relation to other, of others in relation to peoples and society and so on. This structure can be found in multiple life domains, e.g., "I am subordinate (come second) to my family, to my responsibility to my family.") But the dominant-subordinate relationship established with the other is an equitable one in the sense that the person functions as a role model/mentor, caring parent/caring adult child, involved co-worker/respectful colleague, and so on. The collective nature of the intelligence demonstrated applies not only to cognitive tasks, such as study/work projects, but also to the coordinative, hierarchized emotional, and social intelligence/cognition necessary for adaptive socio-emotional/socio-affective function. The person is widely generative in the critical life domains, leading to a sense of accomplishment and self-fulfillment without any self-inflation. The other in this life perspective needs empowering to grow (and to end up being capable of the same perspective). The self is other-activatory.

The person might not have the supportive environment to function in this ideal or might otherwise be incapable of it and falter in undertaking it. The person could lapse into stagnation rather than generativity and in self-absorption rather than other-concern. The other could be misperceived as unworthy of a generative attitude and acts or as someone who should do it on her/his own. The other is disempowered, deactivated, and emptied of what is required to succeed. Instead of being a positive role model, the person might become an absent or negative one. Instead of being a mentor, the person might even become a tormentor. Instead of prompting growth and integration, the person might rejoice in regression and disintegration. Instead of generativity, one might express degenerating behavior toward the other. In this scenario, the self is joyless; the other is, too. The other is not even a subordinate entity to the dominant self; it has been removed from the equation, and the self is subordinate only to the self itself. The other is not just misperceived; it is removed/ciphered to zero. The self suffers in consequence, itself not having any genuine capacity to guide, scaffold, frame, hold for, or contribute to the other in reciprocity, relationality, etc. Rather than the other being absent from the world of the self, given that the other might (will) somehow survive, the self is absent from the world of the self and so is empty, a vacuum, without power, without inertia, without presence, and without being in the world. One could call this degenerativity.

Positive Pole in Eriksonian Development

Generativity is one of the hallmark stages in Erikson's theory, and it concerns helping others and institutions around us grow optimally, from family to work to society as a whole (and the planet/world). It includes directly supporting these people/entities or providing/facilitating indirect support. It includes caring for, teaching, demonstrating/modeling/mentoring, facilitating/framing, guiding/scaffolding, cooperating, working together with, building constructively, and so on. When in the generative mindset, the tasks involved are not considered onerous but part of the array of adult life functions that people engage in normally, with aplomb, and without complaint to the degree possible. The attitude involved is not self-inflationary but self-fulfilling and humble, without self-absorption. The person never experiences stagnation because the responsibilities undertaken are rededicated at each second. Accidents and worse can happen even in 1 second of carelessness. Care is a mantle that is never put aside in the generative self. We constantly promote/empower the other, prompt and instill self-help in the other, and otherwise create a worldview in which we are subordinate to our generative actions while keeping a balance and not sacrificing (naively) the self.

Negative Social-Self Working Schema

The generative self can mutually subordinate the I to the Other, who is being helped through her/his activities, and also mutually subordinate the Other to the I. Other and I are collective/mutually hierarchized and represent a balanced force that must be maintained in balance for the helping of the other to continue. The post-formal sub-stage of multiple intelligence (super-ordinate abstract) hierarchizations permits the broad conceptualization of self in relation to other to take on this form. The person knows her/his priorities, never abandons them, does nothing to sap the energy needed for them, indulges multiply in responsibilities, and never does so in order to receive, because pure giving is pure receiving. The person continuously activates/empowers in generativity. Activities that empower the other help maintain proper perspective of self and other. It is as if one is telling the self – I am me because you are me. I am them because they are me. My me is your me. My me is our we. Your we is my me. I grow you just as you grow me. I grow you just as you grow me in giving me the honor of growing you. I cannot grow if you don't grow. Somehow you might grow without me helping you when given the opportunity, but then it will be more difficult for me to grow myself.

The generative person thinks like this or behaves like this or both. There is no lack of will or lack of good will toward the other. There is no self-stasis, only self-development through the other. There is no empty self-congratulation, only full self-satisfaction in relation to a constructive attitude/action toward the other. It is as if the person is saying – I activate myself not for me, but to activate you. I empower myself not for me, but to empower you.

The ideal approach to generativity emanates fluidly in some people who have had the appropriate environmental support and continue to have it. However, for many of us, being wholly generative in the way indicated is a constant struggle, and some people even self-sabotage/reject any attitude/action of the sort. The other is not propped up/supported, scaffolded/relationally co-engaged, and so on, but the other is isolated from the self, left to flounder/deal with matters alone, and so on.

The other is not construed as any other, and also all others and part of the self and worthy of everything the self can provide it; rather, the other is construed as a manipulative/controlling other or worse. The other is not approached humbly to help, but is approached arrogantly to aggress in one way or the other. The other is not considered an object to empower but one to disempower. The other is perceived as a person (people) who can deflate the self, deactivate the self, deny the self, and even obliterate it. The self has no recourse but to disempower the other, deflate/deactivate/deny the other, and even obliterate it. The self mentors only the self, teaches only the self, activates the self only for the self, and generates only for the self, but all these exercises inevitably fail and leave the self not only without the other but also without the self.

The social-self working schema is asocial and worse. Any positive aspect seen in the other is absent, in that there is no space in the self beyond the fulsome false presence of the positives attributed to the self. At the extreme, there is no negative social-self working schema because there is no other, no generativity in the genuine sense of the word. Or, the other is deemed unworthy of any generative act, a degenerate psychologically beyond help. The other is discouraged from growing and even humiliated, in contrast to the attitude toward the self, which is superficially full of self-praise.

But the self can lapse into self-absorption to the point that everything seems empty and nothing of value is happening in her/his life, leading to stagnation not only relative to the self but also to the other. In this sense, instead of a generative self, one finds a degenerative one. Just as the other is considered not worthy of a generative attitude/behavior, the self ends up feeling the same about the self, with consequent degenerativity in many or all life spheres possible or even likely.

The person having difficulty with generativity might gravitate to the extremes of under-generativity, leaving it aside altogether, or, conversely, over-generativity, heavily investing in it but superficially and too transparently. The former type might adopt a socialized generativity, but without the rigor of having self-generated it genuinely. The latter type might express an undercurrent of dismissal/rejection of the other, seeing an anti-other, instead of a genuine other worthy of genuine generativity.

Attachment, Neo-Eriksonian Development, Therapeutic Implications [Patients and Therapy]

Patient Presentation

The adult struggling with generativity issues will feel barren in a lifeless world, even if there are at least some others around her/him bustling in one way or another with energy, activity, and caring behavior. The adult incapable of generativity will descend into self-absorption either as a displacement to the lacks felt or as a primal self-orientation that has chronically encumbered the person because she/he has always been unable to escape the self-focus of the self. Because of the self-absorption, the person will not help the other in any way through other-enhancing generativity. This would apply to all relevant major life domains/adult functions, including at school/work, in family/social life (if any), and toward society/the planet. The person will be unable to see the connection between the barren feeling felt and the discarding/rejection of the other in terms of generativity/caring. Also, the person will blame the other more than the self for her/his issues. Fellow students/co-workers will be seen as possible competitors instead of having a cooperative potential. There will be no group work, only isolation into the self away from the group. The person will deride the other, deny any giving to the other, hope for the demise of the other, and so on.

The themes in the structures created will be deficient in generativity, whether in terms of the self as a generative agent or the other as a worthy recipient of generativity. The person will always place the self super-ordinate to any other in any life domain of the other. (I give to myself and only myself; the other is there only to take away what I aim to give myself). The person will feel full of the self rather than self-fulfilled, but with an empty self, as well, instead of a filled one, because only the appropriate attitude/actions toward the other, to the degree possible, can instigate a filling self, and this attitude will be absent. The person will take power for power's sake and rob the other of any power but, in the end, feel powerless. The person will be so absorbed with the self that the person will miss what is best for the self, leaving it a shell, at best.

Stagnation will set in, with a fear even of moving psychologically if not physically. To really move on, the person will have to confront the self about the attitude/actions toward the other, who is so intrinsically cast aside/rejected. Without doing so, rather than the humility in genuine generativity, the self will know barrenness in a complete isolation (at least from the other if not all daily functions). Efforts at self-inflation as a displacement activity will fail; the person risks a complete reversal to total self-deflation. The hypo type will be like this, unless there is a socialized generativity in place, but if that does happen, it will not be genuine or committed. The hyper type will be multiply engaged in pseudo-generativities but with the risk of their collapse into the superficiality involved and manifesting an underpinning anti-other attitude/behavior.

Behavioral/Symptom Mental Scanning

Crises related to generativity will be difficult for patients to deal with if they are already expressing a sense of stagnation, self-absorption, and emptiness. People like this will feel a personal barrenness, will not engage in helping others grow, and will resent the attitude of others toward them. They will self-justify and not have self-doubt in these regards, will not invest emotionally in any other in their life, and will have an arrogant, aggressive attitude toward them, using that as a front to preserve an ill-conceived self-isolation and sense of self-importance/inflation. People like this will not see how their life is purely instrumental and not shared, with no core/helping/generativity directed to the other. They might engage in activities that are self-constructive and without any concern for the other.

When asked why he/she is in crisis and need of therapy, adults like this will cite accomplishments but, as well, feelings of barrenness. There will be expressions of personal futility and social "infertility," with queries why they cannot relate positively to the other. But their understanding of positive relations with the other will be especially for self-boosting/inflating and other-bursting/deflating. People like this will describe personal narratives with the I as central in narratives and the other as forced adjuncts. The other will never be the focus of a subplot in the narrative told about any constructive effort aimed at them through endeavors undertaken by people like this. Story lines will contain a dominant hierarchization of the self lording over the other in the abstract superstructure of self-other relations carried by people like this.

Therapeutic Implications

The adult failing to generate generativity will express self-absorption, including self-inflation, and also stagnation in relating to the other, except perhaps instrumentally for self-gain. Power will be a major therapeutic theme, as in – how can I better empower myself/depower the other?

The therapist can address the concept of taking responsibility in a wider sense, which might include helping the other. The therapist should address the growth imperative essential to the human condition and how this implies generativity. The therapist can accentuate that power for power's sake generates an empty feeling and never lets the power-seeker rest, feel peace, or feel plenitude. When life is about power, or any primitive motivation, the horizons one can see in life are limited by the nature of the motivation. If power predominates, the filter used to see the other is power-saturated – how can I maximize it in me and minimize it in the other, and that is all that counts.

The self and other are engaged in a choreographed dance at all levels, and when the rhythms are reduced to stilted and stunted themes, the self is reduced as much as the other. It is as if the person is saying – If I can't see you in your majesty, how can I have any in me? The more I am not humble about myself, the less I am able. The more I do not want to generate fulfillment in the other, the less I am fulfilled. Generating in the other helps to generate the self in me. When I am subordinate to you (without losing me), I am dominant in me. To be dominant in me, I need to subordinate to you (without losing me). We are a team, where both can win. Cooperativity is the highest form of empowerment because both self and other gain in power. My power is for you and your power feeds mine when I help you generate it. Consider gravity – objects exist in reciprocal influence no matter how small is one compared to the other. Moreover, without a second object, a first one really has no gravity – it needs an object to activate its gravity. The best relationship in the gravitational relationship of the objects is some type of equality. This way, neither object can crash into the other and leave lasting scars on its (psycho)geology. We are meant to grow the other. Inherent to our condition is the teaching impulse, the modeling motivation, the mentoring effort. We abhor a vacuum, and a self-world without any generative helping of the other is the worst emptiness possible. Take away my helping gusto and you take away my humanity.

These are the types of themes that can be explored in therapy. The ideal is that the therapist asks the person how she/he can help herself/himself, How can the person fill the sense of barrenness? What is required to help the person help herself/himself, and does this in any way mean the person should start in some way to help the other and help the other learn to help herself/himself? The hypo-generative type will need this kind of approach, and the hyper-generative type will need some sort of de-masking to begin. Both types will need to converge on genuine generativity to help fill their sense of barrenness/stagnation, self-absorption, and emptiness. May the power be with the therapist in these regards.

Stress-Trauma Resilience/Coping

By definition, an attitude of generativity fosters a better stress/trauma resilience/coping. The start of generativity in the 20s–30s creates important links with study/work associates, family/friends, and neighborhood/society members, which could be helpful in the connections available for stress/trauma resilience/coping. Moreover, genuine generativity brings with it a peaceful calm as responsibilities are adopted, such that the person will be less overwhelmed by stress/trauma.

However, if the person is experiencing generativity issues, the normal social resources that might be available will be affected, as will the strengthening of the self to confront the stress/trauma. The person might give up dealing with the stress/trauma, in that stagnation already might have set in. The person might be so self-absorbed that she/he will retreat even further into the self and let the stress/trauma fester and get so out of control that it becomes totally unmanageable. The person might have been so power-centric that all power would be lost in face of a burden of the stress/trauma, revealing the feeble frame in the person.

Therapeutic Strategies [the Other and Change]

Relational Co-regulation

The adult avoiding any generativity will engage with the other only toward boosting self-absorption/inflation, self-empowerment, and also deflation/disempowerment of the other. The growth of the self will be emphasized at the expense of the growth of the other, but the self will wither rather than prosper because of the misappropriation of generativity. The other will be sacrificed for the self, and regulated out of the mind of the person. There will be no co-regulation with the other that is mutual and equitable, growing both the self and other, because the self will be concerned only with growing the self. The self will not care for/help the other without any inclination toward self-gain, will not teach/role model for the other unless there is self-gain, will not scaffold/facilitate learning in the other unless the learning feeds back into the person, and so on. There might be some mutual gain that is supported, but never selfless (yet self-protective) gain for the other. If the other self-absorbs/stagnates because generativity cannot be engaged, the person will not intervene to help get the other underway in growth/generativity. "Co-generativity" is an ideal in relational co-regulation, but it will be stymied by a self-important and imposing self that is letting others even die on the vine psychologically.

Behavior/Symptom Network/Connectivity Change (Horizontal)

The patient in the midst of paralyzing generativity difficulties will be so self-absorbed and in stagnation that there will be no room in the person's psychology for caring for/helping/growing any other. Plights experienced by others (even those who are family/parent/significant others, etc. aside from those with whom one only works with/studies with, etc.) will be ignored/not considered personally relevant. Society ills will be totally out of the question to personally consider and address. The person might be so self-inflating and power-focused that the other is considered only as medium to arrive at self-determined self-enhancing goals.

That said, the patient will query why any personal growth seems so difficult and why others react negatively to her/him, especially if they are needy. The patient will depreciate the other while bloating the image of self. The patient will not even be capable of acknowledging the physically and psychologically weak other who lives in her/his sphere. Nor will she/he realize how this negligence of the other weakens the fabric of the self and its growing potential.

The cognitive structure implicated in sustaining this construction of self and other involves hierarchically arranging dominant-subordinate abstract ideas, but the higher-order structure will be deficient in placing the other in relation to the self in a self-other equilibrium in which each can grow by and through the other and beyond. Power-seeking detracts from personal growth, while empowering growth in the other adds to it. Activating the power in the other in a way that the person does not abuse the power generates a genuinely powerful self.

The hypo style of problems in generativity will skirt generativity attitudes and efforts. However, there might be a socialized style in these regards, but not truly ingrained or sustained. The hyper-generative style will be multiple, pseudo, and variable and without a genuine sense of re-responsibilities. There even might be an anti-generativity attitude subsuming the putative generative behavior, leading to mixed messages for the other rather than genuine generativity/growing for the other.

Behavior/Symptom Growth, Deep Change (Vertical)/Constructing a More Positive Life Story

The patient growing into generativity will be able to self-grow care and concern for the other to the point of growing the other. The person will be able to bootstrap the other to grow optimally, facilitate her/his growth, scaffold/frame, teach/mentor/model, and activate the other to become generative in turn (one day). The person will not undertake these re-responsible tasks expecting any gain or reward for the self except the reward of seeing the other grow (toward generativity). The barren feelings on the terrain of the self will be replaced by the blooming harvest of the other's growth, and the person will be more at peace and positive. The person will be self-protective throughout the process, not over-extending nor being taken advantage of. This will lead to a co-regulatory relational equilibrium with the other, even if the other is a child needing much support, because there is no calculus attached to genuine generativity. The self will drop the self-importance it stores and open to other-importance. The self-generated empowering of the other will take place by having shed the arrogance toward the other. The person will marvel at the growing other and engage in discourse to see that process continue [How are you changing for the better? Is that the best way of seeing things or are there others? That is not homework; it is mind work or mind growth.]

The cognitive frame that allows this new perspective to take hold concerns super-ordinate abstract hierarchizations, such as in the relationship in the self as conceived in its full complexity and in relationship to the other, as well. The person might deploy a logic involving abstract super-structures in which concepts related to various life domains are hierarchized, such as in relating a variegated self to a variegated other, self to work/school, self to family, and so on. In the end, the generative activating self can spread and burgeon when the mind frame that can activate it self-activates a concern for generating the other to its optimal state.

At this point, the person is ready to move to the next phase in development, which concerns midlife consciousness, or what I have labeled catalysis. The generativity instilled in the present age period can seed logarithmically a growth in the self and other that is trans-domain, transpersonal, and meta-systemic. The collective intelligence abstract structures involved are differentiated to the point that self and other coexist, co-define, co-relate, and find co-being through an exponential growth that reevaluates, refines, and redefines one's life course and path toward a transformative shift in personal psychology. The inverse of midlife crisis always might cast its shadow on any such development.

The person becoming generative will tell stories of how growing other people and entities is so rewarding and cannot be matched by any material gain or even self-growth. The person will tell stories about the other being helped rather than how this helps the person. The person will tell the stories told by the other about how they are growing, emphasizing how she/he might have contributed to that process, e.g., by activating it to unfold naturally in the other. The person will feel fulfilled, humble at the growths induced, and not express any gain from the activity, including a sense of power. The person will describe how she/he used to be self-centric and now is much more other-centric, and how she/he used to be engrossed in the self, absorbed to the hilt in the self, and now instead glows at the growth of the other. The person will describe how she/he can teach/mentor/model, and scaffold/frame, but in a way that educates the listener how to do the same or facilitates such. The hypo type will emphasize these and related stories, and the hyper type will also address the altered pseudo nature of past generative attitude/activity.

Consciousness, Theory of Mind, Selves, Responsibility

The adult developing generativity is concerned with developing the other, which opens whole vistas in self-growth, including in helping the other grow optimally. The level of conscious awareness is now at a peak point of the multiple responsibilities that life entails and the need to rededicate to them continually. The person adopts a reverential attitude to the other, society, the planet, etc. and sees them as a sanctuary, with concomitant expressions of sanctity for all life and all humanity. The person is ready for a catalytic amplification of all these themes as they become systematized and multiplied.

The Collective Intelligence Stage Sub-stage of Systematization (39–50 Years): Sub-stage 23

Self and Relational Development [Initial Theoretical Elaborations]

A very brief description of the present step in Young's 25-step Neo-Eriksonian developmental model follows. It is presented again in Chap. 18, to help give a collective overview of the 25 steps in the modeling.

Catalytic (growing others) acts vs. midlife crisis acts (39–50 years). Growing adults carry through with all their responsibilities so that everything around them grows or gets better. But problems could develop for you and cause you to let go all your responsibilities even though you had taken them all on well up to this point in time. You change and act just for the self. You reject loved ones, work, and all your responsibilities. Or, you could keep them and just go through the motions, feeling sad.

Appendix 5.3 gives the brief amount of work already done in prior publications related to the task of developing in depth the Neo-Eriksonian (sub)stage model. The next section of the chapter gives an interim summary that elaborates the contents of Appendix 5.3 with respect to the present sub-stage being considered, of the sub-stage of Collective Intelligence Stage Sub-stage of Systematization.

Interim Summary

The midlife adult has been described as having a midlife crisis but, as with other universally negative views of difficult passages in the life course such as teen age "storm and stress," this perspective on the midlife adult is exaggerated in its negativity. It is more likely that the midlife adult is continuously involved in all her/his generative responsibilities, and they become even more demanding. The workplace expects more executive/managerial functions, children are getting older and more difficult to manage in the preteen and teen years, and time for leisure/volunteer activities becomes more difficult to find. Life satisfaction decreases due to the wear and tear of responsibilities, but they are not abandoned. To the contrary, the person doubles down; takes leadership roles; uses experience to help compensate for the increasing demands on her/him, as well as relying on the web of social connections and other resources accrued; and thinks through better any problems with a super-ordinate abstract intelligence that coheres into an organized system.

In that the prior sub-stage in the present model referred to Erikson's stage of generativity, the present sub-stage can be described as involving "meta-generativities." Moreover, the responsibilities therein increase logarithmically, leading to a welter of Catalytic Acts for this age period. We gladly take on the challenges, relish the fruits of our labor, seek to help others bear similar fruits, and end each day with an inner peace that is well-earned and that we hope to pleasantly spread. We constantly rededicate ourselves to our responsibilities, seek to add to them, or, inevitably, by dint of our responsibilities already undertaken, have more foisted on us. We thus constantly have to reevaluate/refine and readjust/redefine our life trajectory. In doing so, for any one domain, we can transform the life course/path being followed and have it emerge in new directions.

The systemic view created can include quite large collectives of ideas/approaches, and we can value each of them as the overall systemic structure is built. There will be cross-currents across sub-domains in any one domain that one has systematized, and the beginning of cross-domain multiplication/integration will begin. This super-ordinate abstract cognitive facility underpins the successful discharging of our meta-generative re-responsibilities. Our cognitive vision undergirds our behavioral vision.

When the person is having difficulty in meta-generative catalyzing acts, she/he might shirk responsibilities and burrow into the self, being supra self-absorbed and stagnant. This could happen in multiple domains, including with our romantic partner. There might be the usual hypo- and hyper (insincere) types and their complexities. The extreme danger is abandoning all responsibilities and turning against those whom one has supported in our generative responsibilities before the crisis had begun.

Self-Response to Cognitive (Mis)perception of the Other

The midlife catalysis in generativity that takes place in work/family/society means that the person has become an instrumental support for others. At the same time, the person might be overwhelmed in undertaking these responsibilities and put them on hold/abandon them. The self is doubly invested in as the other is doubly abandoned, (doubly in the sense of multiple domains and doubly in the sense of critical junctures for the work/family, others involved). The other becomes not only put on/hold abandoned but also unduly criticized/rejected, leading to confusion (and reflecting the person's confusion). The re-evaluation/redefinition of the self and life trajectory that takes place leads to pining for earlier life periods without the same responsibilities. The self becomes a skeleton of the responsible person that had been and psychologically emaciated as a result. The other risks becoming the same if other supports are not found.

Positive Pole in Eriksonian Development

Having graduated from the generative period into a catalytic meta-generative one in which all our responsibilities become more demanding, we still undertake them with efficacy, balance, and aplomb, humbly giving to the other (with self-protection involved) so they can flourish, and that becomes the primary reward for us in and of itself. We continue to care/model/mentor, frame/guide/scaffold, cooperate/work together/build constructively, and adopt more of a leadership role in doing so. The person can think systematically at a super-ordinate abstract level, which facilitates having this positive view of continual rededication to one's multiple applicable responsibilities. Stagnation and self-absorption are not options or even words in the lexicon in the person's psychology. For people like this, power resides in doing and being for the other and not for any material or self-infatuated gain.

Negative Social-Self Working Schema

The generative self will have a very positive schema of the other and engage in many ways to help and to foster growth in the other. The same applies to the person behaving doubly this way, in catalytic meta-generativity.

However, the person struggling with generativity will view the other as a drain on resources and abandon efforts to help and encourage growth. This might be even worse as the person gets older and wants to self-absorb rather than give generatively of the self. The other could be overly criticized/doubly rejected and be confused by the confused behavior of the person if generativity had already commenced appropriately. The midlife crisis represents a crisis for the other as much as the self.

Attachment, Neo-Eriksonian Development, Therapeutic Implications [Patients and Therapy]

Patient Presentation

The patient struggling with generativity at this more advanced level will present like the patient who presents with the same issues at the prior developmental level but more intensely and broadly. Any flame of sensitivity will be extinguished and the person will be self-absorbed/stagnated to a major degree. People will be let down by the sudden abandonment of any sensitive acts that had already taken place. The sense of barrenness will be pervasive. Perhaps suicidality will be an issue in the person's thought process. The person might engage in classic midlife crisis behaviors including abandoning the romantic partner/parent to the children. The person might justify the action by pointing out the many flaws in the other, rightly or wrongly perceived, and without any proclaimed effort to want to work through the issues with the partner.

Behavioral/Symptom Mental Scanning

The midlife crisis patient will blame everything and anybody for her/his predicaments. The abandoned other might be the unjustly criticized/rejected. The person might protest that the other is at fault and deserves the abandonment/barrenness. Ultimately, the person might become so morose and recognize her/his suicidal potential because of the harms done.

Therapeutic Implications

In meta-generativity, responsibilities are multiplied, and the person who retreats into a midlife crisis will require work on abandonment of the other and a sense of barrenness in the self. The impact on the potential growth of the other should be discussed, as well as the self-infatuation taking place and its potential dangers.

Stress-Trauma Resilience/Coping

Entering a midlife crisis will be detrimental to stress/trauma resilience/coping. The person will be self-infatuated/absorbed and bereft of genuine social support. The person will generally stagnate, feel barren/empty, and not be able to handle external intrusion of any sort on the other-excluded lifestyle.

Therapeutic Strategies [the Other and Change]

Relational Co-regulation

The person ensconced in a midlife crisis will be so self-infatuated that the other will exist in a barren landscape of abandonment. The self will be so inflated that the hurt caused to the other will leave the person unfazed. The other either comes for the ride on the person's terms or is cast aside to make due as best can. The other is left to self-regulate and without any buffering by the person.

Behavior/Symptom Network/Connectivity Change (Horizontal)

The patient in midlife crisis will pull the wagons around the self and justify all actions taken. Movement toward catalytic generativity will be slow and could start by reaching out to any harmed other.

Behavior/Symptom Growth, Deep Change (Vertical)/Constructing a More Positive Life Story

As the patient resolves the midlife crisis, growth into a more mature self who undertakes her/his multiple responsibilities becomes more likely. This will serve to create a lifestyle that leads to psychological maturity/ego integrity and a joy in looking back at one's life. The person will explain how the midlife crisis was a temporary one, and she/he is back on track fulfilling the myriad responsibilities of life in a way that makes grow the other. The person will refer to life's struggles as a learning experience and how her/his struggles can inform/teach others about how to grow; maintain a positive, helpful attitude; etc.

Consciousness, Theory of Mind, Selves, Responsibility

The person struggling with generativity and overcoming it, even later on when the responsibilities involved increase logarithmically or catalytically, can refer to how the landscape of her/his life is so filled and is not barren in any way. The person is heading toward a complete conscious maturity in which the other's growth to maturity is being fostered fully. The person will realize that the midlife crisis that might have taken place was a humbling, humanizing experience and that the true psychological home of the person should be filled with all the others that she/he has helped along the way and had given them the power to help others in their turn.

The Collective Intelligence Stage Sub-stage of Multiplication (50–61 Years): Sub-stage 24

Self and Relational Development [Initial Theoretical Elaborations]

A very brief description of the present step in Young's 25-step Neo-Eriksonian developmental model follows. It is presented again in Chap. 18, to help give a collective overview of the 25 steps in the modeling.

Ego integrity (feeling good about the self and life) acts vs. despair acts (50–61 years). As the years go on, family and relationships grow, work or study continues, and perhaps you help people and society, depending on your situation. You feel comfortable about how life has gone. But if problems happen about this, you could feel very low, depressed, or disappointed. You regret not having given your best in life, not being fully present in everything done, etc. Also, perhaps you get angry, can't do anything, etc.

Appendix 5.4 gives the brief amount of work already done in prior publications related to the task of developing in depth the Neo-Eriksonian (sub)stage model. The next section of the chapter gives an interim summary that elaborates the contents of Appendix 5.4 with respect to the present sub-stage being considered, of the sub-stage of Collective Intelligence Stage Sub-stage of Multiplication.

Interim Summary

The adult who has engaged well in major life tasks faces an elderly period with a deep-seated joy and satisfaction that life has been meaningful and fulfilled. Erikson referred to this age period as involving ego integrity. His theory involved the concept of mutuality in self-other relations, and the ego can achieve the indicated integrity through the other. According to the present model, the underlying cognitive capacity of this age period involves multiple super-ordinate abstract systems. They help the person examine major life domains and find cross-domain linkages that allow for the sense of accomplishments and enjoyments at the prospect of retirement/grandchildren, further work/volunteer activity, leisure, etc., as the case may be.

Life never is perfectly successful, and there are losses to deal with at this age. The person readily comes to terms with them or accepts them in the grand scheme of things. The person reviews the past and its complexities, stresses, and multiplicities, and accommodates to any felt losses by the gains also felt as having taken place. The gains involved could refer to those of others whom one has helped.

Life reflects meaning at multiple levels, including in life tasks, but reaching out to others is part of the existential and spiritual questions we all face, as well. The person might ask who am I and realize the question is meaningless. For example, at this age, the I is multiple; also, "being," in the sense of presence and action to the degree possible, is primary. The better question might be "where have I fit into the people around me and the planet, have I contemplated that with sufficient perspicacity or wisdom, and have I contributed to all this sufficiently, or stimulated others to do that (or both)?" If the answers to these types of questions do not reach a threshold of comfort, the person might feel that the life lived did not have meaning, and despair and disappointment will set in.

The depression might be quite heightened in a hypo type. The hyper type might be quite over-invested in false ego-inflating activity. In the former type, there might be a social conformity assuaging the despair/depression. In the latter type, the deep despair/disappointment might be expressed in a surface anger bristling against the other, who is considered meaningless and without any type of integrity.

Self-Response to Cognitive (Mis)perception of the Other

The person reaching the later adult period and having passed through major life tasks enters into a phase termed ego integrity vs. despair in Erikson's lifespan stage theory. This stage parallels the cognitive one of the present model of Collective Intelligence multiplication in which super-ordinate abstract systems propagate throughout the cognitive architecture of the person. This capacity affords the person the ability to create super-ordinate abstract operational schemes that can relate the cognitive models built for the major life domains lived and themes considered while building, as well, linkages across them. These systems will necessarily include one for the self, the other, and their linkages. The other will be perceived as a co-participant in a life well-lived, perhaps the subject of multiple generativity acts, perhaps as peoples well-respected and even defended, perhaps as a long-term romantic partner, etc. The self will be understood as an actor who made choices to help the other in multiple ways – living a life of support of the other; helping the planet (fauna, flora), too; etc. The person who despairs of a meaningless life with no ego integrity will be disappointed/depressed, and the mood will extend into the core components of the self/I.

It is as if the person is saying – Why did I make those self-centered choices; I lived a life focused on my little pleasures and avoided large stresses instead of seeing the futility of that lifestyle, etc. My life has been joyless and empty instead of satisfying and acceptable? I did not work through troubles but receded into myself and let the troubles take on a permanent life of their own that I assiduously avoided in my self-core. I did not keep my composure, reach out to the other in need, and now feel absolutely alone. I wanted a useful life, but it ended up useless. My focus was on myself and that did not grow with time but became increasingly sad and had feelings of meaninglessness. Too bad I did not see the big picture and see the importance of people, the planet, the smiling child, and the person in need of help. I stood alone and am alone. I saw the other as not worthy of anything from me. I saw people as deserving their aloneness and their insatisfactions. I did not see that they had meaning not only for themselves but also for me. It made me a mean person – perhaps not hateful, but spiteful, rejecting, indifferent, etc. The other is more than I had imagined, and now I can only imagine a future that is forlorn and lonely (even if some people might be around).

Positive Pole in Eriksonian Development

The person having experienced a positive passage through the major steps in the life course, and having taken on the multiple adult challenges with at least a modicum of success while having been sensitive and helpful to the other, will look back on life with satisfaction and a pleasant feeling that could extend even to sublime joy. The person will feel that life has meaning, her/his life had been acceptable, and the other deserves the help received. The person will not decry the inevitable losses in life in this age period, feel morose at the failures that accompanied the successes, despair at a sense of emptiness, or otherwise lament the meaningless of life. Spirituality and pondering one's place in the universe will help.

Negative Social-Self Working Schema

The elderly person who has difficulty looking back at her/his life for the meaningless feeling it projects also will look at the other with a negative attitude. The person will have placed barriers between self and other and regret the sense of emptiness created. Instead of thinking, "I have been worthy of love all my life by the other" and "I have received love from the other all my life," the person will sense an abject failure in these regards and feel loveless and not having loved. The attitude will extend to any other who will be evaluated in any way as not being worthy of help/love. The other might be viewed as a joyless object in the subjective world of the person, a desolate, devastated entity, whose sense of despair is of no concern to the person. But the same desolation/devastation/despair could infiltrate the core self of the person and confirm that life is filled with losses, and never has been satisfying and acceptable, as the social isolation that had been created becomes a daily and endless reality.

Attachment, Neo-Eriksonian Development, Therapeutic Implications [Patients and Therapy]

Patient Presentation

The person expressing a joyless, meaningless sense of her/his life will despair at the losses, emptiness, and isolation experienced. The person might have significant others around her/him but still perceive life in these disappointed, downtrodden terms. There will be little that brings satisfaction, little accepted in the life course, and the life review will be pessimistic and hopeless. The person will not be able to activate the underlying cognitive skill of this age period and create positive super-ordinate abstract systems that are multiplying out and interrelating in links, or, to the contrary, the person will have created a structure in these regards that is marked by the types of negative moods and outlooks described, both for the self and in viewing the other.

Behavioral/Symptom Mental Scanning

The elder adult asked to mentally scan for her/his problems because life seems meaningless will be able to point out that lack of meaning, but might not know why. The person will feel the despair/isolation, but not be able to find solutions, for example, by improving social relations. There will be a give-up/I can't attitude that the therapist will have to deal with. Life will be seen as dissatisfied, dispirited, disappointing, and pointless. The other will not even be acknowledged or noticed in the struggle to find joy, but the therapist can have the patient recreate some joyful moments in the past toward creating a more satisfying affectivity about living and the future.

Therapeutic Implications

The despairing older adult looking back with an empty feeling about the meaninglessness of her/his life will need to scour for moments in the past when she/he had been helpful/caring to other people, when negative choices were possible, but those choices were left aside, when the person could find some satisfaction in the present context and so on. Meaning is what we make of it, much life could still be left for the person to find it, and the person still could be helpful in one way or another. The existential questions related to spirituality, one's place in the world, and so on, could be broached as well. Meaning exists on many planes.

Stress-Trauma Resilience/Coping

The person destitute of meaning in her/his life as the older adult period unfolds will be less capable of dealing with stress/trauma than otherwise would be the case. The resources necessary, both personal and social, will be lacking. The person might not react at all to the stress/trauma, being too depressed/despairing, or the person might be so overwhelmed that chronic anxiety cannot dissipate in any way. The meaningless of life will feel quite exacerbated either way and the ego that much more shattered.

Therapeutic Strategies [the Other and Change]

Relational Co-regulation

The person who despairs at life's emptiness will not have anchored the self to the other in any constructive, positive, helpful way and will be left rudderless on her/his remaining life voyage. The self will be a weary one, with little interactive engagements, joy, and sense of integrity. The I of the self will be by itself and the other will be cast adrift without any relationship to the person. The person will need to find when she/he had experienced any positive relationship with any other. The person could examine the nature of the relationship and how the other interfaced with the self, so the person can have a take-home message toward creating a more positive relational co-relation with another in the time remaining.

Behavior/Symptom Network/Connectivity Change (Horizontal)

The elderly person embedded in desolation at life's meaninglessness will not be able to escape the despairing feeling of desolation and the social reality of perceived isolation and loneliness. The person will be ruminating over the multiplicity of life losses and failures and will regret the emptiness of her/his relations with others. Dissatisfaction will lurk in every corner of life examined. The fractured self will seep with disappointments at life and in the other for failing to improve life. The person will not know how she/he, by herself/himself, can improve it. The therapist will face the great challenge of moving the elderly person out of her/his doldrums. The conundrums of how to proceed will require an eclectic, individualized approach that uses the best-fitting therapeutic tools in the tool box, but common factors will be more important than any technique. The therapist can seek moments of inner peace in the past of the individual and build from there. This will help prepare the last phases of life.

Behavior/Symptom Growth, Deep Change (Vertical)/Constructing a More Positive Life Story

The elderly person gaining some semblance of positivity about the past will be better able to move into the last phases of life. Empty despair will turn toward a fulfilled joy to some extent, preparing for contemplation and acceptance of death. The person will integrate some type of spirituality and a feeling of oneness with life, the past, the present, and whatever the future holds. Wisdom will permeate to a degree the end-of-life cycle and bring a cathartic feeling of universal human and planetary/world connection. The elderly person looking back at a life without meaning can begin to tell stories that reframe some of the experiences in the past more constructively. The person can begin to reach out to people in her/his life, or even neighbors/strangers met in stores, etc. and tell how they are finding meaning in the smallest and presumably insignificant contacts with other people, even with pets of people, etc. Meaning is constructed from these collected seconds of positive and helpful interactions over a lifetime, and the person can rejoice in each of the incidents in the time left of this nature and tell new narratives about the self, the other, and their relationships.

Consciousness, Theory of Mind, Selves, Responsibility

People having issues with the meaningless of life will have difficulty in the foci of their consciousness, relations with other, finding positives in the self, sense of morality and the respect for the sanctity of life, and the humanity of all peoples and the planet. Life will seem to have been wasted, and wisdom will seem something beyond their ken as the last phases of life rear on the horizon. Spirituality will be rejected and asking existential questions avoided. The therapist will examine the range of joyless despair in all the nooks and crannies of the patients' rumination of the past, resignation to the present, and the dread of the future and have them work through toward acceptance and a sense of plentitude to the degree possible. Shedding light helps illuminate life, including in its final phases.

The Collective Intelligence Stage Sub-stage of Integration (61 Plus Years): Sub-stage 25

Self and Relational Development [Initial Theoretical Elaborations]

A very brief description of the present step in Young's 25-step Neo-Eriksonian developmental model follows. It is presented again in Chap. 18, to help give a collective overview of the 25 steps in the modeling.

Cathartic (purifying) acts vs. abandonment acts (61 years and after). No matter the age, the person facing death looks back fondly and faces it without fear. You have a broad, wise view of life, how your life was lived, and what death means. You prepare for death with some form of inner peace and spirituality. But if there are problems this way, you will feel alone and abandoned by life at its last moments, and struggle with inner peace, spirituality, and death itself. You might seek last-minute help.

Appendix 5.5 gives the brief amount of work already done in prior publications related to the task of developing in depth the Neo-Eriksonian (sub)stage model. The next section of the chapter gives an interim summary that elaborates the contents of Appendix 5.5 with respect to the present sub-stage being considered, of the sub-stage of Collective Intelligence Stage Sub-stage of Integration.

Full Summary

The end-of-life phase could be associated with a sense of oneness with humanity, the infinity of the universe, and the unknown or presumed known of the afterlife. The phase could be cathartic, purifying, spiritual, freeing of the struggle and stresses that life has wrought, and freeing of illness/disease and disability/infirmity. It could be a phase surrounded by loved ones, times for reminiscing, remembering the joys of a lifetime, and being thankful for having survived and resolved the many trials and tribulations of life. The person has a broad, wise view of life, how life was lived, and what death means, and so feels an inner peace and spirituality. By this point in time and often much earlier, the person might have developed a cognitive apparatus of super-ordinate abstract logic that is integrated. This acquisition could have developed decades earlier and helped shepherd the person through the toughest of times through the wisdom that it helps facilitate (along with other socio-emotional acquisitions, support, etc.).

The person could be living a phase of psychological completeness/maturity that had lasted decades and with a full undertaking of re-responsibilities, acting on higher-order morality, etc. The person might feel communion with the other, the planet, etc. and experience a deep resonance and reverence with her/his personal sense of holiness and holistic merging with any world beyond the immediate one. The end-of-life is a time of transcendence from earthly realities and bodily concerns, to the best that the mind can do in these regards. Mysteries abound, but at this point in time, answers that are believed about them are accepted graciously. Or, answers to them that soothe the person are constructed, heard, or otherwise incorporated to bring to the person a final peace. The answers in these regards add to the sense of tranquility experienced and contribute to looking forward to death instead of fearing it. The I is an integrated one and is part of the communion with the We that makes for a composed fellowship with one's spiritual source.

However, people struggling with end-of-life issues might feel that the world/other/life/universe has abandoned them. They feel turbulence instead of wisdom, fall back instead of look forward, feel impure rather than purified, feel irrelevant instead of being reverent, feel unintegrated instead of integrated, and feel spiritually alone instead of spiritually transcendent. They are without an overarching vision of the life lived and the fate awaiting them and without any connecting fellowship with any other/humanity, mystery, and the infinity. The self feels miserable even fearful. The other is totally discounted, nonexistent. Instead of catharsis in the end-point experience of life, the person feels shut out and shuts out, self-imploding before expiring, and not allowing any other into the last circle. The other as anything spiritual is extinguished, and is pared down to an anti-other, with no human properties, no interest in the person or for the person (an attitude promulgated by the behavior of the person as much as anything else).

The person might even desire not to have any last relationships, with relational co-regulation excluded as much as the other. The ability to deal with final stress/trauma will be completely negated. The person will not recognize the other, being incapable of perceiving their misery, if present. Rather, the person will be perceiving life as escaping and death as abandonment.

The therapist working with patients like this will try to give some support to the degree possible and seek to salve the hurt as best she/he can. In therapy, the person might be able to make some progress toward acceptance of the other and death and move into some sort of spiritual communion. The therapist will need to let the glimmers toward that light increase by the good will and effort of the patient, if any can manifest, and by being fully present in the moment. The person could develop a last-minute reprieve from the utter banality or even meaningless that she/he had perceived in the life lived. Therapists can help facilitate that growth in the end-state of a human life. End-of-life conflicts can be integrated into better visions both for patient and therapist, taking the context of the life lived into consideration.

Having reached the end of the description of the 25 lifespan steps in development as conceived in the present model, I remind that the typical ages associated with each step are normative, or averages, and that each person's individual developmental trajectory will vary greatly compared to the average. Moreover, as development proceeds into the later steps, everything else being equal, many people will not arrive at the penultimate steps in the way indicated. For example, each of us, as we face end of life issues, will reflect on the past and wonder about what follows death, if anything. However, this does not mean that we will do it with the cognitive sophistication described for the last step of the present model. The same message applies for each step of the model. For example, identity is a constant theme in development, but it might not take place with the cognitive underpinning and complexity described for the step at issue in the present model.

Reference

Young, G. (2011). *Development and causality: Neo-Piagetian perspectives*. New York: Springer Science + Business Media

Chapter 18
Book Conclusions

Abstract This chapter ends the book on a positive note. It refers to the role of causality, development, the present Neo-Piagetian/Neo-Eriksonian model in development, activation-inhibition coordination, and so on and how these notions can contribute to the project of unifying psychology.

The first portion of the book consists of an exposition of the development of laterality and proposes the value of viewing behavior and its causation in terms of activation-inhibition coordination. This portion of the book also examines a stage/sub-stage model in these regards based on my Neo-Piagetian 25-step model, in particular. The second portion of the book explains in great depth for the first time the 25-step Neo-Eriksonian model that parallels the Neo-Piagetian one. This model is much more differentiated than Erikson's eight-stage model, which would give it advantages both in understanding lifespan development and applying it clinically in therapy. It is a normative model developmentally but allows for individual variability.

The clinician could work with the model to better understand patients. At the same time, no theory, treatment procedure, test, diagnostic manual, and so on can be applied straightforward without accommodation to the particular patients being assessed/treated, and much clinical skill is required in this sense to work with the model presented. That said, the extrapolation from the normative situation in psychology, whether in understanding the person or treating the patient, requires scientific rigor in generalization from normative knowledge. Working with this model therapeutically will require scientific acumen and a knowledge base to make using it effective. The second half of the book is aimed at increasing the normative knowledge of patient development, thereby allowing for scientific reasoning to take hold and be applied effectively to any patient at hand.

Generally, the book elaborates on my conceptions of causality (Young, 2016) and my Neo-Piagetian/Neo-Eriksonian 25-step stage/sub-stage model (Young, 2011). It merits its description as the third book in the series of three books on causality and development. The three-book series has the advantage of explaining my Neo-Piagetian/Neo-Eriksonian model in one publishing venue (Springer SBM/International; as well see an article by Young, 2012).

G. Young, *Causality and Development*,
https://doi.org/10.1007/978-3-030-02493-2_18

Also the model is so extensive that it can serve as an integrating framework to hitch ongoing empirical work. For example, the research on executive function (EF) is burgeoning, but can it be explained in terms of qualitative advances in development, as per a (sub)stage model? In this regard, Barkley (2012) had proposed a model of EF development that is compatible with the present model (Young, 2016). The research might show longitudinal associations from earlier to later life, and even over the lifespan, but linear, quantitative findings do not necessarily indicate qualitative shifts in development. This type of research finding could be examined for changes in behavior from one age to the next, and if that is done well, it might be easier to see associations of findings to extant (sub)stage models. However, if these latter models are imprecise, not nuanced, too vague, untestable, invalid, and so on, it makes no sense to try to use them as umbrellas to explain isolated, siloed findings. However, with the better precision, differentiation, testability, and presumed validity of the present sub-stage model compared to the ones it built on (Piaget, Erikson, Case, Fischer, etc.), the project of relating empirical findings on pertinent topics to the model makes more sense. Undertaking endeavors like these will be enriching both to the present sub-stage model and to the empirical enterprise in psychology and further underscore the value of the present model.

The same applies to the book series approach to causality. It offers a vast frame to integrate causality as a unifying theme in psychology. By integrating on an ongoing basis concepts and findings related to causality to the contents of three books in the series on causality and development, including the present one, psychology as a field might acquire more unity.

Young's (2016) review of the causality of behavior was exceedingly comprehensive but did miss a few primary sources. For example, Ryan and Deci (2017) reviewed their self-determination theory, and one chapter presents their causality orientation theory and scales to measure it. In this regard, the autonomy orientation, controlled orientation, and interpersonal orientation are the major "motivational" orientations. However, the nature of these orientations might not be causal in the sense described here.

Also, for determining whether therapy is causally effective, Kazdin (2009) offered criteria to determine if genuine change has taken place in the research on the topic. He emphasized mediators, moderators, mechanisms, etc. Young (2016) did mention equivalent approaches to causality.

Note that the approach of psychodynamic psychotherapy also views causality of symptoms as multi-factorial both among symptoms and reciprocally across symptoms and core conflicts. "[C]ore conflicts can influence symptoms, symptoms can influence core conflicts, and symptom can influence one another" (Cohen, McElhaney, & Jensen, 2018, p. 2). This approach speaks to the network concept that permeates the present book.

Knight (2016) used Erikson's eight-stage lifespan model to link psychodynamic psychotherapy with it. She related each of the eight stages to a virtue (e.g., hope for Trust vs. Mistrust). Also, she re-transcribed the stages into a step model for psychodynamic psychotherapy (e.g., the search for courage in trust). She considered that a patient might need help with more than one-stage passage. My similar work examines the positive and negative themes in development at each step in the 25-step

Neo-Eriksonian model. The 25 themes give a much more detailed and nuanced examination of critical organizers that could be used in psychotherapy than the virtues in Knight's model. Moreover, I have reworked Haidt's foundational moral motives into my Neo-Maslovian model, which is somewhat similar to Knight's virtue approach (see Table 13.1 in Chap. 13).

Beyond these similarities and improvements in the approaches of Knight and myself to patients confronting difficulties at multiple levels or (sub)stages in the Eriksonian/Neo-Eriksonian sense, consider that my models of multiple cognitive and of multiple emotional intelligences address similar matters. In the present yoking concept, conceptual filters/behaviors/problem-solving strategies that are associated with one sub-stage or another of the present Neo-Piagetian/Neo-Eriksonian model can be combined with others according to ongoing/online needs of adaptation. Therefore, the combinations used in this yoking mechanism might end up functionally maladaptive because of a variety of reasons, including poor habits developing along these lines through improper environmental support at one or more sub-stages as development is traversed. In this sense, according to the model, irrationality can exist at multiple levels and in multiple combinations, both in the cognitive and socio-emotional realms or in both together. The complexity of the irrationality that stems from these developmental possibilities greatly complicates both the presentation of the irrationality and how one might proceed in dealing with it therapeutically.

The present model proposes, then, that there are many ways that the person can be irrational, with more pervasive, deeper-seated irrationality associated with the lower levels of model. For example, irrationality that is associated with thinking reflexively only will have quite a different presentation than an irrationality associated with distorted or malign abstract thought. Cognitive distortions themselves are presented too simplistically in the literature in that they can reflect more lower-level or more upper-level sub-stages of the present model. The classic formulation of blockages in development relates to fixation and regression. However, the cognitive distortions/appraisals/socio-emotional filters, etc. associated with each type could be so varied and differentiated according to developmental experiences that the irrationality reflected will be equally complex. Finally, individuals might be living a hypo and hyper type according to difficulties that they have at any one sub-stage of the present model, or multiples of them, further complicating the nature of the distortions, fixations, regressions, etc., in the irrationality presented by the individual.

Causal theory is spreading to the inner and outer reaches of our experience. Causal set theory describes the building blocks of space as events that are related to each other by a web of "cause-and-effect" (Musser, 2018). Integrated information theory describes consciousness emanating from complex, interconnected mechanisms in which their structure encodes a set of "cause-and-effect relationships" (Koch, 2018). Both for the inner mind and the outer universe, causality might be the primary characteristic of the constituents and mechanisms involved. This would support my description of humans as being "Homo Causa," both in how we think and how we understand behavior and its context (Young, 2016). In this regard, Sanefuji and Haryu (2018) found that, in preschoolers, understanding psychological causality in a story picture sequence (e.g., being surprised not to see a teddy bear in its place when it had been taken surreptitiously) related to understanding others' false beliefs according to standard false-belief task performance. To carry this argument further and relate it to the proposed 25-step Neo-Eriksonian sequence that is at the heart of the present book, perhaps creating ourselves as Homo Causa could be one more identity domain in Eriksonian theory and elucidating it and understanding its ramifications could be one more domain in the institution of Eriksonian generativity and so on.

Another concept in Young (2016) that deserves further work relative to the stage/sub-stage model presented in this book concerns the concept of "freedom in being." Essentially, it refers to the product of psychological freedom and the ongoing, indeterminate process of arriving and transcending the present state in this regard. It consists of components, such as having a sense of freedom and holding a belief in free will (Baumeister, 2008). In Young (2016), I related the concept of Freedom in Being to Heidegger's concept of *Dasein*, or Being in the World. Another relevant precursor concept of freedom concerns May's (1981) distinction between existential and essential freedom, which concerns one's freedom to choose and the inner sense of freedom, respectively. A more differentiated concept of freedom relative to all these ideas concerns adding political freedom, or the appraisal that one has it. In this vein, it would be best to speak of "socio-cultural political freedom," because constraints in this regard extend to family, racism, etc. Future work on freedom should elaborate the appropriate psychological freedom types (e.g., functional, or decisional, freedom, as per Lau and Hiemisch, 2017, and ethical freedom, or generalized trust, as per Zagonari, 2016) and the role of related concepts, such as consciousness (Baumeister, Lau, Maranges, & Clark, 2018) and a sense of responsibilities (Young, 2016, and this current book). Finally, future work should examine how various freedom types evolve through the later steps of the present 25-step model in Neo-Eriksonian development, especially those concerning adolescence and adulthood. Furthermore, other concepts relevant to adolescence and adult development could be examined within the passage of these Neo-Eriksonian steps, such as appreciation of advanced moral and ethical values (as per Young, 2017).

Summary of the 25-Step Neo-Eriksonian Lifespan Developmental Socio-affective Model

The following gives the brief description of each step in the current five stage x five sub-stage (25-step) Neo-Eriksonian model by collecting together the brief descriptions made for each in Chap. 13–17. I add a brief introduction and scoring device in order to facilitate their use either clinically, toward making an inventory, or both.

25 Questions on Growth and Problems Over the Lifespan: Explanation and the Questions

Here is a questionnaire with 25 questions for you to answer. Please read each one carefully, and respond on the answer key. The questions are about possible problems you had in growing or developing.

Note

The following explanation of the present questionnaire can be used to help get information from it. It could help whether it is used by: interviewers in the clinical setting, for example, psychiatrists, psychologists; given to respondents directly before they answer, for example, with paper and pencil; or used in research in one way or another, for example, online. The questionnaire administrator can use any section of the explanation for the purposes at hand, or all of it, as might be required. The questionnaire can be given once to get a snapshot, or several times to get a picture of change. The change could be over three different ages, or more, in a longitudinal study. It could be about change before, during, and after therapy, and so on.

The present questionnaire includes 25 questions, and they are based on a model of growth or development from early in life to the end of life. Erik Erikson created a model of eight steps in human growth or development. The eight steps cover all ages from birth to the elderly period. Erikson referred to the steps in growth as "stages." Each step was viewed as very different from the step that grew before it. He thought that each step was formed by combined influences. Growth has biological influences (for example, psychological sexual impulses) and environmental ones (for example, parental). Erikson described each of the eight steps of his model in both positive and negative terms. For example, one stage is about finding "Identity" in adolescence, and that could be easy to do (positive) or it could be hard (negative). Also, the important problem related to each step in growth could end up being both positive and negative, in a mixture (for example, the adolescent is still seeking identity because he hasn't created one yet and is still searching). Also, the major problem (called "issue") at a particular step in growth might not appear at the age it is supposed to. For example, it could become important for the person at any other step. For instance, finding identity is not a problem that is limited to teenagers. Identity problems could appear in adulthood, for example, at mid-life, too.

The 25-step growth model being described to you covers all the ages in development (the model was created by Gerald Young, in 2019). As mentioned, it is built on Erik Erikson's model of eight steps (or stages) in growth. This model covers all the ages of life by adding 17 steps to Erikson's model of eight steps. These steps begin from the early pre-natal period. And they go to the very late elderly period. That is, the steps start to develop before birth, and continue right into the oldest ages.

How do we get to 25 steps in the new model from eight steps in the other model? In Young's model, there are five major growth periods. These growth periods involve the following: (1). before birth/birth; (2). infancy; (3). childhood; (4). adolescence; and (5). adulthood. Each of these five periods includes 5 steps (sub-stages). So there are 25 steps in total in the model (5 periods x 5 steps). Because Young's growth model has 25 steps and not only eight, his model has a lot more detail compared to Erikson's growth model.

So we will examine the 25 steps of life and where you fit in. For example, do you have problems with any of the 25 steps over all the ages of life, and what ages did the problems begin—in the ages when each step starts, or before, or later on? As the person grows, problems can appear at any time. For example, the step of trust develops in the first year of life but problems in trust can develop any time.

Having trust in people is one area where things can go wrong, but there are 25 possible problems described in the 25-step model. The problems or negative side of each step could develop for anybody. So problems could develop for you in any of the 25 steps of the model. Here is the critical question for you—Did any of the listed 25 problems develop for you, such as having problems in trusting people or in finding your identity?

Even though the 25-step model indicates that problems might develop at any age (e.g., trust problems can develop after infancy; identity problems can develop before or after adolescence), the 25-step model sticks to the typical case of problems developing according to the steps that they go with. That is, the questionnaire based on the model gives the average ages when the problems could become very important for you.

So the 25-step model ends up describing 25 steps in growth, with each one having one major problem that can develop in it. Once any one psychology problem develops as you grow, it can last into the steps that follow too, making the problems at later steps even worse. So your growth could involve several problems together from different steps. This will make the combined problems that much harder for you to deal with.

What about the causes of the problems that you might have? The problems could develop because the environment has problems (such as in parenting or poverty). Or, the problems could appear because of problems in biology (such as in brain development). Or, the problems could happen because of problems in psychology (such as poor coping skills for stress). Therefore, Young calls the 25-step model that he created "biopsychosocial." However, mostly, he describes the environmental problems that a person might have (e.g., in parenting). This approach is clear in the questions that you are asked to answer below (later).

It must be very hard to look at yourself to decide which steps in growth have been more difficult for you. Which growth steps in your life have led to problems that are still bothering you? It would be even harder to decide what are your major problems when there are several of them and they make each other worse. Also, it must be very hard to look at yourself for your problems when your problems might appear only after the time or age period they normally do. For example, what if identity becomes a problem in the middle of the life? Also, it surely is hard to figure out the causes of the problems that you might be having. Maybe the environment wasn't a good support when you were growing up (e.g., parents, or there was poverty). Maybe your body or brain was not as best as it could be. For example, you began taking too much alcohol or marijuana that could affect your body and brain. Maybe you just didn't know how to cope with stress.

Whatever the causes, I am especially interested in finding out what are your major problems as defined by Young's model of 25 steps in growth. Erikson spoke of trust in infancy, for example, compared to mistrust. Is that an issue for you? It might be even if you are not sure when trust problems first developed. For sure, you cannot remember what happened in infancy. But maybe trust did not develop well even back then, and the trust problem never left as you continued to grow in childhood. Therefore, the trust problems that might have developed in you when you were very young might still be there. Or, as I said, it could have developed later, for example, you had a bad adult relationship and don't trust any possible partner anymore.

The following presents the 25 exact questions of the questionnaire based on the 25 steps of a growth model that covers all the ages of life, and in a simple way. For example, although trust normally develops in infancy, the list of 25 growth steps mentions trust in a general way that could apply to any age, not just infancy. The list takes the same approach for each of the 25 steps in the model. Maybe a problem is supposed to start in childhood but is only happening now. That is, even though the model is about growth over the lifespan, the list below is not so concerned in finding out the exact age when each of your problems started. Instead, you need to tell me how much each problem that goes with the 25 steps in growth is bothering you right now, even if you are not sure when each problem started. Some questions will make little sense to you because they are about older people and you are younger. Or, you are older and the questions are for younger people. Just try your best and think about each question to see what is bothering you now.

Note that each question refers to "you" to make the questions more personal, but the questions can be about anyone. Each question tells a story that could be about you in every detail or most details, but they could not apply to you at all. The questions give the wording in the original model, for example, Trust vs. Mistrust, but the explanations offered help explain harder words. Finally, the questions give the average ages when the problems in each question appear as childhood and adulthood go on, but these ages are only averages and might not work for you. Just try your best and think about each question to see what is bothering you now. [If you are younger than the age indicated for any one step or question, this step in life or question about it could still worry you as you think about problems in the future or feel that you will be unprepared for it. So do not exclude answering questions on later ages as they still might apply to you.]

Please indicate one of the answers for each question, which are about whether you have problems in the present related to the 25 steps in development. The possible answers go from +3 to −3. The answer +3 means: no problem/doing fine. The answer −3 means: big problem/in crisis. The following 7 points give all the choices that you need to answer all the questions:

Positive side	+3. This is no problem for me. I am doing very well with it; it is quite a positive for me
	+2. Dealing with this well, although in the middle of dealing with it
	+1. Don't really think about it, I just follow advice and think/act like other people do about it who are around me
Negative side	0. I am "not sure" what to say; This question does not apply to me; it's "not applicable"
	−1. This is a problem for me, but I put it aside, on a backburner, because I don't have to or don't want to deal with it
	−2. I am not dealing well with this. It is confusing to me as I try, and is a problem for me
	−3. This is a major problem for me and I am not doing well with it. It is quite a negative in my life

25 Questions on the Steps in Growth

1. **Distance Acts vs. No (Lifeless) Acts (early fetal life)**. Even from very early on, people could be rejected a lot, and even severely abused. Their life is at risk (any torture fits here). If this happened to you, you could react by wanting to kill yourself and behaving to hurt yourself. In general, your behavior is very reflexive, not directed well or on target toward its goal. It is disorganized in its movement, even with wrong distances to targets. Perhaps you feel it's hard to move and feel lifeless.
2. **Nursing Acts vs. Rootless Acts (fairly premature)**. As you grew, starting in the early nursing period, you experienced major abuse and your self was denied or not allowed to grow. You grew feeling that you had no anchor, or were missing roots. You felt helpless and hopeless. Also, you did not feel like caring for yourself. This might have led you to not care for anybody. You felt the same way even when you became a parent (or will feel that way when you have children one day).
3. **Outcome Acts vs. Outcast Acts (that excluded you) (somewhat premature)**. From early in life, you developed simple goals, and tried to reach them. They got you what you wanted. But maybe the environment (parent) did not even support this basic activity and you were disregarded and not allowed to have any goals. You were treated like an outcast, or not belonging to anything, and were not allowed to speak or be what you wanted. Maybe you became the same way, and greatly ignored people and ignored yourself.
4. **Care-Giving Acts vs. Careless Giving Acts (full-term newborn)**. Normally, right from birth, newborns develop a beginning self based on the body and actions, like grasping a finger. But the environment (parent) might not treat the baby well—being negligent and even abusive sometimes. Perhaps the environment (your parent) was uncaring or gave you poor care because of this. So, as you grew, you began to not care for yourself. Or, maybe you went the other way by constantly trying to seek care, but without knowing how.
5. **Emotional Acts vs. Mal-Emotional or Negative Emotional Acts (0–1 month)**. Early in life, babies often are emotionally content. But from early on, you were very emotional, frustrated, unhappy, and even were in rage, fear, or both. The environment (parent) was not supportive, and did not deal well with your emotions, leading you to have further emotional turmoil or trouble. As you grew, you continued to express a lot of negative emotions, or perhaps you went in the opposite direction, showing no emotions and feeling detached.
6. **Dyadic Acts vs. Dys-Dyadic or Poor Interaction Acts (1–4 months)**. Normally, the growing infant is learning how to interact the right way with people. But even then, you experienced a non-supportive environment (parent). It involved too much control, domination, and manipulation. The result was that, as you grew, you did not learn to interact with people the right way. You were not warm or sensitive. Instead, you were clumsy and confused socially, and could withdraw in silence. Or, perhaps you were angry and rejected people.

7. **Trust Acts vs. Mistrust Acts (4–8 months)**. In the first year of life, normally the infant develops a sense of trust or confidence in people. But if the environment (parent) is not supportive, the person might not be able to trust people and create any close relationships. If this happened to you, also you might feel down and without purpose, and be passive or suspicious. Perhaps you became angry inside, too. Or, instead perhaps you trusted blindly anybody else (and were taken advantage of by them).
8. **Sociability Acts vs. Un-Sociability or Poor Sociability Acts (8–12 months)**. Normally, the growing person develops social behavior that helps create positive relationships. This starts in infancy, including in positive attachment to the parent. However, without good parental/care-giver support, a person could develop insecure attachments and not be good socially even after. Social behavior becomes avoidant, fearful, rejecting, or ambivalent. If this happened to you, perhaps you attached to anybody without being careful about it. Or, perhaps you totally avoided any relations, being super wary and isolated.
9. **Autonomy (Independence) Acts vs. Doubt (Dependence) Acts (12–18 months)**. Normally, like the toddler, we become eager and act for ourselves, feel confident in exploration, and feel satisfied in social behavior. But perhaps your environment (parent) did not give you good support of your independent activity, and you ended up feeling dependent and not confident. You found it hard to take initiative and explore. You become inward and dissatisfied. You even felt dominated. Or, you went the other way; and you became defiant, argumentative, and not cooperative.
10. **Interdigitational (Give and Take) Acts vs. De-Digitational (Give or Take) Acts (18–24 months)**. As we grow, we learn to interact with give and take (not just giving or taking). But if you did not receive environmental support (parenting) for this, you might have difficulty in sharing, being concerned for others, and feeling fondness and even love. Instead, you might hate people. As for sense of yourself, you might not feel self-pride and even hate yourself. Maybe you seek too much power or avoid confrontation, so people manipulate you easily.
11. **Super-Ordinate (Well-Coordinated) Acts vs. Dis-Coordinate (Uncoordinated) Acts (2–3.5 years)**. Normally, we feel "together" (the parts of my self are super coordinated) and do not think that we are "in pieces" (not coordinated). But if your environment (parent) was not supportive this way (was controlling, for example), you did not develop to feel together and felt "in pieces." So you put your personal needs in the middle of everything (being "egocentric," self-centered). Perhaps you were somewhat resistant, too. Or, perhaps you always accepted whatever other people wanted.
12. **Initiative Acts vs. Guilt Acts (3.5–5 years)**. The growing person balances being forward (in initiative) and being inward and withdrawing. The person could feel guilty when being too forward. For example, pre-schoolers might have sexual feelings for the parent (of the opposite sex) that are too forward and do not go away, even without knowing it. If the environment (your parent) does not handle this well, you could develop unconscious (unaware) sexual prob-

lems that continue into adolescence onwards, or general problems in initiative (having too much or too little).

13. **Identification and Gender Acts vs. Problematic Identification and Gender Acts (5–7 years)**. In growing, we identify with, or want to be like people who are around, especially parents. This helps you learn about and act like the gender that you prefer. But your environment (parent) might not be supportive about this. This could create problems for you, including not wanting to be like the parent or becoming opposite to how is the parent. Or, perhaps you do not identify with anyone, and have become narcissistic, uncontrollable, etc.
14. **Industry (Putting in Good Effort) Acts vs. Inferiority Acts (7–9 years)**. In growing, normally we enjoy learning, including at school, feel motivated, and develop peer friendships. However, your environment (parent) could have shown little interest in your learning, manipulated you, created harsh rules, etc. This could have led you to lose interest in school and learning, lose self-confidence, have the wrong friends, feel inferior, and even rebel. Or, perhaps you went the other way, and felt too superior, while you became insensitive and lied as needed.
15. **Role/Personality Tryout Acts vs. Role/Personality Confusion Acts (9–11 years)**. The growing person tries out different roles, friends, attitudes, and personalities, both for the challenge and having fun. If you had problems in the environment supporting tryouts such as these, maybe you had a hard time exploring them, or explored them too much but on the surface only. So you became confused in your tryouts, and stopped them. Or, you tried out negative (e.g., anti-social) tryouts in roles/personalities (and you felt different moods, including brooding).
16. **Consciousness (Being Aware) Acts vs. Contra-Conscious (Not Being Aware) Acts (11–13 years)**. Once the thinking of people becomes logical and abstract, such as in the teen years, they can develop an awareness of the self, other people, the environment, society, and their place in the world. If your environment (parent) was not supportive of this type of thinking and opening, you had difficulties in being aware like this. Perhaps you were less conscious and more conforming than normal, or you were conscious but in fanatical or superficial ways.
17. **Identity Acts (Positive Ones) vs. Identity Diffusion (or Negative Identity) Acts (13–16 years)**. The growing person explores different identities, selves, or questions of "Who I am." Your environment (parent) could interfere in creating a positive identity that you like. This could lead you to: (a) confusion in identity; (b) putting off the search for identity; (c) simply adopting identities of other people without thinking about it; (d) adopting negative identities, such as in teenage gangs/delinquency; or (e) adopting many identities, but all surface, false, or fake ones.
18. **Nurturing Acts vs. Mis-Nurturing (Not Nurturing) Acts (16–19 years)**. The growing person engages in caring behavior of other people, to give them support and bring out the best in them. The environment (parent) might not support nurturing, and the person will not nurture or care for people. If this happened to you, this will affect your social relationships. Perhaps you will ignore people,

not like them, and so on. Or, perhaps you will nurture people a lot, but only on the surface and without real caring.

19. **Intimacy Acts (with Partner) vs. (Social) Isolation Acts (19–22 years)**. The growing person gives positive effort, including at work or in school, and with any romantic partner and any children. The person feels a deep, long-lasting love for the partner, if any is present, and feels deeply involved in everything done. Without environmental (parental) support (or with past problems), you could reject romance and feel lonely and empty. Or, you could go through the motions and be fake in any relationship with a partner, even behaving roughly.
20. **Universal (General Concern for All People) Acts vs. Self-Singular (Self-Focused) Acts (22–25 years)**. The growing adult is concerned for all people and desires to care for or help anybody in need. This is especially true for family, but could apply to anyone, too. There is a basic helping moral value felt about everybody. Without getting good support this way, you could become a person who rejects helping others, family and all people included, or only helps them without feeling (or just to get praise).
21. **Meta-Collecting (Seeing the Big Picture) Acts vs. Disillusionment Acts (25–28 years)**. The young adult could see the big picture of the world and all its interconnections at many joined levels. You could develop concern for the growth of all groups of peoples, wanting them capable of helping other peoples. If things go wrong this way, you could ignore or even act against other peoples, detesting them, and feel disillusioned/down. Or, you could help peoples only because you have been taught to, and you do it only superficially.
22. **Generativity (Generating) Acts vs. Self-Absorption (No Responsibility) Acts (28–39 years)**. Growing adults give their best to their responsibilities, from family and relationships, to work and study, to society. The conscious, identity, relating, and helping attitudes of the prior steps in life become real in all activities. If problems come up for whatever reason, you could let go your responsibilities, feel empty, focus only on yourself, and not grow. Or, you might try hard to take your responsibilities, but just on the surface or because of your training.
23. **Catalytic (Growing Others) Acts vs. Midlife Crisis Acts (39–50 years)**. Growing adults carry through with all their responsibilities so that everything around them grows or gets better. But problems could develop for you and cause you to let go all your responsibilities even though you had taken them all on well up to this point in time. You change and act just for the self. You reject loved ones, work, and all your responsibilities. Or, you could keep them and just go through the motions, feeling sad.
24. **Ego Integrity (Feeling Good About the Self and Life) Acts vs. Despair Acts (50–61 years)**. As the years go on, family and relationships grow, work or study continues, and perhaps you help people and society, depending on your situation. You feel comfortable about how life has gone. But if problems happen about this, you could feel very low, depressed, or disappointed. You regret not having given your best in life, not being fully present in everything done, etc. Also, perhaps you get angry, can't do anything, etc.

25. **Cathartic (Purifying) Acts vs. Abandonment Acts (61 years and after).** No matter the age, the person facing death looks back fondly and faces it without fear. You have a broad, wise view of life, how your life was lived, and what death means. You prepare for death with some form of inner peace and spirituality. But if there are problems this way, you will feel alone and abandoned by life at its last moments, and struggle with inner peace, spirituality, and death itself. You might seek last-minute help.

References

Barkley, R. A. (2012). *Executive functions: What they are, how they work, and why they evolved*. New York: The Guilford Press.

Baumeister, R. F. (2008). Free will in scientific psychology. *Perspectives on Psychological Science, 3*, 14–19.

Baumeister, R. F., Lau, S., Maranges, H. M., & Clark, C. J. (2018). On the necessity of consciousness for sophisticated human action. *Frontiers in Psychology, 9*, 1925. https://doi.org/10.3389/fpsyg.2018.01925

Cohen, J. N., McElhaney, R., & Jensen, D. (2018). The empirical examinability of psychodynamic psychotherapy: A reply to Hoffart and Johnson. *Clinical Psychological Science, 6*, 1–6. https://doi.org/10.1177/2167702617751887

Kazdin, A. E. (2009). Understanding how and why psychotherapy leads to change. *Psychotherapy Research, 19*, 418–428. https://doi.org/10.1080/10503300802448899

Knight, Z. G. (2016). A proposed model of psychodynamic psychotherapy linked to Erik Erikson's eight stages of psychosocial development. *Clinical Psychology and Psychotherapy, 24*, 1047–1058. https://doi.org/10.1002/cpp.2066

Koch, C. (2018, June). Toward a fundamental theory. *Scientific American, 318*, 61–64.

Lau, S., & Hiemisch, A. (2017). Functional freedom: a psychological model of freedom in decision-making. *Behavioral Science, 7*, 1–18.

May, R. (1981). *Freedom and destiny*. New York: W. W. Norton.

Musser, G. (2018, June). What is spacetime? *Scientific American, 318*, 55–58.

Nucci, L. (2018). Character: A developmental system. *Child Development Perspectives*. doi: 10.1111/cdep.12313

Ryan, R. M., & Deci, E. L. (2017). *Self-determination theory: Basic psychological needs in motivation, development, and wellness*. New York: Guilford Press.

Sanefuji, W., & Haryu, E. (2018). Preschoolers' development of theory of mind: The contribution of understanding psychological causality in stories. *Frontiers in Psychology, 9*, 955. https://doi.org/10.3389/fpsyg.2018.00955

Young, G. (2011). *Development and causality: Neo-Piagetian perspectives*. New York: Springer Science + Business Media.

Young, G. (2012). A unitary Neo-Piagetian/ Neo-Eriksonian model of development: Fundamental assumptions and meta-issues. *New Ideas in Psychology, 30*, 241–249. https://doi.org/10.1016/j.newideapsych.2011.11.002

Young, G. (2016). *Unifying causality and psychology: Being, brain and behavior*. Cham, Switzerland: Springer International Publishing.

Young, G. (2017). *Revising the APA ethics code*. Cham, Switzerland: Springer International Publishing.

Zagonari, F. (2016). Which attitudes will make us individually and socially happier and healthier? A cross-culture and cross-development analytical model. *Journal of Happiness Studies, 17*, 2527–2554.

Chapter 19
Appendices

Abstract This chapter provides appendices that illustrate the prior work in Chaps. 13, 14, 15, 16 and 17 published on matters related to the Neo-Eriksonian model of development. It consists of 25 appendices or one for each step of the model. The appendices are numbered by the sub-stages of the present Neo-Piagetian/Neo-Eriksonian model of five stages x five sub-stages (i.e., Appendices 1.1–5.5).

Appendix 1.1. Prior Work on the Reflex Stage Sub-stage of Coordination (Sub-stage 1): Self and Relational Development (Earlier Fetal Life)

Cognitive Acquisition

Reflexive movements pair, but not in fixed order (e.g., fingers in mid-position open then flex, or vice versa, but not to any particular stimulus; also applies to arm flexion and extension) (Young, 2011; Taken from Table 20.6, p. 467).

Behavioral Specialization (e.g., in Right Arm-Hand)

Pairs of single reflexive behaviors (*reflex pairs*) not yet linked to activating mechanisms are evident, but do not manifest in fixed order (e.g., in proximal arm flexion and extension, in distal fingers open and flex; either example in reverse) (Young, 2011; Taken from Table 26.1, p. 598; Originally from Young, 1990).

G. Young, *Causality and Development*,
https://doi.org/10.1007/978-3-030-02493-2_19

Socio-Emotional Acquisition

During such behavior, distance alteration or maintenance occurs with respect to targets accidentally present. (At later levels in development, behaviors directly involve stimulus targets) (Young, 2011; Taken from Table 20.6, p. 467).

Positive Social-Self Working Schema

No schemata other than reflex pairings [Nevertheless, if called upon socially, as in late prenatal interaction with massage, musical stimulation, and story telling, the pairings are appropriate in context] (Young, 2011; Taken from Table 24.2, p. 565).

Negative Pole in Eriksonian Development

Distance acts vs. no distance: Distance regulation to target is irregular, too forward, or rarely "near." Without a primary base, behavior is undifferentiated (Young, 2011; Taken from Table 20.11, p. 476; Originally Young (1997); Taken from Table P.3, p. 11).

Theme in Story About Development

Want to live, not hurt self vs. want to die, hurt self (Young, 2011; Taken from Table 14.10, p. 328; Originally from Young, 1997; Taken from Table 10.1, p. 234).

Self-Development

Fetal Life Being not quite a self at this juncture, the moniker "elf" will do to describe the *non-self* (Young, 2011; Taken from Table 13.1, p. 297; Originally from Young, 1997; Taken from Table 3.2, p. 75).

Other(s)' Attitude Based on Cognitive (Mis)Perception of the Other

The child is viewed as an extension of the parent's needs and self so that the parent feels justified to negate, abuse, reject, deny, and behave absolutely, with overt insults and anger toward the child. The attitude is abrasive, negative, and hostile (Young,

2011; Taken from Table 14.2, p. 318; Originally from Young, 1997; Taken from Table 7.2, p. 164).

Appendix 1.2. Prior Work on the Reflex Stage Sub-stage of Hierarchization (Sub-stage 2): Self and Relational Development (Quite Premature)

Cognitive Acquisition

Paired reflexes establish fixed order and firing mechanisms (hierarchy), but with second reflex on target only fortuitously (e.g., the arm extends after tonic neck reflex, touching object; sounds pair by vocal cord activity and lip/mouth/tongue positioning) (Young, 2011; Taken from Table 20.6, p. 467).

Behavioral Specialization (e.g., in the Right Arm-Hand)

Reflexive behavior hierarchies manifest in two ways. First, they become subordinated to specific stimulus sensitivities in firing. Second, reflexive behavior pairs become fixed in sequence but with second component only fortuitously on target (e.g., in proximal ipsilateral arm extension in tonic neck reflex, in distal finger opening to facilitate flexing on contact) (Young, 2011; Taken from Table 26.1, p. 598; Originally from Young, 1990).

Socio-Emotional Acquisition

Reflex pairs now manifest correct activation order, and this can lead to adept nursing behavior (e.g., suck then swallow; smell then turn) in optimal circumstances (Young, 2011; Taken from Table 20.6, p. 467).

Positive Social-Self Working Schema

Reflex pairs better coordinate (e.g., super-ordinate, subordinate) and react to stimuli (Young, 2011; Taken from Table 24.2, p. 565).

Negative Pole in Eriksonian Development

Nursing vs. rootless acts: Basic reflexive survival mechanisms are awry, e.g., in reacting to stimuli or in nursing. Given an absence of physical alimentation, behavior is without orientation or stability (Young, 2011; Taken from Table 20.11, p. 476; Originally Young (1997); Taken from Table P.3, p. 11). [Even if developing ideally, nursing may be too forceful, not tuned, ineffective, etc.]

Theme in Story About Development

Take care of self vs. not care for, ignore self (Young, 2011; Taken from Table 14.10, p. 328; Originally from Young, 1997; Taken from Table 10.1, p. 234).

Self-Development

Premature Self I Motor skills unexpectedly are put to test in fragile, vulnerable prematures. Even nursing acts are problematic. We can speak of a *reflexive pre-self* (Young, 2011; Taken from Table 13.1, p. 297; Originally from Young, 1997; Taken from Table 3.2, p. 75).

Other(s)' Attitude Based on Cognitive (Mis)Perception of the Other

The child's reasoning or position is attacked, criticized, or rejected. The parent overtly denies the possibility of the child being correct (Young, 2011; Taken from Table 14.2, p. 318; Originally from Young, 1997; Taken from Table 7.2, p. 164).

Appendix 1.3. Prior Work on the Reflex Stage Sub-stage of Systematization (Sub-stage 3): Self and Relational Development (Somewhat Premature)

Cognitive Acquisition

The two reflex pair components can more flexibly relate or associate with other movements (reflexive, other), through primitive control schemata, which help better target behavior, even if it is still brusk. This system allows the first sequence of more than two acts, even if limited (e.g., if off center, fingers adjust position slightly to facilitate ensuing grasp; target visually followed, better ensuring tonic neck reflex on appropriate side; coos variable to some extent) (Young, 2011; Taken from Table 20.6, p. 467).

Behavioral Specialization (e.g., in the Right Arm-Hand)

Each component of reflex pair can become associated with simultaneously occurring movement, either reflexive or not, to assure better targeting of second component, thus creating primitive patterns. At this point, the primarily reflex related *primitive schemas* are being formed (e.g., in looking directed tonic neck reflex with subsequent proximal arm extension on appropriate side, in fingers open and move slightly before flexing to grip after non-centered contact) (Young, 2011; Taken from Table 26.1, p. 598; Originally from Young, 1990).

Socio-Emotional Acquisition

With nascent schemata, more target-oriented behavior structures can manifest (e.g., explore, approach, reject), but they are still based on reflex pairs and are more functional and general than uniquely social (Young, 2011; Taken from Table 20.6, p. 467).

Positive Social-Self Working Schema

Primitive schemata form in visual, auditory, haptic, olfactory, gustatory, and kinesthetic activity/exploration; with intermodal system coordinations (Young, 2011; Taken from Table 24.2, p. 565).

Negative Pole in Eriksonian Development

Outcome vs. outcast acts: Target-related appetitive behavior is contextually inappropriate, over- or under-energized, too negative (e.g., avoidance, crying), etc. Because of this foundation, the behavior may promote rejection (Young, 2011; Taken from Table 20.11, p. 476; Originally Young (1997); Taken from Table P.3, p. 11). [Even if developing well in a supportive context, the prematurity of the infant could severely compromise surviving-related behavior and survivability.]

Theme in Story About Development

Be aware of, acknowledge other vs. disregard, ignore other (Young, 2011; Taken from Table 14.10, p. 328; Originally from Young, 1997; Taken from Table 10.1, p. 234).

Self-Development

Premature Self II Survival being more certain, the inherent openness of babies manifests. Contact and information are sought even in the precarious circumstances of the hospital. Given the grounding of behavior in primitive control schemata, there appears to be a psychological self, which we can label the proto-self. Because it is especially action- and target-oriented, it can be characterized as the *corporal proto-self* (Young, 2011; Taken from Table 13.1, p. 297; Originally from Young, 1997; Taken from Table 3.2, p. 75).

Other(s)' Attitude Based on Cognitive (Mis)Perception of the Other

The child's reasoning or position is overtly dismissed with no effort to constructively redirect or guide understanding of the other's viewpoint. The child is told that he or she is "wrong," but there is no effort to explain why (Young, 2011; Taken from Table 14.2, p. 318; Originally from Young, 1997; Taken from Table 7.2, p. 164).

Appendix 1.4. Prior Work on the Reflex Stage Sub-stage of Multiplication (Sub-stage 4): Self and Relational Development (Full-Term Newborn)

Cognitive Acquisition

Organized multiples of systematized reflex pairs controlled by patterned schemata form, with embedding possible (Young, 2011; Taken from Table 20.6, p. 467).

Behavioral Specialization (e.g., in the Right Arm-Hand)

Patterned, *schema*-controlled, ballistic, preprogrammed behavior (i.e., sequential multiples of above) triggered, but not always directly to (on) target; in proximal activity (e.g., pre-reach agitation in front of target moves) and/or in distal activity (e.g., fingers serially extend and flex upon sheet contact on back of hand, with arm and hand agitation producing turning) (Young, 2011; Taken from Table 26.1, p. 598; Originally from Young, 1990).

Socio-Emotional Acquisition

But unlike their paired constituents acting by themselves, these multiples are not necessarily directly to (on) target (e.g., ballistic arm movements to moving target serially performed couched in context of appropriate postural, head positioning; fingers serially extend and flex upon sheet contact with context-related turning possible, if needed; combined sound series) (Young, 2011; Taken from Table 20.6, p. 467).

Positive Social-Self Working Schema

Consistencies in care-giving lead to the formation of bodily components-in-context associations. Patterned schemata fire mechanically (Young, 2011; Taken from Table 24.2, p. 565).

Negative Pole in Eriksonian Development

Care-giving vs. careless giving acts: The care-giver system is not activated appropriately (e.g., newborn too passive or tests care-givers' limits, e.g., too much crying, colicky behavior). Care-givers bring their own agenda, and this may be maladaptive (e.g., indifference, postpartum depression, abuse). The will to receive care/live may be compromised by long-term, ineffective, non-optimal, or emotionally absent care-giving due to problems with infants, care-givers, or their match (Young, 2011; Taken from Table 20.11, p. 476; Originally Young (1997); Taken from Table P.3, p. 11). [Even if the infant has a supportive environment, risks abound in the capacity to elicit appropriate care-giving and be able to accept it.]

Theme in Story About Development

Accept care from other vs. reject care from other (Young, 2011; Taken from Table 14.10, p. 328; Originally from Young, 1997; Taken from Table 10.1, p. 234).

Self-Development

Emergent Self I (Might also Be Called Full Birthing Self) Full-term newborns manifest integrating cross-modal matching abilities tied to corresponding production schemes (e.g., imitating mouth opening). This primary perceptual/representational capacity may be affiliated with perceptual learning, simple classical conditioning, and/or priming in memory. Priming is a nonconscious, facilitative effect in memory and functions to improve perceptual identification of objects. Helplessness and calling behaviors elicit care-giving, making much of the intra-modal world socio-affective. The emerging self seems to be a perceptual intermodal self. Neisser (1991) takes a similar position, for he calls the self in this period the perceptual self, and attributes to it two components – the ecological self and the interpersonal self (Young, 2011; Taken from Table 13.1, p. 297; Originally from Young, 1997; Taken from Table 3.2, p. 75).

Other(s)' Attitude Based on Cognitive (Mis)Perception of the Other

Only part of the child's behavior or argument is treated as indicated in the previous sub-stage (Young, 2011; Taken from Table 14.2, p. 318; Originally from Young, 1997; Taken from Table 7.2, p. 164).

Appendix 1.5. Prior Work on the Reflex Stage Sub-stage of Integration (Sub-stage 5): Self and Relational Development (0–1 Months)

Cognitive Acquisition

Schema-guided reflex combinations integrate or differentiate with exercise to come to incorporate (a) fully reflex-free behavior components (under independent schema control) and (b) the monitoring of movement and/or the moving target. This makes approach and target-related behavior more sustained, smooth, and flexible (e.g., reaching adjustment to swaying target) and allows an element of reversibility in the behavior (e.g., restart movement if context necessitates it), although target-related behavior is still relatively rigid (e.g., no manipulation). Also, fingers move flexibly to facilitate efficient grasping; there are situational/intonational adjustments in cooing. [For Piaget, reflex exercise brings organized patterns of behavior through generalization and differentiation of behavior schemes. Schemes vary with even slight variations in target, so that these are always "new."] (Young, 2011; Taken from Table 20.6, p. 467).

Behavioral Specialization (e.g., in the Right Arm-Hand)

Patterned behaviors above begin to differentiate with practice, as continual monitoring of movement and/or moving target renders movement more smooth and flexible. *Independent schemas* no longer are dominated by reflexes (e.g., in proximal reaching adjustment to moving object, in distal fingers grasp target) (Young, 2011; Taken from Table 26.1, p. 598; Originally from Young, 1990).

Socio-Emotional Acquisition

The reflex-free behavior and continual monitoring of movement and/or target bring with them the first emotions, which concern arriving at relevant ends or the feelings engendered in failure to do so (e.g., quiescence, relief, distress). New emotions emerge with each succeeding cognitive sub-stage in the sensori-motor period (Young, 2011; Taken from Table 20.6, p. 467).

Positive Social-Self Working Schema

Independent schemata that are not reflex controlled allow contextually adjusted, patterned behavior with emotional integrations (Young, 2011; Taken from Table 24.2, p. 565).

Negative Pole in Eriksonian Development

Emotional vs. mal-emotional acts: Evaluations along emotion-related dimensions (e.g., whether goals being interfered with) are inaccurate. Component emotional reactions are problematic. In short, emotional scripts are not functioning normatively (e.g., too damped, too negative). For example, infants manifest distress in unpredictable ways, are not soothed in normal manner, are too fussy, and are never engaged by sensorily interesting spectacles/objects. The same extremes may be evident in other emotions as they emerge in the succeeding sub-stages. As in prior sub-stage [and in all subsequent sub-stages], care-givers may contribute to these difficulties (Young, 2011; Taken from Table 20.11, p. 476; Originally Young (1997); Taken from Table P.3, p. 11). [And if development is proceeding well and the environment is supportive, the newborn might still be expressing emotions inappropriately. However, this can be accommodated by the supporting environment.]

Theme in Story About Development

Appropriate emotion (e.g., directed, adaptive) vs. inappropriate emotion (e.g., rage, fear) (Young, 2011; Taken from Table 14.10, p. 328; Originally from Young, 1997; Taken from Table 10.1, p. 234).

Self-Development

Emergent Self II Infants in the next weeks develop the capacity to integrate separate schemes into more unified structures, building intermodal integration skills. Usually schemes function with concomitant, most basic emotional overtones and are body-focused. We can designate this self the *primary emotional self* (Young, 2011; Taken from Table 13.1, p. 297; Originally from Young, 1997; Taken from Table 3.2, p. 75).

Other(s)' Attitude Based on Cognitive (Mis)Perception of the Other

Despite such behavior, part of the child's behavior or argument is acknowledged or listened to by the parent. There is a differentiation and reversibility evident in the willingness to acknowledge/listen to the child (Young, 2011; Taken from Table 14.2, p. 318; Originally from Young, 1997; Taken from Table 7.2, p. 164).

Appendix 2.1. Prior Work on the Sensori-Motor Stage Sub-stage of Coordination (Sub-stage 6): Self and Relational Development (1–4 Months)

Cognitive Acquisition

Different schemata coordinate but mostly in a parallel, back and forth way. Schema coordination comes to include this rather than a fixed sequence. This can occur across different sensory modalities (e.g., 3-month-olds only imitated vowel sounds matched to an adult's mouth movements, Legerstee, 1990). It allows somewhat more online behavior control after behavior onset and thus better target attainment (e.g., beginning visuomotor coordination before a target but without visually guided reaching, i.e., watch hand while active before a target, but without forward movement to it; watch the palm of the hand while fingers touch target; ballistic reaching to target with some but not constant visual surveillance of movement or grasp the target without looking at it; two independent actions coordinate, e.g., foot scratch, reach; Wolff, 1987). [For Piaget, primary circular reactions concern accidentally discovered effects centered on the body that are repeated, e.g., "coordinated" schemes in sucking the thumb brought to the mouth. Target differentiation increases as schemes accommodate to a newly encountered object once having attempted its assimilation] (Young, 2011; Taken from Table 20.7, p. 469–471).

Behavioral Specialization (e.g., in the Right Arm-Hand)

Through *schema coordination* parallel and back and forth in nature after behavior onset (e.g., vision and appropriate movement), behavior patterns come under even more moment-to-moment control (e.g., in watching arm during proximal reach to target, in watching hand, while distal fingers serially touch target) (Young, 2011; Taken from Table 26.2, pp. 599–600; Originally from Young, 1990).

Socio-Emotional Acquisition

Dyadic exchange begins, because schema coordination comes to include a schema of the infant with another of the (adult) partner (Cohn & Tronick, 1988). By 3 months, infants even become upset when the dyadic flow is interrupted by mother adopting a still face (Cohn & Tronick, 1983). Not only can the infant be shaped by operant by the (adult) partner, but he/ she can do the same in the "game" that is played (Watson, 1973). Similarly, not only can the infant be imitated by the partner, she/ he also imitates, even in a deferred (1 day later) fashion. Neonatally acquired learning skills contribute to these social ones (e.g., see Meltzoff & Moore, 1989, 1992, 1994, for their description of neonatal cross-modally mediated facial and head movement imitation). Later in the development, the shaping processes come to include parallel ones based on classical Pavlovian conditioning, while the imitation ones expand to include expectations, intentions, and social roles (Young, 2011; Taken from Table 20.7, pp. 469–471).

Positive Social-Self Working Schema

Working schemata become increasingly coordinative of the socializing self and the other but only in the sense of partial components of both (e.g., the baby is contented and experiences pleasure) (Young, 2011; Taken from Table 24.3, p. 566).

Negative Pole in Eriksonian Development

Dyadic vs. dys-dyadic acts: Social dialogue is marked by poor synchrony with partner, incorrect reading of partner, misplaced actions, variable reactions, too demanding bids, excessive turning off, deficient learning skill, etc. The pleasure and joy typically inherent in a dyadic interaction with care-givers may be replaced by much frustration, gaze aversion, and disinterest instead (Young, 2011; Taken from Table 20.12, pp. 476–477; Originally Young (1997); Taken from Table P.4, p. 12).

Theme in Story About Development

Active dialogue, involved conversation vs. monologue, one-way conversation (Young, 2011; Taken from Table 14.10, p. 328; Originally from Young, 1997; Taken from Table 10.1, p. 234).

Self-Development

Core, Coordinated Interaction Self Young infants' scheme coordination skills lead to dyadic interchanges. Invariant patterns are established, but especially because of care-giver framing. This permits the infants' inherent active nature to achieve agency through participation in regulatory "games" played, connectedness of one's own actions and transactions, control of emotional reactions in the care-giver, etc. At this point, the self seems to be an *inter-coordinated incipient social self* (Young, 2011; Taken from Table 13.2, p. 298; Originally from Young, 1997; Taken from Table 3.3, p. 76).

Other(s)' Attitude Based on Cognitive (Mis)Perception of the Other

There is a high degree of parental control, subjugation, repression, authoritarianism, opposition, imposition, manipulation, and dominance in the conversation. It is shaped directly by the parent's ideas or agenda. The child has no independent thought but waits for the parent to provide direction. The parent uses language to control the child's physical actions and behaviors. An order is given that directs the path in the conversation (e.g., "You don't have to say that," or "You'd better ... You have to ... You must ...") (Young, 2011; Taken from Table 14.3, p. 318; Originally from Young, 1997; Taken from Table 7.3, p. 165).

Appendix 2.2. Prior Work on the Sensori-Motor Stage Sub-stage of Hierarchization (Sub-stage 7): Self and Relational Development (4–8 Months)

Cognitive Acquisition

Schema coordinates manifest a dominant-subordinate relationship [hierarchy] in terms of a constant temporal order and/ or an interweaving toward a common end. But this is established in context only after behavior onset has produced an accidentally interesting effect, so that a goal is not evident at outset [image schemata, or representations of analog redescriptions of basic perceptions, partake in this process (Mandler, 1992)] (e.g., target behavior with visually directed, i.e., coordinated reaching, or with closed hand reaching preceding opened hand seizure; visually guided finger manipulation of target; simple bimanual coordination with preferred hand reach then other hand grasp, or preferred hand grasps target then other hand fingers it, Rochat, 1989; one hand balances posture while other hand reaches, Rochat & Senders, 1991; self-soothing with one hand in mouth in order to use other in activities, Thelen & Fogel, 1989; babbling with hand raising to call absent adult). [For Piaget, secondary circular reactions involve accidentally discovered effects centered on the environment that are repeated (e.g., reach for and shake rattle), showing that goal schemes can be kept in mind if targets are in view and can be reached without detour (e.g., seek partially hidden, interesting object).] (Young, 2011; Taken from Table 20.7, pp. 469–471).

Behavioral Specialization (e.g., in the Right Arm-Hand)

With *schema coordination hierarchies*, after behavior onset, goal can be established in context (primary releasing stimuli defined), and one schema in above schema coordination becomes primary; thus, there is directed target groping subserved by dominant-subordinate linkage of two schemas (e.g., in visually directed proximal reaching, in watching as distally manipulate target, in simple bimanual collaboration involving (right hand) reach then (left hand) grasp) (Young, 2011; Taken from Table 26.2, pp. 599–600; Originally from Young, 1990).

Socio-Emotional Acquisition

A sense of "trust" develops in infants both in themselves and in the environment, for the dyadic exchanges with the care-giver in the prior sub-stage permit a firmer relationship to consolidate. Complementary infant/care-giver schema hierarchies form in "mutual regulation" (reciprocally, each dominant in "game" played at times) (Young, 2011; Taken from Table 20.7, pp. 469–471).

Positive Social-Self Working Schema

As the infant develops a sense of trust, context-activated goals are added to developing schemata, which take on a hierarchical structure (e.g., components of self are interested in and delighted in other) (Young, 2011; Taken from Table 24.3, pp. 566).

Negative Pole in Eriksonian Development

Trust vs. Mistrust acts: A sense of mistrust in oneself and the social world takes hold, for care-giving is unreliable, intermittent, or otherwise negative (e.g., rejecting, over-intrusive, smothering). Infants cannot create a normal, mutually regulated, hierarchical integration with the care-giver where at times infants are dominant and at times subordinate in a reciprocal balance at play. Emotions that emerge involve fear, sadness, crankiness, etc. (Young, 2011; Taken from Table 20.12, pp. 476–477; Originally Young (1997); Taken from Table P.4, p. 12).

Theme in Story About Development

Trust, confidence in other vs. mistrust, no faith in other (Young, 2011; Taken from Table 14.10, p. 328; Originally from Young, 1997; Taken from Table 10.1, p. 234).

Self-Development

Core Initiatory Self At midyear, we see a more hierarchical behavior (e.g., context-created, purposeful behavior, Piaget; generalized sense of personal agency; Case, 1991), which fosters social initiation, emotional focus, and particularities in relationships. A sense of trust in the surround, especially care-givers, develops when that surround facilitates successful goal-oriented behavior. Erikson's psychosocial stage of trust vs. mistrust also fits here and suggests we call the self of this period the *end-focused trusting self* (Young, 2011; Taken from Table 13.2, p. 298; Originally from Young, 1997; Taken from Table 3.3, p. 76).

Other(s)' Attitude Based on Cognitive (Mis)Perception of the Other

The child's reasoning position is competed with, contradicted, countered, or opposed in an effort to subvert, manipulate, control, or undermine it (Young, 2011; Taken from Table 14.3, p. 318; Originally from Young, 1997; Taken from Table 7.3, p. 165).

Appendix 2.3. Prior Work on the Sensori-Motor Stage Sub-stage of Systematization (Sub-stage 8): Self and Relational Development (8–12 Months)

Cognitive Acquisition

Each constituent of schema hierarchies refines (is added to), and their coordination is more adaptive. Also, primitive representational images of targets permit a systematic, intentional goal from behavior onset and more subtlety in its end-point search (e.g., reach for fully hidden object even if detour needed [object permanence]; exploratory, organized finger manipulation; complex bimanual coordination with preferred hand manipulation and other hand stabilization; babbling and pointing to get adult to get object; alternate gaze between mother and object being offered to her, Messinger & Fogel, 1990, in Fogel, 1991). [For Piaget, the sub-stage of coordination of secondary schemes consists of combining schemes as means to fit new intended ends, as in object permanence tasks.] (Young, 2011; Taken from Table 20.7, pp. 469–471).

Behavioral Specialization (e.g., in the Right Arm-Hand)

Linked schemas above related more systematically, allowing *primitive representation of target*, permitting intentional end-focused goal from behavior onset (e.g., in proximal reach for hidden object, in two-step movement to target, in distal exploratory manipulation either (a) alone or (b) in complex bimanual coordination, with complementary (left hand) stabilization) (Young, 2011; Taken from Table 26.2, pp. 599–600; Originally from Young, 1990).

Socio-Emotional Acquisition

Target images facilitate highly social behavior where liked individuals and friendly strangers are sought out, engaged, and adapted to. Their departure may induce organized search and not only distress and protest (Young, 2011; Taken from Table 20.7, pp. 469–471).

Positive Social-Self Working Schema

Working schemata include self-defined goals, primitive representations such as images of the care-giver, and the desire for intersubjectivity and proximity and contact. The emotional side of the developing cognitive-affective structure includes feelings of affection and comfort (Young, 2011; Taken from Table 24.3, p. 566).

Negative Pole in Eriksonian Development

Sociability vs. unsociability acts: A lack of sociability pervades social intercourse with the care-giver, family, and strangers. Insecurity in the attachment relationship solidifies in either an anxious avoidant or anxious ambivalent-resistant (mixed) fashion. Infants do not share with care-givers sitting as a secure base, fail to adapt to their departure, ignore them, or are ambivalent on their return and are not optimally interactive or are negative with strangers. Thus, we see emotions such as worry, dislike, aggressive displacement, and displacement escape (Young, 2011; Taken from Table 20.12, pp. 476–477; Originally Young (1997); Taken from Table P.4, p. 12).

Theme in Story About Development

Sociability makes other secure vs. not securing other (Young, 2011; Taken from Table 14.10, p. 328; Originally from Young, 1997; Taken from Table 10.1, p. 234).

Self-Development

Subjective Attachment Self Given the emergence of primitive representational images, and the beginning of (hidden) object permanence, intentions come to guide behavior before its onset. Thus, mental states of self and other are better coordinated, producing more friendliness, sharing, and referencing of the other (and indirect agency; Case, 1991). Attachment to the care-giver becomes active (e.g., searching when the care-giver leaves, calling/protesting her or his departure). The self at this level seems an especially *permanent intersubjective self* (Young, 2011; Taken from Table 13.2, p. 298; Originally from Young, 1997; Taken from Table 3.3, p. 76).

Other(s)' Attitude Based on Cognitive (Mis)Perception of the Other

The child clearly is directed to speak or act in a particular way with no constructive explanation given as to why (e.g., "No," "Tell me about ...," "Why don't you ...") (Young, 2011; Taken from Table 14.3, p. 318; Originally from Young, 1997; Taken from Table 7.3, p. 165).

Appendix 2.4. Prior Work on the Sensori-Motor Stage Sub-stage of Multiplication (Sub-stage 9): Self and Relational Development (12–18 Months)

Cognitive Acquisition

Structured chaining of systematic schema pairs leads to the formation of linear plans. These manifest as complex combinations, but especially embeddings, or the use of sub-programs in plans (e.g., resolve embedded hiding behind second screen; repeat novel adult utterance; name object to get adult to seek it. Blake and Dolgoy (1993) found that success on a means-end task (pulling a string horizontally to obtain an object) preceded the acquisition of comment gestures (e.g., point in a book) and request gestures (for adult to function as agent)). [For Piaget, tertiary circular reactions refer to deliberate trial-and-error exploration of new means for established schemes, e.g., pull blanket to get toy on it; return to starting point by reverse or alternate path.] (Young, 2011; Taken from Table 20.7, pp. 469–471).

Behavioral Specialization (e.g., in the Right Arm-Hand)

Through multiplicative embedding of one simple intention or means in another, or in multiplicative combining of two means or ends, diagonal movement to target, in cooperative distal hand use in resolving an embedded hiding, in trial-and-error exploration of means-ends relationship, between distal manual activity and effects on objects (Young, 2011; Taken from Table 26.2, pp. 599–600; Originally from Young, 1990).

Socio-Emotional Acquisition

Toddlers can begin to develop a sense of "autonomous" will, for the sociability and sense of trust of the prior sub-stages are transformed by the current linear plans. The exploration of means-end relationships comes to include their own behavior as means in relation to an end (the "self") to be satisfied, i.e., the focus is now on the toddlers' nascent self, as much as those of others, as the appropriate self in this regard (Young, 2011; Taken from Table 20.7, pp. 469–471).

Positive Social-Self Working Schema

The 1-year-old infant acts increasingly autonomous through planned exploratory behavior eagerly implemented, although this does not happen with explicit plans at the behavior's outset (it is "accidental"). The social other is integral to the working schemata being formed but as an object of sensori-motor activity rather than a pre-conceived representational goal. The primary care-giver who has been sensitive in the first year so that the infant feels "loved" is still sought actively in reunion after a brief separation (Young, 2011; Taken from Table 24.3, p. 566).

Negative Pole in Eriksonian Development

Autonomy vs. doubt acts: A sense of autonomy is stifled, for toddlers develop pervading, overly-dependent behavior, doubt, hesitation, inertia, or lack of self-confidence. Deliberate trial-and-error exploring becomes chaotic, trying, erroneous, imploring (dependency), flat in affect, or with exaggerated fear. Dependent behavior brings with it emotions such as jealousy, greed, and defiance (Young, 2011; Taken from Table 20.12, pp. 476–477; Originally Young (1997); Taken from Table P.4, p. 12).

Theme in Story About Development

Independence, autonomy vs. dependence, self-doubt (Young, 2011; Taken from Table 14.10, p. 328; Originally from Young, 1997; Taken from Table 10.1, p. 234).

Self-Development

Verbal Autonomous Self Linear inner plans in 1-year-olds allow increased autonomous action even if in opposition to care-giver wishes. Also with planning capacities, infants can entertain leaving their care-givers' base to explore and return in a psychological and not only a physical sense. Care-givers co-create meaning with infants through language as they toddle about exploring and returning for refueling. Thus, language facilitates the development of Erikson's autonomy through its distal and shared modalities. The conceptual awareness of self as an independent actor emerges. Thus, we can speak of an *independent autonomous self* (Young, 2011; Taken from Table 13.2, p. 298; Originally from Young, 1997; Taken from Table 3.3, p. 76).

Other(s)' Attitude Based on Cognitive (Mis)Perception of the Other

Only part of the child's discourse is manipulated. Manipulative suggestions are made that flow from that part of the child's psychology that seems to have been judged possibly unacceptable to the parent (Young, 2011; Taken from Table 14.3, p. 318; Originally from Young, 1997; Taken from Table 7.3, p. 165).

Appendix 2.5. Prior Work on the Sensori-Motor Stage Sub-stage of Integration (Sub-stage 10): Self and Relational Development (18–24 Months)

Cognitive Acquisition

A primary plan integrates another plan, allowing mental detours or beginning conceptual reversibility. That is, an embedded secondary plan forms a reversible, branched sequence that can return to the primary master one (e.g., resolve double embedded or invisible hiding or resolve single one with tool; sequentially sort two subsets of a group of objects; form novel two-word utterance using words in other two-word utterances). [For Piaget, the sub-stage of invention of new means through mental combinations occurs via symbols that represent objects/events, e.g., push carriage from side opposite handle, reversing normal procedure when situation calls for it, because symbol guides behavior.] (Young, 2011; Taken from Table 20.7, pp. 469–471).

Behavioral Specialization (e.g., in the Right Arm-Hand)

Organized sequences above being to differentiate into hierarchic branching of embedded, secondary sequential plans followed by return to primary one, which is the structure of a priori *symbolic plans* (e.g., in proximal hitting of rolled ball back to thrower, in resolution of an embedded hiding with a tool distally manipulated in the hand or in double embedded hiding resolution, in using distal hands to set apart one subset of a group and then another) (Young, 2011; Taken from Table 26.2, pp. 599–600; Originally from Young, 1990).

Socio-Emotional Acquisition

With the advent of symbolic sensori-motor-mediated plans and their reversible secondary plans, toddlers can participate in a prolonged interaction either for its own sake (play) or with the seeking of control. Social interchange becomes a complex, subtle, intertwining of negotiation, stratagems, and control dynamics, at times, even in relaxed play. Rogoff (1990) describes the way children of this age begin to engage in guided participation where they actively determine the nature of their social role and the extent of their implication in social discourse (Young, 2011; Taken from Table 20.7, pp. 469–471).

Positive Social-Self Working Schema

Infants at 18 months of age enact symbolically guided, planned activity, but always with a sensori-motor and affective base. They experience appreciation and pride. Others are understood in terms of the plans and with consistent participation in them. The infant varies plans involving them on purpose to see the effect (Young, 2011; Taken from Table 24.3, p. 566).

Negative Pole in Eriksonian Development

Interdigitational vs. de-digitational acts: Mutuality in play is impossible, for young children cannot partake in prolonged, reciprocal, peaceful exchanges, have no facility in smoothly entering such social relations, and are either too overpowering/possessive or too submissive/subjugated when participating in them. Thus, give-and-take social behavior may be avoided. Children evaluate others with contempt, not appreciation, and evaluate themselves with the same and a sense of rejection, not pride (Young, 2011; Taken from Table 20.12, pp. 476–477; Originally Young (1997); Taken from Table P.4, p. 12).

Theme in Story About Development

Share, give-and-take with other vs. not share, give or take with other (Young, 2011; Taken from Table 14.10, p. 328; Originally from Young, 1997; Taken from Table 10.1, p. 234).

Self-Development

Verbal Constancy Self In older toddlers, symbol plans, which permit mental combination, underlie behavior. Also, evaluations emerge due to these plans. Thus, social interchange becomes a complex interdigitation of plans, and a mutual awareness that the other has plans and is aware, producing the beginnings of true role taking and empathy. Toddlers develop self-constancy, whereby they realize that they can actively oppose care-givers and either reinstate their relationship or have care-givers cooperate. Thus, toddlers symbolize the self as a separate entity, seeing it as a willful agent of their symbolic plans. (Toddlers can use the words "I" and "Me" at this age.) In short, the self at this age can be called an *interior implicative self*. Toddlers both implicate (evaluate) cognitively and implicate themselves (interdigitate) socially (Young, 2011; Taken from Table 13.2, p. 298; Originally from Young, 1997; Taken from Table 3.3, p. 76).

Other(s)' Attitude Based on Cognitive (Mis)Perception of the Other

Despite some signs of parental manipulation, etc., suggestions are made in a way that appears to give the child a chance to use them or not (e.g., "You know that you could get what you want if you did it this way.") (Young, 2011; Taken from Table 14.3, p. 318; Originally from Young, 1997; Taken from Table 7.3, p. 165).

Appendix 3.1. Prior Work on the Peri-operational Stage Sub-stage of Coordination (Sub-stage 11): Self and Relational Development (2–3.5 Years)

Cognitive Acquisition

With coordination of symbol plans, young children can regulate a series of actions in a persistent, flexible way in order to achieve a standard, conventional goal. For example, they can build a house of blocks according to a model (Bullock & Lütkenhaus, 1988). They begin to balance two symbol streams, performing dual-objective tasks, such as simultaneously sorting two subsets of a group of objects, although with no fixed strategy. They begin to learn to read and write individual letters, working across the auditory and visual modalities. Also, two-word utterances are coordinated, and past events are incorporated in ongoing autobiographical narratives (Howe & Courage, 1993). Piaget describes children in this period as egocentric, or incapable of decentering from their perspective. In present terms, this means that symbol plan coordinations having the self's perspective as one component automatically fix that component as dominant even with the balancing that can take place: however, this dominance does not reflect a true hierarchical arrangement as in the next sub-stage, because the dominant/subordinate relationship of the element symbol plans is not cognitively gained and flexible, capable of uncoupling in the appropriate context, but cognitively anchored, imposed, and rigid or inflexible (Young, 2011; Taken from Table 20.8, pp. 472–473).

Behavioral Specialization (e.g., in the Right Arm-Hand)

Symbolic plan coordination found, as the child simultaneously holds in mind several symbol plans (e.g., in proximal hitting of rolled ball to side target, in using distal hands to simultaneously sort two subsets of a group of objects, in using memory to begin to learn to draw, write) (Young, 2011; Taken from Table 26.3, pp. 600–601; Originally from Young, 1990).

Socio-Emotional Acquisition

Because there are coordinated symbol plans, whether one analyzes social peer play, pretend play, conversations, monologues, stories, etc., the beginning of superordinate structures is now evident. The target has an overall coherence to some extent, which is accentuated by cohesive relations between its parts (e.g., Halliday & Hasan, 1976). Even groups of neighboring units display more relational rules, as in the development of verbal syntax and its coordination with intonation in utterances (Young, 2011; Taken from Table 20.8, pp. 472–473).

Positive Social-Self Working Schema

In symbol plan coordinations, the child's plans are more focused on the self egocentrically, and the other, while schematized more holistically, needs to adjust. A sense of the other as a loving one grows (Young, 2011; Taken from Table 24.4, p. 567).

Negative Pole in Eriksonian Development

Super-ordinate vs. dis-coordinate acts: disjointed, inappropriately juxtaposed oppositions in social behavior manifest. Children seem incoherent, fragmented, and without refined social skills. Language does not fit context, actions mismatch intentions, and emotions improperly contrast. This may be evident (in different ways) both over long stretches and neighboring behaviors. The normal egocentrism of children is inappropriate or compromised, for the "ego" is dispersed or fractionated (Young, 2011; Taken from Table 20.13, pp. 477–478; Originally Young (1997); Taken from Table P.5, p. 13).

Theme in Story About Development

Self as together, coherent vs. self as not together, fragmented (Young, 2011; Taken from Table 14.10, p. 328; Originally from Young, 1997; Taken from Table 10.1, p. 234).

Self-Development

Egocentric-Centrated Self Symbol plan coordination allows young children to organize cohesive, coherent wholes in behavior (e.g., in language utterances, story events, parallel tasks, and in understanding the social system of the family with its multiple roles; Case, 1991). But coordinations involving the self are egocentrically anchored with no or little flexibility in thought to permit decentration on the other. This cognitive egocentrism leads to a lack of differentiation of the physical and psychosocial features of the other and a lack of appreciation of their perspective. One's own self is an incorporating, coupling one, and so it is labeled the *coupling egocentric-centrated self* (Young, 2011; Taken from Table 13.3, p. 299; Originally from Young, 1997; Taken from Table 3.4, p. 78).

Other(s)' Attitude Based on Cognitive (Mis)Perception of the Other

The parent channels/neutralizes/pacifies the child by disrupting/disorganizing/ confusing the child (e.g., "You're not thinking right"). The parent gives "I don't know" answers to questions. The child directly attempts to keep the discussion going, but the parent does not participate or give an answer to allow the discussion to proceed. Indiscriminate rewards are used to foster a climate of compliance/consumption (Young, 2011; Taken from Table 14.4, p. 319; Originally from Young, 1997; Taken from Table 7.4, p. 166).

Appendix 3.2. Prior Work on the Peri-operational Stage Sub-stage of Hierarchization (Sub-stage 12): Self and Relational Development (3.5–5 Years)

Cognitive Acquisition

Symbol plans evidence dominant/subordinate relations (hierarchies) in preschoolers. For example, in dual (multiple second) time-sharing tasks, generally language is spared relative to tapping. Speech witnesses the subordination of clauses in sentences and events in narratives. Also progress is made in recognizing and producing the written form in alphabet and in counting sequences and in naming them. For Bialystok (1992), alphanumeric entities are formal representations in which the label is affixed to the written form or are hierarchically structured, to use our terminology. The prior period sees the beginning of the development of coordinated plans at the cognitive level (Young, 2011; Taken from Table 20.8, pp. 472–473).

Behavioral Specialization (e.g., in the Right Arm-Hand)

The above pairs develop a dominant-subordinate *symbol plan hierarchization* (e.g., in proximal symbolic fantasy gesturing to help explicate a sentence, in speeded distal tapping interfered with or being subordinate to spared language in dual, time-sharing tasks). This hierarchization also refers to the child placing own plan as dominant in relation to perception of those of parents, others (as in egocentric notions of good drawing, lettering) (Young, 2011; Taken from Table 26.3, pp. 600–601; Originally from Young, 1990).

Socio-Emotional Acquisition

Consequently, in terms of socio-emotional systems, one sees a super-ordinate coherence across behaviors. Three-year-olds can come to hierarchize these super-ordinate coordinations. Thus, in terms of Erikson's theory, their perspective may be hierarchically positioned as dominant (in initiative) over those of others (even at the Oedipal level, if one abstracts from Freud) (Young, 2011; Taken from Table 20.8, pp. 472–473).

Positive Social-Self Working Schema

The child's symbol plans are more differentiated, with an initiative subordinating the other, who is still responded to with an overriding love, however (Young, 2011; Taken from Table 24.4, p. 567).

Negative Pole in Eriksonian Development

Initiative vs. guilt acts: Initiative is damped by (familial) conflict deriving from too intrusive impositions or fantasies. This may even result in the Oedipus. The nascent superego is saturated with guilt related to repressed wishes. Adoption of the same-sex parental identity in a nonvolatile manner is jeopardized (Young, 2011; Taken from Table 20.13, pp. 477–478; Originally Young (1997); Taken from Table P.5, p. 13).

Theme in Story About Development

Initiative, energy, perseverance vs. no initiative, inertia, guilt (Young, 2011; Taken from Table 14.10, p. 328; Originally from Young, 1997; Taken from Table 10.1, p. 234).

Self-Development

Initiative Self Preschoolers' predilection for hierarchizing symbol plans directs them to think of themselves as dominant or with initiative in their daily challenges. The differentiation of the other is from within the children's projected perspective. This can lead to the Oedipal situation of fantasizing about the opposite-sex parent. In summary, we can refer to a *hierarchizing initiative self* (Young, 2011; Taken from Table 13.3, p. 299; Originally from Young, 1997; Taken from Table 3.4, p. 78).

Other(s)' Attitude Based on Cognitive (Mis)Perception of the Other

With a younger child, passive listening without comments or encouragement is a type of pacification-channeling, because the child's thought cannot be advanced, coherent, etc., in and of itself. With an older child, a parent can pacify-channel in more indirect ways (e.g., ignore the child's thought, invalidate it; turn to own ideas after child's speaking turn without acknowledgement of listening). The parent is passive with no verbal or nonverbal expressions, direction, or guidance. The parent may acknowledge her or his listening role (e.g., "Hmm hmm"). The parent parrots or paraphrases the child's comments or requests minor restatements. Minor corrections are given by the parent (in vocabulary, pronunciation, grammar), but with no new information. The parent may make a direct request for information or may ask a direct question (e.g., "Say that again," "What do you think about ..."). The child is rewarded if he or she follows the parent's lead or suggestions or if the (implicit) promise of such is possible. The result is that the same comments or ideas occur during the discussion. No advances in storytelling or thought are made (Young, 2011; Taken from Table 14.4, p. 319; Originally from Young, 1997; Taken from Table 7.4, p. 166).

Appendix 3.3. Prior Work on the Peri-operational Stage Sub-stage of Systematization (Sub-stage 13): Self and Relational Development (5–7 Years)

Cognitive Acquisition

Symbol plan systems emerge from the prior hierarchies, for component symbol plans refine by adding elements and better inter-coordinate in complementary ways. This produces organized rule systems by allowing children to hold things in mind, to begin to use a tentative reversibility in thought pathways about the concrete problems before them, or to return to the starting point in thought in order to select another path for comparison and to use a precursor logic. Thus, children can begin formal schooling and learn to read and write efficiently, all signs of organized rule system mastery. In storytelling, there are higher-order plots with related episodes involving problem and resolution. The simplest concrete operational problems of Piaget are solved (Young, 2011; Taken from Table 20.8, pp. 472–473).

Behavioral Specialization (e.g., in the Right Arm-Hand)

The above symbol plan hierarchies expand as they integrate other symbols into *symbol plan systems.* There is an increasing ability to hold things in mind while solving problems or even undue past learning about a problem, trying to use a primitive logic (Young, 2011; Taken from Table 26.3, pp. 600–601; Originally from Young, 1990).

Socio-Emotional Acquisition

The symbol plan systems of middle childhood enable children to increasingly relate themselves to the personalities, styles, habits, etc., of valued others. This process carries children beyond the initial phases of gender identification that begin earlier in life. In particular, identification with parents' and friends' characteristics accelerates (Young, 2011; Taken from Table 20.8, pp. 472–473).

Positive Social-Self Working Schema

The "I" can take primary perspectives of the self/other through symbol plan systems and Eriksonian "industry precursors," guided by others (Young, 2011; Taken from Table 24.4, p. 567).

Negative Pole in Eriksonian Development

Gender vs. problematic gender acts: Identification with the primary characteristics of the parents is undermined, for the process may be limited to frontal negative attributes (e.g., anger, rejection, confused signals) or dismissed, producing a frontal negativity (aggressivity, avoidance, depression). This attitude may carry over into peer- and school-related activity (e.g., disobeying parental wishes; compensatory over-inclusion of negative peer models in behavior; resistance, under-achievement in schooling). Self-devaluation is seeded (Young, 2011; Taken from Table 20.13, pp. 477–478; Originally Young (1997); Taken from Table P.5, p. 13).

Theme in Story About Development

Accept/identify with parents vs. reject/not be like parents (Young, 2011; Taken from Table 14.10, p. 328; Originally from Young, 1997; Taken from Table 10.1, p. 234).

Self-Development

First-Person Perspective Taking, Unilateral Self Symbol plan systems allow rule systems to be mastered and dimensions of self- and other-ranking to be apprehended. This enables identification with parental attributes and sex-appropriate gender roles. Such perspective taking is accompanied by a clear differentiation of others' psychological characteristics. But a subjective, one-way understanding of the other predominates. Thus, we can speak of a *systematizing primary-perspective self* (Young, 2011; Taken from Table 13.3, p. 299; Originally from Young, 1997; Taken from Table 3.4, p. 78).

Other(s)' Attitude Based on Cognitive (Mis)Perception of the Other

The parent points out a position/option that is different from the child's own without constructive explanation (e.g., "Couldn't it be that ...", or "Yes, but another way is ..."). Or the parent enunciates own thought or position with some explanation (Young, 2011; Taken from Table 14.4, p. 319; Originally from Young, 1997; Taken from Table 7.4, p. 166).

Appendix 3.4. Prior Work on the Peri-operational Stage Sub-stage of Multiplication (Sub-stage 14): Self and Relational Development (7–9 Years)

Cognitive Acquisition

In peri-operational multiplication, children come to solve most of the problems involved in Piaget's stage of concrete operations. Symbol plan systems can combine, chain, or sequence in inter-coordinations, alternating patterns, etc. This leads to improvement in logic, rules, reversals in thought, etc. Children's storytelling involves embedded minor plots which reflect the multiplicative nature of the symbol plans. Moreover, the major and minor plots are resolved sequentially, fitting Piaget's description of thought reversals, where children return to the starting point of their cognition before moving on (Young, 2011; Taken from Table 20.8, pp. 472–473).

Behavioral Specialization (e.g., in the Right Arm-Hand)

In the next step, these systems are inter-coordinated, inversed, alternated, ordered, etc. Such a structure allows a better logic, leading to rule-governed, skillful application (e.g., in art activity, writing, manual dexterity in music). Piaget's *concrete operations* develop in this context (Young, 2011; Taken from Table 26.3, pp. 600–601; Originally from Young, 1990).

Socio-Emotional Acquisition

Children apply their concrete operational logic with its serial symbol plan systems to the "industry" of school and its broad instruction, challenging tasks, and required production of "things" (Young, 2011; Taken from Table 20.8, pp. 472–473).

Positive Social-Self Working Schema

This logical ability grows and others are seen to evaluate the self (Young, 2011; Taken from Table 24.4, p. 567).

Negative Pole in Eriksonian Development

Industry vs. inferiority acts: The problems above are magnified, resulting in a sense of rebelliousness, inferiority, or inadequacy. Chains of fight and/or flight become linked in children's minds, overwhelming their ego's image of itself. A propensity to over control may develop as a defense mechanism, leading to exploitation, manipulation, deception, etc. (Young, 2011; Taken from Table 20.13, pp. 477–478; Originally Young (1997); Taken from Table P.5, p. 13).

Theme in Story About Development

Like to try best/know (e.g., at school) vs. not try best/feel inferior (e.g., rebellious/lazy) (Young, 2011; Taken from Table 14.10, p. 328; Originally from Young, 1997; Taken from Table 10.1, p. 234).

Self-Development

Reciprocal, Second-Person Perspective-Taking, Self-Reflective Self Concrete operations permit school-aged children to think more logically, facilitating the "industry" of school. This logic is also turned inward, for children evaluate their own thoughts, and is also turned toward others, for their perspectives are evaluated. Others are understood to perform the same "other" evaluation (i.e., evaluation of the children themselves). Loevinger calls the equivalent of this stage the self-protective stage. The label *concrete operational secondary-perspective self* seems appropriate here (Young, 2011; Taken from Table 13.3, p. 299; Originally from Young, 1997; Taken from Table 3.4, p. 78).

Other(s)' Attitude Based on Cognitive (Mis)Perception of the Other

Despite some signs of channeling or pacification, a part of the child's discourse is acknowledged/accepted/praised on its own terms. The parent clearly acknowledges the child's answer or comment but without accepting it (e.g., "Yes, I know what you mean," or "I was just going to ask you that."). The parent shows some evidence of warmth and active interest in the child's position, although the conversation is not completely interactive (Young, 2011; Taken from Table 14.4, p. 319; Originally from Young, 1997; Taken from Table 7.4, p. 166).

Appendix 3.5. Prior Work on the Peri-operational Stage Sub-stage of Integration (Sub-stage 15): Self and Relational Development (9–11 Years)

Cognitive Acquisition

In peri-operational integration, a limited logic in imagination comes to glimmer. Children form suppositions about the non-apparent that are amenable to further manipulation, both mental and real, even if such control of suppositions is difficult (Demetriou, Efklides, & Platsidou, 1993). They differentiate optional branches or embeddings of logic in their thought and can deal with them simultaneously or in parallel to some extent, because the ability to hold things in mind forms a larger integral whole and children accelerate in the ability to retraverse a course in thought (reversibility). Thus, in storytelling, plot and subplot resolutions are more fully elaborated and unified, and they occur in parallel, not sequentially (Young, 2011; Taken from Table 20.8, p. 472–473).

Behavioral Specialization (e.g., in the Right Arm-Hand)

Next, this process refines, as the child can use *logic in imagination* in restricted contexts (Young, 2011; Taken from Table 26.3, pp. 600–601; Originally from Young, 1990).

Socio-Emotional Acquisition

With the growth of logic in imagination, preadolescents come to project better their role both in the familiar social world of family and friends and the institutions of school and peer clubs. Roles and personality styles are imagined, applied, modified, and discarded, and attempts by others in doing the same are observed and assimilated (Young, 2011; Taken from Table 20.8, pp. 472–473).

Positive Social-Self Working Schema

The child's working schemata include testing of different roles, with others seen as modelers and accepting of this dynamic (Young, 2011; Taken from Table 24.4, p. 567).

Negative Pole in Eriksonian Development

Role vs. role confusion acts: The social roles imagined in the context of family, friends, school, and other institutions are limited and limiting. These roles are restricted ones, overreactions, compensations of lack, etc., befitting the sense of rebelliousness and/or inferiority developed previously. This emotional cauldron may produce a social (external), role-oriented individual trying to mask internal conflicts (Young, 2011; Taken from Table 20.13, pp. 477–478; Originally Young (1997); Taken from Table P.5, p. 13).

Theme in Story About Development

Personality/role tryout vs. personality/role confusion (Young, 2011; Taken from Table 14.10, p. 328; Originally from Young, 1997; Taken from Table 10.1, p. 234).

Self-Development

Third-Person, Perspective-Taking, mutual self Subteens' logic in imagination leads to multiple exploration. They remove themselves from the self-system. A different self is imagined, and a mutuality in self- and other perspective taking takes hold (third-person perspective taking). An independence from one's own self accrues through immersion in others. Loevinger names the equivalent of this stage the rule-oriented stage. At this level there seems to be a *projecting tertiary-perspective self* (Young, 2011; Taken from Table 13.3, p. 299; Originally from Young, 1997; Taken from Table 3.4, p. 78).

Other(s)' Attitude Based on Cognitive (Mis)Perception of the Other

A glimmer of possibility is left open for the child's position or argument to emerge as being correct but in the context of others. The parent points out relationships between the child's position and (an)other(s), their own, etc., integrating the child's view as one differentiated member of a larger perspective (e.g., "You're right, but ...") (Young, 2011; Taken from Table 14.4, p. 319; Originally from Young, 1997; Taken from Table 7.4, p. 166).

Appendix 4.1. Prior Work on the Abstract (Formal) Stage Sub-stage of Coordination (Sub-stage 16): Self and Relational Development (11–13 Years)

Cognitive Acquisition

With the coordination of streams of logic in imagination in young adolescence, classical Piagetian formal operational problems can be tackled, but with limited success, for the balanced synchronization of the streams is limited, not consistent. In simpler abstract problem-solving, alternative hypotheses are formed, and one variable at a time is allowed to vary, while the other(s) are held constant, because young teenagers can orchestrate their logical thought pathways, even when no physical evidence is available to help in finding solutions (Young, 2011; Taken from Table 20.9, pp. 473–474).

Behavioral Specialization (e.g., in the Right Arm-Hand)

A coordination of logic in imagination is found (e.g., in solving problems by allowing one variable at a time free to vary). This can lead to novel, *abstract, formal thought* in restricted contexts (e.g., genuine craft, interpretation in painting, music) (Young, 2011; Taken from Table 26.4, p. 601; Originally from Young, 1990).

Socio-Emotional Acquisition

The advent of abstract logic allows higher-order conscious awareness in that young adolescents reflect on their behavior, cognitions, past, family, and future. This should lead to overt esteem for the self and others, an opening of the mind to freedom from repressed ideas and absorption in the world of abstract ideas (Young, 2011; Taken from Table 20.9, pp. 473–474).

Positive Social-Self Working Schema

Conscious "I" weighs abstractly (Young, 2011; Taken from Table 24.5, p. 567).

Negative Pole in Eriksonian Development

Conscious vs. contra-conscious acts: Young adolescents can lapse into conscious self-depreciation, a closure to freeing repressed thoughts, cynical ridicule of others and their constructive efforts, and "turning off" free thinking altogether. One reaction to this confusion may be to conform excessively and adopt the role identifications perceived as preferred by parents, peers, teachers, etc. (Young, 2011; Taken from Table 20.14, p. 478; Originally Young (1997); Taken from Table P.6, p. 14).

Theme in Story About Development

Open conscious (e.g., see past, change future) vs. close, confine conscious (Young, 2011; Taken from Table 14.10, p. 328; Originally from Young, 1997; Taken from Table 10.1, p. 234).

Self-Development

In-depth, Societal-Symbolic Perspective-Taking Self Young adolescents can coordinate separate pathways of logic in imagination, precipitating the acquisition of formal abstract thought. Such logic enables creative conscious awareness, where adolescents have meta-cognitions about their cognitions and motives. Past and future are analyzed, linked, and chained or coordinated to give a Janus-like vision in the present. Conscious esteem develops for the self, the other, and ideas. Abstract logic allows one to see the self and other as complex entities functioning simultaneously at multiple conscious and unconscious levels. If confusion sets in, excessive conformity may result. Loevinger terms the equivalent of this stage the conformist stage. At this level, the self may be described as the *abstractly aware conscious self* (Young, 2011; Taken from Table 13.4, p. 300; Originally from Young, 1997; Taken from Table 3.5, p. 80).

Other(s)' Attitude Based on Cognitive (Mis)Perception of the Other

The parent indirectly encourages partially independent, novel thought of other possible dimensions to the story/reasoning position or the way given dimensions may interact (e.g., "Can you think of anything else"; "Why do you say that?"; "What else did he do or say?"; "How does *this* relate to *that*?"). The parent suggests that more may be possible or that there's something important missing (e.g., "Didn't you forget something?"). The parent does not provide information, but hints at a direction so the child can take the lead of the discussion. The parent listens to the child's response and continues the conversation by building on the child's responses or by asking indirect questions (Young, 2011; Taken from Table 14.5, p. 320; Originally from Young, 1997; Taken from Table 7.5, p. 167).

Appendix 4.2. Prior Work on the Abstract (Formal) Stage Sub-stage of Hierarchization (Sub-stage 17): Self and Relational Development (13–16 Years)

Cognitive Acquisition

The above thought process becomes more structured in middle adolescence, for coordinated abstract logic in imagination manifests hierarchical order across streams, permitting a spurt in formal operational thought. Abstract approaches being explored are compared either among themselves or to a more general perspective. Story construction should reflect this by placing plots and/or themes being explored in various relations, juxtapositions, etc. (Young, 2011; Taken from Table 20.9, pp. 473–474).

Behavioral Specialization (e.g., in the Right Arm-Hand)

Abstract approaches explored. First, there is their pair-wise comparison or *abstract hierarchization* (with that of a mentor, between themselves, etc.) (Young, 2011; Taken from Table 26.4, p. 601; Originally from Young, 1990).

Socio-Emotional Acquisition

Adolescents can now weigh multiple variables and logically proceed to attempt to solve problems about the self, the wider world, and their relation. This process can lead to a frontal evaluation of self-identity, ideology, and place in the time course (Young, 2011; Taken from Table 20.9, pp. 473–474).

Positive Social-Self Working Schema

Identity "I" tests and seeks identity (Young, 2011; Taken from Table 24.5, p. 567).

Negative Pole in Eriksonian Development

Identity vs. identity diffusion acts: The search for identity can be subverted, postponed, meander, lead to back alleys, etc., as Erikson described (Young, 2011; Taken from Table 20.14, p. 478; Originally Young (1997); Taken from Table P.6, p. 14).

Theme in Story About Development

Search for identity, inner essence vs. identity cutoff (Young, 2011; Taken from Table 14.10, p. 328; Originally from Young, 1997; Taken from Table 10.1, p. 234).

Self-Development

Conscientious-Conformist Self Adolescents can now weigh multiple variables and logically proceed to attempt to solve problems about the self, the wider world, and their relation. Accentuated by pubertal awakening, this process can lead to an evaluation of self-identity, ideology, and place in the time course. A sense of the real self, truly personal goals, concerns about personal adjustment, and options concerning the self emerge. Loevinger labels the equivalent of this stage the transitional one of the conscientious/conformist stage. One may call the self in this period the *identity-seeking self* (Young, 2011; Taken from Table 13.4, p. 300; Originally from Young, 1997; Taken from Table 3.5, p. 80).

Other(s)' Attitude Based on Cognitive (Mis)Perception of the Other

Part of the child's reasoning is praised, reinforced by the parent directly with a constructive comment (e.g., "That's a really good idea because ..."). The parent encourages the child to continue with her on his position/idea/comment. The parent allows the child to control the pace and direction of the discussion (Young, 2011; Taken from Table 14.5, p. 320; Originally from Young, 1997; Taken from Table 7.5, p. 167).

Appendix 4.3. Prior Work on the Abstract (Formal) Stage Sub-stage of Systematization (Sub-stage 18): Self and Relational Development (16–19 Years)

Cognitive Acquisition

Late adolescents develop abstract systematization where the approaches examined and compared in the prior sub-stage are qualified, or more reciprocally interrelated, leading to super-ordinate models. Stories could reflect this logical advance by a refinement of the plots and themes therein, producing a more structured whole (Young, 2011; Taken from Table 20.9, pp. 473–474).

Behavioral Specialization (e.g., in the Right Arm-Hand)

Second, one may find *abstract systematization* of the approaches, leading to a better-desired outcome (Young, 2011; Taken from Table 26.4, p. 601; Originally from Young, 1990).

Socio-Emotional Acquisition

Late adolescents are permitted to undertake adult-like functions, having acquired a capacity to see themselves systemically in relation to the life course (in terms of love, advanced schooling, and perhaps work and children). Others are related to with responsibility and reciprocal sharing (Young, 2011; Taken from Table 20.9, pp. 473–474).

Positive Social-Self Working Schema

Conscientious “I” undertakes adult(−like) functions (Young, 2011; Taken from Table 24.5, p. 567).

Negative Pole in Eriksonian Development

Nurturing vs. mis-nurturing acts: Responsible adult roles cannot be envisioned. Decisions are not subjected to critical, personal standards. Social relations are more unidirectional or parallel than reciprocal. Work and school activities are not future-directed and may be demeaned. Any nurturing is superficial and considered superfluous (Young, 2011; Taken from Table 20.14, p. 478; Originally Young (1997); Taken from Table P.6, p. 14).

Theme in Story About Development

Nurture, take care of other vs. Not nurture, not care for other (Young, 2011; Taken from Table 14.10, p. 328; Originally from Young, 1997; Taken from Table 10.1, p. 234).

Self-Development

Conscientious Self The capacity of late adolescents for abstract systematization permits systemic understanding; personal and other perspectives can coexist in one integrated structure. Social and societal relationships are seen as components of a larger whole to which the individual must contribute. With this viewpoint come self-constructed standards or criteria applied in critical thought. Loevinger calls the equivalent of this stage the conscientious stage. Late adolescents seem to possess a *maturing conscientious self* (Young, 2011; Taken from Table 13.4, p. 300; Originally from Young, 1997; Taken from Table 3.5, p. 80).

Other(s)' Attitude Based on Cognitive (Mis)Perception of the Other

The child's whole story/reasoning/position is shown to be valid in a constructive way (Young, 2011; Taken from Table 14.5, p. 320; Originally from Young, 1997; Taken from Table 7.5, p. 167).

Appendix 4.4. Prior Work on the Abstract (Formal) Stage Sub-stage of Multiplication (Sub-stage 19): Self and Relational Development (19–22 Years)

Cognitive Acquisition

Young people pass into multiplicative, relativist abstraction, weighing larger systems organized into coherent multiple frameworks. Stories then should manifest creative, balanced combinations (Young, 2011; Taken from Table 20.9, p. 473–474).

Behavioral Specialization (e.g., in the Right Arm-Hand)

Third, inhibition of major self-reinforcing dialectical *relativist abstraction* that could lead to changing inter-approach multiples and thus superior creativity (Young, 2011; Taken from Table 26.4, p. 601; Originally from Young, 1990).

Socio-Emotional Acquisition

Adult functions are vigorously adopted. Youths weigh options and usually settle into an intimate monogamous relationship and steady job/role (e.g., studying/working, constant presence for offspring) (Young, 2011; Taken from Table 20.9, pp. 473–474).

Positive Social-Self Working Schema

Multiplicative, relativistic "I" delves and debates (Young, 2011; Taken from Table 24.5, p. 567).

Negative Pole in Eriksonian Development

Intimacy vs. isolation acts: This pattern continues (responsible adult roles cannot be envisioned), but more so, for multiple adult functions may be foisted on the individual by society. Abandonment of any such functions undertaken, or other self- and other-destructive behavior, becomes possible, yielding sentiments of loneliness, isolation, etc. Instead of a relativist, unique, yet mutual self, there is an absolute, desolate one (Young, 2011; Taken from Table 20.14, p. 478; Originally Young (1997); Taken from Table P.6, p. 14).

Theme in Story About Development

Feel mature, intimate, in adult Function vs. Feel isolated, alone (Young, 2011; Taken from Table 14.10, p. 328; Originally from Young, 1997; Taken from Table 10.1, p. 234).

Self-Development

Individualistic Self The dialectical, relativist thought of youth permits the self to be seen as unique yet engaged in a deep mutuality with differentiated others. Loevinger refers to the equivalent of this stage the individualistic stage. We can call this self the *mutual relativistic self*, for there is a profound non-absolutist immersion in the self, the other, and their relation (Young, 2011; Taken from Table 13.4, p. 300; Originally from Young, 1997; Taken from Table 3.5, p. 80).

Other(s)' Attitude Based on Cognitive (Mis)Perception of the Other

The youth is prompted to expand on the immediate/proximate implications of her or his story/reason/position (Young, 2011; Taken from Table 14.5, p. 320; Originally from Young, 1997; Taken from Table 7.5, p. 167).

Appendix 4.5. Prior Work on the Abstract (Formal) Stage Sub-stage of Integration (Sub-stage 20): Self and Relational Development (22–25 Years)

Cognitive Acquisition

In adults' abstract integration, an empathic universality may emerge, e.g., in values or in stories. This can take place because differentiated branching in abstract logic can come to include harmonization of self and other (Young, 2011; Taken from Table 20.9, pp. 473–474).

Behavioral Specialization (e.g., in the Right Arm-Hand)

Lastly, an empathic, *abstract universality* may prevail (e.g., in painting, music, theorizing) (Young, 2011; Taken from Table 26.4, p. 601; Originally from Young, 1990).

Socio-Emotional Acquisition

If established in terms of self-knowledge, family, and daily responsibility, individuals seek the same for others, expanding their sense of harmonious integration (Young, 2011; Taken from Table 20.9, pp. 473–474).

Positive Social-Self Working Schema

Universal "I" harmonizes (Young, 2011; Taken from Table 24.5, p. 567).

Negative Pole in Eriksonian Development

Universal vs. self-singular acts: Rather than encouraging others' development, the self implodes in self-indulgent acts or worse (Young, 2011; Taken from Table 20.14, p. 478; Originally Young (1997); Taken from Table P.6, p. 14).

Theme in Story About Development

Universal/charity/harmonization/empathy/genuine concern for any other, any community vs. non-empathy (Young, 2011; Taken from Table 14.10, p. 328; Originally from Young, 1997; Taken from Table 10.1, p. 234).

Self-Development

Autonomous Self-Sufficient Self Adults possess abstract integration skills, which enable a universal empathy. They recognize others' need for individualized independence within a framework of reciprocal interdependence. They accept others' conflicts or ambiguities as their own. Loevinger indicates that the equivalent of this stage is the autonomous stage. This self seems an *accepting universal self* (Young, 2011; Taken from Table 13.4, p. 300; Originally from Young, 1997; Taken from Table 3.5, p. 80).

Other(s)' Attitude Based on Cognitive (Mis)Perception of the Other

The adult is prompted to see how her or his story/reason/position fits into a larger picture and may be harmonious with it (Young, 2011; Taken from Table 14.5, p. 320; Originally from Young, 1997; Taken from Table 7.5, p. 167).

Appendix 5.1. Prior Work on the Collective Intelligence Stage Sub-stage of Coordination (Sub-stage 21): Self and Relational Development (25–28 Years)

Cognitive Acquisition

Knowledge sub-domain (generic, attempted collective sub-domain theory/procedure; Pascual-Leone, 1990) super-ordinate coordination (meta-theory, supra-speculation, overarching principle, second-order logical system or hypothesis, etc., building) occurs. It refers to scientific, professional, religious, moral, artistic, complex practical/technical, and other knowledge domains (even oral folk traditions). It involves personal reflection taking place even when comprehension has not been communicated to others or has not influenced others, if communicated (Young, 2011; Taken from Table 20.10, pp. 474–475; Originally Young (1997); Taken from Table 2.1, p. 58).

Behavioral Specialization (e.g., in the Right Arm-Hand)

Pairs of *abstract integration super-ordinate structures* coordinate, juxtapose, etc. (e.g., in musical, architectural, sculptural, or other artistic planning and performance/composition or theory/analysis related to them) (Young, 2011; Taken from Table 26.5, p. 602).

Socio-Emotional Acquisition

Attempted collective sub-domain is coordination accompanied by subtle coordination on principles (meta-collecting abstraction reasoning), which not only engenders superior perspicacity but also a sense of awe about their ideas, flux, and uncertainty (Young, 2011; Taken from Table 20.10, pp. 474–475; Originally Young (1997); Taken from Table 2.1, p. 58). The other deeply engaged as a wholesale community of peoples also elicits this sense of awe in their humanity/potentiality.

Positive Social-Self Working Schema

The self is collective, fused, and coordinative symbiotically with others (Young, 2011; Taken from Table 24.6, p. 567).

Negative Pole in Eriksonian Development

Meta-collecting vs. disillusionment acts: Disillusionment with every society, with all groups, and with any constructive activity for peoples can pervade the individual, for the notion of profiting from collective symbiosis is not entertained (Young, 2011; Taken from Table 20.15, p. 479; Originally Young (1997); Taken from Table P.7, p. 14).

Theme in Story About Development

Feel coordinated/symbolic with every society, e.g., act for community of peoples vs. feel disillusioned with every society, not being for community of people (Young, 2011; Taken from Table 14.10, p. 328; Originally from Young, 1997; Taken from Table 10.1, p. 234).

Self-Development

Post-autonomous Self Meta-collecting reasoning in sub-domain or generic theory-procedure coordination engenders an appreciation of the wholeness of the web of being that allows our participation in this process. Loevinger calls the equivalent of this stage the post-autonomous stage. This self is termed a *holistic meta-self* (Young, 2011; Taken from Table 13.5, p. 301; Originally from Young, 1997; Taken from Table 3.6, p. 82).

Other(s)' Attitude Based on Cognitive (Mis)Perception of the Other

The adult is prompted to indirectly seek or explore alternative scenarios, stories, perspectives, even ones not espoused by the significant other her- or himself and which may be discrepant from the other's own point of view. The person should be encouraging a "collective" attitude/moral/value in this line of discourse as she or he proceeds (e.g., "Is there another way of seeing …") (Young, 2011; Taken from Table 14.6, p. 320; Originally from Young, 1997; Taken from Table 7.6, p. 168). All groups equally deserve emancipation.

Appendix 5.2. Prior Work on the Collective Intelligence Stage Sub-stage of Hierarchization (Sub-stage 22): Self and Relational Development (28–39 Years)

Cognitive Acquisition

Sub-domain hierarchization can manifest, for dominant/subordinate relations established (Young, 2011; Taken from Table 20.10, p. 474–475; Originally Young (1997); Taken from Table 2.1, p. 58).

Behavioral Specialization (e.g., in the Right Arm-Hand)

Then, the post-formal structure takes on a hierarchical relationship, where one component is primary or dominant in the relationship (*post-formal hierarchization*) (Young, 2011; Taken from Table 26.5, p. 602).

Socio-Emotional Acquisition

Progress in this endeavor leads to feelings of generativity. For example, one can become a mentor of some sort to younger individuals (Young, 2011; Taken from Table 20.10, pp. 474–475; Originally Young (1997); Taken from Table 2.1, p. 58).

Positive Social-Self Working Schema

The self knows priorities, is multiply complex, and can give multiply and not for taking (Young, 2011; Taken from Table 24.6, p. 567).

Negative Pole in Eriksonian Development

Generativity vs. self-absorption acts: Generative role models with family, at work, and in the community are sacrificed for self-absorption, a sense of emptiness, and stagnation (Young, 2011; Taken from Table 20.15, p. 479; Originally Young (1997); Taken from Table P.7, p. 14).

Theme in Story About Development

Role model, demonstrate way to others vs. self-absorbed, stagnate (Young, 2011; Taken from Table 14.10, p. 328; Originally from Young, 1997; Taken from Table 10.1, p. 234).

Self-Development

Generative Self With hierarchization of the coordination in the above process, a spreading generativity (e.g., mentoring) is fostered. We can speak of an *activating generative self* (Young, 2011; Taken from Table 13.5, p. 301; Originally from Young, 1997; Taken from Table 3.6, p. 82).

Other(s)' Attitude Based on Cognitive (Mis)Perception of the Other

The prompts given to the person are given in a direct manner, but only for part of, not a full, perspective. The person is encouraged to see where trade-offs, negotiations, bargaining, or give-and-take may apply to certain collective-oriented positions. However, the other instills in the person the idea that one of them is dominant over the other(s) (Young, 2011; Taken from Table 14.6, p. 320; Originally from Young, 1997; Taken from Table 7.6, p. 168).

Appendix 5.3. Prior Work on the Collective Intelligence Stage Sub-stage of Systematization (Sub-stage 23): Self and Relational Development (39–50 Years)

Cognitive Acquisition

Domain systematization can be attempted through mutuality in sub-domain regulation. People can master (or influence) an entire domain, catalyzing its transformation. This can occur through a train of quantitative additions to the field (emergent discoveries) or by a major qualitative change in foundation (paradigmatic shift) (Young, 2011; Taken from Table 20.10, pp. 474–475; Originally Young (1997); Taken from Table 2.1, p. 58).

Behavioral Specialization (e.g., in the Right Arm-Hand)

In the next steps, the components systematize (Young, 2011; Taken from Table 26.5, p. 602).

Socio-Emotional Acquisition

When these advances are radically different from the existing field's direction, we can speak of chaotic attractors and catastrophic inversions, respectively (Young, 2011; Taken from Table 20.10, pp. 474–475; Originally Young (1997); Taken from Table 2.1, p. 58).

Positive Social-Self Working Schema

At midlife, the self can create and work to transform personal, social, work, and community systems (Young, 2011; Taken from Table 24.6, p. 567).

Negative Pole in Eriksonian Development

Catalytic vs. midlife crisis acts: Midlife crisis develops; for instead of emerging as a force in whatever collective is of concern, the adult pays the price for having skirted the collective. The confusions and changes engendered are unconscious attempts to return to prior levels through misapplied catalytic discoveries, shifts, inversions, etc., in thought (Young, 2011; Taken from Table 20.15, p. 479; Originally Young (1997); Taken from Table P.7, p. 14).

Theme in Story About Development

Reevaluate/redefine life course/path vs. crisis/confusion in life course/path (Young, 2011; Taken from Table 14.10, p. 328; Originally from Young, 1997; Taken from Table 10.1, p. 234).

Self-Development

Midlife Self Domain systematization parallels the transitional midlife period. Generativity is more elaborate and systemic. It is coupled with a transformative rethinking of the self and contemplation of the end of those phases where one's potential and dream seemed to have no temporal or physical constraints. We can refer to a *catalytic midlife self* (Young, 2011; Taken from Table 13.5, p. 301; Originally from Young, 1997; Taken from Table 3.6, p. 82).

Other(s)' Attitude Based on Cognitive (Mis)Perception of the Other

The prompts above are direct and are aimed at eliciting a whole new perspective. The adult encourages the person to consider alternative collective positions as being part of a larger system and that all are considered equally valid, legitimate, and in a dynamic relationship with each other (Young, 2011; Taken from Table 14.6, p. 320; Originally from Young, 1997; Taken from Table 7.6, p. 168).

Appendix 5.4. Prior Work on the Collective Intelligence Stage Sub-stage of Multiplication (Sub-stage 24): Self and Relational Development (50–61 Years)

Cognitive Acquisition

Inter-domain efforts may be undertaken (multiplication) (Young, 2011; Taken from Table 20.10, pp. 474–475; Originally Young (1997); Taken from Table 2.1, p. 58).

Behavioral Specialization (e.g., in the Right Arm-Hand)

Multiply out throughout the full system (Young, 2011; Taken from Table 26.5, p. 602).

Socio-Emotional Acquisition

Older adults who span a whole domain may experience a sense of ego integrity or satisfaction and acceptance of their life flow (Young, 2011; Taken from Table 20.10, pp. 474–475; Originally Young (1997); Taken from Table 2.1, p. 58).

Positive Social-Self Working Schema

The elder self-reviews the multiplicity of life and lives (Young, 2011; Taken from Table 24.6, p. 567).

Negative Pole in Eriksonian Development

Ego integrity vs. despair acts: Disappointment with the meaningless felt in life sets in (Young, 2011; Taken from Table 20.15, p. 479; Originally Young (1997); Taken from Table P.7, p. 14).

Theme in Story About Development

Examine/find joy in life's meaning vs. despair at life's emptiness (Young, 2011; Taken from Table 14.10, p. 328; Originally from Young, 1997; Taken from Table 10.1, p. 234).

Self-Development

Ego Integrity Self Inter-domain thought is accompanied by satisfaction and acceptance of one's life course. The self appears a *satisfied ego integrity self* (Young, 2011; Taken from Table 13.5, p. 301; Originally from Young, 1997; Taken from Table 3.6, p. 82).

Other(s)' Attitude Based on Cognitive (Mis)Perception of the Other

The adult encourages the person to see the implications of adopting large systems and to compare them. The adult and person discuss together similarities and differences among them. The adult and person together realize that these sometimes conflicting systems can exist simultaneously (Young, 2011; Taken from Table 14.6, p. 320; Originally from Young, 1997; Taken from Table 7.6, p. 168).

Appendix 5.5. Prior Work on the Collective Intelligence Stage Sub-stage of Integration (Sub-stage 25): Self and Relational Development (61 Plus Years)

Cognitive Acquisition

Perhaps knowledge domains are integrated. In the final phases of life, often there is a wider knowledge that is accompanied by cathartic or purifying experiences (Young, 2011; Taken from Table 20.10, pp. 474–475; Originally Young (1997); Taken from Table 2.1, p. 58).

Behavioral Specialization (e.g., in the Right Arm-Hand)

And achieve full integration (e.g., would a full musical symphonic composition and performance/orchestration qualify for this skill or the graphic work in high-end mathematics, physics, or related science?) (Young, 2011; Taken from Table 26.5, p. 602).

Socio-Emotional Acquisition

The elderly become impregnated by a holistic sense of wisdom and also feel communion or reverence with what they regard as holy. In their most meditative moments, they hope to transcend and feel one with mystery (Young, 2011; Taken from Table 20.10, pp. 474–475; Originally Young (1997); Taken from Table 2.1, p. 58).

Positive Social-Self Working Schema

An integrated "I" is really an integrated "We" at life's end (Young, 2011; Taken from Table 24.6, p. 567).

Negative Pole in Eriksonian Development

Cathartic vs. abandonment acts: The elderly unwisely shut out spiritual experiences, denying any fellowship with humanity, the unknown, and the infinity (Young, 2011; Taken from Table 20.15, p. 479; Originally Young (1997); Taken from Table P.7, p. 14).

Theme in Story About Development

Feel oneness with life, universe vs. feel abandoned by life, universe (Young, 2011; Taken from Table 14.10, p. 328; Originally from Young, 1997; Taken from Table 10.1, p. 234).

Self-Development

Integrated Self In the final phases of life, often there is a wider knowledge, which is accompanied by cathartic or purifying experiences. The elderly become impregnated by a holistic sense of wisdom and also feel communion or reverence with what they regard as holy. In their most meditative moments, they hope to transcend and in consequence to be one with mystery. Loevinger gives the term for the equivalent of this stage the integrated stage. Self-development culminates in a *purified integrated self* (Young, 2011; Taken from Table 13.5, p. 301; Originally from Young, 1997; Taken from Table 3.6, p. 82).

Other(s)' Attitude Based on Cognitive (Mis)Perception of the Other

The other encourages explicit attempts to put all previous systems into an overarching principle, tempered by contextual pragmatic realities, e.g., living with and growing from conflict (Young, 2011; Taken from Table 14.6, p. 320; Originally from Young, 1997; Taken from Table 7.6, p. 168).

References

Bialystok, E. (1992). Symbolic representation of letters and numbers. *Cognitive Development, 7*, 301–316.

Blake, J., & Dolgoy, S. J. (1993). Gestural development and its relation to cognition during the transition to language. *Journal of Nonverbal Behavior, 17*, 87–102.

Bullock, M., & Lütkenhaus, P. (1988). The development of volitional behavior in the toddler years. *Child Development, 59*, 664–674.

Case, R. (1991). Stages in the development of the young child's first sense of self. *Developmental Review, 11*, 210–230.

Cohn, J. F., & Tronick, E. Z. (1983). Three-month-old infants' reaction to simulated maternal depression. *Child Development, 54*, 185–193.

Cohn, J. F., & Tronick, E. Z. (1988). Mother-infant face-to-face interaction: Influence is bidirectional and unrelated to periodic cycles in either partner's behavior. *Developmental Psychology, 24*, 386–392.

Demetriou, A., Efklides, A., & Platsidou, M. (1993). The architecture and dynamics of developing mind: Experiential structuralism as a frame for unifying cognitive developmental theories. *Monographs of the Society for Research in Child Development, 58* (5/6, Serial No. 234).

Fogel, A. (1991). *Infancy: Infant, family, and society* (2nd ed.). Saint Paul, MN: West.

Halliday, M. A. K., & Hasan, R. (1976). *Cohesion in English*. New York: Longman.

Howe, M. L., & Courage, M. L. (1993). On resolving the enigma of infantile amnesia. *Psychological Bulletin, 113*, 305–326.

Legerstee, M. (1990). Infants use multimodel information to imitate speech sounds. *Infant Behavior and Development, 3*, 343–354.

Mandler, J. M. (1992). How to build a baby: II. Conceptual primitives. *Psychological Review, 99*, 587–604.

Meltzoff, A. N., & Moore, M. K. (1989). Imitation in newborn infants: Exploring the range of gestures imitated and the underlying mechanisms. *Developmental Psychology, 25*, 954–962.

Meltzoff, A. N., & Moore, M. K. (1992). Early imitation within a functional framework: The importance of person identity, movement, and development. *Infant Behavior and Development, 15*, 479–505.

Meltzolff, A. N., & Moore, M. K. (1994). Imitation, memory, and the representation of persons. *Infant Behavior and Development, 17*, 83–99.

Messinger, D., & Fogel, A. (1990). *The role of referential gazing in object exchange*. Paper presented at the International Conference on Infant Studies, Montreal, April.

Neisser, U. (1991). Two perceptually given aspects of the self and their development. *Developmental Review, 11*, 197–209.

Pascual-Leone, J. (1990). Emotions, development and psychotherapy: A dialectical constructivist perspective. In J. D. Safran & L. S. Greenberg (Eds.), *Emotion, psychotherapy and change* (pp. 302–335). New York: Guilford Press.

Rochat, P. (1989). Object manipulation and exploration in 2- to 5-month-old infants. *Developmental Psychology, 25*, 871–884.

Rochat, P., & Senders, S. J. (1991). Active touch in infancy: Action systems in development. In M. J. Weiss & P. R. Zelazo (Eds.), *Newborn attention: Biological constraints and the influence of experience* (pp. 412–422). Norwood, NJ: Ablex.

Rogoff, B. (1990). *Apprenticeship in thinking: Cognitive development in social context*. New York: Oxford University Press.

Thelen, E., & Fogel, A. (1989). Toward an action-based theory of infant development. In J. Lockman & N. Hazen (Eds.), *Action in social context: Perspectives on early development* (pp. 23–64). New York: Plenum Press.

Watson, J. S. (1973). Smiling, cooing, and "the game". *Merrill Palmer Quarterly, 18*, 323–339.

Wolff, P. H. (1987). *The development of behavioral states and the expression of emotions in early infancy*. Chicago: University of Chicago Press.

Young, G. (1990). Early neuropsychological development: Lateralization of functions - Hemispheric specialization. In C. A. Hauert (Ed.), *Developmental psychology: Cognitive, perceptuo-motor and neuropsychological perspectives* (pp. 113–181). Amsterdam: North Holland.

Young, G. (1997). *Adult development, therapy, and culture: A postmodern synthesis*. New York: Plenum Press.

Young, G. (2011). *Development and causality: Neo-Piagetian perspectives*. New York: Springer Science + Business Media.

Index

G. Young, *Causality and Development*,
https://doi.org/10.1007/978-3-030-02493-2

E

F

Printed by Printforce, the Netherlands